TIME OUT OF MIND

Also by Ian Bell

Once Upon a Time: The Lives of Bob Dylan
Dreams of Exile: Robert Louis Stevenson – A Biography

TIME OUT OF MIND
THE LIVES OF BOB DYLAN

IAN BELL

PEGASUS BOOKS
NEW YORK LONDON

TIME OUT OF MIND:
THE LIVES OF BOB DYLAN

Pegasus Books LLC
80 Broad Street, 5th Floor
New York, NY 10004

First Pegasus Books hardcover edition 2014

ISBN: 978-1-60598-628-9

10 9 8 7 8 6 5 4 3 2 1

Printed in the United States of America
Distributed by W. W. Norton & Company, Inc.

For Amanda, who has heard it all . . .

Contents

I don't know him because I don't think there *is* any *him*.
I don't think he's *got* a self!

CHAPTER ONE

Time Is an Enemy

IT HAD BEEN A STRANGE TRIP, BRIEF AS A LUCID DREAM. AT ONE INSTANT Bob Dylan was no one from nowhere; at the next he was prophet-designate. In the depths of a bone-freezing New York winter a ragamuffin from the Minnesota outlands was notable only for his unfeasible ambition. By the following year's end, as a gilded decade commenced in earnest, all the talk was of poetry and poets, of a prodigy with a supernatural facility in the songwriter's art. In the capsule history, genius suffered no birth pangs. Everything that happened to Dylan happened at the speed of recorded sound.

For a brief while in the 1960s he had seemed to alter daily, changing in manner, speech, style, sound and physical appearance almost as casually as most men changed their button-down shirts. No sooner had the image of one Dylan emerged from the emulsion than the outline of another was becoming visible. His identity, such as it ever was, had resembled a shimmering ghost. In the beginning, 'Bob Dylan' was less a person than a manifestation, a series of gestures.

For him, a single decade would become a life sentence, but in truth he had spent little enough of the 1960s in the public eye. By common consent it had been his era, once and ever after, and yet somehow, for much of the time, nothing to do with him. As late as late October 2012 a 71-year-old was still being badgered by an interviewer from *Rolling Stone* magazine for his reflections on 'his' decade, the one with which he was 'so identified'.

Dylan granted he had been *there*, as though times and places were one and the same, but said none of it had meant that much to him. As he told the journalist: 'I really wasn't so much a part of what they call "the Sixties".' The assertion sounds strange but rings true. You can pick out dates to prove it. For years on end, even – especially – at the height of his influence, Dylan had been silent, elliptical, gnomic or just absent. Hindsight says that his had been a comet's path. After the first dazzling flare he had all but disappeared from view.

A folk and blues record had been released and ignored in March of 1962. Critical acclaim had begun to form in a bubble around him with the appearance of *The Freewheelin' Bob Dylan* in May of the following year. True fame, the global kind, had descended with a trio of extraordinary albums issued in the space of 14 months in 1965 and 1966. Then he had exhausted himself, and shredded his nerves, and self-medicated, and crashed a motorcycle, and changed his way of thinking, and retreated into family life, and ducked from sight as though dodging a bullet: theories had abounded. The chronology says simply that he quit the concert circuit and the hoopla.

Three years and a matter of weeks: that, properly speaking, had been it for 'the voice of a generation'. His time spent clad in the Nessus-robe of the 'protest singer' had been briefer still. After girdling the globe in a few mad months in 1966 for the sake of audiences stranded somewhere between admiration and outrage, Dylan had withdrawn from the stage, injured several times over. He did not return for the best part of eight years. By the decade's end he had become a country crooner, of sorts, one liable to call an ill-assorted collection of standards, covers and pastoral experiments his self-obliterating *Self Portrait*. Estranged fans had taken it as a bad joke. The fact remains that an artist whose name is entwined, supposedly, with the 1960s and the decade's concerns was involved only briefly with either. As the 1970s began he was, resolutely, a private citizen who sometimes – but not too often – wrote songs.

Even at fame's apex he had not created many truly big hits, as these things are measured, not for himself. None of the albums recorded during 'his' decade reached number one in his homeland. No chart-topping singles appeared under his name. Often enough the record industry's shiny gold and platinum certifications would arrive only after years of steady sales. Dylan had acquired vast influence among his contemporaries. He was talked about endlessly by the journalists, academics and self-designated radicals who wanted to bestow significance on pop music. Some people spent a lot of time – a peculiar enough notion – trying to explain him and his work. Too often, however, 'Bob Dylan' was a cipher, the blurred face in a piece of monochrome footage deployed just to mark a date.

His '60s had amounted to three fast, torrid years at the eye of the storm. The rest had been preface and footnotes. Some of the latter had been strange, some private, some important, but their meaning had only begun to become clear when the decade was done. For long stretches, Dylan had simply not been around. Assumptions, myths and guesswork had stood in his stead. In the 1960s, he had compressed time. By the 1970s, as 'youth culture' awoke to a hangover and worse, time seemed to stretch ahead of him, demanding to be filled.

There is plenty to be said, of course, about what Dylan had done along the way. He had challenged the folk tradition with his embrace. He had inspired the imitative flattery of a horde of singer-songwriters. He had destroyed the assumptions of Tin Pan Alley and raised the craft of song to the level of literary art. Then he had given the academicians of literature a few problems of definition and assimilation. Dipping out of sight, refusing the assigned roles, he had produced some of his finest work and some of his worst. But still those who treated history as a public-relations exercise for one big idea or another refused to let the 1960s go. When clocks began to tick again, Dylan's reputation was marooned in time.

His talent, at once undeniable and oddly indefinable, produced a paradox. He inspired a great many people to attempt songwriting, but no one truly followed in his train. You could not trace Dylan's influence on pop, folk or 'rock' in the way you could delineate Louis Armstrong's profound effect on jazz, or name the borrowed Beatles chord changes in countless pop-type songs. Any number of performers took a crack at mere Dylan imitation, especially in the early days, affecting what they took to be his mannerisms or his diction, settling themselves beneath their harmonica racks and their political assumptions. None survived the inevitable mockery. Dylan, ran the consensus, was not to be copied. Musically, lyrically, there could never be a school of him, or a movement – now there was an obnoxious idea – made in his image. By the time the '60s were over, when he was eluding all categories, even the person in possession of the name no longer knew quite what to make of 'Bob Dylan'. But that had been a problem from the start.

**

How does it feel, as all the best questions begin, to sing the same songs over and over, decade after decade? Dylan's keenest admirers will tell you that he does no such thing. Those who persist in calling a busy performance schedule his never-ending tour argue that the true and profound meaning of Dylan's art is to be found on the public stage, in an idea of creative indeterminacy, in songs that are continually reworked, revised and remade. Some advocates of the view go as far as to claim that Dylan's tours – certain of them, at any rate – will one day stand revealed as his real body of work and as central cultural events of the past half-century. They are comfortable with hyperbole. But these fans find their Dylan in his concerts, in hundreds of bootleg recordings drawn from hundreds of shows, in a precise definition of performance art and in the idea of creativity eternally in flux.[1] The songs of this Dylan are forever provisional. They never end. They will only conclude, in some manner, when he is no longer around.

It's a seductive notion, a grand theory, and the perfect excuse for evasions and omissions. It keeps the game of interpretation alive, year upon year. What could be said about a cunning, complex song such as 'Tangled Up in Blue', first heard on the 1975 album *Blood on the Tracks*? That would depend on the version under discussion and there are lots of those available to the patient fan. Verses of the song have come and gone down the years. Pronouns have been switched around. Tantalising changes of emphasis have been effected. Dylan's angle of attack, emotional, verbal and musical, has altered. And the song itself – if it even remains a singular entity – was/is constructed around the nature of time and identity.

Cultural and literary theory of the modern sort opens its jaws and swallows these hors d'oeuvres whole. They are perfect for the times. For Dylan, meanwhile, they provide the solution to another familiar problem. The youngster who once railed against even the idea of interpretation is now the old man whose songs, it sometimes seems, can mean just about anything. Or rather, they can mean something to every variety of someone. There is a critique and a critical school – literary, linguistic, musicological, philosophical, theological, historical, sociological – for every occasion. The priestly sects, academic and amateur, come hurrying over the fields in their droves to pronounce on the words that fall from Dylan's mouth. And if those words are not always exactly, demonstrably his own – this era's fan obsession – so much the better. There is a *lot* to be said about intertextuality, originality, plagiarism, tradition, allusion, inspiration, codes, ciphers and the collapse of authorial hierarchies. Anyone who simply likes to listen to a Dylan song now and then is therefore missing the point, or so he or she is liable to be told. In the twenty-first century, Dylan offers limitless scope for the never-ending *tour d'horizon*.

Still, if it's Monday night, 19 November 2012, it must be Philadelphia. At the Wells Fargo Center, a sports and entertainment complex renamed to mark a banking group's escape from the great financial crash, Dylan offers that same 'Tangled Up in Blue' as his fourth number of the evening. According to his own bobdylan.com, this means the song has been performed on 1,273 occasions. That's a lot more creative flux and rewriting, you might think, than one defenceless poem can easily stand. The truth is that while Dylan never exactly repeats himself in performance, that while he has tinkered often enough with words and arrangements, he does not do so nightly, or monthly, or yearly. Arguably, his shows have not changed to any significant degree in the twenty-first century. Nevertheless, by 2012's end he will have heard himself deliver a version of 'Tangled Up in Blue' 1,275 times. To what purpose?

It's a living, certainly, and a pretty good one. In 2012, it would have cost you close to $300,000, reportedly, just to secure Dylan for your festival. He can still sell $600,000 worth of tickets while filling an amphitheatre in Berkeley, California.[2] Self-evidently, his performances meet a demand from audiences no longer greatly interested in music albums for their own sake. Putting on a show is simply what he does, having found no better, lasting alternative over the years. It's something, consequently, over which he believes he exercises no real choice: 'the road', in Dylan's accounting, is where he mostly exists. It means he is better travelled than almost anyone now living. The view from a tour bus isn't perfect, but this artist knows his America far better than most. When the chance arises and the mood takes him he walks around, big towns and small, exploring the heartland. He has seen a lot of changes, seen things appear and disappear, and seen what time can do. That might be relevant to 'Tangled Up in Blue', the well-travelled song of departures and arrivals.

Just before Philadelphia, *Rolling Stone* has published its interview.[3] In the piece, Dylan notes that he 'saw and felt a lot of things in the Fifties, which generates me to this day. It's sort of who I am.' But those times, the people, places, ideas and beliefs they contained, are long gone. The '60s, the era dominated culturally by a music industry that took transience and novelty for granted, wiped them out. Bob Dylan wiped them out. The songs made by the youth who emerged from the late 1950s continue, however. 'Blowin' in the Wind', the kid's first calling card, closes the Philadelphia show. That's performance number 1,145.

What kind of charge can the song still contain? Even the younger members of Dylan's audience, their perceptions fresh, are unlikely to be hearing 'Blowin' in the Wind' for the first time. Its alluring melody might still provoke an emotional reaction. The singer's ability to wring the sense of a contemporary meaning from words that are half a century old might still be arresting. The contrast between the verses of youth and a septuagenarian's gnarled, attrited vocals is, for some of us, invariably affecting. But in this, time is no illusion. It has done its work on Dylan, his songs, and on how those songs are heard. He has played Philadelphia 30-odd times in his career. In 2012, there's 'Highway 61 Revisited' (1,777 performances), 'Ballad of a Thin Man' (1,057), 'Like a Rolling Stone' (2,006) and, perennially, 'All Along the Watchtower' (2,101). The roughest arithmetic tells you that many millions of people have experienced these songs in concert halls and arenas. To those for whom it matters most, the entrancing novelty of 2012's show in Philadelphia is the chance to hear 1964's 'Chimes of Freedom' receive only its 54th public performance, if bobdylan.com's busy researchers are right.

But what, as they say, is that all about? Dylan resists the legend of the never-ending tour fiercely. Something about the idea seems to offend him. In the *Rolling Stone* interview, but not for the first time, he asks rhetorical questions of those who wonder over his attachment to the life of the itinerant performer. 'Is there something strange about touring?' he asks Mikal Gilmore, his interviewer. 'About playing live shows? If there is, tell me what it is. Willie [Nelson]'s been playing them for years, and nobody ever asks him why he still tours.'

It's a fair point. But if the giving of concerts is just one of those quotidian things, why does Dylan's faithful website transcribe the set list for each and every show, or track the public performances of each and every song all the way back to 1960 and the Purple Onion pizza joint in St Paul, Minnesota, where the 19-year-old Dylan picked up a pitifully few dollars a night for singing the likes of 'Man of Constant Sorrow' and 'Sinner Man'? That kind of detail, that extreme attention to the minutiae of an existence, appeals most to those who keep alive the disputed myth of an Odyssean tour-without-end. Some of the fans have near-metaphysical notions about Dylan's activities, yet he – or whoever acts in his name – is both dismissive and complicit.

Anyone who has ever written so much as a postcard has to pay attention, at some point, to the person who did the writing. Who was she? What was he thinking? The poet who inters his earliest verse in the file marked 'juvenilia' also inters his younger self. Yet Dylan, in his 70s, elects to confront the words of a 20-something nightly. In some fashion he contends with time itself and leaves you to wonder what the songs still mean to him, if they can still mean anything. He says this to Mikal Gilmore: 'A performer, if he's doing what he's supposed to do, doesn't feel any emotion at all.' He engenders feelings, in other words, but is – the old, alleged virtue of the allegedly authentic folk stylist – impersonal. Can that be true?

*

Each October, it begins again, the now annual, odd and faintly comical ritual. In 2011, bookmakers judge Dylan their 'second favourite'. After a lot of late and heavy betting, the singer is even installed briefly as a cert in a race that is no race, a contest never intended as a contest. Where once there had been idle speculation over a mere possibility advanced by a few eccentric enthusiasts, now real money is being laid by people prepared to believe that a popular singer and songwriter could – should? – win the Nobel Prize in Literature.

Why not? He already has an (honorary) Pulitzer Prize, awarded in 2008 for his 'profound impact on popular music and American culture, marked' – there are no prizes for writing these citations – 'by lyrical compositions of extraordinary poetic power'. The college dropout meanwhile has degrees granted by serious people at serious universities: from Princeton in 1970 and from St Andrews, Scotland's oldest such institution, in 2004. In fact, despite the 1963 Tom Paine Award debacle, when his tipsy, freestyle approach to free speech outraged liberalism's arbiters thanks to an attempt to understand John F. Kennedy's assassin, Dylan has acquired more scrolls and trophies than one man can easily store. By 2011 his name is attached to France's green gilt *Commandeur des Arts et des Lettres* medal, Spain's Prince of Asturias award, an Oscar, a Golden Globe, fully 11 Grammy awards, induction ceremonials in all the appropriate halls of musical fame, and to his homeland's National Medal of Arts. This last – though Dylan didn't actually show up for the affair – was bestowed in 2009 by President Barack Obama himself. So much for the insurrectionary '60s, then.

At the end of May 2012, as the Nobel chatter resumes and tireless commentators return to the vexed topic of pop stars and poetry, Obama reappears to wrap a blue-and-white ribbon around the neck of a stony-faced artist. The commander-in-chief confers what is, for Americans, the most precious piece of costume jewellery available, the Presidential

Medal of Freedom. Dylan honours the occasion by looking like a hostage. The dark glasses remain in place, even in the White House, but a smile is nowhere to be seen. Perhaps this is because a do-or-die pianist from the Marine Corps Band has just played 'Don't Think Twice, It's All Right'.

A statement from the administration is the usual thing: 'considerable influence on the civil rights movement of the 1960s . . . significant impact on American culture over the past five decades'. Dylan is on line with the novelist Toni Morrison, the astronaut John Glenn, former secretary of state Madeleine Albright and others, dead and alive, accounted great and good. Obama says nice, sentimental things and, looking down from his six-feet-and-one-inch eminence, calls Dylan (5' 7") a giant.

Sometimes it seems as though he does little else but receive awards. Late in 2012, he tells his interviewer that he turns down most of what he is offered simply because he lacks the time to collect each and every prestigious ornament. Here is an artist who does not struggle in obscurity. Validation, as the language of the age would have it, is not required. Still, every other media report of the White House event persists in describing Dylan as a folk singer. He has not been one of those, by a generous estimate, since 1964. But for those who know nothing of an ancient musical tradition, and who probably couldn't care less, 'folk' is another of those '60s things.

As 2012 draws to a close, it is announced that Dylan's song 'The Times They Are a-Changin'', 48 years old, will be among the 2013 'inductees' to the Grammy Hall of Fame. He has meanwhile emerged, without offering comment, from another round of Nobel speculation (once again, the ante-post second favourite has failed to place) and endured another controversy, this time over his paintings and the charge, now familiar, of plagiarism. His 35th studio album, *Tempest*, issued in September, has won a lot of praise, some of it preposterous. Now the announced wonder of the hour involves a venerable '60s star who, miraculously, can still make serious, intriguing music. For Dylan, it seems, there is no escape from his decade.

Posterity might one day take a different view. The lists of such things remind you, for example, that while nine Bob Dylan albums were released in the 1960s, exactly as many appeared in the following ten years. (If you include the vindictively titled *Dylan*, a collection of leftover cover versions released in retaliation by a spurned record company, the score for the 1970s is in fact ten.) Equally, if chart success is any kind of guide, the artist did far better in the aftermath of 'his' era, with three of the American number-one albums that eluded him throughout the '60s, than he had before.

Still journalism preserves its shorthand note: 'Dylan/ protest/ voice/ folk/ his generation'. These days, the laptop addendum might skip ahead: 'Wilderness years/ late renaissance/ astonishing'. The perception behind the precis endures for several reasons. One is that a decade as tumultuous as the '60s, as purportedly singular, seems still to demand a defining voice. Half a century on, the documentary sequences possess a soundtrack that is beyond cliché: the moptop quartet, the Stones and 'Street Fighting Man', a Motown track, and always, as though on an infernal loop, Dylan. Most often he can be heard singing a prophecy-song of changing times when the times foretold are long gone, the prophecy disproven and discarded. Whether this misrepresents history is beside the point. He has become part of the received narrative. No one ever asks the actor when he would like the play to end.

Equally, the chronology of one phase in Dylan's later career catches the eye for several of the wrong reasons. There came a time when he measured every height with his fall, when his work, like his reputation, suffered a decline so precipitous it seemed unstoppable. Between the appearance of the hectoring evangelical Christian album *Saved* in June of 1980 and 1997's *Time Out of Mind* the test was to find a good word to say about Dylan's works, then to find more than a handful of people likely to give a damn. In the second half of the 1980s his albums hovered in the suburbs of the *Billboard* 200, peaking at 54 (*Knocked Out Loaded*) or 61 (*Down in the Groove*). A 'return to form', declared in repeated triumphs of journalistic hope over experience, might see him graze the top 20, as with 1983's *Infidels*, or aim for the edge of the top 30, as with *Oh Mercy* (1989). Then the collapse would resume. When the best Dylan seemed capable of producing was a brace of eccentric albums of ancient folk and blues tunes in 1992 and 1993, even the staunchest of old fans were no longer buying it, whatever it was supposed to be. In his live works, meanwhile, he was careering from the high peaks of adulation on an avalanche of lousy reviews.

The twenty-first century would decide that *Good As I Been to You* and *World Gone Wrong* are, in reality, fine and fascinating things, born of love and deep knowledge. Beyond the public gaze, they were the beginnings of Dylan's artistic redemption. At the time, they sounded like the voice of a wounded man groaning in the wilderness. They sounded, moreover, like the last resort of a poet in the purgatory of contractual obligation. Here, self-evidently, was a songwriter, the most esteemed songwriter in the world, who could no longer write. Notoriously, Dylan failed to release a single original composition between September of 1990 and September of 1997. So who wouldn't have preferred to remember the candescent racket of 'Like a Rolling Stone'?

Lists of hits and misses do not begin to tell the story. Amid all the dross of 17 lost years in the '80s and '90s there were numerous works of lasting worth. Invariably, however, they were buried, like nuggets in deep silt, on albums that were inept or misconceived. *Knocked Out Loaded*, from 1986, is a lazy, execrable thing that nevertheless contains 'Brownsville Girl', one of the most inventive, complex and involving compositions to have appeared under Dylan's name. Even on the original vinyl record it seemed to come, at the start of side two, as though from nowhere, a narrative woven in patterns so intricate it still puzzles and enthrals admirers. But the track released was itself a shadow, arguably, of an even better original. The fact spoke to another perverse and self-destructive artistic habit.

In the 1980s and 1990s collectors of bootleg recordings began to grasp how completely Dylan could misjudge himself. It is another way of saying that a once-unerring artistic confidence had evaporated. Time and again, the songs he left off his albums were self-evidently superior, superior beyond the limits of relative worth or personal taste, to most of the things he chose to release. It became another Dylan puzzle. This ritual of self-harm had begun with *Infidels* and the decision to omit 'Foot of Pride' and 'Blind Willie McTell' (in either of its spellbinding incarnations) from the record. By 1989, *Oh Mercy* and the suppression – no other word seems right – of songs such as 'Series of Dreams' and 'Dignity', the pattern was plain. Both albums as released, for all their intermittent glories, were bedevilled by a lack of conviction. The artist's worst enemy was the artist himself. Then his ability to write anything at all began to desert him.

He had long lost the glorious facility of youth. No doubt he had heard too many people speak too often, too ponderously or too reverently, about his art. Clearly, he had thought about it himself, often enough, while clarifying his language for 1967's *John Wesley Harding*, or while distilling the essential spirits of *Blood on the Tracks* in 1974. By the mid-1980s, when he was struggling to assemble the half-hour's worth of music he would call *Down in the Groove*, he had mislaid even the ability to be professionally glib. It amounted to this:

Bob Dylan was no longer capable of composing, unaided, a single wholly new Bob Dylan song. The album was a wretched affair.

It should have been journey's end for a performer in Dylan's line of work. Beyond a band of diehards, he was no longer taken seriously. Worse, an artist who had always been impatient with the recording process no longer seemed to take his own records seriously. The next release documented parts of a tour – the wrong parts, but the error was by now predictable – with the Grateful Dead in the summer of 1987. Public gratitude was not much in evidence, if record sales were a guide, and the diagnosis of creative death was confirmed. Somehow Dylan was contriving to make each new album worse than its predecessor. The only rational explanation for *Dylan & the Dead*, so it seemed, was cynicism.

As though to emphasise the scale of the decay, the singer had meanwhile allowed his record company and his management to pass implicit judgement with 1985's multi-disc *Biograph* compendium. The exercise, involving 53 famous or previously unreleased recordings spanning a 20-year period, was not intended to shame Dylan. It was, among other things, the first move in a long campaign to reclaim his work from the bootleggers. Nevertheless, the contrast between tracks discarded in the '60s and '70s and the stuff he was passing as fit for consumption in the 1980s was damning. *Biograph*, an expensive set, sold at least as well as anything purportedly new to which Dylan was then putting his name. In most cases, it did better.

Real Live, a redundant document from a European tour, had been lucky to reach number 115 in the American chart at the end of 1984. *Empire Burlesque* had reached 33 in the summer of '85, but the pricey *Biograph* matched that when winter came, and went on to sell vastly more copies than Dylan's latest product. *Knocked Out Loaded* and *Down in the Groove* would follow: knocked down, then out. Such was the standard verdict. Most talented performers in popular music start out as small fry, as 'cults', and proceed with luck, work and judgement to achieve fame. Dylan was heading in the opposite direction. To all appearances, he was a spent force.

Did he care? Did he notice? Stray comments from the period suggest a stoical acceptance that his moment as an unlikely star had come and gone. For all that, whether obliged by contract, financial need or stubborn defiance, he continued to release those derided albums. The 1980s would see seven such artefacts emerge from the recording studios. *Infidels* and *Oh Mercy* might each have redeemed Dylan's reputation, but each was defaced – another unavoidable word – by its maker and those around him. The rest were very easy to forget.

In one sense, it needn't have mattered. On any fair reading Dylan's reputation would have been secure thanks only to the songs composed and sung between 1962 and 1978. In his business, particularly at the artistic end of the trade, a 16-year career is nothing at all to be ashamed of. Plenty of performers have made money for decades from work achieved in less time. The Beatles, those reproving deities, had hung together for barely seven years as recording artists, after all. Elvis had counted out most of his days among the living dead. But the seeming creative extinction of Dylan in the late 1980s was peculiarly poignant because it seemed both complete and inexplicable.

He had been perplexing for long enough. As far as the forgiving fans who stuck around were concerned, that was part of the contract. In 1969, there was the 'country' singer of *Nashville Skyline*; in 1970, the baffling anonymous artist of *Self Portrait*. After two of his most successful works, *Blood on the Tracks* and *Desire*, Dylan had ended the 1970s by surrendering his autonomy to God and evangelical Christianity. But at no time had he seemed wholly lost to art, bereft of ideas or a sense of direction. It hardly mattered, when the rot set in, that bootlegs told a more complicated story. As far as most listeners were concerned, Dylan drifted aimlessly through the second half of the 1980s and the first half of the 1990s. His records were poor or worse and few cared. Nothing important of him remained.

This meant, among other things, that it became silly to talk of Dylan the artist, Dylan the poet. Much attention was still being given to what he had done in better days, but by the 1980s many of the books and articles being published were sounding an elegiac note. The first edition of Robert Shelton's long-delayed *No Direction Home: The Life and Music of Bob Dylan* appeared in 1986, when those liable to wonder what all the fuss was about were being offered *Knocked Out Loaded*. In 498 pages of text, the biography contained only 13 pages dealing with Dylan's activities between 1980 and 1985. It ended by wondering whether the artist would follow 'Rimbaud's route' – and throw in his hand – or whether he would manage the Yeatsian path to 'even greater creativity toward old age'. Shelton was not prepared to guess.

The music business can offer at least ten comebacks for every penny. Most draw their inspiration from the creative agency of accountants, from managers sniffing a moment ripe for nostalgia or from the chance to exploit another greatest-hits package. Only rarely do performers renew themselves. Writers, equally, are reluctant to be reborn in late middle age. Lazarus never did explain how the trick was done. Nevertheless, Shelton covered his bets well enough. The late poetry of W.B. Yeats might certainly count as one parallel with Dylan in his second coming; all those old or ageing blues players who were 'rediscovered' in his youth could stand as another set of precedents. Equally, you could dismiss all such comparisons. When Dylan rose again, he did it on his own terms.

Among his contemporaries there is a short list of those who have simply ploughed on – Neil Young, Paul McCartney, the egregiously avid Stones – and a vastly long list of the faded and fallen. His case was different. Beginning with his initial work on *Time Out of Mind* in 1996, and pressing on to *Tempest* in 2012, he forged another of those 16-year careers, became still another 'Bob Dylan', and vindicated himself. Critics fell into the habit of exhuming and adapting a famous line from Minnesota's F. Scott Fitzgerald and his unfinished *The Love of the Last Tycoon* (1941).[4] As it turned out, there was a second act in at least one American life.

In these pages it will be argued, among other things, that in the process Dylan created a body of work – less sumptuous, less startling, less intoxicating – to match any of the products of his 1960s. He did it, moreover, while contending with everything, the whole accreted legend, the multiplicity of identities, that 'Bob Dylan' had come to mean. He did it while contending with age, with the fact of time, and with the burden of memory.

So we look again for the answer to the old, plain and perplexing question: how did he do that?

*

The Swedish Academy does not publicise its discussions or chat about the tastes of its 18 members when they are done selecting the Nobel laureate in literature. Dylan has been nominated each year since 1997, and each year the arguments over his place on the bookies' lists have resumed. How can one whose art depends on pop music be suitable for the highest honour available to a writer? Where Dylan is concerned, the game is now ancient: poet or not? If a poet, of which variety, and by which criteria? Specifically, how can poetry be said to exist if it fails to 'survive' on the page?

Some still talk and write as though the very question demeans the august prize. Some of Dylan's own admirers meanwhile dismiss the entire debate, as though to clear the ground for bigger claims. *Of course* he is not a poet, they will say, but he is the greatest songwriter in a golden age for songwriting and that alone is a big enough thing. Talking to the fan magazine *Isis* in 2005, the author and Dylan scholar Greil Marcus made the familiar point. The prize is for *literature* (it turns out). Our boy sings, performs, and writes *songs*. Besides, said the scholar, Dylan has plenty of awards and no shortage of money. Marcus argued that 'thousands' of novelists were more deserving. Elsewhere, he had said confidently that Dylan's songs are not 'true literature'.[5]

Dylan doesn't need the Nobel and the Nobel doesn't need Dylan: point taken. But even implicit questions need answers. If you cannot place him among the poets, where would 'Desolation Row' figure in the development of post-war popular songwriting? It's very hard to say. If you cannot set Dylan among writers of verse, what has all the fuss, 50 long years of it, been about? For some critics, that's even harder to say. And what is this thing, this self-evidently exclusive thing, we call literature (if the Swedish Academy so pleases)? Where American poetry is concerned, a mid-century professorial parlour game, sometimes still misidentified as a 'New Criticism', has done its reductive work on art.

Tomas Tranströmer, an octogenarian Swede for whom the honour is long overdue, wins the Nobel in 2011. A year on, the honour and eight million kronor go to Mo Yan, the first Chinese novelist to be recognised, a writer controversial for his failure to be politically controversial in his homeland. In the present context, the fact leaves a trace of irony. On each occasion, nevertheless, there is no sign that Dylan gives a damn. He accepts his honours, when time allows, but shows no inclination to argue over definitions of his work.

Tranströmer, though, is a *real* poet (who once wrote of 'Jangling tambourines of ice', and elsewhere of being 'north of all music'). His status is not in dispute: anything but. The Swedish master, formerly a psychologist, makes sparse, dazzling arrangements of words to be delivered and received, uttered and heard. So what is it that Dylan does, exactly? Mo Yan's fictions are rooted in folk tales and given what is described routinely as a 'hallucinatory' edge. So why does that sound so familiar? The Nobel, it is sometimes forgotten, is *in* literature. Lexicographers, paid to think twice, will not stretch the definition of the thing beyond 'the art of composition in prose or verse', or 'the art of written work'. Academicians are a little harder to describe.

Judging by some of the press discussion over a song and dance man, a lot of people still define literature by a process of elimination. The only agreed truth is that no one else in Dylan's 'field' – which would be? – could even merit consideration as a candidate. In this game he is too big, or just too old, to be contained within mere popular music, yet simultaneously insufficiently literary to stand alongside others who pattern words obsessively. Where the recent history of the Nobel is concerned, Dylan might also be, quite simply, too American.

Gordon Ball, the Professor of English and Fine Arts at the Virginia Military Institute who first proposed Dylan for the 1997 Nobel, had attempted to deal with some of the arguments in his nomination letter for 1999. Backed by an international committee of like-minded academics, the editor and friend of Allen Ginsberg had reminded the Nobel judges that, in honouring the Italian playwright Dario Fo in 1997, they had already recognised an artist whose work 'depends on performance for full realisation'. Ball had then recalled the prize given to W.B. Yeats in 1923, despite, as was said at the time, 'a greater element of song than is usual in Modern English poetry'. Thereafter the professor had invoked the praise given by Yeats to Rabindranath Tagore, a previous laureate, who was, said the Irishman, 'as great in music as he is in poetry'. Ball could no doubt have piled up more evidence for his thesis. The literature award has been given in years past to historians and philosophers. There is no obvious, definable reason why Dylan's way with words should be accounted the wrong way. But it would be unwise to risk money on the argument.

Remarking on the speculative betting generated by the 2011 Nobel, the permanent secretary to the Swedish Academy, one Peter Englund, compared Dylan to 'a literary UFO'. It was a neat way to dismiss a phenomenon and an inadvertent confession. Englund, and perhaps the Nobel Committee itself, didn't know what to make of Dylan. This said nothing about the singer, but it amounted to a slightly depressing comment on the guardians of world literature in the twenty-first century. Dispassionately, their response throughout has been puzzling. Either they want to say – but do not dare – that the Nobel must not be sullied by popular song, or they don't want to get into arguments liable to raise questions about their criteria, and hence about the nature of literature itself.

In March of 2013, nevertheless, an interesting fragment of news goes around the world. It seems that Dylan has been elected to join the elite group, generally 250 strong, of the American Academy of Arts and Letters. To most observers of such matters in the United States, this is not just another scintillating bauble to add to the pile in the artist's crowded trophy cabinet. There is more to it than a hearty handshake and a souvenir photograph. For better than a century the academy has had a reputation, never denied, for disdaining popular culture and anyone deemed too modern for their own or society's good. Once upon a time, those who ran the institution would not have deigned even to notice Dylan's existence.

In 2013, in contrast, he is offered honorary rather than full membership simply because the academy cannot decide whether he is worthy – though there is apparently no longer any doubt about that – because of his music or because of his words. 'The board of directors considered the diversity of his work and acknowledged his iconic place in American culture,' says Virginia Dajani, executive director. 'Bob Dylan is a multitalented artist whose work so thoroughly crosses several disciplines that it defies categorisation.'

True enough. So again you wonder, whether the artist cares to or not, why the organisers of the Nobel are so fearful of cultural UFOs. He has been central to American culture for half a century. He is as 'literary', say millions of listeners and several shelves full of earnest books, as they come. Still the struggle to decide what he is, and what he is worth, and how he is to be placed in anyone's canon, goes on.

*

In November of 1965, the 24-year-old Dylan had told Joseph Haas of the *Chicago Daily News* that he was spiritually non-aligned, that he reserved the right to make his own choices in life. 'I just don't have any religion or philosophy,' he had said. 'A lot of people do, and fine if they really do follow a certain code. I'm not about to go around changing anything. I don't like anybody to tell me what I have to do or believe, how I have to live.'

Oblivious to the contradiction, the young singer then proceeded to extol the 'amazingly true' I Ching, the ancient (if stubbornly cryptic) Chinese divination manual he pronounced 'the biggest thing of all'. By February of 1974, nevertheless, Dylan was explaining himself again to Ben Fong-Torres of *Rolling Stone*: 'Religion to me is a fleeting thing. Can't nail it down. It's in me and out of me.' In the autumn of the following year, on the opening night of the Rolling Thunder Revue, he was questioned about belief in the deity by Allen Ginsberg. As Barry Miles, later the poet's biographer, reconstructed the exchange, the answer was as follows:

God? You mean God? Yes, I do. I mean I know because where I am I get the contact with – it's a certain vibration – in the midst of – you know, I've been up the mountain, and – yes, I've been up the mountain and I had a choice. Should I come down? So I came down. God said, 'Okay, you've been up on the mountain, now you go down. You're on your own, free. Check in later, but now you're on your own. Other business to do, so check back in sometime. Later.'[6]

'Later' turned out to involve the passage of just a few short years. By then it would cease to be a question, as it happens a wholly redundant question, of whether Dylan entertained a belief in God. Instead, he would 'accept Christ' sincerely and embrace the belief that Jesus is the Messiah. It's fair to say that the artist would surprise and dismay a few people with his decision. Early in 1979, nevertheless, he would be baptised by full immersion in a California swimming pool and begin to tell his audiences what it meant to be born again. Most would not thank him for it.

Oddly, perversely, his fans and critics would in later years treat Dylan's involvement with evangelical Christianity as a kind of phase, as though the artist had taken a holiday from himself. Somehow ignoring a host of songs over better than three decades, they would study the small print and ignore the contract, concluding – the relief was palpable – that he had got the thing out of his system with three quick albums, 1979 to 1981, before returning to 'secular music', his true calling. Of all the nonsense ever talked about Dylan, this error counts as monumental. Given the artist's habit of delivering statements of faith, albeit reluctantly, whenever he is pressed on the matter, given the apocalyptic imagery that runs through song after song, given that many of those songs are impossible to understand if you discount religious belief, calling Dylan 'secular' is like calling the Dalai Lama a careers adviser. This artist cannot be understood without his God. Church membership is neither here nor there.

He was a religious writer for much of the 1960s, though it took a while for most people to notice. By the beginning of the 1980s, he had come to occupy a precise area in the unending realm of faith. Most followers of the major religions would consider Dylan's beliefs to be paradoxical. Some would call them nonsensical, others blasphemous. His statements and his songs nevertheless support a simple description. He remains a Jew, but a Jew who accepts Jesus and believes, furthermore, that Christ will return any time now. Fireworks and more will follow.

Dylan is, as these things are described, a messianic Jew.

It renders him part of a small minority, but it also makes him typically American, one of those millions who have assembled creeds of all sorts from whatever was to hand and persuasive since before the republic was founded. After all, Dylan's acceptance of Christ at the end of the '70s happened at precisely the moment when evangelical Christianity was sweeping America. The history of his entire career says that he changes as the nation changes (and vice versa). In 2012, his latest album, *Tempest*, would again be coloured by the language of belief. For example, almost at random:[7]

I love women and she loves men
We've been to the west and we going back again
I heard a voice at the dusk of day
Saying, 'Be gentle, brother, be gentle and pray.'

Or:

Low cards are what I've got
But I'll play this hand whether I like it or not
I'm sworn to uphold the laws of God
You could put me out in front of a firing squad

Or:

They waited at the landing
And they tried to understand
But there is no understanding
For the judgment of God's hand

By the time *Rolling Stone* was being allowed its traditional audience in honour of the new album in September 2012, the artist had all his lines, of defence and attack, by heart. Faith as a general notion was not denied; the specifics, some of them liable to test the patience even of believers, were kept vague. For Dylan, the ambiguities and self-contradictions, weighed to the ounce, had become part and parcel of what it means to believe. A touch of the Sermon on the Mount wouldn't go amiss, however. Asked if his 'sense' of faith had changed, Dylan replied:

Certainly it has, O ye of little faith. Who's to say that I even have any
faith, or what kind? I see God's hand in everything. Every person, place
and thing, every situation. I mean, we can have faith in just about
anything. Can't we?[8]

This from one who had just laid claim, in the same interview, to
transfiguration. Who could say if he had any kind of faith, but who
could gainsay him if he claimed to detect the hand of God in everything?
Eschatology is one of the big words used to mark last things: it has
been Dylan's specialist subject for decades. It counts as the most
important fact of the last 30-some years for the man and his writing.
But here he was deploying it, just as in the good old days, to twist the
skull of a hapless journalist. For all that, when he faced a question
about whether he found the experience of touring 'fulfilling', Dylan
gave what sounded like an entirely straight answer. 'Well, what kind
of way of life is fulfilling?' he asked in return. 'No kind of life is fulfilling
if your soul hasn't been redeemed.'

*

His career has passed the half-century mark with no sign that he
means to desist or surrender to age. After so many nights and years
on the road his voice is a magnificent ruin, a thing of wonder and
dismay to which notes and words must these days be moulded with
care. The words keep on coming for all that. Whether he has
appropriated certain of those words has become, in a strange way,
almost irrelevant. As with his prose, as with his paintings, the word
plagiarism is heard, but the uses to which Dylan puts borrowed lines
and images in songs interest more people than they trouble. His
motivations are more fascinating than his pillaged sources, though
there is a whole cottage industry devoted to spotting those sources.
None of that explains why a writer who was the most fecund of them
all has need of such stratagems.

He writes a book that is miscalled a memoir and seems to sit back
and wait until every allusion, hidden quotation and filched gem of
prose or poetry is discovered. He calls the book *Chronicles*, accepts praise
for a style that would not have shamed Mark Twain, and hears himself
being corrected for mistaking – some people are less kind – the facts
of his own life. Then the lists of debts owed begin to arrive: Twain,
Jack London, Proust and many more besides. He begins to show his
paintings and begins to receive a little grudging praise. Then he

produces a series, 'The Asia Series', that the gallery describes as 'a visual journal of his travels' when he knows, as everyone with any interest in Dylan or art soon knows, that in several cases he has done no more than copy famous photographs that he could have copied anywhere, at any time. It is as though he is determined to confuse every issue.

That might even be the case. Back in those headlong 1960s days he was praised on all sides for his originality. The entire point, so it seemed, was that there was no one like him. Now, time and again, intermingling his work with the work of others, he risks exposure by a simple question: who was Bob Dylan anyway? Often enough he seems to be hoping that someone, some accusing voice, will tell him.

*

Only rarely do biographical studies of Dylan resist the temptation to judgement. Even the most reverent works are provoked into petulance, bitterness or disappointment here and there. A contrary individual has done plenty of things, personally and artistically, to upset someone, somewhere, at some time. Sooner or later, he pisses everyone off. Dylan's unstable identity, the sense he gives that what passes for a personality is never better than a veneer, has guaranteed a rough ride down the years for devotees and sceptics alike. Add the fact that he is as driven as any authentic artist, obedient first and foremost to creative instinct, and you have a recipe for perplexity, then dismay, sometimes for a kind of anger.

Who has Dylan not betrayed? They form a queue, decade upon decade: the folk crowd, the radicals, the literary cliques, the godly, the secular, the politicians and priests, the journalists, the myth-makers, the prisoners of nostalgia and those who believe, desperately insistent, that with genius comes a sacred responsibility. Almost every word written about Dylan has been written by someone who knows exactly what he should be doing, or should have done. This alone makes him interesting.

None of it truly matters, of course. The making of a bad record is not a moral issue. If art is the topic, personal behaviour is irrelevant. Artistic choices are matters of fundamental opinion. You don't like that song? Listen to something else. His latest opinions distress you? Find another hero. What Dylan is, and why he is what he is, and why that should matter at all, comprise the only worthwhile puzzle. To this day, several pieces are missing.

CHAPTER TWO

Written in My Soul

ON THE THIRD FRIDAY IN JANUARY 1975, BOB DYLAN RELEASED HIS 15th studio-made album in a dozen or so years. *Blood on the Tracks* was neither expected nor suspected. Its author had been back in business as a public performer, by his lights, for just over a year, but nothing had prepared his audience for this new work. Of all the things of which he was thought capable – as always, an improbably long list – unburdening himself, purging himself publicly, was not his style. Dylan didn't do that.

Planet Waves, issued in the previous January, had been his first attempt in 40 long months at a fully rounded set of self-composed songs. The effects of a willed absence had been evident: rust had penetrated the artistic mechanism. Critical hyperbole, the special blend reserved for Dylan, had helped to give him his first number-one album in America, but sales had waned quickly. The set had soon enough felt thin, underweight, oddly mannered and hesitant. For no immediately explicable reason, it failed to repay much attention. Public demand for the latest Bob Dylan was limited.

Somehow there was a stiffness in the musical joints, an unpersuasive, metronomic rigour to The Band's best efforts, and a vagueness to Dylan's memory where an ineffable vocal line was concerned. If 'Tough Mama' or 'On a Night Like This' were what remained of '66, and of the Woodstock basement, the performers who reassembled in the early 1970s had forgotten the meaning, verb and adjective, of 'rock'. Two acute and forbidding pieces, 'Going, Going, Gone' and 'Dirge', were lost in the shuffle on *Planet Waves*. Those who had grown up with Dylan, desperate to hear again the old, unalloyed genius after some testing times, had tried and failed to kid themselves. The album's ecstatic and ribald handwritten sleeve notes, later removed, had been more fascinating than most of the songs. 'Back to the Starting Point!' Dylan had scrawled. 'Yeah the ole days are gone forever and the new ones aint [sic] far behind . . .' But the promise of the 'cast-iron songs & torch ballads' of Planet Waves soon faded into another of those fascinating false dawns.

Reviewers had taken a keen interest in the writer's apparent willingness to appease the confessional urge, but with a couple of exceptions – the transparently autobiographical 'Wedding Song', the 'anthemic' (in pop's crude coinage) 'Forever Young' – the tracks could not bear the weight. Unlike the singer-songwriters he had licensed, Dylan allowed only hints of intimacy. He mentioned places familiar from the standard bio and set scenes, glittering like little recovered jewels, that might have sprung from memory. But such songs – 'Something There Is About You' and 'Never Say Goodbye' – had merely invited Dylan's audience to treat allusion as fact. Had Planet Waves been produced by any other artist, reviews would have ranged from 'not bad' to 'pretty fair'. The competition Dylan had provided for himself, the unrelenting competition with which he would have to contend for decades to come, rendered the album a middling affair. Irrespective of anything supportive critics wanted to believe, he was still falling a long way short of his best. Whatever the problem, Planet Waves was not the answer.

The 1974 'comeback' tour, launched in Chicago in that same January amid an all-outlets media pandemonium, had meanwhile amounted to misdirection, to a sleight of hand. The tour had embraced 21 cities in Canada and the United States, but musically it had gone nowhere at all. Audiences had been delighted, predictably, and critics had swooned to see the artist back on tour – 'live', as they say – for the first time since 1966. For most, striking matches or waving their twinkling cigarette lighters in comical obeisance, it had been enough just to celebrate and bear witness. But as the accompanying album, Before the Flood, had made plain, there was nothing subtle about this returning hero.

He and The Band, performing together and apart – in theory, billing was shared – had gone at the rearranged Dylan songs with a metaphorical wrecking ball. There had been plenty of sound and fury, but the significance of the performances had been slight. On the recordings approved for release – certain bootlegs, to be fair, are more intriguing – Dylan sounds as if he wants to get through the ordeal with all possible speed. With the exception of the double-edged 'Forever

Young' and intermittent performances of 'Wedding Song', the *Planet Waves* compositions disappeared from the set as the tour progressed. They were not granted space amid the famous hits on *Before the Flood*. Such choices told their own story.

Dylan, though on guard against an epidemic of nostalgia, instead gave lucky customers the old stuff in new guises. He took their money, a lot of money, but soon enough disdained the praise. Talking to Cameron Crowe for the 1985 *Biograph* box set, he spotted his own mistake. On the tour he had played 'Bob Dylan' to his utmost, nothing more, and gained plaudits for mere 'energy'. Looking back, he called that absurd and 'sort of mindless'.

No doubt Dylan also remembered that while sales of *Planet Waves* had struggled to reach 600,000 copies by the close of 1974, at least 5 million applications for concert tickets – some estimates run to double that number – had been received. A Dylan still singing those '60s songs was preferred to his best recent efforts in the studio. Close to 700,000 people across America had been desperate just to see him and lucky enough to have their wishes granted; what they heard was of less importance. The biggest cheers, night after night, had been for 'Like a Rolling Stone'. By its end, the sole useful function of Tour '74 had been to show Dylan how *not* to stage public performances. It was a lesson he would digest in 1975 with fascinating consequences.

*

Some questions had seemed to hang in the air, for all that, as he reappeared on stage for top dollar and the undivided attention of those still transfixed by a shared past. They were not artistic questions, as such, but they had to do with this artist's place in an altered world. A lot had happened in the eight years of his seeming absence. The consoling Aquarian mythology of the 1960s had disappeared like so much fairy dust – he had been prescient about that – and no one was yet hailing glad conservative morning in America. If anything, the opposite was true. As the American political system was shaken to its roots, the very survival of the Republican Party seemed to be at stake. The common mood was sour; faith in the nation was in short supply. Vietnam had lurched towards a kind of peace – for American enlisted men, at least – but the conflict's apparent conclusion in 1973's Paris Peace Accords bore no resemblance to a US victory. It tasted very like defeat for the nation that had never before lost a war.

When Dylan and The Band took to the road at the start of '74,

America's last moon mission in the twentieth century was over and done. The Arab oil embargo was rattling the economy and corroding business confidence. Many of those who had found their identities in the impulses of the counter-culture were heading for the hills and retreating to communes. Meanwhile, the affair of the Pentagon Papers, the vast Department of Defense study copied by the analyst Daniel Ellsberg and part-published by the *New York Times* in the summer of 1971, had demonstrated an astounding, dispiriting truth. Four American administrations – those of Truman, Eisenhower, Kennedy and Johnson – had lied systematically to the people about their activities and intentions in Vietnam. In October of 1973, thanks to charges relating to bribery and the evasion of taxes, the vice-president himself, Spiro T. Agnew, had been obliged to resign.

Then, capping all, there was the aftermath of a strange episode in a Washington office and apartment complex named the Watergate. A vast unravelling at the heart of the state was set in motion by an affair that had seemed, for long enough, like a footnote to the list of America's worries. At first, no one – no one who was anyone, at least – had given a damn. Afterwards, the folk myth of heroic journalists righteous for truth against the odds would fill the void where a body politic once had stood.

So a 24-year-old watchman, Frank Wills by name, had come across five burglars inside the Democratic National Committee's Watergate offices on the night of 17 June 1972. So the cops had been called and made their collars in the wee small hours. And so what? At first it hadn't sounded like the biggest crime on record. True, a quintet resplendent in business suits and surgical gloves with sophisticated bugging equipment to hand did not qualify as run of the mill, but these were early days for the great American conspiracy theory. Even journalists suspicious of President Nixon took a while to join the dots.

Then, amid wave upon wave of revelations, chiefly from the *Washington Post*, hell broke loose. By the first week of 1974, most Americans knew something – and some knew many things – about Watergate, the presidency, and the state of America's democracy. These were headlines read around the world.

First, belief in the nation had been tainted by a war whose conduct and point, if any, had seemed to tear the country apart. Loyalty to the idea of America right-or-wrong had been tested beyond the breaking point. All the draft dodgers taking refuge in Canada and elsewhere in no sense represented a majority, but there was a nagging symbolism in their defiance. To conservatives they represented betrayal, but that in itself was troubling. The other side of the political coin said that too many of America's claims had proved counterfeit. Certain veterans of the fighting in Indochina, authentic heroes among them, had become prominent in anti-war protests.

Then there was the Watergate thing. To all the doubts over probity in foreign policy were added devastating allegations: that the president re-elected in a landslide as recently as 1972 was out of control, that he had engaged in a conspiracy against the constitution, that his deeds had been criminal. Whatever Americans thought of the man in charge, the office of president, and all it represented, remained near-sacred. In one sense, Richard Milhous Nixon stood accused of sullying faith itself. The crisis was without precedent.

*

Each night on his tour Dylan would win blistering cheers for a certain famous line among several famous lines in his song 'It's Alright, Ma (I'm Only Bleeding)'. This was not mere lazy, reflexive counter-culture approval. In city after city, not a soul was in any doubt that, sooner rather than later, even the President of the United States would have to stand naked before the people. In early 1974, those enemies against whom he had raged and cursed for so long were closing in on Nixon. This time, they had the law on their side.

Dylan had performed his song as usual at the Coliseum in Denver, Colorado, on the evening of 6 February. As usual, those once-prophetic lines had caused whoops and cheers. That very day the House of Representatives in the 93rd Congress had approved a resolution 'providing appropriate power to the Committee on the Judiciary to conduct an investigation of whether sufficient grounds exist to impeach Richard M. Nixon, President of the United States'. A little less than a fortnight later, just after Dylan's tour had ended, the Senate committee investigating the labyrinthine Watergate affair would end its public hearings. The 39th president had nowhere left to hide. Impeachment was inevitable if he failed to resign.

When the articles of impeachment appeared at the end of July, they could not have been more damning. But then, how else could a president fall if not thanks to 'high crimes and misdemeanours'? In the matter of Watergate, Nixon had obstructed justice, violated his oath and his constitutional duty, then conspired 'to cover up, conceal and protect those responsible and to conceal the existence and scope of other unlawful covert activities'. There was more.

This president had commissioned lies, condoned lies and been party to the withholding of evidence. He had bought silence and attempted to influence witnesses, tried to misuse the power of the CIA and, not least, 'made false or misleading public statements for the purpose of deceiving the people of the United States' into believing that White House misconduct had been investigated.

Nixon had abused his power shamelessly and repeatedly by attempting to tamper with both the tax service and the FBI in an effort to confound 'enemies'. Finally, thanks to his disdain for subpoenas, he had been flagrantly in contempt of Congress. It would take decades of careful, assiduous PR work to bring this sepulchre back to any semblance of whiteness. Candour, poetically enough, would have nothing to do with it.

Nixon would go nowhere near a jail, of course. Few at the time were surprised by that. Awash with self-pity, apparently still sustained by his most famous lie – 'I'm not a crook' – he would resign in August and receive a pardon from his successor, Gerald Ford. Some 70 minions, bagmen, burglars, dirty-tricks artists and bit players would be less fortunate.

The shock to American belief in America was profound. Some of that was echoed – anticipated and echoed – in 'It's Alright, Ma'. That he had sensed the impending disillusionment fully a decade before the Watergate crisis was taken as confirmation of Dylan's genius. According to a *Newsweek* report in January of '74, his performance of the song on the tour's opening night in Chicago 'even inspired one man to rip off his clothes and declare his presidential candidacy on the spot'. But Dylan had written 'It's Alright, Ma' in 1964, and detected the rot, and foreseen contempt for authority figures, when his own understanding of political engagement had begun to alter. Those existentialist lines – 'But even the president of the United States / Sometimes must have to stand naked' – had not been intended as a comment on judicial process.

A decade later, the arena crowds could cheer his intuitions all they liked. He would not, could not, resume the cursed role of spokesman. There was nothing in his recent repertoire that resembled 'It's Alright, Ma'. If audiences applauded what sounded like a judgement on Nixon, they were indulging in nostalgia for the brave old world of protest. And nostalgia, as Dylan would tell the *Los Angeles Times* in 1992, 'is death'. Even amid the tumult of a constitutional crisis, he would not be lured into making political pronouncements. Those days were gone.

Vietnam and Watergate were reason enough for protest and what America, quaintly, would sometimes term 'social comment'. But when had Dylan last risked a simple statement of honest opinion? His songwriting no longer allowed such a thing. Even before the great exhaustion of 1966, even before the flirtations with Nashville and the desperate, nomadic search for privacy, he had denounced that conceit (and by implication denounced his younger self). In his now unshakeable opinion no one who claimed to know the truth, least of all a mere singer, deserved serious attention: the act of making the claim was proof of bad faith, of ignorance and illusion. Equally, pronouncements on issues of the day were antithetical, somehow, to creativity. Passing controversies, slogans and ideologies and positions, had nothing important to do with the permanent truths of art.

Such, at least, had been Dylan's reasoning. Fundamentally, he didn't want the job. He had tasted 'leadership' and the experience had horrified him. To be expected to think in a certain way, to speak and perform in a certain pre-approved manner, was more than he could bear. A clumsy couplet in 'Wedding Song' on *Planet Waves* was blunt enough: 'It's never been my duty to remake the world at large / Nor is it my intention to sound a battle charge.' He would not have that kind of greatness thrust upon him. By the early 1970s, only a deity could have dented his indifference.

It remains a mistake, nevertheless, to imagine that Dylan somehow relinquished his intelligence, or that politics, politics in the broadest and deepest sense, would disappear entirely from his music simply because he cancelled his subscription to this cause or that movement. His objections were specific: he was no one's glove puppet. He would not be taken for granted. This didn't mean he ceased to think or, however subtly, to voice his thoughts.

That summer Dylan was on his farm in Minnesota, drafting and redrafting a song about deceit, general and particular. 'Idiot Wind' would range across the bleak territory of a broken marriage and tear through the storm of dishonesty sweeping the republic. *Blood on the Tracks*, the album he would record later in the year, would be categorised as 'personal', confessional, autobiographical. Dylan was too acute, too artistically slippery, to fall headlong into that trap. 'Idiot Wind' would descend sometimes into vicious petulance, but the old knack for finding a universal allegory in a personal circumstance survived. While justice kept its appointment with Nixon, Dylan was shaping an image of democracy's decay that would stagger Allen Ginsberg. In a 1976 interview with Peter Barry Chowka for *New Age Journal*, the poet argued that the song was 'one of Dylan's great, great prophetic national songs, with one rhyme that took in the whole nation'.

Idiot wind, blowing like a circle around my skull
From the Grand Coulee Dam to the Capitol
Idiot wind, blowing every time you move your teeth
You're an idiot, babe
It's a wonder that you still know how to breathe

*

A few weeks after his tour's end in Inglewood, California, on 14 February 1974, Dylan was back in New York, studying painting and pondering the state of his marriage. If half the rumours reaching the press and TV were true – by August, even *Rolling Stone* would see fit to make note of the gossip – he had done himself no favours and hurt Sara Dylan deeply with his failure to resist the sexual temptations available to a superstar on the road. The album he would write and record later in the year would persuade many listeners, meanwhile, that the couple's problems ran deeper than a few casual betrayals.

Who really knows, or has the right to know? There is the unanswered question of cause and effect. Unhappiness caused by infidelity, or vice versa? There is the fact that Sara Dylan has kept her memories and thoughts to herself, held fast in absolute privacy. There is the fact that those who read *Blood on the Tracks* like an open letter harbour a naive idea of what pronouns might (or might not) signify in a song. Finally, there is the fact that Dylan has said only a few enigmatic things down the years to explain – to appear to explain – what happened to his first marriage.

In 1978, notably, he would tell the *Dallas Morning News* that the study of painting was the true beginning of his estrangement from Sara. It was during his lessons, Dylan said, that 'our marriage started breaking up'. She ceased to understand him, he would recall. For whatever reason – that part would remain obscure – she no longer grasped what he was saying or thinking. Dylan, meanwhile, 'couldn't possibly explain it'.

You could call it a strange tale. In this anecdote, the most famous 'break-up album' of them all arose from insights gleaned during the studies that helped to cause the break-up. Further, the meaning of separation and loss is explored – in several of the songs, at least – through methods acquired in the classes that hastened separation and loss. There is no such word as meta-irony, but there ought to be.

Blood on the Tracks is something more than the diary of a divorce, but if Dylan's account was correct his songwriting was revived and transformed in the second half of the 1970s by a tangle of events, illuminations and misapprehensions. The strange part is that once you have read his explanation, it colours every subsequent experience of the marvellous entangling songs. In blue, mostly.

The teacher in question, an enigmatic, grouchy, Ukrainian-born multilingual septuagenarian named Norman Raeben, would contribute only a little to his pupil's painterly skills but have a lasting effect on his perceptions. Dylan would characterise him as uncompromising and wholly unimpressed by fame. Supposedly, if you can believe such a thing of an encounter set in New York City in 1974, Raeben had no real idea that a famous singer was one of the less-gifted beginners in his studio on the 11th floor at Carnegie Hall. That part of the anecdote is questionable. For his part, Dylan was, let's say, more familiar with the famous concert venue than most.[1]

For a couple of months, nevertheless, the pupil worked dutifully, from 8 a.m. or so until 4 p.m., five days a week, under the irascible Raeben's guidance, and spent the rest of his time pondering the deeper meaning of the artist's dictums. Striving to show a class full of off-duty cops, bus drivers, young acolytes and rich old ladies how to look and truly see, the tutor was raising questions about identity, intuition, perspective, illusive time and unmediated creativity. So Dylan believed, at any rate. *Blood on the Tracks*, on his accounting, was a direct result of Raeben's urgings and of an erstwhile college dropout's return to school.

In one sense, Raeben was repeating the offer made by Joseph Conrad in the preface to *The Nigger of the Narcissus* (1897). His task, wrote the novelist, was 'to make you hear, to make you feel – it is, before all, to make you *see* . . . If I succeed, you shall find there according to your deserts: encouragement, consolation, fear, charm – all you demand; and, perhaps, also that glimpse of truth for which you have forgotten to ask.' Raeben added an insight of his own on the relationship between time and the visual image that was, for Dylan, more startling and infinitely more suggestive. Of itself, this was odd.

As the singer explained to several interviewers a few years later, time ceases to exist within a painting – the flower doesn't wither, the clouds don't move – but continues for the oblivious observer. Which is the illusion? Dylan would also sometimes stress the difference between seeing the parts of a picture and grasping the whole. His stroke of genius was to apply these ideas, trite enough in themselves, to his own art form in 1974.

Like Conrad's fiction, a song is time-bound; it begins and ends. In music, time in its several senses is everything. *Blood on the Tracks* would dispute the fact. What made the triumph odd, however, was that Dylan treated the illumination as something new, and forgot – or was persuaded to forget – that he had mastered time before, most notably in 'Visions of Johanna' on the 1966 album *Blonde on Blonde*. In that song, too, he had played fast and loose with pronouns, permitted identity to become provisional, transposed or overlaid scenes, and allowed the perception of time to become fluid. But in 1974 he and everyone else seemed to forget all the things he had ever known of her, him, them, it, then and now.

Listen to 'Visions' and state who 'he' is. State the time, in any given verse, in relation to subjective time in any other verse. The *Blonde on Blonde* song, like several others on the album, exploits film grammar rather than paint to achieve the effect. But the fact of its existence acts as an overdue reminder that one of Dylan's achievements in *Blood on the Tracks* was not without precedent, whatever the writer chose to believe. The important achievement, especially in the mutability cantos of 'Tangled Up in Blue', was formal. It had to do with language, specifically diction, and emotion. Dylan in his high-'60s swagger, fascinated by dissociation and chaos, had not even paused to consider such a connection. Back then, words had poured from him in a near-spontaneous flood. Older, becoming wiser, he tried to canalise emotions by formal means, through tenses and verse structures, in order to find sense in the shapes he gave them. But life, not the rhetorical gambits of Norman Raeben, caused *Blood on the Tracks*.

The insights of Dylan's mentor have not brought the late painter – who died of a heart attack in December 1978 – much in the way of a posthumous reputation. Art was not revolutionised, it seems, by his interest in synchronicity, or by his insistence on an intense way of seeing. The attention paid to Raeben these days is, rightly or wrongly, most often due to his brief association with Dylan. The singer would nevertheless assert that *Blood on the Tracks* possessed no sense of time thanks to Raeben. Instead, the record contained a 'code' – always a word to feed to certain fans – in its lyrics. You might wonder whether 'code' is itself a kind of code, of course, in Dylan's involuted language. The single known fact is that the album was conceived, written and recorded while his relationship with Sara was cracking and crumbling. To deny that the songs are entirely autobiographical is not to deny that they are drawn, some of them, from life.

One claim is beyond dispute: the verses of any song are parts, inescapably, of the whole. *Blood on the Tracks* does not stoop to anything as banal as a 'concept' – its maker, unlike certain of his contemporaries, didn't fall for that one – but it possesses a coherence that is formal, emotional and tonal. Art is united in the person, or at least in the persona created. Dylan had begun to ask how the constituent elements of an album might function together.

*

Early in 1974 he had purchased a 100-acre farm on the Crow River, in north-western Hennepin County, Minnesota. The spread, close to the small town of Hanover and perhaps 40 minutes from Minneapolis, had also become home to his brother, David, and to David's family. After his experiences with Raeben had caused Sara to cease to 'understand' him, Dylan took refuge in his home state, amid the landscape he knew best. Hopes of a pastoral idyll were fading with his marriage, but at the farm there was a studio for painting, a slow tributary of the Mississippi flowing by, and freedom from all the freaks and grasping obsessives bewitched by 'Bob Dylan' who were liable to render Greenwich Village uninhabitable. In the summer he came to Minnesota, without his wife but not entirely alone. For part of the time, at least, a young woman named Ellen Bernstein, an employee of Columbia Records, was with him.

Dylan was 33 years old, a revolutionary who had outlived his revolution, a family man whose family's core was disintegrating, a formerly instinctive artist struggling to reawaken his instincts, and a performer who seemed, on the evidence of the late 1960s and early 1970s, to have exhausted most creative possibilities. Any one of those facts might have served as a good place to begin to start again.

That summer he began to fill a small, cheap notebook – red, as you are always reminded – with verses enough for seventeen songs, though only ten were placed on the album and only a dozen have seen the light of day. The notebook contained more than he would need. As his subsequent editorial decisions would demonstrate, one mark of the concentrated, distilled quality of *Blood on the Tracks* is that Dylan never intended to allow it to sprawl, in that pre-digital age, into another of those tricky double albums.

As it was he would push his luck, technically, with a piece of vinyl running to almost 52 minutes of playing time when the experts in these matters decreed, as they still decree, that 22 minutes a side represents the outer limit of acceptable audio quality. A longer single album was close to an impossibility. By the time he was satisfied with his verses, and had begun to play the songs for friends and acquaintances, the hour's worth of material at his disposal was insufficient for a two-record set, but too much for one disc. Choices were required.[2]

Many critics and fans would later contend that the marvellous 'Up to Me', at over six minutes, was dropped because it was 'too similar' to 'Shelter from the Storm'. Discussing the former in his 1985 notes to the *Biograph* compendium, Cameron Crowe would certainly label it a 'companion piece' to the song used on *Blood on the Tracks*. It is hard, however, to connect the apocalyptic imagery of 'Shelter from the Storm' with the strange remembered road movie that is 'Up to Me'. Besides, the recordings made by Dylan in New York in September 1974, the ones he fully intended to release before second thoughts intervened, are hardly a musically diverse bunch. The same three or four chords are favoured; open tunings are everywhere in evidence; lyrics with a religious flavour – the only real connection between the two songs – are scarcely rare. The evidence suggests that Dylan dropped a great piece for entirely pragmatic reasons.

It is even possible that the sequencing of the songs on the finished record, a source of much speculation and analysis, was a hard-headed concession to the engineers who would have to master the disc. 'High-frequency content' survives best on the outer edges of such an artefact. You finish sides with lighter, shorter tracks if you want to maintain sound quality. 'Up to Me' did not fit that bill. To suggest such a thing of any Dylan work is blasphemy, of course.

The first sessions for *Blood on the Tracks* were held at A&R Studios at 799 7th Avenue in New York. Previously known as Columbia's Studio A, it was the successor to the hit factory where Dylan had once upon a time recorded six of his finest albums. The first session was held on 16 September, with the artist taking on the duties of producer and the vastly experienced Phil Ramone – the R in A&R – in charge of the engineering.

On that first morning Ramone encountered and promptly hired the multi-instrumentalist Eric Weissberg and his band Deliverance for the evening's session. They had all the necessary skills. Weissberg could read music and play any instrument liable to be required for recordings in the folk(ish) style. Much good it did him. Dylan arrived and almost immediately began to play, allowing Deliverance little time to notate the music. His tunings were meanwhile strange and unfamiliar, but he made no allowances. Mistakes didn't seem to trouble him. If his shirt buttons rattled audibly on his guitar's body, or if the sound of scraping fingernails could be heard, Dylan ignored the distraction. Spontaneity, aided by a good deal of wine, was once again his guiding principle. He had worked hard on his songs, rewriting or discarding verses, determined to stay true to Raeben's principles. Deliverance, like so many musicians before, would have to shift for themselves.

Ten songs were recorded during the first session. Half a dozen of those, it seems, were somehow put on tape with the aid of Deliverance. Takes of 'Idiot Wind', 'Lily, Rosemary and the Jack of Hearts' and 'Meet Me in the Morning' passed muster. The remainder were set aside. On the next day, Dylan decided that henceforth he needed only the help of the band's bassist, Tony Brown, and an organist who had worked on *Highway 61 Revisited* named Paul Griffin. Most of the members of Deliverance had been fired, in other words. 'You're a Big Girl Now', 'Shelter from the Storm' and 'You're Gonna Make Me Lonesome When You Go' were then added to the list of takes meeting the artist's specifications.

Not for the first time, Dylan was working at lightning speed. He was working, in fact, much as he had done in his very first sessions under the guidance of John Hammond, back in the winter of 1961, in those selfsame studios. He knew no other way, and didn't care to learn.

The *Blood on the Tracks* songs were now clear in his head. He expected trained musicians to be able to keep up, no matter what. Nevertheless, his approach to the making of an acknowledged masterwork was a reminder of a curious fact. Dylan had made his name and found fame as a recording artist and yet in reality he was no such thing, at least not as the term is commonly understood. He disliked the entire process and compromised with it grudgingly. In this, he was as much of a purist as the old folk crowd.

In Dylan's mind, the studio destroyed the essence of music. He consented to overdubs, for example, only with extreme reluctance. As Deliverance were quick to realise, the technical deficiencies in a recording counted for nothing alongside the vitality, the substance, the living heart of a performance. Dylan took a lot of risks, in short, to preserve his idea of real music-making. It would take him decades to come to terms with the consequences of his convictions.

On the afternoon and early evening of the 18th, Dylan made a couple of attempts at 'Buckets of Rain', the half-hopeful track destined to close the finished album, with only the steel guitar player Buddy Cage for company. During the next session, running from Thursday night on the 19th into the early hours of Friday morning, with Tony Brown serving as lone accompanist, Dylan attempted almost three dozen takes of various songs and achieved five he thought good enough to count as finished articles. It seemed he had done it again, just as in the old days: an entire album in something less than a working week. And not just any album.

It was then that he realised that he had made more music than a single vinyl disc could accommodate. 'Up to Me', a song most people would have saved at all costs, was removed from the running order. It would remain hidden until the release of the *Biograph* box set a decade later. As is too often forgotten, however, an album based only on the sessions recorded in New York was even longer, by a good couple of minutes at least, than the album that would eventually see the light of day. Test pressings of *Blood on the Tracks* were made regardless; artwork was commissioned. A new Dylan album would be ready for the Christmas holiday market.

Then the artist had second thoughts. The standard account holds that while on a December visit to the farm in Minnesota he was convinced by his brother that the album as planned, the album that was set and ready to go, lacked a necessary commercial edge. What was said, if it was said, has been elaborated by a lot of people who were not present. David Zimmerman supposedly argued that the record was too stark, too bare, too daunting. Given that Dylan had set out to make a plain, unadorned and low-key album, this should not have counted as a problem. When, for that matter, had he ever abandoned work on the advice of his beloved brother? The precise origins of the anecdote are elusive. In his 2001 biography of Dylan, Howard Sounes identified the artist himself as being 'still unhappy about approximately half the tracks he had recorded in New York'.[3] Then, and only then, did brother David suggest a local solution.

But who cares? The masterpiece called *Blood on the Tracks* is the commercially available version you can buy readily. The test pressing, the so-called *New York Sessions* bootleg, is lovely, startling and arguably superior, especially where 'Idiot Wind' is concerned. But Dylan's decision to re-record, and to do so with a group of local unknowns, speaks of a creeping indecision, an early symptom of the self-doubt that would afflict him in the years to come. *Blood on the Tracks* in either incarnation would have stood as a remarkable achievement, yet he doubted himself, or was talked into doubting himself.

As it was, he demonstrated yet again that the juvenile medium of pop was capable of an unsuspected maturity. In the 1960s he had shown that popular songs could aspire to the status of literature, that – at worst – a song could be crammed full of metaphors, images and ideas more usually associated with poetry than with teen romance. In that decade, Dylan had shown what could be done with the slippery notion of sensibility. With *Blood on the Tracks* he turned his 'break-up' into a meditation on time, impermanence and loss. One of his subjects – he had a few – was the essential isolation of the human individual, the ache that love couldn't cure. As in all the best poetry, this was shown, not stated. Those stories by Anton Chekhov, the ones he would mention as inspiration almost 30 years later in his book *Chronicles: Volume One*, remain entirely plausible candidates for Dylan's model.

At a place called Sound 80 Studios in Minneapolis, close to his Dinkytown stamping-grounds from his very earliest days as a student dropout and apprentice folkie, Dylan repaired the perceived flaws in *Blood on the Tracks* with a little borrowed 1934 0042G Martin guitar and the help of a pick-up band of local musicians (who never did receive credit). Five tracks were replaced, though whether the substitutes count as an improvement is a matter of opinion. Some such as Clinton Heylin have quibbled, persuasively enough, over a few rewritten lines; others over a 'loss of focus'. This writer contends that the final version of 'Idiot Wind', alone among the released recordings, edges a little too close to melodrama. It is, as Heylin has also observed, 'overwrought'. The control shown by Dylan elsewhere on the record, the delicacy of emotional interplay, is lost. He lets rip; he allows what sounds in places like self-pity and spite to get the better of him.

When the album appeared, several of the better-known rock critics expressed disappointment, if not disdain, picking out allegedly sloppy musicianship. In Britain, the *New Musical Express* even called the accompaniments 'trashy'. *Rolling Stone*'s reviewer, Jon Landau, wrote of 'typical shoddiness'. On occasion, the bizarre hybrid form styling itself 'rock journalism' was shown to be just as empty-headed as Dylan had always alleged. Wisdom prevailed in the end, shortly followed by unquestioning reverence. The record-buying public in America and Britain had meanwhile voted for *Blood on the Tracks* en masse, turning it into a big hit on both sides of the Atlantic.

*

Blood on the Tracks is the musical and literary equivalent of the painter's penetrating gaze. An album of popular songs – a suite would be the fancier description – was ideal for Dylan's concentrated purpose. It counts as an obvious fact, but one often overlooked, strangely enough, when the arguments over poetry resume. The artist would discover the truth for himself when he tried to become a film-maker. He had encountered it in the mid-'60s, to his immense frustration, when embarking on the novel that wound up in disarray as the 'prose experiment' *Tarantula*. Song was the only medium in which he truly functioned artistically. Only in songs could verbal compression be combined with narrative, the internal logic of imagery – his imagery above all – and the emotional colouring of melody. That much is, or ought to be, self-evident. But in Dylan's hands, on *Blood on the Tracks*, song became something more expansive than poetry. The usual charge against his art should have been turned on its head. The problem, if it ever was a problem, was not that his 'poems' failed to 'work on the page'. The printed page was an utterly inadequate expression, a hollow echo, of the performed songs. Write about what Dylan wrote and you have not begun to say even the half of it. Everything said about this artist's work is paraphrase.

Between September and December of 1974 five *Blood on the Tracks* songs were remade. The effect, in several cases, was to depersonalise the works slightly, as though Dylan was putting a safe distance between himself and the belief that he was engaged in naked autobiography. Any judgement remains a matter of opinion. Perhaps he wanted to prevent his audience from getting the wrong idea about private truths and public art, or perhaps he realised that he had gone too far, revealed too much, and invaded his own privacy.

Equally, a song such as the long ballad-fable 'Lily, Rosemary and the Jack of Hearts', recorded first in New York with just Dylan's guitar, is not easily explained, even as metaphor, as the story of a marriage. Those who care to take the alleged esoteric wisdom of Tarot cards seriously might find a nuptial allegory in the verse-movie. There is also an obvious sense in this tale's plot that life is a performance and a game, that fate is the luck of the draw. Dylan is happy enough, meanwhile, to find symbolism in a frontier story: you don't call your elusive man of mystery the Jack of Hearts for nothing. But you could equally argue that the writer is as interested in extending his beloved ballad tradition as he is in supplying puzzles for critical analysis.

He had dabbled often enough before in gambling songs. The fourth poem from his 'Some Other Kinds of Songs' on the sleeve of 1964's *Another Side of Bob Dylan* had taken its inspiration, and a line or several, from the old blues piece 'Jack o' Diamonds (Is a Hard Card to Play)'. Whether Dylan knew it from Blind Lemon Jefferson, Tex Ritter, Odetta or Mance Lipscomb is neither here nor there. Playing card imagery had long been his stock-in-trade, as it would remain. 'Lily, Rosemary' does not fit easily, for all that, with the supposed 'break-up' theme of *Blood on the Tracks*.[4]

'Shelter from the Storm' is another of the album's songs that could be represented as an allegory on mystical bonds, but in no possible sense is it a literal account of marital relationships. Dylan might now and again mythologise his existence and its travails, but if autobiography lies in these verses it is buried so deep as to be invisible. At best, you could say that he has given the most profound aspects of marriage a fictional setting, slap in the middle of a landscape that is part biblical, part western and part apocalyptic. The song contains one of his very finest couplets: 'Well, I'm livin' in a foreign country, but I'm bound to cross the line / Beauty walks a razor's edge, someday I'll make it mine.' But the writer who wants to 'turn back the clock to when God and her were born' is not talking about a long-married couple drifting apart.

Such truths did Dylan no good, in any event. *Blood on the Tracks* was filed instantly under 'autobiography', where it has remained. It was deemed a record about a break-up, 'lost love', pain, loneliness and redemptive hope. It is all those things, of course, but it is more than that. Dylan, you suspect, couldn't help himself. His songs had always enlarged the meaning of personal experience. He had never believed, like so many of the singer-songwriters who followed in his wake, that an event was of consuming importance simply because it had happened to him. *Blood on the Tracks* had to do with what it meant to be human, with the struggle of those born alone to communicate with one another. In his otherwise-hyperbolic original sleeve notes for the album, the journalist Pete Hamill had rightly called this 'the quarrel of the self'.

Interviewed by *Rolling Stone* in 1978, Dylan said of the song 'Tangled

Up in Blue': 'What's different about it is that there's a code in the lyrics, and there's also no sense of time. There's no respect for it. You've got yesterday, today and tomorrow all in the same room, and there's very little you can't imagine not happening.' Such was the art and craft underpinning the work. It made the confessional aspects of the song and the album almost incidental.

*

Once again, the Dylans attempted to repair their marriage. Love and pride endured, it seems, despite the self-knowledge gained in the writing of the *Blood on the Tracks* songs, and despite the profound bitterness revealed in certain verses of 'Idiot Wind'. It was one odd, ironic aspect of the album: Dylan had achieved a new 'mature' understanding of the human condition, but in his own life he continued to flounder.

He drifted from coast to coast, listening to music, attending parties, performing at a schools benefit in San Francisco organised in March by the promoter Bill Graham. Sara was with him at the show, but whatever hopes she or Dylan entertained for their union were soon confounded. As spring turned towards summer he was in the south of France, spending six weeks with his friend the painter David Oppenheim, and celebrating his 34th birthday with a bout of hedonism that Oppenheim would call 'pathetic and superb'. Interviewed by the (now extinct) fanzine *Fourth Time Around*, the painter would also remember his friend as lost, confused and despairing, afraid even to sleep alone.

Dylan had expected his wife to join him in Europe, but he was disappointed, bitterly so. He called her frequently, to no avail. By now, the message was very clear. Her patience was at an end, her tolerance and support all but gone. The couple would not be divorced finally until the summer of 1977, amid horrific rancour, but by that time only the formalities remained. There would be other attempts to find ways to renew their vows before the lawyers intervened, but Sara's refusal to drop everything and fly across the Atlantic was an unmistakable declaration. By the middle of 1975, to all intents and human purposes, the marriage was over.

In France, looking out over vineyards under a pink sky, Dylan once again pulled himself together. His marriage had failed, but his work remained. He decided to remind people of what, in essence, he was. At that moment, work was all that truly remained for an artist who could not be sustained by celebrity alone. In some strange way he was renewed by the fact. The old tenacity, the defiance of every circumstance,

46

reasserted itself. When people ask how it is that this artist endures, decade after decade, one simple answer is stubborn pride.

The summer of 1975 found him in familiar New York haunts, particularly the old Bitter End club on Bleecker Street in the Village, close to the corner with LaGuardia Place and a short walk from his Houston Street loft. For reasons best known to its owners – who would soon acknowledge the mistake – the old joint had been renamed The Other End. Or rather, the club had been absorbed in February of 1974 by its newly acquired adjacent sibling. Crucially, the latter possessed a liquor licence. There Dylan was soon drinking his wine, listening to music, and meeting old friends such as Ramblin' Jack Elliott and Bobby Neuwirth. For a few weeks he was granted the illusion of privacy in a public place. Those with whom he chose to socialise were allowed to approach the presence; the curious and importunate were kept at bay. It was as much as he could hope for.

Dylan was also beginning to wonder what he could do next in his perplexing career. Concert performances built around the *Blood on the Tracks* songs would have been a fascinating proposition, but the notion seems never to have crossed his mind. The writing and recording of that album had each been singular events, born in the moment, and born of the pressure of experience. The achievement was impossible to repeat and he had no desire to try. As usual, Dylan had begun to move on.

A work finished was not a work forgotten, exactly, but already his acclaimed new album was, for him, a thing of the past. As he began to join performers on stage at The Other End, nevertheless, an idea of performance was beginning to form in his mind. He was striking up new acquaintances and soaking up the old communal energy of the Village. Plenty of celebrities had begun to cluster around the club that summer, but the ambience was – or so they and Dylan chose to believe – a world away from the superstar nonsense, the stadiums, limousines, private jets and idolatry, that had marred the 1974 tour with The Band. Perhaps there was another way for him to take his music to the people, and to deal, finally, with the entities he had named Bob Dylan.

*

Just as *Blood on the Tracks* was being released in January of 1975, Dylan decided to allow portions of the celebrated basement tapes to see the light of day. Not once would he manage a convincing explanation for this remarkable change of heart. He had long dismissed the great songs recorded casually in the vicinity of Woodstock in upper New York State during the summer and autumn of 1967 as being of no account. In late 1969 he had told *Rolling Stone* that the tracks were merely demos, that he had been 'pushed into coming up with songs'. Even when afflicted by writer's block in the first years of the decade, when partial bootlegs of the tapes were becoming commonplace, he had declined, with a single near-pointless exception, to draw on a catalogue that included 'This Wheel's On Fire' and 'I Shall Be Released'.

Talking in April of '75 to Mary Travers (she of Peter, Paul and Mary) on KNX-FM Los Angeles for his first radio interview since 1966, Dylan was less than illuminating. A couple of months before Columbia's *The Basement Tapes* received its release, he said:

> The records have been exposed throughout the years so somebody mentioned it was a good idea to put it out, you know, as a record, so people could hear it in its entirety and know exactly what we were doing up there in those years.

Given that he had taken charge of the project, the 'somebody' was almost certainly Robbie Robertson, The Band's guitar player. Dylan had played no real part in the archaeological effort to collect and restore the old tapes. It seems likely, in fact, that he had no clear memory of exactly what the reels of disdained recordings contained. Hence the entirely misleading claim that record-buyers would hear the Woodstock work 'in its entirety'. *Blood on the Tracks*, an international hit, had just spent a fortnight at the top of the *Billboard* album chart: Dylan had no need of product to satisfy the record company, no requirement for further acclaim. Nevertheless, his attitude towards the 1967 recordings was curious, as it would remain.

Robertson, for his part, sounded disingenuous when he got around to attempting to explain how *The Basement Tapes* came to be released. He failed even to offer a convincing explanation for his own motives. Interviewed by *Crawdaddy* magazine for its March 1976 edition, the guitarist was certain only that the legal version of the basement recordings had not been produced to 'combat' the tenacious bootleggers. Robertson said:

> All of a sudden it seemed like a good idea. I can't tell you why or anything. It just popped up one day. We thought we'd see what we had. I started going through the stuff and sorting it out, trying to make it

stand up for a record that wasn't recorded professionally. I also tried to include some things that people haven't heard before, if possible . . . I just wanted to document a period rather than let them rot away on the shelves somewhere. It was an unusual time which caused all those songs to be written and it was better it be put on disc some way than be lost in an attic.

It was one thing to refuse to look back, but Dylan had a large blind spot where this part of his work was concerned. Several of the songs had provided hits for other artists. A good number had been praised to the skies by the usual critics. Who writes 'I Shall Be Released' and acts as though it's a bagatelle to be rearranged and added, almost as an afterthought, to a makeshift greatest-hits package? In April of 1975, nevertheless, Dylan was still telling Travers that the basement songs were 'written like in five, ten minutes, you know' while he and his musicians were 'drying out' in their rural retreat. No big deal, then.

If he had been paying more attention, Dylan might have thought twice about some of the choices made by Robertson. After a wave of approbation for *The Basement Tapes* from critics primed for genuflection – the *New York Times* burst a corset and called the set 'one of the greatest albums in the history of American popular music' – questions were asked. Why had tracks recorded primarily in basic stereo been collapsed into mono if not to give a fake 'primitive' patina to the sound? Who thought it clever to add overdubs of drums, keyboards and guitar to several performances on this 'historic document'? How come one-third of the twenty-four tracks offered were by The Band – who would receive commensurate royalties – when most buyers were interested, first and foremost, in the songwriter of the age? By 14 August, *Rolling Stone*'s gossip column, 'Random Notes', was reporting 'a Columbia insider' to the effect that Dylan had demanded $1 million for consenting to the album 'because he wanted to help out The Band, who he reportedly said was [*sic*] having financial problems (denied by a Band spokesman)'. It was soon discovered, in any case, that half of the recordings selected by Robertson to represent his group's contribution had either not been made in 1967, or had not originated in the improvised studios of Woodstock.

The original basement tapes ran to between 120 and 130 recordings, depending on how false starts, stoned jokes and a handful of allegedly 'missing' titles are calculated. These days, after sterling remastering work by the bootleggers, a compendium with 124 takes is easy enough to obtain. Yet, for the sake of The Band, Dylan's fans were obliged in 1975 to do without 'I Shall Be Released', 'The Mighty Quinn', 'I'm Not There', 'Sign on the Cross', 'Silent Weekend', 'All You Have to Do Is Dream' and even the glorious fun, interruptions and all, of 'I'm a Fool for You'. That was before anyone mentioned the numerous traditional songs and cover versions attempted in 1967. Dylan's performances could have filled a couple of fine vinyl double albums easily.

Despite it all, and in defiance of the approbation granted to the work, he gave no sign that he cared. Subsequently he would fail to disguise his contempt when attempts were made to identify those covert, subterranean recordings as the founding artefacts for an ill-defined musical movement known as Americana. He would have no taste whatever for the grand cultural theories piled around the monuments raised to this phase of his career. Something about the circumstances surrounding the Woodstock recordings, or perhaps just the recordings themselves, had left him dissatisfied and defensive.

You can easily believe, of course, that the success of *Blood on the Tracks* could have been enough to persuade Dylan finally to countenance an album based on the tapes. The former gave plenty of cover, commercially and creatively, for the latter. Nevertheless, a simple fact is worth repeating: even in the worst of times, paralysed by writer's block and self-doubt at the end of the 1960s and the beginning of the 1970s, he had refused to exploit the great songs of 1967 seriously.

His only concession had come in the autumn of 1971, in the depths of his creative drought, when Columbia had proposed the mistitled double-album stopgap *More Bob Dylan Greatest Hits*. Dylan had suggested that one side should contain previously unreleased material, but on this occasion the company had been oblivious to the appeal of 'the legendary basement tapes'. He had therefore re-recorded three of the 1967 songs in an afternoon and put them on an album that did not contain too many certifiable hits. That had been the limit of his interest.

Few others would have hesitated in lean times to fortify flimsy albums with 'Too Much of Nothing' or 'Goin' to Acapulco'. Nevertheless, eight years after the fact, with *Blood* fast becoming established as one of his finest achievements, no one was liable to accuse Dylan of desperate measures, or of recycling his own legend. In any case, the bootleg industry and a host of cover versions had already settled the matter. The reviews for *The Basement Tapes* were preordained, if not already written. The only person who seemed to dissent was Bob Dylan.

According to Rob Fraboni, the studio engineer given the job of restoring the original basement recordings, the artist spent next to no time overseeing the work. It was all one to him, it seems, whether the original, spooky stereo sound captured by The Band's Garth Hudson was rendered into that spurious 'authentic' mono at the behest of Robbie Robertson. Above all, Dylan appeared not to care about the songs involved. If 'copyright issues' between himself and his estranged manager, Albert Grossman, had ever been at stake, they were no longer relevant by the summer of 1975. Dylan simply refused to take seriously all the praise that had been showered on his compositions. Omit 'I'm Not There'? Sanction an album that misrepresented the work done at Woodstock and the legends born of that work? As he seemed to say, 'What of it?' In a way, he had a point. The legal double album entitled *The Basement Tapes*, since greatly improved by a 2009 remastering exercise, would stand in its own right as a significant event in pop's small universe.

There is, in any case, rubbish aplenty in the remainder of the mythologised bootleg corpus; enough of it, certainly, to rebut some of the extravagant acclaim and the socio-historical theorising. The Woodstock recordings embrace a fair number of duds and worse. There are numerous tracks to which no serious (or sober) artist would lend his name. Nevertheless, Dylan's disdain even towards the official release and what it was supposed to represent stands as an early example of the wilful artistic self-harm that would become commonplace in the succeeding decades. But nothing in his world is forever.

After touring South America, Central America and Europe in 2012, Dylan returned to the US in the autumn of the year. At first his concert set seemed to follow the structure that had become familiar to audiences across the world throughout the year. Then, at a casino's 10,000-seat arena in Uncasville, Connecticut, as though out of nowhere (appropriately enough), Dylan opened with one of his less-favoured songs. Why choose 'You Ain't Goin' Nowhere', a 45-year-old tune from a body of work he had often disparaged? Only he could say. Before long, however, the song had become one of Dylan's regular opening numbers. As the tour drew to a close in Brooklyn, New York, at November's end, there it was again, a piece of the past redeemed.

CHAPTER THREE

A Wanderer by Trade

IN 1975, FOR ALL THAT THE WORLD KNEW, THE SUCCESS OF *Blood on the Tracks* had replenished Dylan's self-confidence. Certain of the reviewers had hedged their bets, or grumbled vacuously over 'production', but half a million copies of the album had been sold within three weeks of its release. Critics changed their tunes soon enough. By the summer of the year it appeared that Dylan's old, weird amnesia had been banished for good. Not only had he created a record to surpass *Planet Waves* easily, he had done something inimitably new, once again, with the songwriter's art.

The cascading popularity of FM radio in the mid-1970s, with its so-called 'integrity programming' and its allegiance to 'album-oriented rock', was perfectly timed for the newly 'mature' artist. The length of a track was no impediment to the free-format AOR stations and the hippy DJs who refused to treat music as the next best thing to ambient noise. Ambitious recordings were no longer being chopped in half routinely, as had been the fate of 'Like a Rolling Stone', for the sake of airplay. Songs from *Blood on the Tracks* that would never have been granted a hearing as singles by traditional stations – even 'Tangled Up in Blue' only made it, just, to 31 in America – were given reverent attention. Each play demonstrated that Dylan was as powerful a writer as he had ever been. Surely he no longer had reason to fear the permanent loss of his creative faculties? He would choose a strange way to prove it.

While the likes of Patti Smith and Bette Midler congregated (and squabbled) at The Other End, while Bobby Neuwirth resumed his duties as courtier and master of ceremonies, Dylan began to wonder what might be made of all the talent that was gathering around him each night. The bass player Rob Stoner came to his attention, as did a teenaged multi-instrumentalist named David Mansfield. Mick Ronson, formerly the guitarist with David Bowie's Spiders from Mars band, came to call. Neuwirth was by now using his own club performances as de facto auditions for Dylan. The guitar player Steven Soles was invited along; the Texan who called himself T-Bone Burnett, another guitar player, arrived in town at Neuwirth's behest for 'more fun than the law allows'.[1]

Watching Ramblin' Jack Elliott perform on the first Thursday night in July would even prompt Dylan to give the dutifully awestruck club crowd a fine performance of an entirely new song called 'Abandoned Love'. Known for long enough as 'St John the Evangelist' thanks to a verse that the writer, typically, would later discard, the remarkable piece – in this performance, at any rate – would do Ramblin' Jack's own set no favours. As ever, that amiable man would raise no objections. Soon enough, under the guise of guest appearances during performances by Neuwirth, the artist was performing regularly.

Patti Smith, with whom he developed an affinity and a friendship in this period, had only just begun to complete the long transition from fringe performance poet to bandleader. She had yet to release an album when Dylan saw her perform her own 'Redondo Beach', a soon to be famous version of Them's 'Gloria', and the old Stones hit 'Time Is On My Side' at the end of June. He was taken with Smith in large part because of her honesty, her humour and her utter fearlessness as a performer. Though she would decline an invitation to sign up as cabin boy on Dylan's next voyage, she was given a better insight into his thinking than most of his old New York friends and colleagues. A 1975 feature in the short-lived *New Times* captured a moment: 'She and Bob Dylan sit at the top of tile stairs at a hush-hush Greenwich Village party, trading whispers like two schoolboys.' Smith would recall the conversation. Dylan 'had been in hiding for so long', she would tell Barry Miles in 1977.

> And he was working out this Rolling Thunder thing – he was thinking about improvisation, about extending himself language-wise. In the talks that we had there was something that he admired about me that was difficult to comprehend then, but that's what we were talking about. That's what we were talking about on the stairway . . .[2]

'This Rolling Thunder thing', when it came to fruition at the end of October, would involve transporting the human contents of an idealised

Greenwich Village club around the small towns, colleges, theatres and arenas of the Eastern Seaboard. It would attempt to rekindle the bohemian fantasy that had been the young Dylan's first inspiration. Rolling Thunder would assert an idea of what music and performance were *for* in a straightforward rejection of everything the imperial progress of Tour '74 had come to represent. It would be, in one sense, a last attempt to expose the figure of 'Bob Dylan' to scrutiny by the man who bore the name.

The 31 shows in Rolling Thunder's first incarnation would amount to a kind of erratic developing essay on identity, on disguises, on human contact. The concerts would also be, by turns, pretentious, acute, self-indulgent and enthralling. Rolling Thunder would become a piece of theatre, a radical artistic gesture, a travelling circus, a movable movie set, a gypsy caravan and the realisation, intermittently, of a superstar's old dream of creative emancipation. That was the general idea, at any rate.

Perhaps Dylan could just hit the road with a bunch of friends and allies, roll from town to town, play wherever he wanted, whenever he wanted, and be free at last of the entertainment industry's assumptions and diktats. There was only one way to find out. Strangely enough, the artist who had scorned the counter-culture and all its otiose free-form rhetoric was about to launch an enterprise that seemed, at least in its first phase, to be the culmination of every misty-eyed '60s hope. Romantic chatter, from participants and the media, would hang over the tour like a cloud of peculiarly fragrant smoke.

As Joan Baez later informed *Rolling Stone*'s dogged reporting team, the Rolling Thunder thing would be an 'offbeat, underground, weird medicine show'. Roger McGuinn, formerly of the Byrds and also along for the ride, would contribute the inspired opinion that 'this tour is like better than tripping out'. The poet and Dylan votary Allen Ginsberg, never knowingly undersold as a snake-oil salesman for blind optimism, would proclaim on behalf of the 100-strong expeditionary force that 'We have, once again, embarked on a voyage to reclaim America'.[3] First, in a gesture that counts as typically perverse, the artist found himself a writing partner.

Dylan had never before felt the need for a collaborator. He had worked with the prowling ghosts of the long-dead often enough in adapting or appropriating old songs. Richard Manuel of The Band had provided the melody for 'Tears of Rage' during the recording of the basement tapes, just as the group's Rick Danko had contributed to

'This Wheel's On Fire'. Refusing credit for his contribution, Dylan had helped McGuinn out on 'Ballad of Easy Rider' – with an opening couplet and a half scribbled on a napkin – for the soundtrack to the 1969 film. He had also part-written the banal 'I'd Have You Anytime' with George Harrison at Woodstock late in 1968. Before the release of *The Basement Tapes*, however, none of these works had been allowed anywhere near a Bob Dylan album. Amid the composition of hundreds of songs, he had never sought a full-time writing partner. Dylan flew solo: the persona was well established and intrinsic, or so it seemed, to his art. How could there be equal billing when he had no equals?

Jacques Levy, six years Dylan's senior, was nothing if not a resourceful character. A trained clinical psychologist and psychoanalyst – useful skills, perhaps, in the entertainment business – he had already acquired a certain reputation as the director chosen by critic-impresario Kenneth Tynan to launch the witless 'erotic revue' *Oh! Calcutta!* on Broadway in 1969. With a musical based on *Peer Gynt* in mind, Levy had then done some writing with McGuinn, the best-known example being 'Chestnut Mare', an enduring piece whose precise relationship with Ibsen's poem-play remains to be explained. Later in life, the dramaturge would become a professor of English and drama at a college in upper New York State. On his death in 2004 an obituary notice in the *New York Times* would describe him as a 'lovable, brilliant, irascible, inspiring, principled rebel hipster, charismatic sweetheart of a man'. When he bumped into a famous acquaintance one summer day in lower Manhattan in 1975, Levy was presented with a proposition: would he care to help Bob Dylan out with some songs?

In another version of the story, the two met at The Other End, having been introduced previously by McGuinn. During their conversation, so it seems, Dylan suggested a collaboration. At Levy's loft apartment, just around the corner on LaGuardia Place, they then set to work on a half-finished song named 'Isis'. Who then wrote what as the pair worked through the night is very far from clear.

Dylan's motives are equally obscure. Interviewed by Bill Flanagan early in 1985 for the book *Written in My Soul* (1986), the artist was asked why he had not persisted instead with 'what you'd tapped into with *Blood on the Tracks*'. The answer:

> I guess I never intended to keep that going. It was an experiment that came off. I had a few weeks in the summer when I wrote the songs. I wrote all the songs for *Blood on the Tracks* in about a month and then I

recorded them and stepped back out of that place where I was when I wrote them and went back to whatever I was doing before. Sometimes you'll get what you can out of these things, but you can't stay there. Co-writer. That was probably an album where I didn't have anything and I wasn't even thinking about making a record. I think I ran into Jacques downtown and we went off and just wrote some songs.

'I didn't have anything': was that truly the case? He had written 'Abandoned Love', after all, such as it then was, and composed a better song during his trip to the south of France in late spring. In each version of the tale of his first efforts with Levy, 'Isis' was already begun. Equally, Dylan's typically casual assertion that 'we went off and just wrote some songs' did not quite match Levy's memory. He would tell the writer and editor John Bauldie that the pressure on the pair during the writing process was 'tremendous'.[4] Dylan was not just messing around.

Nevertheless, the fact that in this of all years he felt the need for a co-writer is hardly insignificant. It is as though the masterpiece that was *Blood on the Tracks* had drained him in some peculiar way, or that the effort had been so singular it was impossible to repeat. Dylan, having 'stepped back out of that place', might have felt no desire, if that's the word, to accept the further emotional consequences of the Raeben method. *Blood*, his artistic life's blood, had been the only word for the experience. In any case, and contrary to public appearances, he was not quite as certain of his restored gifts as he might have seemed.

Consider the claims Dylan would make about the insights gleaned from his art teacher in 1974. In April of 1978, the journal *Rock Express* would learn that he had understood how to explore 'all the different selves that were in there'. In November of the same year, *Rolling Stone* would be told of an artist who had managed at last 'to do consciously what I used to be able to do unconsciously'. By helping Dylan to put mind, hand and eye together, Raeben, it was asserted, had given him conscious control of unconscious impulses. What had become of all that when the new songwriting partners were trading lines for unreliable topical songs, or sketching out their corny verse fictions? Collaboration involves an inevitable, if partial, surrender of artistic identity. The Dylan of *Blood on the Tracks* had disappeared, or had been suppressed. Perhaps he was too much to bear.

In the second half of July 1975 Dylan would fill an album of songs with Levy's help. Certain of the recordings would become, as they remain, much admired. For all that, it is open to question whether Dylan's songwriting was enhanced by the partnership. A better question might involve asking why this singular intelligence felt in any need of support, and why a supposedly reborn writer would seek out a passing supplier of words. The artist who embarks upon such an arrangement has either made a calculation involving the sum and its parts, or he is none too sure of himself.

Each of the songs created by Dylan and Levy, first in New York and then at the artist's house on Lily Pond Lane in the village of East Hampton, out on the Long Island shore, are treated still as works by the former. A couple of the pieces are held by some fans to be among the most significant of all 'Bob Dylan' songs. No one, it seems, thinks twice about it, as though Dylan's imprimatur is as close to authorship as makes no difference. Nevertheless, in another interview with Flanagan, this time a 2009 promotional effort arranged and published by his own bobdylan.com, the artist would state flatly that Levy 'wrote the words' for at least one song. 'I just sing it,' Dylan would maintain of the piece entitled 'Joey'. It was his way of abdicating responsibility for an item of verse reportage that succeeded artistically but came up short – and not for the first time in Dylan's career – journalistically.

When the album *Desire* emerged in January of 1976, only two of its nine songs would be wholly in the artist's name. Ginsberg, contributing stray thoughts in fervid sleeve-note jottings, would not linger long over the question of authorship, or whether such a thing mattered. In the poet's ecstatic prose, these were 'Dylan's Redemption Songs! If he can do it we can do it. America can do it.' Levy had a 35 per cent copyright share, by contract, in those seven featured works, but the appraiser from the Jack Kerouac School of Disembodied Poetics found only 'the culmination of Poetry-music as dreamt of in the '50s & early '60s . . . poet alone at microphone reciting-singing surreal-history love text ending in giant "YEAH!" when minstrel gives his heart away & says he wants to stay. Dylan will stay here with us!'

And so, relentlessly, on. Ginsberg knew all about Levy. Neither the poet of *Kaddish* nor anyone else could calculate the division of labour in the writing of the lyrics for *Desire*, but the assumption of sole authorship by a lone genius persisted. Precisely because Ginsberg knew all about Levy, however, he was obliged at length to concede that a 'Half-month was spent solitary on Long Island with theatrist Jacques Levy working on song facts phrases & rhymes, sharing information seriousness'. The seer, jotting down notes, did not explain how Dylan could have spent his time both 'solitary' and in intense collaboration.

So who wrote the songs? Or rather, who contributed which idea, and wrote which part, if the artist with his name on the album could later all but disown 'Joey', or if the 'theatrical' opening to 'Hurricane' was not, in fact, wholly his doing? Ginsberg would describe another track, accurately enough, as 'a short novel in verse, old-fashioned Dylan surrealist mind-jump inventions line by line, except D. says he's reading Joseph Conrad storyteller'. So where was Levy in the making of 'Black Diamond Bay', the best of all the jointly written songs to emerge from *Desire*?

Submitting amiably to questions from fans on a 'social news and entertainment' website late in 2012, Levy's son Julien, still to be born at the time of the collaboration, gave a partial account of his father's side of the story.[5] It did not entirely clarify matters.

> The writing process I think worked in some version of Dylan spitting out things he'd been working on on guitar or piano, and my dad would spit out whatever struck him as a response to the music. Or maybe they had a plan, and my father would jot down lyrics and they'd refine it with music, bit by bit, adding here, subtracting there – chiselling away at it until it was a fully-realised song.

Julien Levy then suggested that even the song 'Isis', a set of verses that has received scrutiny inordinate by most standards, far less by the standards of those who pan for their gold in Dylan's streams of consciousness, was strictly a co-production, right down to its venerated first line. Levy also maintained that, in his father's view, there was rather less to the piece, vaunted symbolism and all, than met the ear.

> Dylan invited my dad over to work on some songs, my dad showed up, they got to work. Dylan said he had a little piano thing he had been working on and he started banging out those first piano chords to 'Isis'. My dad just spat out, 'I married Isis on the fifth day of May . . .' and Dylan loved it, so they just kept going with it like that, creating this story until it reached a conclusion. By the time it was done, Dylan loved it, and was so excited that he ran downstairs to the local bar and read the lyrics out to whoever was just sitting there. It was on the strength of that that they decided to keep writing together.
>
> My dad always talked about how there was no special symbolic

meaning behind any of the images in 'Isis', that it was just a fun, adventurous kind of cowboy story.

The 'local bar' was undoubtedly The Other End. That apart, Julien Levy's account of his father's recollections casts a cool light – amid much affection for Dylan – over the figure of the artist in this moment. Here's our excited poet, rushing off to regale the drinking classes with his latest molten verses. Here's the overlooked collaborator, who has been the catalyst for the process from its first line, maintaining after the fact that nothing more than a fun cowboy story had been achieved. Jacques Levy also told the journalist Larry 'Ratso' Sloman that the 'Isis' melody was at first 'almost a dirge'.[6] It would not be much improved when the artist decided to enter the recording studio.

In his account of the Rolling Thunder tour from its gestation to the end of its first phase, Sloman quoted Levy to the effect that writing with Dylan was 'a totally co-operative venture' and that it was 'impossible to remember' who had contributed which line to a song. Nevertheless, it is a notable fact that after the end of 1978 the co-written works would disappear entirely from Dylan's concert repertoire for the best part of a decade. Talking to Paul Zollo from the magazine *SongTalk* in the spring of 1991 – though the interview would not be published until the winter issue – the artist failed to shed much light on the matter.

> We both were pretty much lyricists. Yeah, very panoramic songs because, you know, after one of my lines, one of his lines would come out. Writing with Jacques wasn't difficult. It was trying just to get it down. It just didn't stop. Lyrically.

Between fits of knowing laughter, Dylan would further observe that 'Isis' was 'a story that meant something' to Levy. 'Yeah. It just seemed to take on a life of its own, as another view of history.' In this interview Dylan made it clear that the song so often treated as a personal statement, the song he would sometimes announce from the stage as being 'about marriage', was nothing of the kind. His memory of the writing instead turned on the need to prevent a piece that could have gone 'just about any way it wanted to go' from getting 'too close'. He was asked the obvious question: too close to whom? Answer: 'Too close to me or him.'[7] The lingering implication was that such a risk had been averted, both for the artist and for the writing partner to whom a cowboy story had 'meant something'.

Desire remains a perplexing thing because it has no settled style, because a distinctive authorial voice is hard to spot, and because Dylan claims or refuses credit for authorship as and when it suits him. In pop music, generally speaking, the last detail is of no importance: songs are written to order, to suit the artist or the occasion. In terms of art, in terms of poetry, in terms of certain songs to which several varieties of symbolic and personal importance have been ascribed, it amounts to a puzzle. At moments throughout the Rolling Thunder adventure Dylan would present himself in terms of a theatrical conceit that would one day become familiar. Here he was, 'live and in person', yet also, physically, masked and anonymous, that hideously famous 'Bob Dylan' face shielded sometimes by strange plastic armour, or painted ghostly white. So was he making the words of Jacques Levy merely seem to be his own? If so, a lot of fan-babble since has been ill-advised.

One warm afternoon in late June or early July, meanwhile, a 25-year-old violinist with extravagantly long hair and a feigned gypsy look who went by the name Scarlet Rivera was stepping out of her Lower East Side apartment, instrument case in hand. She was planning to visit a friend before commencing rehearsals with what *People* magazine would later understand to be 'an obscure 10-piece Latin band that paid her $100 a week'.

'Then this car comes up and cuts me off,' Rivera (born Donna Shea in the Romani heartlands of Chicago) would tell the magazine early in the following year. 'Some ugly green car. The guy driving asked me if I really knew how to play the violin.' The violinist couldn't make out the face, but recognised a famous profile. 'Actually he had this woman next to him ask me. He asked her to ask me for my 'phone number, but I told her to tell him that I didn't give out my number to somebody stopping me on the street.'

'Come downtown and rehearse with me,' Dylan then reportedly said. 'I'm heading uptown,' Rivera replied before roguishly demanding a ride to her destination. Once she was inside the car, Dylan turned downtown. Nevertheless, the two got on well, it seems, and spent the rest of the afternoon and evening at his rented rehearsal studio, playing songs of his that she had never before heard.

One was entitled 'Isis', another was called 'One More Cup of Coffee', a third 'Mozambique'. Dylan was no longer likely to say that he 'didn't have anything' in the way of songs. 'One More Cup' was, in fact, all his own work, written in May of 1975 as he reached his 34th birthday during that desolate and debauched stay with David Oppenheim in the south of France. Dylan would tell Paul Zollo in the spring of 1991 that he had been inspired by a visit to a 'gypsy' festival, but that 'the verses came from someplace else'. It was a place, no doubt, where marriages end. 'No gratitude or love,' said the parable's first verse. 'Your loyalty is not to me / But to the stars above.'

Dylan's tale involves a few arresting coincidences. One is that the festival – in reality a religious pilgrimage – takes place in the small tourist town of Saintes-Maries-de-la-Mer, amid the marshes and lagoons of the Camargue, each 24 May. That date, it will be recalled, is Dylan's birthday. The object of veneration among the thousands of Romani people who gather, moreover, is the statue of their adopted saint. They know her as Sainte Sara, *Sara e Kali*, 'Sara the Black'. The name alone would have possessed a special resonance for Dylan. Each May, the saint's effigy is carried from its shrine to the Mediterranean shore in a re-enactment of what one legend says was her arrival in Gaul, perhaps as a black Egyptian maidservant to one of the Three Marys – Magdalene, Salome, Jacobe – who had sailed from Alexandria after the crucifixion of Jesus with their uncle, Joseph of Arimathea.

All of this must have worked on Dylan's imagination as he stood where Hemingway and Picasso had stood before him, contemplating another birthday and his estrangement from his own Sara. Her name, it seemed, had mystical associations that he would soon enough enlarge and explore. *Sara e Kali*, a saint not recognised by the Church of Rome, would meanwhile find herself in the service of the gods mumbo and jumbo thanks to the blasphemous 'theory' that she served not only Mary Magdalene but the offspring of Christ supposedly born in Gaul.[8] A more interesting fact is that the Manouches, as the French know the Romani, had their origins in the Indian subcontinent, that the rituals for *Sara e Kali* relate to the worship of the Hindu goddess Kali, and that they have a common linguistic root in the name: Kali, from *kāla*, meaning blackness, time, death and change. Thus: 'One more cup of coffee 'fore I go / To the valley below.' Whether Dylan knew all this ethnographic detail or not – his songs concerning his wife suggest he had more than an inkling – he had been deserted, as he believed, by a woman associated with a goddess.

The glimpse of Rivera's affected 'gypsy' style as she walked a New York street was serendipitous, then, but almost guaranteed to engage Dylan's attention. The musical flavouring that her fiddle would give to *Desire* was, equally, more than just an experiment or an artist's whim. The journalists who would style the Rolling Thunder Revue a 'gypsy caravan' got closer to the contents of Dylan's imagination than they realised. He had met the Romani 'king' in the Camargue. The aged personage had never heard of the singer, but the possessor of, allegedly, 12 wives and 100 children had been another unwitting contributor to 'One More Cup of Coffee'. After they had rehearsed, Rivera, for one, understood that Dylan was ready to record, and perhaps to perform. Whatever the collaboration with Levy involved, however it bridged the gulf between partners, intentions and abilities, the process was beginning to bear fruit. The crop would vary in quality somewhat.

If a larger plan was emerging, meanwhile, it amounted to this: yet again Dylan would trust to instinct and to luck. Auditioning musicians found on the street was hardly standard practice. Picking co-writers on the basis of chance meetings on corners or in Greenwich Village bars was not risk-free. Recruiting a band and a supporting cast from club-dwellers and drinking pals was surely tempting fate. To do all this with no apparent thought for the roles to be filled, the cost involved, the structure of the performances to be given, the personnel to be managed, the music to be made or the compatibility of those being hired was nuts. It was exactly what Dylan did, nevertheless, in the summer and autumn of 1975, with only charisma, ample funds and a couple of ideas to sustain him. His break for artistic freedom would become a gargantuan and costly undertaking. Then again, making money from the Rolling Thunder notion was his second thought, not his first.

He might well have felt the need for help with his writing in such a circumstance. Levy meanwhile seems to have had no qualms about his fitness for the work, or over his right to be treated as a partner, with that 35 per cent share – since he wrote none of the music – in the songs produced.[9] Nevertheless, if Dylan had misplaced some of his self-assurance at the end of the '60s and the start of the '70s, he had not lost his habit of assuming that anything he cared to attempt would come good in the end, somehow or other. Not for the first time or the last, he was ready to take a risk.

Whether Dylan's troupe of friends, acquaintances, hired hands and hangers-on understood his logic is less certain. Suddenly the ascetic self-discipline that had characterised the making of *Blood on the Tracks* was gone. It was as though he needed the change for the sake of his rest. Equally, you could find prior evidence for a recurring pattern in

Dylan's behaviour to explain his improvisations in mid-1975. He had been this way before, veering from the hard, painstaking graft of *The Times They Are a-Changin'* in the second half of 1963 to the drunken, album-in-a-night exercise that was *Another Side of Bob Dylan* on 9 June 1964. Later he had switched, suddenly and without warning, from the bacchanalian improvisations with The Band in the spring and drowsy summer of 1967 to the austere, sculpted delicacy of *John Wesley Harding* towards the end of that year. It amounted almost to a personality trait: tension and release, tension and release. Besides, who could have borne a career forever on the raw edge of existence, devoted only to the universe of *Blood on the Tracks*?

In the summer of 1975, Dylan's planning might as well have been based, as perhaps it was, on the opaque Chinese wisdom of the I Ching and its cosmic bar codes. One discarded version of the song 'Idiot Wind' certainly made explicit reference to the oldest of self-help manuals. By the summer, Dylan was improvising, trusting to luck and fate, whatever they represented. It caused him no intellectual problems; quite the reverse. Even before God made His appearance at stage right, the artist was as susceptible on occasion to esoteric waffle as the next counter-culture survivor, despite his advertised aversion to all things hippy. Within a couple of years he would be explaining to a reporter from *Rolling Stone*, for one example, that Jesus had taken on 'the bad karma of all the people he healed'.[10] His own sleeve note for the *Desire* album – written as though to prove that the world can never have too many Allen Ginsberg impersonators – would announce that Dylan had 'A WHOLE LOT OF KARMA TO BURN'. This time, Indian religions would take the fall for his understanding, if any, of causality and eternity. In practice, he was rolling the dice.

As Rolling Thunder coalesced around him, mere ancient wisecracks seemed to have become his creative strategy. 'Chaos is a friend of mine,' he had said back in 1965, dictating still another entry in pop culture's dictionary of quotations. 'It's like I accept him; does he accept me?' Nora Ephron and Susan Edmiston, his interlocutors from the *New York Post*, had been further informed that 'Truth is chaos. Maybe beauty is chaos.' In 1975, Dylan's album and his tour would test this seductive, risky theory to its limits.

General confusion became a characteristic of this phase in his career, and of the Rolling Thunder carnival. The roadshow was intended as some sort of statement, but what was said meant different things to different participants. Dylan would take inspiration, some of the time, from a pair of French movies. One was Marcel Carné's *Les Enfants du Paradis* (1945), the other François Truffaut's *Tirez sur le pianiste* (1960), otherwise known as *Shoot the Piano Player*. The young playwright Sam Shepard, a former lover of Patti Smith hired by Dylan to 'work on a proposed film with the Rolling Thunder Revue' by 'providing dialogue on the spot' – though that idea 'very quickly dissolved into the background' – would be questioned specifically about his knowledge of the works when he arrived amid tour rehearsals in October.[11]

Both pictures are, to summarise grotesquely, studies in performance, revolving around ideas of acting, disguise and identity. Carné's piece of romantic 'poetic realism', written by the poet Jacques Prévert – of whom Dylan was well aware – involved the tale of four men in pursuit of the same beautiful woman. One man was an actor, one a mime artist, one a master criminal, and the fourth, it is generally supposed, the allegorical representation of Nazi occupation in the person of a villainous aristocrat. You could equally describe the four as aspects of human desire. Only the mime artist, played by Jean-Louis Barrault, was entirely pure in heart, his whitened face an unblemished canvas. Whatever else he took from Carné's romance – interconnected relationships, unattainable love – Dylan would seize on that idea.

In fact, he took a great deal more. In this instance, the artist would not be shy about his influences. Carné, still a very-much-alive 69-year-old when Dylan's troupe began to shoot over 100 hours of film for what became *Renaldo and Clara*, would be reminded, if he cared, that there is no copyright in ideas. Whiteface? Check. 'Woman in White', a flower motif, certain resonant passages of dialogue, the old contrast between performance and backstage reality, the actual and the imagined? Dylan overlooked very little. On the other hand, he would not attempt to conceal the fact. The only small details he would miss, according to most critics of *Renaldo and Clara*, were Carné's cinematic daring, his lyricism, his staging, his ability to inspire magical performances and his self-knowledge.

Shoot the Piano Player is a crime story, in the main, but it too turns on the erasure of identity. As depicted by Charles Aznavour, the piano player is another figure attempting to escape from his past. Who is he exactly? 'Bob Dylan' liked that kind of question. Beneath the gangster movie plot, the picture veers abruptly between tragedy and farce, at one minute sedate, the next furiously paced. There is an improvisational quality, too, in *Piano Player* that must have appealed to Dylan, not least given Patti Smith's comments on the origins of

Rolling Thunder and her claim that he was 'thinking about improvisation'. Though Shepard's job would amount to nothing important, he was not misinformed. Not content with preparing for an album and plotting a tour, Dylan had a movie in mind. Obviously, Bob Dylan would be its star, but someone else would pretend to play 'Bob Dylan'.

*

Saigon had fallen – or been liberated – in the last days of April amid humiliating scenes of panic. The overloaded choppers had staggered from the compound of the Defense Attaché Office and the roof of the US embassy while the People's Army of Vietnam and the National Liberation Front closed in. Military radio had played Irving Berlin's 'White Christmas', oblivious to any and all symbolism, as a signal to Americans that the evacuations had begun and that it was time finally to leave.

Before the end, President Gerald Ford, broom to Nixon's dust, had ordered the evacuation of 2,000 orphans, a mere handful of the tens of thousands of children set adrift from their homes and parents, Caucasian, black or Asian, during the upheavals of America's longest war. Over 100,000 Vietnamese adults – civilian employees, common-law wives, dependants, the rich and formerly powerful – had also managed to escape, but many more desperate people had been abandoned as the US withdrew its last representatives. Reprisals and massacres had been feared before the helicopters had scurried away. There had been a concern, too, that the people of the city would turn against their former protectors once it became clear that the Americans were deserting the country. The last US Marines had left the embassy just before 8 a.m. on 30 April.

What had it all been worth? Even the question soon began to sound banal. Vietnam had dominated the lives of Dylan's generation. It had defined and divided them, for or against, for better than a decade, with eight miserable years of fighting at its heart. Combat deaths, at a minimum 47,000, had almost matched the number of American dead on the battlefields of the First World War and easily exceeded the total of those killed in action in Korea. In one manner or another, 58,000 young Americans had died in South East Asia and over 300,000 had been wounded. It would take years for America to come to terms with Vietnam, far less to honour the fallen. Returning veterans felt they were spurned, at best ignored. In 1975, many of them believed that their country didn't want to know about them, what they had done, or why – willing or not – they had done it. Suddenly the country seemed to be repressing every memory.

Three million had served; a million and a half had seen combat. For all that, the entire military might of the US had failed against a small and often primitive nationalist movement, a 'fourth-rate power' in the hubristic words of Henry Kissinger. Too often, the psychological effects on those young Americans who otherwise survived were profound, indelible. It took a distinct collective effort to set their experiences and their memories aside. That, nevertheless, became the burden of the veterans' complaints while the politicians pretended to draw their strategic lessons.

The larger effect, the abiding effect, was a wholesale loss of faith in government. Until they began to hear and believe that amends could somehow be made for Vietnam through still more military power and preparedness, Americans doubted their leaders. If you got your news from rock and roll, as so many young men in combat had got their news, Dylan's doubting songs and his spurning of politics could seem like good, simple common sense.

By 1975, in any case, the erstwhile New Left was old news. In January, an attempt by the remnants of the Weather Underground to bomb the Department of State building had been a last gesture by one fragment of a fractured movement. Perversely, radicalism had seemed to draw its only strength from Vietnam. With the war's end, people drifted away from left politics, new or old. Feminism seemed more relevant and more valuable to many women. Environmentalism struck others as a more important cause than any. The escapism implicit in 'alternative lifestyles' seemed more attractive to a lot of people than street protests. Radicalism survived, of course, but it became diffuse. By 1975, the self-contradictory appeal of single-issue politics was everywhere. This was the audience for whom the 34-year-old Dylan was making a record and preparing a tour.

*

The first recording session for *Desire* was held on 14 July, just before Dylan and Levy retreated to quaint but filthy-rich East Hampton on Long Island's South Shore to resume their songwriting workshop. The session at Columbia's New York studios was a fruitless affair, at best a testing of the waters. Nothing would be kept for the album. Instead, a trivial and slightly unpleasant Dylan-Levy joke at the expense of the lesbian radical-feminist novelist Rita Mae Brown – 'How'd you ever get that way?' – took up a large part of a long night. For reasons best known to himself, the artist would persist with the 'comic' song 'Rita May' [sic], but a reported seven attempts to achieve a usable recording on the 14th pointed to a problem. A later version of the track would wind up as the ignored B-side to a flop single at the end of 1976, but the song's sole claim to anyone's attention was in demonstrating that the writing partnership was successful only fitfully. More than once during the collaboration, whether at Levy's urging or because he had nothing better to offer, the artist would lower his standards. Some of the results would end up on *Desire*.[12]

Dylan's explanation for the absolute failure of a night's work had less to do with the songs than with the music. Rivera, the borrowed band of the Traffic founder Dave Mason, sundry backing singers and some fine session players had been unable to give him the sound he wanted. Disappointment and frustration, it is sometimes asserted, then caused Dylan to think seriously about assembling his own ensemble. Given that Rolling Thunder was already sounding in his head, however, it was all but inevitable that he would have to get around to picking a few musicians. And why stop at a few?

Several unsuccessful attempts were also made on that first night to capture the song that would become known as 'Joey'. Dylan might later seek to distance himself from the work, but here was another problematic aspect to the writing partnership. Levy, naturally enough, had his own interests and enthusiasms. One of those arose from an indulgent view of the blood-spattered wiseguys and cynical goodfellas of organised crime in New York City. In the figure of the gangster Joseph 'Crazy Joe' Gallo, Levy detected – presumably by ignoring every readily available documented fact – a kind of folk hero. Dylan, always a sucker for a righteous outlaw, went along with it; most New Yorkers who knew anything about the Mob would be less forgiving. As romantic fiction, the song would have required no justification. As a presentation of historical truth, involving a recently dead hoodlum with whom Levy had been acquainted, it was less dubious than laughable. This would be pointed out forcefully.

Dylan should in any case have known better. He understood the multiple complications of topical song. They had caused him to quit the public-comment game, after all, with an undisguised relief. Back in 1963–4, his 'The Lonesome Death of Hattie Carroll' had achieved emotional truth at the expense of several facts. With 'Joey' he and

Levy would sentimentalise reality, as pop music does, and make a cartoon cliché of Italian American life. Was that worth a memorable chorus? The finished version of 'Joey' remains one of the better musical things on *Desire*, but its tangential relationship with truth, its fake mythology and synthetic emotions, were echoed in some fairly dismal writing, certainly on Levy's part. As one couplet has it, 'Sister Jacqueline and Carmela and mother Mary all did weep / I heard his best friend Frankie say, "He ain't dead, he's just asleep."' Any self-respecting director of a real gangster movie would have dumped that last piece of dialogue. Creative-writing tutors would have winced in honest collective pain, meanwhile, at the B-minus fake-archaic 'all did weep'.

The fact that Dylan-Levy, joined at the tediously hip, were also turning out material as risible as 'Rita May' should have alerted the artist to the risks he was running. No one else was likely to care. For fans and acolytes, a Bob Dylan song was a Bob Dylan song, a nonpareil beyond all categories. Only the artist could take responsibility. Instead, he and Levy would in one instance produce what they regarded as a piece worth keeping after playing an aimless word game. It seems the contest was to see who could find the most rhymes for Mozambique. Magnifique – as an example of professional writing technique – the song was not. Undaunted, Dylan took the resultant effort into the recording studio.

A fundamental question would thereafter be set aside by most fans when *Desire* topped the American charts and lingered there for fully five weeks. Were the results of these cooperative songwriting ventures actually much good? Levy's vaunted theatrical instincts and Dylan's taste for the 'cinematic' would be – and still are – much discussed. A hit is a hit, meanwhile, but the texture of the verses themselves, the lines, couplets, images and rhymes, would too often slip through the critical net. Even in its best moments, the writing on the album is rarely startling and never audacious in the quicksilver manner Dylan had once made his own. Sometimes the lyrics read and sound like sentiment-by-committee, imagery-by-numbers.

Dylan, so often the victim of the authorial fallacy, invited a difficulty never predicted by practitioners of literature's numbing less-than New Criticism. The personal pronouns in his songs were no guarantee, he said to us, that the writing was ever an exercise in autobiography. What happened, then, when 'Bob Dylan' took the stage to sing 'I married Isis on the fifth day of May' if the line, pronoun and all, had been cooked up by someone else entirely? What happened to the strange, free-standing consciousness that had been Dylan's conspicuous gift to popular music? His songs – another pronoun – didn't come from a Tin Pan Alley production line: such had been the pledge from the start of his first assault on an industry. Now here he was in 1975, knocking out tunes with an off-Broadway talent-for-hire, yet performing as though each couplet, good or bad, was his. All of the acknowledged Dylan-Levy compositions appear in the former's *Lyrics: 1962–2001* (2004). They are each registered for copyright purposes by one of Dylan's publishing companies. The big book, well worth study for all its flaws, is a testament to the long, enduring career of an unexampled talent. The song index alone runs to a dozen pages and would be longer by far if the book was brought up to date. But the writing of *Desire* complicates arguments over art and the artist.

If Dylan had needed no help to compose the great songs of the 1960s, or of *Blood on the Tracks*, where stood the co-authored mock-ups, the hollow exercises in rhetoric and role-playing, for which Jacques Levy claimed co-paternity? Had the songs been better, no one would bother to ask. Despite the multitude of fans who will hear not a word against it, *Desire* is what is sometimes called a patchy affair.

A fortnight after his first attempt to secure useful recordings, Dylan was back in the studio, supposedly in search of a 'bigger sound'. He organised this quest, if organised is the word, as though throwing an after-hours party, seeming to gather up everyone and anyone who came to mind or happened to be around. The predictable result was a shambles as twenty-one musicians, six guitar players among them (not including the artist), tried to sort themselves out. Production, in the traditional manner, even in the casual manner favoured by Dylan's old mentor John Hammond, was absent. A luckless Columbia staff man by the name of Don DeVito was granted a producer's responsibilities but precious little executive power in Studio E. No one, least of all Dylan, was in control. Eric Clapton, always a staunch admirer of the artist and no stranger to the foibles of superstars – he had patented a few notable idiosyncrasies of his own – was among the baffled guests who could not believe what was going on, or what was *supposed* to be going on.

Dylan's old, deep-rooted refusal to pay heed to the realities and demands of the recording process all but destroyed the sessions of 28 and 29 July as ingenious engineers struggled to find space on their 16-track machines for the competing demands of so many instruments and vocalists. The feat could have been accomplished – the Beatles had mastered bigger problems with far less sophisticated equipment – but that would have required more effort than Dylan, addicted to spontaneity, convinced that the best music somehow just happened, was prepared to expend. This heroic delusion would hamper his efforts to record his songs for many years to come.

The artist could claim, rightly enough, that some of his best music had been produced during lightning raids on the studios. *Bringing It All Back Home* had required only three days of his time in 1965; *John Wesley Harding* had needed just as little effort in 1967. *Blood on the Tracks* might have cost Dylan the equivalent of a full week in 1974, but that was due only to the second thoughts that had caused him to remake the record. He didn't like to hang around. He did not believe, in any case, that recording captured the reality of music – an unhelpful prejudice if you made your living by selling records – but previous triumphs thanks to 'spontaneity' would blind him to his self-created problems. The first serious sessions for *Desire* were prime examples.

As predicted, times were changing. Pink Floyd had been lavishing six months of work in 1975 (for whatever reason) on the album *Wish You Were Here*. Queen's preposterous 'Bohemian Rhapsody' had required three weeks of labour and, notoriously, 180 overdubs on a single brief passage of music before taking its place on that year's *A Night at the Opera*, an album thereafter touted, as though the fact was a badge of honour, as the most expensive collection of tunes anyone had then assembled. Dylan's dissent from this obnoxious orthodoxy was well known and honourable but not necessarily useful. In London that summer a scruffy sort with 'I Hate' scribbled on his ragged Pink Floyd T-shirt was about to join a motley crew called the Sex Pistols. John Lydon and his comrades would mock the decadence of the music industry and its 180 overdubs something rotten. But that little incident wouldn't help Dylan to get a record made. Of the forty-five takes captured on 28 and 29 July, only one song attempted, entitled 'Romance in Durango', would make it to the album.[13]

As ever, he got there in the end. Having wasted his own and everyone else's time, Dylan listened to reason – articulated, it seems, by the bass player Rob Stoner – and stood down most of his army of helpers. After the chaos, the album the artist would release was finished soon enough, but he persisted to the end with minor songs. One was a Dylan-Levy piece entitled 'Catfish', dedicated to a star baseball player who bore the nickname, a track that seemed to have been destined from the start for the netherworld of strictly limited interest. Another song, written by Dylan alone, was called 'Golden Loom'. With a better melody it might have repaid attention, but the writer appears to have lost interest soon enough. Both tracks would turn up on 1991's *The Bootleg Series Volumes 1–3 (Rare & Unreleased) 1961–1991* as mere curiosities. Nine songs, fifty-six minutes of recorded music, remained from the sessions to become *Desire*. It was, for the first time in a long time, a near self-explanatory title.

*

From its first assertive notes to its conclusion eight minutes and thirty-two seconds later, 'Hurricane' is a thrilling thing. If facts are of no interest, the song fulfils every dream of justice and vindication ever nurtured because of Bob Dylan. Scarlet Rivera's violin soars like an exultation for the downtrodden; the drums hammer like a mob at the door; the artist sings as though now, finally, he is interested neither in irony nor in the concealment to be had from ambiguity. He wants to tell you a story, a true story.

The fiddle is 'slightly off-key', of course, say people who don't often listen to fiddles, or attempt to imagine what might be involved in accompanying Bob Dylan. Life's fact-checkers, meanwhile, cannot vouch for the narrative's every last word, to say the very least. Some claims made on behalf of a boxer imprisoned for almost two decades for his part in a triple murder are simply wrong. Certain omissions by Dylan-Levy from 'the story of the Hurricane', Rubin Carter, amount to shoddy journalism. But these objections are born of hindsight and also omit certain truths. At first hearing, *Desire's* long opening track was astonishing, a triumph of compressed narrative, of vernacular writing, of sheer polemical intensity. Despite every off-handed rebuttal, every denial of interest for long years on end, here was Dylan back with a protest song, with an inescapably political song.

You could bear in mind, of course, that he had never ceased to be a political being. The refusal of a spokesman's role, the rejection of ideological conscription by '60s types who wanted only slogans and anthems, was not the same as refusing to think politically. As a performer who owed everything to black music, and as a human being, Dylan had never ceased to despise racism. Nor had he ever lost his non-theoretical aversion to injustice generally. Like Woody Guthrie, his first and last hero, Dylan's instinct was always to back the individual against anyone's version of the system. Numerous songs written after he 'quit politics' – from 'It's Alright, Ma' to 'I Shall Be Released' to

'Idiot Wind', to name only three – could be set on repeat play to prove it.

'Hurricane' was explicit, however. The song was rooted in reality and in recent history. Its only precedent in Dylan's post-'60s career was 'George Jackson', and 'Hurricane' was better, melodically if not lyrically, than the 1971 song. Until certain doubts began to creep in, 'the story of the Hurricane' sounded like a flawless, righteous indictment of racist policing and a corrupt legal system. The important fact, the fact that unites the songs written for Jackson and Carter, was that racial bigotry had not evaporated from American life with the civil-rights movement. By the mid-1970s, too many had chosen to overlook this truth. The artist and his co-writer had not.

Dylan and Levy had both taken an interest in Rubin Carter and his campaign against conviction. Dylan, like a number of people in the public eye, had been sent a copy of the boxer's book *The Sixteenth Round: From Number 1 Contender to Number 45472* (1973). The very subtitle would be disputed by those who pointed out that when Carter was arrested he was in no sense first in contention for 'the middleweight crown'. Where a bloody triple homicide was concerned, the detail was trivial. In the 'acknowledgements' to his book, the fighter had written from the notorious Rahway State Prison in east New Jersey of 'the corrupt and vindictive officials who played their roles to a T in this tightly woven drama to bury me alive'. He had Dylan's attention, you must suspect, from page one.

The story goes like this. In the early hours of 17 June 1966 two armed men entered the nondescript Lafayette Bar and Grill on East 18th Street in Paterson, New Jersey, Rubin Carter's home town. Without ceremony, the pair opened fire. A bartender and a 60-year-old male customer died instantly; a female customer would die of an embolism four weeks later thanks to multiple wounds. A second male customer, Willie Marins, 42, survived the attack, despite being shot in the head while standing by the pool table. He and the 51-year-old female witness Hazel Tanis would tell the police that the gunmen were black. Neither witness would identify Rubin Carter or his co-accused, John Artis.

On the night of the killings, the intimidating, shaven-headed boxer, nicknamed 'Hurricane' thanks to his ferocious fighting style, was 29 years old. His once-promising career, encompassing 27 wins in 40 fights, 19 by knockout, was fading. He had gained his shot at that middleweight crown at the end of 1964 and had lost in Philadelphia on a unanimous decision. In May of 1965, he had endured the hiding of his life at the hands of the Nigerian Dick Tiger, as Carter himself confessed, in the smoky haze of New York's Madison Square Garden. In five fights before the shootings in 1966, the Hurricane had lost twice, won twice (against lowly opponents), and registered a draw. When the murders happened, his title hopes were gone.

It is also fair to say that Rubin Carter had not been a model citizen. Dylan-Levy would overlook the fact in their song, just as Dylan had failed to mention the six hostages who died during George Jackson's attempt to escape from San Quentin Prison in California in 1971. As with the dead radical, however, it was always possible to argue that Rubin Carter had been the victim of hellish circumstances, and that every circumstance had been a consequence likely to befall any black man in a white world. Such was the consistent view of the author of *The Sixteenth Round*. 'In Paterson,' as Dylan would sing, 'that's just the way things go.'

In his later career, Carter would emerge as an eloquent campaigner for penal reform and human rights. In Canada, for a dozen years after 1993, he was executive director of the Association in Defence of the Wrongly Convicted, given credit for addressing several miscarriages of justice. On the occasion of his second autobiography, Nelson Mandela would contribute a foreword testifying that the former boxer's 'rich heart is now alive in love, compassion and understanding'.[14] So who could truly say which was the real Hurricane, or decide which parts of the biographical record were relevant to the paramount claim that he was 'falsely tried' and wrongly convicted in a 'pig-circus'?

Still, facts are facts. Carter was in a reformatory for assault and robbery by the time he was 14. He was kicked out of the army in 1956, marked down as 'undesirable' after four court-martial proceedings. He was afterwards a mugger capable of serious black-on-black violence and the owner, it is alleged, of a fearsome temper. Before the Lafayette killings, he had spent 11 of his 29 years in confinement. The suggestion that before the slaughter he was militant for civil rights, 'a revolutionary bum' in the words of the song, is also disputed. There is nothing in Carter's books, nor in the annals of civil rights, to support the claim that in 1966 he had a functioning political bone in his body. Nevertheless, interviewed by *Penthouse* magazine for the edition of September 1975, the Hurricane would assert:

I'm not in jail for committing murder. I'm in jail partly because I'm a black man in America, where the powers that be will only allow a black man to be an entertainer or a criminal. While I was free on the streets – with whatever limited freedom I had on the streets – as a prizefighter, I was characterised as an entertainer. As long as I stayed within that role, within that prizefighting ring, as long as that was my Mecca and I didn't step out into the civic affairs of this country, I was acceptable. But when I didn't want to see people brutalized any longer – and when I'd speak out against that brutality, no matter who committed the brutality, black people or white people – I was harassed for my beliefs. I committed no crime; actually the crime was committed against me.

In *The Sixteenth Round,* Carter would admit, perhaps boast, that in childhood he had taken to fighting 'like a duck takes to water'.[15] He would also confess to having knifed a man repeatedly – in self-defence against a predatory paedophile, he said – and to having been classified as a juvenile delinquent. Nevertheless, there was room enough in his text for accusations against cops and judges for fomenting 'prefabricated lies to tear me down'. In Carter's account of his early years, he had adhered only 'to the first law of nature – self-preservation'.[16]

It was a description of an unjust world that might have been made to appeal to Dylan's quixotic faith in nature's outlaws, those individuals forced to defend themselves against the real criminals, the ones who never get caught and never go to jail. A superstar's reflexive romantic bias didn't mean the boxer was guilty of a multiple killing staged – or so the cops quickly persuaded themselves – in instant revenge for the murder of a black bartender in a place called the Waltz Inn. It didn't make Rubin Carter innocent, either.

A minor criminal called Alfred 'Al' Bello had been a couple of blocks away from the Lafayette Bar 'prowlin' around' with burglary on his mind on the night of the shootings. Bello would later testify that as he drew near to the dive – supposedly in search of a pack of cigarettes – he almost ran into a pair of black males. One was armed with a shotgun, one with a pistol, and both were laughing. Bello said he took to his heels as the men got into a white car.

The petty crook was nevertheless one of the first to reach the murder scene, along with a woman named Patricia Graham (later Patricia 'Patty' Valentine) who lived above the bar and grill. She also told the cops she had seen a couple of black men climbing into a white car, a Dodge Polara, before driving north. A second neighbour, Ronald Ruggiero, heard the shots and later said that as he looked from his window he saw Al Bello running westwards on Paterson's Lafayette

Street in the direction of 16th Street. The description of the car given by Bello and Valentine would change at Carter's second trial.

Nevertheless, Carter's car was, supposedly, a match for the getaway vehicle. Having been pulled over once that night and allowed to proceed because a third man, John 'Bucks' Royster, had been with them, Hurricane and Artis were stopped for a second time and taken to the murder scene. This took place within half an hour of the shootings. No fingerprints were taken; no tests were made for gunshot residue; no one who had witnessed the events surrounding the killings identified the pair. When Rubin Carter was hauled to Paterson's St Joseph's hospital, a horribly wounded Willie Marins, blinded in one eye, indicated that the boxer was not one of his assailants. A cop then found a shotgun shell and a .32 calibre round in Carter's car. Both items were later declared, wrongly, to be compatible with the murder weapons. The officer who made the find waited the best part of a week before turning in his evidence. Artis and Rubin, having passed polygraph tests, had meanwhile been released.

Months later, Bello told the police – and why the delay? – that he had not been alone while sniffing around a sheet-metal works for a burglary opportunity. An individual named Arthur Dexter Bradley had acted as his accomplice. This pair then proceeded to identify Carter as one of the armed men they had seen outside the bar. Bello meanwhile identified 19-year-old Artis. Inevitably, Carter and his companion were arrested and indicted.

In May of 1967, what Dylan-Levy would describe, correctly, as 'the all-white jury' found the accused guilty, but declined to recommend the electric chair. In 1974, after Carter had sued his way out of a state psychiatric hospital thanks to 'cruel and unusual punishment', Bello and Bradley, located by the *New York Times*, suddenly claimed they had been cajoled and bribed into lying. This time they said they had *not* seen Carter and Artis near the Lafayette Bar. It was then that the Hurricane sent Dylan a copy of *The Sixteenth Round*. In May of 1975, the artist paid a visit to the fighter in prison. After taking notes and talking with Carter for hours, Dylan seems to have promised to write a song.

In late October of that year, just before 'Hurricane' was released as a single, he told the ever-attentive *Rolling Stone* of his conviction that Carter's 'philosophy' and his 'were running on the same road, and you don't meet too many people like that, that you just kinda know are on the same path as you are, mentally'. The remark would be quoted for years to come in arguments over Dylan's involvement in the case.[17] Of more interest, as a measure of his attitude and belief, were a couple of the things that Dylan said next. He made large claims.

> I never doubted him for a moment. He's just not a killer, not that kind of a man. You're talking about a different type of person. I mean, he's not gonna walk into a bar and start shooting. He's not the guy. I don't know how anybody in their right mind is gonna think he was guilty of something like that.

Then:

> There's an injustice that's been done and you know that Rubin's gonna get out. There's no doubt about that, but the fact is that it can happen to anybody. We have to be confronted with that; people from the top to the bottom, they should be aware that it can happen to anybody, at any time.

Dylan and Levy were not the only ones to be moved and angered by Carter's tale. In 1975, the fighters Muhammad Ali and Joe Frazier, no strangers to racism, would speak out fiercely in the Hurricane's defence. Ali, in his second spell as heavyweight champion of the world, would dedicate his contest against Ron Lyle in May to the Hurricane. The champion thereafter became co-chairman of the Hurricane Defense Fund, established to aid Carter with his legal costs. In September of 1975, Ali led a march to City Hall in Newark, New Jersey, to publicise Rubin's cause. Other prominent people – the writer Norman Mailer, the actor Burt Reynolds, the singers Harry Belafonte and Johnny Cash among them – signed up to the national committee of the Hurricane Trust Fund.[18] The veteran Chicago novelist Nelson Algren, the author of *The Man with the Golden Arm* (1949), had meanwhile begun to research the case after being commissioned in 1974 to write a magazine article.

In the summer of 1975, aged 66, failing in his powers but fascinated by the town, Algren would even move to Paterson in an attempt to understand the murders. As the poet and playwright Joe Pintauro would later remember, this 'dedication to the lost cause of clearing the boxer Hurricane Carter from a murder rap . . . drained Nelson's energy and emptied his pockets. The Hurricane Carter case turned into a quicksand of unresolvable complexities and Hurricane was never cleared. After years of effort, Algren finally converted his commitment into material for his novel *The Devil's Stocking*, but by then he had grown old and tired.'[19]

The novel was published posthumously in 1983, but Algren's weariness was understandable. The case was a horrible tangle of claim and counterclaim. Thanks to recantations, undisclosed deals between prosecution and witnesses, and to apparent lying by Bello and Bradley, the new trial that had been denied to Carter in 1974 was granted. In March of 1976, the New Jersey Supreme Court overturned his conviction on the grounds that the prosecution had withheld the tape of an interview with Bello proving he had been promised leniency for his misdoings in return for testimony. Hurricane and Artis were freed on bail, with most of the bail money posted by Muhammad Ali. The New Jersey prosecutor soon re-indicted the pair.[20]

In November 1976, after Bello yet again changed his mind and again claimed to have seen Hurricane and Artis near the Lafayette, the boxer was convicted for a second time. The judge had allowed testimony describing angry black people gathering outside the Waltz Inn after the shooting – by a white man – of the black bartender on the evening before the Lafayette murders. The prosecution claim that revenge had been the motive for the killings was therefore deemed to have been supported. Neither Bob Dylan songs nor famous novelists were of any help. Rubin Carter's conviction was not overturned finally until 1985.

The last decision did not mean, contrary to what Nelson Mandela would choose to believe, that the boxer had spent 'twenty years in prison for a crime he did not commit'. It did not mean, as Dylan would sing, that the Hurricane was an innocent man. Prosecutors could have tried his case for a third time, but declined to make the attempt. The final ruling said only that 'grave constitutional violations' of the petitioner's rights had occurred. Some chose to describe those abuses as 'technicalities', but a 1988 attempt by New Jersey's prosecutors to have the case reviewed was thrown out by the United States Supreme Court. Bello, a confessed alcoholic, was in any case the sole remaining witness who had placed Hurricane and Artis at the murder scene. Whatever the truth, innocence – or guilt – was not established and Carter has made no attempt in the years since his release to obtain redress from the authorities. He has also continued to insist that he played no part in the killings.

Down the years Dylan-Levy have been accused, variously, of naivety, of the worst excesses of radical chic, of promoting a liberal conspiracy theory, and of inspiring a disputable Hollywood film, *The Hurricane* (1999). The last part is true. On its release, Norman Jewison's movie was deemed particularly egregious by observers of the fight game for suggesting that Carter had only lost his middleweight title bout against Joey Giardello in 1964 because of racial bias among the judges. Even Rubin didn't make that claim.

Meanwhile, a piece of dialogue in the song, supposedly an exchange between Bello and Patty Graham/Valentine, was said by the latter never to have happened. The claim that Carter was 'far away in another part of town' when the killings took place is disproven by his own alibi, placing him in a bar called the Nite Spot just a few blocks away. The general charge of racism is meanwhile hindered by the fact that the jury in the second trial contained two black members, and by the fact that the case was examined on behalf of the state of New Jersey by a black legislator who found the claim unjustified. Racist language attributed in the song to police officers was never documented.

Equally, the idea that Carter spent his spare time placidly riding horses, as the song describes, 'where the trout streams flow and the air is nice' cuts no ice with those who recall a frequenter of the Nite Spot and similar louche joints. Finally, there was a report carried by the UPI press agency on 8 June 1976. It began: 'A woman [Carolyn Kelley, who had persuaded Ali to take an interest in the case] who was instrumental in the movement to win Rubin "Hurricane" Carter a new trial charged from her hospital bed Monday she was beaten by the former boxer at a Maryland hotel.' Carter denied the claim and no indictments were issued.

In the Dylan-Levy song, a story is told that leaves no room for ambiguity. Dylan's music strikes its chorus, time after time, like the sound of cell doors slamming shut. In 1975, the artist was immune to doubt, electing to begin what would be one of his bestselling albums with eight and a half minutes of livid rage and righteous denunciation. Under his direction, the first phase of the Rolling Thunder Revue tour would become, in large part, a campaign to secure Rubin Carter's release. 'Hurricane' would be played at every show along the way. So what if Dylan was utterly wrong?

'Topical song' contains this curious dichotomy: it claims the status of historical truth and art simultaneously. Artists who weave poetry from facts have long wrestled with the ensuing paradoxes. Was Macbeth a weak and murderous usurper, or was the real man as pious and peaceable a King of Alba as a ruler could be a thousand years back? Perhaps it doesn't matter much to an audience struggling with the complexities of Shakespeare's *The Tragedy of Macbeth*. If, on the other hand, you have co-written a hot-off-the-presses documentary song asserting that a blameless man has fallen victim to a sickness in your society, facts count. They count because you say they count. When racism and heinous murders are at issue, those facts are everything. That is part, an intrinsic part, of your story. But if other facts then say that no final judgement in the case of the Hurricane was ever possible, what remains?

*

Dylan's instincts should never be underestimated. One fact concerning the song 'Hurricane' was not in dispute in 1975. Whatever happened at the Lafayette Bar and Grill, whoever was guilty or innocent, the Dylan-Levy account was only too plausible. That was the essence of the song's power. In 1966, and for many years afterwards, Paterson was a melting-pot town with more than its share of ethnic tensions.[21] The Lafayette was alleged, meanwhile, to have been a home-from-home for white racists. That might have made it a target for a revenge attack at 2.30 a.m. on a June night, but it also helped to explain the world inhabited by black men such as Rubin Carter.

One author of 'Hurricane' might say that injustice could 'happen to anybody', but it wasn't quite true. Details within the verses were used at the time, as they are used still on certain websites, to dispute a bigger argument about law, race and power.[22] Dylan and Levy took the figure of Carter and used what they knew about the case – and there was more than just 'poetic licence' involved – to say something about America. Was the Hurricane an early victim of racial profiling? In his case, the jury (no joke intended) is still out. The song nevertheless posed a question: what kind of country is it that allows ethnic identity to become a standard tool of criminology, of law enforcement, and of penal procedure? One answer: a country that considers itself white. Dylan-Levy's news was not always welcome news, therefore. That might explain why the flaws and failures of their song were seized upon with such zeal. But facts, as mentioned, are facts.

The General Social Survey (GSS) is a remarkable American project. Since 1972, the National Opinion Research Center at the University of Chicago has been harvesting flecks of data from every aspect of daily existence to compile this ever-changing portrait of the nation. In

1972–3, when Rubin Carter was deep in the fight to overturn his conviction, the GSS disclosed encouraging news. As it turned out, only 3 per cent of Americans still believed that whites should have 'first chance' at a job; only 13 per cent endorsed racially segregated schools.

This was considered progress, but not all of the findings could be viewed in the same rosy light. As the authors of a 2009 paper from the Harvard Kennedy School put it, 'just 1 in 4 (25 per cent) said that they would not vote for a qualified black presidential candidate nominated by their own party'.[23] 'Just' might stand, no doubt, as a plausible statistical measure in the social sciences. The paper further recorded that in the early 1970s 'only a third of Northern whites endorsed the idea that whites have the right to keep blacks out of their neighborhood, compared to 53 per cent of Southern whites'. Clearly, the word 'only' must also carry greater weight with sociologists than with some of us.

The Harvard paper continued: 'Fully 86 per cent of white respondents rejected school busing as a tool for achieving school desegregation. Only about a quarter of white respondents thought the government was spending "too much" on assisting blacks, but most felt that such spending was already at the right level. Third, in 1972 74 per cent of whites nationwide agreed that "blacks should not push themselves" where they are not wanted.'

A few statements could be rephrased. You could as well say, for example, that at the beginning of the 1970s one in four Americans – from a survey involving all ethnic groups – thought too much money was being spent for the benefit of the recent descendants of slaves. Three Americans in every four were averse to black self-assertion, or – if 'push themselves' means anything – to political action by black people. Equally, 'fewer than 15 per cent of whites nationwide' – not just in the South, in other words – still hankered after a racist education system. The 'idea that whites have a right to keep blacks out of their neighborhoods' enjoyed the support of 40 per cent of the population in 1972. In 1973, laws to prohibit racial discrimination by people selling their homes were still being opposed by 65 per cent of whites.

The authors of the Harvard paper, alert to the claim that Barack Obama's election to the presidency in 2008 had brought America to a 'post-racial' moment, also noted that in the year of his first triumph 'a nontrivial proportion of whites nationwide, 28 per cent, still support an individual homeowner's right to discriminate on the basis of race when selling a home, and even nearly 1 in 4 highly-educated Northern whites adopt this position'. The manifold assumptions behind the tiny comparative word 'even' could justify an entire field for study.

When Rubin Carter was publishing his first book and fighting his courtroom battles, the '86 per cent of white respondents' opposed to the use of school buses in the battle against segregation found their cause célèbre in the city of Boston. Efforts there to enforce the Racial Imbalance Act of 1965 by moving children to shared classrooms were met with protests and riots. Thanks to busing, one black lawyer was attacked with the sharp end of a flagstaff bearing the Stars and Stripes; vengeful black teenagers then put a white man into a coma. The General Social Survey had already identified the roots of the argument. Most white people were sufficiently progressive as to abhor outright segregation in schooling. They welcomed black faces among their children. But not *too many* black faces.

Dylan-Levy had not plucked a glamorous controversy from the air, then, or manufactured a conflict to suit their unexamined Village-liberal attitudes. The so-called 'incarceration boom', the disproportionate jailing of young African American men, began in the mid-1970s. The General Social Survey meanwhile did not, and does not, see fit to gather data from anyone detained in a penal institution. So who really knew about the reality?

Even before mandatory sentencing – 'three strikes and you're out' – blacks made up 41 per cent of inmates in state or federal prisons in 1970, at a time when African Americans were 11.1 per cent of the general population.[24] The comparable figures as the twenty-first century began would be 72.7 per cent and 13 per cent respectively. In seizing on the case of the Hurricane, Dylan-Levy had seized on a bigger truth. Carter, right or wrong, was emblematic of the fact that, despite all the civil-rights struggles to which Dylan had once given his clamant songs, something foul was going on. In 'Hurricane' the familiar prophetic voice told of a society in which, by the century's end, one in five black men in their 30s who lacked a college education would instead have a prison record.[25]

Does any of that count as an excuse for error by writers declaiming on issues of truth and justice? Dylan would be forced to re-record his 'Hurricane' – the result was a marked improvement – after Columbia's lawyers fretted that Bello and Bradley might sue over the unsubstantiated claim that they had 'robbed the bodies' at the Lafayette. In 1982, Dylan-Levy would also be on the receiving end of a complaint under the heading 'Patricia Ann Valentine, Plaintiff-Appellant v. CBS Inc.

D/B/a Columbia Records, Bob Dylan A/K/a Robert Zimmerman, Jacques Levy and Warner Bros. Publications Inc.'. 'D/B/a' stands for 'doing business as', but neither at first hearing nor on appeal would the courts do business with Miss Patty Valentine's claim for redress because, she said, of 'common law defamation, invasion of privacy, and unauthorized publication of her name in violation of a Florida statute'. She had not been named in the song, as she alleged, as a party to a conspiracy.

Instead, back in reality, 'all the criminals in their coats and ties / Are free to drink martinis and watch the sun rise'. Dylan had placed himself back in the arena of political argument, where beliefs too often pass for facts and facts are always open to interpretation. Even critics of 'Hurricane' accept that if Dylan-Levy had presented audiences with a piece of pop fiction, something akin to Elvis Presley's 'In the Ghetto' or Marvin Gaye's What's Going On, applause would have been universal. The song spoke of truths about America that were hard to dispute.

On its own terms, in contrast, the piece drew its electrifying charge from the fact that it concerned the fate of a real man. There was, in any case, a bigger fact. Whatever the errors committed by Dylan-Levy, the Hurricane was never shown to be guilty beyond reasonable doubt. The very worst that could be said might be covered, instead, by the old Scottish verdict of 'not proven'. The legal 'technicalities' that saw him freed existed for a reason, as Judge Haddon Lee Sarokin of the United States District Court for the District of New Jersey made clear when he set aside the convictions of Carter and Artis in November 1985.[26]

In his judgment, Sarokin observed that the prosecution had been 'predicated upon an appeal to racism rather than reason, and concealment rather than disclosure'. Throwing out the revenge theory, attacking the suppression of evidence, dismissing the reliability of Bello 'after his unbelievable series of recantations and recantations of his recantations', the judge said: 'This court is convinced that a conviction which rests upon racial stereotypes, fears and prejudices violates rights too fundamental to permit deference to stand in the way of the relief sought.' Sarokin also shredded the state's claim that the ammunition allegedly discovered in Carter's vehicle matched the murder weapons. He noted that police had tried and failed to halt an actual white getaway car on the night in question. Freeing Carter, the judge went on to say that 'to permit a conviction to be urged based upon such factors, or to permit a conviction to stand having utilised such factors, diminishes our fundamental constitutional rights'.

82

So Dylan-Levy got some facts wrong. They were not quite as unreliable, it transpires, as those paid to administer and enforce the law in New Jersey in the aftermath of the Lafayette killings. The fact that the septuagenarian Rubin Carter is 'not innocent' in 2013 is somehow enough, for some amateur criminologists, to convict a man time and again in their virtual courts, and to condemn a song. This might be what Dylan-Levy had in mind when they wrote of being 'ashamed to live in a land / Where justice is a game'.

In his own book on the Carter case, the late Paul B. Wice, a professor of political science at Drew University in Madison, New Jersey, wrote that it 'shows what can happen when police and prosecutors do not act professionally, critical witnesses lie, and the justice system is unwilling to correct its errors or admit its mistakes'.[27] Perhaps it also shows what a songwriter, sometimes, is for. In 'Hurricane', the old, mistrusted idea that poetry is truth was illuminated to glorious effect. Rubin Carter was not always the best of black men. That didn't make him a guilty black man.

*

On the *Desire* album, 'Hurricane' is followed instantly by 'Isis'. It makes for an uncomfortable contrast. You have to muster a certain tolerance for a labouring melody to indulge the song that supposedly 'meant something' (or other) to Jacques Levy. Here's one occasion when Scarlet Rivera's plangent fiddle amounts to little more than exotic colouring, a tinting of the dull negative, mere tone. You must then summon patience towards symbolism, if it truly exists, for symbolism's sake. Then, sometimes, you must remember to ask why you cared about Bob Dylan to begin with. With 'Isis', collaboration brought out his worst – which is to say most portentous – side. Compare this piece of mock-epic verse with 'Shelter from the Storm' from *Blood on the Tracks* and you see why two pairs of hands were less capable than one. 'Isis' has the feel of something manufactured from New Age bric-a-brac.

The song is peculiarly of its time. In the mid-'70s, notoriously, all manner of hocus-pocus masquerading as esoteric wisdom was being granted shelf space. A blockage in the counter-culture's intellectual plumbing, long predictable, would cause Dylan-Levy's fable of tomb raiders, mysterious hidden treasure, a 'mystical child' and Mexican-type pyramids – icy ones, too – to be taken very seriously. Stuff was backing up everywhere. Deliver a fun cowboy story that could be taken as the description of a numinous 'quest' way out west and the fans of

Carlos Castañeda's visionary hokum would be on you like stoned coyotes.

Whether the Peruvian American's adventures in shamanism and ready-to-wear enlightenment ever took place is a subject for continuing debate among those who still care. The pertinent fact, according to the always reliable internet, is that his 11 books would sell 28 million copies in 17 languages, and that stacks of those were bought, read and believed in the 1970s. The Castañeda phenomenon, one marker of the intellectual mutations afflicting the remnant counter-culture, was peculiar but far from unusual. While middle America was panicking over fuel shortages amid the OPEC oil embargo of 1973, while rationing was being introduced and gas stations were running dry, those who fancied themselves as seekers after truth were on an intellectual vacation. In the aftermath of the crisis, automobile sales fell in America for the first time in decades. The economy stagnated amid crazy inflation – hitting 12.3 per cent by the end of 1974 – while the aptly named 'misery index' (inflation plus unemployment) rose ever upwards. Many people, some of them boasting an education, looked for alternative ways to exist, think and believe. Sometimes it seemed as though any alternative would do.

You could take your pick: religions of every variety, ancient or newly hatched; primal therapy for your childhood trauma; crystals for your delinquent chakras; the I Ching and Tarot cards – Dylan dabbled with both – to plug you into the collective unconscious. You could be healed by colours, or by channelled 'energy', or be brought to instant cosmic consciousness by one of the frequent flyers from a passing UFO. The presence of those visitors among us had been demonstrated, at least to his own satisfaction, by Erich von Däniken in his wildly popular book *Chariots of the Gods?* (1968). By the middle of the 1970s, the volume was well on its way to selling 63 million copies around the world. In 1977, Steven Spielberg's movie *Close Encounters of the Third Kind* would make many millions of dollars from the wishful thinking of the selfsame, ready-made audience. Other questing souls were poring over the mistranslated 'prophecies' of Nostradamus, or taking up with the Scientologists, or seeking out the signs and wonders promised by the evangelical communes of the burgeoning Jesus movement. The last of these developments, the latest of America's recurring religious revivals, would acquire a significance for Dylan before long.

In the meantime, he was singing in 'Isis' of a treasure-seeker crossing the wastelands to 'the pyramids all embedded in ice'. Out in communal

America, in the 'intentional communities' springing up haphazardly in the backwoods and desert regions, a belief in pyramid power – another miracle founded on infallible 'energy' – was already well established. 'Seeking', just as in the Dylan-Levy tale, was also in vogue. The counter-culture was turning inwards, prodded by a growing band of shrinks, seers, saints and mountebanks. It was all a long way from the civil-rights struggle and political engagement. The spiritual fashions of the 1970s could be taken as evidence of a deep disenchantment: those heading for the communes would not have disagreed. In place of a generation's refusal to believe in their elders or in governments, there was a willingness to believe just about anything. Whether thanks to Levy's influence or to Dylan's own foggy understanding of what was afoot, 'Isis' played to a certain crowd.

It was of no moment that plenty of people were trading in this stuff, in music and in print. By 1975, parts of the pop world were being crushed beneath the weight of 'wisdom' as the oxymoronic expression 'New Age thinking' passed into the language. The depressing thing about 'Isis' was and is the fact that Dylan fell for it, or seemed to fall for it. There had been signs before – on *John Wesley Harding*, on *New Morning* – but here was his spiritual side exposed for all to see. It counted, fittingly enough, as an omen. With this piece he then persuaded others to take his apparent seriousness seriously. No doubt he half-believed it himself.

None of this should mean that 'Isis' is necessarily a bad song, of course. Mysticism and allegory are old news in literature; poetry is not verifiable scientifically. On the album, nevertheless, these mannered verses and this piece of music seem only to stifle the power of 'Hurricane'. Perhaps it is simply the jolting difference between the secular ballad written for Rubin Carter amid his real plight in a real prison cell and a windy tale set to a mythographic cliché. Perhaps it is just that even now the 'Isis' melody seems forced, lacking in conviction, dull.

On the Rolling Thunder tour Dylan was capable of transforming this song 'about marriage' in his performances, at least if the Montreal footage from the film *Renaldo and Clara* is to be trusted.[28] Dispensing with his guitar, wielding his harmonica like a personal weapon, speeding the song's tempo, prowling around the stage and singing as well as he had ever done, Dylan turned the fake-mystical western without much of a tune into something memorable and, by its lights, authentic. For all that, the film of a venomously precise performance in early December serves only to demonstrate the weaknesses of the studio version recorded in New York on 31 July. On stage, Dylan's sheer driven energy helped to distract attention from what could not be concealed on the album.

So what kind of famous song – more particularly, what kind of Bob Dylan song – is this? Why Isis? Why give the female lead in this little cowboy story the name of an Egyptian deity if, in the Levy version, there was no symbolic intent? Interrogating the theatre director during the Rolling Thunder tour, Larry Sloman would try to call in evidence the sensationally inept Jesus-meets-Isis D.H. Lawrence tale *The Man Who Died* (1929).[29] (Specimen: 'He crouched to her, and he felt the blaze of his manhood and his power rise up in his loins, magnificent.' The fantasy ends with the actually immortal observation that 'Tomorrow is another day'.) Levy would not entertain the suggestion of a relationship. The song, he claimed, had nothing to do with an Egyptian goddess. Those pyramids had been introduced, supposedly, only as a substitute for the Grand Teton mountain range. The locale for 'Isis' was therefore 'the hills somewhere in Wyoming or something'. The story had arisen, said the trained psychotherapist gamely, only because of some sort of unconscious connection. Despite his presumed expertise in such matters, Levy did not speculate on the nature of the connection.

In June of 1985, during a syndicated satellite radio interview, Dylan persisted with the transparent conceit that 'Isis' was as much a mystery to him as it was to anyone. A caller was told that he had written the song with another person, that 'I think half the verses were mine and half the verses were his'. Somehow, 'it just sort of ended up being what it was. I really don't know too much in depth what it would mean.'[30] If the junior writing partner was misinformed, then, or if he had failed somehow to notice that his co-author might possibly have chosen his strange song title for a reason, where was Dylan heading with this stuff? God-wards, more or less.

In old Egypt, Isis was, as another song might have put it, a friend to the poor. Slaves and sinners enjoyed her patronage. She was the mother goddess, a protector of children and of the dead. Her vast wings afforded shelter and her 'lap' was identified with the throne of the kingdom. She taught mortal women how to grind corn and weave; she taught people how to combat illness and how to marry. She was the sister and consort of Osiris, the creator of civilisations, later the ruler of the underworld. Cults of Isis have persisted to the present day, some of them exotic enough to be at home in certain parts of California, but she is not often identified with Sara Dylan.

In his vastly influential *The Golden Bough* (1890–1915), the Scottish anthropologist J.G. Frazer writes of Isis-worship developing from the fertility cult of 'a rustic Corn-Mother adored with uncouth rites by Egyptian swains' to the religion of 'the true wife, the tender mother, the beneficent queen of nature, encircled with the nimbus of moral purity, of immemorial and mysterious sanctity'.[31] Only a short leap was required after Christianity's appearance, it seems, to transport prospective worshippers from Isis to the matching cult of the Madonna. Dylan would follow.

The American Joseph Campbell, pioneer of comparative mythology and propounder of the belief that myth is central to all human society, drew heavily on Frazer's work, and from Freud and Carl Gustav Jung, for his claim that storytelling has followed a pattern – 'the hero's journey' – in almost every culture and at almost every point in history. Campbell called it 'the one, shape-shifting yet marvellously constant story'.[32] In his *The Hero with a Thousand Faces* (1949) he traced fully 17 stages in this 'monomyth', during which the heroic sort is called to adventure, meets his mentor and experiences an ineffable 'threshold passage'. So far, so 'Isis'.

Thereafter, as though trapped in a mythopoetic board game – or, indeed, stuck inside the average Hollywood action movie – the hero has to find his allies and guides, face ordeals, resist temptations, brave enemies, have his dark night of the soul, survive a final, truly big test, and win the boon he was after to begin with. Then he returns, celebrating, resurrected and fit for his place in society. This is, after a fashion, the Dylan-Levy song.

In *Primitive Mythology* (1959), the first volume in a tetralogy he would entitle *The Masks of God*, Campbell would observe that Isis and Osiris, siblings and spouses, were born 'during the sacred interval of those five supplementary days' that fell between one 360-day Egyptian calendric year and the next. The 'five intercalated days . . . were taken to represent a sacred opening through which spiritual energy flowed into the round of the temporal universe'.[33] So: 'I married Isis on the fifth day of May'? So: 'things would be different the *next time* [my italics] we wed'? If that was the idea, Dylan-Levy were adrift with their Egyptology. The five added days in the ancient calendar did not fall anywhere near the month we know as May.

Nevertheless, in *Occidental Mythology* (1964) Joseph Campbell would identify Isis – along with Venus-Aphrodite, Cybele, Ishtar and others besides – as a version of the pre-Christian 'Mother of God'.[34] As in *Primitive Mythology*, she was recalled as 'the natural mother of all things', 'adored throughout the world'. This was the 'Isis of Ten Thousand Names'. Involve her in a song 'about marriage', therefore, and you have stepped just a little way beyond the usual romantic clichés.

Campbell's influence was approaching its height in the 1970s: *Primitive Mythology* alone went through 11 reprints during the decade. No one had yet paid serious notice to the fact that his 'hero's journey' template appeared to exclude ordinary mortal women almost entirely, or that a host of modern, post-Enlightenment narratives have nothing in common with his supposedly universal pattern. On the opening page of *The Hero with a Thousand Faces*, Campbell had written, near ecstatically, that 'myth is the secret opening through which the inexhaustible energies of the cosmos pour into the human cultural manifestation'. In the 1970s, this sounded like a claim worthy of study to those inclined towards New Age mysteries, not least because Campbell would also argue that almost everything important about the species – religion, philosophy, art, science, dreams, 'social forms' both primitive and historic – had come boiling forth from 'the basic, magic ring of myth'. Only later would critics begin to ask what any of this actually meant, or presumed to describe. A claim so gigantic was impossible to support with evidence. Precisely because the claim was so gigantic, however, it caught on.

The Arthurian tale of the Grail quest fits the Campbell mould, but then so does the movie *Star Wars* (1977), a picture written by George Lucas – typed, at any rate – under the direct and acknowledged influence of *The Hero with a Thousand Faces*. In fact, any number of numbingly predictable three-act Hollywood hero-vehicles still echo the allegedly primal myth, but only because their writers and directors have taken Campbell's account of man's journey for, so to speak, gospel. Dylan-Levy's little tale might therefore seem to be in a direct line of descent from pop culture's versions of the mythologist's theories. But what is interesting about 'Isis', once you survive its lacklustre melody, is that the song does no such thing. Dylan, Levy, or both together, subvert the entire idea.

Campbell prescribes a meeting with a goddess – the 'Queen Goddess of the World', indeed – and sees nothing amiss with casting Woman as Temptress whose lure has to be 'surpassed' by the hero. Dylan-Levy seem to subscribe to this notion – 'What drives me to you is what drives me insane' – but their story ends with their hero's return to his Isis. As for the quest's reward, the treasure and boon: the tomb in the song is empty. As the artist sang: 'There was no jewels, no nothin', I felt I'd been had.' The Dylan-Levy song is close to a parody, in fact, of Campbell's theory. Their protagonist's return, having dumped his dead companion 'down in the hole' and having 'said a quick prayer', does not fit with the allegedly immemorial narrative. In the slightly amended version given in *Lyrics: 1962–2001*, the relevant verse, by far the best in the song, runs:

> She said, 'Where ya been?' I said, 'No place special'
> She said, 'You look different.' I said, 'Well, not quite'
> She said, 'You been gone.' I said, 'That's only natural'
> She said, 'You gonna stay?' I said, 'Yeah, I jes might'

Successful or not, 'Isis' showed Dylan to be dabbling with ideas on the border between poetry and religion. Whether of his own volition – he picked the title, after all – or because Levy had given 'Isis' its direction with, allegedly, that first line, Dylan was striking out on a new course. However you read the tale, it treats the union of two people as a metaphysical, even *sacred* bond. In 1975, this was new for Dylan. It went far beyond the more-or-less conventional pieties of 'Wedding Song' on *Planet Waves*. It also aligned the artist, fast approaching the end of his actual marriage, with the credulous transcendentalist wing of his post-'60s generation. Only one outcome was likely.

In fact, *Desire* provided evidence that he was a lot closer to encountering his God in 1975 than anyone cared to notice at the time. After the throwaway (if only) 'Mozambique', a track that probably justified its existence because it involved the only truly uptempo pop song from which a useful recording had been extracted, came 'One More Cup of Coffee'. The refrain, 'One more cup of coffee for the road / One more cup of coffee 'fore I go / To the valley below', seemed like an obvious enough comment on death and possible resurrection. The next track all but shouted its meaning, yet few bothered to listen.

'Oh, Sister', the album's fifth song, was instead regarded as an attempt – an obtuse and maladroit attempt – to come to grips with emerging feminism. Such it was, in part. As such, it was a big improvement on the entirely witless 'Rita May'. But Dylan-Levy did more than attempt to address, in a self-serving kind of way, the Women's

Liberation Movement and second-wave feminism in the United States in the 1970s. The authors had awoken late to that, in any case. By 1975, books such as Kate Millett's *Sexual Politics* and Germaine Greer's *The Female Eunuch* (both 1970) were long established as bestsellers, the visible and vocal expressions of a global upheaval. Dylan, never previously mistaken for a born feminist, was only crashing the party, clumsily, when he sang, 'Oh, sister, am I not a brother to you?'

In reality, the Dylan-Levy song, if it counted as any sort of serious response to feminism, embodied an ancient sort of paternalism in the joint authors' treatment of their 'sister'. As Michael Gray pointed out in his *Song & Dance Man III* (2000), and more explicitly in his *The Bob Dylan Encyclopedia* (2006), with this piece 'Dylan's religious focus is on its way to the conventionally Christian'.[35] You could even argue that Dylan and his focus have arrived intact at that righteous position with 'Oh, Sister'. Then you would find yourself agreeing with Gray's rueful observation that 'it's hard to understand how we could have ignored [this] at the time'.

No one figured Dylan for a believer in 1975. No one wanted to believe it, *despite* the words coming out of his mouth. Mystical 'Isis' was one thing, a reflection, perhaps, of the decade's spiritual fads and fancies. *Christianity?* Here it was, nevertheless. Each of the first three verses of 'Oh, Sister' ended, respectively, as follows:

Our Father would not like the way that you act
And you must realise the danger . . .

And is our purpose not the same on this earth
To love and follow His direction? . . .

We died and were reborn
And then mysteriously saved . . .

Whatever the definitions of sisterhood and brotherhood, this was paternalism from the biblical source, with Emmylou Harris providing dutiful backing vocals as Rivera's violin played second fiddle to the preacher. The 'theory' that Dylan was instead engaged in a kind of songwriter's call-and-response with Joan Baez because of something she *might* have written seems flimsy. When you begin to talk of being 'mysteriously saved' you are not raking over old love affairs. Religious or not, the result was twee.

On the album, in another unsettling contrast, the long ballad called 'Joey' followed. If 'Hurricane' was held to be controversial because of its disputed relationship with the truth, here was real myth-making, though not in the sense understood by Joseph Campbell. The Joseph in this song, 'Mad Joey' Gallo, might have been portrayed as a victim of his society and of his times, just like Rubin Carter. Dylan-Levy, or Levy alone, might have been attempting to depict an individual 'Always on the outside of whatever side there was', an honourable man seeking only 'peace and quiet', hounded by the police and gunned down while trying 'to protect his family'. The merest brush with the facts of the career of a lifelong vicious mobster dispelled that nonsense. The facts, in any case, were no secret.

Musically, 'Joey' strikes a nicely wistful, elegiac note, even if the 'Little Italy' accordion might test the patience of a few Italian Americans. Once again, it is possible to assert that if Dylan-Levy had stuck to outright fiction they would have stayed clear of trouble. This piece of Mafia chic was asking for that trouble. Americans, New Yorkers above all, were hardly ignorant of organised crime by the middle of the 1970s. The testimony of the informer Joseph Valachi during the 1963 McClellan Hearings had exposed the existence of the Mob's ruling 'Five Families'. Those hearings had led to the Racketeer Influenced and Corrupt Organizations legislation in 1970. The 1972 House Select Committee on Crime had then investigated the connections between gangsters and horse racing. Thanks to the word of another informer, one Joe 'The Baron' Barboza, allegations – vigorously denied – had been made against the original superstar, Francis Albert Sinatra. 'Joey' said nothing new about hoodlums. Its treatment of bloody reality was the problem.

The fact that Francis Ford Coppola's film of The Godfather had appeared in 1972, and had brought forth a masterful sequel in 1974, is clearly relevant. Call it an influence. The first film of the eventual trilogy was based on Mario Puzo's 1969 novel. That had taken its title, in turn, from an expression first heard publicly during Valachi's 1963 testimony. There was something to be said, thought author and film-maker, about honour beyond the law, about bonds of loyalty transcending society's demands, about working to survive and surviving to work. Dylan-Levy followed along behind. As the latter would tell Larry Sloman, one of the 'wonderful' things about the co-written songs of Desire was that they gave Dylan 'a chance to do some acting'.[36]

On one reading, Coppola created an allegory of American capitalism.

According to several other readings, he romanticised, even glorified, men of unspeakable violence who corrupted everything they touched. A fair verdict might be that the director managed both feats. Where's the contradiction, after all? The movies are explicit in portraying the corruption and the destruction, physical and moral, to which inevitably corrupted 'honour' must lead. Equally, the pictures are fiction: parallels might be drawn and interpretations made, but Coppola and Puzo were free to reject them. Nevertheless, when you cast Marlon Brando, Al Pacino and Robert De Niro as your stars, Hollywood's dazzling lustre overwhelms most of the distinctions between light and shade, squalid and heroic.

When you name your song for a real person and employ documented incidents from his career, a burden of proof descends. If you have made your reputation as a truth-teller, meanwhile, responsibilities are unavoidable. Dylan-Levy did not linger much over moral gradations. They made an outlaw hero not from a Billy the Kid, a figure mired in legend, but from an individual who had been shot to pieces – back, elbow, backside – in that clam house on New York's Mulberry Street in 1972. They (or Levy) even introduced an improbable godfather of their own at Gallo's grave, come 'to say one last goodbye to the son that he could not save'.

The real Joey had launched a Mob war and died as a result. Whatever his literary pursuits in prison, whatever his friendships with incarcerated black men (who 'seemed to understand / What it's like to be in society with a shackle on your hand'), he was a hit man, an enforcer, a racketeer preying on the weak, and an individual party to certain scenes of mayhem that might well have inspired passages in *The Godfather*. Gallo read Tolstoy; it didn't make him a hero.

As though to demonstrate how deluded celebrity folk can be, 'Joey' appeared while America was enduring a justified panic over rising crime rates. In 1960, 288,460 crimes of violence had been recorded, 9,110 of them murders. By 1970, the equivalent figures were 738,820 and 16,000; by 1975, still climbing, the numbers said 1,039,710 and 20,510.[37] The romanticising of Gallo in such a circumstance was crass. To call 'Joey' 'just a song', to argue that all artists blur the difference between truth and fiction, to say that art has its prerogatives, does not answer the case for a singer with Dylan's pedigree, even if he did not contribute a line to the finished piece. The argument would ring hollow, in any case, when in 'Hurricane' he was hammering away at the need for unpolluted truth and demanding an end to lies.

In his *Village Voice* comment on *Desire*, early in March 1976, Lester Bangs would peel 'Joey' apart.[38] Otherwise forgiving of outrageous outlaw behaviour (much of it his own), Bangs made the obvious point that certain New York gangsters had been given sufficient cause to 'blow away' Joe Gallo. The crook had been the opposite of an innocent man swept along by events. Crazy Lester didn't care for the song at any price – 'ponderous, sloppy, numbingly boring' – or for Dylan, most of the time. Among other things, a writer long disenchanted with his former hero had decreed *Blood on the Tracks* to be an instrument, variety unspecified, of self-abuse. The artist scrambled most of the big Bangs theories about 'rock' and its ineffable potency.

In the *Voice*, the journalist nevertheless asserted that Gallo had been a wife-beating thug who was fed the anti-psychotic drug Thorazine routinely, by the same suffering wife, after his release from prison. Bangs also managed to speak to Jacques Levy, who appears not to have mentioned that Dylan might have contributed little, if anything, to the lyrics of 'Joey'. Instead, the co-writer asserted, as if it was news, that, 'You know, Bob has always had a thing about outlaws.' Levy then asked if anyone would call John Wesley Harding 'a small-time hoodlum' (in point of fact, the real Wes Hardin was a murderous medium-scale hoodlum). Dylan's collaborator further defended Gallo as no psychopath and, indeed, right on cue, as 'a victim of society'.

Bangs, for his part, offered the view that Dylan was simply lazy, that *Desire* was 'an exploitation record'. In answer to the wholly rhetorical question, 'What is Dylan thinking?' relentless Lester got the jump on his own last coma – 30 April 1982, wrong drugs in the wrong order at the wrong Manhattan time in an apartment above a Chinese restaurant – by asserting of the artist that 'he is not thinking at all'. In the case of 'Joey', there was some truth in the statement. The only journalistic trick missed by Bangs involved another simple question. When even the murdering subliterates of the Mafia knew an individual by playful nicknames involving 'mad' and 'crazy', what hope was there for the usual, folk-type liberal Greenwich Village defence of a poor boy forced to live outside the law?

In *Rolling Stone*'s review of the album, also in March, Dave Marsh would demonstrate that the once-deferential magazine was no longer awestruck on demand. Reviewers, some of them, were losing patience with Dylan's presumed right to please himself. *Desire* had become an odd and confused piece of work. Of 'Joey' and the artist, Marsh – who otherwise praised the album highly – wrote that the track was 'musically seductive', but argued that

> his neatest ellipsis is to avoid all mention of the public execution of Joseph Colombo [the crime family boss survived the execution attempt], which the evidence suggests the Gallo mob ordered. In which case it is hardly relevant that Joey Gallo did not carry a personal weapon [reports of his killing state that he drew a handgun when the attack began] and much more understandable that he himself was gunned down in front of his family. Gallo was an outlaw, in fact, only in the sense that he refused to live by the rules of the Mob . . . Is an intellectual Mafioso really that much more heroic than an unlettered hood? This is elitist sophistry of the worst sort, contemptible even when it comes from an outlaw radlib like Bob Dylan.

Sheer fiction saved the record. Clinton Heylin describes 'Black Diamond Bay' as 'something of a lost gem', apparently because Dylan has never played the song in concert.[39] If the artist pays no attention, why should we? A degree of neglect for the piece might also have arisen from first impressions – everyone's first impressions – of the *Desire* album, when any long ballad was liable to wind up becalmed in the wake of 'Hurricane'. 'Black Diamond Bay' was nevertheless a striking piece of art and craft to begin with. It grows in stature with the years.

The song is beset with literary associations, chiefly involving Joseph Conrad, and is weighed down by its apparent debts. Dylan-Levy didn't just set a few bits of a novel to a tune, but the temptation to justify the artist in terms of literature has often beguiled the citationists who treat all references as cultural price stickers, marks of artistic worth and quality. If Dylan shows that, for a wonder, he has read a serious work or two, he becomes a serious proposition. On the other hand, the parallels between 'Black Diamond Bay' and at least one of Conrad's later books are hard to ignore.

Allen Ginsberg would make the first move in the allusion-hunting game with his *Desire* sleeve note – presumably based on a conversation with Dylan – exulting in those 'surrealist mind-jump inventions line by line, except D. says he's reading Joseph Conrad storyteller'. For whatever reason, some who paid attention to the song then made an erroneous connection with *Heart of Darkness* (1899). The idea would have been intriguing, save for the fact that the connection doesn't exist; there is no match. The clear family relationship, in structure, bits of plot and lots of set dressing, is with 1915's *Victory*, the finest of Conrad's pre-modern melodramas. In the book, as in the song, structure is paramount.

You can well believe that the song sprang, in some form, from Dylan's reading. Its other, better reason to exist was as a continuation of his investigation into the possibilities of metaphysical ballads that began with 'Lily, Rosemary and the Jack of Hearts' on *Blood on the Tracks*. The two songs have a lot in common but several important differences. At eighty-four lines, seven and a half minutes and seven expertly constructed verses long, 'Black Diamond Bay' might meanwhile count as another good example of Dylan's 'cinematic' writing, or what Michael Gray has called, accurately enough, his 'movie-spinning'.[40] The description, a self-confessed species of faint praise, overlooks what might be involved in creating a drama that lasts only 450 seconds, with a startling, audacious inversion of perspective at its end. Dylan-Levy got that from Joe Conrad, but its use in the song is a feat of technical daring.

Mercifully, 'Black Diamond Bay' owes nothing whatever to anything Joseph Campbell had to say about primal narrative, mythic or otherwise. There is no hero, certainly no epic journey, least of all a spiritual rebirth. Instead, the song owes everything to Conrad's use in *Victory* of doubled perspectives, physical and moral, and to the idea of fate, blind and mute, that permeates *Blood on the Tracks*. In 'Black Diamond Bay', good and evil contend; people scurry around on their plots, affairs and petty human errands; the volcano explodes regardless. The End.

Back home, at the song's actual end, the narration is halted by a new voice, possibly a version of Dylan's own, as he sits at home alone in LA, drinking beer and 'Watchin'' old Cronkite on the seven o'clock news'. Nothing much happening; some earthquake somewhere; some flotsam; just 'another hard-luck story that you're gonna hear'. After the long preceding *fin de siècle* drama 'there's really nothin' anyone can say'. There is no mystical revelation to be had from this version of the human condition.

Dylan-Levy handle all of this brilliantly. They pinch details from Conrad – period, island, gambling room, a Panama hat – but adapt only fragments of *Victory*'s plot to get the gist they need. In the novel, a narrative that at first seems realistic, if preposterous, turns out to be nothing of the kind. The reader who sees beyond heroes and devilish villains is given an allegory. In the song, in place of Conrad's tale of

Heyst the 'forgotten cast-off', the son a disillusioned 'philosopher', one who becomes locked in a struggle with an evil hotelier, Schomberg, for the heart and soul of a teenage girl, Lena – performer in a 'ladies' orchestra', no less – we get high, sardonic comedy. Conrad was writing about faith, love, fate and the challenge of evil. Dylan-Levy offer up a tale of human vanity getting what it deserves. One self-involved character, 'the Greek', is even trying ineptly to hang himself while the volcano explodes, the lava flows and the island sinks out of existence. This is, if you are that way inclined, very funny.

'Black Diamond Bay' has more sheer vivacity than the rest of the songs on *Desire* combined, 'Hurricane' always excepted. If Dylan did not perform it in concert that might have had something to do with the dispassionate, stoic and comical secularism of a piece that makes 'Isis' and 'Oh, Sister' seem fatuous. Even the stratagems and conceits of high literature are given a kind of comeuppance. Conrad's genius in *Victory* was in the management of viewpoint: first that of a sailor, then that of Heyst as teller of the tale, then the perspective of Heyst within himself, then a position within a neutral, authorial denouement. Dylan-Levy cut through it all to leave us with a bored guy drinking beer and watching the news. This, says the song, is how we these days understand ourselves: through a screen, through a background filter, through bland announcements that somewhere far off something might have happened that might have mattered to someone, but not to us.

> It seems there was an earthquake that
> Left nothin' but a Panama hat
> And a pair of old Greek shoes

On the remainder of *Desire* Dylan otherwise indulged his abiding need to play cowboy in a piece called 'Romance in Durango' and chose to end the album with a song to his wife. The former track was a (mostly) vigorous piece of writing that would have fitted well enough with the handful of sun-baked verses Dylan had conjured up for Sam Peckinpah's *Pat Garrett and Billy the Kid* (1973). Clinton Heylin, among others, has made the association: the movie had been filmed in the western Mexican state of Durango, after all.[41] On the other hand, 'Romance', theatrical or 'cinematic' according to taste, bears several of Levy's fingerprints. As the 'theatrist' would tell Larry Sloman, 'I love stories and plots.' Would Dylan have written of 'Hoofbeats like castanets on stone', or had his hero promise that 'Soon you will be dancing the fandango'? Let's hope not.

The questions act as another reminder, nevertheless, of the issue of authorship in seven of the works on *Desire*. Heylin records Levy's claim that most of the lyrics in 'Romance in Durango' were the director's own work. On the other hand, Michael Gray says that in an 'utterly marvellous' piece, with 'its skilful concentration of language', Dylan 'as often before . . . says more with less'.[42] So who gets the credit or, if needs be, the blame? With most other songwriting collaborations the issue would not arise. In the old Tin Pan Alley partnerships, above all in the miraculous half-century working relationship between Jerry Leiber and Mike Stoller, a composer operated with a lyricist; the labour was divided. In Dylan-Levy, both participants came up with words, to varying degrees. Since one of the pair was Bob Dylan, a creative singularity, a writer sometimes identified as a poet, authorship is relevant.

Inevitably, *Desire* gives the sense of an artist who is not always wholly at one with his material. 'Romance' feels, for whatever the word is worth, like an example. Dylan has a genuine secondary talent for covering other people's songs, but this album is an entirely different case. On at least one occasion, by his own account, he provided none of the lyrics. In other cases, such as in the Durango romance, his contribution is said to have been minimal. To this day, nevertheless, everything on *Desire* is treated, pored over and 'analysed', as a product of his strange, personal and individual genius. Shakespeare's efforts as a script doctor occupy one of literary scholarship's discrete categories. Pablo Picasso's intense and intimate relationship with Georges Braque in the moment of Cubism – and Jacques Levy was no Braque – gets its own shelf of monographs. With *Desire*, everything is held to be Dylan even when the artist makes no such attribution. The mistake is odd, but persistent.

Musically, in any case, 'Romance in Durango' was a cliché, a skeletal melody that sounded like a parody of Tejano and exemplified one of the album's real problems. The artist had not over-exerted himself with these tunes. The record would be a big hit; the Rolling Thunder tour that preceded *Desire*'s release in the first week of January 1976 would be a wayward triumph. But here, even after *Blood on the Tracks*, were more signs of a falling away, of a creative decline. Dylan could not manage all of the words. In the studio, he could no longer ride waves of chaos to glory. And he could not invariably contrive, borrow or adapt the melodies he needed to make the most of the lyrics he had assembled on the fly with an eager collaborator. The Dylan who could manage such feats unaided was otherwise engaged.

It tells us something, perhaps, about the part played by Sara Dylan in his existence. It might remind us, too, as we weigh out the hits and misses in an artist's career, that talent exists within a human life, not in ideal, temperature-controlled isolation. Dylan was heading in strange directions even as he produced another big hit of an album. He was becoming unmoored, adrift, even as he seemed to pull *Desire's* last song from his back pocket. There was no doubt, however, about who had written this one.

Dylan's confederates in the studio were given no hint of the existence of 'Sara'. He made the recording used on the album in the early hours of 1 August, after six consecutive attempts, while his visiting wife, not forewarned, sat listening. In a manner that could not be matched by anything on *Blood on the Tracks*, Dylan exposed himself utterly. He seemed to plead for his life.

Jacques Levy would tell Larry Sloman that 'Sara' had been written at the house in East Hampton. In *On the Road with Bob Dylan*, 'Ratso' Sloman would describe the night of 31 July/1 August as a quiet session in which a good deal of time was spent listening to playbacks of previous recordings.[43] Then, it seems, Dylan turned to his wife, said, 'This is for you,' and performed 'Sara'. As noted, it was not done in the single take pop legend might have required. Nevertheless, the song was greeted by those present, in Sloman's account, in the kind of silence generally described as 'stunned'. The only important biographical detail is that Sara Dylan remained 'impassive'.

What she felt is, as ever, not recorded. The song's appeal is, intensely, a matter of taste. There are clichés enough within it. But here, equally, are scenes from a marriage, viewed through one man's tired eyes. Here are family moments, intimate thoughts and deep feelings, private – you might have thought – and personal, offered in a manner that was, for this artist, entirely unprecedented. The song ends with Dylan's keening words, 'Don't ever leave me, don't ever go.'

Many fans find 'Sara' intensely affecting; a few of us wince. How a notably guarded woman might have felt about having her marriage acted out before strangers in the middle of a New York night tends to be overlooked. Clearly, Dylan was so caught up in his emotions he did not see fit to ask permission – for when did he ever? – for such an exercise. Through all the years of their union he and his wife had made their privacy paramount. Now all of that was cast aside simply because he felt the need.

You could call 'Sara' one of the great love songs. You could also call it a piece of sentimentalised emotional blackmail. If Levy was right about the moment of composition, Dylan was springing a surprise he had prepared beforehand. Sara, trapped by the performance, might have had reason for her impassivity. He, bereft, simultaneously acknowledging that the marriage was over yet begging for it to continue, could put his side of the story before millions of people in a Bob Dylan song. She had no such opportunity, even if – though you must doubt it – she had wanted such a thing. The fans who hear only an expression of profound love assume that Sara Dylan must have been deeply moved when first she heard the song. But what was she supposed to say or do? Try again, yet again, to make the marriage work, no doubt. For a short while the song would seem to achieve its purpose, but the recording session remains one of the strangest episodes in Dylan's career.

The paramount rule of his art had been that plain truth is never to be offered, that enigmas have a value for their own sake. This was, over and above everything, how he worked. Precisely because he had avoided explicit autobiography he had achieved universal meaning. Dylan was a creative ellipsis. Now, suddenly, he was telling the world frankly, among other things, of how his wife had helped to get him off heroin in New York at some point (presumably) in 1965.

I can still hear the sounds of those Methodist bells
I'd taken the cure and just gotten through
Stayin' up for days in the Chelsea Hotel
Writin' 'Sad-Eyed Lady of the Lowlands' for you

This, surely, was too close to any bone. Who tells the world such things? Not, or so it had been presumed hitherto, Bob Dylan. We might also remember, however, that 'Sad-Eyed Lady' had in fact been written, according to plenty of witnesses, in a recording studio in Nashville, Tennessee, on a night in mid-February 1966, when the artist was struggling to put together the album he would call Blonde on Blonde. The cure, one cure at any rate, might well have been endured just as he described, but the writing was done in Tennessee, not in New York. The author had said as much himself on more than one occasion.[44] Sara Dylan, recipient of a poet's adoration, undoubtedly the begetter of that great 1966 song, might well have paused in 1975 to wonder what became of the facts.

*

Fake platinum and spray-painted gold weave their spells. Because *Desire* went on to be a big hit, because it remains beloved, because Dylan went on to give it a context with the Rolling Thunder tour, it has been granted a free pass in most of the many assessments of his work. Set it beside *Blood on the Tracks*, however, and treat it song by song. You could call the *Desire* collection 'diverse'; you could also call it incoherent. It refuses to settle, thematically or stylistically. Then ask yourself – though this is not much of a guide to anything – about Dylan's own devotion to the fruits of his collaboration with Jacques Levy.

He has declined to perform four of the album's nine songs since 1976. 'Oh, Sister' made it to 1978 before disappearing from the artist's concert repertoire. 'One More Cup of Coffee' – entirely his own, significantly or not – has popped up intermittently, as has, very rarely, 'Romance in Durango'. 'Joey' was revived briefly in the summer of 1987, largely thanks to the urgings of Jerry Garcia and the Grateful Dead, but a handful of live performances in that dismal period served only to prove how very little Dylan could remember of all the words he had not written. The song turned up again, like a freak winter weather event, at a show in Toronto on 14 November 2012, but that was probably just a case of the playful artist keeping his band on their toes.

Desire is not central to his body of work. That might be because of the album's curious creative origins, or because it evokes memories of public controversy and private misery. Equally, the artist who has always been his own best critic – in hindsight, at any rate – has probably made a judgement. These days, Dylan has well over 600 self-composed songs to choose from when he takes his abraded vocal folds before a microphone on the public stage. The nine songs from *Desire* do not, generally speaking, meet his specifications. Clearly, he is not attached to them, personally or professionally. Yet in 1975 these songs represented the course he had chosen after the cold, mostly calm perfection of *Blood on the Tracks*.

Where did it all begin to go wrong for Bob Dylan? Late in 1975, the question would have seemed ridiculous. Surely this was the year, if any, when the tide of genius returned, when every claim ever made about him could be reasserted. The fact remains that after Dylan's first triumphs in the 1960s doubts had crept in periodically, in waves. Soon enough they would affect the artist himself. Before too many years they would overwhelm him. Perhaps it was inevitable: there is no such thing as an unblemished career save for those who die too soon, or take the Rimbaud route of creative self-annihilation. Knowing what the 1980s and 1990s would bring, it can therefore be asked of Dylan: when and where?

Some would select the long absence from public performance after the motorcycle crash in July of 1966. Others would nominate the supposed nadir of the *Self Portrait* album four years later. In fact, of course, he recovered from each of those setbacks to demonstrate, whether in the basement tapes or in *Blood on the Tracks*, that his creativity was intact. From the mid-1970s onwards, however, something began to happen to the man himself, to the interlocking series of personality changes he had accepted as the next best thing to an identity. It was as though he began to lose the signal. His private frequency seemed to disappear in the static.

Perhaps the failure began in a pre-dawn moment on 1 August 1975, just after he had sung his song to his wife. Then, at the last, probably just before 4 a.m., he got a final take he thought was good enough for 'Isis', that mystical rumination 'about marriage'. Then, barring a little overdubbing, he concluded he had made an album from all the studio chaos, the hack collaboration, and the familiar, fragile sandpainting known to him, as to everyone else, as Bob Dylan. Patti Smith barely understood the half of it when she spoke of improvisation. Henceforth, the artist would spend long decades trying to work out why his art had ever truly mattered to him.

*

With *Desire* complete and its last, discrepant track still echoing in their heads, Dylan and his wife took their children to the Minnesota farm for a holiday. As in 'Sara', as in so many troubled marriages, the presence of the youngsters enabled the parents to coexist, or so it seemed, for a while longer. Dylan was nevertheless set on returning to the road, even if his wife's heart must have faltered at the prospect. Did she protest? There are no facts to be had concerning these private matters; only guesswork is possible. One guess would nevertheless be that any lingering hope of saving the Dylan marriage was not likely to be enhanced by his return to the old, vagrant, insufferable rock and roll lifestyle. It is equally possible – and mere speculation, once again – that each of these people was resigned to the inevitable. A holiday for the sake of the children, the pretence accepted by estranged couples in every age and place, was probably the best that could be managed.

In early September, Dylan summoned a minimal three-piece band – Scarlet Rivera, the bassist Rob Stoner, the drummer Howie Wyeth – for a TV engagement in Chicago. As ever where broadcasting was concerned, the artist's sole motivation was a sense of personal obligation. He did not do these things because he enjoyed them. To this day, the old man will not countenance the possibility of being seen on the giant Jumbotron screens that are otherwise deemed essential parts of the stadium-rock experience. In 1975, an appearance on *The World of John Hammond*, a Public Broadcasting Service (PBS) tribute to his first producer, mentor and teacher, was Dylan's way of paying a debt.

In the footage he looks about as comfortable as he ever did in a TV studio. The band, given scant notice and little chance to rehearse, are meanwhile learning, as all his musicians have had to learn, that keeping up with the boss demands intuition, quick wits, daring and an ability to improvise. On this night – or rather, in the early hours of the morning – their efforts are not entirely successful. He makes no allowances: none. In one sense, Dylan takes these skilled players for granted. In another sense, he trusts them implicitly. As ever, he thinks it redundant to look ahead before he makes his leaps.

In the WTTW studios in Chicago, on 10 September, 'Hurricane', a rewritten 'Simple Twist of Fate', and 'Oh, Sister' – dedicated to 'someone out there tonight . . . She knows who she is' – are performed with a kind of distracted intensity. Dylan, sweating visibly, manages to look pained throughout, as though he should be anywhere but under the TV lights. Somehow, nevertheless, he leaves the viewer with the sense that without his unwilling presence a cold vacuum will be all that remains. In these scraps of footage Dylan reveals himself, yet again, as a necessary artist. The Chicago renditions give no real clue, of course, of what is to come. That would be too easy.

CHAPTER FOUR

Thunder on the Mountain

Shower arose from the N.W.   hard thunder   caught us in a
verry hard rain
> John Ordway, Lewis and Clark expedition, June 1805

Michael contended against Satan in the rolling thunder . . .
> William Blake, *Milton*, 'Book the First'

SOMETHING TO DO WITH RAILROADS? SOMETHING TO DO, PERHAPS,
with the relentless, fruitless mid '60s high-altitude bombing campaign
waged by America against North Vietnam? Was this roadshow inspired
by the Shoshone celebrity shaman who had given his name to a very
successful book amid all the New Age outpourings of 1974? Was it a
borrowing from the title of a 1972 album by the Grateful Dead's
drummer? Or did the Rolling Thunder Revue acquire its designation
just as the artist described?

> I was just sitting outside my house one day, thinking about a name for
> this tour, when all of a sudden, I look up into the sky and I hear a boom.
> Then, boom, boom, boom, boom, rolling from west to east. Then I figured
> that should be the name.[1]

Larry Sloman, reporting manfully for *Rolling Stone*, would describe
Dylan punching the air, 'like a prize-fighter', to illustrate the sounds
he remembered having heard at that moment. The artist's description
of the event was, in any case, just as good as any other. The tour's
chosen title was an apt enough metaphor for rock music, for the
explosive noise that could seem, sometimes, to fill the air, to echo,
resonate and decay. The tag also seemed to catch the sense of a changed

emotional climate in an America hovering on the edge of its 200th birthday, its 'Bicentennial', after all the civil-rights upheavals, the long nightmare of the war in South East Asia, the disgrace of Watergate and the economic turmoil enveloping working people as the western world's long, paradisal post-1945 boom came to an end. Rolling thunder: an approaching disturbance in the atmosphere. It was not a sound that could be ignored easily.

You can read too much into such things, of course. Where the Rolling Thunder Revue was concerned, many did. Amid the sophomoric philosophising and the grandiose claims of consciousness-raising effects – Dylan was less guilty of the offence than Ginsberg and certain others, to be fair – it was just a concert tour. A lot of cocaine was taken along the way. Groupies descended on the strolling players like hungry camp-followers. Egos grew inflated or became bruised according to the mood or the occasion. As with any concert tour, some nights were a *lot* better than others. The artist had meanwhile prepared a new album whose sales would prosper wonderfully in the wake of all the attention. Ginsberg, typically, might have announced to Sloman that the revue was 'the vision of the Sixties becoming real', but we should be wary of the gilded legend.[2]

Most of the big names in attendance, and some of the smaller fry, had a well-developed sense of how to sell a show and a healthy respect for the magical powers of hyperbole. Bobby Neuwirth, that satellite forever in Dylan's orbit, the acolyte who traded ineradicable ebullience against his modest talents, would give *Rolling Stone*'s Nat Hentoff both barrels full of bullshit as the first phase of the carnival neared its end. In this version, the entire Rolling Thunder project had materialised at the bottom of a glass or three one night at The Other End. Neuwirth, co-conspirator with Dylan back in the days when the artist was subjecting hapless victims to his rhetorical 'mindfucks' in Village bars, laid it on thick for Hentoff, but he knew no other way. If Dylan was involved, nothing else could possibly compare with what had been devised.

Me and Bob and Ramblin' Jack decided we were going to go out and tour in a station wagon, go out and play Poughkeepsie. That didn't turn out to be possible. So we did this instead. And this ain't no Elton John show, you know. This ain't no fucking one-fourth of the Beatles show or nothing like that. This show, we got it all, man. Between us we got it all. And it just gets better and better and better.[3]

Neuwirth, joking or not – probably not – was invoking the erratic cross-country trip Dylan and three stoned courtiers had undertaken in a powder-blue station wagon in February 1964. By the 1970s, the odd little journey had become part of the artist's expanding mythology, a Kerouacian (supposedly) expedition into the American heartland long before *Easy Rider* and the peregrinations of all the happy, hippy pilgrims. Neuwirth had joined that 1964 trip as a substitute sidekick just as it neared its end. Late in 1975, somewhere in New England, he was telling the man from *Rolling Stone* – 'I think you have to see Neuwirth to remember his singing,' Hentoff would note, dropping dry sand on his page – the fantasy tale of how Dylan had almost played little old Poughkeepsie, that blameless butt of New York snobbery and jokes. Instead, here were a group of elite performers who just got 'better and better and better'.

In another version of Rolling Thunder's genesis, Dylan had been contemplating this kind of tour for a long time. There is only anecdotal evidence for that claim, and not much of it. Howard Sounes asserts in his ample 2001 biography – without the usual copious documentation – that 'For years Bob had been talking to friends about a touring-revue show, maybe travelling by train, playing small towns'.[4] Sounes concludes that Dylan's juvenile fantasy of itinerant musicianship and carnival life, the one best expressed in his 1963 song 'Dusty Old Fairgrounds', had stayed with him. If so, all those talks with 'friends' – The Band's Robbie Robertson was doubtless one, though he mentioned the matter only after Rolling Thunder had come and gone – failed to lead anywhere in particular.[5] Tour '74, Dylan's first real effort at live performances since 1966, had found no use whatever for small towns or railroad trains.

On the first page of his book about the revue, Larry Sloman merely offers a strictly rhetorical 'who knows?' in answer to the question of inspiration, adding that 'a hundred different versions' were available according to who was doing the talking. In his Dylan biography Robert Shelton, only partly confirming Neuwirth's tall tale, wrote that the idea 'took fire' during the hot summer nights of 1975.[6] Sean Wilentz, in his *Bob Dylan in America*, would later quote an anecdote from Roger McGuinn's blog in which the artist and the former Byrd are tossing a basketball around in California in the spring of '75. Out of the blue, apropos of nothing at all, Dylan announces a desire to do 'something different', 'something like a circus'.[7]

People magazine, having interviewed the artist for a cover story just before the tour began, was given a clear idea by *someone* of what the Rolling Thunder Revue would entail. Dylan was not named as the source, though the journalist was astute enough to mention, as an afterthought, that he 'creates in a genre in which minimal art is almost impossible'. Nevertheless, according to *People*, the 'itinerary would detour the megabuck impresarios, the multiseat superdomes, the computerized ticket networks and re-create the modest small-club mini-tours that characterized the years when he first left Hibbing, Minn.'[8]

Ramblin' Jack Elliott's biographer meanwhile offers a verbatim statement by the artist, presumably one drawn from Elliott's memories of the night in question.[9] As they drank together on 3 July after the Other End show in which 'Abandoned Love' was first performed, Dylan had sounded his old friend out about a notion. Thus: 'Neuwirth and I were just talking about an idea, where we'd get a bus and travel around and sing and do little concerts in little halls.' Ramblin' Jack was then asked, as though the question was necessary, if he was 'in'. Neuwirth had, not for the first time, embroidered his story just a little, but Elliott was as good a source as any. He could identify the when, if not the why. As to that, Sloman, writing after the tour's end and publishing in 1978, was probably closest to the truth. No one but the artist truly knew or yet knows what he heard in the thunder.

Shelton would assert – but only assert – that Dylan 'tried to bring it all back home with the Rolling Thunder Revue'.[10] In the biographer's mind 'it' meant Greenwich Village in the early 1960s and everything the Village scene had signified to those who were involved. That might have been a part of it, judging by the cast Dylan would assemble in October. Those such as Neuwirth, Elliott and Ginsberg certainly wanted to believe that the lost hope of 'the last movement' (as the artist himself described it to Shelton in 1971) could be found again. A kind of Beat-folk aesthetic was no doubt involved. There was a belief, too, that Dylan was repaying old debts, personal and musical, to certain of his old Village cronies by inviting them along for the ride. One problem is that several of the suggestions intended to explain the origins of Rolling Thunder contradict several of the other suggestions. Sentiment, a desire to revisit the past, might well have touched Dylan after a few brandies during after-hours sessions at The Other End, but it does not sound like a wholly compelling motive.

He was always nostalgia's sworn enemy and always more ambitious than that. By October, he had a movie running through his head, new songs to sing, a new band in rehearsal, Rubin Carter's cause to further, and certain half-formed notions about performers and the nature of performance that he needed to convey. Neither a Gerde's Folk City reunion tour nor a counter-culture revival show could have been looming large in his thoughts. Old friends and colleagues would play significant roles in the Rolling Thunder Revue, but *roles* they would remain, whether the players knew it or not.

Levy would meanwhile 'direct' the affair while attempting to bear in mind that, as ever, Dylan did not take direction. Sam Shepard would sign on to write dialogue for the proposed movie before discovering, almost instantly, that the thing was to be improvised, guided only by the star's intuitions, thus rendering any script entirely redundant. Ginsberg, called at four in the morning after having had no contact with Dylan for four years, would be recruited as a kind of on-call bard only to find that there was no demand, not even once, for his services on the concert stage.[11] Neuwirth would perform, of course, as a kind of part-time master of ceremonies and full-time court jester. In 2004, in a foreword to a reissue of Shepard's *Rolling Thunder Logbook*, T-Bone Burnett would write of 'a bus full of musicians and singers and painters hurtling through the dead of night fuelled by White Russians and other things, making a movie, writing songs, and playing' – at least when they got it right, as the guitarist conceded – 'some of the most incendiary, intense and inspired rock 'n' roll, before or since'.[12] That was just one side of the story.

As one of the core group of musicians who did the real work on stages that could sometimes be crowded with upwards of 30 people, Burnett knew the whole tale as well as anyone. Rolling Thunder shows were not brief affairs. The ten-piece band that came to be known, whimsically, as Guam – with Neuwirth included in their number for no obvious reason – could be called upon to play for the best part of five hours during the two-act concerts. Musicians aside, the retinue also included the usual stage, sound and lighting people, road managers, accountants, assistants of various sorts, and – lest any of the artistes grew too starry-eyed about their bohemian journey into the heart of authentic America – an eight-strong platoon of security personnel. In addition to Dylan, Guam, Jacques Levy, Scarlet Rivera, Ginsberg, Jack Elliott and a series of guest performers, Les Kokay has put names to 75 people who were entitled to claim Rolling Thunder service medals.[13] Whatever the tales told about his gypsy caravan, the artist was not travelling light.

Among the multitude would be two entire film crews engaged for the task of attempting to capture the contents of Dylan's mind on celluloid. One would be led by Howard Alk, the cinematographer who had been involved intermittently in the editing of *Eat the Document*, the artist's botched attempt to make sense of a mass of documentary footage from the 1966 world tour. Charged with supplementing – or surpassing – Alk's efforts with the second crew was Mel Howard, later to be given credit as producer of the finished (more or less) film that Dylan would call *Renaldo and Clara*. Shooting began 'spontaneously' before the troupe had even left New York.

Lou Kemp, Dylan's boyhood friend from Camp Herzl, the Zionist summer school in the Wisconsin woods, was meanwhile handed the mind-boggling task of getting this entire ragtag army on the road and delivering it to its selected destinations, if possible in absolute secrecy. The star, for one example, would be booked into hotels under the name Phil Bender. Kemp had tagged along as a companion, and sometimes as Dylan's protector, on parts of Tour '74. Rolling Thunder, in which his authority as designated tour manager became both official and onerous, was a very different kind of job. Though Kemp shared his role as 'co-captain' with the experienced promoter and technical director Barry Imhoff, it was a notable change of pace from the old pal's day job running the family fish-shipping business. Or perhaps not.

Dylan had thrown around invitations to this adventure without appearing to think twice about the consequences. On the other hand, he seemed to know exactly what he wanted from his revue. Whatever Neuwirth or anyone else had to say about old times and collective endeavours, it was his show. Dylan could have taken to the road with the finest musicians money could lease or buy. By the middle of the 1970s, as the first chaotic *Desire* sessions had demonstrated, there was no shortage of people prepared to lend their talents to his cause. A few, such as Patti Smith and Leonard Cohen, would have the self-possession and the common sense to keep Rolling Thunder at arm's length, but they were the exceptions. Most others flocked to Dylan whenever he said the word. He had given the impression, nevertheless – what with picking up violin players in the street – that he was selecting his confederates according to whim. Some of those who joined him on the tour were big names with big reputations. Others, like Scarlet Rivera, were complete unknowns before they stumbled into Dylan. Clearly, it all made sense to him. Or rather, as so often before, he would make sense of it in due course, whatever it amounted to.

For all that, Rolling Thunder's reputation as one of Dylan's boldest and most satisfying ventures into public performance was earned. The revue might have been chaotic. It might have misfired more than once. It might have seemed like self-indulgence, a caprice, a superstar's flight into the fantasy of artistic liberation, a project dependent on big money that seemed to scorn the big-money amorality of the entertainment business while – let's not forget – pushing still another album. Often enough, nevertheless, it worked.

In its second incarnation in 1976, Rolling Thunder would end dismally, in (at best) a kind of pyrrhic victory for the artist's thrawn determination. It would lead Dylan nowhere in particular as a writer. It would count, in that regard, as a failed experiment. That might be one reason why the star kept the work achieved in the late autumn and early winter from the great mass of his audience until 2002, when at last he sanctioned *The Bootleg Series Vol. 5: Bob Dylan Live 1975, The Rolling Thunder Revue*. Even that fine album emerged as little better than a sampler, despite its extravagant title, excluding as it did most of the other acts who were reckoned to be integral to the touring shows. Only three duets with Joan Baez made it to the official release.

On the other hand, you could bear in mind that Dylan made no effort whatever to repeat this 'legendary' exercise, as though to assert that if lightning won't strike twice, thunder cannot follow. When had he ever repeated himself? Before the twenty-first century, when the difference between the groove of touring and a well-worn rut became hard to discern, Dylan had no patience whatever for the idea that he might, now and then, retrace his steps. The revue meant a lot to him while it was happening; when it was gone, it was gone. Yet if performance-in-the-moment truly counts as one large part of his art, this version of willed amnesia is of no small importance.

Sometimes, when by some combination of luck, alchemy and temperament it worked, Rolling Thunder was glorious. The glory rested, furthermore, on an artistic strategy that would become profoundly important in Dylan's career. The stage became the place where he would reinterpret and reimagine his songs, musically and lyrically. Sometimes the transformations were drastic indeed. That, above everything else, would become the lasting point of the touring revue. In effect, Dylan rewrote himself. In the process, he found one alternative to the wearisome, dispiriting process of making records. He had chewed on the idea before, but in 1975 he swallowed it whole. A song need not be, could not be, a single, immutable thing.

*

Dylan had kept certain of the *Desire* musicians hanging around after the last of the recording sessions. He had also taken up residence at the Gramercy Park Hotel on Lexington Avenue and begun to welcome others to this new base of operations. According to Don DeVito, Columbia's representative at the tapings, the artist had been dropping hints since mid-July that he had concerts in mind.[14] Nevertheless, the band members who joined him for a fortnight's rehearsals in New York in mid-October – very ragged rehearsals they were, too – reportedly had no inkling that they were preparing to hit the road. They certainly had no idea about the sort of trip Dylan had in mind. The procession of famous names who began to appear at the rented studio space might have counted as a clue, you would think, but since Dylan was unforthcoming the musicians, it seems, did not enquire further. Instead, if the *Renaldo and Clara* soundtrack and bootleg recordings of their ramshackle efforts are anything to go by – why mere rehearsals were taped at all is still a mystery – they thrashed away at song after song in an effort to satisfy their enigmatic boss.

Among the celebrity faces materialising in Midtown Manhattan was one who would be given a co-star's co-equal billing in Dylan's cherished film project, yet later describe it as 'monumentally silly', a series of 'mind movies' enacting 'whatever dream [he] had had in the night'. That winter, for the benefit of the journalist Nat Hentoff, she would dismiss the artist's venture into art cinema as 'a giant mess of a home movie'.[15] A lot of sober American critics – the Europeans were more forgiving – would soon enough concur with her judgement of the near-four-hour piece Dylan would call *Renaldo and Clara*. It left a question unanswered, however. So what was Joan Baez doing in the film, and on the tour, a long decade after being discarded with brutal finality by the artist with whom she had once discussed marriage and children?

We have her word for that last part. By all accounts, nevertheless, the once and future Queen of Folk came straight from the airport to a party at Gerde's before joining rehearsals. Baez, for one, was under no possible illusions about the nature of the job on offer. Attempting to rebuild her finances that year, she had been about to embark on a tour of her own when the message from her old lover came. Some skirmishing had followed – no one ever doubted her pride – but in the end she had taken the deal. Quoted by Hentoff in his *Rolling Stone* piece, Baez would explain that she had 'told the people dealing with the money that although it seemed like fun, they'd have to make it worth my while to change my plans'. Thanks to Dylan, the revue of course had 'integrity', she would tell the writer. Nevertheless, her lawyers had worked out a contract, 'a very detailed contract'.

Baez was not a special case. Roger McGuinn had also postponed a tour at Dylan's behest that autumn. The singer who owed one large part of his career to 'Mr. Tambourine Man' – and another part to Jacques Levy, his erstwhile co-writer on 'Chestnut Mare' – was a sincere enthusiast for Rolling Thunder, as he would remain. Yet, as the former Byrd would explain to the writer Sid Griffin, he had refused Dylan's offer and then, after a change of heart, had instructed his agent to have his own shows called off. As McGuinn would then put it: 'They arranged to do that and worked out a deal where I got a fee for the whole tour . . . But let me tell you, this was *not* about the money!'[16]

No doubt that was true for one and all. Admiration for Dylan was not to be circumscribed by tawdry concerns. On the other hand, these were professional musicians who did not expect to be asked to donate their talents for free for weeks on end, irrespective of anyone's breezy idealism, the media's myths, or the naivety of fans. Idealism, even the stars' own idealism, was not a professional imperative. You still have to wonder, nevertheless, why Baez came running for the sake of an artist who had cast her aside, one who had not only broken her heart but left her disillusioned in 1965. The popular explanation is that somehow she was still in love with Dylan and still capable of believing that the old 'integrity' could flow through him. She was not so trusting, however, that she would neglect the small print of her very detailed contract.

Things were more complicated than they seemed. One suggestion made by Ramblin' Jack Elliott's biographer is that the original Dylan-Neuwirth plan to 'just get a bus and travel around and sing', first proposed on 3 July, was conceived as a small and simple affair.[17] As Elliott heard it, the trip would be just the three of them – and Joan Baez. In this account, she had been central to the madcap scheme from the start. So had Dylan simply taken her consent for granted, or was Rolling Thunder created from the outset around the otherwise astonishing assumption that he and she could work together again, if not in harmony – they never quite managed that – but in some rediscovered spirit of mutual tolerance?

Perhaps Baez sensed an opportunity of her own at a time when, by her confession, she was trying to restore her public profile. Perhaps, just as a decade before, there was a mutual benefit to be had from the adventure. Why did he invite her, after all, given their shared history? One answer seems simple enough. 'Dylan and Baez Together Again': that headline would certainly sell some tickets for the begetter of the Rolling Thunder Revue among fans eager for another taste of the good old '60s days. It would not do his nominated co-star any harm either, of course.

In 1987, in the first of her autobiographies, Baez would describe one of the little *Renaldo and Clara* vignettes she found so risible.[18] In this scene, wearing a faded satin dress borrowed from 'an old gypsy lady' and expected to produce dialogue out of thin air, she would ask and answer her own questions. Such as: why had Dylan never told her about Sara? Such as: what would have happened if she and the artist had married 'way back then'? Her answer: the relationship would have failed because she was 'too political' and because he lied 'too much'. In Baez's recollection, Dylan said nothing at all during this excruciating impromptu scene, certainly not while the cameras were running. Improvisation, oddly enough, was not his forte, in her opinion. In point of fact, he would reply – diffidently, it's true – that he had married the woman he loved. On a cold, grey November day he would stand at the bar in the rural restaurant, one of Arlo Guthrie's haunts, smiling fixedly but 'embarrassed', digesting news that was, Baez would write, no news at all.

The scene at Mama Frasca's Dream Away Lodge – in western Massachusetts, not in upstate New York, as Baez seemed to believe – would not be the main event of the day for most of those present. A lot of eating, drinking and off-the-wall singing would go on while Ginsberg wandered around reading *Moby-Dick* in memory of Herman Melville's recent departure from the area. By then the troupe would have played two shows at the Springfield Civic Center, only the fifth stop on the tour. In the restaurant in the little town of Becket, in Berkshire County, Mama Frasca would be far more interested in her female guest than in Dylan. After chicken, spaghetti, liqueurs and some ad hoc filming, Guthrie would play old rock and roll songs on the house piano.[19] It would make for a convivial day. Just like the artist, however, Baez would stand at the centre of her own small, private drama on the Rolling Thunder tour.

*

In Manhattan, while Dylan and Baez rehearsed, Larry Sloman noticed a couple of small details. They did not to strike the reporter as particularly odd. In fact, they involved two tiny gestures recorded by the writer as though they were only to be expected and somehow only fitting. In the middle of the 1970s, the bastard genre called rock journalism was still struggling to shed its deference towards the demigod geniuses of pop music. (Sloman's own book would aid the process greatly, ironically enough.) What the writer saw was Dylan in need of a cigarette and a cigarette appearing instantly, as if by unspoken command. Earlier, when the artist had shown symptoms of thirst, he had simply *pointed*, without a word, at a container of fruit juice. Sloman could perhaps have mentioned a line from a song that ought to have appeared on *Blonde on Blonde* in 1966, but inspiration passed him by. The line goes: 'Yes, you, you just sit around and ask for ashtrays, can't you reach?'

Dylan was at the point in his life when the idea of fetching his own cigarette no longer occurred to him. The notion that he should even have to ask for a drink had become strange. In October of 1975, he was just 34, still a young man, but he had been one of the bigger stars for better than a decade, for most of his adult life. This made him a perfectly normal member of the pop industry's elect, but strange, perfectly so, to almost everyone else on the planet. Unlike most of the rock aristocracy, however, Dylan was proposing to venture out on the road amid the palpable fiction of a communal, cooperative enterprise. He was about to present himself, albeit as the main event, as one of a company of touring players.

There was a creative need behind his desire, but the desire involved an impossibility. It also involved the weird, evolving phenomenon the twenty-first century would know simply by the shorthand 'celebrity'. Here was one artist beloved by many people who could never be one of them. Here was one, they said, who 'spoke' to them, but he could no longer speak, not in any simple, unmediated fashion, to a single one among them. For a poet, it was a bizarre predicament. Still some wonder why he donned masks or blanked out his face with deathly white makeup on the Rolling Thunder tour. Like the blank-eyed self-effacing painting of himself he had made for the cover of *Self Portrait*, it was one way, perhaps the only way, to say, 'Listen to the music.'

It didn't solve the riddle. The fact of Bob Dylan could no longer be undone. The artist would toy with an impossibility during the Rolling Thunder Revue while insisting on the centrality, in all things, of the intimidating name on the marquee. He would play around, indeed, with Arthur Rimbaud's declaration, 'I is another,' donning his masks and his whiteface as though to disown each and every one of his colliding multiple identities while insisting on the words he sang in Bob Dylan's name. This time, sometimes, he would manage the feat triumphantly. But it would certainly be the last time.

*

One week before the expeditionary force set off, a party was held at Gerde's Folk City in honour of Mike Porco, the restaurateur turned club owner who had nurtured the young Dylan – though at no great financial cost – and helped him to secure his cabaret card back in the grubby, glorious days of 1961. Porco would sell Folk City before long, but as October drew to a close in 1975 he was delighted to have the Rolling Thunder crew join him for his 61st birthday celebrations. Fond memories could be rekindled; thoughts of the good old days, thoughts held in some quarters to be among the revue's motive forces, could be given another airing. Honour could be done to Porco and to the past.

It didn't quite turn out that way. Among those present, the spectre at the feast, was the ruin of the handsome man who had once been Phil Ochs. That October, so lost to unquenchable alcoholism as to be delusive and dangerous – psychotic, in the usual parlance – he had less than six months left before suicide became an invitation impossible to refuse. Once he had championed Dylan only to be spurned and mocked – yet sometimes praised beyond the skies – in return. Ochs, still on occasion presenting himself as a 'topical singer', was another kind of remnant of a shared past. In 1975, he was a reminder that not all memories were golden, that not everyone from the old Village had survived intact, if they had survived at all.

By October, Ochs had been banned once and for all from The Other End. Sometimes, without any of Rimbaud's fancy poetic conceits, he believed himself to be another person entirely, a character by the name of John Butler Train. This individual, he would insist, had murdered the 'real' Phil Ochs. He began to carry weapons, hammers or knives, habitually. He was near to destitution and too often violent. Some old friends were in genuine fear of this character. That night at Gerde's, wearing Dylan's hat, desperate for attention and desperate to be added to the list of former comrades joining the Rolling Thunder Revue, Ochs turned in a shambolic performance that was, reportedly, by turns sad, brave and profoundly disturbing. In the footage that would appear in Dylan's film *Renaldo and Clara*, capturing the final images of Ochs as he prepared to take the stage, he looked like the very sick man he was. There was no chance whatever of his being allowed to enlist with

THUNDER ON THE MOUNTAIN

the troupe. The artist's whims, if whims they were, did not test each and every boundary of sympathy, or of common sense.

He had been an obsession for Ochs from start to finish. In the beginning, Phil had simply exulted ceaselessly, joyfully, over Dylan's talent. The *Highway 61 Revisited* album had caused this old-style singing activist to laugh in sheer delight at its daring. Ochs had defended Dylan resolutely against the obtuse Stalinist folk-left crowd after the great Newport '65 'betrayal'. Amid all the doctrinal hair-splitting over electricity and popularity he had been eloquent and loyal. For thanks, the artist had dismissed this best of fans as a mere 'journalist', booting him out of a limousine for the crime of failing to praise an inferior pop single sufficiently. Ochs, always painfully sincere and desperate for friendship, could bring out the cruelty in Dylan for reasons the former never understood and the latter never bothered to explain.

Later, as incessant boozing turned every thought into a toxic mash, Phil would talk about Bobby endlessly, but the talk could alternate without warning between the old admiration and a vicious, drunken hatred. A *Rolling Stone* article at the end of August, a piece devoted entirely to Dylan's return to the Village, had described the first performance of 'Abandoned Love' on 3 July. Almost in passing, the reporter had noted: 'A staggeringly drunk Phil Ochs stopped by and yelled at Dylan for a few moments. Dylan didn't seem to mind.'[20] The incident could probably stand as a metaphor, if one were needed, for the artist's relationship with a lot of people, fixated fans above all. He didn't make Phil Ochs crazy, but his music and the fact of his genius didn't help. Love and maddened anger were never too far apart.[21]

As ever, Dylan travelled on. One last stab at rehearsals would be attempted on Cape Cod, during a few days spent at a plush, secluded place called the Sea Crest Beach Motel in the northern end of the Massachusetts town of Falmouth. It was about a 30-minute drive away from the first concert venue. Incongruously, a fund-raising mah-jong tournament involving 165 little old ladies – or 'nice Jewish mommas', as Sloman would call them – was in full swing when the revue descended on the place. One evening, ready or not, the prim tile-tossers were treated to a few numbers by Rolling Thunder members, for the benefit of the cameras, and to the otherwise surreal spectacle of 'one of America's foremost poets, Mr Allen Ginsberg' reading from *Kaddish*, his long and passionate elegy – 'Proem, Narrative, Hymmnn [*sic*], Lament, Litany and Fugue' – for his own Jewish mother.

In her memoir, Baez would remember the mah-jong but place the event in Portland, Maine. 'They didn't know how to respond to this world-famous literary figure with the long beard,' Baez would write, 'who started out mildly enough but ended up shouting about bearded vaginas, his eyes growing round and wild behind his glasses.'[22] Wild, perhaps, but whatever Baez heard that night her brief sketch was not entirely fair to *Kaddish*, or indeed to the Jewish women in the audience. The great poem is visceral, even gruelling, but deeply felt and, for some people, intensely moving.

At the motel, Dylan looked on silently as the cameras rolled and these elderly Jewish women, so much like his own mother Beatty Zimmerman, listened to the threnody for poor, crazed Naomi Ginsberg. As his biographer would write, 'It was as if Allen was finally reading it to Naomi herself.' No one doubted that the audience found the performance hard going, but Sam Shepard, for one, would remember the poet receiving a burst of applause at its end. Baez, who came on next to leave the women 'charmed' with the tedious, venerable 'Swing Low, Sweet Chariot', must have forgotten the detail.[23]

*

The Rolling Thunder Revue opened on 30 October in Plymouth, Massachusetts, in one of those little venues that were supposed to be the concert party's reason to exist. The War Memorial Auditorium, seating perhaps 1,800 with the addition of temporary seating, was hardly a club, but it made an opening statement – the one that would count – about Rolling Thunder's intended ethos. The town itself, where zealous if seasick Pilgrims had anchored their *Mayflower* in 1620, meanwhile provided a symbolic touch as America prepared for its 200th birthday. A decade before, Dylan had performed his '115th Dream' on the *Bringing It All Back Home* album as a comedy wandering sailor fresh off the famous boat. One couplet contained a joke that had faded somewhat, for the writer at least, in the intervening years: 'I said, "You know, they refused Jesus, too" / He said, "You're not Him."'

The first of the Plymouth shows was sold out, as was the second. On Halloween, the second night, he had his plastic Bob Dylan mask on, masquerading, but the disguise was a weird affair. All agree that the thing was transparent and seemingly moulded to his face. Sloman – who was present for most of the tour before getting himself fired – would make mention of sequins. In other words, you could see through this mask, it took the shape of 'Bob Dylan', but it was camouflage. Whatever the gesture was intended to convey, it was not conducive to

THUNDER ON THE MOUNTAIN

the playing of a harmonica. On each of the occasions Dylan appeared in his plastic contraption he was soon forced to rip it off – and perhaps that was the whole point – in order to make music.

The shows had a shape and a structure to which they would more or less adhere for the remainder of the year. That much was Levy's doing. Lighting cues, an intermission, support acts, curtains opening and closing, the slow revealing of the star as he emerged from the darkness: these were theatrical devices, simple as vaudeville, but powerful. Nevertheless, 'theatrical' was hardly a novelty in rock music by the middle of the 1970s; if anything, it was becoming the kind of curse that only punk's avenging angels could lift. Exactly a year before Dylan's opening in Plymouth, David Bowie had been in the middle of an extravagant seven-night run at New York's Radio City Musical Hall during his Diamond Dogs tour. The people wanted 'theatrical'? The angular Englishman had delivered it by the gross ton. On his vast stage Bowie had contrived a cityscape complete with skyscrapers, a movable catwalk, a giant hand, numerous dancers, a cherrypicker crane to raise the star on high, even some music: catching an audience's attention no longer came cheap. Dylan and Levy were seeking something that was the opposite of grandiose, street theatre in contrast to the grand rock operatics of Bowie, but they were at one with the times. A single performer with just a guitar and a harmonica would have failed those new Dylan-Levy songs. That was a matter of opinion, of course.

The pattern of the first shows, the pattern that would remain, can be described easily enough. Guam would open with perhaps half a dozen non-Dylan songs amid Neuwirth's banter. Ronee Blakley, the artist and singer who had spent part of the previous summer starring in Robert Altman's *Nashville* – she was another who had cancelled a tour for Dylan's sake after being noticed at The Other End – would generally take a solo spot or two. Ramblin' Jack Elliott would then perform a short set, in the early days of the tour with only his own guitar for accompaniment, before stepping aside, without preamble or introductions, as the artist strode from the gloom of the wings to deliver a pointed 'When I Paint My Masterpiece' with Neuwirth vocalising at his side. On the first night in Plymouth, by Sloman's account, this 'ironic song about the limitations on artistic achievement' became a 'heraldic [*sic*] triumph'.[24]

Got to hurry on back to my hotel room
Where I've got me a date with Botticelli's niece

117

TIME OUT OF MIND

She promised that she'd be right there with me
When I paint my masterpiece

Most who saw the shows have maintained down the years that even multiple bootlegs (Dylan's crew taped everything), footage from *Renaldo and Clara* and the 2002 album *Bob Dylan Live 1975* do not give an adequate impression of the Rolling Thunder Revue. On-the-spot journalists such as Sloman tended, as reviewers do, to piece together their notes from phrases like 'and the crowd goes wild'. As with a lot of Dylan's concert work, a determined effort of deduction, grasping at echoes and old shadows, nevertheless allows the semi-educated belief that, some of the time, something special was going on. Crudely, the artist did not disappoint. Often enough, he did a lot more, singing with a sureness and commitment that revealed the strained, stentorian efforts of Tour '74 for the contrivances they were, a commitment that could often dispel any doubts over the *Desire* material. Dylan's fearlessness in reworking his own songs, even the works treated as holy relics by too many fans, was meanwhile remarkable in itself. *Live 1975* is proof enough that, at their best, the Rolling Thunder ensemble justified all the glowing reports.

Dylan would perform perhaps five numbers with Guam as his first offering. Then the yellow stage curtain, a curious affair designed to mimic a proscenium arch, emblazoned above with the name of the show and decorated below with joke images of jugglers, strongmen and gymnasts, would fall: intermission. The homage to Carné's *Les Enfants du Paradis* was plain enough to anyone who knew the picture. Then, just before the curtain rose again, two familiar but invisible singers could be heard. As the tab went slowly upwards, 'an amazing sight' was revealed: Dylan and Baez together again. Here was Jacques Levy's cherished *coup de théâtre*, corny as hell but undoubtedly effective. 'Close your eyes and it could have been Newport in 1963,' said a certain dazzled journalist.[25] That was, no doubt, the general idea.

Invariably, the pair would commence their evening's collaboration with 'The Times They Are a-Changin'', or with 'Blowin' in the Wind'. The degree of calculation was self-evident, though few in the audiences cared. Dylan was employing Baez to evoke memories. He might have been averse to nostalgia, but he was not afraid to risk the disease for the sake of the show. After four or five songs together, he would leave Baez to continue with the help of Guam and sometimes with the aid of Roger McGuinn. Often, as though in a display of pride, she would perform her own 'Diamonds & Rust', a wistful song (one of her few compositions) about that long-gone affair with the star of the show. McGuinn would then offer a song or two: 'Chestnut Mare' or 'Eight Miles High', another big hit for the Byrds. Finally, Dylan would return for a half a dozen more songs, never forgetting 'Hurricane', before proceedings were brought to a close, on almost every occasion, with 'Knockin' On Heaven's Door' and a rendition of Woody Guthrie's 'This Land Is Your Land'. There were no encores.

Things would change as various celebrity guests joined the tour for one night or more, but not by much. After the first shows had granted the audience close to five hours of music-as-theatre in exchange for their $7.50 tickets, Levy managed to tighten things up a little. Nevertheless, Rolling Thunder was always a long night. Dylan's own, unimpeded performances might embrace no more than a dozen songs and last not much more than an hour in total, sometimes to the annoyance of paying hecklers who had not come to see Ramblin' Jack Elliott, McGuinn or Ronee Blakley, but that was the deal. Rolling Thunder was a revue. It said so on the last-minute posters that appeared just before tickets were briefly put on sale by hall managers sworn to secrecy – any breach would result in cancellation, or so ran the promoters' threat – weeks before. Audiences saw and heard what Dylan wanted them to see and hear, even if that meant listening to Bobby Neuwirth or Mick Ronson's glam-rock guitar. Anyone whose patience wore thin could always spend their time wondering what the artist meant by it all.

He gave them plenty to ponder and digest in Rolling Thunder's first phase. *Desire* had not yet been released, after all. Thanks to Columbia's twitchy lawyers, the final version of 'Hurricane' had been recorded only six days before the revue's opening night. It would not be in the stores until November, when the tour was deep in chilly New England. Around half a dozen of the pieces Dylan performed in the concerts would be entirely new to audiences who tended to learn every syllable of his work by heart. It seemed inescapably obvious, too, that he was amending the style of his old songs to suit both his new band and his new material. Revision, as in rethinking and rewriting, had become the order of the day. For Dylan, Rolling Thunder was still another new beginning. *Blood on the Tracks*, whose songs were given only minimal exposure on the tour, was already far behind him.

Reviews were pretty good; some were very good indeed. Though Lou Kemp tried to keep most of the reporters at bay – and seemed to enjoy giving Sloman a tough time – any Dylan tour was a media event. The idea that he, Neuwirth, Elliott and Baez could ever have gone rolling around the back roads of America like merry prankster troubadours untroubled by baggage of any description had always been a nonsense. Dylan and the Rolling Thunder troupe could not even alight on small towns like Plymouth, Durham in New Hampshire, or Augusta in Maine without causing a fuss. In fact, precisely because such places never saw an authentic superstar the fuss became inevitable. Legends, as someone probably said, are not born but made. Spontaneity can take a lot of planning.

Dylan, though, was as disloyal as ever in his performances to any key in which any given song might once have been recorded. Sometimes – and this is apparent on bootleg recordings – the key would change from night to night. Sometimes it could change in the middle of a song. Tempo could also seem entirely arbitrary, a matter of the artist's intuition or mood. It is a tribute to the Guam musicians that they learned an essential thing about Dylan as a performer: he did what *felt* right, in the moment. By common consent a weight of responsibility therefore fell on Rob Stoner, the bass player, to watch the maestro's every muscle, anticipate the impending changes if he could, and guide his colleagues. The artist's instincts became the band's instructions. They could not rely on what they had learned or thought they knew about a piece of music. It was unprofessional behaviour on Dylan's part, in the usual sense, but it was art. Most of the time.

Here began the generation-long audience game of spot-that-tune. Writing of the very first show, for example, Sloman would describe a rendition of 'It Ain't Me, Babe' – entirely correctly, if recordings of the Halloween concert and subsequent tapes are a guide – as 'almost *bossa nova*'. *Live 1975* opens with an account of 'Tonight I'll Be Staying Here With You', to take another example, in which every word of the *Nashville Skyline* original save the chorus has been rewritten, while a wistful melody has been pummelled into the shape of a rock song. 'A Hard Rain's a-Gonna Fall' meanwhile became the unlikeliest of candidates – though the transformation was unimpeachable – for retooling as a ferocious, straightforward piece of rock and roll. Even the newer pieces from *Desire* were not immune to this seemingly arbitrary treatment. In fact, they seemed to be prime candidates for refurbishment only weeks after they had been recorded, as though Dylan was already bored with their musical settings, or – more likely – already dissatisfied with what had been managed in the studio.

So it was that in 1975 yet another theory about the artist began to emerge. This one held that he did not mess around with favourite songs just to keep himself awake. Instead, he was creating art anew while the audience looked on. After the so-called Never-Ending Tour was inaugurated in June of 1988 and began to become a fixture in the lives of Dylan's most devoted fans, the theory grew steadily more elaborate. The artist, so we heard, was asserting that a song only truly exists in performance. He was reminding us that no song – no piece of art? – is ever complete in any real sense. Dylan was demonstrating that concerts and concert tours were creative works in their own right. 'Bob Dylan' and what he was presumed to intend were parts – this kind of chatter caught on quick – of a construct.

It would all become very complicated indeed, its richly satisfying post-structuralist debates undermined just a little only when, now and then, Dylan did in fact seem a tiny bit bored with 'Blowin' in the Wind' number several-hundred-and-counting. A better bet was that he was wedded from the start to the practices of his real spiritual fathers, the bluesmen, those musicians who failed to repeat themselves because they didn't know how to manage such a thing. Like Dylan, they did not understand music in those terms. If each moment in life was different, each performance, or at least each tour, must surely reflect the fact. The precise, album-perfect copy was the real 'construct'. The attempt to play the same song in precisely the same way night after night, city after city, was the truly eccentric and truly noxious habit. It was also camouflage, by no coincidence, for superstars who were supremely bored and utterly cynical. The problem with Dylan's method, if it can be called a method, is that the artist has to be brave and brilliant to pull it off. He also has to care. In the autumn and winter of 1975, Dylan cared.

*

Out on the road, barely a week into the tour, Larry Sloman would run into a bitterly angry Sam Shepard. The playwright was discovering that there was less to his contracted role, if there was anything at all, than he had been promised. He was thinking of quitting – as he did, before too long – mostly because 'they' had made 'some assurances to me in terms of money' and those assurances, he said, had not been fulfilled. In Sloman's account, Shepard would rage against the 'anti-money, anti-establishment position' that allowed the unnamed 'they' to 'rip you off and it's all right 'cause it's an anti-materialist thing'.[26]

The point would become a source of press speculation. How much was Dylan spending on this 'guerrilla tour', this vagabond's gesture of artistic dissent, and how much, in fact, was he making? Taxed on the issue by *Rolling Stone*, Lou Kemp would say only that 'everybody's on salary. We've got 70 people to house, move and take care of. We gotta pay for this film that's being shot and that's costing an arm and a leg. So far Dylan has not seen a penny. He's the only one who hasn't gotten paid yet.'[27]

Expenses must certainly have been high, with ten members of Guam on the payroll and 15 people assigned to movie-making, plus all the rest. Equally, the romantic idea that Dylan was to play only small 'theatres' would fade quickly after the tour's first week. Columbia had refused to underwrite the revue; some of the big names had entirely satisfactory contracts; a lot of bills had to be met. By the fifth show in Providence, Rhode Island, the 'low-key' Rolling Thunder Revue was playing to crowds of 12,000 in a single hall. *Variety*, the entertainment industry's inimitable journal of record, had already taken note of an apparent change of heart in its edition at the beginning of November, its headline asking sweetly if Dylan was suddenly 'interested' in money.

Venues capable of containing audiences ranging in size from 10,000 to 16,000 (as in Toronto) became the rule rather than the exception. With tickets priced at a standard $7.50 – towards the high end, but not unreasonable, though they would later rise to $8.50 – most journalists could do the arithmetic.[28] By now, Larry Sloman was under orders from his *Rolling Stone* editors to keep a close eye on the box office and the money that was assumed to be rolling in.[29] In the mid-'70s, the cry of 'sell-out' was still a curse. It did not simply mean that every last precious ticket had been sold. So where was the 'integrity' invoked by Joan Baez? Like Dylan's revenues, a lot of it would wind up, albeit briefly, on the cinema screen.

The fact told a story of its own. The original notion cooked up in the Village of four old friends hopping aboard a bus to 'travel around and sing' as the ragamuffin mood took them had become a slightly comical memory even before the New York skyline was out of sight. There was certainly a Rolling Thunder bus. It became home from home for most of the troupe, even if that meant exhausted souls taking turns to grab one of the few bunks available amid all the drinking, drugs, revelry, singing, squabbling and snoring. Depending on the anecdote, life on the bus was either one long party or hell on wheels. Dylan, in contrast, travelled in his own private motorhome and didn't often socialise with most of the employees.

In an obvious sense, he couldn't be blamed for that: everyone wanted a piece of 'Bobby'. A lot rested on his shoulders during this tour. Those songs didn't rewrite themselves. Jacques Levy might have been investing the concerts with a theatrical structure while everyone worked hard for the sake of protracted shows. But to the artist fell the job of filling that giant 'Bob Dylan'-shaped hole at the centre of everything. He was entitled to respite and to privacy. If nothing else, his mystique demanded it. Still, that deluxe motorhome destroyed anyone's lingering illusion that Dylan could ever again be first among bohemian equals.

He had last fulfilled that role at the end of April 1962, when the first recording sessions for *The Freewheelin' Bob Dylan* began. The old Village days, when all were broke and all were hustling for work, could only have been revived if the democracy of poverty and youthful ambition had been restored. In what sane world was that remotely possible? Then as now, fame in pop music was built on hierarchies, not on egalitarianism. For all its musical strengths and all its dazzling performances, the Rolling Thunder Revue was an alternative-lifestyle fiction sold to big crowds who still wanted to believe in the promise, whatever it once had meant, of 'Bob Dylan'.

If he was making any money at the box office, the artist's honest excuse was that the 'evolving' movie was indeed costing what his fish-merchant friend called an arm and a leg. Dylan was bearing the entire monumental cost. It is a pity, therefore, that he failed to pay enough attention to what was going into his picture. Keeping Sam Shepard happy and writing scenes worth filming would have been cheaper by far than all those clumsy improvisations shot on a wing, a prayer and the artist's dime. Soon enough – in the middle of May 1976 – Dylan would be handing an importunate Allen Ginsberg $15,000 in recognition of his work on *Renaldo and Clara*. The older poet would reckon he was entitled to the cash for 'acting in [the movie] and setting up the scenes and dialogue'.[30] Even those who admire the film might struggle to justify that invoice. Those who admire Ginsberg can meanwhile ask themselves what happened to all that anti-materialist Buddhist 'non-attachment', all that radical '60s rhetoric.

The incident gives a rough clue, nevertheless, to the kind of money Dylan must have been paying to Baez, McGuinn and all the others working for love and whatever else was specified in their contracts. The Guam band was a big, expensive proposition in its own right.

Ravaged Elvis Presley, his last studio recordings behind him, was also out on the road that year. He too could summon better than 30 individuals to the stage, what with a six-piece band, eleven singers and a small touring orchestra, all flogged onwards yet again by the insatiable Colonel Tom Parker. But a ticket to see Presley was costing $10 in 1975 and the King was due to mark New Year's Eve in front of 60,000 people at the Pontiac Silverdome, a football stadium in Michigan, picking up $300,000 personally for just an hour's work.[31]

Dylan was trying to face in two directions. On the one hand, he wanted his modest, understated, friends-making-music show with its 'anti-money, anti-establishment position'. On the other hand, he was trying to run a big, even grandiose touring ensemble on a scale Elvis would have recognised while footing the bill for a horribly expensive movie. 'Theatrical', like the picture business, didn't come cheap. How much was he making? Plenty and not enough.

*

What with cocaine on demand, the adrenalin rush of performance, the looming, ever-watchful cameras and the usual oppressive intimacy of life on the road, almost everyone involved with Rolling Thunder went a little crazy. Often they had a real camaraderie, it's true, but there were some big personalities among them, with egos to match. Baez, with her own guaranteed spot on the bill and a pleasantly superior dressing-room – fruits of that detailed contract, no doubt – could be imperious. Neuwirth's needling humour was not to all tastes on all occasions, especially after drink (or whatever) had been taken. As Joni Mitchell would observe on first boarding the bus, they could seem like 'cruel people being cruel to each other'.[32]

This troupe were under an unspoken obligation to behave as a tightly knit group – as if life on the bus allowed any other choice – but they were also expected to defer instantly, automatically, night after night and day after day, to a wholly unpredictable individual. Musicians by trade, they became hostages by habit, like all touring bands. The difference for the Rolling Thunder ensemble was that its members would also find themselves turned into actors, after a fashion, for scenes in a movie Dylan did not readily discuss, far less explain. Some of those involved failed even to realise that one day they would be listed as 'characters' – though this might have been the artist's droll choice after the fact – in *Renaldo and Clara*.

Neuwirth as 'The Masked Tortilla'? T-Bone Burnett as 'The Inner

Voice'? Ginsberg as 'The Father', David Mansfield as 'The Son', and the visiting old Canadian rocker Ronnie Hawkins – this was surely labouring a point – as the unholy ghost, 'Bob Dylan'? But then, everyone involved in Rolling Thunder was a character, in the several senses of that word. The fact that they had to come up with their own lines while their lives became anecdotal, if not 'legendary', was presumably part of the point the artist was trying to make about existence as performance. The interesting question is whether the nominal director – the name 'Bob Dylan' would occupy that role in *Renaldo and Clara*'s credits – exempted himself from his own strictures.

Plymouth, Dartmouth, Lowell, Providence, Springfield, Burlington: the old New England towns, the places where America began, came and went as the Bicentennial approached. From the start, Ginsberg had been promoting the idea that the semi-evolved film should attempt some sort of comment on the state of the nation, but an idea so coherent and obvious suited neither the tastes nor the talents of Dylan's movie-making collective. *Renaldo and Clara* would wind up, as cineastes rarely say, as a bit of this, a bit of that and a portion of something else entirely. The film would combine those inept improvisations with remarkable concert footage and an assortment of interviews. For many, the old cliché about the whole and the sum of its parts would spring to mind. It became a tour movie, in short, with pretensions. Anything worth saying about the American experience would be said, as ever, in Dylan's songs.

At Lowell in Massachusetts, during the tour's third stop, he had paid homage at Jack Kerouac's grave. It turned out to be one of *Renaldo and Clara*'s best sequences. Ginsberg had recited one of his lost friend's favourite poems, Shakespeare's 97th sonnet: 'How like a winter hath my absence been / From thee, the pleasure of the fleeting year! / What freezings have I felt, what dark days seen!' The poet had then quoted a few lines from Kerouac's *Mexico City Blues*, in its turn a Dylan favourite. Sitting cross-legged on the grass, the two men had then improvised a slow blues with guitar and harmonium. Momentarily, Dylan had paused to pick up a fallen autumn leaf and store it in his pocket. The lurking, ever-present movie camera had caught it all, of course, but Dylan, clearly moved, had seemed able to ignore the apparatus for once. The nature of the debt had altered with the years, but he owed much to the Kerouac whose work had once set him afire, and helped to set him on the road.

Still the Rolling Thunder Revue pressed on. Whatever the financial concerns behind the scenes, Dylan seemed to the paying public to be enjoying himself. Suddenly he was almost garrulous on stage. His song introductions began to resemble a comedy turn. In Providence, Rhode Island, the audience was told that 'Isis' was 'a true story'. Just before the opening bars of 'Romance in Durango', innocent customers were invited to remember that 'raw lust does not hold a candle to true love'. In Burlington, Vermont, the venerable, much-analysed 'A Hard Rain's a-Gonna Fall' was dedicated 'to all psychology students'.

On 15 November, at the Niagara Falls Convention Center, 'When I Paint My Masterpiece' was delivered, supposedly – and why not? – 'for Gertrude Stein and Modigliani'. In New Haven, Connecticut, before 'It Ain't Me, Babe', the audience was informed: 'This song is dedicated to da Vinci.' At one show, 'Oh, Sister' was performed 'for Henry VIII'; at another, Dylan decided that 'Durango' was for 'D.H. Lawrence, if he's here tonight'.

In Hartford, Connecticut, the artist said of 'The Lonesome Death of Hattie Carroll': 'I wanna dedicate this to Wallace Stevens from Hartford, a great renowned poet. Wherever you are now, we wish you the best of luck.' In Quebec, the song was performed for the benefit of 'the great French poet Arthur Rimbaud'. In New York's Madison Square Garden, on the final night of this wandering vaudeville tour, 'I Dreamed I Saw St. Augustine' would be sung 'for Herman Melville, who's sitting . . .'

It wasn't all comedy. Almost without fail, something was said by Dylan, night after night, about the plight of Rubin Carter. The show staged in Worcester, Massachusetts, on 19 November was typical: 'This song is called "Hurricane". If you got any political pull you can help us get this man out of jail and back on the streets.' Dylan would also tell a New England crowd of learning 'that Massachusetts was the only state that didn't vote for Nixon. We didn't vote for him either.'

Perhaps the funniest moment came in New Haven on 13 November. A shout – 'Bob Dylan, Bob Dylan' – had gone up from someone in the crowd. The artist, preparing to perform a revised 'Tangled Up in Blue', had replied deadpan: 'No, I don't think so. I think you've got me mistaken for someone else.'

In New Haven, meanwhile, Joni Mitchell joined the show and the motley crew on the bus. She would stick with both all the way to the 'Night of the Hurricane' at Madison Square Garden, reputedly becoming the sole participant in the revue to pay her own way. Bruce Springsteen was also to be seen at the Veterans Memorial Coliseum in New Haven on 13 November, but the chances of a performance ended, it seems, when Dylan ruled out an appearance (what with one thing and another) by the full E Street Band. On 2 December the Maple Leaf Gardens in Toronto, an ice-hockey arena capable of accommodating more than 16,000 customers, would see performances by Ronnie Hawkins, plus Mitchell, plus Gordon Lightfoot, all in addition to the existing vast cast and their leader. Some 54 songs were performed by various artists during that second Toronto show. Things, it could be argued, were getting out of hand. Only Leonard Cohen brought a breath of elegant good sense to proceedings when he declined politely to participate in the Montreal concert on 4 December on the grounds that it would be 'too obvious'.

At some point, just to complicate matters further, the film-makers Alk and Howard decided – or so Howard later asserted – that it would be a nicely 'creative' idea to bring Sara Dylan and her husband together for the sake of the movie. It led to uncomfortable scenes and a degree of slapstick backstage when, more than once, the artist's girl of the hour was hustled out through one door while his wife entered through another. Sara Dylan had neither the taste nor the aptitude for life on the road. By then she and Dylan were married in name only, joined as parents – when he had the time – and by what once had been held in common. How he persuaded her to drag herself from California to New England in such a circumstance remains a mystery.

Nevertheless, *Renaldo and Clara* thus began to develop into the tale, roughly speaking, of a triangular relationship with, supposedly, mythological overtones. Dylan played Renaldo (obviously), alongside Sara/Clara and Baez as 'The Woman in White'. Sympathisers would argue that the piece thereby achieved emotional tension and coherence, particularly in its original near-four-hour version. They could never explain away the fact that amateur actors – Sara Dylan had some slight experience, it's true – tend invariably to produce amateur dramatics. Dylan might have had complicated ideas for his picture, but he, of all people, seems not to have realised that complexity is best expressed by professionals.

*

Rubin Carter wasn't getting out of jail any time soon, despite anything Bob Dylan might have to say about the matter. The struggle to win the boxer a second trial would end horribly in December 1976 when he and John Artis were once again convicted, but on the 'Night of the

Hurricane' – Monday, 8 December 1975 – hope still remained. Thanks in part to Dylan, Rubin's case was a cause célèbre liable to attract celebrity liberal attention even, or especially, from those who did not necessarily understand every last detail. As the *New York Times* would report, all of a sudden any number of 'prominent political figures' had found time to show support for Carter and claim places on the guest list at Madison Square Garden. Famous athletes commanded excellent seats while 'among the show-business personalities' the likes of Candice Bergen, Ellen Burstyn, Dyan Cannon and Melba Moore were spotted. There would be more speeches at the Garden than the artist would tolerate in normal circumstances, but he was given little choice. On this night, despite his best efforts, 'Mr Dylan' – the *Times* house style altered for no man – was a long way from the 'reaffirmation of the old Dylan rootlessness', as the paper described it, that had been part of Rolling Thunder's avowed point and purpose.[33]

John Rockwell, the writer of the piece, found it necessary, in fact, to dish a little dirt amid some judicious praise for the Carter benefit. Rolling Thunder had grown into an arena show, like it or not. Its size, wrote the journalist, had 'provoked some cynicism and charges of hypocrisy, especially since Mr Dylan's friends and tour members have been more enthusiastic than usual with their populist rhetoric and assertions of Mr Dylan's selflessness'. Rockwell continued:

There are reportedly three films being made, at least some which may well make money, and Mr Dylan is apparently thinking of renewing the tour in Europe two months from now. The stories of warm good feelings among tour members have been partially purchased by a skulking, in-crowd exclusivism, and there have been persistent tales of dissension and ego clashes, too.

Dylan was damned if he did and damned if he didn't. If he stepped away from public life his absence was mourned or condemned. If he got involved only 'populist rhetoric' was worth mentioning. No one had said a word about hypocrisy when he and The Band were cleaning up amid a huge demand for tickets during Tour '74. They had played the Garden twice during that campaign, to great acclaim. In any case, from whom 'reportedly' had the tale of three films come, with the supercilious assurance that one or more could 'well make money'? What was being implied by the use of the phrase 'partially purchased', far less the description of 'skulking, in-crowd exclusivism'? Mr Rockwell was naming

THUNDER ON THE MOUNTAIN

no names and making no claims on his own behalf, but he was happy to clothe gossip in the affectless style of the *New York Times*.

A lot of it happened to be true, of course. There was an undeniable contradiction between much of the Rolling Thunder chatter and the economic realities of staging the biggest little tour anyone had seen. The artist had been fooling himself, and therefore his audience, by pretending that 'the old Dylan rootlessness' could be dusted down, that the mythical minstrel boy could sing as and when he pleased, answering to no one. But what – for Mr Rockwell didn't say – was he supposed to do? Retreat again into the old seclusion and wind up being labelled as a weird recluse, victim of a thousand mad 'theories'? Tour as the Stones had been touring in 1975 – six nights at the Garden in June – with the arrogance of decadent princelings, with their mocking giant inflatable phallus, their circus elephants, their truckloads of Merck coke and their habit of keeping audiences waiting for hours? Had *Variety* ever wondered if the Stones were 'interested' in money? If Rolling Thunder had succeeded in anything, it had succeeded as one musically vibrant rebuttal – others were being prepared at that very moment – to the decayed nonsense 'rock' had become by the mid-'70s.

Dylan had met Rubin Carter again on 7 December and performed at the Correctional Institution for Women – confusingly, men were held there too – in Clinton, New Jersey, where the boxer was then an inmate. It had been a strange affair, afflicted with what Larry Sloman would describe, inimitably if unhelpfully, as 'a strange vibe'. The band had played, Ginsberg had recited, Joni Mitchell and Joan Baez had been followed – to the delight of the otherwise unimpressed inmates, who gave her a standing ovation – by the soul and R&B singer Roberta Flack. 'Hurricane' had then been given one of its final performances for the benefit of the TV news cameras. A press conference had followed in which, as so often, Carter had made his case with eloquence and passion. For all that, there had been a sense of artifice, even of something a little phoney, about the affair. It was a sense best captured, ironically enough, by an infamous photo opportunity staged for *People* magazine.

The Clinton prison was no maximum-security installation: Rubin was no longer being treated in that manner. The joint had no bars to speak of, no gloomy, echoing cell blocks. A scene was therefore contrived between Dylan and Carter involving a floor-to-ceiling gate normally used simply to close a hallway. The prisoner was placed on one side, his would-be liberator on the other. The photograph acquired was a fake, in other words, and the 'bars' an implausible prop. The magazine would nevertheless run the image across two pages late in December. Why did Dylan go along with the stunt? Presumably because he thought it might do Carter's cause some good. Did that, too, count as hypocrisy?

The 'Night of the Hurricane' was advertised just over a week before the event. Tickets, said the ad in the *Times* Sunday 'Arts & Leisure' section, were to be sold only through the Garden box office. As a consequence, thousands of fans had queued through the small hours for a pair of the 14,000 available seats. On Monday night these faithful souls would see Dylan appear, as he had appeared throughout the tour, in a hat resembling a pale fedora that was decked, as usual, with flowers. The crowd would wonder, as other crowds had wondered, what the white face paint signified. They would hear a telephone call from Rubin Carter relayed through the hall's public-address system. They would be treated to several unnecessary speeches and in turn treat Muhammad Ali, once again heavyweight champion of the world, to the unprecedented experience of being booed to the rafters for his attempt to turn Hurricane's night into a lame pitch for a no-hope Tennessee politician. Above all, mercifully, the audience at the Garden would hear the artist at something close to his best.

Dylan had been reluctant to bring his show to New York. The revue's premise might have been long lost, but it seems he could sense the reaction he was liable to receive from disdainful *Times* critics and others besides if he turned up at the city's biggest venue with his gypsy ensemble. George Lois, a Madison Avenue advertising executive who had taken up Rubin Carter's cause, was obliged to beg the artist – 'I went up to New Haven and got down on my knees,' Lois would tell *Rolling Stone* – to act against his better judgement.[34]

Backstage, there would be a brief moment of hysteria thanks to a rumour, a rumour Dylan would come close to announcing as the truth, that Carter was about to be released. Out front, Robbie Robertson would join the band for 'It Takes a Lot to Laugh, It Takes a Train to Cry', the song dedicated mockingly to Albert Grossman, that exorcised ghost of a former manager, 'who won't be our next president'. Effortlessly, Dylan would prevent his show from turning into anyone's political rally. He at least had learned something since the 1960s. If the press or anyone else wanted a truly political point, it would be there in the Rolling Thunder Revue's customary closing song, Woody Guthrie's 'This Land Is Your Land'.

*

So what had Dylan intended and what, in fact, had he done? A home-grown version of *Les Enfants du Paradis* would be one slightly odd answer. It happens to be true, but the fact does not sit well with the usual descriptions of Rolling Thunder, or the usual dismissals of *Renaldo and Clara*. If nothing else, the director deserved credit for his taste. At a stretch, you could even transpose the film's central plot situations to the tour – and the movie, and the album – Dylan devised. He had said *something of the sort* to Sam Shepherd, after all. That does nothing to explain the artist's motives, however, in making these works.

Despite all its contradictions, Rolling Thunder did become a kind of anti-tour by a performer who still seemed to flinch at the self-exposure involved in public appearances. You could say, too, that he was experimenting with form – if a rock and roll tour counts as having form – and trying to see if there was a new way (or a very old way) to reach audiences. He was conducting an audit of his own life and career, very possibly, through all those roles and masks, with some of those who had played their parts in his existence as his cast, with the cameras rolling. Perhaps, equally, he didn't know quite what the hell he was doing, or what he wanted, but was content to follow his instincts in the hope of finding an answer. That sounds like him. Not for the first time, you remind yourself: no one made him do it. In this phase of his life, nevertheless, a new question became pertinent.

Dylan had won the sort of creative freedom granted to very few: what did he mean to do with it? He had followed his first ambitions ruthlessly and won his prize. Now what? The people demanding his return to active service on the ideological front lines had grown fewer, but the campaign for Hurricane Carter had shown that those shrill types were still around. They had attached the label 'protest' to the song written for the fighter almost instantly, while Dylan-Levy had intended, instead, a kind of campaigning journalism. The difference was overlooked. It was tangential, in any case, to art.

Campaigning, even on his own terms, was not an occupation liable to hold the artist's attention for too long. He might also have begun to wonder whether Rubin Carter, ruthless in his desperation, was not using 'Bob Dylan' much as everyone else, given half a chance, had tried to use Bob Dylan. Spiritual kin the two men might have been, but the Hurricane never did show much interest in the music being made on his behalf. During the prison concert, Rubin had paid attention only when the song written in his name was being performed. His favourite Dylan song, the boxer had declared when pressed, was 'It's

Alright, Ma (I'm Only Bleeding)'. That seemed to be simply because the verses spoke to Hurricane Carter – so he said – about the plight of Hurricane Carter.

For all his comical travails, Larry Sloman was no slouch as a reporter. As he had come away from the press conference at the Clinton prison, he had wondered about the Hurricane's polished performance for the assembled press. Troubled, Sloman reached what still seems a valid conclusion. Carter was no murderer, the journalist thought, but 'he sure as hell might be a damn good con artist'.[35] Given the distance he would put between himself and Rubin's case in the year ahead, when the campaign to have the boxer freed was a long way from over, Dylan might well have been inching towards a conclusion similar to that reached by Ratso. At the very least, a few second thoughts were very probably in order. Carter was fighting for his life but doing so with the guile of one who understood how to gain and keep the sympathy of nature's liberals. He was not culpable on that account, necessarily, but the sight of Rubin working a room full of journalists could make a person uneasy. Patently, for whatever reason, the artist's devotion to the cause was ebbing. Within less than two months 'Hurricane' would receive its final performance.

So what was Dylan's role to be, if any, in his field of art and within his industry? What was his choice? Things had changed; America had changed. Spokespersons on behalf of generations were falling out of fashion as the last of the counter-culture disappeared into squalor while cocaine and smack became the seductive and unforgiving drugs of choice. It was a poor exchange, whatever Dylan thought about the politics and political movements of the '60s. To that extent, at least, there was probably something in the claim that Rolling Thunder was a last hurrah for the spirit of Greenwich Village. The artist's great knack had been to make startlingly new music from the sense of old times and other places.

Blood on the Tracks had demonstrated his continuing artistic potency. *Desire* would prove to the world that he was still capable of surprising changes of direction. By the mid-'70s, nevertheless, a simple fact of life had to be addressed: he and his audience, his first audience at any rate, were so much older than before. As a generation, they were no longer being swept along by the old sense of infinite, unstoppable change, by the unexamined '60s belief that just about anything was possible. There was disillusionment, damage, cynicism amid the retreat into all those New Age fairy tales. America's 1976 Bicentennial, advertised as a moment of national reaffirmation and renewal, would meanwhile be the briefest respite from a nagging sense of foreboding. Perhaps Vietnam had done more damage to the country's once invincible optimism, its formerly incurable faith in American exceptionalism, than anyone truly realised. Before long, the question would become commonplace: had the republic's best and most potent years come and gone?

For Dylan, weary for so long with grand statements about his life and his songs, there were the usual strange parallels. They could have said much the same things about him. That had a lot to do with his origins and his age, of course, born in the middle of the country and growing up in the middle of the American century. But the arc of his career, rising amid the great national prosperity and seeming to fall away as national optimism fell away, as the promise of the '60s fell away, as the great upsurge of rock and roll fell away, seemed to trace the graph exactly. Nothing so pessimistic was said when *Desire* was perched at the top of the album charts, of course, but it would be said before too long. Soon they would begin to say that Bob Dylan's best years, the years of effortless creativity, were behind him, long lost and gone forever.

*

So what was the Rolling Thunder Revue in its best and brightest moments? In January 1976, back in London, Yorkshire-born Mick Ronson gave as good an account as any of the ties that had bound the first of the tours together. The guitarist also said something important, by his lights, about the nature of Dylan's art. Even in Ronson's inextinguishable Hull accent, it counted as a testament of faith.

> With Bob, you just know. If there was something he was looking for in a song, you'd try to find it without being told. And that's the thing about Dylan. I'd follow him anywhere, no questions asked. That whole tour was this huge, huge adventure. A real treasure hunt. There was Joan Baez. McGuinn. Ginsberg – he's a grand lad, is Allen. There was Dylan. And there I was, too. For a lad from Yorkshire like meself, it were truly out of this world . . . There'll be nowt like it again. Fookin' nowt.[36]

*

There was one thing more, a casual statement that soon enough would sound like a presentiment. Back in October, interrogated by *People* magazine, the artist had been taxed as usual on the subject of 'the Bob Dylan myth'. He had been as evasive as ever. He had never learned to enjoy this line of questioning. Finally, however, he came up with an answer. The myth of 'Bob Dylan'? 'It was given to me – by God.'[37]

CHAPTER FIVE

The Palace of Mirrors

DESIRE WAS RELEASED ON 16 JANUARY 1976 AND HELD BY MOST CRITICS and fans to be a triumph. A second concert was staged for the benefit of Rubin Carter on the 25th at the Astrodome in Houston, Texas, and derided as a shambles. 'Hurricane' was performed publicly for the last time at that badly organised and thinly attended show. Dylan had surely done all that he could with the song, with bohemian vaudeville and with the Rolling Thunder Revue. Outbreaks of press cynicism towards certain of his alleged superstar pretensions aside, responses to the tour had otherwise been gratifying. The artist should have quit while he was ahead.

There were some decent arguments urging him onwards. Only one part of America, far less the world, had been granted the chance to witness the latest 'new Dylan' at work. Given the media attention afforded to Rolling Thunder, there was, presumably, a demand waiting to be met. Equally, the ad hoc nature of the tour in the autumn and winter, not to mention the impossible financial strain involved in adding two film crews to the payroll, had left a big hole somewhere between gross and net. A lot of money had been made, but a lot had been spent. In January of 1978, the *Los Angeles Times* would put the cost of *Renaldo and Clara* at $1.25 million.[1] There were sound economic reasons, therefore, for mounting a spring campaign. In Dylan's specialised line of work, those have rarely proved to be the best reasons.

Desire was a big hit, however. Soon enough it was the artist's third number-one record of the decade. That should have been the main thing. However much the 105 to 110 hours of film stock expended on the *Renaldo and Clara* project had cost him, Dylan was not about to go broke with an album sitting at the top of the charts. *Desire* had also been accepted, almost instantly, as an appropriate follow-up to

Blood on the Tracks. This might seem to show that the wisdom of crowds is overrated, but critics and record buyers probably had a point. Dylan could easily have painted himself into a tight corner with his masterpiece. Hiring Jacques Levy might therefore have been something more than a caprice.

If Dylan had intended consciously to put *Blood* behind him, what was supposed to follow? If Levy's claims can be taken at face value – and Dylan has seemed to confirm certain of them – the collaborator certainly nudged the artist in the direction of structured narrative, fictional and documentary. Left to his own devices, Dylan would not repeat the experiment, but in 1975–6 it served his purpose. Besides, as Gertrude Stein, recipient of a couple of enigmatic dedications during the autumn tour, would probably not have said, a hit is a hit is a hit.

All of the songs on *Desire* were treated as Dylan songs. Jacques Levy's presence was noted, but his contribution was not often examined closely. Most reviews were shaped around 'Dylan this' or 'Dylan that', the artist first, last and always in splendid creative isolation. 'Not only is he writing better than ever,' *Billboard* would assert confidently, 'but his songs seem to reflect a new Dylan.' Reviewing the album in *Rolling Stone*, Dave Marsh would state, none too helpfully: 'It's not altogether clear just what Jacques Levy contributed to the songs. In many ways, they are of a piece with Dylan's other work.'[2]

The remark was itself of a piece with several reviews, but likely to baffle anyone familiar with all the work that had gone before. The *Desire* songs, for better or worse, were a disparate bunch with no clear or obvious precedents, least of all in terms of the music. As far as the words were concerned, the case for resemblances was hard to make. 'Hurricane', whether 'protest' or not (not), bore no real relationship to a song such as 'The Lonesome Death of Hattie Carroll'. 'Joey' was not another crack at 'Only a Pawn in Their Game'. Marsh believed that 'Isis' could have sat easily among the songs of *John Wesley Harding*, by virtue, no doubt, of its presumed mythic or indeed 'symbolic' content. The belief remains hard to fathom. Yet again, the words sung by Dylan – even if they were not necessarily his words – were being subjected to a refined variety of analytical torture. Each question became one question. What did the new songs signify in terms of 'Bob Dylan', that enduring monolith? The *Rolling Stone* critic, for all his reservations, would still decree *Desire* to be 'important'.

'The Night of the Hurricane II', to give it the full ungainly title employed on the posters, had the hallmarks of a flop sequel from the instant the decision was taken by promoters to move the show from a giant dome in Louisiana to a giant dome in Texas. The concert would be the last significant gesture made by Dylan on Rubin Carter's behalf. A $10,000 donation from the venue's owners aside, however, the event would fail to raise so much as a thin dime for the cause. The Madison Square Garden concert, in contrast, had earned around $100,000 for the Hurricane's legal defence fund. In Texas, despite a $12.50 ticket price and a tribe of famous musicians donating their services for free – 'expenses' aside – only a rancorous, complicated argument over what happened to all the money would be left to show for the humanitarian effort.

Carter, perhaps significantly, is said to have been deeply involved in organising the Texas benefit even *before* the New York concert, despite the fact that very few people in Houston knew about his case and fewer still cared about some local New Jersey controversy.[3] As it was, with an audience of 66,000 expected only some 30,000 tickets were sold. Air-travel bills of $45,000 for musicians, promoters, friends, hangers-on and anyone else who could cadge a ride, plus an eventual collective hotel tab of $36,000, were meanwhile on the wrong side of frugality. In the end, claimed expenses would run to over $428,000. Ticket revenues were put at slightly less than $380,000.

The concert programme had promised Bob Dylan and the Rolling Thunder Revue 'also starring', in descending order, Stevie Wonder, Isaac Hayes, Dr John and Shawn Phillips, the Texan singer-songwriter. There would also be 'many other surprise superstars'. The programme itself contained a long letter from Rubin asking concert-goers to write to the governor of New Jersey on the prisoner's behalf, reprinted newspaper clippings concerning the Carter affair, and the lyrics of 'Hurricane'. No amount of rhetoric prevented a fiasco.

The sound in the Astrodome was abysmal and the concert ran, as these things do, for hour upon endless hour. Neither the star, the billed acts nor the 'surprises' – Stephen Stills, Carlos Santana, Richie Havens – seem to have impressed the locals greatly. If the pop reviewer from the *Houston Post* was any guide, the Rolling Thunder legend did not travel well. There was an omen in that. According to *Rolling Stone*, Bob Claypool's verdict on the revue et al. was that 'they stunk. A lot of people left even before Dylan came out. It was boring. People were leaving in floods. A gross event. Weird bullshit.'

If true, it was a dismal moment at which to give 'Hurricane', that song born of rage and compassion, its last performance. It soon transpired that 'Sara' too had been dropped from the set once and for all, though the loss in that case was not great. In any case, the marriage song, whatever it was worth, had failed in its purpose. 'Idiot Wind' would take its place in the concerts given in 1976. The significance of the gesture hardly needed to be decoded.

*

Of itself, the Astrodome debacle did not seem to trouble Dylan greatly. The blame had not been his, not directly. Whether the public and the press saw things that way was another matter. For several months the artist had been identifying himself very publicly with Rubin Carter's campaign. After all the legal problems, the 'Hurricane' single had been rush-released, at Dylan's insistence, and become a minor hit, reaching number 33 on the *Billboard* chart. More to the point, the song opened and announced the *Desire* album. To a great many listeners that seemed, reasonably enough, like a perfectly clear statement of the artist's concern and commitment. The name 'Bob Dylan' still counted for something.

The Houston programme, with that name biggest and boldest at the top of the bill, had been plastered with Rubin's campaign literature. At Madison Square Garden on 8 December Dylan had behaved as though the scandal of the man's incarceration was a matter of the greatest urgency. After the Astrodome he seemed, quite simply, to walk away.

He had other things on his mind, no doubt. Perhaps he believed he had done enough. Perhaps, equally, he had begun to develop just a few private doubts about Carter's character and methods. It had never been Dylan's habit, in any case, to linger in the vicinity of failure. The Houston show, even on the most generous possible interpretation, had failed badly. Nevertheless, the truly significant fact is that the artist ceased to perform 'Hurricane' just as the boxer's fight against conviction was approaching a crucial moment. As coincidences go, that one tests credulity.

On 9 February, with Carter and John Artis convicted yet again, Rubin received two consecutive life sentences. Dylan, like all the celebrities who had made speeches or taken those choice seats at the Garden, was nowhere near the courtroom. Hurricane's battle would go on until 1985, but the singer who had been so vociferous, so righteous, was no longer prepared to offer so much as one song. So what became of 'an innocent man in a living hell'?

Dylan began instead to plan for a tour that would take Rolling Thunder around the cities of the Gulf of Mexico and out into the Midwest. Some of the places chosen were not his traditional territory – fans of the erstwhile folk singer had long tended to be concentrated on the coasts – but an artist with a number-one album doesn't often pause over such considerations. Equally, Dylan did not pause this time around over the alleged attractions of the 'small theatres' that had generated so much chatter in 1975. The venues for almost all of his 26 dates between 18 April and 25 May, Lakeland in Florida to Salt Lake City, Utah, would be in the 7,000 to 12,000 capacity range. Some were a good deal bigger than that. Dylan was 'interested' – and why not? – in making some money.

Tour rehearsals began early in April at the Belleview Biltmore Hotel in Clearwater, Florida. Dylan had already wasted some time at The Band's studio, Shangri-La, in Malibu, California, messing around – judging by some of the bootleg recordings – with Eric Clapton. Between them, the pair had managed to come up with a poor version of a dismally inconsequential Dylan song called 'Sign Language', a piece the Englishman would nevertheless see fit to record for his own *No Reason to Cry* album. Even back in Malibu, where Sara spent most of her time at the big, eccentric fantasy house Dylan had part-designed and built on the Point Dume peninsula after the cherished Woodstock establishment was sold in 1973, he had not been at home often. That life was at an end. His infidelities were continuous, relentless, utterly casual and conducted, as any amateur psychologist would have observed, with just a hint of desperation. The pattern of behaviour would not alter once the tour had begun.

He brought Guam and most of the Rolling Thunder ensemble back together in Florida. To his evident dismay, however, Ramblin' Jack Elliott discovered that his services were no longer required. Instead, the satirical country singer and self-styled 'Texas Jewboy' Kinky Friedman would join the touring party. Ramblin' Jack never discovered the reason for his dismissal, nor what became of precious old friendships. Noting Friedman's presence, he simply put two and two together. Dylan, with his own thoughts to manage, meanwhile chose to spend as little time as possible with his musicians.

At first, this seemed like a natural reaction to the grim news from New York that Phil Ochs had hanged himself finally on 9 April. Dylan was badly affected, it appears, though whether by guilt because of the way he had often treated a former comrade and fellow musician or by sheer, impotent sadness it is impossible to say. He must have wondered, for all that, if his failure to accept Ochs into the Rolling Thunder community had been some version of a last straw for a man in desperate trouble. There had been no other realistic choice after that bizarre October night at The Other End, but what of it? Isolating himself in Florida, the artist had reason to ponder the impossible hopes that so many still attached to the idea they had of 'Bob Dylan'. For his part, he began to keep strictly to himself. Communications with the Rolling Thunder troupe would henceforth be limited. Dylan's reticence became, on many occasions, a stony, indifferent silence. The erstwhile bohemian ensemble were employees and given no cause to forget the fact.

Something else had changed. As the first Florida shows would make clear, songs from *Desire* were to be less prominent than before, despite – or because of? – the album's success. Pieces from *Blood on the Tracks*, transmuted and transformed, with 'Idiot Wind' providing the culmination of the basic set, would begin to return in numbers. The change in tone and attitude, impossible to avoid with the inclusion of that venomous diatribe venomously rendered, would become steadily more marked. In point of fact, more songs from *Bringing It All Back Home* and *Blonde on Blonde* would be performed during the spring concerts than the remaining works from *Desire*. The touring company would still travel under the banner of the Rolling Thunder Revue; most of the same people would still be involved; but the difference between one season's work and the next would be profound. *Hard Rain*, the live album that would become the official record of the tour, boils still with splenetic fury.

Dylan was on edge, on *the* edge, trapped suddenly in a misconceived tour, his marriage all but ended, his private life an aimless mess. Critics would notice the results, of course, and much of the time would not care for them. Southern audiences, equally, would often be short on enthusiasm. In due course Dylan would suffer the humiliation of having shows cancelled – Lake Charles in Louisiana, Houston and Dallas in Texas – thanks solely to miserable ticket sales. For some, the uncompromising performances would be very hard to take. Soon enough, word of mouth, travelling fast, would count against the artist, hit album or no hit album. The tour would meanwhile become an act of sustained wrath. As though trying to wring a secret from the instrument, Dylan would take to playing lead guitar. Or rather, for he never attempted to pass himself off as a virtuoso, he would take to attempting to play electric lead guitar.

THE PALACE OF MIRRORS

It would stand as an example of symbolism as the little universe of rock and roll understood the word. It would count, for all the artist's ineptness with his instrument of choice, as the outward expression of inner turmoil and an assertion – this much every musician understood – of status. He was the star, take it or leave it. The trouble was, to paraphrase one of his own terrible jokes from a later period, that Dylan was not necessarily one of the few guitarists around whose playing was better than having no guitarist at all.

Itemise each of the elements of the second Rolling Thunder tour and you have a recipe for an unholy mess. Strangely, it wasn't quite like that. The artist was continuing to put his songs through a process of wholesale revision. This time the work was being rethought to suit his mood, and indeed his idiosyncratic guitar playing. Even the sacred 'Like a Rolling Stone' was turned into a severe, visceral thing during a failed attempt at the Belleview Biltmore to produce footage for a proposed NBC TV special. Here the flower-decked fedora was gone, replaced by a voluminous yellow bandana that made its wearer look like a guerrilla fighter just arrived from the mountains. The song itself was, more than ever, a half-spoken, raging soliloquy, slower than before but deeper emotionally than it had been in a long time.

Dylan had turned an artistic profit from his anger often enough before, but in the spring of 1976 he seemed to be going for broke, like a man with nothing left to lose. It seemed that finally all of it, 'Bob Dylan' first and foremost, had become too much for him. He should have been on top of the world with the success of *Desire*. Instead, he was lashing out. In the process, he would produce music of an integrity that only came to be understood, far less appreciated, after the Rolling Thunder Revue was long gone.

The first attempt at a TV film having ground to a halt thanks to his furious dislike of the staging and much else besides, Dylan found himself committed to providing – and to paying for – a concert documentary while trying to keep his own show on the road amid dire spring weather. It was not a happy tour. The artist poured booze down his throat and his emotions into his performances, but failed to achieve a cure. When Sara turned up in New Orleans just before the show at The Warehouse on 3 May the battle between husband and wife resumed, sometimes in public. She left within a matter of days while Dylan endured the miserable humiliation of cancelled concerts in Texas and the pressure of preparing himself for the TV special. It had been conceived as a big-deal, prime-time affair, with a live album planned to appear simultaneously. Given that the tour had been treated with disdain in several quarters, it was hard to see what Dylan could produce to salvage the situation.

When at last Rolling Thunder reached the chosen venue at Colorado State University's Hughes Stadium to the north of Denver, the rains were coming down hard. The biblical deluge refused to stop. It poured for days; the stadium was open to the skies; the mountain air was freezing; and the artist was soon in a foul, black mood. Just as he was deciding that Rolling Thunder would play on, downpours or not, and that the film would be made come what may, his wife reappeared with his children and his mother in tow. It was the eve of his 35th birthday and he was in the middle of another affair. None of this was ideal.

In their second-to-last show as an ensemble, soaked and freezing to the bone, real sparks and shocks coming from instruments that refused to stay in tune, the Rolling Thunder Revue played as though every cliché about last stands and dependent lives was a statement of fact. As a show it was anything but faultless, but it was a fiercely determined, even principled gesture. Unless you are precious about musical precision, you can hear as much on the *Hard Rain* album. Though TV critics would struggle to see much art in the fire and ice of the NBC special, you can still perceive the ragged glory of Dylan and his band on the film, too. At Fort Collins, Colorado, the local crowd, at least as cold and wet as the band, understood what they were witnessing and responded accordingly.

It would count as the lasting mark of this last, impassioned phase of Rolling Thunder. A lot of people, accustomed to the musical purée that passed for rock and roll in the first part of the '70s, had missed the point of the spring tour and would go on missing the point for many years. Those who were alert and eager for what was just around the corner caught the first sulphurous whiff, the first snatches and glimpses, from Dylan and his musicians when they were under siege in Fort Collins. It wasn't punk, not by any stretch of the imagination, but in 1976 something of the spirit the artist had possessed in 1966 was recaptured and that was the next, better thing.

At Fort Collins, Sara Dylan meanwhile watched her estranged husband perform 'Idiot Wind' and 'Shelter from the Storm' in a manner, vicious and yet proud, defiant yet regretful, that provided a summation for the songs, for the tour and for their marriage. After one more show at a half-empty Salt Palace in Salt Lake City, a place far better suited to basketball and hockey, it was over. Dylan moved on without a backward glance. He had a whole other movie to complete.

*

After half a century and more, it is just about possible to divide this artist's work into three broad categories. Some of the things he does are accepted instantly: a 'Blowin' in the Wind', a 'Mr. Tambourine Man', a *Modern Times*. Other manifestations of his art take a while to gain recognition from his audience before the hosannas are heard: the 1966 tour, the country music, the *Street-Legal* album, his evangelical songs. In one small corner of hell, however, there are pieces of work so utterly tainted by critics' first impressions, so encrusted with the residue of received opinion, they seem beyond all hope of redemption. The prose experiment *Tarantula* would be one example, the *Self Portrait* album a second and the film *Renaldo and Clara* a third. Each has been treated unfairly.

Most who claim to know about the book have never read it closely, if they've read it at all. The album has rarely been given a proper hearing by people who take their cues in matters of taste from the award of tiny paper stars by critics who seem always to know what Dylan should have been doing instead (generally speaking, whatever it was he was doing before). The movie, by and large, has simply not been seen.

That doesn't make it a lost masterpiece any more than a good word for *Self Portrait* transforms the set into the greatest thing Dylan ever recorded. Nevertheless, the film he and Howard Alk began to assemble after the last echo of Rolling Thunder had faded away is not without merit. To indulge in special pleading: the sheer depth of the artist's faith in this work should at least give more people pause. Dylan believed in the thing, and believed absolutely. He was passionate about it. He knew perfectly well that many people wouldn't get it. Yet he persevered. It is surely worth enquiring after the reason.

Anyone who says that *Renaldo and Clara* was simply a vanity project does not know much about the subject of their accusation – Dylan has scrapped better work than his peers could manage on their best days – or what the film cost him. He more or less abandoned *Eat the Document*, but he stuck with this one. His adventures in cinema have often been unhappy, to say the least of it. The question is therefore worth asking. Why did he care so much about a work that cost him so much time, money and effort and earned him only derision?

It would not see the light of day until 1978. The earliest edit would have taken an entire working day out of any viewer's life, but even in its first released version, at close to four hours in length, there was the implicit assertion that Dylan did not mean to be bound by Hollywood's definition of the average attention span. He would lose that battle twice over, first when the long version was massacred by the critics and again when he sanctioned a near-meaningless two-hour edit late in 1978. By then it would be too late. *Renaldo and Clara's* dismal reputation had already been made.

So what do you get if you chance upon this work? In parts, a truly terrific concert movie. Should Dylan ever wish to pander to an audience that cares nothing for fancy ideas and improvised acting – a big enough constituency, then – there are still the makings of a remarkable, straightforward Rolling Thunder documentary within *Renaldo and Clara*. Given the sheer quantity of footage gathered during the tour, much more must be available than has been seen. Equally, the soundtrack to the 232-minute picture as it stands could form, with just a little attention, the album still desired by those who saw the revue or are these days obliged to traffic with bootleggers. Such projects were not even close to what Dylan had in mind. Still, they count as a start.

Second, there remains a lot of *cinéma-vérité* material that is not without charm, drama or human interest. Evangelists raging on Wall Street and reproachful statues of Jesus, Allen Ginsberg reading his *Kaddish*, the scene at Kerouac's grave, interviews with journalists, the singer David Blue playing pinball while telling old stories about the Village: these are neither meaningless nor dull. The fault with the film, the great fissure at its heart, is the attempt to fuse all the other elements into an enveloping drama while forgetting, or failing to understand, dramatic structure. The maker of *Renaldo and Clara* seems not to have understood that idea well enough even to subvert it. The fact that most of Dylan's actors were rank amateurs might have been supportable if he had kept their parts simple and coherent. Movies made with non-professionals have worked often enough. Here the director, struggling to weld together different kinds of cinema, overwhelms his players with a ton of ill-explained big ideas while failing to support the actors with useful dialogue, or with any sense of actions and consequences.

Come 1978, Dylan would devote a lot of time to interviews in an attempt to persuade audiences to give his film a chance. He didn't always help his case. Ron Rosenbaum of *Playboy* would be lectured on 'the essence of man being alienated from himself and how, in order to free himself, to be reborn, he has to go outside himself. You can almost say that he dies in order to look at time and, by strength of will, can return to the same body.'[4] Jonathan Cott of *Rolling Stone* – who found *Renaldo and Clara* 'adventurous and mysterious', 'intimate and evanescent' – would be told that 'Art is the perpetual motion of illusion'.[5] Dylan, who wouldn't try to take this tale to Poughkeepsie, went on (and on):

> I've had this picture in mind for a long time – years and years. Too many years . . . Renaldo is oppressed. He's oppressed because he's born. We don't really know who Renaldo is. We just know what he isn't. He isn't the Masked Tortilla. Renaldo is the one with the hat, but he's not wearing a hat. I'll tell you what this movie is: it's like life exactly, but not an imitation of it. It transcends life, and it's not like life . . . I'll tell you what my film is about: it's about naked alienation of the inner self against the outer self – alienation taken to the extreme. And it's about integrity.

Even in the mid-'70s, this kind of talk was hardly guaranteed to sell a movie to the average Bob Dylan fan, far less the average popcorn-muncher, even if the music was better than pretty fair. It is worth observing, too, that this artist would *never* have discussed his songs in such a manner. He had always understood, instinctively and perfectly, just how destructive such chatter can be. Struggling to explain *Renaldo and Clara*, he sounded like nothing so much as an extra-intense Dylan 'scholar' picking the symbolic bones from the carcass of 'Desolation Row'. You could speculate, in fact, that the picture might have done just a little better at the box office had he kept his high-flown thoughts to himself.

What was almost touching in such interviews, nevertheless, was Dylan's intense belief in the film. In a forgiving mood you can argue that it starts pretty well, with Dylan in his strange transparent mask singing 'When I Paint My Masterpiece', Neuwirth in tow. Then comes a scene in a hotel lobby with reliable Larry Sloman trying to get a room, Blue chatting at his pinball table, then Dylan as our hero sitting in a garage playing his guitar, then a scene – the scene – at The Other End. All of this could pass for intriguing. But suddenly there's Bobby Neuwirth in a silly Zorro mask, then Sara Dylan and Baez as (presumably) whore-goddesses. Joan Baez grew tired quickly enough of that last juvenile conceit and you can hardly blame her. Long before the supposedly symbolic triangular relationship has manifested itself, the last of a viewer's hope has fled. The Dylan fan sticks it out, if she or he is honest, for the same old reason: the music. When the final credits are followed by the usual bland legal statement that 'persons and events in this film are fictitious; their relationship to other persons and events is unintentional' the only fair response is sarcasm.

Interviewed by the *Los Angeles Times*, and still maintaining that he had another movie in mind – 'If we could make a deal with a studio . . .' – Dylan already had certain excuses prepared. If the film had flaws, it turned out, those had been the fault of others. Clearly, the difference between the movie in this director's head and what wound up on the screen was vast. That wasn't his fault, however.

> The film could have been much better if people could have had a little more belief, been a little freer. There was a lot of conflict on this film. We had people who didn't understand what we were doing, but who were willing to go along with it. And we had people working on the tour who didn't understand and weren't willing to go along with us. It hurt us. It was good for the show, but it hurt the film.[6]

Interviewed at around this time by the Canadian weekly *Maclean's*, Dylan would attempt to maintain that no one in the audience would have guessed the fictional scenes had been improvised had he not said as much. Later in the conversation, a little self-knowledge would begin to manifest itself. Though the chances of his beloved movie failing had not been mentioned, he said:

> Whether it's a failure or not, I don't know. It could be. Maybe the movie isn't for everybody. Maybe there are only two or three people in the universe who are going to understand what it's about.[7]

Even at his most defiantly romantic, the loner against the world, Dylan had not gambled for a career in music by backing those odds. Over the years he would spend a lot of time claiming to be misunderstood and claiming that he didn't care. In reality, rejection of his work never sat easily with him. When *Renaldo and Clara* paid its brief visit to cinemas he would suffer one of the sharper rebuffs in his creative life. Years later, kind souls and diehard fans would attest that he was right, that he had been misconstrued, that (among other things) he had managed a homage to bohemianism itself with his movie. Obscure and ancient Beat experiments would be adduced. His remarks about Carné and Truffaut, remarks both sincere and calculated, would thereafter keep a few people busy. That wasn't wholly unreasonable. Like an eager film-school student, Dylan had obviously studied the use of motifs, the implicit arguments over the nature of identity, the jump cuts and the sequencing evident – perhaps only too dazzlingly evident – in *Les Enfants du Paradis* and *Shoot the Piano Player*.

The result, in a strange way, was like *Tarantula* all over again. He had wanted to write a novel; he was, so they said, a genius with words. So why couldn't he just write a novel? He loved movies; he believed he understood movies; some of his songs, they said, were very like movies. So why couldn't he just make a movie? Perhaps because Dylan's gift for songwriting had seemed to come without effort for so long, he fooled himself into believing that any art could be conjured easily.

A better verdict might be that with *Renaldo and Clara* he came closer to making his dream-movie than most critics were prepared to allow. There have been worse films. Given a chance he would, no doubt, have learned from his numerous mistakes. But he was Bob Dylan, songwriter. A great many people were very clear about that. They were not prepared to allow the artist to abdicate from the duties they had defined. In effect, the reaction to *Renaldo and Clara*, like the reaction to *Tarantula*, was an attempt to put him in his place, to force him back to his true calling. In 1978, after his picture was released at last, no studio would be found to offer him a modest budget and a sound stage to call his own.

*

The day had not yet dawned when Dylan could be summoned to the White House to play for presidents. On 4 July 1976, on America's 200th birthday, he was neither seen nor heard. A few weeks later he would succumb to an aimless interview with *TV Guide*, a journal of cultural affairs then at its multimillion-selling peak, in an effort to support the *Hard Rain* concert film. 'I sometimes dream of running the country and putting all my friends in office,' Dylan would tell the man from the magazine. 'That's how it works now, anyway.'[8] Beyond that, he had nothing to say about the state of the nation. He took no public part in the celebrations for the birth of the republic or its two centuries as democracy's shining light.

Bob Hope was on TV wrapping himself in the flag in an NBC

'spectacular' that July weekend. On the Fourth itself, President Gerald Ford, Nixon's hapless substitute, was in Philadelphia addressing patriots as distinguished as the actor Charlton Heston. Ford was declaring: 'It is right that Americans are always improving. It is not only right, it is necessary.' In New York Harbor, Vice-President Nelson Rockefeller was reviewing a fleet of tall ships while six million people, or so the *New York Times* estimated, looked on. That night fireworks would light up the Statue of Liberty. Across America, as the newspaper reported, it was 'A Day of Picnics, Pomp, Pageantry and Protest'. Restored steam locomotives were meanwhile pulling a travelling historical exhibition entitled 'the American Freedom Train' around the country. Not a city, town or village in America was untouched by the festivities. The nation was awash with speeches and souvenirs.

Gil Scott-Heron, the radical self-styled 'bluesologist', maker of *Winter in America* and *From South Africa to South Carolina*, introduced one of the few audibly sceptical voices amid the summer's celebrations with a piece entitled 'Bicentennial Blues'. In it he nominated 1976 as 'A year of hysterical importance', one in which the public had been 'bludgeoned into bicentennial submission'. Scott-Heron reminded anyone who happened to be listening that the facts of racism, poverty and injustice had 'got by' too many Americans, not least those contemplating a vote for the 'Hollyweird' Ronald Reagan, then just a grinning former conservative governor of California. On the weekend of the Fourth itself, Scott-Heron was performing his 'Bicentennial Blues' poem, all eight minutes and forty seconds of it, before a Boston audience for a concert album, *It's Your World*. His was not the voice of the majority.

The year had opened with another nuclear test in Nevada. Inflation, still perilously high at 5.75 per cent, had nevertheless subsided a little; official unemployment stood at 7.7 per cent. One day before the Bicentennial itself, the Supreme Court had ruled that the death penalty, suspended during the four previous years, was not inherently 'cruel or unusual' and no offence to the constitution that bound together 218 million Americans. Crime was still a preoccupation for politicians and the media – 'wars' on wrongdoers abounded during political campaigns – but making a living was the main concern for hard-pressed law-abiding citizens. Another long recession had ended, statistically speaking, in 1975, but the economy remained weak as the country staged its birthday party. Only with federal help had New York City survived a brush with bankruptcy. Amidst it all, something was stirring.

The novelist Gore Vidal had observed the essentials of the phenomenon in an essay published in the year before the Bicentennial. Describing his experiences delivering provocative 'State of the Union' lectures to audiences caught between bemusement, amusement and outrage, Vidal had written of encountering among his fellow Americans a 'general hatred of any government'. He told of 'the message that I got from one end of the country to the other: we hate this system that we are trapped in but we don't know who has trapped us or how'.[9]

Among conservative Americans, the mood was being articulated loudly. Some believed they had found an answer to their problems. Reagan's failed challenge to Ford for the 1976 Republican presidential nomination would be remembered long afterwards as the prophetic moment. Earlier in the decade, right-wing institutions such as the Heritage Foundation, the Conservative Political Action Conference and the American Conservative Union (all founded in 1973) had sprung into existence. By 1976, the influential monthly magazine *Commentary* had completed its shift from left to right and confirmed itself as the house journal of what would come to be known as neo-conservatism. Political reaction would produce action in due course. Preposterous as it might have seemed at the time, the not-so-strange death of '60s liberalism was all but complete.

Dylan gave no sign that he noticed or cared. This didn't make him immune, however, to what was going on in his country. Congressional Democrats had done predictably well in elections in 1974 in the aftermath of Watergate. Their party's candidate, Jimmy Carter of Georgia, would win the presidency on 2 November 1976. During his nomination acceptance speech in New York on 15 July, the new candidate (or his speechwriters) would misquote 'It's Alright, Ma' comprehensively, asserting that 'We have an America that, in Bob Dylan's phrase, is busy being born, not busy dying'. The artist would respond like a jaded elder statesman through the august pages of *TV Guide*. 'People have told me there was a man running for president quoting me,' Dylan would say. 'I don't know if that's good or bad. But he's just another guy running for president.'

Carter's eventual victory would prove to be a kind of illusion and the briefest of respites for liberal Americans. In time, their Democrat president would become even less popular than Nixon, a phenomenon unthinkable in 1974.[10] As the artist had mentioned almost casually to *People* magazine back in October, 'The consciousness of the country has changed in a very short time.' Out in the American heartland political conservatism and yet another evangelical Christian revival were growing in strength, hand in glove. And Dylan had always harboured a weakness for a deity.

*

In November, on Thanksgiving Day, he would appear at Winterland Ballroom in San Francisco for what was billed as The Band's 'farewell' concert. It was a last farewell, in reality, to the youthful comradeship that had once bound the group together. When Dylan's former backing musicians returned to touring in 1983 it would be without Robbie Robertson, the guitarist whose perceived high-handedness and self-regard – there were plenty of other allegations – had alienated his colleagues long before the affair known as *The Last Waltz* was being organised. By 1976, in any case, Robertson had decided he was weary of life on the road. The other members of the quintet would continue to believe, in contrast, that he had broken up The Band for purely selfish reasons, furthering his own career – under the guidance of one Albert Grossman – while keeping a tight grip on their joint legacy.

Many years later, all of drummer Levon Helm's bitterness towards Robertson would spill forth in his autobiography. Among other things, Helm would contend that he received not a cent from the show, album and Martin Scorsese documentary movie each known as *The Last Waltz*. In an afterword to his book published after his passing in 2012, Helm would be quoted by his co-writer claiming that Rick Danko, The Band's bass and fiddle player, had died prematurely because of sheer overwork (the 1999 autopsy settled for drug-related heart failure). In Helm's disgusted opinion, Danko had worked too hard for too long because 'he had been fucked out of his money'. Levon said:

> People ask me about The Last Waltz all the time. Rick Danko dying at 56 is what I think about The Last Waltz. It was the biggest fuckin' rip-off that ever happened to The Band – without a doubt.[11]

Dylan would remain forever fond of Levon – the feeling was reciprocated – but in late 1976 these were not his problems. For the purposes of album, movie, money and valediction, Robertson appeared to have enlisted any prominent musician who had ever been associated with The Band. There were a couple of others, vapid Neil Diamond conspicuously, whose relationship with anyone other than the guitar player was hard to identify. On Thanksgiving night at Winterland there were poets, turkey dinners for 5,000, ballroom dancing, seven high-end 35-mm cameras and a crew of experienced cinematographers to meet Scorsese's demand that every last second be captured on film. Joni Mitchell, Muddy Waters, Van Morrison, Neil Young, Eric Clapton, Ronnie Hawkins, Paul Butterfield and Dr John were among the performers. There was no possible doubt, however, about the identity of the star guest.

Dylan did his job in the end, but not without almost wrecking the entire production. At the last minute, so it was said, he announced that he would not be filmed. As the tale was afterwards told, he did not want his appearance to steal any thunder due to the concert sequences in *Renaldo and Clara*.[12] Since Warner Bros. had only agreed to finance Scorsese's lavish array of cameras because of a promise that Bob Dylan would be in the movie, this posed a problem for Robertson and the show's promoter, Bill Graham. The Band were no longer a hot item in their own right by 1976. The $25 tickets for the evening had only begun to move, in fact, after Graham had leaked details of the guest list to the *San Francisco Chronicle*.[13] Only some feverish negotiations during the intermission – while almost everyone else busied themselves with vast drifts of cocaine – and the intervention of one of Dylan's lawyers saved the show, the movie and the album.

The Last Waltz would duly become known as 'the greatest concert film ever made'. Very fine it is too, in places. Dylan's performance was as good as most and far better than some, if a long way short of his finest. 'Baby, Let Me Follow You Down' (twice) and 'I Don't Believe You' were done with sufficient conviction. One of those ineradicable anecdotes-with-no-source prefaced with the word 'reputedly' probably catches the artist's real attitude best. In this tale, Neil Diamond is leaving the stage. 'Follow that,' he supposedly says to Dylan. The artist replies, 'What do I have to do, go on stage and fall asleep?'

*

He was not exerting himself unduly. Whether because he was still refusing to admit the truth about his marriage or because he knew the miserable truth beyond doubt or dispute, Dylan had fallen into a fit of indolence. He still had *Renaldo and Clara* to see to, but he was not giving his full attention to the editing process. He would turn up here and there – at The Band's concert, at a riotously intoxicated Leonard Cohen recording session in June of 1977 – but in terms of his career history only one fact would be pertinent. Between the release of *Desire* in January of 1976 and the summer of 1978, Dylan would fail to produce an album in the studios. *Hard Rain*, the record intended to document the 1976 spring tour, had been released in September of the year, doing only modestly well in America but reaching number three in Britain. A mostly pointless single from the album, 'Stuck Inside of Mobile with the Memphis Blues Again' (with the entirely pointless 'Rita May' as its B-side), had failed utterly in November. The rest, save for the sound of approaching lawyers, was silence.

The end was ugly, the aftermath worse. In the papers she would lodge during the divorce, Sara Dylan would state that in Malibu, at the still 'unfinished' Point Dume house with its copper onion dome, the quarrels became ceaseless. She would further assert that she began to fear her husband, that she locked doors against him and his volcanic temper. The real issue was other women. Sara would claim that in February of 1977 one turned up at her breakfast table who seemed to be living on the estate. His wife gained the impression, as lawyers say, that Dylan wanted this latest flame to reside in the main house. In the ensuing argument, so it was alleged, he struck Sara on the face and ordered her out of the house. This would be the story released subsequently to the press by one of Sara Dylan's lawyers.

Court papers would be sealed, however, after she filed for divorce at the beginning of March. We therefore do not know Dylan's response, if he had one, to the central allegation. What is known is that Sara Dylan moved out immediately and hired Marvin Mitchelson, one of the many celebrity lawyers who seem to constitute a major part of the Southern Californian economy. The community property laws of that state meant the artist was always likely to lose heavily, in financial terms, in any divorce settlement. Mitchelson would make sure of it. Sara, in any case, knew just about all there was to know about Dylan. There were plenty of stories she could have told. Some of those involving the couple's recent married life were not pretty. She had – and there's no denying it – tolerated a lot and suffered for her tolerance. It was in Dylan's interest to yield.

When the divorce papers were filed Sara demanded custody of the five children, child support, alimony, the Malibu house and, the most expensive item of all given Californian law, a division of Dylan's wealth. The papers listed the 'Malibu complex; other and diverse property including residence, farmlands and acreage in New York City; East Hampton, Woodstock and Greene County, New York; Minnesota and New Mexico; and undetermined interests in publishing companies, subsidiary and residual recording rights, royalties and literary copyrights'. Sara also wanted a restraining order against her husband. In the bloodless language of the filing, the 'respondent, Robert Dylan, is hereby restrained and enjoined from harassing, annoying, molesting, or in any way interfering with the peace and quiet and personal privacy of the petitioner, Sara Dylan'. Her demands would fail in only one detail. Because the artist could claim, accurately, to be working on *Renaldo and Clara* in Point Dume's editing suite – and because he wanted desperately to keep the house – he would be allowed to go on living there. Beyond that, it was no contest.

Early speculation would put the settlement figure at $6 million, then at $10 million. Later estimates, taking into account those property assets around the country, ran to $36 million *plus* a continuing half share of the royalties – pick a figure – for songs written and recorded between 1965 and 1977, with the proviso that a further payment would be due to Sara Dylan in the event of Dylan's catalogue being sold.[14] He appears not to have put up much of a contest, if he put up any contest, over the money. That part of the final rupture between himself and Sara was settled quickly and, to all appearances, amicably. The real fight would be over the custody of the children.

His love for them was never in doubt, but somehow Dylan persuaded himself that he, of all people, with his habits, women, fame, fans, creative life and professional obligations, was entitled to believe he could care for his brood. Sara would be ferocious in her determination to disabuse him of that idea. Yet again, his understanding of his several competing identities – Bob Dylan the artist, Bob Dylan the rock star, Bob Dylan the doting father and others besides – was inadequate, worse than naive. Children aside, nevertheless, the divorce was settled at the end of June.

'Sad Eyed Lady of the Lowlands' had not foretold this. There had been no mention of Californian community property law in 'Sara'. In hindsight it was self-evident, nevertheless, that the years of Dylan's real contentment had been those eight years after 1966 when he had hidden from stardom and stayed away from touring, living with his family at Woodstock or on Cape Cod. For the private man who carried the name, picking up the burden of 'Bob Dylan' had been a big mistake. On the other hand, no one had put a loaded gun to his head, or deceived him into thinking that the rock and roll 'lifestyle' was an inevitable adjunct to rock and roll music. He had made his own choices. Among other things, he alone had decided that his brush with old

Norman Raeben had caused his wife to cease to 'understand' him. And plainly, above all, Sara Dylan had been expected to tolerate more than was tolerable, even in a celebrity union.

Still, by the summer of 1977 a central part of his former existence had removed herself from his life. Another muse – for Sara had been that, if she had been anything – was gone. He would still sing the songs he had written because of her, but their essential, original meaning was gone. As so often before and since, Dylan retreated to his farm in Minnesota. Still another girl was with him.

*

He would write a group of songs that summer, just as he had written songs in 1974. This time, however, he would not rush into the studios, as he had done with *Blood on the Tracks*, to turn his writing into an album at the first opportunity. It might have been better if he had.

On 16 August 1977, while Dylan was on the Minnesota farm, news broke that Elvis Presley had died in Memphis. The artist was distraught for days, yet he couldn't have been entirely surprised. The grotesque condition of the only king of rock and roll had been plain for the world to see for long enough. Presley's late concert performances, sweating at the slightest exertion and straining at the seams of those preposterous jumpsuits, had become a joke to everyone but the blue-rinsed, middle-aged faithful. For all that, few had truly understood the depths of Presley's drugged, bloated degradation. Peter Guralnick, foremost among his biographers, would describe a performer who was scarcely able to sing or follow a melody in his last shows in 1977, 'a man crying out for help when he knows help will not come'.[15] Dylan had known, as most observers had known, that something was seriously amiss in the strange world that Elvis inhabited. Still the death came as a profound shock to the artist.

A part of his past, and therefore of his world, had been eradicated. Perverse as it sounds, the loss of Presley mattered almost as much to Dylan as the loss of his marriage. Or perhaps, possibly, it counted as another of those last straws. Elvis, the music, the lost world of the 1950s, the hope and defiance and unstoppable energy, had been essential to the person Dylan was, or believed himself to be. If those sound like childish, self-involved notions, the truth about this artist is misunderstood. He was of a generation, perhaps the last such generation, for whom pop music was part of the meaning of existence. It's not a big guess to say that Dylan grieved for himself when he grieved for Elvis. According to what he would tell Robert Shelton almost a year later, he suffered 'a breakdown' when he heard about the death.[16]

> I went over my whole life. I went over my whole childhood. I didn't talk to anyone for a week after Elvis died. If it wasn't for Elvis and Hank Williams, I couldn't be doing what I do today.

Dylan seems to have worked hard in Minnesota, but he put the work aside, for whatever reason, when he returned to California determined to reclaim his children. It was as though they represented the one loss, the last loss, that could not be borne. His relationship with Sara, civilised and businesslike as the divorce had gone through, struck an unnavigable reef of animosity. Even her decision to take the kids on a holiday to Hawaii had caused him to believe she was plotting to move them beyond his reach. These parents were in territory familiar to the survivors, poets and superstars or not, of many broken marriages. For the Dylans, it all became as hideous and pointless as any suburban trauma, dragging on week after week in hearings and negotiations between lawyers. The full tabloid tale of court orders and accusations – find your 'expert', find your 'evidence' – serves no one now. In the end, inevitably, Sara Dylan won the day and established herself somewhere in Beverly Hills. The artist got his children for the holidays.

*

Renaldo and Clara saw the flickering light finally with a pair of premieres, in New York and LA, in the last week of January 1978. The *Village Voice* would set no fewer than six critics on the movie and five of those would struggle to come up with a decent word to say for the production. The journal's James Wolcott would observe that so many reputations went down with the film it was like watching the defeat of the Spanish Armada. Mark Jacobson would begin his review by casually wishing Dylan dead for lending his name to a picture that failed to supply true confessions.[17] Long after the event, the journalist would concede that the review 'came out a little more negative than I would have liked'. What 'came out' began

> I wish Bob Dylan died. Then Channel 5 would piece together an instant documentary on his life and times, the way they did for Hubert Humphrey. The way they do for Chaplin, or Adolf Hitler. Just the immutable facts.

Seeing all those immutable facts about Elvis made his dying worthwhile. The high points. What a sum-up. You don't get much gray, but like the reporter in *Citizen Kane* found out, gray doesn't necessarily amount to shit.[18]

You could say the same about certain movie reviews. Sometimes you begin, just about, to understand the artist's contempt for journalism. Along the way – having said, with spectacular nastiness, that 'Dylan had a good reason to beat Sara' – Jacobson complained because the movie was longer than *Citizen Kane*, because it 'revealed' nothing new about Dylan, because it was a 'rich kid's vanity project', and because – this seemed to be the film's real offence – the poor critic didn't get it. Years later, he would confess that 'you will always write things you wish you didn't'. There is one infallible solution for that problem.

In America, in any case, *Renaldo and Clara's* reputation was left bleeding in the dust. The *Village Voice* was only the shrill soprano in a chorus of lousy reviews. Writing in the *New Yorker*, Pauline Kael complained that the movie was both a failed and a dishonest drama, guilty of employing the star's former lover (Baez) and wife as a kind of 'tease'.[19] Critics lined up to trash the picture while film fans eager for a production with a song in its heart took their pick that year from *Grease*, *The Buddy Holly Story* and *Animal House*.

In Europe, *Renaldo and Clara* was at least treated with a degree of respect, perhaps because Dylan himself had long been treated as a serious artistic proposition by Europeans, or perhaps because European film critics, with their auteur theories and their art-house cinema loyalties, were always liable to give an earnestly pretentious director a break. In truth, Hollywood's commercial imperatives still counted for less on the old continent than on the new. Bernardo Bertolucci's *1900* (1976) had run to 245 minutes in the *short* version. Jan Troell's *The Emigrants* (1971) and its sequel, *The New Land* (1972), had between them demanded 395 minutes of a viewer's time. In any case, *Renaldo and Clara* would be given an out-of-competition screening at the Cannes Film Festival in May and, lest it be forgotten, win the Interfilm Award at the Mannheim-Heidelberg International Film Festival later in the year. A minority of people, European people, had the temerity just to enjoy the picture.

It made no difference. The film, given only a limited release to begin with, was gone from American movie houses within a few weeks. A further messy edit sanctioned by Dylan towards the end of the year, cutting the running time to two hours and giving more room to the concert footage, did a little better, but it was not enough. Within a few years the director would withdraw the film from distribution entirely. Those who wanted their 'Bob Dylan' as they understood him were not to be denied.

He was in no hurry to keep them happy, but suddenly he had no choice. Poverty did not beckon, exactly, but with millions spent on the Point Dume house, millions more on the movie, and tens of millions awarded to Sara, Dylan was obliged to go back to work, like it or not. So he reasoned, at any rate. In May of 1978, he would even confess to the *Los Angeles Times* that he had 'quite a few debts to pay off'.

> I had a couple of bad years. I put a lot of money into the movie, built a big house . . . and there's the divorce. It costs a lot to get divorced in California.[20]

Clearly, the divorce was the big ticket on the list. The briefly controversial switch to large venues during the autumn and winter tour of 1975 had been excused, after all, by the need to divert revenues to *Renaldo and Clara*. No one was obliging Dylan to subsist meanwhile in a vast mansion on a big Malibu estate. The settlement made on Sara was the debt that could not be avoided. But he did not intend to go broke, or even to change the style of living to which he had grown accustomed, on that account.

After the embattled heroics of the spring tour, a revival of Rolling Thunder was neither plausible artistically nor attractive financially. Perhaps the artist just decided that a trip abroad would do him a power of good. It's more likely that his newly chosen manager, an individual accustomed to producing concerts for the likes of Presley and Sinatra or managing the likes of Neil Diamond, made the traditional showbiz suggestion. If Dylan needed to raise some money, Jerry Weintraub would happily organise the kind of world tour that was the closest approximation to a licence to print the stuff. Japan, the Far East, Europe, the United States: dozens of concerts and millions of tickets for the sake of one man's divorce settlement. Set beside this operation, the Rolling Thunder troupe were Boy Scouts up against the US Marines.

It's not an insignificant detail. In 1978, Dylan would chase the bottom line. All the talk of small clubs, folk roots, bohemia and being happy just to sing and play anywhere for anyone might never have happened. This time musicians would not be selected on a whim and a prayer. This time there would be no messing around with old pals, art cinema or campaigns for the wrongly convicted. Everything would be bent to a single end. Dylan's accountants could no doubt have supplied all the reasons, priced to the last penny. Those fans who wanted to believe that he existed as a creative singularity inside a bubble called genius would have to cope, as best they could, with this fact of the artist's life: he liked to talk about living just for the music, but he was not eager to retreat to a poet's garret. Being rich was very much easier, and a lot more agreeable, than being poor. Dylan was not about to give it all up. American reviewers would not call this 'the Alimony Tour' for nothing.

Rehearsals began towards the end of 1977 in a rented Santa Monica factory space he called Rundown Studios. Bootlegs dating from the last week in December of that year still do the rounds. Some of the recordings contain rough accounts of what were then new Dylan compositions, but he still had no plans – none he would reveal, at least – for an album. On this occasion, mercifully, Jacques Levy's services had not been required for the writing process. At first it would seem that the musicians who began to arrive at the studio were not needed either, what with the distractions of the fight for custody of the Dylan children and the impending movie premieres. Work did not start in earnest until the end of one year and the beginning of the next.

Dylan was now remodelling his old songs habitually, even obsessively, on the basis of experiments in rehearsal. It was as if he realised that he would need some sort of artistic stimulant if he was to remain fully conscious through nine months, ten countries, four continents and one hundred and fourteen shows. By the time it was all over, someone would calculate – these show-business legends always wind up being expressed in suspiciously round figures – that Dylan had played to two million people. By the end, nevertheless, only a very few Americans would believe they had seen the best of him.

Back in Santa Monica he had prepared himself, his eight-piece band and three backing vocalists – the membership of both altered somewhat as the weeks passed – by trying out certain of the new songs and by trying to make the old songs sound new. What began to emerge was not always bad but it was, invariably, weird. With Rolling Thunder, Dylan had moulded his music to suit the musicians he had chosen. At Rundown, he took another step: the nature of the band, girl singers, sax player and all, dictated the 'arrangements'. Unkind souls, American reviewers in particular, would later conclude that Elvis had been too much on the artist's mind. Words such as 'Vegas' and 'lounge act' would be employed. Dylan drew the line at a jumpsuit – though sequins would be sighted – but tolerated several other indignities.

The tour began at the Nippon Budokan in Tokyo on 20 February. Three nights in the capital were followed by three nights in Osaka and another five nights back in Tokyo. Within the space of a couple of weeks, Dylan had already made a ton of money with a show that was, in effect, a greatest-hits package – a revue of a different sort – complete in places with a flute, of all things. The first night saw only a couple of novelties in the space of 28 songs. 'The Man in Me', never performed in concert after being recorded for the *New Morning* album in 1970, put in an appearance. 'Tomorrow Is a Long Time' and 'One of Us Must Know (Sooner or Later)', two wildly different songs from two very different years in the '60s, emerged from the artist's filing cabinet. Japanese audiences seem to have struggled at first with the new arrangements, but the shows sold out regardless. At the start of the tour the feeling was inescapable, nevertheless: this was Dylan cabaret.

Forgiving fans of bootlegs would for years insist that the live album *Bob Dylan at Budokan*, recorded by the Japanese outpost of Columbia for regional distribution only, was not properly representative of what was going on during this stage of the tour. In truth, the differences from show to show were marginal. The problem was less that the music was bad – some of it has a certain strange charm to this day – but that it was pointless. It sounded at times like a Dylan tribute act in a resort hotel. Money was the only possible excuse. For the bassist Rob Stoner, veteran of Rolling Thunder from start to finish and de facto bandleader, the excuse wasn't good enough. When Japan, New Zealand and Australia had been ticked off the list and 'the Far East' deemed conquered, Stoner quit the tour. For Dylan, this was inconvenient. He was planning to snatch a few days – as ever, only a few – and turn those nine new songs into an album.

*

Street-Legal would be album number 18 of those recorded in a studio and number 23 in the grand total if, that is, the rather fine triple-disc compendium *Masterpieces*, released only in Australasia and Japan in March 1978, is included.[21] By that year, totting up the titles was becoming tiresome, certainly for Dylan. He had long since acquired the habit of treating each new set publicly as just another album, part of the routine, even a chore. The fact that he would spend only four days in April on the recordings that became *Street-Legal* was symptomatic. He could devote weeks to rehearsing for a concert tour yet expect a modern album – modern even by the standards of 1978 – to be achieved just by rolling the tapes while the band played.

Dylan wanted to record his latest group of songs 'live' in an era in which, almost as a matter of habit, artists were assembling tracks from discrete recordings of their constituent parts. With almost two months free between concerts, he was also maintaining – in later interviews it would be stated as a matter of fact – that he had only those four days in which to cut the album. There was no technical reason, however, why his wish for unmediated performances could not have been granted. All that was required was for Dylan to accept that it was impossible to make such an album at the record industry's equivalent of a moment's notice, especially when he was employing a pretty big group of musicians. He couldn't or wouldn't see it. To defer to technology, even to deign to take an interest in technology, seemed to Dylan to amount to surrender and betrayal. In time, the attitude would become near-fatal to his recorded work. It almost killed *Street-Legal*.

'Almost' is the disputable word. Some who concede that the resultant album was a mess and an audiophile's nightmare, at least in its first released form, still rank *Street-Legal* high in Dylan's canon.[22] Of notable critics, Michael Gray has been perhaps the most assertive – and the most honest – writing that this set amounts to 'one of Dylan's most important, cohesive albums', a collection of 'astonishing complexity and confidence, delivered in one of Dylan's most authoritative voices, and extremely badly produced'.[23] In 1978, most American reviewers would have wondered what Gray was on about, or on. For them, abysmal production was the least of it. Where *Street-Legal* was concerned, critical opinion in Europe and America would be wide oceans apart.

Perhaps because it yielded an unlikely hit single in the United Kingdom and across Europe in the shape of 'Baby, Stop Crying', European buyers and reviewers were always more enthusiastic towards the album than Americans. *Street-Legal*'s chart placings – number two in the UK, eleven in the US – would make the divergence stark. The additional fact that Dylan's six nights of concerts at London's Earls Court Exhibition Centre in June would be viewed by the British press as historic triumphs while his American shows were scorned (on a good night) set a small critical tradition in stone.

When the album was released in June, Robert Christgau of the *Village Voice*, grading music like chicken portions, would award Dylan C+ and remark that the 'divorcé' was 'too in love with his own self-generated misery to break through the leaden tempos that oppress his melodies'. The reviewer would then wonder if Dylan intended 'his Neil Diamond masquerade as a joke'. By 1983, to take another tiny example, an extensive Dylan entry in the so-called *Rolling Stone Encyclopedia of Rock & Roll* would note *Budokan* and the 1978 world tour as examples of Dylan 'redoing his old songs with some of the trappings of a Las Vegas lounge act'. The entry would fail even to mention *Street-Legal*.

In *Rolling Stone* itself, after kicking off his review with the splendidly eccentric claim that Dylan's 'Señor (Tales of Yankee Power)' 'is really just a pastiche of the best moments' – best moments? – 'of the Eagles' *Hotel California*', Greil Marcus would tear *Street-Legal* apart. The artist had never sounded 'sillier' or 'so utterly fake'. One track was 'intolerably smug', another simply 'creepy'. As for the singing, Marcus would write, 'it's simply impossible to pay attention to it for more than a couple of minutes at a time'. Besides, 'all that raw chanting in big halls . . . has at once produced a new vocal style, and destroyed Dylan's timing and his ability to bring emotional precision to a lyric'. Comically, way back in 1978, just four short years after his return from an eight-year lay-off and long before the Never-Ending Tour had done real damage to his voice, the artist would be accused of giving far too many concerts. At its indignant, petulant heart, the review would accuse Dylan of 'not giving a damn whether a record is good enough for his audience'.[24]

Such commentary did its work. After its release in June, *Street-Legal* would wind up as the first fully realised Dylan studio album since 1964 – *Dylan* and the *Pat Garrett & Billy the Kid* soundtrack aside – to fail to reach the US top ten. Later it would be identified as, at best, a relative failure after *Blood on the Tracks* and *Desire*. Its lack of thematic unity – as though *Desire* had possessed such a thing – would be held against it. The musical settings provided by that big, brassy band and the backing vocalists would be held to suffocate the lyrics. The contrast between verbal complexity in some of the songs and a certain maudlin, sexist sentimentality in others would be picked out – Marcus would set that ball rolling – as a deep flaw. The charge sheet would say that the writing didn't hold together, that the 'slick' music jarred and that the production was diabolical. The case would have some merit.

In 1978, on first hearing, you were invited to wonder if *Street-Legal* had been produced at all. Clearly, there was a big difference between what Dylan heard while the band played and the sounds struggling technicians managed to capture from the space at Rundown. Those 'technical issues' were at the heart of the problem. Dylan had elected to use his bare-bones Santa Monica rehearsal hall and a mobile recording truck rather than bother to find a professional studio that could accommodate live performance. The technicians' attempts to adapt Rundown while an impatient star nagged were hurried improvisations at best. What emerged from the resulting murk at the former rifle factory was the worst of both worlds: live performances in collision with 24-track technology when neither was organised to meet the needs of the other. To top it all the final mix would be, politely, a strange affair.

The average record buyer cared nothing for these details and neither did Dylan. The difference was that the customer expected the artist and those around him to take care of tedious technical matters. The fan wasn't supposed to pause and wonder why the sound was thin, the vocals too often indistinct, the drums sometimes a mere suggestion in the distance. Dylan, who had spent most of the '60s ignoring the mysteries of the new-fangled stereophonic mix, was at home only in the multidimensional universe of live performance. That wasn't available in your local record store. Even the release of *Desire* in the then-fashionable quadraphonic format – for those who could afford the gear – had failed to bridge the gap between Dylan's reality and what vinyl could deliver. Something had to give, but it wouldn't be the artist. The still-debatable reputation of *Street-Legal* was one result.

Set all that aside. Make allowances for those 'technical issues'. The album remains a disjointed affair. Some of the writing is thrilling and some not much better – for Marcus was not entirely wrong – than Dylan-by-numbers. 'Changing of the Guards' is an indisputably (says this writer) great song while 'Is Your Love in Vain?' is risible, even embarrassing. Seriously: what was anyone supposed to make of 'Can you cook and sew, make flowers grow / Do you understand my pain?' There is something of a gamut to be run, in other words. 'No Time to Think', at over eight minutes, is a track that defies the usual description of the artist-as-poet. Overly rhetorical it might be, but it works well enough on the page; less well, hardly at all in places, as a piece of music. 'New Pony' is a standard blues metaphor to a standard blues riff and strikes this listener, at every hearing, as tiresome and bombastic.

'Baby, Stop Crying' veers between sounding like a corny lament and a description of a domestic scene you would not want to witness. Perhaps, in strict fairness, that was the driving idea behind the song, but the performance seems forced and false.

'Señor (Tales of Yankee Power)' is the album's second great song. It is also a constant reminder of what *Street-Legal* might have been. Who is the personage addressed, God or overlord? The song begins:

> Señor, señor, do you know where we're headin'?
> Lincoln County Road or Armageddon?
> Seems like I been down this way before
> Is there any truth in that, señor?

And ends:

> Señor, señor, let's disconnect these cables
> Overturn these tables
> This place don't make sense to me no more
> Can you tell me what we're waiting for, señor?

Michael Gray has called this 'a classic post-Vietnam song' while pointing out the 'Christ-gesture' of 'Overturn these tables'. That reading is entirely fair.[25] Gray understands the song as a marker on the last stretch of Dylan's road to becoming a declared Christian. The entire album is meanwhile understood in terms of salvation lost and found. On its own terms, this counts as a solid argument.

Nevertheless, to read *Street-Legal* entirely in terms of Dylan edging towards God remains something of a stretch. If religious imagery is the only guide, it needs to be remembered that the artist had been inching towards the idea of salvation for better than a decade without taking the final step. Or rather, he had been doing so without choosing to make a formal declaration of faith and allegiance. A trawl through the basement tapes will turn up plenty of examples of the 'spiritual Dylan'. *John Wesley Harding* is meaningless if you ignore its religious content. A sense of God runs through *Planet Waves* and through *Blood on the Tracks*. As Gray himself pointed out, He is there plainly – though strangely He was overlooked at the time – in *Desire*'s 'Oh, Sister'. Hindsight says it would have been odd if *Street-Legal* had contained no further sightings, or fresh evidence that Dylan was becoming ripe for a full-blown conversion. He had been a religious writer, one way or another, for years. None of this compensates for the album's flaws, however. That miracle was not achieved.

One problem in writing about Dylan and religion, whether in the context of 'Señor' or any other song, is that the artist had never denied God. In the '60s he had made all the then-usual statements about churches and organised belief and why they were probably not needed. He had not said, not once, that he did not believe, or even that he doubted. God was invoked repeatedly; religious assumptions were Dylan's assumptions. Take, for one example, the forever overpraised 'Masters of War', probably written at the end of 1962 or in the first days of 1963. Its approach to war and imperialism, though utterly simplistic, is not so far distant from the approach taken in 'Señor'. Its moral world turns on the betrayal of Judas and the forgiveness of Jesus. Christ is more forgiving than the singer, of course, but there is no scepticism towards the proposition that He exists and forgives.

Dylan caused confusion in the '60s by persistently denying his Jewish origins, by engaging in satire, by assailing hypocrisy, by finding himself conscripted on behalf of a counter-culture that placed no value on church-going after the alternative spiritual supermarket was declared open for business. Things can become confusing when you have the likes of Allen Ginsberg pouring his patent medicine essence of misunderstood Buddhism in your ear, when people on every side are talking about 'karma', and when there is a wife with a taste for all things New Age waiting patiently at home. But an outright non-believer? The Dylans did not raise their children in that manner. He had been coming to terms with the Jewish faith of his ancestors since at least the beginning of the 1970s.

This did not, specifically did not, make him a potential recruit for Jesus – he would resolve the contradiction to his own satisfaction before long – but it was proof enough of his inclinations. Not a single song from the 1960s or the 1970s justifies the supposition that this artist was ever far from God. If Dylan embarked upon a spiritual journey, it was a short trip. *Street-Legal* merely refined his theological position a little.

'Changing of the Guards' is a degree more complicated than anything else on the album and all the better for it. Christ pops up here, too, as a kind of spiritual superhero on behalf of the meek, anticipating the saviour Dylan would embrace before long. Here too, set in the landscape of mythology and Tarot cards, with an Isis figure for a heroine – perhaps the writer had been reading his D.H. Lawrence after all – are the end times: 'Merchants and thieves hungry for power', 'destruction in the ditches', 'Renegade priests and treacherous young witches', 'dog soldiers' in the 'palace of mirrors'. The last verse will promise peace, the fall of false idols and even the conquest of 'cruel death' itself. First, pronouns having been switched, Christ militant will have a word.

Gentlemen, he said
I don't need your organization
I've shined your shoes
I've moved your mountains and marked your cards
But Eden is burning
Either get ready for elimination
Or else your hearts must have the courage
For the changing of the guards . . .[26]

In that context, the shuffling of Tarot cards within the song becomes a little puzzling. There is no doubt that Dylan is using the imagery of the old esoteric poker deck extravagantly, though perhaps with less credulity than fans of all-knowing allegorical pictograms would like to believe. Certainly there are explicit references to cards from both the Tarot's 'major arcana' and the minor, whether Fortune, Death, the Moon, the Chariot ('on the wheels of fire') or the Tower. The King and Queen of Swords are in the deck, too, as is the Three of Swords with that 'heart-shaped tattoo'. A lot depends, however, on the pack being employed. For example, the card known as the Tower in English – hence Dylan's reference – is generally called *La Maison Dieu*, the House of God, in the sixteenth-century *Tarot de Marseille*. Equally, many Europeans have a peculiar tradition that the pack is best used just to play games. Perhaps they are not alone.

Did Dylan believe in Tarot? He might well have been a believer in trumped-up anglophone notions of divination. Some fans would love to think so. Interviewing the artist in London in June, Robert Shelton would certainly mention his 'fascination' with the pack.[27] If Dylan possessed a real faith in the cards, he could even have picked up the idea, entirely spurious, that the Tarot has an Isis connection. Like much else that was exotic and unverifiable, this version of cartomancy caught on widely in the 1970s among those packing for their spiritual journeys.

Equally, the artist might simply have decided that a song with a mock-prophetic intent, even a serious mock-prophetic intent, could stand a little esoteric colour. He wasn't picky. For Dylan, arresting images were, as they remain, pictures worth a couple of thousand words, functioning as a language in their own right. Asking how Tarot squared with the Christian element in 'Changing of the Guards' is probably a fruitless exercise. What we know is that this artist responds first to imagery that he can put to his own use. The verbal fantasy landscape painting evident in 'Changing of the Guards' isn't so different, as a matter of technique, from what Dylan had achieved in 'A Hard Rain's a-Gonna Fall', or from what he would achieve in 'Jokerman'. It might also explain why in due course he would respond with such intensity to the Book of Revelation.

Imagery, not religion, gives 'Changing of the Guards' its power, but that's just the difference – one that Dylan would soon forget too easily – between a poem and a sermon. As far as faith goes, however, what matters about the song is the attraction of the messiah figure for this supposedly Jewish writer. Hitherto, the serious uses to which Dylan had put religious language had been justifiable, more or less, in terms of the Torah. Even this song might have been excused, had there been a need, as a version of Jewish messianic prophecy, of which there is an abundance. Yet looking back it is possible to see just how open Dylan already was to the claim that prophecy had been fulfilled. In London that summer Shelton would assert proudly, 'He knew I wouldn't ask him about God.' The enquiry had been made too many times before.

Street-Legal's third great song, hampered by its routine arrangement, encumbered by the girl singers whose presence would become a persistent distraction in the years ahead, is 'Where Are You Tonight? (Journey Through Dark Heat)'. This is another definitive rebuttal to the claim that Dylan's writing had begun to falter. It is evidence, probably superfluous, that his need for Jacques Levy's help on *Desire* had been personal rather than professional. Again, however, if evidence is required that here was a man lost in life and in the toils of spiritual conflict, most questions are answered.

> I fought with my twin, that enemy within
> 'Till both of us fell by the way
> Horseplay and disease is killing me by degrees
> While the law looks the other way

You can understand 'the law' in the conventional sense of the forces encountered by a man forever on the road – one idea that never grows old for Dylan – or you can understand it in the Jewish sense on which the writer was raised. It could be a reference to coppers; it could be a reference to the Halakha, the body of laws for religion and for life. You can take the journey itself as spiritual or as another reworking of the shifting narrative trail traced in 'Tangled Up in Blue'. You can spot the images of personal loss or find something a good deal deeper in the idea of an individual struggling with 'that enemy within', himself, his 'twin'. You can take it, above all, that this Dylan is a man who is approaching God yet is still, given recent events in his private life, somehow incomplete.

There's a new day at dawn and I've finally arrived
If I'm there in the morning, baby, you'll know I've survived
I can't believe it, I can't believe I'm alive
But without you it just doesn't seem right
Oh, where are you tonight?

*

Dylan was back on the road by the first day of June. Fully seven nights at the Universal Amphitheater in Los Angeles awaited before he and his musicians were due to cross the Atlantic. Soon enough the artist would be praising the wonderful perceptiveness of British audiences as a heartening contrast to the treatment he could expect at home. In *Rolling Stone*, Cameron Crowe would report that Dylan's performances had 'won over many doubters' by the end of the LA run, but the burden of the piece would be the tale of 'glibly professional' shows that 'left most die-hard fans and reviewers puzzled'.[28] The journalist would quote an unnamed 'prominent musician' as a surrogate for majority opinion. 'There were things that killed me and there were things that really pissed me off,' the bravely anonymous critic would remark. 'He could take this show to Vegas and not change one note.'

The important fact that Dylan could wear 'specially tailored' clothes, switching between 'a black studded pants outfit or one with a white sequined thunderbolt design' – both verging on the criminal, it's true – would go into the *Rolling Stone* notebook. The drastic rearrangement of many favourite songs would be observed. That Dylan had taken to styling himself 'an entertainer' while indulging in 'earnest between-song patter' would be added to the charge sheet. Crowe would even remember witnessing the *artist shaking hands with members of the audience.* An alleged visit by Dylan to (of course) Las Vegas, supposedly to watch a performance by Neil Diamond, was the only explanation given for this new 'concert stance'. What's plain is that the short hop to damning conclusions, hard on the heels of the reviews for *Street-Legal*, had been achieved.

Britain, too, had made up its mind long before the artist arrived. The difference was that the vote had been cast almost unanimously in Dylan's favour before a note was heard. But then, the perverse islanders liked *Street-Legal*. Their music press had not stooped to asinine abuse of the record. Instead, music journalists had rummaged in the superlatives drawer for the old folder marked 'Best Since . . .' In the UK, the album would become his biggest seller since *New Morning*.

Dylan had not played in Britain since the last day of August 1969 and the Isle of Wight festival. Everyone, artist and audience, had chosen to forget the 'mixed reception' given to that show with The Band, irrespective of any virtues captured by bootleggers. One performance aside, Dylan had not toured among the British since 1966. Tickets for his run at Earls Court therefore sold out instantly to people who had queued for days; many more could have been sold. Audiences were warm, forgiving, ready to enjoy themselves and eager for him to succeed. In fairness, he didn't let them down. He and his band had performed better than pretty well in Los Angeles, but in London there was a meeting of minds between the artist and his public. Quoted – or roughly paraphrased – by *Melody Maker* after the last Earls Court show, Dylan said:

> Doing these concerts here has made me realise about British audiences. They're really something different – they actually come for the words and the songs. That's what's missing back home. There they tend to come for . . . not so much the music, more the sideshow.[29]

This was not mere flattery from a gratified artist. The Earls Court audiences were not dissuaded in the slightest by new arrangements of old songs, or dismayed by alleged hints of 'Vegas'. Veterans of Dylan shows would long afterwards maintain that these were among the best concerts he ever gave in Britain. *Melody Maker*'s Ray Coleman would write that 'Different lines of his songs came over with fresh force', that 'Rarely, if ever, has the song ['Just Like a Woman'] been so brilliantly blown apart and knitted together again', that 'his harmonica solo was a riveting joy'. The journalist would remember the notes of the solo 'bringing the ecstatic crowd to its feet with a mighty roar'. Coleman, who did not insist that the last night was necessarily the best of Dylan's London run, would even give a special mention to a performance of

'Señor'. The contrast with the reception the artist would receive in his native land in the autumn of the year would count as remarkable. Either the English capital got very lucky, or the tour lost something important when it returned to the States, or Dylan was dead right about prevailing attitudes back home.

What can be said for certain is that an authentic hero's welcome still awaited him across Europe. He painted his newest masterpiece in Rotterdam, Dortmund, Berlin, Nuremberg, Paris and Gothenburg. As in London, the latest incarnation of Bob Dylan was accepted without reservation by the French over five nights at the 10,000-seat Pavillon de Paris. David Bowie and Bob Marley had managed only a couple of nights apiece there in the preceding weeks. Europe also allowed the artist and his band – between whom there now existed a genuine rapport – to behave like overgrown cultural exchange students. They took in the sights. Dylan even paid a visit to the Anne Frank House in Amsterdam.

Back in England, he made amends for the Isle of Wight. The 'Picnic at Blackbushe', staged on a Hampshire airfield that had once housed the RAF and, later, the US Navy, had been fully expected to draw big weekend crowds. It was supposed to meet part of a huge and lucrative British demand for Dylan after the adulatory reports of the Earls Court shows. A back-of-the-envelope calculation based on ticket sales said that an impressive 100,000 customers could be expected. On Saturday, 15 July, according to predictably cautious police estimates after the event, something like 200,000 turned up; the real figure was undoubtedly greater. Some of the horde might have been eager to see Graham Parker and the Rumour, Eric Clapton or Joan Armatrading, but the day's headline act and unquestioned star, resplendent in a top hat borrowed from a hotel doorman, was Dylan. As darkness fell and bonfires began to spark into life in every corner of the site, he commenced a near-three-hour performance that would include six of the nine *Street-Legal* songs. If your taste runs to coincidence, 'Señor' was followed, not for the first time on the tour, by 'Masters of War'. With everything from a solo version of 'Gates of Eden' performed in a pool of blue light to 'Forever Young' with Clapton playing along, Dylan's set culminated in what had become his standard encores. Again, the juxtaposition seemed to make a point: first, 'Changing of the Guards', then 'The Times They Are a-Changin''. The reception from the vast tribe on the airfield was, in that word favoured by benign reviewers down the decades, rapturous. All that remained was to persuade America to take the same view.

It didn't happen. The final American stretch of this world tour would be a very long haul. Dylan would seem to run out of energy or patience as concrete stadium succeeded concrete stadium in the course of 65 shows. He and his musicians would perform in thirty-one states and three Canadian cities before delivering their valedictory encores at the bizarrely named Hollywood Sportatorium in Florida on 16 December. Harmony within the band would be disrupted, meanwhile, when the artist took up with Carolyn Dennis, one of the singers – in what would become a significant relationship for both of them – after already getting himself involved with another of the vocalists, Helena Springs. For better or worse, Dylan could and did please himself in these matters.

It made little useful difference to performances that would cease to be fresh, confident or assured before the last hike of the globe-spanning expedition was far advanced. Instead, Dylan's singing would too often seem to bear out the criticisms levelled against the vocals on the album by Greil Marcus. The new arrangements would also lose their original poise and conviction. Monstrous world tours are the enemy of art, as any performer who isn't too busy counting the money comes sooner or later to realise. Dylan was more alert to the problem than most, but with too many minds already made up thanks to reviews of *Street-Legal*, and with all the cracks about alimony, Elvis and lounge acts, some of his shows would fail to sell out.

For all that, the artist, apparently unable to think of anything better to do with himself, remained undaunted. By the end he was talking to his musicians of concerts in 1979, of touring ever onwards. After all, he was still making a lot of the money he believed he needed. A gross figure of $20 million for the 1978 tour receipts is generally mentioned. As with Rolling Thunder, Dylan was never likely to quit easily when he was doing what he thought he wanted or needed to do. Critical disdain meanwhile had a tendency to make him more stubborn. As the long pilgrimage neared its end, he began to tell stories, bizarre or revealing according to taste, from the stage. In Jacksonville, Florida, on 13 December, his preface to 'Ballad of a Thin Man' became an elaborate reworking of vintage Dylan hokum. It was that or a comical parable on the relationship between an embattled performing artist and his audience.

> The carnivals [they] used to have in the '50s, every carnival used to have a geek. Do you know what a geek is? A geek is a man that eats a live chicken, right before your eyes. He bites the head off, eats that. Then he

goes ahead, eats the heart, drinks up the blood, sweeps up all the feathers with a broom. In them days, it cost a quarter to see him . . . Anyway. The geek pretty much kept to himself most of the time. Nobody never did get too tight with the geek. But one day I was having breakfast with the bearded lady and she says, 'Stay away from that man.' I say, 'Why?' She says, 'Because he looks at everybody else in the world as freaky, except him. He thinks that he's just earning a living, and what he's doing is pretty straight . . .'

The singer then proceeded to claim that being stared at on the streets of Nashville for having long hair in 'about 1964' had 'reminded' him of the geek and inspired the song. In Lakeland, Florida, two nights later the introduction to 'Señor' was stranger still. This artist objected to the myths surrounding Bob Dylan except when he was inventing the best of them.

I was riding on a train one time from Durango, Mexico, to San Diego. I fell asleep on this train. I woke up about midnight and a lot of people were getting off the train. The train was in the station, pulling up to the platform at a place called Monterey. So a bunch of people were getting off the train. On to the platform, the steps, this man gets up to the train. Everybody else gets off. He come down the aisle and took a seat across the aisle from me, wearing nothing but a blanket and a derby hat.

So I was sitting there. I felt a very strange vibration. I was staring into the window, which was like a glass mirror. And I could not help myself any longer, I had to turn around and look right at this man. When I did I could see that his eyes were burning and there was smoke coming out of his nostrils. I immediately knew this was the man I wanted to talk to. So I turned around to the mirror for a while to figure out something to say. And when I had it all together I turned around and he was gone.

By late 1978, for all that, touring and self-doubt were taking a toll. As winter came on, Dylan and most of the band came down with flu. By the time they reached San Diego on 17 November he was still feeling sick, disorientated and exhausted. The performance that night was hard going. Almost exactly a year later, on 27 November 1979, back in the same city, Dylan would tell his audience – a supportive one, on this occasion – of how it had been. This parable was also intended to explain what had become of him and his music in the intervening months. Dylan would relate that it had all happened towards the end of the 1978 concert. Someone in the crowd, he would say, 'knew I wasn't feeling too well'.

> I think they could sense that. And they threw a silver cross on the stage. Now usually I don't pick things up in front of the stage. Once in a while I do, but sometimes, most times, I don't. But I looked down at that cross. I said, 'I gotta pick that up.'
>
> I picked up that cross and I put it in my pocket. It was a silver cross, I think maybe about so high. And I put it . . . brought it backstage with me. And I brought it with me to the next town, which was off in Arizona, Phoenix. Anyway, when I got back there I was feeling even worse than I'd felt when I was in San Diego. And I said, 'Well I really need something tonight.'
>
> I didn't know what it was, I was using all kinds of things, and I said, 'I need something tonight that I never really had before.'
>
> And I looked in my pocket and I had this cross that someone threw before when I was in San Diego. So if that person is here tonight, I want to thank them for that cross.[30]

The audience in San Diego's Golden Hall in 1979 would exult when Dylan mentioned the cross. They would be unusual witnesses to his performances that year, rare examples of a crowd being as one with the singer and the statements he had begun to make from the concert stage. His story of the silver cross would be part of his introduction to a song called 'Slow Train'.

The San Diego crowd would not flinch, unlike other spectators, when Dylan then discoursed on newspaper stories about 'people in Turkey revolting', 'Russians don't have any food', 'all that trouble in Ireland', and the Islamic revolution that had just destroyed the Shah's regime in Iran. This audience would not shake their heads in bewilderment when Dylan said, 'They got a funny bunch of people over in Iran. They have a religion called "Muslims", you know?' The artist would remind this crowd that 'the Bible says, "Vengeance is mine, sayeth the Lord" . . . We know this world as we see it is going to be destroyed. Christ will set up his kingdom in Jerusalem for a thousand years. We know that's true.' In San Diego, where some in the audience had become personally acquainted with the artist by the end of 1979, they would only shout a loud 'Amen!' to all of that.

CHAPTER SIX

God Said to Abraham . . .

I know thy works, and thy labour, and thy patience, and how thou
canst not bear them which are evil: and thou has tried them which
say they are apostles, and are not, and hast found them liars . . .

Revelation, 2:2

LATE IN 1978, SO THE STORY GOES, GOD FOUND BOB DYLAN IN A
hotel room in Tucson, Arizona. Stranger things have happened. The
deity had hovered in the haunted wings from the beginnings of the
singer's career, but the relationship, ebbing and flowing, was always
tricky. Sometimes in the early days it had seemed that the songs mocked
belief; sometimes that only the hypocrisies of institutions were held
culpable. At other moments, particularly in his apprentice work, Dylan
had appeared to adopt the tropes of the old hellfire blues without a
second thought, as many did. Nevertheless, to the sort of people who
understood the *sort* of thing being said in the songs they liked best, it
was unthinkable – beyond belief, in fact – that an artist without an
ounce of deference in him, one who took nothing at face value, one
who saw the masters of war conscripting God to their side, could simply
and sincerely believe all the old Bible crap. In the late 1970s, unbelievers
formed a devout majority of the artist's fans.

By the time he got to Tucson, it made no difference. On or around
19 November, Dylan sensed 'a presence in the room that couldn't have
been anybody but Jesus'. Then the artist felt a hand placed physically
upon him: 'I felt it. I felt it all over me.' Then his 'whole body' began
to tremble. The room itself seemed to move. 'The glory of the Lord,'
as he would later testify, 'knocked me down and picked me up.'
Describing the experience two years later, Dylan would deny that he
had been 'down and out' or miserable at the time. Supposedly he had

173

been 'doing fine' and was 'relatively content'. But he had been hearing a lot about Jesus. Later, perhaps a month or so later, he would indicate to 'a very close friend' that he was 'willing to listen' to the Christian message.[1]

That's the tale, at any rate. As with so many Dylan stories, it requires the suspension of doubt, if not of disbelief. He turned to evangelical Christianity: this much we know. But he had been making God-noises for years before that silver cross flew from the darkness to lie glittering, presumably, in the radiance of the San Diego spotlight. *Desire*'s 'Oh, Sister', if it was not Jacques Levy's doing, was hardly the work of an artist oblivious to the deity. It was one example among many.

The sequence of supernatural events is also as neat as a movie plot: first the cross appearing amid Dylan's gloom, then the Pauline moment in a hotel suite. The anecdote involving the little silver cruciform trinket is an interpolation, in any case, of statements gleaned from a single concert bootleg, not from any of Dylan's statements-for-the-record of what led him to become a Christian. When he felt like talking on stage he came up with a lot of strange stuff. There are no witnesses to say that the story of the cross was any more true, or any less metaphorical, than the story of the geek.

You needn't question that Dylan experienced *something* profound, meanwhile, to wonder why he never actually identified the time or place of his transformation. Tucson? Judging by his 1978 concert schedule, it's close enough. Dylan would certainly say, and later regret saying it, that he 'truly had a born-again experience'.[2] The last tiny mystery is this, however: if Jesus made personal, room-rocking contact on a winter's night, why was there any need for evangelical tutelage? That, nevertheless, was what Dylan sought and what he got.

*

In its edition of Saturday, 3 November 1979, the *San Francisco Chronicle* carried a review by Joel Selvin of the opening night of Dylan's latest concert tour. As soon became clear, the rock critic – as certain showbiz writers were then styled – was not entirely impressed. One clue was in the headline above the piece. It read: 'Bob Dylan's God-Awful Gospel'. The artist was about to suffer for his new-found faith.

'These are strange times,' Selvin began. 'Gas costs a dollar a gallon. Someone built a pyramid in San Francisco. And Bob Dylan converted to Christianity.' Clearly, the last sentence was taken to be a self-explanatory illustration of how peculiar some portents can be. Dylan had come to God and God had emerged with a celebrity scalp. Amid weird events, this was the weirdest. The reviewer continued:

> The ironies flew thick and fast Thursday at the Warfield Theater, where Dylan took the capacity crowd by surprise with an opening-night performance composed exclusively of his singing praises to the Lord.
>
> He never touched the likes of 'Blowin' in the Wind', 'Don't Think Twice', 'Mr. Tambourine Man', 'I Shall Be Released', 'Just Like a Rolling Stone' [sic] or any of the many other songs that secured his fame and allowed him to sell out each of his 14 Warfield shows far in advance, with tickets scaled sky-high at $15 and $12.50 apiece.

Having warmed up, Selvin described an audience behaving 'with admirable restraint'. Catcalls and boos certainly 'echoed throughout the 2,200-seat former vaudeville palace', but for the most part the audience sat through a two-hour concert in 'stunned silence', granting only 'modest, polite applause' to Dylan's 17 songs.

The review thereafter was quietly murderous. First Selvin noted, as an odd but interesting truth, that Dylan 'displayed no joy in singing the gospel according to Bob'. While he gave 'humble thanks for his own deliverance', he was 'short of convincing', the writer decided, in his humility. There was no 'beatific aura'. His hatchet well whetted, the journalist then went seriously to work. The observations were brutal, given the topic at hand, but not necessarily inaccurate.

'Anesthetized by his new-found beliefs,' wrote Selvin, 'Dylan has written some of the most banal, uninspired and inventionless songs of his career for his Jesus phase.' The lyrics were founded on 'ridiculous rhymes and images', the message was neither uplifting nor joyous, and Dylan was content merely to repeat that temporal existence suffers a 'dearth of meaning'. Then Selvin headed for the big finish.

> Dylan . . . once wrote songs that expressed the outrage and alienation felt by an entire generation. His desertion of those ideals in favor of fundamentalist Christian theology symbolizes the confusion and chaos that generation found in its search for answers.
>
> Years from now, when social historians look back over these years, Dylan's conversion will serve as a concise metaphor for the vast emptiness of the era. Dylan is no longer asking hard questions. Instead, he turned to the most prosaic source of truth on Earth, so aptly dubbed 'opium of the masses' by Karl Marx.

All those years from then, it is possible to look back and say that, in fact, Dylan was asking hard questions indeed. For one thing, his choice was not a metaphor for anyone's emptiness but his own. Nevertheless, you could also say, as Selvin said, that as pieces of writing the 'gospel' songs from the album *Slow Train Coming* were simplistic, even banal. This most complicated of writers had surrendered complexity for the sake of personal salvation and composed doggerel to express his gratitude. He had elected to subordinate himself. Worse, the bounty of song he had gained in return was pitiful. He was saved, but his art, the art that counted for so much to so many, seemed all but lost. Whatever else is still believed of Dylan's encounter with the triune God, it need not involve poetry.

Christ didn't make a Gerard Manley Hopkins of the artist when He interceded. Jerry Wexler, the best studio producer then available, a Jewish atheist unimpressed by news of Jesus, could not alter the fact. Many who bought the album, Christian or otherwise, would disagree sincerely, but those were some dull, ill-written songs. Worst of all, they floated on fervent waves of righteous cliché. 'Gotta Serve Somebody' could have been written by any one of a host of godly, ghastly Californian hacks trading rock and roll's sins against future redemption at the end of the '70s when all the drugs began to wear off. *That* was our chief objection, back then.

> You may be a construction worker working on a home
> You may be living in a mansion or you might live in a dome
> You might own guns and you might even own tanks
> You might be somebody's landlord, you might even own banks

The Nazarene, in the Bible's account, was alert to class, to what it means and what it does to humanity. In 'Gotta Serve Somebody' Dylan's late-American born-again conservatism requires the fiction that all will be as one, brick-hauler and mansion-dweller alike, when the judgement bell sounds. The distinction between the meek and the rest is abolished. The song is explicit: 'You may be rich or poor, you may be blind or lame.' It became the most notable feature of *Slow Train Coming*: no trace of human compassion, not an ounce, not even a hint. 'Human' had ceased to be the preoccupation of a writer who had once found an inexhaustible fascination in the chaos of mortal existence, in what we are. Selvin was right about the absence of any sign of joy in this 'gospel singer'. As represented by the artist, being saved was not a lot of fun.

Dylan's idea of redemption involved the least-worst choice: accept or go straight to hell. Even among the godless, who didn't necessarily know any better, his pitiless relish at the prospect of eternal suffering for those not saved was akin to a parody of superstar heaven. Most other versions of Christianity would have been far easier for audiences to accept, even in 1979, even in a San Francisco that did not yet blink at a misused Marxian cliché in the local newspaper.

A word is missing, nevertheless, from Selvin's famously damning (in some circles) review. The word is 'Jewish'. Dylan might have affronted the remnant counter-culture with his 'doses of Bible-thumping'. At the time, few paused to wonder how his discovery of a messiah, the veritable confirmation of ancient prophecies, would sit with the faith into which he had been born. It was, after all, the faith that held the worship of such a messiah-type to be, straightforwardly, idolatry.

Most of the tales of born-again Bob are shaped around the alienation of the secular erstwhile Christians who had once bought his records. The meaning of his conversion for Dylan himself, and for his fugitive, vaporous identity, is far more interesting. Selvin, like several of the reviewers who witnessed that first gospel tour, accused the artist of betrayal, as though a sincere conviction could also amount – the joke within the joke – to bad faith. The deeper truth is that Dylan believed he was reuniting the fragments of his identity, this Jew in a Christian world, through messianic Judaism. Some would account that a delusion and the most complete betrayal of all. For him, nevertheless, it was very real. And how did that happen?

*

On 13 November 1979, Dylan and his band were performing the 11th show in their hard-fought 14-date run at the Warfield Theater in San Francisco. The former governor of California was meanwhile in New York City. At the old vaudeville joint on Market Street, where the quizzical ghost of Charlie Chaplin ambled, Dylan was achieving a version of a song called 'Covenant Woman' that is still admired by some bootleg fans. At the Hilton New York, in a gargantuan dormitory-tower looming over the Avenue of the Americas, the genial ex-governor was announcing his candidacy for the presidency of the United States.

While Dylan and his troupe were asking 'When You Gonna Wake Up?' and the singer was assuring his fans that 'God don't make promises He don't keep', Ronald Reagan had this to say:

I believe this nation hungers for a spiritual revival; hungers to once again see honour placed above political expediency; to see government once again the protector of our liberties, not the distributor of gifts and privilege. Government should uphold and not undermine those institutions which are custodians of the very values upon which civilization is founded – religion, education and, above all, family. Government cannot be clergyman, teacher and patriot. It is our servant, beholden to us.

Reagan, by then 68, went on tell his party and prospective voters that a 'troubled and afflicted mankind' was pleading with them to keep a rendezvous with destiny, uphold familiar moral principles and become 'that shining city on a hill' surveyed, planned and claimed outright by their putative Puritan forebears. Back in San Francisco, Dylan was singing a song entitled 'Do Right to Me Baby (Do Unto Others)'. One part went: 'Don't wanna burn nobody, don't wanna be burned / Don't wanna learn from nobody what I gotta unlearn'. Afterwards, the artist thanked those who had applauded and said: 'You know you read about that situation in Iran, but we're not worried about that because we know the world is going to be destroyed. We know that Jesus is coming back.' Candidate Reagan was not yet ready to share that news with the electorate.

*

Dylan was in a bad way towards the end of the 1978 world tour. Sheer exhaustion played its part, of course, but his recreational habits were not what any doctor ordered. The usual lurid allegations of drug use and hard drinking have been made. Anomie is not, in any case, a condition that is diagnosed easily or often. Dylan had done the proper, professional thing and repaired his finances in spectacular style during all those months on the road. Whatever his habits, he had imposed an unusual degree of discipline on himself. But, city by city, sports arena by sports arena, the early enthusiasm had given way to a kind of self-disgust. He was making money at the expense of his music.

Dylan was perfectly capable of doing what was expedient, but he was no hypocrite. Besides, he understood the law of diminishing creative returns. When it became obvious that an artist had ceased to care about his work, customers stopped showing up. They were fickle enough to begin with. Barely four years after the deluge of ticket applications for Tour '74, the final American leg of the excursion around the world had been a hard sell from the start. In 1978, sceptical concert-goers who knew nothing else knew Dylan as the pretentious creator of that dumb unwatchable movie, as the maker of the 'lazy' album *Street-Legal*, as the formerly dissentient street poet who had 'gone Vegas' with his chick singers and his slick band. If his performances seemed only to confirm those accusations, Dylan was done for. As 1978 began to give way to 1979, with his silver cross in his pocket, he was asking a lot of questions about himself, his art and his life. Jesus picked his moment to show up.

The truth was probably more complicated. Dylan was undoubtedly at a low ebb, but his band was full of people who had 'received Christ'. The guitarist Steven Soles and the young multi-instrumentalist David Mansfield were both enthusiastic converts to Christianity in its evangelical Californian guise. Roger McGuinn had gone with God, as had Johnny Cash (in that case a short trip) and assorted members of bands such as Poco, America, Santana and others besides. Helena Springs was a believer. Carolyn Dennis had been raised on gospel. Mary Alice Artes, still another companion – 'girlfriend' barely begins to describe a member of the circle of women around Dylan at this point in his life – had just been born again. She was, it seems, the 'close friend' to whom he turned after his experience in or around Tucson. There was no shortage of people in Dylan's life for whom evangelism mattered. In the spiritually promiscuous milieu of late-'70s California, non-belief was fast becoming the devilish exception. Christianity, modernised and glamorised, was the rising faith in the music business. In any case, Dylan had never been a non-believer.

Even a cursory examination of his work since 1967's *John Wesley Harding* showed evidence of an interest in matters of religion at every step of the way. Several of that album's songs would not have existed without the Book of Revelation and the Book of Isaiah. *Blood on the Tracks, Desire* and *Street-Legal* had been flecked and stained deeply with biblical imagery. The fact that Mary Alice Artes was connected with the Vineyard Fellowship, a small but fast-growing evangelical group in the San Fernando Valley, only provided what seems, in one version of hindsight, like the last link in the chain.

In January of 1979, after a Sunday service, Artes spoke to Kenn Gulliksen, a leading pastor at her church. It was, to begin with, familiar stuff about how she wanted to 'rededicate' her life to Jesus rather than persist with a different kind of superstar relationship. Then Artes asked if there was anyone available to have a serious talk with her 'boyfriend'. Her boyfriend turned out to be Bob Dylan. Two other pastors, Larry

Myers and Paul Emond, were dispatched – their precise velocity has not been calculated – to an apartment in the West LA suburb of Brentwood.

Dylan had been seen wearing a cross of some description during the final dates of the 1978 tour, but as he later told the story he had not rushed into the arms of Christ after his hotel room experience. When the Vineyard pastors arrived at the apartment he was 'kind of sceptical' but 'also open'. Though he had a lot of questions – chiefly to do with the perplexing nature of the claimed Messiah – he 'certainly wasn't cynical'.[3] What did the preachers mean by 'son of God'? What was the meaning of this claim 'dying for my sins'?

These were Jewish questions. Conversion to Christianity had a baleful, immemorial significance for many of Dylan's people because, historically, it had so often been accomplished through persecution. In modern times, equally, conversion was often derided by faithful Jews as a purely self-interested attempt at assimilation, a surrender to the majority culture for the sake of acceptance or a career. It was also apostasy. Jews simply did not buy the fundamentalist claims made on behalf of the wonder-working Essene from Galilee. In any case, Dylan had not been raised as a secular Jew. He had studied; he had learned his Hebrew; he had enjoyed his weeks and months at a Zionist summer camp. His parents had been leading lights in Jewish organisations. As a child he must have asked about the differences between himself and all the Christian kids. In 1971, he had spent some time 'investigating' what Judaism meant to him and had paid a visit both to Jerusalem's Western Wall – on his 30th birthday – and to the Mount Zion yeshiva, Diaspora Yeshiva Toras Yisrael. In January 1979, Dylan was asking basic questions of the messengers from Jesus. In essence, they led to one question: how could he *be* Jewish and become Christian? The answer, when it came to him, would be a little out of the ordinary.

Larry Myers would remember his first encounter with the artist. Speaking in 1994, he recalled meeting 'a man who was very interested in learning what the Bible says about Jesus Christ'.

> To the best of my ability I started at the beginning in Genesis and walked through the Old Testament and the New Testament and ended in Revelation. I tried to clearly express what is the historical, orthodox understanding of who Jesus is. It was a quiet, intelligent conversation with a man who was seriously intent on understanding the Bible. There was no attempt to convince, manipulate or pressure this man into

anything. But in my view God spoke through His Word, the Bible, to a man who had been seeking for many years. Sometime in the next few days, privately and on his own, Bob accepted Christ and believed that Jesus Christ is indeed the messiah.[4]

Conversion was not easy, Dylan would say later, and you are inclined to believe him. Interviewed by an Australian journalist in 1980 he would call the process 'painful' and compare it to a baby learning to crawl, observing:

> You have to learn to drink milk before you can eat meat. You're reborn, but like a baby. A baby doesn't know anything about this world and that's what it's like when you're reborn. You're a stranger. You have to learn all over again.[5]

In the same interview, Dylan would make the guess – 'gently', as the journalist noted – that 'He's always been calling me. Of course, how would I have ever known that?' Yet even after talking to the two Vineyard pastors he remained reluctant to commit himself to fully fourteen weeks of intensive Bible study.[6] Then, in his telling, he woke early one morning feeling compelled to show up at the classes in the fellowship's improvised school in the town of Reseda, 30 or so miles from his Point Dume compound.

*

In the 1960s and 1970s secularism in art, pop and rock was taken for granted. John Lennon's 1966 remark, wholly uncontroversial in Britain, that the Beatles were 'more popular than Jesus' – and that the disciples were 'thick and ordinary' – had defined one side of the argument. The bonfires made of the band's records in some Southern states that year had formed the evangelical rebuttal. Rock and roll was not virtuous, not chaste, not obedient, not respectful and not necessarily in accord with each and every commandment. Dylan, it was presumed, would never surrender himself to mere uncritical faith, or to the 'conservative values' that seemed always to be part of the deal. Sing a white man's gospel? Preach like some polyester-clad TV hellfire evangelist? Actually believe that Armageddon was imminent (turn right at Tel Aviv) and insist that only those born again in Christ could hope to be saved? For the hip, record-buying true believer this was blasphemy, or a hideous joke, or (yet again) the last straw. Ostentatious faith was the preserve of those who embraced every right-wing cliché available. For Bob Dylan to squander his art on the banalities of the modern revival show was preposterous, depressing, insulting, or more evidence that he had lost his wits. 'Christian rock' was a contradiction in terms. In 1979, as always, the deep-dyed Dylan fans were convinced they knew him better than he knew himself.

This was foolish. Hindsight says that the only surprise lay in how long it took for a highly moral and moralising writer to act on all the clues in certain of his most self-righteous songs. Wasn't Dylan insistent on fundamental truth? Didn't he mistrust the surface appearance of material things? Wasn't his a restless intelligence forever seeking a deeper understanding of existence? Had he ever said a single word, in any case, to suggest that he harboured doubts about the omnipresence of a deity? And wasn't he given to saying that something was very wrong with the flimsy world of man? By converting to Christianity, Dylan stuck the counter-culture's note of scepticism back in its bottle and cast all upon the waters.

From start to finish his verses have been littered with the language of religion. 'I'd Hate to Be With You On That Dreadful Day', a poor song assembled from damnation clichés in 1962, might never have made the cut for an album, but it was unambiguous. He was barely 21 when he sang:

Well your clock is gonna stop
At Saint Peter's gate
Ya gonna ask him what time it is
He's gonna say, 'It's too late'

Amid the basement tapes there was, conspicuously, 'Sign on the Cross' and a singer 'worried', though Jewish by birth, by what the Roman insult pinned to Christianity's symbol might have signified. As mentioned, *John Wesley Harding* is studded throughout with religious imagery, each instance – at least five dozen of those, they say – recorded scrupulously by adherents. During his remarkable researches for *The Bible in the Lyrics of Bob Dylan*, researches so assiduous they could only have been pursued by a Protestant theologian who happened to be a fan of the artist, the late Colbert 'Bert' Cartwright found no fewer than 387 biblical allusions in the 246 Dylan songs and sleeve notes published between 1961 and 1978. Significantly, perhaps, Cartwright also recorded that the references were apportioned almost evenly between the Bible of the Jews and the Bible known to Christians.[7]

Even five decades after he started out, his commitment to specific creeds having abated somewhat, Dylan was still declaring that he was trying to get to heaven before they closed the door. The righteous anger had dissipated slightly, but still he invoked the 'Spirit on the water / darkness on the face of the deep' on the 2006 album *Modern Times*. He still talked of paradise and belief; clearly, contrary to every nonsensical rumour, he still believed. The only surprise is that anyone had ever reached any other conclusion.

In 2012, late in the day, Dylan would introduce the album *Tempest* to interviewers with the explanation that he had set out to write something else entirely. His initial ambition, he would say, had been to write ten purely religious songs, songs akin to the old 'Just a Closer Walk With Thee', but the concentration required had eluded him. In the course of the ritual interview with *Rolling Stone* that October, Dylan would further assert that 'Rainy Day Women #12 & 35', *Blonde on Blonde*'s apparent ode to the sacrament of dope back in 1966, had been misunderstood – people are strange – by those 'that aren't familiar with the Book of Acts' and what it truly means to be stoned. At one point he would claim the ability to see God's hand in all things, yet tease his interviewer with the thought that people can have faith 'in just about anything'. Few of them would explain their lives and careers as an example of actual 'transfiguration', however. Dylan did so in the interview in all (apparent) seriousness before accepting, as a statement of the obvious, that his songs are shot through still with biblical language.

Of course, what else could there be? I believe in the Book of Revelation. I believe in disclosure, you know? There's truth in all books. In some kind of way. Confucius, Sun Tzu, Marcus Aurelius, the Koran, the Torah, the New Testament, the Buddhist sutras, the Bhagavad-Gita, the Egyptian Book of the Dead, and many thousands more. You can't go through life without reading some kind of book.[8]

Of all the books you could stumble across, and of all the 27 accepted texts in the New Testament compendium, the one attributed to the fevered cave-dwelling John of Patmos is, let's say, a revealing first choice. The Christian Bible's big finish – visionary, apocalyptic, supremely resistant to a single interpretation – is a poem made for a certain kind of poet, and for a particular sort of believer. This piece of theologically incoherent art has a specific contemporary resonance, equally, for born-again Americans with a taste for prophetic utterances who set their spiritual watches by the end times, 'rapture', Armageddon and vindication. Several of those who were influential within the Vineyard Fellowship in the 1970s and 1980s were of that persuasion and industrious in spreading the news. By the twenty-first century, if not before, Dylan had come to believe that 'disclosure' is to be had from John's verses and all they portend. So God, presence and idea, had permeated the singer's every fibre and utterance in 1979. It was a very particular version of God, however.

*

Dylan then studied in the School of Discipleship under Kenn Gulliksen and at least four other competent pastor-teachers, including myself. We met in a comfortable conference room that was part of a suite of offices, which served as the church offices. The church worship services were held on Sunday afternoons in the sanctuary of St. Paul's United Methodist Church in Reseda, so it was necessary for us to occupy offices elsewhere. There was a real estate firm occupying the first floor suite of offices. Bob attended the intense course of study along with other students for three and one-half months.

Larry Myers, 1994[9]

In one of its histories, the Vineyard Fellowship says that the church 'finds its roots in the unique period of the 1970s when a lost generation met a sovereign move of God. This generation that included a counterculture and anti-establishment dynamic sought a living faith, marked by simplicity of structure, vitality of contemporary music, personal experience of God's love, and an invitation to make a real difference in a lost world.'[10] When Dylan encountered them they were a friendly bunch, too, and fond of music. They were very fond of famous musicians. That isn't quite the whole story, however, of this version of neo-charismatic third-wave church-planting evangelical Christianity.

The fellowship had not been in existence for long when Dylan came its way. Gulliksen had been an assistant pastor with Calvary Chapel, a group of evangelical churches founded on a belief in the 'inerrancy' of the Bible and on *sola scriptura*, the conviction that 'the Old and New Testaments are the Word of God, fully inspired without error and the infallible rule of faith and practice'. In 1974, Gulliksen and his wife had moved from Texas to Los Angeles to launch a new ministry. Bringing together various Bible study groups, he soon began holding Sunday services among the downtrodden of Beverly Hills. Believing that God had instructed him, the pastor gave the name Vineyard to his emerging congregation. In 1977 or 1978, Gulliksen joined his forces with those of another disaffected Calvary Chapel 'affiliate' named John Wimber, an individual who was to prove charismatic in every sense, though Wimber did not assume the organisation's leadership fully until 1982.[11] One way or another, in any case, the Association of Vineyard Churches, these days an international movement claiming 1,500 outposts, was born.

In his 'three and one-half months' of study Dylan was exposed to specialised teaching. The Vineyard is keen, to take the most conspicuous example, on what is known as kingdom theology, the belief that all history turns on the struggle between God and Satan, a struggle that will be concluded by the second coming of Christ, but only after the Antichrist, paradoxically enough, has brought a deceptive peace to humankind. (Critics denounce radical versions of this thinking, which take the struggle to be altogether literal, as 'militant Biblicism' and 'holy war theology'.) For now, the kingdom is here, it is argued, but not complete, a matter of 'the already and the not yet' as believers say. Some of those believers have a taste for 'signs and wonders', for evidence of supernatural events involving the laying on of hands, for the alleged healing of the sick and the casting out of demons. A minority are not averse to glossolalia, to 'speaking in tongues'. At times in its short history the Vineyard movement has also produced a remarkable number of individuals blessed with the gift, albeit not the unerring gift, of prophecy.

It is taken for granted that humanity is born in sin. It is believed – and Dylan went for this one in a big way – that the Devil is real, actual and everywhere active among us. Chiefly, however, and to simplify greatly, everything is pinned on the return of the Messiah and the End of Days, the time of punishment and reward. The idea is taken for granted among most dispensationalist evangelicals, though they quibble over precise definitions of 'the rapture', that moment when the Almighty will snatch true believers from the face of the earth. Apparently there is some argument over the precise timing of this event, whether amid, before or after 'tribulation'. Another part of the Vineyard creed, not the least important, is 'justification' before God, accomplished by faith in Jesus alone.

Dylan did not hesitate over that aspect of belief. But then, after a more intensive course of study than he had endured since high school, it seems he did not hesitate over much that he was told. In his gospel songs he would part from other Vineyard adherents only in seeming to skip over the benign manifestations of this version of Christianity. The central tenet, the cleaving to a messiah first and last, gripped him. It grips him still. Everything in the Bible is the literal truth. This world is coming to an end. Judgement will follow.

It speaks to character. Dylan is a dogmatist until the minute he changes his mind. When he is in thrall to one idea all competing ideas are, by definition, false or – that word from his youth – phoney. It is as though he starts from the assumption that Bob Dylan would not take an interest in anything that isn't supremely important.

So his beloved antique folk and blues music ceases to be just a thing of abiding wonder and becomes a key to life's mysteries, something akin to a philosophy, even a creed. It is notable that when he ceased to preach, if not to believe, Dylan began to tell interviewers that music had always been the most meaningful thing in his life.

Equally, when he declined to be used on behalf of political causes in the 1960s there would be no appeal against his judgement that all organised politics is a deceit and a waste of time. By 1984, he would be framing his opinion in the terms he understood best: 'politics is an instrument of the Devil.'[12] Dylan might refuse to be anyone's leader, but he does not hesitate to lay down the law. When he accepted the evangelical Messiah as fundamental to the nature of existence, therefore, there could be no deviation, no doubt, no holding back. Say this much for the artist (or for his state of mind): any thoughts of the likely damage to his career did not impede him in the slightest. As Robert Hilburn of the *Los Angeles Times* would be informed in November 1980: 'When I believe in something, I don't care what anybody else thinks.' That was never entirely true, but as a declaration of faith it would stand.

Gulliksen assigned Myers as a full-time guide and minder to the most prominent of the Vineyard's show-business converts during the artist's studies in the 'school of discipleship'. The measure was intended, supposedly, to protect Dylan from the media types clustering daily in Reseda. In 1999, when he was entreating believers to 'intercede for Bob, to pray without ceasing that God will access his heart so that he will be open to responding again to the truth', Gulliksen would give an insight, unwittingly no doubt, into the Vineyard's real attitude towards the catch it had made for Jesus. As to celebrities, the pastor – who had by then returned to the Calvary Chapel flock – said:

> The three best known of that decade were Martin Luther King, John Kennedy, and Bob Dylan. Two of them were killed and Dylan was the only one left. So you are not talking about just a celebrity, you are talking about 'the' remaining celebrity.[13]

The Vineyard church was both star-struck and pragmatic. You could also mention opportunistic. Music, smiles and 'contemporary worship' were intrinsic to its effort to connect with the 'counterculture and anti-establishment dynamic'. Who better embodied all of that than Dylan? If the main business at hand was the winning of converts among the entertainment-industry types of Southern California – and among their millions of fans – he was the perfect advertisement for the Vineyard Jesus. The pastors cared about Dylan's soul, too, of course. As Myers saw fit to insist, as though he might have said it once or twice before, it would not have crossed their minds to 'attempt to convince, manipulate or pressure this man into anything'. Heaven forfend.

The Book of Revelation was at the heart of everything Dylan learned. Or rather, the interpretation placed upon the visionary writings ascribed to 'John of Patmos' by the Vineyard folk was central to what was taught in the conference room of a real-estate business. Modern textual analysis suggests there might in fact have been three Johns at work in compiling the Patmos book, and that the trio were not always in agreement theologically, but such details were no impediment to students in the San Fernando Valley who heard they were getting a glimpse, 1,900 years after the prophecies were inscribed, of an imminent apocalypse. In Dylan's childhood pointless Cold War civil-defence advice had urged him to 'duck and cover' when doomsday arrived. That, he learned in 1979, would be worse than foolish when the angelic trumpeters, the scorpion-tailed locusts, the Four Horsemen, the False Prophet, the Whore of Babylon and the Archangel Michael hove into view. It was all true. Once 'decoded' the Book of Revelation told it, as Californian evangelicals probably said, like it was, or certainly would be.

The decrypting of an inerrant biblical text was a fruitful line of research. Beyond question, it also helped some people to sell a great many exciting books of their own. This meant that students such as

Dylan could spend as much time on contemporary 'interpretations' of things the Bible could be made to say as they spent on Scripture itself. A flood of speculative literature had been unleashed amid the fashion for being born again. Modern American religiosity gets much of its reputation, in Europe at least, from its appetite for this theological equivalent of junk food.

The Late, Great Planet Earth (1970) by Hal Lindsey ('with Carole C. Carlson') is an uncomplicated sort of work. It takes 'dispensational eschatology' for granted. It therefore does not quarrel with the possibility, never mind the argument, that the Bible is not necessarily prophetic in a simple, predictive sense. Lindsey's glossing of holy writ is never so dull. He treats the good book as a cosmic countdown. All the stuff that's in there, suitably interpreted, will happen in this world and in our times. So what might bring about rapture, tribulation and the Second Coming?

The author invites readers to look closely at current (*c.* 1970s–'80s) events. The Antichrist is just around the corner if he's not actually already in charge of the conspiracy known as the European Economic Community. Meanwhile, there's an awful lot of bad stuff – earthquakes, famines, wars – going on. And what about those Soviets (strangely earning no mention whatever in Scripture)? They would probably invade Israel if they could; in fact, that's probably exactly what they will do. All real evangelicals know what that would mean: Armageddon, scheduled by the inerrant Bible for a hillside 20 miles outside of Haifa. In Lindsey's somewhat provisional reckoning, meanwhile, the messiah was supposed to return within a generation of the refounding of the State of Israel. Quick: fetch a calendar.

Dylan was not the only sophisticated, intelligent and well-read individual, before or since, to fall for the claptrap that passeth understanding. In fact, he was in no sense unusual. Doubts have been cast over how much of *The Late, Great Planet Earth* Lindsey wrote in a mundane, physical sense – the prolific but elusive Carlson also worked on a follow-up, *Satan Is Alive and Well on Planet Earth* (1972) – but the Wikipedia oracle maintains that 28 million copies of *The Late, Great . . .* apocalypse fantasy had been sold by 1990. Lindsey, the self-styled Christian Zionist, was meanwhile an influential presence in and around the Vineyard church, for a while at least. Dylan studied his book closely. Then he studied it again. Judging by his subsequent statements, the artist took this pseudo-scriptural disaster-movie synopsis very seriously. Its bizarre predictions became the core of his end-of-the-world view. Doom seemed to matter rather more to him than the Beatitudes.

*

He was only one part, though a well-publicised part, of a religious revival. Or rather, Dylan was caught up in still another of America's periodic upsurges of demonstrative faith amid all the usual omens of decadence, decline and fall. It had become almost a national habit. In their 2004 book, *The Right Nation*, John Micklethwait and Adrian Wooldridge make the telling point that revivalism has rarely been absent from the history of the republic. 'Some people think America is in the middle of its Fourth Great Awakening,' they write, 'but the truth is that these great awakenings have been so frequent and prolonged that there has never been a period of sleep from which to awake. Revivalism does not need to be revived; rather, it is a continuous fact of American life.'[14]

Statistics tell one part of the modern story. In the course of the 1970s membership of the evangelical Southern Baptist Convention grew by 16 per cent, that of the Assemblies of God by 70 per cent. In contrast, the established churches fell back: the United Presbyterian Church saw the number of its adherents diminish by 21 per cent; membership of the Episcopal Church fell by 15 per cent. By 1980, the two dozen largest individual churches in the United States were evangelical in style or doctrine, with immense wealth and huge numbers of potential volunteers ready to further God's work through the right candidate. The Christian Broadcasting Network was the fifth-largest cable TV network in the country, boasting 30 million subscribers.[15] Preachers of the 'Religious Right' such as Jerry Falwell and Pat Robertson had meanwhile become significant political players, men entirely at ease in the media and the corridors of power. Voters were being registered by the Right in their tens of thousands.

In 1979, just as Dylan was joining the choir, the Moral Majority was founded to articulate a collective conservative rage against the 1973 Supreme Court *Roe v. Wade* decision on abortion, against gay rights, against women's rights, against affirmative action and – a perennial favourite – obnoxious 'liberal' textbooks. There was a simultaneous demand from the evangelical lobby for a rewriting of the Constitution to permit 'voluntary' prayers in schools. Such attitudes had long been part of the fabric of American life, but in the late 1970s and early '80s they began to dominate public debate. Evangelicals had once made it a point of principle to steer clear of organised politics. When they took up the challenge – more in anger than in sorrow, it seemed – the effect on the lordly Republican Party was revolutionary. Utterly uncompromising in any matter capable of being defined as an issue of religious belief, the new conservative Christians began to talk as if they alone were authentically American, the sole heirs to the nation's first principles and founding ideals. Faith and ideology began to seem indistinguishable.

It is a mistake, then, to view Dylan's experiences only through the prism of Bob Dylan. His conversion is significant for what it meant to his art, for the nature of the faith he chose, and for what it said about his identity as a Jew. But his response to born-again religion was entirely of its American place and time. The Vineyard's teachings – Dylan's understanding of them, at any rate – came with an amount of political baggage. It is no coincidence that he too became – what shall we say? – less tolerant in his outlook just as conservatives were beginning to wield a renewed influence in his country. When Dylan began to preach, such people were convinced they had found their candidate for president.

In many ways, Ronald Reagan and Bob Dylan were not so very different. (I've typed funnier sentences, but not many.) Both men could fairly claim to have sprung from the small-town heartland, from the tradition of Democratic politics, and from the role-playing business of entertainment. Both were susceptible to nostalgia for a lost American past. Both possessed personalities that were, at best, opaque. Both made a point of being extraordinarily hard to decipher. After the first youthful flush of enthusiasm for justice and liberty, Dylan did not set out to bring down anyone's evil empire, Satan's aside, but in 1979 he and the man running for president shared a talent. In neither case was it possible for anyone easily to state the real nature of the person.

Reagan began as a faithful believer in Franklin Delano Roosevelt and ended up as the patron saint of American neo-conservatism. Once a Hollywood trade unionist opposed to nuclear weapons – though an FBI informer against 'Commies' too – he heard the chimes of conservative freedom just before Barry Goldwater made his doomed run for the presidency in 1964. Reagan had been helped along on his political path by the California business types who became his mentors and sponsors, but he had only joined the Republican Party formally in 1962. In his new political home, he wasted no time, opposing both Lyndon Johnson's Civil Rights Act (1964) and the Voting Rights Act

(1965). Reagan took the unapologetic view that it was an individual's right, when selling or renting a property, to discriminate against 'Negroes'. That kind of record did a presidential candidate no harm in the Southern states.

By the end of 1979, Reagan had the votes of the Religious (which is to say Christian) Right sewn up. Most evangelicals had come out for Jimmy Carter, the devout Sunday school teacher, in '76. But the belief that 'Satan had mobilised his forces to destroy America' – not to mention the Carter administration's threat to deprive their schools of tax-deductible status on the grounds of discrimination – cooled the ardour of these Christians.[16] They persuaded themselves that the Carter White House and Democrats generally were a threat to 'traditional moral values'. Reagan understood the Religious Right perfectly. He especially knew how to sound as though he understood everything about them, their hopes, fears and iron beliefs. Whether he was ever truly one of them is open to question, however.

His mother had adhered to the Disciples of Christ, a Protestant church blending Presbyterian and Congregationalist traits, but one with an overriding insistence on the acceptance of Jesus Christ as Lord and Saviour. If needs be, Reagan could speak the Christian Right's language. His upbringing in religion had in fact been entirely conventional, but by the end of the 1970s the candidate was a supreme exponent of the art of blending folksy nostalgia for a former, better, more moral America with the evangelical conviction that the country was going straight to hell for want of faith. By the time he achieved the presidency he was calling himself born again, though this did not seem to involve attending a church with any great frequency.[17]

Reagan made everything simple. Sometimes he could even make reactionary politics sound like an affable comedy routine. Paradoxically, the ability to fake likeability came naturally to him. There is no doubt, for all that, that this candidate had sensed a mood in the country. Suddenly the conservative zealot who had been dismissed by liberals throughout the '60s, even after his coup in winning the governorship of California handsomely in 1966, was looking and sounding like a mainstream politician. Or rather, he was being accepted by voters across middle America as the reassuring voice of their mainstream opinions. To begin with, even the patricians in his own party didn't believe it was possible. Reagan's adopted state had taught him a lot.

Contrary to any impression given by Hollywood, California had been a home-from-home for evangelical belief long before the Dust

Bowl migrants began stumbling in with their meagre possessions and their old-time religion during the 1930s. The astoundingly popular preacher and faith healer Aimee Semple McPherson, nominally a Pentecostalist, had set up shop in Los Angeles after the First World War. By 1923, her gigantic Angelus Temple in Echo Park, boasting the biggest set of church bells on the West Coast and a pair of 30-foot-high 'Jesus Saves' neon signs to pull in the customers, was capable of seating over 5,000 people. Others in the City of Angels were busy with their missions and moral crusades, whether to establish Prohibition or kick out a mayor. While McPherson was performing her miracles, Pastor Robert P. 'Fighting Bob' Shuler was broadcasting to radio audiences from the bastion of his Southern Methodist church in the Downtown business district. Shuler specialised in vicious attacks on all the usual scapegoats, whether politicians, Jews, Catholics, black Americans, or ungodly books. His chats were hugely popular. Beyond the Hollywood Babylon, Angelinos were morally, socially and religiously conservative.

Interestingly enough, that hasn't changed much. In August of 2005, a survey was released by the Barna Group showing that Los Angeles contained a greater number of evangelical adults than any other American metropolis.[18] As the researchers put it: 'The city that produces the media often criticised or boycotted by evangelicals is also home to nearly one million of those deeply devout Christians. In fact, there are more evangelical adults in the Los Angeles market than there are in the New York, Chicago and Boston metropolitan areas – combined!' The survey, based on interviews with 24,000 individuals, also estimated that California as a whole was home to almost two million committed evangelicals. There were plenty of them around when Dylan made his choice of faith. They were prominent features, too, of Californian society in the 1950s and 1960s. In conservative Orange County, in particular, there was a lot of talk about God's purpose for America while Beats, freaks and guitar-playing hippies disturbed the peace. In those days, amid unprecedented economic growth in the state, only one condition remained to be fulfilled to allow the rise of Ronald Wilson Reagan.

Its theological justification was always vague. Naive readers tend to conclude, in fact, that the New Testament contains nothing to suggest that the pursuit of riches is reconciled easily, if at all, with Christianity. There is no 'prosperity gospel'. Nevertheless, when Reagan began to harbour political ambitions in the mid-1950s the idea was becoming common ground between some evangelicals – others, to be fair, objected vehemently – and Republican political operators trying to complete the conservative circle. The simple idea was to prove that it was all right to get rich. Soon enough, in fact, pastors and politicians alike could be heard arguing that the defence of wealth and American capitalism was a Christian's civic duty. As ever, biblical texts could be found as required. In 1947, a struggling Oklahoma preacher named Oral Roberts had come across the second verse in John's Third Epistle. 'I wish above all things that thou mayest prosper and be in health, even as thy soul prospereth,' it reads. Roberts, soon to become filthy rich in the God business, had been delighted to hear that. Elsewhere, notions of 'divine reciprocity' were beginning to be combined in the 1950s and '60s with the so-called laws of faith. 'Give and it will be given back unto you' could be combined conveniently with 'ask and ye shall receive'. All of this was going on while Dylan was singing of freedom's bell 'Tolling for the luckless, the abandoned an' forsaked'.

In due course, Reagan's presidency would provide happy days for those capable of reading Scripture as a guide to financial planning. By the time he was announcing his candidacy and Dylan was preaching to the unconverted at the Warfield Theater in San Francisco, evangelical Christianity was identified – had indeed identified itself – as a reliable front-line battalion in the conservative political insurgency. Politics and the deity had become entangled. By the twenty-first century no one among the 'empowered evangelicals' of the Vineyard would think it odd in the slightest if a 'conversation with God' involved a request for a job, admission to a particular college, or even a sports car.[19] Presumably it is not polite in such a circumstance to mention voodoo. For his part, to his perhaps eternal credit, Dylan would complain in a 1986 interview that he had 'heard a lot of preachers say how God wants everybody to be wealthy and healthy. Well, it doesn't say that in the Bible.'[20] The remark would be prompted by a mention of the word 'conservative'.

Candidate Reagan was, if a little belatedly, opposed to abortion, in favour of capital punishment, no friend to the environmentalists, an opponent of the long-contested Equal Rights Amendment intended to guarantee equality for women, a supporter of prayer in schools, and, as already noted, a chuckling character who had spoken out against civil-rights legislation. By 1979, most of this met the requirements of most of the people with whom Dylan had allied himself. Reagan would go on to designate 1983 as the 'Year of the Bible'. In 1982, by way of a preface, Congress would pass a joint resolution recognising the book as beyond doubt the Word of God, further declaring that it had made 'a unique contribution in shaping the United States as a distinctive and blessed nation and people'.

It is sometimes forgotten that Reagan's most famous speech, one culminating in an assault on the Soviet 'evil empire' – while rejecting a freeze on the nuclear-weapons programmes that were liable to hasten one version of Armageddon – was in fact delivered to a gathering of the National Association of Evangelicals. In March 1983, the president gave this crowd what they wanted to hear with his thoughts on abortion, prayer in schools and 'the tried and time-tested values upon which our very civilization is based'. In his terms, the battle with godless state Communism was 'not material but spiritual'. Twice, to the audience's evident delight, the president declared that 'America is in the midst of a spiritual awakening and a moral renewal'. It was, indeed, 'a renewal of the traditional values that have been the bedrock of America's goodness and greatness'. It was no accident that this politician had inaugurated the presidential 'tradition' of concluding speeches with the phrase 'God bless America'.

That Reagan was the choice of most of the people most of the time during the '80s is beyond argument. In 1980, in his third attempt to become president, he was awarded 50.7 per cent of the popular vote against Carter's barely respectable 41 per cent. In 1984, Reagan's mandate was renewed with an unambiguous landslide, granting him 58.8 per cent of the vote to swamp Walter Mondale's 40.6 per cent. That result counted as Republican vengeance for Lyndon Johnson's crushing of Goldwater in '64, 61.05 per cent to 22.58 per cent, but the Reagan presidency had a greater significance. Just six years and three months after Richard Nixon's disgrace and resignation had seemed to destroy the American Right, here they were, back, hugely popular, grinning contentedly, and in charge. With God on their side.

This – conservative, faith-driven, patriotic, disinclined to listen to bad news or to complicated explanations – was the America in which the artist found himself born again. The liberal rock critics would just have finished savaging a Bob Dylan album entitled *Saved* when in 1980 the remains of Fritz Mondale's political career were being buried, piece by charred piece, in a shallow grave. Back at the Warfield in San Francisco on 9 November, five nights after the election, Dylan would perform a song he had been playing since a show in Toronto in April. 'Ain't Gonna Go to Hell for Anybody' is not one of his works that reads well on the page and it would not find a place in the artist's

Lyrics 1962–2001 (2004). By November of 1980, meanwhile, Reagan had no use for a campaign song. Still, Dylan sang:

> I can persuade people as well as anybody
> I got the vision but it caused division
> I can twist the truth as well as anybody
> I know how to do it, I've been all the way through it
> But it don't suit my purpose and it ain't my goal
> To gain the whole world, but give up my soul.
>
> But I ain't gonna go to hell for anybody
> I ain't gonna go to hell for anybody
> I ain't gonna go to hell for anybody
> Not for father, not for mother, not for sister, not for father, no way!

It is almost as if the artist picked his Jesus moment. Perhaps Dylan was proving himself to be just another ordinary American after all. You could also say, however, that he discovered convenient truths at a convenient time. He could twist those truths as well anybody. If you are one of those who understand Dylan's career in terms of calculated moves and deliberate 'reinventions', the 'born-again phase' can seem like a very neat set of coincidences, even if it did not work out exactly according to plan.

Equally, he didn't need to be told that the '60s were over and done, that his participation in the events of the decade had been misunderstood and misrepresented, that his allegiance to the counter-culture had been provisional at best, that his patience with hippies (and the rest) was always limited, that his true loyalty was to the old music, rooted in Christianity, of the heartland. On that reading, his conversion was more than just a statement of belief. This was not the theological equivalent of making a baffling country album in Nashville. Dylan was throwing in his lot with a distinctive American constituency just as that constituency was blessing Ronald Reagan.

An obsession with God was, as it remains, part of the nation's character, the paradoxical result of being founded on Enlightenment principles. Giving liberty to all religions, the Founding Fathers – a couple of them might have been dismayed – encouraged every possible variety of faith to emerge and compete in the belief market. The result, perplexing to most of the rest of the world, was a liberal theocracy, a spiritual free-for-all in which, nevertheless, His presence was one of the things held to be self-evident, thereby rendering America a special case among nations. Among the western democracies, the United States is uniquely religious. In 1979, just for once, Dylan was part of the majority.

These days, American evangelicals often claim to fear for the future of their movement. Their political power has diminished sharply since Reagan's era. In one pastor's account, 'evangelicalism as we knew it in the twentieth century is disintegrating'.[21] Which is to say that a mere 20 million people, 7 per cent of the population, identify themselves as belonging to evangelical churches. Only those raised to take America's religiosity for granted could understand the fundamentalist talk of crisis. In 2001, the American Religious Identification Survey (ARIS) found that 76.5 per cent of people called themselves Christians; in 2002 the Pew Research Center put the number at 82 per cent. By 2008, ARIS noted an increase in those with no religion, up from 8 per cent to 15 per cent in 18 years, but still found 76 per cent of respondents calling themselves Christians. Such, so it seems, is the catastrophic decline.

In 2012, meanwhile, the Pew Forum on Religion and Public Life discovered that fully 41 per cent of Americans had switched religion at least once in their lives, but also found that 36 per cent attended a religious service at least once a week. ARIS further reported, in 2008, that 45 per cent of Christians (and 34 per cent of the adult population) considered themselves to be 'born-again or evangelical'. Belief that there is 'definitely a personal God' took care of 69.5 per cent of Americans, while a further 12.1 per cent went for a 'higher power'. A mere 2.3 per cent decided that there is 'no such thing' as God. By European standards, each and every one of those statistics remains remarkable.[22]

In the years after Dylan accepted Christ, evangelicals would turn the American Protestant world upside. By 1986, according to Gallup polls, 31 per cent of the population, fully 55 million people, were 'comfortable' to be called born-again or evangelical. Between the mid-1970s and the mid-1980s, according to the data provided by the General Social Survey, the proportion of Americans 'strongly affiliated' to religion went up from 38 per cent to 43 per cent. Dylan was catching a wave, in other words. The only thing that made him different from any other entertainer enduring a spiritual crisis, inhaling a dose of premium-grade fervour, or hitching his star to popular sentiment, was a matter of origins.

*

The death of Dylan's father Abram ('Abe') Zimmerman at the age of just 56 in the summer of 1968 affected the singer profoundly, they say. It appears also to have awakened, or reawakened, an interest in his Jewish heritage. In the years that followed he visited Israel several times and studied Judaism with apparent intensity. That should probably count as predictable: this was the faith of his fathers and, after a fashion, he would return to it. But that heritage suggests an issue mentioned too rarely when talk turns to born-again Dylan: just why did this Jew become a Christian? What was in it, spiritually speaking, for him? And why a Christian with a pronounced taste, utterly alien to Judaism, for world-ending collective punishment?

If he truly needed a route to God, the disavowal of his own identity was shocking to a lot of his fellow Jews. It was no small matter, to put it mildly, for one of his background, however 'secular', to accept Jesus as Messiah and personal saviour. Nor did Dylan take up with Christianity in one of its self-effacing, ingratiating forms. The hard-line evangelising brand he adopted isn't known for sweet ecumenical reason, or for genuine tolerance, despite the Vineyard's energetic attempts to embrace pop-style music and laughter. Its revealed truth allows no exceptions, no 'you're right from your side and I'm right from mine'.

Judaism is in error and Jews will not be saved unless and until they accept Christ. Ditto Muslims. (These days the Vineyard advertises itself as 'uniquely poised and prepared to bless Muslims'.)[23] Ditto Hindus, non-reborn Christians, Buddhists, Jains and all the rest. Ditto you-name-it. Hence the usual list of forbidden human states and choices: drink, drugs, adultery (tricky for Dylan), homosexuality, abortion. The Vineyard Fellowship, the church that gave the singer his full-immersion baptism and consequent rebirth-in-Christ, was entirely hardcore behind its handy 'Satan shields'. Yet for Dylan, descendant of those who had fled a Tsar's pogroms, acceptance of Jesus was a wholesale rejection of his historic identity and of his family. He had rehearsed the same gesture amid all his other evasions during the '60s, telling journalists that he was not Jewish, or that he didn't 'feel' Jewish, or that his origins were of no importance. By the end of the '70s, it was as though he was trying to discard a part of himself entirely, once and for all. Dylan, so it seemed, was making an irrevocable break with the past. This time he was leaving Hibbing, Minnesota, behind for good.

The obvious point is always worth repeating: Bob Dylan was born a Jew, which is to say born of a beloved Jewish mother. In the religion's law, that's what counts. Perhaps it didn't matter much to Dylan in his childhood and youth, but the faith was an enfolding fact of his life. He was raised Jewish, too, in a place that knew few of his people. In 1941, year of his birth, religious affiliations in Hibbing were divided between overwhelmingly preponderant Roman Catholics and Lutherans of various flavours. Nor were Jews gathered in numbers in Minnesota as they were in the great cities. The North Country was far from the communities in which American Jewry achieved its cultural critical mass. Still: Robert Zimmerman was Jewish, circumcised and named within days of his birth. At 13, he had marked his religious majority and become a *bar mitzvah*, a son of the commandment, thanks to an old rabbi shipped in from New York to help the boy memorise his texts. In May of 1954 the congregation had chanted the old words – 'This is the Torah which Moses placed before the children of Israel' – and Robert was given responsibility for his own religious observances.

You can throw these things aside, no doubt, if you fail or cease to believe. Discarding them for the sake of Christianity, the sect that has been the source of so many Jewish woes, is another matter. Besides, as far as Judaism is concerned the prophesied events presaging the coming of the Messiah have not occurred. Demonstrably, it is argued, those events did not occur in the first century. So Jesus/Yeshua ain't Him.

For good measure, the Christian idea of the Trinity, the belief that God is divisible, counts as heretical for Jews. The belief that it is the Messiah's job to save the world from its sins is also rejected. Jews have no truck with the idea that God could be made flesh, or with the weird notion of praying to this Jesus. They are opposed profoundly to what is called replacement theology, 'supersessionism' – the Messiah's advent means that older stuff can be dumped – and its motives. For most, it is very simple: anyone who claims that Jesus is his saviour is no longer properly a Jew. In this contest over the one God, the gulf between the two sides cannot be bridged. The solution adopted eventually by Dylan would be no defence against the charge of apostasy. For those who believed as his forefathers had believed, it would only make matters worse.

In any case, the artist did not 'receive Jesus' thanks to just any New Testament study group. Irrespective of any peculiar political alliances then being formed between the American Christian Right and Zionism, the Vineyard crowd were not inclined to split theological differences.

To accept one supernatural story, Dylan had to reject alternative versions. The Vineyarders were happy to welcome allcomers as grist to the conversion mill, but for evangelicals the deal rested, obviously enough, on one unbreakable condition: the acceptance of Jesus as Messiah.

It's just possible that Dylan saw things differently. He might have felt that the gulf between the Torah and Christian fundamentalism was neither wide nor important. If so, he had part of a point. As one rabbi and scholar has put it: 'To be a Jew means first and foremost to belong to a group, the Jewish people, and the religious beliefs are secondary, in a sense, to this corporate allegiance.'[24] The writer adds, however, that the 'contrast with Christianity is self-evident'. Christians are defined by their beliefs. And Dylan found himself believing, head over heels, before he was ducked in a California swimming pool. The act of submersion and submission could not be overlooked or ignored. Those 'flesh-colored Christs that glow in the dark' are powerful still, it seems.

Others had followed the twisting path before Dylan. Conversion to Christianity by Jews had become a minor American phenomenon in the '70s thanks in part to the relentless work of the evangelicals. Al Kasha, a former Brill Building songwriter and a double Oscar-winner in the early part of the decade, was a celebrity Angelino who had parted from his Brooklyn Jewish roots for the sake of born-again Christianity. Thanks to his work for CBS Publishing in the 1960s and to the songs he had written or co-created for numerous performers – Aretha, Jackie Wilson, Bobby Darin, Neil Diamond, Donna Summer and more – Kasha was a music-industry player. That wasn't what interested Dylan.

Though having become an ordained Southern Baptist pastor after 'praying to receive Jesus' during a bout of agoraphobia, Kasha was also what is known as a messianic Jew, a follower of Christ who nevertheless considered himself Jewish. In 1979, he and Dylan met at the Vineyard. Subsequently, the artist would become a regular participant in the 'Bible study' held at Kasha's Beverly Hills home. In 2011, the evangelical journalist Dan Wooding was given one version of Dylan's conversion. Kasha said:

> Bob's nature is that he's a very much a seeker and he was interested to see why a fellow Jew would come to know Christ. He started at the Vineyard church and then, when we met there, he came to a first Bible study. And at the second Bible study he gave his life to the Lord.

I prayed the prayer of confession, which he repeated, about his sins and that Jesus was the Son of God and is God . . . I pointed out to him in John 4 that 'salvation shall come through the Jews' and that Jesus came to this earth as a Jew. I'm a Jewish believer now going on since 1978, so it's a long time. That Bible study started in '79 and never ended until this past year.

Bob would stay until three or four o'clock in the morning asking me questions beyond my knowledge. The interesting thing is that he felt a comfort that I was a fellow songwriter.[25]

Presumably it was in Kasha's home, therefore, that the artist made the decision, 'privately and on his own', alluded to by Larry Myers in 1994. If that's the case, Jesus was accepted in the presence of a Jewish convert. In a later interview with Wooding, Kasha would say that Dylan 'came to the house every week for six months' – given the artist's known whereabouts in the first half of 1979, this can't be exactly true – and that he was baptised near Malibu by 'Vineyard people'.[26] The composer would also claim that Dylan wrote Slow Train Coming 'mostly in our home. I gave him a key and I'd be sleeping upstairs with my wife and he'd come in at three or four o'clock in the morning, and I'd hear him picking as he felt a kind of holy spirit comfort.' At this point Dylan was also writing under the gaze – supervision might be a better word – of his Vineyard pastors. Myers was sticking closely to him. Whether the artist was actually having his songs vetted for their fidelity to the church's understanding of Scripture is unclear. That's how they would sound to many listeners, nevertheless.

In his interview with Wooding, Kasha would have a couple of other interesting things to say. In 2011, when the popular account still insisted that Dylan had long since put aside his born-again experiences, his former host would be able to state, with apparent confidence, that the singer 'has never renounced his faith'. As Kasha explained it, 'once you're saved, you're saved forever'. But he also had this to offer:

If you want to know the truth, and I always try to be as honest as possible, I think some Christians took advantage of him. They would tell him, 'Go out and sing for nothing.' Why should he sing for nothing if he's being paid by other people? So I think that that bothered and hurt him.[27]

Cajoling Dylan to work for free – but with no gain for the Vineyard? – does not sound like the worst kind of naked exploitation. Nor does it sound like the whole story of his parting from the fellowship. Thanks to long and sometimes bitter experience, Dylan was sensitive to anyone trying to take advantage of his name and fame, but a few free shows would not have killed him. It might even have counted as that favourite celebrity hobby 'giving something back'. Disenchantment, if that's what it was, would come later, in any case, and probably had more to do with the fact that some in the Vineyard sect proved too eager to drop his name when advertising their spiritual wares.

Dylan had begun to put Scripture into rhyme – the most generous description of the *Slow Train Coming* songs – almost from the instant Jesus had shaken up his hotel room. His band had heard versions of 'Slow Train' during the last days of the 1978 tour. The audience at the Hollywood Sportatorium in Florida had meanwhile been granted the sermon entitled 'Do Right to Me Baby (Do Unto Others)' on the global roadshow's final night, 16 December, as a strange sort of preface to the Judaic 'Forever Young'. Jesus was accepted into Dylan's life in January of 1979 and work on the album began in the Muscle Shoals Sound Studio in Sheffield, Alabama, on Monday, 30 April. In the interim, therefore, the artist was putting the Word into bad verse and interrogating Al Kasha on 'why a fellow Jew would come to know Christ'. Plainly, conversion had not answered every question.

This might have been Dylan's meaning when in May 1980 he told a journalist that being born again 'is a hard thing', a 'painful' thing. Joy and exultation were not mentioned at any point in the interview. Dylan also said that 'I'm becoming less and less defined as Christ becomes more and more defined'.[28] The person disappearing had once been Jewish. Dylan was supposed to relinquish himself in being born again – that was, for what it was worth, the idea – but he did not quite manage it. Instead, he effected a distinctive sort of compromise. It holds to this day.

When the album *Saved* appeared towards the end of June 1980 its inner sleeve carried a quotation from the Bible. The verse from Jeremiah (31:31) reads, 'Behold the days come, saith the Lord, that I will make a new covenant with the house of Israel, and with the house of Judah.' Why this passage? There are complicated arguments over these two 'houses', over the ten lost tribes of the ancient Kingdom of Israel who might (or might not) have emerged from captivity to become the Gentile 'multitude of nations', and other arcane issues besides. One point is more or less agreed: for house of Judah read 'the Jewish people'. Dylan was pointing to God's deal with humanity, but drawing specific attention to himself, a Jew, and to the 'new covenant' that had been offered to him and his community. You could say the artist had been searching the small print for a way to justify his position. On the *Saved* album, typically, he would find a personal meaning in God's promise and express it in the song 'Covenant Woman'.

> Covenant woman got a contract with the Lord
> Way up yonder, great will be her reward
> Covenant woman, shining like a morning star
> I know I can trust you to stay where you are

Jews for Jesus and messianic Judaism are not one and the same thing. Members of the former organisation, founded in 1973, are one part of the latter movement, but the movement itself is more diverse than the activities of a single group of evangelicals might suggest. There are those born Jewish who recognise Yeshua as the Messiah but refuse to recognise him as God, or who draw the line at the strange idea of a three-in-one deity. There are also those who accept the claims made for Christ, but who detect the unwelcome hand of Protestant evangelicals interfering in Jewish debates. Jews for Jesus, it is often alleged, is just another front for Christian missionaries engaged in the age-old effort to detach Judaism from its faith, traditions and roots.

Whether Dylan understood as much, or cared, in 1979 and 1980 is not clear. Whether the differences truly matter is, equally, not our problem in these pages. In its modern form, the phenomenon of Jews accepting Christ had only been evident for a few years when Dylan was writing *Slow Train Coming*. Nevertheless, it seemed to solve the problem he had posed to Al Kasha. Through messianic Judaism he was able to go on living as a Jew and regarding himself as a Jew while recognising Jesus as his saviour. Everything he has said and done since involving religion, whether turning up at Hasidic synagogues for the High Holidays or extolling the Christian Book of Revelation, accords with a dual affiliation. At a press conference in Hamburg at the end of May 1984, Dylan would be asked, 'Bob, are you Christian or Jewish?' The entirely truthful answer: 'Well, that's hard to say.' Pressed on the matter, the artist would simply respond, 'It's a long story.'

When messianic Judaism first began to appear in the early 1970s its proponents differed from earlier 'Jewish Christians'. The young men who established Beth Messiah in Cincinnati and Beth Yeshua in Philadelphia might have launched their congregations as offshoots of familiar Christian 'missions to the Jews', but they soon asserted their independence. The point, as the converts realised, was to be both Jewish, even ostentatiously Jewish, and Christian. These followers of Jesus were not prepared to be assimilated. As their critics still argue, they wanted it both ways, retaining most of the outward forms of traditional Judaism while participating in the all-singing, all-dancing evangelical charismatic Christian revival. The messianic Jews would retort, as one history of America's alternative religions has put it, that they were 'working to "make things right" and bring together the truth and beauty of both religions: the faith in Jesus, or Yeshua, with the belief in the special role of Israel in history and the traditional symbols of Judaism'.[29] That's probably a fair enough summary of Dylan's position in the months after his conversion.

Perhaps predictably, Christian evangelicals and some messianic Jews have described the coming together of two traditions as uncomplicated, as though recognition of Jesus solved every possible problem. In a 2006 book on Dylan and the Protestant God, for example, Stephen H. Webb, a professor of religion and philosophy at Wabash College in Indiana, makes this faintly audacious statement:

> Many people attracted to the Vineyard were Jewish, and they actually became more Jewish when they became Christian. Like many evangelical churches, the Vineyard emphasized Christianity's connection to Judaism and treated authentic Judaism as compatible with Christian faith in Jesus the Messiah.[30]

They actually became more Jewish? You could call that a large claim. If you happened to be Jewish, even of the messianic persuasion, you could probably call it a few other things. Webb, who describes Dylan as 'best understood as a musical theologian' and as one of the rare American artists 'to develop an essentially conservative view of Jesus', does not give much attention or weight to the singer's Jewish upbringing.[31] The professor, himself from an evangelical background, prefers to believe that Dylan was in some osmotic manner rendered unconsciously Christian by his surroundings years before he (or anyone else) came to terms with the fact. Given numerous other known facts, particularly the facts of the artist's life in the aftermath of his time among the Vineyarders, that counts as presumptuous, but not untypical of evangelical Christian attitudes. So the Vineyard 'treated authentic Judaism as compatible with Christian faith in Jesus the Messiah'? By setting aside just one small technicality, presumably, after the church had decided what was 'authentic'. Dylan was never so cavalier.

In the 1970s, politics was also at work. The pioneering young 'Jewish believers in Jesus' (as the contemporary compromise term has it) were avowedly conservative refugees from counter-culture decadence. Drugs, alcohol, sex before marriage: these delights were forbidden. The attitude was appealing, predictably, to the Christian evangelical movement. The 1967 Six Day War and the 1973 Yom Kippur War, fought out by Israel and its Arab neighbours, had meanwhile given right-wing charismatic Protestants a renewed interest in any Jew who might be won for Christ. The evangelicals' obsession with imminent Armageddon – among the 'dispensationalist' wing, that is – played a very big part in encouraging a collaboration.

The Christians were afflicted by the old notion, cobbled together from two faiths, that the Jews had to possess their own country before Jesus could return and the last battle could commence. Israel therefore became essential to the promised final showdown between good and evil, even if Judaism's conception of *Acharis HaYomim*, the 'End of Days', doesn't quite accord with the fantasies of the 'Armageddon lobby'. Dylan's 1983 song 'Neighborhood Bully', defending Zionist Israel against allcomers, would be one expression of the new alliance. Israeli governments were meanwhile delighted to fund hundreds of 'familiarisation' trips to the biblical lands for evangelical pastors at a time when the Christian Right was influential in Washington. Jews prepared to accept Jesus and charismatic worship were part of a grand political bargain as the last days of this planet earth, 'rapture' and all, approached. Unswerving American conservative support for the Zionist-dominated state, it is too often forgotten, has a 'theological' basis.

In the summer of 1984, even after his supposed return to secular music, Dylan would still be confirming his belief in the literal truth of the Bible, still talking about Revelation and end times – though those had been postponed for 'at least 200 years' – and still discussing 'the new kingdom'. He would assure his interviewer that he could 'converse and find agreement with' Orthodox Jews and Christians alike.[32] Dylan's quoting of Jeremiah on the *Saved* sleeve, his song 'Covenant Woman', his public statements and much else besides, had by then provided plenty of evidence of his messianic Judaism. It was no private eccentricity. Nothing else explained his choices or his rhetoric.

In July of 2005, the Union of Messianic Jewish Congregations (UMJC), a grouping founded in 1979, significantly or not, would publish a statement attempting to define its collective beliefs. The statement would speak of 'congregations and groups committed to Yeshua the Messiah that embrace the covenantal responsibility of Jewish life and identity rooted in Torah, expressed in tradition, and renewed and applied in the context of the New Covenant'. Boldly, the UMJC would assert that together 'the Messianic Jewish community and the Christian Church constitute the ekklesia, the one Body of Messiah . . .' Further: 'Messianic Judaism embraces the fullness of New Covenant realities available through Yeshua, and seeks to express them in forms drawn from Jewish experience and accessible to Jewish people.'[33]

That might have counted as a working definition of Dylan's Christian faith were it not for the fact that, as ever, he resists definition. In the summer of 1986, for example, a slightly startling report would appear in the New York Daily News. This would state that Dylan had spent 'parts of the last four years' living and worshipping among Hasidic Jews in Crown Heights, Brooklyn. Members of the community would tell the newspaper that the artist had been 'taking instruction from Talmudic scholars and listening to talks by Lubavitcher Rebbe Menachem Schneerson'. Pressed on Dylan's activities, a spokesman for the Chabad-Lubavitch sect would reply: 'He is a very private person and we respect his wishes to remain so. You never know when he will drop in – he can come or go at any time.'[34] In fact, by that date the diarist for New York magazine had already published a small, overlooked item (on 6 June 1983) to much the same effect and received a 'no comment' from Dylan's representatives. By the end of 1983, nevertheless, one of the Lubavitch rabbis would be talking freely to Christianity Today about the 40-something student who had made his way to Brooklyn.[35]

All of this could be reconciled with messianic Judaism, no doubt, but for one difficulty. Among other things, Chabad-Lubavitch, perhaps the biggest of the Hasidic sects, styles itself as a Jewish 'outreach' operation. As such, it has devoted a good deal of its time and energy over the years to counteracting Christian missionary work among Jews. Dylan's presence in Crown Heights between 1982 and 1986 would come about as the result, direct or indirect, of a determined effort to reclaim him for Judaism. A Lubavitcher from Minnesota, one Rabbi Manis Friedman, an individual later to be condemned universally for voicing grotesque opinions on child sex abuse, would get most of the credit for waging the campaign to win the artist back for the home team.[36] Hence the widespread belief in the early 1980s – a belief not discouraged by Columbia Records – that Dylan had given up on the born-again Christianity fad and returned to his secular (if Jewish) ways.

This, though, is where things become a little more interesting. The venerable Menachem Mendel Schneerson, who would be 84 in the summer of 1986, was a determined evangelist for Judaism, but also, simultaneously, a keen promoter of efforts to 'hasten the messianic age'. By the time Dylan came to make contact with the Chabad-Lubavitch sect, many of Menachem Schneerson's followers would be proclaiming the belief, unprecedented in Judaism, that the rebbe *was* the Messiah. Within the wider faith the assertion would prove controversial, to put it no higher, but it remains the case that the sect has failed to replace its rabbi since his death in 1994 – again, a decision without precedent – while claims made for his status have accumulated, both in Israel and in America. A headstone beside his open-air mausoleum in the New York borough of Queens refers to Schneerson in Hebrew as 'the Messiah of God'. Some have further alleged that he acknowledged this supposed fact while still alive.

As it is, the idea of a dead Messiah is unthinkable to traditional Jews. In 1996, the Rabbinical Council of America passed by an overwhelming majority a resolution declaring: 'In light of disturbing developments which have arisen in the Jewish community, the Rabbinical Council of America in convention assembled declares that there is not and has never been a place in Judaism for the belief that Mashiach ben David (the Messiah, son of David) will begin his messianic mission only to experience death, burial and resurrection before completing it.'

The fact remains that by the time the *Daily News* carried its report on his four years of intermittent study and worship in Crown Heights, fully a decade before the council spoke out, Dylan would be spending a lot of his time with people who believed the Messiah was among them. In 1986, bluntly, the artist would be listening to talks from the alleged Messiah himself. So the figure of a saviour and the idea of salvation would linger in Dylan's life and thought while Chabad-Lubavitch worked to reclaim him for Judaism. Whether He turned out to be Jesus or an aged rabbi, what would matter most for the artist during and after his Vineyard interlude was this ineluctable figure, this mystery, the Messiah. In practice, it would amount to a subtle change in theological emphasis. In his interview during the summer of 1984, irrespective of the shifting balance of religious allegiances in his own mind, Dylan could sound for all the world as though he was still as one with the evangelicals on a central point of belief. As he would tell *Rolling Stone*'s Kurt Loder:

> But what's going on today isn't gonna last, you know? The battle of Armageddon is specifically spelled out: where it will be fought, and if you wanna get technical, when it will be fought. And the battle of Armageddon definitely will be fought in the Middle East.[37]

Little more than a year later, it would seem to most readers of *Spin* magazine that the bloodcurdling theme had persisted. In September 1985, Dylan would lay it all out for Scott Cohen.

> The messianic thing has to do with this world, the flesh world, and you got to pass through this to get to that. The messianic thing has to do with the world of mankind, like it is. This world is scheduled to go for 7,000 years. Six thousand years of this, where man has his way, and 1,000 years where God has his way. Just like a week. Six days works, one day rest. The last thousand years is called the Messianic Age. Messiah will rule. He is, was, will be about God, doing God's business. Drought, famine, war, murder, theft, earthquakes and all other evil things will be no more. No more disease. That's all of this world.[38]

In this interview, Dylan would recite his lessons and recite them almost word for word. The point is that these were the lessons, wholly unexceptional, of conservative Judaism, not of the Armageddon-obsessed Christian evangelicals. Talking to *Spin*, Dylan would fail to make that distinction clear. The battle at the End of Days due to be incited by Messiah refuseniks is not a major part of Jewish teaching. Instead, the passing of 6,000 years is seen almost as a stage in human development. In his telling of this version, you'll notice, Dylan would make no mention of a Technicolor apocalypse, clashing armies, mass destruction and the promised eradication of one-third of humanity. The six-from-seven schema mentioned was lifted by the fundamentalist Protestants for the seven 'dispensations' – this one is number six, of course – which an ingenious God has devised, supposedly, to run tests of obedience on humanity. But by 1985, if not before, Dylan would have transferred his allegiance to old Jewish prophecy.

He would tell Cohen that when the time came there would be 'a run on godliness', that people were 'gonna run to the Jews' for the word of God and that Jews, embroiled in worldly things, 'ain't gonna know'. That sounds like Schneerson talking. Nevertheless, thanks to the Lubavitchers, Dylan would discern an important difference between the big fireworks promised in *The Late, Great Planet Earth* and his own tradition's long-held views on the messianic age. You could equally say that he would make a choice of superstitions, that he would wind up choosing between two irrational fairy tales to make his life seem more rational. But they would be his choices.

Dylan would be consistently inconsistent in the years ahead. He does not practise systematic theology. He does favour obedience to instinct and emotion. He is as creative in the matter of fundamentalist superstition as he is in everything else. That he remains the religious fundamentalist he became in early 1979 is, meanwhile, self-evident. His habits of thought are eclectic, however. As we have seen, the Book of Revelation, a text not easily reconciled with Schneerson's teachings, far less with the rebbe's alleged status as Messiah, would go on exercising a profound fascination in all the decades to come during the long effort to unite art with faith. Dylan is a messianic Jew but, thanks to Chabad-Lubavitch, a lot more Jewish than Christian.

The singer Helena Springs, who knew him as well as anyone in 1978 and 1979, would later assert that in converting the artist was simply 'exploring Christianity. He didn't give up being a Jewish person, but he learned how to pray. And when he'd learned all he could learn, he went on to something else.'[39] These days, Dylan makes his observances in synagogues, not churches, while proclaiming his belief in Revelation to passing journalists. Just to keep professors of comparative religion on their toes, he is also the unabashed author of an album entitled *Christmas in the Heart*. As ever, he does not care who is left puzzled.

In 1979 and 1980 he would accept the Vineyard's fire-and-brimstone sermons with little apparent argument. Soon enough, nevertheless, he would begin to prowl again through the thickets and lush pastures of esoteric wisdom. It seems likely, too, that Dylan failed – and who can really blame him? – to get every version of the end-times tale straight in his head. For all that, the single, fixed messianic idea became embedded in his Judaeo-Christian thinking in 1979 and it would not shift.

You could give Dylan, or Chabad, some credit for sophistication. As it turns out, there is a way to read Revelation simply as a rewrite of old Jewish apocalyptic literature. You can make the argument, too, that one of the rewriters, stuck on an island off the Turkish coast in the first century, was a good messianic Jew whose lurid allegory was intended as propaganda to prevent the cult of rabbi Yeshua from opening itself up to Gentiles, as the apostle-apostate Paul was then demanding.[40] With all that in mind, someone who might have been burned by importuning twentieth-century evangelical Californian Protestants could these days treat Revelation as 'essentially an anti-Christian polemic' and as good Jewish literature.[41] For someone with a messianic outlook, the strange book's code – a Dylan word, if ever there was one – conceals the story of a persecuted Jew's struggle to proclaim the Messiah while remaining Jewish. The controversies over Menachem Schneerson would then be relevant. The puzzles over Bob Dylan's meandering path to faith would certainly be relevant.

A lot of points need to be stretched to reach that conclusion. For one, Dylan didn't know any of that stuff when he went under in a Santa Monica swimming pool. Mainstream Judaism finds Revelation interesting, at best, but unacceptable. There was a lot of apocalyptic literature around, in any case, when the book was being written. Many scholars meanwhile reject the anti-Christian interpretation of the text. Cut away all the possibilities and you are left with the simple fact that Dylan's top text to this day is the finale of the Christian Bible. His faith is messianic; religions are secondary.

So the joke is hardly worth resisting. One at whom the word 'messiah' had been tossed so often for the sake of irony or a tabloid headline acquired a conviction involving the alleged real deal. At the end of another strange decade Dylan was living, writing and performing as though in the last days of the world. But try explaining that to a rock and roll audience.

CHAPTER SEVEN

Wade in the Water

DYLAN COULD HAVE DONE WITH THE SERVICES OF JERRY WEXLER ON *Street-Legal*. For the want of a competent producer a great album was almost lost. With Wexler in the Muscle Shoals control room for *Slow Train Coming* a poor group of songs unlikely to bring anyone to Christ was turned into a hit record, earning Dylan a Grammy award in the process. The producer didn't deserve the entire credit – he would have no such success in his second attempt – but his presence in Sheffield, Alabama, was a reminder that the artist's approach to recording was sometimes redeemed by the intercession of a guardian angel who could sense an incipient rhythm and read a VU meter. It would take Dylan a long time to learn the lesson.

The individual whose name and face appeared on the record sleeves didn't like making records: you could call that an obstacle. He had no patience for the increasingly complex and painstaking work involved. He distrusted overdubs, headphones and all the technological voodoo. For preference, defying the evidence of his own ears when playbacks said he was making a mistake, he performed live with the band. In a radio interview in 1984 he would complain, a little extravagantly, that being in the recording studio was 'like working in a coalmine'.[1] In the spring of 1979, Wexler, the born unbeliever, a man whose personal interest in the content of Dylan's latest set of lyrics approached zero, was a godsend. For years afterwards the producer would tell the story of how the artist 'in an access of evangelism . . . pulled out the Bible and started to hit on me'. Wexler told him to forget it. Dylan was 'dealing with a confirmed 63-year-old Jewish atheist', one who had never once believed in any god, 'not for a hot minute'.[2] The artist, to his credit, 'cracked up' when he was rebuffed. You sense, nevertheless, that the producer was making a stand in this small trial of strength. His autonomy in the studio, if not his soul, was at stake.

Whatever he thought of religion, Wexler understood something about gospel. You don't produce Aretha's *Amazing Grace* (1972) unless you know a few things. If you can also claim to have invented rhythm and blues – or at least to have come up with the term while working for *Billboard* after the war – you can probably locate any studio sound required, even when the client is an eccentric poet who suddenly wants to proselytise. In reality, Wexler's deep knowledge of gospel music was not truly essential to *Slow Train Coming*, but his intuitions where the stubborn artist was concerned mattered greatly.

Dylan's new-found faith, though disconcerting, had not the slightest influence on the veteran producer during the making of the album. In fact, Wexler's lack of interest in any version of God might have been the dispassionate favour the artist needed. The additional presence of the Muscle Shoals Rhythm Section keyboard player and producer Barry Beckett was a bonus. Whatever anyone thought of the songs, no one was going to quarrel with the sound that was achieved. For Wexler and Beckett, that was a point of honour. For Dylan, with the unhappy memory of *Street-Legal's* reception still fresh, it might have been the whole idea. He could be his own worst enemy in the struggle to get the sound he wanted, but want it he did. Rock and roll's first and only poet was about to offer his fans a set of lyrics that many would find hard to swallow. He surely knew as much. An immaculate sound would act as a diversion, if not as a disguise. The sentiments in the words were impossible to disguise.

The producers were aided immeasurably, as was Dylan, by the guitar of Mark Knopfler. Many great musicians had coped with the artist, or failed to cope, over the course of 18 studio projects before *Slow Train Coming*, but the Dire Straits leader seemed from the start to have a better understanding of what he was up against than most. Knopfler had finished working with Wexler and Beckett on his band's second album, *Communiqué*, not many weeks before. At the end of March he had found himself coming under Dylan's scrutiny during the third and last Dire Straits performance in Los Angeles in the midst of a tour of Europe and America. After the show Knopfler had accepted the invitation to play on *Slow Train Coming* without hesitation, despite the fact that he and drummer Pick Withers had to be in Germany 12 days after the end of the Alabama sessions. They too would be a little taken aback by the nature of the songs on which they were expected to play.

Dylan could count himself fortunate, nevertheless, that the guitarist found the time to lend some light and shade to his album. In later years Knopfler's playing would sound mannered and self-referential, but in 1979, if your thoughts didn't run to J.J. Cale, he was the freshest thing around.

Such were to be the saving graces of *Slow Train Coming* after the muddle and mess of *Street-Legal*. Dylan would have the professionally made album he wanted, with the unimpeachable – if sometimes overly 'tasteful' – playing that might keep a certain kind of critic off his back. Wexler and Beckett would take care of the technicalities he detested. Knopfler would play with a rare, intuitive sympathy, asking questions of the melodies without burying them beneath self-aggrandising displays of virtuosity. The rest of the musicians would take their cues smoothly from the guitar. Helena Springs, Carolyn Dennis and Regina Havis would set aside any disagreements between themselves – what with one Dylan-related thing and another, Springs and Dennis were not in harmony away from the microphone – long enough to achieve the singing the artist understood as gospel. The rest was up to him.

It is possible to admire *Slow Train Coming*, in a distant sort of way, and still detest the thing. It is possible, just about, to set aside any views you might have about deities, for or against or none-of-the-above, while finding it impossible to be agnostic about the album Dylan chose to make. Many people detect no chilliness at its adamantine heart, the rest of us – correctly, of course – can sense nothing else. The singer and writer Nick Cave probably put it best in 1997 (while naming *Slow Train Coming* as his favourite album of any description). The work, Cave said, is 'full of mean-spirited spirituality. It's a genuinely nasty record, certainly the nastiest "Christian" album I've ever come across.'³ The album beloved by some is, to others among us, a gesture of artistic subordination and a specimen of arid and often puerile dogmatism. That's just for starters. Once you pause to consider Dylan's words and his delivery of those words, the hour of judgement is at hand.

There are four dozen mentions of God, Lord, Jesus, He, the Man and Christ in the 12 songs prepared for *Slow Train Coming* (nine would be used). The Devil and/or Satan gets around a dozen mentions. Pass no opinions on the theology: that's a lot. Not one of those songs achieves the annunciative power of 'The world is charged with the grandeur of God' (Gerard Manley Hopkins), or the simple purity of 'Faith – is the Pierless Bridge / Supporting what We see . . .' (Emily Dickinson). Not one song comes close, for that matter, to the radiant imagery,

Dylan-via-Poe, of 'My love she's like some raven / At my window with a broken wing'. Nothing on the album approaches the visionary expansiveness of 'I Shall Be Released'. If you take the Dylan of *Slow Train Coming* on his own terms, as a religious writer, you will listen in vain for signs of transcendence or notes of joy. Instead, the album is a narrow, confining, self-involved work that does not begin to address a straightforward creative problem: how many times can you say the same few things?

Slow Train Coming would be treated ever afterwards as the first in Dylan's 'gospel trilogy'. The assumption would be made that within a few brief years, the spiritual breezes having shifted, he simply turned his attention back to the garden of earthly delights and deliriums. That's not remotely true. 'Trilogy', equally, is stretching things where the third nominated album, *Shot of Love*, is concerned. 'Gospel' is meanwhile just a lazy way of saying religious, or of making vague reference to a stream of biblical quotations and allusions. Dylan's music, his 'gospel sound', bears only the faintest resemblance to the genre as it was understood in 1979. Gospel is and always was a broad church, but *Slow Train Coming* is a Christian rock album with inflections and affectations.

How would Dylan have proceeded in the years ahead if his allegiance to the Vineyard had endured? *Slow Train Coming* and its successor, *Saved*, would cover all the angles where his monosemous preaching was concerned. There were, after all, few enough angles to begin with. In this manifestation, religion – his version of religion – offered slim pickings for a writer. After *Slow Train Coming*, the *Saved* album would strike a great many listeners, Christian or otherwise, as redundant. You can only suspect that Dylan made a quick return to 'secular' music simply because he had nothing left to say about the meaning of religion. Any new and dramatic spiritual upheavals were incidental. 'Get saved or be damned' is not, in fact, a theme you can develop until kingdom come.

It points to a problem with what Dylan was choosing to believe in 1979. A great many religious writers in every era have managed to say plenty about the mysteries, problems and rewards of faith. This artist, fresh from his 'three and one half months' of study, was wrapping up the arguments in short order with pontifical authority. The question arose: who did he think he was, exactly? That question probably helped to explain several uncharitable reactions to the album. Many would not care for Dylan's 'Bible-thumping': so much was inevitable. But even those who were prepared to sympathise, prepared to understand that the artist was attempting to testify to a life-changing experience, couldn't help but be struck by his lack of humility. Some people spend their lives wrestling with the secrets of Scripture; study consumes their existence. Dylan considered himself learned enough to preach and lay down the law after just 14 weeks. Only a mail-order diploma would have been quicker.

No one had paid much serious attention to the religious allusions in his work before this album. Some of the references had been obvious enough, but they had failed to alter perceptions of the counter-culture's prophet. Few had heard his mother's anecdote about the big Bible kept open on the lectern at the Woodstock house throughout the writing of *John Wesley Harding*. Among those who cared before 1979 the religious motifs and borrowings had been regarded as just more leavening in the lyrical dough. But even if such details had been widely noticed or known, even if Dylan's interest in religion had been common knowledge, none of it would have qualified him to preach. Barely five months had passed between the commotion in an Arizona hotel room and the first day's attempts in the Muscle Shoals studio to nail an acceptable version of a song entitled 'Trouble in Mind'. In those few weeks Dylan had gone from being the naive soul asking about the meaning of the crucifixion to one dealing out the fundamentalist cards. He had, even by his standards, a lot of nerve and it would not go unnoticed when the album was released in August. He had set about the mysteries of religion much as he had set about mastering the folk tradition: Bob Dylan had to know, or appear to know, everything. In reality, either he had acquired a lot of scriptural knowledge on his own time – so why bother with discipleship school? – or the teachings he had absorbed in a few classes were utterly simplistic. Listen to the album.

'Trouble in Mind', the product of the first, failed Muscles Shoals session, a song assembled from biblical quotations by way of Vineyard pamphlets and Hal Lindsey's fantasy literature, is as good an example as any of Dylan's method in the writing of *Slow Train Coming*. Genesis, Jeremiah, 1 John, Luke, Matthew and the (possibly) Pauline Epistle to the Ephesians are pulled apart for lyrics. Satan as the 'prince of the power of the air', soon to be a recurring figure in Dylan's rhetoric, puts in an early appearance. The title is meanwhile lifted from a blues song that was at least half a century old by the time it suited the writer's purpose, a song covered by everyone from Victoria Spivey to Janis Joplin to Sam Cooke. It had also been recorded by Big Bill Broonzy

– Dylan's most likely inspiration – for Folkways in the mid-1950s.

So far, so Dylan. Half the songs on *John Wesley Harding* could be deconstructed according to the same crude principles. But what is achieved here? 'Trouble in Mind' would wind up, in some countries, as a B-side to the hit 'Gotta Serve Somebody', but it was neither worse nor better than most of the things on *Slow Train Coming*. All that ancient wisdom for this?

> So many of my brothers, they still want to be the boss
> They can't relate to the Lord's kingdom, they can't relate to the cross
> They self-inflict punishment on their own broken lives
> Put their faith in their possessions, in their jobs or their wives

Set aside the proposed equivalence between wives and possessions. Even Luke 12:15 doesn't make the connection, though it should be remembered that by Dylan's time fundamentalists were beginning to reject the nineteenth-century belief in families and marriages enduring eternally (and blessed they were) in the afterlife. Some among the born-again were doing away with gender, too, as a feature of the world to come. That possibility might not have been to Dylan's taste. Nevertheless, his kind of Christians were strangely silent on the subject of heaven.[4] You could excuse them for failing to describe the unknowable and indescribable. You could also suspect that they were much more interested in apocalyptic fantasies. If so, they had found their singer. Even for a non-believer, it is faintly startling to realise that in all of *Slow Train Coming* there is but one solitary mention of the promised life hereafter. In 'Gonna Change My Way of Thinking', heaven is described simply as 'A place where there is no pain of birth'. That, existentially speaking, is it. And when Dylan got the chance to rewrite the failed song decades later for Mavis Staples he expunged all mention of this paradise.

In 1979, in a musically dismal piece such as 'Trouble in Mind' and throughout the album, his concerns were narrow and contemporary, his writing grisly. 'They self-inflict punishment on their own broken lives' is a metrical abomination even by the standards of Dylan's personalised poetics. 'Broken lives' is a Vineyard-by-numbers phrase: for the church, everything in this world is 'broken'. But such is the nature of the album: lumps of Scripture go into the stew alongside desiccated fragments of an old Bob Dylan persona, shavings from evangelical tracts, a few dashes of conservative pepper and the cheaper cuts from the Lamb. It doesn't matter what you believe. The result is indigestible when it is not tasteless. *Slow Train Coming* became a hit album, but had it not been for the skills of Jerry Wexler, Beckett, Knopfler and the rest, Dylan's career would never have risen again. As it was, he had to be denied thrice by fans and critics before he began to get the message. The problem was not faith, as such, but the horrifying spectre of Bob Dylan the fanatic.

'Gotta Serve Somebody' would become the hit, Grammy-winning single. Since Dylan has elected to believe that biblical data are not to be doubted, a ponderous melody resolves itself around a single dialectic in the verses. You serve the Lord or the Devil: there is no alternative. No one would call this sermon too complex. 'Precious Angel', the best track on the album, might sound like a love song to Mary Alice Artes in thanks for her part in the artist's conversion. In fact, it turns out to be a report from the front line in the 'spiritual warfare' favoured by those who espouse kingdom theology. This Dylan, unlike every previous version, does not risk ambiguity: 'Ya either got faith or ya got unbelief and there ain't no neutral ground.' 'I Believe in You', a lachrymose affair, sets Bob the Believer in the evangelical Christian's favourite pose as the victim of ignorance and scorn. Those hoping for the best would later attempt to reimagine the item as a set of verses with a dual meaning, personal and spiritual. The interpretation would fail.

> I believe in you when winter turn to summer
> I believe in you when white turn to black
> I believe in you though I be outnumbered
> Oh, though the earth may shake me
> Oh, though my friends forsake me
> Oh, even that couldn't make me go back

Self-pity, an abiding if occasional weakness in this artist, never makes for a good noise. In 'I Believe in You', as elsewhere on *Slow Train Coming*, Dylan's writing wilts under the pressure of his determination to be right with God in all things save syntax, imagery and metaphor. In 'When You Gonna Wake Up?' and 'Slow Train', meanwhile, the old ruses of the protest singer are revived shamelessly for the sake of reductive arguments that would have gratified candidate Reagan. Dylan was as entitled to his opinions as he was to deploy cheap politics, that 'instrument of the Devil'. Still, the purely Christian justification for 'Slow Train' remains difficult to state.

WADE IN THE WATER

All that foreign oil controlling American soil
Look around you, it's just bound to make you embarrassed
Sheiks walkin' around like kings
Wearing fancy jewels and nose rings
Deciding America's future from Amsterdam and to Paris

'When You Gonna Wake Up?' is explicit. The state of the nation – dire, of course – is here described as a direct consequence of the failure to understand why the 'Man up on a cross' died. Reagan and most of those who had created Reagan, the Religious Right, the Moral Majority and the entire conservative insurgency, would not have demurred from any of it. Such was their default argument in every policy debate. Lack of faith, in Dylan's song, means

You got men who can't hold their peace and women who can't control
   their tongues
The rich seduce the poor and the old are seduced by the young

Thanks to America's failure to wake up and heed the Word, a noted adulterer then sings histrionically of

Adulterers in churches and pornography in the schools
You got gangsters in power and lawbreakers making rules

In several senses save the important one, *Slow Train Coming* remains a breathtaking piece of work. Dylan even elects to frighten the children and encourage a few Creationists with 'Man Gave Names to All the Animals', an Edenic little comic song whose sole purpose, it seems, is to get the serpent into paradise and invite infants to guess the name of the creature blighting their born-sinful little lives. For some, Sunday school is eternal punishment. It is not a track you would want on your conscience, far less on your CV. As an attempt to lighten the mood of the album it feels like what it is, a contrivance with a preconceived purpose.

Nothing daunted, Dylan decides to end the set with a personal challenge to the Antichrist. Who can stand, after all, against a vengeful Bob? In fact, the pilgrim gives a fine and heartfelt performance on 'When He Returns'. The song also involves the best-written set of verses on *Slow Train Coming*, though that isn't saying a great deal. The track does make a real connection, however, between Christ's Dylan and all the Dylans who went before. The argument, as in so many earlier and better works, is between truth and deceit.

How long can you falsify and deny what is real?
How long can you hate yourself for the weakness you conceal?

All will be resolved – cue that refrain – when He returns. Somehow, nevertheless, even familiar Dylan questions are enfeebled by the purpose to which here they are put. They are no longer his questions. *Slow Train Coming* sees an artist abdicate art's duty to truth in deference to a higher power. Such was the baptismal transaction, freely accepted. At times on the album, when he is not snarling theatrically in a calculated simulation of old performances, Dylan seems almost relieved to be handing over the job of deciding what is false and what is real. There is an irony in that. Christianity had indeed relieved him of many burdens. It had stilled the buzzing noise of perplexity and human variety. What is missing from the nine songs chosen for *Slow Train Coming* is any sense whatever of life's complexity, any evidence of doubt or difficulty, any suggestion that faith can be perplexing. Once you see what Dylan is about – after 30 seconds or so – everything that follows on the album is predictable. Those who wrestle with faith tend to tell you that the struggle is never simple. The writer of *Slow Train Coming* disagrees. In consequence, there is nothing surprising or challenging in the songs. His God, set in His ways, was not the best writing partner Bob Dylan ever came across.

*

Bob Dylan at Budokan had been released just a week before the first of the *Slow Train Coming* sessions. Recorded over two nights near the start of the 1978 world tour, it had captured only the faintest hints of the music Dylan and his band would achieve once they hit their stride on that expedition, but neither he nor the record company had worried about misrepresentation. The double album had appeared in Japan and Australasia, the markets for which it had been conceived, fully eight months before Dylan arrived in the Muscle Shoals studio, but a flood of imports and a couple of bootlegs had concentrated Columbia's finest minds. No one had paused to wonder if another live album was justified barely a year and a half after *Hard Rain*. It would not be the last time that Dylan's reputation would suffer thanks to a casual attitude towards concert souvenirs.

Several reviewers had been dumbfounded by what seemed to be – and in certain cases were – *Budokan's* wilfully kitsch arrangements. Few had given Dylan credit for adopting an audacious approach to what was, in essence, another greatest-hits package. In Britain, where the 1978 tour had been welcomed as revelatory, there had been mystification (the album still reached number four in the charts) followed by unease. In America, all the 'Vegas lounge act' jibes had been heard again, helped along by photographs that appeared to show Dylan honouring the dress sense, if not the spirit, of late Elvis. Almost alone, *Rolling Stone's* Janet Maslin had been brave enough to say that, overall, she liked the thing. She had called the double album 'a shock, a sacrilege and an unexpectedly playful bonanza'. *At Budokan* was 'spotty', Maslin had conceded, but liberating for artist and audience alike. Then the journalist had picked exactly the wrong words to explain this latest 'new Dylan'. Given the story that was about to unfold, she could not have been more mistaken. 'The fire and brimstone are behind Dylan,' Maslin had written, 'if only because his adolescence, and that of his principal audience, are things of the past.'[5] Brimstone and fire were about to become gluts on the Dylan market. The artist was aflame with his new beliefs. By the second week in May, the tedium of overdubs behind him, he had a record to prove it. Finally he would be telling the world nothing but God's honest truth.

A couple of cruciform images – a pickaxe, a telegraph pole – would dominate the finished album's sleeve. Dylan paid close attention to the design. The record's title was meanwhile a straightforward evocation of numerous holy rolling trains in the American musical landscape, from Curtis Mayfield's 1965 hit 'People Get Ready' – a song Dylan and The Band had attempted back in the Woodstock basement – to the old standard 'This Train'. A spiritual entitled 'The Gospel Train' had made the salvation express a key part of American revivalist iconography as far back as the 1870s, though the idea was older: Nathaniel Hawthorne had published his parodic short story 'The Celestial Railroad' in 1843. A century later, Woody Guthrie had borrowed from 'This Train' for his semi-autobiographical *Bound for Glory* (1943), while Sister Rosetta Tharpe had set about the song with her electric guitar in the early '50s, helping rock and roll, the devil's latest music, on its way. Dylan would broadcast that version on his *Theme Time Radio Hour* show in the middle of the twenty-first century's first decade, when he and the world were older.

The nearest ancestor to his own 'Slow Train' was probably Guthrie's adapted/borrowed 'Little Black Train', a tune Woody had recorded for the pioneering folk promoter Moses 'Moe' Asch in 1944.[6] That song warns bar-room gamblers against trying to cheat their way through life and tells 'silken bar-room ladies' that 'worldly pride' will do them no good when the time comes for the 'final ride'. All that can be done, as Dylan's song also argues, is to 'get ready for your savior'. In one of the sometimes-sung variant verses of 'Little Black Train' we hear of a young man 'who cared not for the gospel light, until suddenly the whistle blew from the little black train in sight'. The train-as-metaphor had exercised a fascination for many nineteenth-century Americans as they contemplated their place amid the vastness of a newly claimed country. The railroad was an obvious symbol of the 'straight and narrow path' as passengers were carried inexorably along thanks to an all-powerful engineer and a benign conductor.[7]

In the summer of 1979 there was nothing even slightly ironic about Dylan's album, its title, or the drawing on its sleeve of an antique train arriving in a frontier landscape while the track is still being prepared by a pioneering evangel with a cross-shaped pickaxe. Dylan was immune to doubt. Rumours of his conversion were beginning to emerge, but disclosure had only ever been a matter of time. His choice would be believe-it-or-not news far beyond the little world of rock music. At the end of May, while the artist was dealing with the lawsuit brought by Ms Patty Valentine over her appearance in 'Hurricane' – and dropping Satan's name into his deposition before the hearing – Kenn Gulliksen felt able to share the glad tidings with the *Washington Post*. Whether the pastor had been authorised to do so is an interesting question, but at the time it hardly mattered. Dylan had already begun to make plans to take his new songs out on the road. He had no intention of trying to hide. Gulliksen would soon be among the first of the Vineyarders to deny that pressure had been applied on the singer to perform only religious material in his concerts. That was, they would say, entirely his own idea.

One simple fact needs to be borne in mind: *Slow Train Coming*, the work of the long-derided born-again Bob Dylan, would be a big success, his last truly successful album in America for a very long time to come. In its first year on release it would sell more quickly than *Blood on the Tracks*. The evangelical album would be certified platinum – one million copies sold in the US – within only nine months. *Blood*, the masterpiece 'everyone bought', supposedly, would not achieve that status until the end of the '80s.

Given the usual depiction of Dylan's conversion to Christianity as a three-act tragedy for his reputation, the initial commercial success of that 'mean-spirited spirituality' counts as puzzling. It cannot be argued, for one thing, that *Slow Train Coming* owed its popularity to America's religious revival. Conservative church-goers remained to be convinced, at the very least, that music so long synonymous with sin could have redeeming qualities. The words might be fine and well – if you could make them out – but temptation lurked down in the grooves and in the inflaming coital rhythm. Dylan, the Jewish convert so recently identified with left-wing causes, could not count on those believers. Besides, the success of *Slow Train Coming* would not be confined to America. The album would reach number three in the US, but number two in the UK, where the Christian evangelical market was never, to put it kindly, the biggest in all creation.

When *Slow Train Coming* entered the US album charts in September, those who were dismayed or disgusted by its unforgiving preaching could take their pick. Either people liked the record and accepted the sentiments, or they liked the noise and, sadly for the Christian Dylan and his critics alike, didn't give a damn about what was being said. In any event it is a mistake to allow the reactions of a few disdainful reviewers, then or now, to obscure the facts. We should not be distracted either by subsequent events in Dylan's born-again career. On its release *Slow Train Coming* was more popular by far than a lot of his albums.

He had reason to be optimistic, then, as he began tour rehearsals at the end of August. If the mood took him, he was entitled to believe that he was, of all things, the voice of a generation once more and the leading shining light of a genuine movement. Just not *that* generation, or *that* movement. Whether he understood that he was accepting the kind of spokesman's role he had rejected back in the '60s is a still unanswered question. Perhaps, instead, Dylan knew he was about to be tested sorely. Such was a true believer's lot, after all. Whatever happened, he meant to put out the Word.

His second decade as a writer and performer was drawing to a close. You can only wonder if he could still recognise himself. Or rather, you wonder which self he still recognised. Whatever else it signified, the first, hot flush of Christian belief amounted to a willed amnesia in an individual whose habit of selective recall had become ingrained in his youth. Forget all the glib talk, still persistent, of masks, 'reinvention', superstar games and role-playing. By 1979, Dylan had set aside at least half a dozen complete identities. The acceptance of Christ, accomplished with relief and little hesitation after the busted marriage, the bad recreational habits, the endless womanising, the creative confusion, the relentless pressure of impossible expectations and the sheer ennui that is the default state of genius, was an attempt at absolute eradication. What else could it be? By definition, you had to be extinguished as a person in order to be born again.

The religious experience required to achieve that state might have been as old as humankind, but in 1979 the phrase was of recent origin. Jimmy Carter had attracted a lot of media attention just by describing himself as 'born again' while running for the presidency in 1976. Dylan, you suspect, grasped the idea instantly. It was, after all, a sanctified version of what he had always done. Clearly, the question he did not ask himself when he underwent baptism was whether it was truly possible to erase a person and start again. The faith of his forefathers said that it was impossible for anyone born Jewish to cease to be a Jew. Typically, Dylan would not be deterred from making the attempt, whatever the critics or anyone else said about his new songs.

What the critics actually said was more or less predictable. The reviewer for Britain's *Melody Maker* commenced as he meant to go on by announcing, as though passing sentence, 'Dylan has switched roles once too often.'[8] This time around, 'Dylan as a Bible-puncher is just too much to swallow.' Several other writers found the views expressed on the album as unpleasant as the splenetic manner of their expression. The contrast between sheer intolerance and professions of faith in a religion founded on love was mentioned more than once. The artist's newly conservative politics – from one who had supposedly turned his back on political causes – did not go unnoticed. In New York, John Lennon caught 'Gotta Serve Somebody' on local radio in the first week of September. The domesticated former Beatle sneered at Dylan serving as Christ's flunkey. Lennon, in those days talking mostly to himself, called the track's production mediocre, the vocal performance pathetic and the words 'just embarrassing'.

Writing in the magazine *New West*, Greil Marcus gave some initial credit to the professionalism behind the album's music and to Dylan's singing, but observed, 'What we're faced with here is really very ugly.' There was nothing new about the use of religious imagery in the artist's work, Marcus explained, but here it was being employed just to sell a received and 'pre-packaged doctrine'. In *Slow Train Coming* the mysteries of revealed religion were reduced to a brutish proposition: 'Jesus is the answer and if you don't believe it, you're fucked.' Inadvertently or not, the critic confirmed Dylan's declaration in 'Precious Angel': 'there ain't no neutral ground'. Marcus retorted that the artist was 'falsely settling all questions' by claiming 'that redemption is a simple affair'. The review concluded:

> American piety is a deep mine and, in the past, without following any maps, Dylan has gone into it and returned with real treasures: *John Wesley Harding* is the best example, but there are many others. *Slow Train Coming* strips the earth and what it leaves behind is wreckage.[9]

Perhaps surprisingly, Dylan was not entirely friendless. *Rolling Stone's* editor, Jann Wenner – who was not necessarily the best critic Jann Wenner ever hired – decided that *Slow Train Coming* qualified for the 'best since' laurel, that honour granted traditionally by any reviewer who can't quite decide how to evaluate a disconcerting Dylan album. On this occasion Wenner concluded, for reasons he neglected to explain, that *Slow Train Coming* was the very best thing Dylan had managed since *The Basement Tapes*. The editor had listened to the new album 'at least 50 times' and failed to cure himself of the conviction 'that it might even be considered his greatest'. Dylan's work was at risk of being damned with loud praise. This was the 'overwhelming' record 'that's been a long time coming, with an awesome, sudden stroke of transcendent and cohesive visions'. Wenner ended his two-page review with the immortal sentence 'I am hearing a voice.'[10] The editor liked it, then. On the other hand, he was far from alone. Few of those who hated the born-again maker of the million-selling *Slow Train Coming* would ever ponder that mystery, far less explain it.

The band selected to join the artist on tour was composed of safe choices and, in the main, stout Christians. Jim Keltner was a reliable if predictable drummer, so reliable he turned up on every other superstar session (former Beatles a speciality) during the 1970s. Dewey 'Spooner' Oldham was a Muscles Shoals keyboard player and songwriter with an impressive pedigree who was hired on Jerry Wexler's recommendation. Tim Drummond, the bassist and sole non-believer in the group, was another of the producer's choices, one who had helped to give *Slow Training Coming* its rhythmic solidity. Fred Tackett, already a contributor to Little Feat's music, was no Mark Knopfler as a guitarist, but he was no slouch. In essence, this was a band of session players, trustworthy pros, but Dylan was sticking with the belief that nothing musical would be left to chance. On this occasion the artist's requirements as to 'gospel' would be fulfilled by the singers Regina Havis, Helena Springs and Monalisa Young. Next to faith, professionalism was Dylan's new favourite word.

After five or so weeks of sometimes chaotic rehearsals, the ensemble's first performance, bizarrely, was on the tiresome TV comedy sketch show *Saturday Night Live* on 18 October. With Bill Murray pulling his knowing faces, strange Andy Kaufman challenging women in the audience to wrestling matches and Monty Python's Eric Idle acting in the vague role of 'host', Dylan and his band performed 'Gotta Serve Somebody', 'I Believe in You' and 'When You Gonna Wake Up?' Perhaps in an effort to kill off the 'Vegas' jokes once and for all, the artist appeared in a short pale-blue jerkin so inoffensive he could have been taken for a janitor. Judging by the tape, his New York audience were not exactly roused to a revivalist fervour by the new songs. That, however, was the real puzzle of born-again Dylan. What did he expect? Asking people to heed nine religious songs on a single album was one thing. Insisting that they listen to nothing but his brand of 'gospel' through entire concerts when he had a back catalogue overflowing with vastly better work was either brave, deluded, or presumptuous. Nevertheless, that was to be the deal when the tour opened at the Warfield on Market and 6th streets in San Francisco on 1 November.

Contrary to certain legends, there were some good nights on the first of Dylan's 'gospel tours'. Four shows in Santa Monica *after* the Warfield run went down very well indeed. Even in San Francisco, it stretched credulity to suggest that every last person paying $12.50 for a ticket to the old theatre was outraged, or even disappointed. The concerts had sold out quickly and completely. After Joel Selvin's review in the *San Francisco Chronicle* on 3 November locals preparing to attend the 12 remaining shows could have been under no illusions about what to expect. *Slow Train Coming* was a bestseller; 'Gotta Serve Somebody' had been given a lot of airplay. Those who can take the lumbering songs argue further, rightly, that the artist and his band performed immaculately in these winter concerts. Just as in 1966, when every last stop on a world tour was depicted fancifully as a blood-curdling confrontation between artist and audience, most of those who would afterwards claim to have been affronted by Dylan's god-awful gospel had paid good money for the privilege. People are strange, but not entirely, collectively perverse. The artist and his musicians were certainly put to trial by ordeal by some audiences, but Dylan would have a point – up to a point – when in 1985 he blamed Selvin's review and others like it as the badmouthing that 'hurt us at the box office'.

In 1979 I went out on tour and played no song that I had ever played before live. It was a whole different show, and I thought that was a pretty amazing thing to do. I don't know any other artist who has done that, has not played whatever they're known for . . . Yet it got all kinds of negative publicity. The negative publicity was so hateful it turned a lot of people off from making up their own minds.[11]

Clearly, group prayers before performances and the ministrations of Larry Myers did not quite have the desired effect. The Vineyard's point man had been assigned to Dylan as a kind of personal chaplain or spiritual chaperone for the tour. If you believe one version of events, the artist himself had requested the pastor's company. Like Gulliksen, Myers would ever afterwards deny having interfered with the singer's decisions and claim, in fact, to have given all the pre-conversion hits a clean bill of health on Christ's behalf. In fact, Dylan seems to have needed no reassurances on that score. He had no intention of performing any of the songs he was 'known for'. To all appearances, the art he had made in his old life held no interest for him. With *Slow Train Coming* barely arrived in the stores, he had begun to write still more songs affirming his relationship with the deity. The new work was being 'shared' with Myers as it came to fruition, but there is no evidence that the pastor aspired to become God's answer to Jacques Levy. Whether he kept an absolute vow of silence in all things is another matter. What does a spiritual adviser do if not advise? The songs would not amount to much, in any case, in the great scheme of Dylan, but such bursts of creativity were always sure signs that he was preoccupied with the task at hand.

He didn't say a great deal to audiences during the first few shows in San Francisco. The catcalls and booing reported by Joel Selvin brought no response until the fourth night, when Dylan announced through the fug of dope hanging over the crowd that 'we all know we're living in the end of the end of times. So you'll need something strong to hang on to.' Much the same line was repeated on the next two nights, but Dylan said little else. On 10 November he stated: 'The rabble says the preaching of the cross is foolishness. To those who perish [it is], but to those who are saved it is the power of God.'

It was proof that the artist had changed somewhat, but it hardly amounted to a full-scale, thundering sermon. If it had been on Dylan's mind to preach, he took a while to warm up. In reality, the apocalyptic little speeches that would overshadow the music on this tour, the 'gospel raps' or 'Jesus raps' as aficionados describe them, were in many cases the artist's righteous responses to what he took to be provocation. When it came to spreading true religion, he was no rock and roll John Donne, no amplified Jonathan Edwards. He wasn't even a poor man's Billy Graham. To begin with, a declaration that the End of Days is upon us and the occasional assurance that 'God don't make promises He don't keep' were about the extent of Dylan's excursions into theology. Only on the 14th did it become clear that the former topical singer had revived one of his old Greenwich Village writing tricks and begun to delve into the daily papers for inspiration. Fifty-two Americans had been taken hostage in their country's Iranian embassy on 4 November. The fact, shocking enough in itself, became a part of Dylan's text for the remainder of the tour, but only as the basis for an injunction to audiences to ignore the trivia of this world. Once again, compassion went missing.

> We read about all the trouble, you know Iran, Great Britain, Russia, Red China and the United States. But we're not going to be bothered by all that because we know the world is going to be destroyed and we look forward to the approach of the Second Coming. And if the gospel is hid it is hidden to those that are lost. So anyway, we're hanging on now to a stronger rock. One made before the foundation of the world. That real, that true . . .'

On the next night, Dylan elaborated just a little with 'Christ will set his kingdom up for a thousand years; we know that it's true. So it's a slow train coming, but it's picking up speed.' The train, set rolling nightly with real gospel songs from the backing vocalists, would never truly leave North America. In fact, it would not be until April of 1980 and the third of the born-again tours that Dylan would risk performances in Canada and his old stamping-grounds on the Eastern Seaboard. Europe would not be considered until the summer of 1981, but the concerts that year would illustrate the kind of reception Dylan might have faced had he turned up at Earls Court with just hot gospel and 'played no song that I had ever played before live'. Only nine of the twenty-five songs he would perform in London on the first night – 26 June 1981 – would be drawn from the 'gospel trilogy'. There would be lots of old favourites in the set. But there would still be a great many empty seats in the godforsaken Earls Court barn after slow ticket sales and rumours of cancellations.

On the last night in San Francisco, nevertheless, there was evidence that even in that bastion of sinful American liberalism not every customer was alienated by the Religious Right's singing preacher. The shock among the first-night audience when it became clear that God was all they were going to get had dissipated. On one bootleg from 16 November, the cry 'God loves you, Bobby!' can be heard from the crowd. An artist who is clearly at ease is interrupted three times over by applause as he introduces 'Slow Train' and chats about 'what a horrible situation this world is in' and how 'God chooses the foolish things in this world to confound the wise'. Then it's back to global destruction and Christ establishing His thousand-year kingdom, lion bedding down with lamb, slow train coming. *Pace* the *San Francisco Chronicle*, Dylan is delighted with this night's audience. 'Have you heard that before?' he asks of the millennial prophecy. Applause is his response. 'Have you heard that before?' More applause. 'I'm just curious to know: how many believe that?' The last question is greeted with still more applause. Later in the show, Dylan can be heard thanking 'all you people for all the letters and all the cards and all the encouragement'. He even declares that he loves San Francisco, despite there being 'a lot of things wrong with it'.

Interviewed 20 years later, the band's organist, Spooner Oldham, would confirm that the roughest nights in San Francisco were at the very start of the run. He would reckon that for the first three nights half the audience had been perfectly willing to applaud while the other half did their booing. Oldham, though he failed to notice the walkouts that certainly took place, would also mention protests outside the theatre, 'folks out in the parking lot with placards'. After the opening nights, however, things calmed down: 'all the rebels didn't come back, or accepted it'.[12]

In addition to the songs from *Slow Train Coming*, Dylan had been giving the Warfield audiences the largest part of a whole new album during these shows. Titles such as 'Saved', 'Solid Rock', 'Saving Grace', 'Covenant Woman', 'In the Garden', 'What Can I Do for You?' and 'Pressing On' didn't require much elucidation. Whatever they meant to San Francisco's paying customers, they were patently what the Vineyard crowd, clustered backstage nightly like virtuous groupies, had ordered. Or so you might assume. Their consistent claim would be that they played no part in deciding the nature of the concerts. Given that they were an energetically evangelical bunch whose avowed purpose was to save souls for Christ, not least the souls of dope-smoking Californians, that doesn't seem to make much sense. But even if the godly didn't try to tell Dylan his business, at least one witness believed the Vineyard's 'Jesus-type people' were 'pressuring him about a lot of things'. As Helena Springs would remember, 'They were not allowing him to live. I remember one time he said to me, "God, it's awfully tight. It's so tight, you know?" He found a lot of hypocrisy in those Jesus people that he had gotten involved with.'[13]

If that's the case – and who knows? – perhaps it is worth thinking twice about the claim by Larry Myers and others from his church that Dylan alone was responsible for the decision to perform only religious songs on the tour. Let's say the assertion is as honest as you would expect from a pastor. The implication is, therefore, that the Vineyard, a church well versed in the use of pop-type music, was more than happy for Dylan to sing all the big hits. If that is the case, the church's leadership might not have been wholly delighted to see their most famous convert refusing to perform his most famous songs, the ones that caught and held all those millions of fans. The dire 'negative publicity' for god-awful gospel of which Dylan would complain was no aid to a church on a recruitment mission from God and a church, moreover, that had no desire to be perceived as odd, sectarian or extreme by mainstream America.

The artist was valuable to the Vineyard because of his immortal soul – what could have counted for more? – but his fame and the songs that had made him famous were worth something too. You can only pause to wonder about the enthusiasm these LA evangelicals might have summoned if a homeless hobo Dylan had wandered in off the street with a beat-up old guitar and begun to sing about his precious angel. Such, though, was the nature of celebrity Christianity and religion's dalliance with rock music at the end of the 1970s. What you were mattered to the Lord, but who you were counted for a lot among those engaged on a membership drive for the Jesus lifestyle choice. The situation was not beneficial, necessarily, to either party.

After San Francisco, Santa Monica was easy. The four shows there were staged as benefits for the evangelical Christian relief charity World Vision International. The audiences were therefore predisposed, to put no fine points on the matter, to welcome the songs and anything else the star might have to say. After all, some of them inclined to the notion that anything popping into the head of a true believer was liable to be divinely inspired. The Vineyard types, led by Kenn Gulliksen, were out in force to provide impeccably moral support. Dylan seemed to be buoyed by the atmosphere generated by those he took to be of his kind and mind. His statements, those 'Jesus raps', thus began to pass beyond the outer fringes of common Christian discourse.

On the first night, 18 November, he said: 'I don't know what kind of God you believe in, but I believe in a God that can raise the dead. Will raise the dead, does raise the dead, all the time.' On the second night, he became garrulous, not to say delirious, as though each piece of his new esoteric wisdom was swirling brightly if confusedly in his head. Dylan wasn't quite talking in tongues – he had already written 'Mr. Tambourine Man' – but there was a strange, ecstatic quality to the way he spoke about the world's coming end. In part, he said:

> All these sad stories that are floating around. We're not worried about any of that. We don't care about the atom bomb, any of that, 'cause we know this world is going to be destroyed and Christ will set up His Kingdom in Jerusalem for a thousand years, where the lion will lie down with the lamb.
>
> You know, the lion will eat straw that day. Also, if a man doesn't live to a hundred years old he will be called accursed. That's interesting, isn't it? And we don't mind, we know that's coming. And if any man have not the spirit of Christ in him, he is a slave to bondage. So you need something just a little bit tough to hang on to.
>
> This song's called 'Hanging On to a Solid Rock Made Before the Foundation of the World'. And if you don't have that to hang on to, you better look into it.

The tour as it unfolded had this much in common with '66: the star did not take kindly to being heckled. His sense of Christian charity had its limits; his humility was never his distinguishing feature; his temper was not always mastered easily. Whatever he liked to pretend, years of stardom had left Dylan with one near-unconscious habit of mind: he was accustomed to people hanging on his every word. When he spoke, they listened. They listened to anything and everything he had to say. By 1979 he had spent years rebuffing their demands for his words of wisdom. He could handle that pressure. What he could not handle were jibes, jeers and the impertinent souls who refused to heed him or his tidings. Bob Dylan himself, to whom all attended, was bringing news of Jesus: who could be deaf to that? Who could abuse the messenger or the message? Quite a few, as it turned out. In 1966, stoned (but not in that sense) and embattled, the artist had developed some well-honed put-downs, often comical, for dealing with those who rejected the electric heresy. In 1979, he was often at a loss when Scripture failed to do the trick. Sometimes he got furious. Whether he was angry on his own or on Christ's behalf it is hard to say.

By the recorded sound of things, Tempe in Arizona was the worst. Once again you wonder what possessed – in the mundane sense – a bunch of college students to fork over their cash when by then every fan or casual listener knew all about Dylan and his God. By the last week in November the artist's determination to devote his concerts to religious music was no longer news. At the University of Arizona's Grady Gammage Memorial Auditorium they bought their tickets regardless and made a den for Daniel.

As before, there were some happy enough to applaud Dylan's preaching. The noise generated by the rest – hooting, bellowing, calling repeatedly for 'rock and roll!' – in the end caused the star attraction to have the house lights turned up. 'I wanna see these people,' he said with a familiar sneer. On the second night, the reception was deemed to be so unrelentingly hostile Dylan refused to play his usual encores. Instead, he gave the crowd a good five minutes of a 'rap' involving the Antichrist and a false (but unnamed) guru before 'When You Gonna Wake Up?'. The sin of this 'false deceiver' from the Far East (or thereabouts) was to tell his followers that 'what life's all about is life is to have fun'. Not in Dylan's book it wasn't. When his audience shouted for rock and roll, he replied: 'You wanna rock 'n' roll, you can go down and rock 'n' roll! You can go see Kiss! You rock 'n' roll all your way down to the pit!'

An introduction to 'Solid Rock' (still being called 'Hanging On to a Solid Rock Made Before the Foundation of the World') became a still longer disquisition on, variously, the woman taken in adultery, the Devil's status as 'the God of this world' and the state of the American nation as judgement approached. Viewed dispassionately, statement by statement, Dylan was raving. He delivered himself of his thoughts in even tones, but the thoughts were tangential to known reality, a stream of higher consciousness, an interior monologue that somehow had escaped into the world. At one point he said:

Every time God comes against a nation, first of all he comes against their economy. If that doesn't work, he comes against their ecology. It ain't nothing new that's happening. He did it with Egypt. He did it with Persia. He did it with Babylon. He did it with the whole Middle East. It's desert now; it used to be flourishing gardens. All right. If that don't work, if that don't work, he just brings up another nation against them. So one of those three things has got to work.

Now, Jesus Christ is that solid rock. He's supposed to come two times. He came once already. See, that's the thing. He's been here already. Now, He's coming back again. You gotta be prepared for this. Because, no matter what you read in the newspapers, that's all deceit. The real truth is that He's coming back already.

And you just watch your newspapers. You're gonna see, maybe two years, maybe three years, five years from now, you just watch and see. Russia will come down and attack in the Middle East. China's got an army of 200 million people. They're gonna come down in the Middle East. There's gonna be a war called the Battle of Armageddon which is like some war you never even dreamed about. And Christ will set up His kingdom. He will set up his kingdom and He'll rule it from Jerusalem. I know, as far out as that might seem, this is what the Bible says.

'Five years from now' have come and gone, of course. The Russia of which Dylan spoke, meaning the Soviet Union, has also expired, replaced by a disobliging Orthodox Christian oligarch state. The Middle East remains in desperately bad shape, as ever, but the evangelical prophecies tacked on to the historical fact of modern Israel's founding are utterly threadbare. Dire pulp fictions such as the interminable *Left Behind* series have made their millions and had their moment. Trusting and devout readers are still waiting to be raptured. Dylan, like the world, has moved on, in his case thanks mostly to Chabad-Lubavitch. If he has learned anything as a messianic Jew it is that time-limited predictions – two years, three years, five years – are a very bad idea. In 1979, obedient to the spirit moving within him, he was shooting his mouth off with the best of the prophetic evangelicals and trying to put the fear of a wrathful God into students who didn't want to know. They might have been what he called 'a rude bunch', but they were a bunch who knew the difference between his great songs and his religious songs. He preached on regardless, his voice a self-satisfied drone that would not be stilled.

Despite all this – indeed, because of it – the audience kept up its racket. Several people had the temerity to shout, more than once, that

Dylan – Bob Dylan – should just shut up. At one point a born wit called out 'Praise the Lord with puke!' Again and again, they demanded rock and roll. One way or another, the sermons were pointless. The artist was talking to himself.

It could be argued, fairly, that Tempe was an exceptional case, that even during these shows the hecklers were noisy but not necessarily a majority. As had happened with the protesters at the Manchester Free Trade Hall in 1966, the vociferous students of Arizona U probably drew attention to themselves and earned a hellish reputation for the entire tour. When evangelicals or open-minded fans turned out – as they did on the next two nights at the Golden Hall in San Diego – Dylan often found welcome support. It remained the case, nevertheless, that the Tempe audiences spoke and scoffed for many as the decade drew to a close. Either they had no interest in what the artist was peddling, or they despised it. Dylan was transgressing the unwritten rule that said 'rock and roll' – he rarely played any such thing – must come first and last. Music for its own sake was the shared article of faith, and religion wasn't necessarily the offending issue. If he had devoted his songs and speeches to a purely political cause Dylan would probably have received much the same treatment in Tempe as he got for sermonising. Religion, his unforgiving brand of religion, didn't help, however.

He was planning to make still another album in a break between concerts. It was not a good idea. A worse idea was to set about recording and releasing another set of born-again songs less than a year after *Slow Train Coming*. On the one hand, Dylan could tell himself that the first of his Christian works had achieved impressive sales. On the other hand, the concerts in Tempe and elsewhere should have shown him that the market for his evangelical goods was strictly limited. What good would he be to Christ – or to the Vineyard, as his pastors no doubt calculated – if he alienated his core audience? The last thing he needed, in either event, was a lousy album. *Saved* would be beyond saving.

Ten studio albums had been released in his name in the 1970s along with ten vinyl sides of concert recordings and two 'greatest-hits' packages (though *Masterpieces*, it is true, had only been released officially in Japan and Australasia). In under five years seven pieces of Bob Dylan product had found their way to market. You could say he had been hearteningly prolific. You could also say that he and his record company were testing the theory that the public's appetite for

Dylan was unlimited. They were also putting to the test the proposition that an artist famous for never repeating himself could inflict as many startling transformations as he liked on record-buyers without suffering any sort of adverse reaction. The 1970s had begun with the baffling shock of *Self Portrait*. The decade had encompassed the luminous art of *Blood on the Tracks*, the radical experiments of Rolling Thunder and the blurred visions of *Street-Legal*. It was ending with Dylan in the role of a prophetic Christian evangelist. So package that *oeuvre* as a branded back catalogue. One way or another, it was a lot for the dedicated fan, far less the average record-buyer, to take in.

By the decade's end, in any case, the music industry had changed, but Dylan had not been responsible for those changes. In that fact lay the clear distinction between his 1960s and his 1970s. In the latter decade he had simply gone his own way. He had achieved number-one albums in his homeland, three of them, for the first time in his career. His inimitable music and his perplexing reputation still fascinated his contemporaries. Yet by 1979 it was difficult, even impossible, to claim that Dylan's work still lay at the heart – or anywhere close to the heart – of contemporary music. Religion and the controversies over religion had made it plain: he was no longer vital to what was going on in wider society. Who was selling records out there? America had got the hang, finally, of punk, but the acts shifting units in conspicuous quantities were the likes of Supertramp, Dire Straits, Van Halen, Elvis Costello, The Police, The Eagles, Led Zeppelin, Pink Floyd, Tom Petty and the Heartbreakers, and the purveyors of disco. Several of those acts and artists owed a great deal to Dylan, but by the decade's end he was detached utterly from them and, increasingly, from the audiences they served. Even the singer-songwriters he had helped to create, for better or worse, were lost to self-regard and introspection. Dylan did not partake of their kind of solipsistic pop. He had long been indefinable. The risk, real and present, was that he would become irrelevant.

The point was approaching when a new Dylan record would cease to be an event. That point was closer, in fact, than he could have realised. The derisive reviews he could expect by the decade's end, even from the once loyal *Rolling Stone*, were a sign of the times. Dylan was no longer indulged. It was no longer taken for granted, eccentric though the notion had been to begin with, that his every word and deed was of lasting import. If anything, thanks to the 'Vegas' slurs on the reputation of the '78 tour and the relentless sermons in *Slow Train*

Coming and his new songs, he was distrusted. Reviewers did not so much criticise his work but, increasingly, dismiss artist and work alike. Bit by bit in the 1970s, Dylan had lost the loyalty of 'his generation'. If they were not always older and wiser, they behaved, invariably, as though they were wise to him.

He would never be truly pre-eminent again, never again bend popular culture to his will, never be quite the same source of fascination for a mass audience. With the album he would begin to record in Muscle Shoals on 11 February 1980, Dylan would cease truly to matter for years to come. But then, *Saved* would be a very bad album indeed.

*

How bad? When the tally in 2013 amounts to thirty-five studio-made albums contained in one large, mixed bag, anyone inclined to cut the legend of Bob Dylan down to size is spoiled for choice. In a career of such longevity, stinkers are inevitable. When it was released in the last week of June 1980 *Saved* had the singular distinction of *looking* like a terrible album even before a note was heard. It was as though someone had commissioned a very public announcement: this one's a horror. Honesty in advertising is always to be welcomed, of course.

Tony Wright was and is a very fine cover artist. His work before and after his assignment for Dylan in the designs for Marianne Faithfull's album *Broken English* and Steve Winwood's *Arc of a Diver*, elegant and imaginative in each case, are proof enough of that. With *Saved*, Wright did his job, as directed, and gave the world a glimpse into the songwriter's mind. The painter could not be held to blame for what lay within. There was no error, no interference: buyers were given the singer's message precisely. As the illustrator's website has explained things, 'Dylan had searched for an artist to interpret a dream or vision he'd had. He described exactly what he'd seen and knew exactly what he wanted to see.'[14]

So one gigantic, bloodied hand of Christ with a finger pointing down to a small forest of supplicating hands in a lurid blaze of red, yellow, black and green was Dylan's image of what his album's title was supposed to signify. God was in his dreams. God might even have been causing religious visions. According to taste, the suggestion is either inspiring or disturbing. It does not alter the fact that the original cover for *Saved* – Columbia would later replace it with a generic image of the artist – looks like the kind of crass, overbearing poster favoured by noisy fundamentalist churches struggling to win congregations. It is

God propaganda, evangelical literalism, born-again banality. You could not call it dishonest, however. This was Dylan's idea of the deepest secrets of existence.

A pity about the album, then. Some still try to make a case for it, now and then. One argument runs that there is nothing wrong with songs that sound well enough on tour bootlegs. The problem must be, surely, that Dylan rushed things – another four-day raid on the studio, plus a day for tinkering and revisions – with a band that was road-weary. A better conclusion might be that the songs are simply not up to the task they are supposed to perform. It is not a small task. It has challenged religious artists for centuries, after all. How do you convey the radiance of faith, the actual illumination of belief, to anyone who has not shared the experience? No one save the already devout truly claims that Dylan succeeded with the nine songs (eight his own) on *Saved*, an album that sounds as if it was made by musicians filling a quota. There is sacred music from around the world, from spirituals to oratorios to the *pizmonin* of Judaism, that allows glimpses of religion's meaning even to non-believers. Dylan himself would in time come close to creating work worthy of such company. But not on this record. *Saved* is just a poor, rushed and, indeed, uninspired rock album. What's telling is that Dylan seemed not to be able to hear what was going on even while the project faltered and died.

Saved's fans, and there are a stout-hearted few, point out that this is a kinder, gentler, more personal group of songs than the stern *Slow Train Coming* set. The best that can be said in reply is that the second of the religious albums is at least true to its title. This is the story, over and over, of one man's gratitude for salvation, one man's conviction that anyone who is not saved is in deep, eternal trouble. The album's lyrics are constructed from a personal biblical concordance that might well resonate with fellow believers, but the use to which the source material is put is clumsy. Crudely, Dylan lets his Bible do the talking when what we seek, presumably, are verses which are distinctively his. Once again, the writing, as writing, is poor. The fact might even explain why Dylan had pillaged Scripture so often for so many years. On this evidence, he found authentically original religious language hard to summon. When he did achieve the feat the results would bear no useful resemblance to the songs of *Saved*. Christ might have raised him up to make the album, but the effect on his art was not miraculous. The younger, devilish Dylan still had all the best tunes.

On *Saved* only 'Pressing On', honestly fervent, is worth the bother.

Some of the harmonica elsewhere is nice enough and Dylan is, for the most part, in decent voice. To say more is to take a very minor album seriously simply because of the name on the label. *Saved* would fully earn its reputation as one of the worst things Dylan had done. Only the British, saintly in their tolerance for anything the artist chose to throw at them, would pay the album much attention by granting it a brief stay at number three in their album chart.

*

Shortly after the labours on *Saved* were complete, Dylan and his band flew to Los Angeles for the Grammy Awards. Quite why he was named as best 'rock' vocalist of the year on the strength of the moderate success of 'Gotta Serve Somebody' is a mystery that only those who hand out music-industry trinkets could explain. The honour could be accounted as some sort of compensation, perhaps, for the fact that, barring a couple of unsuccessful nominations in the folk and country music categories, Dylan's revolutionary work of the 1960s had been ignored completely while it was being achieved. Granting him an award to mark his decline was a kind of poetic injustice offered to a poet who was ceasing to function. Dylan would emerge, in time, as a religious writer of real distinction. The punishing irony in 1980 was that religion had done his writing no good at all.

That didn't stop him from taking his songs from God back out on the road, or from preaching at the audiences he encountered along the way when they seemed to object to his message. Again, however, reactions were not uniform. Far from the sinks of iniquity on the coasts, in the heartland the reception given to Dylan's 'gospel' was often respectful and sometimes enthusiastic. It was one small sign, perhaps, of the coming culture wars, so called, in what was soon to become 50–50 America, a nation split evenly and neatly – or so the cliché goes – over issues of faith, morality and politics. As with all clichés, there is some truth in the description. Dylan was already on one side of the divide, but he struggled to express the fact coherently. On 20 May, at the Franklin County Veterans Memorial Auditorium in Columbus, Ohio, he spoke to the audience like a man trying to bond dire daily reality to his mystical eternal truths. The result was weird. For him, everything that happened in the world was a sign of some sort. The trouble was that he couldn't say, as he rambled aimlessly, how the signs connected with the things he claimed were signified.

You see all the race riots and things that have been going on? Well, let me tell you the '80s are gonna be worse than the '60s. Anyway, if you want the word of God in you, I don't know about making it grow . . . I don't know too much about farming, but when the Bible talks about planting seeds on the wayside . . . And I know some of you out there are on the wayside. You hear the word of God, you gonna know you're saved, you're gonna receive all the gladness and joy . . .

Saved was released just after the last of the preaching shows had drawn to a weary close in Dayton, Ohio, on 21 May. Towards the end, potential audiences had been arriving at an unforgiving judgement: one final concert had been cancelled. Dylan had used up most of the available goodwill. Clearly, this shepherd had mislaid his flock. Contrary to anything the Religious Right chose to believe, the majority, moral or not, did not possess an infinity of patience for pietistic hectoring. In that regard, the majority were wise. Dylan's most devoted fans can overpraise the gospel bootlegs all they like – the subset of Christians among them are predictably enthusiastic – but the songs from *Slow Train Coming* and *Saved*, unvarying in their intent, grew pretty old pretty quickly. These were songs *about* religion. Specifically, relentlessly, they were about Bob Dylan and religion. They did not enlarge or illuminate the religious experience for anyone else.

In 2003, Sony/Columbia would sanction an attempt to rehabilitate Dylan's music for his God with a tribute album entitled *Gotta Serve Somebody: The Gospel Songs of Bob Dylan*. As a genre collection, it would be well received. An admiring *Billboard* would report that the five songs from *Slow Train Coming* and the half dozen from *Saved* 'seem like gospel standards now'. For his contribution, Dylan would record an entirely rewritten 'Gonna Change My Way of Thinking' (complete with zany dialogue) with his old flame Mavis Staples, but the album would remain of minority interest. That was the fundamental problem, after all, in 1979 and 1980. Paying customers knew there was more to the finest songwriter of his generation than he had been willing or able to offer for the sake of the Lord. In the end, audiences were not prepared to be toyed with, harangued, lectured, or bored into rigidity. There were not enough hip evangelicals in the world, far less in Dylan's own Christian country, to even up the odds on his side.

In America, *Saved* failed to penetrate the top 20, sticking fast at 24. It was probably lucky to rise so high. Even the 1973 ragbag collection *Dylan*, a set thrown together by a vengeful Columbia from the artist's discards when he took up with a rival company, had done better than that. The corporate suits in New York, never enamoured of their trophy artist's decision to walk the paths of righteousness so publicly, were confirmed in their dark suspicions when the album's gaudy sleeve began to set the discount bins aglow. That giant celestial finger was pointing the direction for Dylan's sales figures. But no one yet knew that *Saved*'s fate was the merest bitter taste of things to come.

Columbia made it clear, however, that there would be no rush to release another evangelising album. They could not prevent Dylan from making such a thing – his contract guaranteed complete artistic control – but there was more than one way to crucify a music-industry heretic. Ostentatious corporate apathy generally did the trick. Had the company men realised what lay ahead, they might have attempted a little gentle diplomacy instead. History shows, in any case, that for the next 17 years no Dylan album would trouble the higher reaches of the US charts. Four of his works would fail even to reach the top 50. For much of that time most observers would deem it impossible for his fortunes ever to be restored. *Saved* was a bigger disaster than any of those involved in its making realised.

It would become clear soon enough that the 1970s had been Dylan's commercial peak. As the decade ended, his luck had run out even as his piety had increased. Suddenly God and artistic self-doubt together had pitched him into a deep trough. If the experience did not destroy his faith in Christ, not to begin with at least, it tore apart his faith in his own abilities.

*

Ronald Reagan was about to sweep to a decisive victory in the New Hampshire Republican primary just as *Saved* was being recorded. The coincidence was neat. *Time* magazine, publishing on 10 March, would report the relieved candidate's triumph as 'Ronnie's Romp!' Despite appearances, no hyperbole would be involved. The result would amount to a startling turning of the tide. Reagan had lost to George Bush (the elder, as we should say) in the Iowa caucus in January. In that poll the belief among Republican Party patriarchs that the former California governor was unelectable had seemed to be confirmed. New Hampshire, with the reliably right-wing Manchester *Union Leader* newspaper leading the charge, would say otherwise.

Whether Reagan could beat Jimmy Carter, with opinion polls giving the incumbent a comfortable advantage, would remain a big question for most of the rest of the year. The landslide in New Hampshire, generally explained by a nationally televised debate staged just a week after *Saved* was recorded, would show clearly that something important was going on. Reagan would proceed to win the primary with 50 per cent of the Republican vote in the Granite State against his main rival's 23 per cent, while the Iranian hostage crisis corroded belief in the Democratic president. Just as Dylan was pressing on with his evangelical faith in a mighty, world-ending conflict, Cold War conservatism was preparing to claim its decade and settle the argument with the evil Soviet empire.

Vietnam was already being consigned to a rapidly rewritten history. Americans who could afford to uproot themselves were on the move from the old rust-belt conurbations to states where the sun shone all the year round, heating bills were manageable, self-reliance was prized, jobs were plentiful, government was distrusted, ethnic tensions were easier to ignore and politics, like religion, was reduced to its convenient fundamentals. The electoral map was being transformed. In the conservative think-tanks the first order of business was to prove, as often as it took, that Lyndon Johnson's Great Society programmes and the rest of the bleeding-heart '60s guff had failed. In office, Reagan would put the last of those programmes to the sword. In their place a faith in unfettered markets as deep as any of Dylan's messianic beliefs would sustain governments for the rest of the century and beyond. Meanwhile, the symbionts who styled themselves neo-conservatives, disillusioned Democrats prominent among them, were identifying Reagan as the candidate best able to restore American pride and end concessions to the Soviet tyranny. Such people were spoiling for a fight. Vietnam veterans were not conspicuous among them. The deep thinkers of the right did not attend wars in person.

So what if Dylan had not 'turned his back on politics'? What if, to be precise, he had adhered to early-'60s radicalism and therefore declined to shoulder the political baggage of conservative Christianity, Levantine Armageddon and all? Even as an exercise in counter-factual fantasy history, these questions are not idle. Dylan had made his own choices at every step of the way. Sticking with the Left, old or new, he could have gone on playing the folk clubs and small halls for half a century, enduring the periodic humiliation of 'rediscovery' while turning out righteous secular anthems for those who still cared. Instead, Dylan in the 1980s would become the perfect echo of his age: fitfully creative, decadent, 'famous for being famous', flitting from style to vapid style, with a surface assurance that hid a world of doubts.

The summary is almost a travesty, but not quite. The point is that this of all artists would simply reflect the decade in which he wound up becalmed. If that was a coincidence, it counts as an odd one. Creativity would not desert Dylan entirely; far from it. Art was about to reappear, in fact, even as the dismal reception for *Saved* was despoiling his reputation. Henceforth, nevertheless, the art would be hard won.

*

After a summer spent on the Minnesota farm and on his new 70-foot schooner, *Water Pearl*, in the Windward Islands, Dylan recalled his band and returned to the Rundown space in Santa Monica. He had a new group of songs to hand. Several of them suggested that he had begun to think hard, perhaps for the first time, about the real meaning of religion. It was as though reactions to his tour and his album had thrown him back on himself. Hitherto he had responded viscerally and emotionally to the experience of being born again. He had expressed his gratitude and his relief. He had become the Christian triumphalist scorning and denouncing those who would not accept the truth. In a righteous fever, he had testified and raved. But Dylan had not paused to contemplate seriously the truths he had accepted.

A couple of his new songs approached greatness. One in particular seemed to arise from, rather than for, the faith he had accepted. It was the song of a man on the ropes, one exhausted by the struggle to recognise himself after the dislocations and upheavals of two decades. In one sense, it was classically religious art. The singer asks who he is and what he is worth; he finds his answer in Christ. But the genius of this piece, the breakthrough after the charmless, overweening certainties of *Slow Train Coming* and *Saved*, was in showing that such faith is not an infallible panacea. Saved or not, an individual could remain flawed, trivial in the scheme of things, despairing and profoundly lonely. The truth conveyed was in the idea of acceptance. For the first time since his conversion, a song had come from the kind of writing that first got the singer known as a poet. Anyone wondering how Dylan could sound so desolate while believing himself saved should meanwhile note a relevant detail. The song is in the present tense. It was written, as the listener is meant to understand, *after* the author was born again.

In 1985, when Christianity was supposed to be behind him, Dylan would say the song was 'inspired'. Talking to the journalist Cameron

Crowe for the booklet designed to accompany the *Biograph* box set, the artist would claim that writing 'Every Grain of Sand' 'wasn't really too difficult. I felt like I was just putting words down that were coming from somewhere else, and I just stuck it out.' The Dylan who was alleged to have returned to the secular world would then turn his remarks into something that sounded very like a sermon.

> Make something religious and people don't have to deal with it, they can say it's irrelevant. 'Repent, the Kingdom of God is at hand.' That scares the shit out of people. They'd like to avoid that. Tell that to someone and you become their enemy. There does come a time, though, when you have to face facts and the truth is true whether you wanna believe it or not. It doesn't need you to make it true . . .

'Every Grain of Sand' is often tracked back to William Blake. In fact, that's a little unfair to Dylan. The Blake of the Pickering Manuscript, a believer with a unique theology – deism without the Deists, more or less – begins his paradoxical 'Auguries of Innocence' with a pair of images intended to contain the universal within the particular. Dylan reverses the idea. Blake's opening, the only relevant verse, runs:

> To see a World in a Grain of Sand
> And a Heaven in a Wild Flower,
> Hold Infinity in the palm of your hand,
> And Eternity in an hour.

Dylan's song, in contrast, describes the discovery of the presence of Jesus, 'the Master', in *every* grain of sand. Blake sees his heaven contained in a single flower; Dylan perceives God 'in every leaf that trembles'. It is a fine distinction, but essential to grasping a song in which the writer is locating himself within infinite creation. Blake is observing infinity in the palm of his hand; Dylan is placing his afflicted, penitent self amid the minutiae of existence at every level. He is no more (or less) important than any leaf or 'every hair . . . numbered like every grain of sand'.

Blake has provided an image of multiplicity. Dylan's net is cast wider. There are echoes in 'Every Grain of Sand' of that other Dylan, the God-driven Welsh atheist Dylan Marlais Thomas, and of his 'Jesus poems' above all. There are also cadences and metaphysical fragments oddly reminiscent of John Donne. There is biblical quotation: the numbered hairs are from Matthew 10:30. There are, equally, those seemingly effortless bits of borrowing and conflation that had gone missing during *Slow Train Coming* and *Saved*. Thus:

Oh, the flowers of indulgence and the weeds of yesteryear
Like criminals, they have choked the breath of conscience and good cheer

The injunction to be 'of good cheer' turns up time and again in the New Testament like some apostolic catchphrase. Conscience, equally, is held out repeatedly, in gospel after gospel, as the essential key to virtue. There is an allusion too, no doubt, to Matthew 4:13–20 ('the sower soweth the Word') and the parable of seed falling on stony and noxious ground. Quite how flowers and weeds can behave like criminals isn't obvious, but Dylan's poetry-reading habits in his youth, that era when fashionable opinion held him to be first cousin to Arthur Rimbaud, might provide one explanation. He knew his way around the works of Charles Baudelaire. The jump from *Les Fleurs du Mal/ Flowers of Evil* to the song's 'flowers of indulgence' is not so great. In his youth, Dylan certainly knew and invoked François Villon's fifteenth-century ballads. The 'Ballade des dames du temps jadis' is the best remembered of them all. Its refrain, '*Mais où sont les neiges d'antan?*' has long been translated as 'Where are the snows of yesteryear?' Dylan at his best doesn't use a word like yesteryear accidentally. So Villon's snows become weeds, those flowers of former sins reduced to spiritual waste by passing time, by wasted time.

It's brilliantly done. It is not brilliant, however, because the writer reminds us that he reads a lot. 'Every Grain of Sand' is authentically human, both as writing and as an expression of faith, in a way that so many of Dylan's 'gospel' songs are not. The lovely harmonica solo on the *Shot of Love* track is a finer testament to belief than all the merciless, browbeating evangelical verses. Nothing on *Slow Train Coming* or *Saved* approaches poetry like this song's last verse.

I hear the ancient footsteps like the motion of the sea
Sometimes I turn, there's someone there, other times it's only me
I am hanging in the balance of the reality of man
Like every sparrow falling, like every grain of sand

One coincidence is worth observing. When Dylan made an attempt to record 'Every Grain of Sand' at Rundown at the end of September he asked Jennifer Warnes to sing it with him. She was at that time involved with Leonard Cohen, another friend and fellow Jew who was perplexed by Dylan's embrace of Christianity's alleged Messiah. What's striking is that when 'Every Grain of Sand' was being written in 'that area where Keats is', in 'like 12 seconds, or that's how it felt', Cohen was slaving, in his usual painstaking way, over the dozens of verses that would be condensed finally in 1984 to form the song 'Hallelujah'.[15] The Canadian was another who had toyed often enough with Christian imagery, most famously in the evocation of Jesus-the-sailor in 'Suzanne', but his act of worship in 'Hallelujah' was contemporaneous with Dylan's 'Every Grain of Sand' and a counterpoint to it, Judaism answering to Christianity.

Cohen's famous song is an injunction to praise in the face of all doubt, a 'broken hallelujah' from a man who allows only that 'maybe' there is a God, a man who doesn't know the name he is supposed to have taken in vain, but who still finds a blazing light in every word no matter how the words are understood. The parallels with Dylan's song are as striking as the differences. Dylan seemed to know it, too. When the so-called Never-Ending Tour was barely a month old in July of 1988, he would give the first of two performances on the road of 'Hallelujah' at the Forum de Montréal in Quebec. The experience would seem to stir something deep within him. In seventy-one concerts that year, two renditions of Cohen's work would be answered by just two performances of 'Every Grain of Sand'. Dylan and his friend in the tower of song understood one another.

That didn't ease the artist's plight in 1980. The radiant version of 'Every Grain of Sand' recorded with Jennifer Warnes would not appear until 1991 and the release of *The Bootleg Series Volumes 1–3*. The album on which the song could first be heard would in the meantime turn out to be even more of a flop than *Saved*. Dylan was entering a period in which his great songs would fail, time and again, to save the albums for which they were written. For most of that time he would only have himself to blame. Sometimes, too often, he would refuse even to allow the greatest songs to appear on those albums. Most of the catastrophes would have nothing to do with his religious beliefs, whatever the beliefs happened to be in any given year. It is beyond question, however, that Dylan's precipitous decline in popularity began when he was born again.

*

At the beginning of November, he took his band back to the Warfield Theater in San Francisco for another long run of concerts. Spooner Oldham had withdrawn from the troupe and Willie Smith had arrived to take care of keyboards. The platoon of backing vocalists, swollen to five members during the last of the spring concerts, had been reduced to a trio: Clydie King, Carolyn Dennis and Regina Havis. The first of these women had by then joined the long list of those who were important to Dylan for reasons that were not simply professional. There were other changes. First, this short tour, just 19 concerts, was advertised, somewhat disingenuously, as 'A Musical Retrospective'. Second, the artist no longer felt moved to preach to his audience. Third, though plenty of the religious songs were performed, these would be the first Dylan shows since December 1978 which did not depend entirely on 'gospel'. The shows, by no accident, were the better for it.

On the first night in San Francisco, Dylan's third number was – lo and behold – 'Like a Rolling Stone'. During the last show almost a fortnight later 'Mr. Tambourine Man', complete with the voice of Roger McGuinn, and 'Knockin' on Heaven's Door' were raised from the crypt. As though another bout of willed amnesia had passed, 'Girl From the North Country', 'Just Like a Woman' and 'Señor' were also heard. Either Dylan had accepted the fact that he could not disown his entire career, or he had given up the unequal struggle to force purely religious music on his audiences. He still took time during the final concert to attack the reviewers who had, he said, misrepresented and defamed the previous year's Warfield shows, but he was coming to terms with reality. He might be able to extinguish all the Bob Dylans who had gone before; history and public memory would not be denied. There was also a career to be considered. He had given unadulterated evangelism his best shot, but it was no longer sustainable. His spirit was willing, but his sales figures were weak. Perhaps more significantly, on the fourth night of the Warfield run Dylan slipped in a song that he would perform on 16 occasions in the months ahead. Another kind of faith was being restored.

All right, we're gonna try something new tonight. Don't know how it's gonna come off, but we'll try it anyway. A lot of people ask me, they want to know about old songs, and new songs and stuff like that. This is a song I used to sing before I even wrote any songs. But this is a real old song, as old as I know . . . So this is how I guess you call one of them old folk songs I used to sing. I used to sing a lot of these things.

Well, I hope it brings you back, I know it brings me back. This is 'Mary and the Wild Moor'. I guess it's about 200 years old.

The English broadside ballad goes back at least to the early nineteenth century and probably emigrated from the London stage to America in the 1820s. Dylan wasn't entirely accurate in claiming that he was doing something new by singing it – he had performed the old song 'The Water Is Wide' as a duet with Joan Baez during some of the Rolling Thunder shows – but he was close enough. His recourse to the folk tradition would become fundamental to his practice in the years ahead. As he said in San Francisco, 'I hope it brings you back, I know it brings me back.' That would not happen overnight. There were tough times ahead.

*

Why did Dylan turn to fundamentalist religion so suddenly, as it seemed, and with such absolute conviction? Because he was predisposed towards superstitious faith from childhood? Because, bloody and bowed, he had worn out one Bob Dylan and stood in need of another? In this argument, two schools of wholly unsystematic thought can be identified. One says, with the support of numerous lines and verses from a host of songs, that Dylan had always inclined towards religion. It was the biggest of his open secrets and there was nothing sudden about his embrace. In this version, all that truly happened when he encountered the Vineyard people was the decision finally to reveal his deepest convictions and express them, temporarily, through a particular creed. The trigger was the addictive idea of the Messiah and what that idea seemed to explain. The argument holds, essentially, that while the experience of conversion might have been shattering, Dylan had always been ripe for faith.

The parallel view says simply that religion was the prop with which he tried to shore up his fragmenting identity. 'Bob Dylan' needed to be refurbished and he had tried most other things. In the summer of 1978 he had undergone a difficult, multimillion-dollar divorce and a deeply unpleasant fight over the custody of his children. Sara and his family had been at the centre of his world and suddenly, thanks to him, they were gone. Relentless hedonism, in its several guises, had proved no substitute. Art being pitiless and greedy, these traumas did his music a power of good, for a while, but Dylan was left as an aimless and profoundly vulnerable individual, so the argument goes, and easy prey for those peddling supernatural answers. It was simple for the Vineyard, offering order amidst the chaos of his life, to take advantage of his weakness.

But was that really all it took? Was he no smarter in the end than all the unhappy teenagers busy being reborn all across the western world? It sounds too simple and it does Dylan no credit. It makes him sound, for one thing, like just another unhappy sucker taken in by the latest fad. Embracing faith, he also rejected a great deal. He was not wholly passive during the process. Only he could attempt to rid himself of every previous Bob Dylan and only he could decide what to do with a born-again identity. It is clear, too, that he had thought often enough about religion. No one was spinning him a line he had not heard before. Interviewers had been asking Bob Dylan for his deepest thoughts on God for years. One way or another, he had read a great deal of Scripture long before the Vineyard's special-forces team were summoned. The history of his public utterances on the subject is a fascinating study in its own right.

In October 1975, long before his decision to embrace Christ, *People* magazine had already been informed of where the artist thought he stood. 'I don't care what people expect of me,' Dylan had said. 'Doesn't concern me. I'm doin' God's work. That's all I know.' In September 1976, interrogated by that noted theological journal the American *TV Guide*, Dylan had become lyrical – had anticipated the lyrics of 'Every Grain of Sand', in fact – in describing his ability to detect the presence of God 'in a daisy . . . in the wind and rain'. 'I see creation just about everywhere,' he had said. 'The highest form of song is prayer. King David's, Solomon's, the wailing of a coyote, the rumble of the earth.'

He felt no obligation to be consistent in his statements, however, before or after he converted to Christianity. By March 1978, amid an interview in Brisbane, Australia, destined for Britain's *New Musical Express*, Dylan had explained to Craig McGregor that he harboured 'no dedicated religion'. He had not, he said, 'gotten into that'. Barely ten months before his apparently whole-hearted embrace of evangelical Christianity, Dylan had added: 'No dogma. I don't usually do that; I usually play my guitar. I don't know why, I've never gone on any of them guru trips. I've never felt that lost.'

By the time 1979 was almost at an end, nevertheless, the selfsame artist had been able to tell the Tucson radio station KMEX that he had been lost and found. Moreover, he had said: 'I don't sing any song which hasn't been given to me by the Lord to sing.' In May of 1980,

Dylan had explained the theocratic world to a journalist from New Zealand's *The Star*, saying, 'God will stay with America as long as America stays with God.' To the same interviewer the artist had granted the knowledge that 'There's a difference between knowing who Christ is and being a disciple of Christ and recognising Christ as a personality and being of God. I'm more aware of that than anything and it dictates my very being.' As his concert tour reached Syracuse, New York, in that same month, the artist had preached to his audience:

> I know a lot of you never heard of Jesus before. I know I hadn't up till a couple of years ago. Jesus tapped me on the shoulder, said: 'Bob, why are you resisting me?' I said, 'I'm not resisting you!' He said, 'You gonna follow me?' I said, 'Well, I never thought about this before!' He said, 'When you're not following me, you're resisting me.' John the Baptist baptised with water; Jesus baptises with fire. Fire and the Holy Spirit. Oh, so yes: there's been a change in me. I wonder what it is?

In the middle of November 1980, amid the concerts in San Francisco, the *Los Angeles Times* was being given the hitherto private explanation for what had become a public truth:

> I truly had a born-again experience, if you want to call it that. It's an over-used term, but it's something that people can relate to. It happened in 1978. I always knew there was a God or a creator of the universe and a creator of the mountains and the sea and all that kind of thing, but I wasn't conscious of Jesus and what that had to do with the supreme creator.[16]

In some narratives, the performances of songs such as 'Like a Rolling Stone' during the Musical Retrospective tour and the decision to allow a few non-religious songs to appear on the follow-up to *Saved* is taken as evidence that by early 1981 the evangelising fever had begun to break. Reduced to the barest essentials, the story goes that the born-again Dylan would begin steadily to disappear within a couple of years. By the time his album *Infidels* appeared in October 1983 it would be presumed that he had returned to secular music and to a secular, albeit 'culturally Jewish', existence. The description doesn't quite fit the facts. Dylan would be photographed praying at Jerusalem's Western Wall in the summer of 1983, for example, dressed in tallith (prayer shawl) and tefillin (phylacteries) on the occasion of a son's bar mitzvah.

That would not be the behaviour of a Christian, obviously enough. Nor would it resemble the behaviour of a man who had turned his back on organised religion or on the Abrahamic God.

The evidence for a return to old secular ways would be at best circumstantial, based partly on altered habits of worship, partly on the fact that his songs would cease to contain – or so it would be said – overtly biblical themes, and partly on the fact that Dylan would become less eager than before to talk theology in interviews. Yet even if you don't buy the story of a previous visit to the Western Wall as it is told in Dylan's book *Chronicles* – a trick, in his telling, to throw off the press by posing as a Zionist – prayers to mark a son's coming of age are hardly the mark of a suddenly irreligious man. The conclusions that would be reached in the early 1980s, still prevalent, remain flimsy. Too often they would be achieved by misreading or ignoring the contents of too many of the later songs. Wishful thinking would be involved.

As the years passed, Dylan would take pains, playful or resentful, to avoid being pinned down. The experience of identifying himself publicly and completely with a creed during his association with the Vineyard left its mark. Belief is, in any case, by definition, a private matter. Why should he be picked out? Nevertheless, in the autumn of 1993 the Reuters news agency would be told that 'A person without faith is like a walking corpse'. Soon afterwards Dylan would begin to say, in apparent contrast, that he placed his only real faith in music. In September 1997, he would declare to the *New York Times*: 'I believe in a God of time and space, but if people ask me about that, my impulse is to point them back towards those songs. I believe in Hank Williams singing "I Saw the Light". I've seen the light, too.'

In the selfsame round of promotional interviews, David Gates of *Newsweek* would be granted 'the flat-out truth'. Dylan would say: 'I find the religiosity and philosophy in the music. I don't find it anywhere else. Songs like "Let Me Rest On a Peaceful Mountain" or "I Saw the Light" – that's my religion. I don't adhere to rabbis, preachers, evangelists, all of that. I've learned more from the songs than I've learned from any of this kind of entity.' Nevertheless, during a press conference in Rome in 2001 he would be asked if he looked to religion for comfort. Dylan's answer: 'I try. Who would I be if I didn't try?' Eleven years later he would talk about an experience he would choose to call transfiguration and claim that every last word was true. And he would still be nominating the Book of Revelation as one of the most important texts in his life.

WADE IN THE WATER

The gulf in understanding between those who fail to believe and those who claim to have been born again is impossible to bridge. You cannot argue rationally with revealed truth, or with someone who claims that a rowdy Jesus turned up in his hotel room. You can run the pop-science tests of plausibility, wonder about Dylan's susceptibility to weak magnetic fields, remember that he had disordered his senses more than once in the usual Rimbaldien style, and then bear in mind that religious experience is sometimes associated with profound depression. In the end, it's all guesswork. William Blake said that as a child he saw angels hanging from the trees, that as an adult he talked to 'friends in Eternity'. Most other people said – for what else could they say? – that he was mad. Yet Dylan chose to believe things that did not seem crazy to millions of his fellow Americans, or to millions of fellow believers around the world. All you can offer as an opinion is that most of his religious writing was not his best writing. Doubt mattered to his art.

What can be said with certainty is that Dylan's embrace of evangelical Christianity was no momentary aberration. Irrational as he often sounded in this period, he was perfectly serious, perfectly attuned to his impulses and feelings. After all, he almost threw away a career for the sake of religion. The need for belief can and should be seen, moreover, as part of a pattern in his life and art, as the necessary polar opposite to the spark of doubt. What truly matters where religion and Bob Dylan are concerned is that the search for faith has endured through each and every one of his fragile, transitory identities. It might be the biggest fact of them all.

CHAPTER EIGHT

Jokerman

IN 1974, THE YEAR OF RICHARD NIXON'S RESIGNATION, ONLY ONE American in every five was prepared to be recognised as a Republican.[1] By January of 1981, Ronald Reagan was secure in the White House, sustained by the rhetoric of neo-conservatism and fomenting what his admirers would call a revolution. The reversal of fortune for liberalism was, as it remains, startling. To all outward appearances the era in which Dylan had grown to maturity and flourished as an artist was eradicated. All the brave, impetuous rhetoric of the counter-culture had come to nothing. To watch Reagan exercise his folksy magic on TV was to imagine that the '60s had never happened. Sometimes it seemed that the memory of the decade was only being kept alive by conservatives who blamed it for all of society's woes. Reagan was an adept teller of that tale.

While governor of California this president had sent in the National Guard to suppress Berkeley's protesting students in 1969. Justifying himself, he had later made a famous statement: 'If it takes a bloodbath, let's get it over with. No more appeasement.' That was not the crafted persona of the former movie star – kindly, smiling, slow to anger but ever righteous in defence of liberty – who took the oath of office on the 20th day of 1981. But who could gainsay Reagan? Though the turnout had fallen short of 53 per cent, he had wiped the floor with Jimmy Carter in the November general election, taking 44 states and 50.8 per cent of the popular vote against the Democratic leader's 41 per cent. Whatever Dylan had meant when he sang of times changing, it surely wasn't the 69-year-old Reagan he had in mind.

Nevertheless, middle America had spoken, loud and clear, while the artist was getting ready to return to the Warfield in November 1980. Among other things, those fabled average Americans had lost patience

250

had the ability to call on the services of almost any musician he cared to mention. In the end, the record Dylan made was better than *Saved* – which is saying absolutely nothing – but it was the roughest, ragged sketch of the work it might have been.

It was time to move on: Dylan could always sense that truth. At the Warfield Theater on 15 November 1980, he had cajoled Mike Bloomfield to the stage. The guitarist who had stood with Dylan during the tempest of the Newport Folk Festival in 1965, who had helped to make *Highway 61 Revisited* the gravitational force of 1960s music, played with real vehemence that night on 'Like a Rolling Stone' and on a new song, 'The Groom's Still Waiting at the Altar'. Though every date he mentioned was wrong, Dylan had told the audience the story – had told *a* story – of how he and his guest had first met. A fine tribute had then been paid to the blues prodigy who 'just played circles around anything I could play'. Afterwards, Dylan invited Bloomfield to join the band on a permanent basis, or so it was said, but the guitar player had ceased to be fit for that kind of work. Heroin had claimed all of his attention years before. Three months after the show, Bloomfield, just 37, had died of an overdose.

Eras sometimes end several times over, with every appearance of finality. In January 1981, *Playboy* had published a long interview in which the unmistakable, disobliging voice of John Lennon could be heard pronouncing on everything under the sun and all parts beyond. Asked at one point if he found it 'distressing' that Dylan had become a born-again Christian, Lennon had replied:

> For whatever reason he's doing it, it is personal for him and he needs to do it. But the whole religion business suffers from the 'Onward, Christian Soldiers' bit. There's too much talk about soldiers and marching and converting. I'm not pushing Buddhism, because I'm no more a Buddhist than I am a Christian, but there's one thing I admire about the religion: there's no proselytizing.

There had been no opportunity for Dylan to respond, even if he had felt so inclined. On 8 December 1980, a deranged fan by the name of Mark David Chapman, an individual with a direct line to God and a grievance against Lennon's 'blasphemy' in once comparing the popularity of Jesus with the popularity of the Beatles, had put four bullets from a .38 Special into the singer on a wintry New York street. Another small part of Dylan's universe had been chipped away.

Afterwards he had been entitled to wonder about the things that might have been passing through the disordered minds of some of his own alleged fans. If peace-loving retired Beatles attracted homicidal losers, what lay in wait from those who hated what once they had loved about Bob Dylan? He had seen his share of fixated admirers and obsessive true believers. If he had read *Playboy*'s interview with John and Yoko, however, he might also have noticed his old, distant friend and sometime rival scorning the worship of dead heroes. 'God willing, there are another 40 years of productivity to go,' Lennon had said. Not for him. In this, as in so many things, he and Dylan had parted company.

*

A vastly better album could have been assembled from *Shot of Love*'s outtakes than the album the artist chose to release. Bootlegs, legal and illegal, still prove the point. Listen to those tracks once or twice and it becomes an indisputable point. Dylan worked on the set, on and off, from the first recording of 'Every Grain of Sand' late in September 1980 all the way through to the final sessions of May 1981. For him, that was a long stretch and an unprecedented effort. In the end, all the labour served only to show that there was a fine balance to be struck between his belief in spontaneity and the need for second thoughts. It was a balance Dylan could not achieve. What killed *Shot of Love*, in essence, was that he got bored with his own best songs long before the album was complete. Given too much time to think, he wound up ripping the heart from the work. A precedent was established.

The biggest loss was a song entitled 'Caribbean Wind'. Next among the gold discarded for the sake of dross was a piece called 'Angelina'. 'The Groom's Still Waiting at the Altar', a track that succeeded in its lyrics as often as it failed musically – through no lack of trying – would be restored to *Shot of Love* when the CD format came along. The summary judgement remains, nevertheless, that Dylan lost the ability to catch quicksilver. If he tried to get through the loathed recording process in one as-live rush he was betting everything on a single throw of the dice and liable to lose. If, on the other hand, he tried to imitate the painstaking habits of his contemporaries, if he submitted to the industrial processes of the music industry, something inside of him died.

Bruce Springsteen's *The River* was the number-one album in America when Dylan and his band took the stage at the Warfield. It had been a year and a half in the making. Dylan could disparage that kind of obsessive effort – and disparage Springsteen, in those days – but if sales were any guide the results spoke for themselves. *Shot of Love* consumed eight and a half months of the artist's life, if mixing and overdubs are taken into account. A great many rehearsals were staged at Rundown before tapes rolled. Producers came and went. For the first time in his career, driven to distraction, Dylan became one of their number. He had never spent so long making a record. Yet the upstart Springsteen had put in twice as much effort and emerged with the prize. *The River* was at number one for the entire month of November 1980. *Shot of Love* got to number 33 late in August 1981.

Dylan simply could not work in the way others worked. For him, the songs existed in their moment. Others could rave about some old, discarded piece of tape. If the essence of a song couldn't be caught in the first moments of creativity it was dead and gone. With *Shot of Love* Dylan tried and failed to cure himself of the attitude. He tried different studios, different arrangements, different groups of musicians. Yet he could not find an environment to suit his preferred methods. In the making of the album he simply wound up fiddling and tinkering, attempting numerous versions of numerous songs in numerous styles. That was one clue to all the problems he would face in the 1980s. He didn't truly know what he wanted.

In 1981, at least two Bob Dylans had begun to contend for possession of the microphone. The album's biggest failure was in the attempt to unite them, to mix the overtly religious and the apparently non-religious. Dylan still had his Christian faith and wrote accordingly. But he had also realised – it is not clear exactly when or how – that there were other things he wanted to say, or rather other ways in which he wanted to be heard. 'Every Grain of Sand', by far the best thing on the album – though a good argument can be made for the alternative version done with Jennifer Warnes – is the paramount case in point. It is, unambiguously, a religious song: most listeners get that far. Those who notice the hymn-like quality it shares with Leonard Cohen's 'Hallelujah' are noticing what is obvious and true. But this is no joyous celebration of simple belief. It would not have suited the Vineyard's evangelising purposes. This song stresses what Dylan explained when he said that conversion was difficult and painful. 'Every Grain of Sand' is an acknowledgement that when the believer raises his gaze from the pages of his Bible, when he pauses in his praises, life goes on, difficult and perplexing. *Slow Train Coming* and *Saved* had not paid much attention to that fact. *Shot of Love*, in construction and intent, is concerned with little else. Yet only in this one song does it succeed in achieving its purpose. 'Every Grain of Sand' is, aptly, the album's single redeeming feature. Dylan could have spent the rest of his eternity in the studio and he would still have failed to transmute the other songs he chose to release into anything of real value. A couple, 'Heart of Mine' and 'In the Summertime', are bearable: that's about the best you can say. The rest dishonour Dylan's art and do no credit to his faith.

The detail is not incidental. The artist's travails amid his 'Christian trilogy' did not arise, as he seemed to want to believe, simply from secular prejudice. His problems had a lot to do with the kind of faith he was expressing and, above all, with the way in which he chose to express it. Too often, the godly Dylan sounded like the opposite of a Christian. Besides which, the music wasn't up to much. Paul Nelson, one of the best critics he ever had, noticed as much in a *Rolling Stone* review of *Shot of Love*. Throughout most of the album, Nelson wrote, 'Bob Dylan sounds more like an irate child who's just been spanked than a grown man who's found the answer of answers.' Nelson had begun his review with this:

> Truth be known, my initial reaction was just another example of the old and familiar Bob Dylan syndrome: i.e., because the man's past achievements have meant so much to so many of us, we tend to give his newest work the benefit of every doubt. No more. For me, it stops right here. Unfortunately, except for 'Every Grain of Sand', *Shot of Love* seldom gets any more interesting than that first listening. Quite the opposite, in fact.[5]

The reviewer went on to assault the tenor of the album. It was not an attack on the music or the songwriting – though Nelson got around to those – but an attack on the artist himself. This Dylan, bathed in God's love or not, was simply unpleasant, a sanctimonious egomaniac.

> By not appreciating the genius of Bob Dylan's current material, we're supposedly crucifying him, even though he's awfully handy with the hammer and nails himself. Dullards that we are, we can't understand God. We don't understand Dylan. Our love is no damn good ('Watered-Down Love'). We're barely alive ('Dead Man, Dead Man'). Therefore, each and every one of us can go to hell.
>
> Well, fuck that. Sinning against God and sinning against Dylan are two different things.

The last remark was certainly true, though its truth was a fairly recent discovery for some critics. The fact was that Christianity had done nothing to diminish Dylan's familiar self-righteousness. The sometimes vicious character he had displayed for much of the '60s was intact on *Shot of Love*. The difference was that this time around the artist gave no credence to scepticism, or – 'Every Grain of Sand' always excepted – to humane doubt. The Dylan of the 1960s had set himself against proscriptive authority, against anyone who had tried to tell anyone else how to live or think. Finally he had gone over to the other side and a couple of almost-secular love songs couldn't disguise the fact. Dylan had once stood up for the kind of liberty-loving individualism that Reagan invoked as a principle but disdained, as his treatment of the Berkeley students had shown, in practice. On *Shot of Love* there was a singer announcing that 'Revolution even ain't [*sic*] no solution for trouble', inveighing against 'The glamor and the bright lights and the politics of sin', denouncing those who 'laugh at salvation' and marking the line between the saved who were 'the property of Jesus' – in the truly awful song of that name – and those who were not. In this version of spiritual warfare, anyone who 'Mocked my God, humiliated my friends' was an enemy. The artist was as brutal towards that kind of foe as he had ever been while skewering hapless journalists with righteous wit in the '60s. This Dylan might have had good Christian grounds for associating social breakdown with the absence of faith, but his analysis, if that's the word, was just the Religious Right's boilerplate rhetoric with a rhyme scheme attached. He surely knew as much. So when did Bob Dylan 'turn his back on politics', exactly?

'Caribbean Wind' was the song that could have made the difference, the song that makes so much else on *Shot of Love* sound juvenile and petty. Predictably, the version that would be released with the *Biograph* box set in 1985 in no sense represents the song in its best incarnations, lyrically or musically. It is inferior to the version Dylan performed at the Warfield on 12 November – for the first and last time in concert – and a lesser work to the much-bootlegged account captured at Richard Perry's Studio 55 in Los Angeles at the end of the following March.[6] The relevant point is that in *any* version this song, in all its multiple renderings and mangled transcriptions, revisions and rewrites, is still preferable to everything else on *Shot of Love* save 'Every Grain of Sand'. In the struggle to pin down 'Caribbean Wind', Dylan lost track of it entirely. One consequence, as Clinton Heylin has explained, is that even the last-gasp attempt released on *Biograph* does not accord with the words printed in Dylan's *Lyrics 1962–2001*.[7] That's the least of the complications. For example, the rather fine Studio 55 variant – not the first, not the last – begins with the arresting

> She was well-rehearsed, fair-browed and blonde
> She had friends who were busboys and friends in the Pentagon

On *Biograph*, the song begins with just the *tiniest* alteration:

> She was the rose of Sharon from paradise lost
> From the city of seven hills near the place of the cross

The second couplet has nothing to do with John Milton, who makes no mention of the rose of Sharon – hence Dylan's lower-case rendering of 'paradise lost' – or with Tom Joad's sister in John Steinbeck's *The Grapes of Wrath* (1939). It has everything to do with Song of Solomon (2:1). The leap from the Pentagon to Scripture is not small, but that was just part of Dylan's difficulty. With apocalypse looming (again) in all versions of the song, he was trying to find a way to express the tensions between physical and spiritual desire, between the need to trust and the readiness to distrust. He was also trying to display these ideas within the structure of the narrative, much as he had done in 'Tangled Up in Blue', by switching points of view and juggling with timeframes. As with that song, the result of all the tinkering was a tangle of competing and sometimes conflicting versions.

Dylan would tell Cameron Crowe, author of the *Biograph* notes, that 'Caribbean Wind' started life on St Vincent in the Windward Islands after 'a strange dream in the hot sun'. It also began to emerge, as Dylan would admit with uncharacteristic frankness, when he was 'thinking about living with somebody for all the wrong reasons'. No name would be given. In *Lyrics*, if it matters, you can read: 'Would I have married her? I don't know, I suppose . . .' The uncertainty, the tentativeness, was echoed at every step of the song's composition. As Dylan would explain to Crowe,

> That one I couldn't quite grasp what it was about after I finished it. Sometimes you'll write something to be very inspired, and you won't quite finish it for one reason or another. Then you'll go back and try and pick it up, and the inspiration is just gone. Either you get it all, and

you can leave a few little pieces to fill in, or you're always trying to finish it off. Then it's a struggle. The inspiration's gone and you can't remember why you started it in the first place.

The writer calculated – though he seemed none too sure – that by the end he was wrestling with four different sets of lyrics. Of the *Biograph* version he could only concede that 'maybe I got it right, I don't know. I had to leave it. I just dropped it.' Frustration clouded his judgement. There were several candidates on *Shot of Love* clearly more deserving of being 'just dropped'. It was one thing to despair of a song that had given him so much trouble, quite another to stick with lesser works just because they had surrendered without too much of a fight during the recording process.

'The Groom's Still Waiting at the Altar', a track that was discarded but later restored to the album, sits somewhere between the fistful of outright failures on *Shot of Love* and 'Caribbean Wind'. Again, there are differences between the words as recorded and those in print under Dylan's name. As lyrics, in either rendering, they are powerful indeed. 'Prayed in the ghetto with my face in the cement, / Heard the last moan of a boxer, seen the massacre of the innocent' is not a bad opening by anyone's standards. Nevertheless, the usual Dylan-friendly dose of finical textual analysis will not alter the fact that musically the track is bombastic and pedestrian, an inadequate notion of R&B inadequately rendered. Praising the written words does not justify the track. Where Dylan is concerned, this annoying little truth is too often forgotten. Some rate the song highly, nevertheless, but even judging by one decent recording from the handful of live performances it was given in 1980, it fails to convince. Yet *still* its place on the album should never have been in doubt.

And then there was 'Angelina'. The history of this song could almost persuade you that the Devil really was causing mischief in Dylan's world. He – the artist, not the evil one – knew how good the piece was. He knew the album needed its lyrical weight amid tracks that were either insubstantial or routinely savage. It was planned as *Shot of Love*'s closing track even after 'Caribbean Wind' was discarded.[8] In the end, 'Angelina' joined the discards for no better reason, supposedly, than to satisfy the technical demands of vinyl and keep the album's running time to the 40-minute mark. Rhymes that were both audacious and wonderfully absurd – concertina/Angelina/hyena/subpoena/Argentina – and a dizzying depiction of an allegorical landscape straight from

Revelation-the-movie: these were dumped wholesale, along with a fine melody and a lovely Dylan performance, just to spare the runts in the *Shot of Love* litter. That the artist was obliged to make choices is hardly the issue. The choices he made were catastrophic and baffling.

Why songs such as 'Caribbean Wind' or 'Angelina' had to make way for the likes of the strange, half-hearted and entirely pointless 'Lenny Bruce' remains one of the bigger mysteries. The artist has not explained himself. It's not so much that Dylan does any disservice to the dead comedian, just that, in his writing and in his performance, he sounds as though he couldn't care less about the supposed martyr for free speech half-remembered in an indifferent eulogy. It is truly hard to believe that the author of 'Angelina' and 'Caribbean Wind' could have written the likes of 'Lenny Bruce is dead but his ghost lives on and on / Never did get any Golden Globe award, never made it to Synanon'. Why go through the motions?

On one ingenious reading, meanwhile, the album's title track was 'inspired' by John Lennon's death. It's the kind of interpretation you need to want to believe. Dylan was reported to have paid a visit to Yoko Ono in New York a month after the murder, though the claim resists documentation. The real problem is that the verses of 'Shot of Love' contain only a couple of lines that could be applied, directly or remotely, to Mark David Chapman and his victim.

There's a man that hates me and he's swift, smooth and near
Am I supposed to set back and wait until he's here?

At a press conference in Travemünde in (West) Germany in July 1981, Dylan would observe that Lennon 'was actually shot by someone who supposedly loved him. But what kind of love is that? That's fan love. That's what hero worship can breed, if you worship a man in that kind of way.' So the mere words shot and love would turn up in a reply to a journalist. How the actions of a crazed and armed fan could be discussed in any other way is difficult to fathom. In reality, the song 'Shot of Love', raising the curtain on another album packed with Dylan's millennialist melodramas, comprises a set of simple oppositions. Such is the sermoner's basic technique. The singer needs an inoculating shot of God's love to protect him against the world's vices. He doesn't need a shot of heroin, codeine or whiskey for what he's got. He has seen 'the kingdoms of the world' and been left afraid.

JOKERMAN

What I got ain't painful, it's just bound to kill me dead
Like the men that followed Jesus when they put a price upon His head

If this was a tribute to the agitator for universal peace and love, it was set out in terms Lennon would have struggled to understand. In his next response to the press in Travemünde, in any case, Dylan would give short shrift to the deceased's most famous hymn to secular morality, the dreaming ballad that contemplated the absence both of heaven and of hell. Dylan wouldn't waste words: 'I never liked that song.' 'Shot of Love', if it has anything at all to do with John Lennon, might just be taken as a graceless rebuttal to a murdered man's beliefs. Should that be the case, the title wins no marks, given the circumstances, for good taste.

Dylan's song was not redeemed, in any case, by the production assistance of the veteran Robert 'Bumps' Blackwell. (He had happened to drop by the studio. Ringo Starr and Ron Wood did the same and wound up recording 'Heart of Mine'. This is how the album was made.) It was fruitless to attempt to turn the artist into a second-rate R&B performer, pointless to believe that even a little of Blackwell's old Specialty Records precision would establish a meaningful difference between a groove and Dylan's religious rut. The songs he was casting aside offered all the clues for which he was searching. Why spurn them for the sake of weary, preconceived ideas about the way a pop album should be assembled?

The question could have been asked several times over of *Shot of Love*. Any one of eight songs could have made room for 'Angelina', the best candidate – given an abundance of choice – being 'Watered-Down Love'. But such arguments, like much of the album, are trivial in the end. Paul Nelson got it right. The credit Dylan earned in better works is not transferable and *Shot of Love* does not deserve the benefit of the doubt. To excuse it as 'underrated', as is the habit of fans who find justifications for any shoddy thing made in the artist's name, is just special pleading. The important fact is that Dylan had begun to misjudge his own gifts utterly.

As though to crown the humiliation, he allowed the album to go on sale with a ghastly 'pop art' cover image that almost made the sleeve of *Saved* seem justifiable. Another biblical verse, Matthew 11:25, would be quoted. 'I thank thee, O Father, Lord of heaven and earth,' it runs, 'because thou hast hid these things from the wise and prudent, and hast revealed them unto babes.' The speaker doing the thanking

261

is Jesus, not a contemporary songwriter, though whether God would have accepted responsibility in any event for some of the statements on Dylan's album is a question for theologians. *Shot of Love* became his second big failure in succession for good reasons.

*

That year, like a nasty premonition come true in the aftermath of John Lennon's murder, a stalker was plaguing the artist at Rundown and elsewhere. Had he been in the mood to think in such terms, Dylan might have noticed an unpleasant irony. By most measures, he was a waning star. According to the harshest judgements made of *Saved*, judgements that were about to be repeated, he no longer deserved all the attention he had once received as of right. Yet here he was with the least desirable of superstar accessories, a devotee so fixated, persistent and threatening it would take security guards, cops and a restraining order to get a woman named Carmel Hubbell out of Dylan's life.[9]

Like Lennon's killing, the incident was a reminder of how savagely weird parts of what remained of the counter-culture had become. That June, while Hubbell was trespassing repeatedly on Dylan's Point Dume estate, NBC was broadcasting the first televised interview with Charles Manson, instigator of the hideous 1969 murders of the pregnant actress Sharon Tate and four others, and of a helpless Los Angeles couple named LaBianca. While Hubbell was making death threats to Dylan's security staff and calling herself 'Ms Manson', the imprisoned leader of 'the Family' was on TV evading Tom Snyder's questions about the slaughter of innocent strangers. 'Well,' Charlie Manson said at one point, effortlessly sinister, 'if I could get some help from the doctor then I could get my mind straightened out a little bit and I [could] come back and play like a human.'

It probably escaped Dylan's notice, but the frenzy incited by this individual had been inspired in its turn by a fanatical belief in certain prophecies supposedly contained in the inerrant Book of Revelation. Manson was also a believer in the imminence of the apocalypse (to be inaugurated, in his version, by racial war). The Family's leader had been confirmed in his psychotic convictions by an ability to interpret songs from the Beatles' 1968 *White Album* as evidence either of Christ's return, or as 'programming' for the final conflict. Seven people and an unborn child had been murdered, in other words, thanks to a crazed misreading of mostly banal Lennon-McCartney lyrics. Rock music, having taken itself far too seriously for too long, had been accepted by some of its most demented enthusiasts as one kind of gospel. On the other hand, Manson had not toured America to sing and preach *his* unforgiving version of Revelation and nightmarish global destruction.

Dylan's concert schedule for the rest of 1981 was designed to give *Shot of Love* all the help the artist could provide. Albert Grossman, his unlovable former manager, was meanwhile suing for certain royalties he maintained were due under contracts that had always been more generous to the representative than to his client. Albert had never lacked gall. Dylan had paid him a lot of money during their partnership and was still handing over a large chunk of his earnings under a previous settlement, thanks entirely to the legal fiction that Grossman had made a contribution, any sort of contribution, to the songs and recordings. A counter-suit was lodged. The case would come close to winding up as the music world's Jarndyce and Jarndyce, Bob v. the Bear, no quarter asked and none given, but the cash equivalent of a double-platinum album for lucky lawyers. For the most part, Dylan left his team to deal with the problem. Nevertheless, the willingness of a man who was anything but a spendthrift to sign big cheques for legal services was evidence of a deep animosity. Grossman had made off with the artist's money once too often.

After a handful of warm-up concerts in Illinois, Michigan and Maryland, Dylan and his now-familiar band arrived in Toulouse at the end of the second week in June for the first of 23 European concerts. On his previous visit to the continent in 1978 acclaim had been near-universal. This time the tour, while not exactly inglorious, was granted a qualified welcome. In London, where six nights at Earls Court were planned in the confident belief that 1978's triumphs would be repeated, ticket sales were slow. The fault did not lie with the artist and his musicians. The kindest explanation is that all the publicity generated by Dylan's adoption of evangelical Christianity had poisoned the well of public affection. *Slow Train Coming* and *Saved* had both been hits in Britain, but by the summer of 1981 audiences had probably heard as much from that version of Bob Dylan as they wanted to hear. Whatever it represented in heartland America, evangelical preaching had long since ceased to be part of the British mainstream. On the first night at Earls Court there was slow handclapping when Dick Holler's '60s hit 'Abraham, Martin and John' was performed in the wake of 'Slow Train' and a Carolyn Dennis rendition of the gospel song 'Walk Around Heaven All Day'. By the third night, though his high-register singing and his daring treatment of works such as 'Mr. Tambourine Man' had received favourable coverage, Dylan seemed to be on the verge of admitting defeat where his religious works were concerned. He told his audience:

> This is a new song off a forthcoming record album. I hope it's on the album anyway. It's called 'Dead Man, Dead Man, When Will You Arise'. I wrote quite a few new songs. I thought I'd play them because I don't know how much longer I'll be playing new songs. People wanna hear the old songs. I was thinking of cutting out all the new songs. So I can play . . . I'm gonna play just older stuff. This time here in London I'm gonna play all the new songs in case they never get heard again.

Given that the tour was only being staged for the sake of his new *Shot of Love* songs, this was disingenuous. It was also a tacit admission, however, that Dylan was perfectly well aware of how completely he had squandered the confidence of many fans. It might not have counted as an emblematic moment, but on the last night at Earls Court a bottle was thrown from the audience after a run of three religious songs towards the end of the show. The missile struck Dylan's guitar, prompting him to retort, 'You're gonna have to go out a long way to hurt me.' Despite what he chose to believe or pretend, it wasn't just a case of the old against the new. All performers with a back catalogue full of well-loved hits have to cope with that mixed blessing. The issue was the nature of songs such as 'Dead Man, Dead Man'. Few audiences, Dylan's audiences least of all, cared for this sort of remonstrance:

> Satan got you by the heel, there's a bird's nest in your hair
> Do you have any faith at all? Do you have any love to share?

Famously, Dylan had left audiences angry, disillusioned or apathetic before, but religion had altered the argument. It was, as the artist might have understood, fundamental to the way he was regarded and the way he wished to be regarded. The fact that 'gospel' formed only one small part of his 1981 concerts in Europe did not get Dylan off the hook. Who was he kidding? Throwing a bunch of old hits out into the crowd did not solve the basic problem. He might have believed that his first duty was to God, but audiences had a quaintly selfish attachment to the mesmerising, multifaceted art of Bob Dylan. If service to Christ meant endless attempts to rewrite the same redemption songs, non-believers (and non-Christians) would find their entertainment and illumination elsewhere. Dylan's resentful little speech in London was a recognition of the truth.

In effect, he gave up. When he reached North America in October, performances began to deteriorate and the purely religious songs began to seem like gestures to appease the star's pride. Group prayers were still held before the concerts, but they prepared the band for performances of 'Maggie's Farm' and 'I'll Be Your Baby Tonight' as much as they affirmed the truth of 'Gotta Serve Somebody' and 'Solid Rock'. The commitment Dylan had given to his religious works at the Warfield in San Francisco two years before had all but ebbed away. By the time he reached New Orleans in the second week in November he was even improvising fragmentary movie scenes, as of old, for Howard Alk, his cinematographer on *Renaldo and Clara* and editor of *Eat the Document*. It showed a certain lack of imagination. No one who became involved in the filming seems to have known what they were doing, or why. Dylan might simply have been providing a little work for Alk, but all concerned forgot – or chose to forget – that impromptu hit-and-run movie-making had paid few dividends hitherto. The artist invented a 'scene'; Howard pointed his camera. It was a desultory effort, in any case.

Like still another all-purpose symbol of what had become of the 'spirit of the '60s', Dylan's old friend and colleague was in the throes of a heroin and cocaine habit. Alk had been living on the Point Dume estate for some time, but his marriage had failed at last. His mood was dark and his future bleak. Early in January 1982, Howard Alk was found dead of a heroin overdose, allegedly deliberate, at Rundown. Dylan's reaction was to shut up the rehearsal studios and abandon any plans to go back on the road. Personally and artistically, he was running up a lot of losses.

*

In an uneasy promotional interview for *Shot of Love* organised by Columbia at the end of the Earls Court run, Dylan had told Dave Herman and an audience at WNEW-FM in New York that he 'couldn't see much difference' between conservatism and liberalism in America. What he meant was that he had failed to notice much of a rightwards drift in opinion, despite Reagan's election and the rise of the Moral Majority. Nevertheless, Dylan had also said that 'personally' he didn't believe in abortion except when a woman's life was at risk. On the other hand, he did believe that gun control 'would make it harder for people who need to be protected'.

There is no way to prove that the artist would have held different opinions in the '60s and '70s, but plenty of evidence to suggest that gun-happy anti-abortionists had never been exactly his kind of people. Suze Rotolo, his first serious lover in Greenwich Village, seems to have endured a termination towards the end of their relationship, an event that had upset him greatly, but Dylan had made no attempt to prevent the procedure. His 1963 song 'Ballad of Hollis Brown', the one telling of 'seven people dead / On a South Dakota farm' thanks to a shotgun wielded by a father driven to kill his family and himself by hellish poverty, had meanwhile evinced no obvious sympathy for 'people who need to be protected' by firearms in the home. Dylan's 'Only a Pawn in Their Game', composed after the assassination of the civil-rights worker Medgar Evers in Mississippi, could have been written to promote gun control. The author might have decided he was blind to political differences, but by 1981 it was a selective blindness.

Talking to Herman, he had complained about 'a whole world full of sickness', a sickness he had blamed on film, TV, the print media and his own music industry. Each, he had said, 'caters to people's sickness'. Dylan had been talking, as was by then his habit, about ailments of the moral and spiritual kind and how they affected behaviour: about sin, in short. He had not offered specific examples. If the whole world was sick because it lacked faith and the blessings of God's truth, there was no need to give details.

On 30 March in Washington, Reagan had been shot by a character called John Hinckley with a revolver bought in a Dallas pawnshop. Three others had been wounded that day, including the presidential press secretary James Brady, who had been left paralysed by his injuries. Such was the context for a disc jockey's questions about gun control and the context, equally, for Dylan's answers. He could remember the 1963 Kennedy killing clearly enough. He might even have remembered the poetry he had tried to compose in the aftermath of the Dallas murder, writing of Jackie Kennedy crawling on all fours to escape the stricken presidential limousine, of the endless news bulletins, of how 'I am sick t my soul an my stomach'. By 1981, Dylan could say only that 'I don't think gun control is making any difference at all'. In one sense, he made an elementary point: in that year firearms were owned by around 49 per cent of households.[10] But the belief that guns were intrinsic to the American way of life was part and parcel of the new conservatism – 'sweeping across the world', as Herman put it – that Dylan had said he could not even detect. Instead, he had argued: 'Guns have been a great part of America's past. So, there's nothing you can do about it. The gun is just something which America has got, lives with.'

When his interviewer had mentioned that 'the abortion question is becoming one of the major political controversies at home', Dylan had replied that the issue was 'just a diversion', that it distracted people from 'the bigger things'. When Herman had said that this all sounded a little 'conspiratorial', the artist had agreed. Then he had expressed surprise because Herman doubted that the fearsome arguments boiling up everywhere in America over reproductive rights were 'calculated'.

It had been a clever, not to say chilling, attempt to give an opinion while dismissing the entire issue of human rights and wrongs as irrelevant to God's 'bigger things'. In fact, while Dylan was trying to extricate himself from the risk of controversy, abortion was dividing communities across his country. A clinic was about to open in Fargo, North Dakota, for example, amid picket lines and bomb scares. Dylan had once known the small city pretty well. It was just across the state line from Minnesota and only 200 miles from Hibbing, his home town. In Fargo, as a classic study would describe, something close to civic warfare would break out in the autumn of 1981 between those bitterly opposed to 'the intrusion of secularism, narcissism, and materialism' and those confronting 'the forces of narrow-minded intolerance who would deny women access to a choice that they see as fundamental to women's freedom'.[11] Dylan could construct his exotic conspiracy theories, but at a time when 'theocons' were working hard for the recriminalisation of abortion he would pick his side. Thus: 'I personally don't believe in it.'

Faith had changed him in many more ways than one. There was nothing new about his habit of confounding expectations. It could even be argued that the fault lay with all the fans and critics who had long taken too much for granted and projected too many of their own precious assumptions across the opaque screen of his personality and his songs. Abortion and gun control were real, contemporary issues, however, and in the end there was nothing ambiguous about the opinions the artist was prepared to articulate.

*

For a while, nevertheless, silence seemed to descend upon him. In 1982, not for the first time, he made himself scarce. Dylan created no albums on his own behalf that year, contenting himself in June with the vague idea of recording a set of duets with Clydie King, his heart's companion of the moment, before deciding that Columbia was not an outfit equipped to deal sympathetically with the results. (The company didn't much care for the project, in other words.) In January, he played bass, for whatever reason, on an Allen Ginsberg session. In March, he was inducted into the Songwriters Hall of Fame. In June, just after the King session, he turned up for a brief performance with Joan Baez at a 'Peace Sunday' anti-nuclear rally in Pasadena without offering public comment for or against the cause. Beyond that, there was nothing much to report. In any usual sense, Dylan stopped working. To all appearances, in fact, he even stopped writing. Sailing in the Caribbean on *Water Pearl* that summer he might just have come up with the beginnings of a song, but the world would not hear the marvellous thing called 'Jokerman' until November 1983.

Dylan paused, it seems, to contemplate a few things. One was religion. Based on no real evidence other than two failed albums in a row, there was media speculation that he must, surely, have begun to reconsider his position as an evangelical Christian. In its gossip column for the issue of 15 March 1982, *New York* magazine ran with a slight story from an unnamed 'source' claiming that Dylan would not be presenting the National Music Publishers Gospel Song of the Year during the following week, either because he wouldn't 'have time to do it', or because the 'evidence is that is over'. The 'interpretation' offered by this anonymous spy in the camp was that 'the New Testament and Jesus were a message he thought he got, but that he was still testing'. Nevertheless, if the New York *Daily News* got its dates straight in June 1986 with the claim that Dylan had by then been studying among the Chabad-Lubavitch community for four years, the 1982 rumours were part-right guesses.

The Vineyard folk could hardly argue. Such was the play they had made of their infinite respect for Judaism and their claim that Jewish and Christian traditions could be reconciled like strayed siblings, the artist's study of the Torah was not a habit to which they could object, even if – a proposition always to be doubted – Dylan had been prepared to listen. Paul Emond, one of the Vineyard first responders sent to minister to the artist early in 1979, put the best complexion possible on the state of spiritual play as far as the evangelicals were concerned when he was quoted in a 1984 *Christianity Today* article.[12] Emond said:

I don't think he ever left his Jewish roots. I think he was one of those fortunate ones who realised that Judaism and Christianity can work very well together, because Christ is just *Yeshua ha'Meshiah* (Jesus the Messiah). And so he doesn't have any problems about putting on a *yarmulke* and going to a *bar mitzvah*, because he can respect that. And he recognises that maybe those people themselves will recognise who *Yeshua ha'Meshiah* is one of these days.

As a statement, Emond's apparently definitive comment was as carefully worded as a press release. Mere 'Jewish roots' – as though Dylan could have possessed any other kind of roots – were preferred to ancestral Jewish faith. The artist was meanwhile 'one of those fortunate ones', a Jew who realised he had been in error, rather than a Jew who had taken a detour via Christianity. In this description, Dylan only donned traditional dress and attended ceremonies to indulge those he respected, not because he gave credence to what was going on during the rituals.

Warming to his theme, Emond ceased to be entirely generous to everyone with 'Jewish roots'. Denying that Dylan had any desire to return to Judaism, the pastor maintained that meetings with Chabad-Lubavitch had taken place only at the movement's request. In this telling, the Vineyard's special relationship with Jews seemed a little less warm than the church liked to claim. Emond said: 'They can't take the fact that he was able to come to the discovery of his messiah as being Jesus. Jews always look at their own people as traitors when they come to that kind of faith . . . When one of their important figures is "led astray", they're going to do everything they can to get him back again.'

There was some truth in that. It is also true to say that in Dylan's shoes Emond would not have hesitated to 'really capitalise' on his reputation for the church's sake, at least according to what *Christianity Today* was told. So how did the Vineyard feel about the possibility that their prize convert was slipping away? Chabad had indeed put in a lot of work to win Dylan back for Judaism. In a neat, near-comical contrast with Emond, Rabbi Kasriel Kastel of the Brooklyn Lubavitch centre denied that the artist had ever forsaken his Jewish faith. 'As far as we're concerned,' Kastel said, 'he was a confused Jew. We feel he's coming back.' The rabbi explained matters by adding that Dylan had been 'going in and out of a lot of things, trying to find himself'. To that end, the Hasidic sect had 'just been making ourselves available'. No pressure, of course.

Dylan had never said that in accepting the Christian Messiah he had ceased to be a Jew. It's a small detail, but easily forgotten. First, he knew that Judaism was not something he could renounce in any manner recognisable to other Jews. Second, his embrace of Christ had been based, almost from the start, on the difficult idea of messianic Judaism. The balance of his allegiances might have shifted, but Dylan remained a Jew whose understanding of faith depended, at least in part, on Christianity, especially on the Book of Revelation, that Christian text with its roots in Jewish apocalyptic literature. He would spend a lot of time with members of the Chabad movement in the years ahead, and join his former wife Sara in Los Angeles in March 1982 on the occasion of their son Samuel becoming a *bar mitzvah*, but Dylan would acknowledge no contradiction.[13] In the early '80s he would drift away from the Vineyard, yet cling to aspects of Christianity and fail to declare himself – perhaps because he believed there was no need for a declaration – as Jewish. What's most striking is the single consistent feature in all of Dylan's dealings with religion. At no point has he felt bound to give absolute allegiance to a single creed, church or sect. These too are the things of man, peripheral to faith and the search for meaning. Nevertheless, if his interest in Judaism was revived at the start of 1982 it meant that unadulterated 'gospel' music was behind him.

That moment had passed, in any case. You can take the cynical view and judge that he had made a hard-headed commercial decision. Purely evangelical music was losing Dylan audiences, sales and a lot of critical respect. Whether he was being persecuted for his beliefs is open to doubt, despite all his complaints, but he was certainly being mocked. On this accounting, given the choice between Christian preaching and a career, he chose the career.

A more generous judgement might be that Dylan had recognised and begun to address a real artistic problem. The fundamental issues of faith were few in number. He had stated them repeatedly in three – or two and a half – albums. A broader and deeper kind of discourse needed a different kind of songwriting. There is no doubt that he was under pressure to relent, not least from his record company, but he had his own thoughts on the matter. For all that, God would never be far, ever after, from Dylan's words and music.

*

In 19 days and nights in 1983, between 11 April and 17 May, he made an album that was both the best and the most troubling thing he had done since *Street-Legal*. *Infidels* would involve one of the finest studio bands he had worked with in many a year. Thanks to Mark Knopfler, it would be better produced, for whatever the fact is worth, than a great many of his records. There would be only a couple of real duds among its eight songs and only a modest amount of controversy over what the artist had to say in those songs. The album would seem, for a while at least, to have restored Dylan's critical and commercial fortunes and to have earned its success. There would be nothing terribly wrong with what was offered on *Infidels*. The problem would lie with what was withheld.

Once you know what this piece of work could have been and should have been, the album becomes maddening. When you begin to consider the choices made and the reasons why those choices were made, the puzzle called Bob Dylan grows ever deeper. If you pause to attend to the works absent from the finished product, the temptation to drop the artist a stiff note of protest, even 30 years too late, grows strong. If ever a Dylan album cried out for the restoration and refurbishment services of the people involved in his archival Bootleg Series, it is *Infidels*. The self-doubt evident on *Shot of Love* here becomes pathological.

With *Infidels* a pattern was established that would influence critical reactions to the artist's work through all the decades to come. Thanks to countless bootleg releases, legal and otherwise, two Dylans would seem to co-exist, one actual and one potential, one the author of the albums as they were set before the public, the other an artist reconstructed from the counterfactual history of what might have been. When countless concert recordings began to be thrown into the mix, dozens of them preferable to the albums sanctioned by Dylan, arguments over his reputation and worth would grow ever more tortuous. Certain fans and students would enjoy the never-ending archaeological effort for its own sake. For some, the collecting of illicit tapes and the ensuing Jesuitical debates over this or that outtake would become a consuming hobby, even a career. To have knowledge denied to the common herd was part of the fun, it seems. For others of us, it would all become just a bit tedious. Why couldn't Dylan stop screwing around with his work? The fact would remain, nevertheless: without a knowledge of certain bootlegs – not, God help us, all of them – an understanding of the art and the artist would become hard to achieve. That truth would be as relevant to the worst of his albums, ironically enough, as it would be to the best. *Infidels* was far from the worst, but it could have been a lot better.

No such thoughts arose when the vinyl disc appeared at the start of November 1983, of course. Only a few, led by Knopfler, knew what Dylan had done and what he had refused to do. To anyone who lacked that insight it was simply the best album he had released in at least five years. Some still contend that *Infidels* is superior to anything he had managed since 1976's *Desire*. When the album appeared a couple of reviewers, befuddled by cask-strength hyperbole, called it his best since – a pair of words that surely deserve to become a compound adjective – *Blood on the Tracks*. The man in the vinyl mine at *Rolling Stone* got his mention of the 1975 masterpiece into his first sentence, then wrote of Dylan's 'stunning recovery of the lyric and melodic powers that seemed to have all but deserted him'.[14] Not everyone agreed. Some reviewers continued to be dismissive, less of the music or the production than of certain sentiments expressed, but the American record-buying public was more forgiving than it had been towards any Dylan release since *Street-Legal*. That was fair. All in all, *Infidels* is not a bad piece of work.

There was a degree of sheer relief evident in the album's reception. Many critics gave it the benefit of all sorts of doubts simply because at first it seemed – an important word – that Dylan had been cured at last of his religious delirium. One song, 'Neighborhood Bully', struck a few listeners as an alarmingly right-wing piece of Zionist rhetoric, but most put aside their concerns. Another track, 'Union Sundown', sounded a little strident in its analysis of America's labour relations and economic misfortunes, but at least the writer was taking an interest in the world around him. There were odd, even eccentric touches. Did Dylan truly believe that 'man has invented his doom' just by landing on the moon? Could it have been him or a character in a song declaring, 'a woman like you should be at home / That's where you belong / Taking care of somebody nice'?[15] Neither question was treated as a big deal. Even when a bit of sustained attention proved that the artist had not in any sense left religion behind, *Infidels* was exempted from scorn.

Perhaps it had something to do with the set's teasing title. Perhaps it was because Dylan was no longer brandishing a religious affiliation like an all-areas backstage pass. Perhaps he had been right all along about prejudice and born-again belief. For whatever reason, the album was granted an acceptance that had not been available to its immediate predecessors. Even when it was made explicitly obvious that the artist was still gripped by his Antichrist fixation – 'sometimes Satan comes as a man of peace' – *Infidels* was deemed 'secular'.

'Jokerman', the opening track, helped matters somewhat. This was, unambiguously, one of Dylan's great songs, recognised as such from the moment the album was released. It was also one of those great Dylan songs that did not yield its meaning instantly, if at all. Most who liked it didn't quite know what the hell (and so forth) it was supposed to be about *specifically*, but that didn't matter. The evangelical Dylan had forgotten the art of writing in this manner, in this meshing of melody and images to create something that seemed to make a sense of its own even when the sense could not be defined. He did not perform the trick to perfection with each of the *Infidels* songs, but in 'Jokerman' and in a few other places hope was restored.

Dylan, conscious of his deficiencies as a technician, had considered a number of people for co-production duties before inviting Knopfler to return to the combat zone. A couple of the big names who would be mentioned as rival contenders for the honour still boggle minds. Asking what Frank Zappa or David Bowie would have done with or to the artist's work is like asking what might happen if the laws of physics could be suspended. Knopfler, clearly the best candidate, recommended his own keyboard player, Alan Clark, and the sound engineer Neil Dorfsman. The latter had handled the recording of Bruce Springsteen's *The River* and the 1982 Dire Straits album *Love Over Gold*. Both of those vastly successful collections had been recorded at the Power Station studio on West 53rd Street in New York; Dylan followed suit. If the former ConEdison plant and its miraculous acoustic properties had generated millions of sales for Knopfler and the usurper Springsteen, the artist wanted all the benefits they had enjoyed.

He didn't have to be reminded of what had become of *Saved* and *Shot of Love*. Columbia had given him another five-album contract in July 1982, but Dylan needed to regain both his credibility and his authority within the company. He had pushed his luck hard, several times over, in the preceding decade and a half among people whose idea of poetry began and ended at the bottom line. Having Bob Dylan on the roster was good for Columbia's image, in theory, but the lawyers who ran the empire from the Black Rock building on a corner of Manhattan's 6th Avenue put their real faith in the miraculous transmutation of cheap vinyl into gold. Dylan had been failing to weave that brand of magic. In April 1983, as he commenced work on

Infidels, corporate lawyer number one was about to sack corporate lawyer number two as a war between the company's president, Walter Yetnikoff, and his deputy, Dick Asher, came to a head. Neither man could have been mistaken for a born music lover, nor for an individual in instinctive sympathy with artists.

Dylan wasn't happy with them and they were not happy with Dylan. Performing at the Stade de Colombes in the Paris suburbs on 23 June 1981, he had expressed grumbling irritation over the fact that he was touring to support *Shot of Love* while Columbia, inept or apathetic, was failing to get the record into stores. The album, Dylan had told the French crowd, 'should be coming out sometime soon. If you know exactly when, you call up the record company I record for, *whatever one that is today.*' (My italics.) The plain truth remained that *Shot of Love* had expired like a mayfly. That fact, in turn, might well have had a bearing on Dylan's rediscovery in 1983 of the joys of 'secular' song and the art of disguised meanings.

Dick Asher would be remembered as a typical major label corporate philistine in an article published in 2008 by Simon Napier-Bell, former manager of the Yardbirds, Wham! and several other groups.[16] As he recalled the incident, the Englishman had just entered the executive's office for a meeting when a secretary announced that Bob Dylan was 'on line one'. The artist, as Napier-Bell would write, had just made 'a couple of albums full of evangelical zeal but they'd bombed'. Dylan's contract had come up for renewal – this would be around the time *Shot of Love* was being recorded, in other words – and Asher was not eager to take the call. As Napier-Bell remembered it, the conversation as it began 'wasn't too interesting'. Then the executive began to yell into the phone:

I've told you, Bob – no fucking religion! If you can't agree to that, the deal's off . . . Look, I'm telling you. There'll be no fucking religion – not Christian, not Jewish, not Muslim. Nothing. For God's sake, man – you were born Jewish, which makes your religion money, doesn't it? So stick with it, for Christ's sake. I'm giving you 20 million bucks – it's like baptising you, like sending you to heaven. So what are you fucking moaning about? You want 20 million bucks from us? Well, you gotta do what we tell you. And what we're telling you is . . . No Torah! No Bible! No Koran! No Jesus! No God! No Allah! No fucking religion. It's going in the contract.

If indeed it did go 'in the contract' a great many of the earnest things written and said since about Dylan, Christianity, Judaism, philosophy, the trials of faith, religious art, the fate of humankind and gospel music might deserve to be erased. No one need go that far. Demonstrably, the artist did not abandon his complicated beliefs. Did he get his company orders, however? In Napier-Bell's account the orders could not have been more explicit. And did Dylan obey Asher in exchange for 20 million pieces of silver? One reading of the *Infidels* lyrics says that might well have been the case. Napier-Bell's ability to give a verbatim account of things allegedly said better than a quarter of a century before their transcription verges on the supernatural, of course. Nevertheless, the gist is clear enough. With a witness present, one of the top men at his record company gave it to Dylan straight: 'no fucking religion', not if he wanted a $20 million deal. You could call that interesting.

What can be said with certainty is that after *Shot of Love* he began to write about matters of religion in a manner that would not be confused easily with religious writing. He hid his meaning and purpose, hid them well enough to fool a lot of critics and, presumably, executives so dim-witted they could tell him to stick with Judaism 'for Christ's sake'.[17] That happened to be the artist's intention, more or less. Napier-Bell would further observe, dryly, that as a devout atheist he had no personal objections to Asher's rant, though 'it seemed tough that a contract should include such specific restrictions'. That, nevertheless, was his description of the exchange. If it was accurate, Dylan began to record *Infidels* under the thumb of a corporate lawyer type whom the English observer called 'a very dull man indeed'.

Some details can be added. When the album was almost complete, for example, the artist would make several statements to the journalist Martin Keller that were markedly less forthright than before. Almost defiantly, Dylan would assert that *Shot of Love* was his favourite among all the albums, that the song of the same name was his 'most perfect song', that it defined him and showed anyone who was interested where his 'sympathies' lay. Despite 'Neighborhood Bully' and 'Union Sundown', he would also maintain, in the familiar manner, that 'I don't write political songs. Political songs are slogans. I don't even know the definition of politics.' When the talk turned to the issue of religion, on the other hand, Dylan would become downright evasive. Whether thanks to Asher's expletives or to his own evolving beliefs, his opinions would not be calculated to please the holy rollers of the

Vineyard church, or the ascetic rebbes of Chabad-Lubavitch. They would cheer a lot of his old fans, however.

> You can turn anything into a religious context. Religion is a dirty word. It doesn't mean anything. Coca-Cola is a religion. Oil and steel are a religion. In the name of religion, people have been raped, killed and defiled. Today's religion is tomorrow's bondage.[18]

Faith was not denied, never that, but it was given the kind of spin to which faithless, secular types could assent without turning a hair. Dylan would perform the same trick with nuance when asked about the search, if any, for his Jewish identity. 'My so-called Jewish roots are in Egypt,' he would say. 'They went down there with Joseph, and they came back out with Moses . . .'

> Am I looking for them? Well, I don't know. I ain't looking for them in synagogues with six-pointed Egyptian stars shining down from every window, I can tell you that much.

Three months or so later, just before *Infidels* was due to be released, Dylan would take another crack at explaining where he stood on the issue of religious belief. He would also try to tell the *Los Angeles Times* why his musical 'gospel' moment had passed. He would not 'disavow any of that', but he would scarcely testify lustily for the Lord, either. Noticeably, his unfortunate if entirely unconscious habit of placing himself on the cross-but-one next to Christ would endure.

> I don't particularly regret telling people how to get their souls saved. I don't particularly regret any of that. Whoever was supposed to pick it up, picked it up. But maybe the time for me to say that has just come and gone. Now it's time for me to do something else . . . It's like sometimes these things appear very quickly and disappear. Jesus himself only preached for three years.[19]

If he did win a contract worth $4 million an album, Dylan spent some of the money wisely. In addition to Knopfler and his colleagues he invited Mick Taylor, the best guitarist the Rolling Stones ever had, to join him at the Power Station. The two had been friends for a while, probably having met at the Roxy Theatre in Los Angeles in January 1982 when Taylor was performing in a Bluesbreakers reunion tour with John Mayall and Fleetwood Mac's John McVie. The blues guitar player was a good choice to support and complement Knopfler. Dylan's next smart move was to call up Lowell 'Sly' Dunbar and Robbie Shakespeare, drums and bass respectively, a pair already long established as the rhythmic heart of modern reggae. All in all, it was a crew few recording artists could match, or afford to match.

At least 16 new Bob Dylan songs were recorded during the *Infidels* sessions amid the usual plethora of cover versions, traditional numbers, jams and phantom titles. Eight tracks would survive to give a vinyl album the near-standard duration of almost forty-two minutes. Of the eight original songs discarded, two would be retrieved for later albums, in one case because the artist was by then desperate enough to risk the woeful number entitled 'Death Is Not the End'. (Listen to it once or twice and you begin to pray for an end that is certain and swift.) The second tune reserved for recycling, 'Clean-Cut Kid', was a kind of mid-period sub-Dylan protest song to do with the malign effects of a wicked society on the innocent mentioned in the title – 'they made a killer out of him' – that did not detain the artist for long in 1983 and would never amount to much. Of the remaining half-dozen works, one piece was entitled 'Julius and Ethel', a song recalling the notorious Rosenberg case and the Brooklyn couple's execution in 1953 for espionage. These days there is little doubt that Julius attempted to pass America's nuclear secrets to the Soviet Union; his wife's guilt is less certain. In the 1980s, nevertheless, arguments over the case were still dividing opinion between left and right. Dylan took the accurate if uncomplicated view that the 1950s had been a weird and paranoid time in which America became a strange, bewildered and fearful place, but his song was no 'Hurricane', nor even a 'George Jackson'. The author has never sanctioned its release in any form and its existence is not acknowledged by bobdylan.com. That might simply be because it is not a good song. 'Juvenile' would be one description.

Now that they are gone, you know, the truth it can be told;
They were sacrificial lambs in the market place sold –
Julius and Ethel, Julius and Ethel.

Now that they are gone, you know, the truth it can come out;
They were never proven guilty beyond a reasonable doubt –
Julius and Ethel, Julius and Ethel.

That left five tracks. Versions of each would turn up on *The Bootleg Series Volumes 1–3* in 1991, but that release would not solve the puzzle of what Dylan had done to *Infidels*. Two songs, 'Lord Protect My Child' and 'Tell Me', probably deserved to wind up on a 'rare and unreleased' compilation; two more, 'Foot of Pride' and 'Someone's Got a Hold of My Heart', should be listed on the charge sheet among the bigger crimes of omission the artist has committed. Even these lapses are dwarfed by the failure to allow the release in 1983 of the song called 'Blind Willie McTell'. Its absence from *Infidels* has set Dylan against everyone who has ever heard the work and bothered to pass comment. At the time, Mark Knopfler, fighting hard for the song, was aghast. His opinion still wins the listener's vote. Fans and those who write about Dylan meanwhile debate whether 'Blind Willie McTell' was just the best thing he did in the 1980s or among the best things he has ever done. In that context, discussions of whether the version captured on *The Bootleg Series Volumes 1–3* is slightly superior or mildly inferior to a widely circulated, frighteningly powerful 'electric' rendition feel like casuistry.

Perhaps the real judgement on the artist is this: anyone who wants to hear how *Infidels* could (or should) have turned out has no choice but to reassemble the album from a range of sources, as though from spare parts. In this day and age, that's no big deal. It was not especially difficult in the 1980s to hunt down outtakes and alternate takes: the better-known 'acoustic' version of 'Blind Willie McTell' was doing the rounds within a year of *Infidels* being released. The point is that Dylan is supposed to be known as a maker of albums as well as of songs, of artefacts with an artistic coherence and a considered design. The making of albums might be redundant in a pick-and-mix digital era, but it has been Dylan's line of work for half a century. If *Infidels* had been a painting he would have stood accused of putting a boot through the canvas.[20]

As it was, he shredded his entire artistic scheme for the sake of one track, 'Union Sundown', mourning the fact that the land of the free market was losing out in capitalism's race to the bottom. The song was an alert anticipation of globalisation and its discontents, but it was no 'Blind Willie McTell'. Few of Dylan's works save, perhaps, 'Visions of Johanna' and 'All Along the Watchtower' are as instantly haunting as this.

Seen the arrow on the doorpost
Saying 'This land is condemned

All the way from New Orleans
To Jerusalem'
I travelled through East Texas
Where many martyrs fell
And I know no one can sing the blues
Like Blind Willie McTell

It sounds at first like an evocation of the Passover story in the Book of Exodus. Egypt is the land condemned to suffer ten plagues; the Israelite slaves are meanwhile instructed to mark out their homes with a lamb's blood so that God will spare them. As Exodus 12:7 has it: 'And they shall take of the blood, and strike it on the two side posts and on the upper door post of the houses . . .' It could also be that Dylan has in mind the 'hobo signs' that were common during the Depression. These were the crude, coded marks left by rambling men in chalk or coal on fences, walls and doors to guide their comrades. A circle with an arrow through it meant 'Don't go this way'. Two parallel arrows across the circle said 'Get out fast'.

A third possibility is that with the phrase 'this land is condemned' Dylan is making poetic use of a common piece of legalese. By the right of eminent domain – in Britain, by the right of compulsory purchase – authorities acquire private land for public use, but only after it has first been 'condemned'. In the nineteenth century, the ruthless hustlers who built America's railroads got their hands on this useful power and abused it mightily. In Dylan's context it has more to do with what became of African Americans and their farms in the Southern states after the Civil War as vengeful whites, deprived of their plantations and their slave economy, set about subjugating and robbing blacks once more. The land earned by the sweat of newly freed slaves who had dreamed of their '40 acres and a mule' was stolen wholesale. If legalised theft didn't do the trick, though often enough it was sufficient, the Klan and the lynch mob were at hand.[21]

Dylan being Dylan, it is better than possible that all three ideas are concentrated in a few words. Thus: a land condemned by God because of slavery; a land where it is dangerous to stray; a land stolen from its people. At the heart of 'Blind Willie McTell' is a meditation on what became of America thanks to the war between the states and the causes of that war. So the writer lifts us aloft in a few bare lines to look down on a landscape somewhere, at some shifting point in time, in the American South.

There are places called Jerusalem, most of them vanishingly small, dotted throughout the region – in Alabama, Georgia, Arkansas, North Carolina, Tennessee – and beyond. Nat Turner, leader of a slave revolt in 1831, was executed at one such town (since renamed Courtland) in Virginia's Southampton County. Equally, the biblical allusion could be straightforward, intended to encompass the entire Judaeo-Christian world. It's more likely that everything lying between a city of sin and the city of God has been condemned. Then, as though a movie camera has soared and dipped, we are in the dark lands of East Texas, 'where many martyrs fell'. A song making a connection between the treatment of black Americans and enslaved Israelites, as many spirituals did, has plenty of history on its side. In this verse, Dylan might also have had in mind 'Fallen', a well-known (if very bad) nineteenth-century poem by the once-popular lecturer and hymnist John Lawson Stoddard. The horrors inflicted by lynch mobs are central to its theme. (Stoddard was also an early advocate of the Jewish right of return to Israel, interestingly enough.) In part, 'Fallen' runs:

> Where history's Martyr dared to break
> The power that held a race in chains,
> I see the ghastly lynching-stake,
> Where brutal mobs their vengeance take,
> And, since no law their course restrains,
> Gloat o'er their writhing victim's pains.

Where racism was concerned, the history of East Texas from the post-Civil War Reconstruction to the middle of the twentieth century was as vile as any among the Southern states. As one scholar explains, 'At the dawn of the twentieth century, East Texas was notorious for lynching and was considered one of the worst regions in the state, leading the state in 1908 with 24 deaths.' In 1910, when Blind Willie McTell was a child, 'more than 100 blacks had been lynched in the Lone Star State'.[22] Most died in East Texas, it is explained, in an area which then stood third among those regions of the United States in which lynchings were commonplace. After Mississippi and Georgia, where McTell was born, Texas as a whole was the state that gave itself over most eagerly to lynch law, accounting for 468 victims between 1885 and 1942.[23]

This, dense with history, thick with connections, is just the first verse. Dylan has here embarked on the kind of historical writing that would become a distinguishing glory of his later career, his era of consuming interest falling – very broadly speaking – in the years from the Civil War to the undated orphan birth of the blues. When he cast the song aside he would lose the thread he had discovered in 'Blind Willie McTell' for the best part of a decade. He would pick up this narrative again only when he remembered the art of 'learning to go forward by turning back the clock', as the fascinating sleeve notes to 1993's *World Gone Wrong* would explain.

It is almost as if 'Blind Willie McTell' was removed from *Infidels* because Dylan himself wasn't ready for the challenges implicit in the song. Here he sets the agonies of black Americans squarely at the centre of the country's history. Inevitably, he is laying out all the reasons for the civil-rights movement and, therefore, for his own earliest work. In this song, the inescapable fact of slavery defines both the nation and the singular cultural gift, the music that grew from the blues, it gave to the world. This, Dylan is saying, is what we come from: look and listen. The long bondage of black America, rendered here in terms both physical and spiritual, was the abiding horror that gave birth to the music that altered the country. African Americans were the enslaved children of God. So what were whites?

It is a moment of high sophistication in Dylan's career. It makes the arguments of a song like 'Neighborhood Bully' seem crude and fatuous. At no point in 'Blind Willie McTell' is the listener's sympathy or tears demanded. Dylan doesn't bother to *tell you* that a historic crime without precedent or parallel was committed in the land of the free. He is insisting instead on its centrality, its near-biblical significance, and its expression in the music that has penetrated every fibre of American culture.

His first four verses resemble panels in an altarpiece, both sombre and glowing. In the second verse the scene is an encampment. Whether this is a stopping place for runaway slaves, a revival meeting, or one of the travelling tent shows that criss-crossed the south for 70 years is left unclear. It could be any and all of the three. History says, nevertheless, that the minstrel and variety companies run by the likes of F.S. Wolcott and Moses Stokes gave Ma Rainey, Ida Cox, Bessie Smith and many others their starts. At one point, Dylan sings that 'Them charcoal gypsy maidens / Can strut their feathers well'. Bessie Smith's very first job as a teenager with the Stokes travelling troupe, just before the First World War, was as a dancer on the chorus line.

Dylan's narrative is not linear. The third verse lies in the heart of darkness, but it reverses time. It harks back to William Tecumseh

Sherman's pitiless Savannah campaign during the Civil War, his 'March to the Sea' in the winter of 1864 that set the South aflame. That happened for the reasons set forth in eight astonishingly evocative and impeccably concise lines. Dylan begins with the Union's attempt to raze the Confederacy and traces the line of cause and effect back to captive tribes.

> See them big plantations burning
> Hear the cracking of the whips
> Smell that sweet magnolia blooming
> See the ghosts of slavery ships
> I can hear them tribes a-moaning
> Hear that undertaker's bell
> Nobody can sing the blues
> Like Blind Willie McTell

The fourth verse contains scenes from a later South. There's a young man 'dressed up like a squire' with a bottle of bootleg whisky and a woman in tow. There's a chain gang on the road and the rebel yells of the Ku Klux Klan in the distance. Racism is resurgent. The verse could be placed in any of the decades after Reconstruction, but inevitably the bootleg booze suggests Prohibition, the 1920s and early 1930s, when the Klan were once again busy and the chain gang, that favourite punishment in the Southern states with blacks its special victims, was a common sight on the highways. Blind Willie McTell made his first recordings, it should be noted, in 1927.

At the song's close, Dylan draws as much of a moral as he intends to draw. 'God is in his heaven', indeed, as Robert Browning's line from 'Pippa Passes', long since reduced to cliché, has told us, but all's not right with this world. Browning took his inspiration, in any case, from the Bible's placing of the Lord God above and humanity below. The song takes this old revealed truth and makes it a cause for doubt. We can aspire to the kingdom, but whether this deity cares to intervene is a question the narrator will not answer.

Is it the same narrator as the one heard at the song's beginning? There is a possibility of doubled voices, as in *Desire*'s 'Black Diamond Bay' when it turns out that the speaker is not doomed within some Conradian episode but sitting at home in LA drinking beer. In 'Blind Willie McTell', the last personage is 'gazing out the window / Of the St. James Hotel' after announcing that God's creation seems to contain only 'power and greed and corruptible seed'. Is this just the voice of a storyteller, one who has only heard of those who saw the arrow on the doorpost and the big plantations burning? There is no possibility of proof in such an argument. It can only be said that the voice heard in this song is better understood as the voice of a hovering collective memory surveying the landscapes of a shared past. Multitudes are contained within it.

Michael Gray has pointed out, nevertheless, that Dylan's work connects to McTell himself through a couple of related songs, Willie's own 'The Dyin' Crapshooter's Blues', recorded late in 1940, and the old, ubiquitous 'St. James Infirmary'.[24] The latter piece was not attempted by the bluesman until 1956, but both songs form part of a vast musical tangle extending from venerable British folk song to 'Streets of Laredo', the late-nineteenth-century piece 'Those Gambler's Blues', McTell's 'Dyin' Gambler Blues', and many more besides. Both 'Crapshooter' and 'St. James' involve doubled narration, as Gray describes, and both depend on the imminence of death suggested in Dylan's last verse. In a footnote, meanwhile, Sean Wilentz observes that there was a St. James Hotel in Selma, Alabama, both before and after the Civil War, and another in New Orleans at around the same period.[25] (Dylan could equally have been speaking in his own voice at the window of a deluxe modern joint. That last idea is possible, but somehow it doesn't seem likely.)

The final verse of 'Blind Willie McTell' is, in one sense, a wholly conventional ending. It says: this has been the American past. It asks: wasn't it hellish and is it not in the nature of humankind to descend into savagery? That's Dylan's nod to his born-again evangelical studies. The reference to 'corruptible seed', fallen humanity, is direct from 1 Peter 1:23: 'Being born again, not of corruptible seed, but of incorruptible, by the word of God, which lives and stays for ever.'

So why Blind Willie McTell? He was no antique curiosity from the pre-history of American music. A neat, sometimes godly man who liked to preach and never forgot to dress well, he drank a fair bit, especially towards the end of his life, but made pretty decent money for years as a polished, professional travelling musician. He had a good head for business, too, by all accounts. McTell played the songs, any kinds of songs, that people would pay to hear. It might even be a mistake to call him a bluesman. Like many of his contemporaries, Blind Willie performed blues, ballads, spirituals, ragtime, show tunes, hillbilly songs and original songs. If anything, he tended at times to steer clear of the earthier versions of 'the Devil's music'. After following every clue and trail, Michael Gray has called him a 'human jukebox and local hero'.[26] No one ever said McTell had made a pact with Satan at the crossroads at midnight, or suffered the attentions of a hellhound on his trail. He was a fine guitar player in the Piedmont fingerpicking style of the eastern states, but he was a pragmatic working pro, not a tortured artist. He favoured a Stella 12-string guitar as much for the volume he could extract from the instrument as for its musical possibilities. McTell did not endure the chain gang or moan the blues. His was a respectable life, mostly, and he sang with a clear, respectable diction, albeit in a slightly nasal voice. He never made a hit record, but a couple of his things, 'Statesboro Blues' in particular, would become popular among the folk revivalists of the '60s and beyond.

Blind from birth, possibly as a result of maternal syphilis, McTell was as much the white world's victim as any African American born in the South near the start of the twentieth century. His ancestry contained an irony that was also common enough: his great-grandfather had been white. But it is simply not plausible to claim that Willie suffered as badly as many of the abused sharecroppers and common folk of his era. He did not match the stereotype and nor did he suffer the violent, degraded end inflicted on some of his peers in the music business. He coped very well, it appears, with his blindness. In fact, according to contemporaries he had for compensation astonishing hearing, not to mention perfect pitch, and a remarkable sense of direction. Educated at the State Blind School in Macon, Georgia, and in private institutions, he learned to read both books and musical notations in Braille.

It is hard, then, to depict Willie McTell as the quintessential voice of the blues in the old, outworn sense. He was no importunate hobo or singing convict. There is nothing harrowed or harrowing about his music. You can't even say – though the game is futile in any case – that he was the best blues musician who ever lived. So why, of all the dozens of black people living and dead to whom he owed a debt, did Dylan pay homage to Blind Willie McTell?

It's not clear that he did. What's truly tantalising about the song is that it has nothing to do, in terms of biographical fact, with the man named in the title. Its scenes have no direct relevance to McTell's life. Musically, there are those patently obvious opening piano chords straight from 'St. James Infirmary', but that tune was hardly Blind Willie's property. It is almost easier to name the blues and jazz people who didn't perform the standard as it is to name those who did, but he was not prominent among the latter. As for Dylan himself, the invocation of McTell seems to amount to this: the artist is putting all of that faith of his into music, his own music and the music of tradition. It is, in this song, the only thing that's left to be trusted in a fallen world. He is calling on Blind Willie in the way some people call on saints: you can all but hear it in his voice. Dylan does not say that this was the very best of the bluesmen. Pushed for a judgement on that score, he has generally tended to nominate Robert Johnson. What the song does state, over and over, is that no one could sing the blues *like* McTell.

Why would that distinction matter? One explanation could be that Dylan was making a case for creative affinity, declaring that Blind Willie was, in the very deepest sense, his kind of musician, one who bore witness to origins and the meaning of art without being reduced to complaint or bluster or mere reportage. For McTell read Dylan, in other words, right down to a shared if erratic religiosity. A better idea, perhaps, is to take Blind Willie as an example of prototypical genius seeming to emerge from nowhere. This was the miracle attributed to the young Dylan – who was he, where the hell had he come from? – but the writer who was approaching his 42nd birthday when he made the song his first order of business at the first *Infidels* recording session knew better. Willie McTell had been 'rediscovered', like so many of his contemporaries, because he had first been ignored by a white world. That world, with its minstrel shows and movies and rock and roll, chose to forget his music's origins and the reasons why, back to slavery and beyond, it had come into existence. All those aged 'obscure' bluesmen of Dylan's youth had come from somewhere, after all, but they and their music were things America had tried to forget. In reclaiming the man, the artist was reclaiming the past. He was making Blind Willie McTell emblematic.

In 2006, interviewed by the novelist Jonathan Lethem, Dylan would dismiss the song as released, both in its official and unofficial versions. By then he had begun to play 'Blind Willie McTell' in his concerts, but only 'because I heard The Band doing it'. He would compare the bootlegs of the *Infidels* outtakes to 'taking a painting by Manet or Picasso – goin' to his house and lookin' at a half-finished painting and grabbing it and selling it to people who are "Picasso fans"'. Where many of the bootleg recordings are concerned, he had a point. Does the artist have no say in the matter? As so often, however, Dylan's memory would then become a little vague. 'Most likely it was a demo,' he would say, 'probably showing the musicians how it should go. It was never developed fully, I never got around to completing it. There wouldn't have been any other reason for leaving it off the record.'[27] In 1984, closer to the event, he would tell *Rolling Stone*'s Kurt Loder that the song was discarded because 'I don't think I recorded it right'.[28]

As ever, Dylan's answers would be occasions for still more questions. Neither version of 'Blind Willie McTell' sounds anything but 'right'. Whether the song could have sat easily alongside the other tracks on *Infidels* is another matter entirely. That consideration might, in the far realms of guesswork, have been a reason for setting aside the work. Another guess sometimes heard is that Dylan believed his own vocal performance had been a failure. If the song was truly 'half-finished', on the other hand, you can only speculate and marvel at the vision that eluded the artist.

'Someone's Got a Hold of My Heart' should have been on the album; 'Foot of Pride' should have been on the album. In both cases, the arguments are, for this listener, straightforward. In the former case, Dylan knew he had a song of value. He would rework it when he came to make the album *Empire Burlesque* as 'Tight Connection to My Heart (Has Anybody Seen My Love)' and make the piece the opening track on a set that would need all the help it could get. Like 'Foot of Pride', the song works by transposing Dylan's biblical imagery to his version of the modern (if pre-apocalyptic) world. Here there is still 'fucking religion' aplenty, but it is not insisted upon, not in a manner liable to trouble a Columbia executive. The dismissive allusion to the blood of Christ might, on the other hand, cause grief to a toiler in the Vineyard.

> I been to Babylon and I got to confess
> I could still hear the voice crying in the wilderness
> What looks large from a distance
> Close up is never that big . . .

> Never could learn to drink that blood and call it wine
> Never could learn to look at your face and call it mine

'Neighborhood Bully' should not have been on the album; 'Man of Peace' should not have been on the album. The former work, as was noticed instantly, was more than just a defence of Israel's right to exist.

Instead it was an attempt to justify the most right-wing variety of Zionist 'security' policy and would be recognised for what it was, as if for irony's sake, even by Israelis. Robert Hilburn of the *Los Angeles Times* would discover as much when Dylan came to play two concerts in Israel in 1987. Ron Maiberg, editor of a magazine called *Montin*, would tell the American critic that the song 'portrays Israel as a helpless neighbor in a neighborhood full of bullies, which is a very right-wing political view here and it depresses me that Dylan is speaking for them'. Another prominent local journalist, Robert Rosenberg, would agree that 'it's a right-wing song in strictly Israeli jargon'. Nevertheless, this writer would 'understand completely how Dylan, visiting here, takes a look around at the region . . . at the vulnerability of the country and says, "Yeah, you've got to be a neighborhood bully to survive." It is not an unnatural reaction.' For what it's worth, the song would not be performed in either of the concerts in Israel.

> Well, he knocked out a lynch mob, he was criticized
> Old women condemned him, said he should apologize
> Then he destroyed a bomb factory, nobody was glad
> The bombs were meant for him. He was supposed to feel bad

There is probably little point in recording that the reasons for decades of conflict between Israel and its enemies have been just a little more complicated than Dylan chooses to believe. It is worth observing, however, that the artist's reaction to Middle Eastern affairs would have gratified the Religious Right in America and cheered their conservative allies in Israel. Equally, as though it needs to be stated, there was once upon a time a Bob Dylan who would have abhorred this species of dim-witted propaganda. Nowhere in 'Neighborhood Bully' is it so much as suggested that anyone who was not an Israeli could have suffered in the region's endless bloody confrontations. Asked about the piece a year or so after it was recorded, Dylan tried to say that it was not 'political' because he had no allegiance to any of the 'maybe 20 political parties' in Israel. He also tried to say that he didn't deserve to be labelled – stuck with 'some party-political slogan' – because 'I don't know what the politics of Israel is'. He thought he knew enough to come out swinging on one side, however. Coming from the writer of 'Masters of War', the *Infidels* song is indeed depressing. Given what was sacrificed to allow it to remain on the album, the track, pedestrian enough just as a piece of music, is doubly dispiriting.

'Man of Peace' is meanwhile just a throwback to the overt, dismal proselytising of *Saved*. It is a rerun of a favourite born-again argument, founded on the distinctly weird contention that 'Good intentions can be evil', that the Antichrist – who might turn out to *seem* like a great humanitarian or philanthropist – is among us even now. (As though, as ever, we've nothing else to worry about.) The song does not begin to compete even with Dylan's better evangelical songs.

'Sweetheart Like You' is a good song, despite its touches of not-so-latent sexism. 'Union Sundown' is a little confused but not catastrophic and rocks along in fine style. 'Don't Fall Apart On Me Tonight' stands up well even now. 'License to Kill' and 'I and I' have their merits, though even their merits are nothing special. In the end, one song of those Dylan allowed himself raises the entire *Infidels* album above the commonplace. A very strange song it is, too.

'Jokerman' took part of its inspiration, according to the writer, from Caribbean legends of 'these spirits they call *jumbis*'.[29] The usual spelling, if it matters, is either *jumbee* or *jumbie*, while the weird tales of the creatures' shenanigans vary greatly from island to island. It seems the stories also derive from a bewildering variety of ethnic and religious sources. Some of these evil dead busy themselves with vampirism, some with lycanthropy, some with basic possession of the living, some with sucking out the brains of unsuspecting passers-by. In other words, *jumbees* are malevolent spirits, in one guise or another.

Dylan's mention of these entertaining folk myths could be ignored as just another of his vague explanations for the creative process were it not for the quantity of things he seemed capable of believing in 1983. His interviewer was told that 'Jokerman' is 'very mystical', as indeed it is. In the islands, the 'shapes there, and shadows, seem to be so ancient', Dylan said. But then he *seemed* to say that the spirits themselves had 'sorta inspired' the song. Even for him, that was fanciful. Yet when he had been asked by another journalist not long before if he believed in reincarnation, this same writer had answered, 'Yeah, I do. I don't think there are any new souls on earth.'[30] It was not the first time he had affirmed such a belief. So what did he not believe? The chances of laughing all of this off as a playful Dylan hoax diminish slightly when you realise that he was talking about *jumbees* just after insisting, in the same interview, that the Bible is the literal truth and that 'the battle of Armageddon definitely will be fought in the Middle East'.

You needn't take him seriously – or the *jumbees* might get you – but it is worth pausing to think about what might have been going on in the mind of the author of 'Jokerman'. With that exercise complete, you can ask how such a very strange concatenation of beliefs, ideas, images and emotions could result in a song that is as powerful as any Dylan ever recorded. If what goes into a piece of work is any guide to what comes out, 'Jokerman' should be no better than the usual 'mystical' prophetic nonsense. Instead, the song is potent enough to make you think twice about the allure of apocalyptic myth, messiahs false and real, and what evil means to those who daily detect its existence on every side. Dylan made art from the oddest materials.

The Jokerman has various guises: born with a snake in each fist, shedding his skins, 'a man of the mountains', a cloud walker, a benign demagogue, a twister of dreams, yet a 'Friend to the martyr, a friend to the woman of shame'. Fair of face, worthy indeed of a Michelangelo, yet obedient only to 'The law of the jungle and the sea', the Jokerman rides a milky white steed and bears witness to a world tearing itself apart amid 'Nightsticks and water cannons, tear gas, padlocks / Molotov cocktails and rocks behind every curtain'. This joker also witnesses the birth of the Antichrist:

It's a shadowy world,
Skies are slippery grey
A woman just gave birth to a prince today
And dressed him in scarlet

He'll put the priest in his pocket,
Put the blade to the heat
Take the motherless children off the street
And place them at the feet of the harlot

This is Revelation for the 32-track age, for the video age. With *Infidels*, in fact, Dylan acknowledged the existence of newly born MTV and the advent of the promotional clip. In the film for 'Jokerman' he supplied, among other things, the basis for what remains one of the most arresting examples of a peculiar genre, even if he did keep his eyes tight shut for most of the movie. Images and his lyrics emblazoned across the images communicated ideas in a dizzying rush: Albrecht Dürer's self-portrait as Christ, a Turner, two Michelangelos, William Blake, Hieronymus Bosch, Picasso, Georgia O'Keefe, Munch and varieties of primitive art. Amid it all were newsreels and still photographs from a troubled world: dead Kennedys, Martin Luther King, Hitler, Ronald Reagan mocked, the first American combat troops into Vietnam, a nuclear blast, and mankind making its big mistake by 'touching the moon'.

One set of verses from the song was reserved for a series of images of all the previous Bob Dylans. The artist was not entirely happy with the notion that a photograph could illustrate even a single ambiguous line from a song, but he played along. You sense that, grumbling or not, he knew what he was doing. Even if the video's 'concept' was not his – George Lois, the advertising man who had fought so hard for Rubin Carter, deserved most of the credit – the conjunctions between life and art were surely no coincidence. The folk singer, the artist of 1965–6, the creator of Rolling Thunder: on the TV screen, one identity followed another.

So swiftly the sun
Sets in the sky
You rise up and say goodbye
To no one

Fools rush in
Where angels fear to tread
Both of their futures,
So full of dread,
You don't show one

Shedding off
One more layer of skin
Keeping one step ahead
Of the persecutor within

Perhaps because of the video, or perhaps because he has so often been represented as a trickster, image manipulator and inveterate myth-maker, 'Jokerman' has sometimes been taken as Dylan's song about his own legend, a track intermingled with a certain scepticism, all of a sudden, towards Christ's active role, if any, in the world. It seems unlikely, to say the least, that the number could cover all those bases. When this messiah witnesses the arrival of the Antichrist, the Deceiver, He seems utterly passive.

JOKERMAN

Oh, Jokerman,
You know what he wants
Oh, Jokerman,
You don't show any response

If this is the usual Jesus, He isn't doing His job. If this is Dylan getting carried away with his Christ-fixation, meanwhile, it all makes precious little sense, even given the endlessly perplexing nature of the song. It might be better to ask, first, why 'Jokerman', then to ask why, chorus after chorus, the incarnated, uninvolved deity would 'dance to the nightingale tune'.

Perhaps because this a song about gods, not God, a song about humanity's ability to touch the divine without hope of a guarantee that this world will be spared its usual biblical fate. Christ, if Christ it is, has a lot of humanity in him in 'Jokerman'. He also carries the traces of many of the gods worshipped by man before the nativity. He dances? That's an ancient idea. Those Caribbean spirits who 'sorta inspired' Dylan took (or take) possession of people during frenzied dances. Divine madness achieved in dancing is a notion common to cultures around the world. The old English carol, medieval in origin, called 'Tomorrow Shall Be My Dancing Day' took this stately notion and presented a Jesus whose entire time on earth could be understood as an enactment of a celestial dance. The modern hymn, 'Lord of the Dance', simply exploits the conceit. In fourteenth-century England, they sang:

Before Pilate the Jews me brought,
Where Barabbas had deliverance;
They scourged me and set me at nought,
Judged me to die to lead the dance.

Then on the cross hanged I was,
Where a spear my heart did glance;
There issued forth both water and blood,
To call my true love to my dance.

Dylan's Jokerman has within him the tension Nietzsche perceived between the Apollonian and Dionysian, order and disorder, law and misrule, intellect and instinct, mind and body. This god-figure dances to keep the world turning, dances to a tune supplied by John Keats and poetry's nightingale. Meanwhile, He stands on water, walks on cloud and avails himself of whatever human vice is to be had in Sodom and Gomorrah. Freedom, of that variety, is 'just around the corner'. Yet still, 'with the truth so far off, what good will it do?' The same figure is simultaneously obedient to 'the Book of Leviticus and Deuteronomy', Judaism's rule books, and to 'the law of the jungle and the sea' underpinning earthly existence. Necessary order and divine disorder: the human dialectic. But still, how could a messiah be a joker?

Dylan has been at his Tarot again. This time there is not much ambiguity about the hand played, but the pillaging of the esoteric deck has interesting resonances within the song. In the standard Rider-Waite pack the Joker is known as the Fool, numbered zero if he is numbered at all. In older French and Italian sets of cards the Fool was rendered as some version of 'Madman'. The figure was depicted, furthermore, either as a kind of holy fool, divinely deranged, or as the ragged Wildman of the Woods, the last descendant of pagan Dionysus. Commonly, even today, the Fool is shown as the possessor of a small dog. So:

Resting in the fields,
Far from the turbulent space
Half asleep near the stars
With a small dog licking your face

Near the stars might allude neatly to Oscar Wilde's boast on behalf of those who rest in the gutter yet can see beyond grim reality; of the wee dog, there can surely be little doubt. Yet how would that fit with Dylan-plays-Christ? The former has kept dogs (rarely small) but Scripture makes no mention of Jesus in the company of pets beyond the familiar texts on sheep, lambs and straying flocks. The hound is in the song for a reason, nevertheless, and it can only be a Tarot-related reason. It is certainly a fact that the animal is present in an alternate 'Jokerman' take, one that gathers the Fool and his Dionysian antecedents together. As Dylan sings in this earlier, better version:

So drunk, standing in the middle of the street
Directing traffic, with a small dog at your feet

Perhaps he's just fond of animals and gave us a Tarot joke to be going on with, interpreting until kingdom come. There are several points of difference between the two versions of the song, nevertheless, and one of these indicates a fascinating moment when the writer clearly had second thoughts about the truth he meant to convey. In the track as released, the earthly struggle between good and evil is conveyed as follows:

> Well, the rifleman's stalking
> The sick and the lame
> Preacherman seeks the same
> Who'll get there first is uncertain

On the bootlegs, meanwhile, Dylan can be heard to sing:

> Well, a preacherman talkin'
> 'Bout the deaf and the dumb
> And a world to come
> That's already been pre-determined

There were sound and obvious metrical reasons for getting rid of 'pre-determined'. By the time he settled on his preferred version, however, Dylan might also have decided – indeed, did decide – that he had no wish to pursue the kind of basic theological point that was otherwise transubstantiated meat and drink to the evangelicals. Whether he was heeding Dick Asher's alleged $20-million threats or changing his own way of thinking, whether he had returned to secular views or not (not), there is a world of difference, in fact and logic, between what is pre-determined and what is uncertain.

There is plenty of doubt in 'Jokerman'. That's what helps to make it a great Bob Dylan song. The doubt is neither existential nor cosmological. For the artist, the fundamental issues had been settled, once and for all, before 1983. But in this song he is asking learned questions. What is a god who becomes a man and lives among men? What difference does it make to the existence of men? How does a messiah function 'when He returns' and the Antichrist is disguised by good deeds and clad in the scarlet of the Whore of Babylon? (Revelation 17:4: 'And the woman was arrayed in purple and scarlet colour, and decked with gold and precious stones and pearls, having a golden cup in her hand full of abominations and filthiness of her fornication.') In Dylan's belief, Christ does not, because He cannot, 'show any response'.

Give the writer credit for audacity, despite it all. As albums containing 'no fucking religion' go, *Infidels* opens with a remarkable piece of work, a marvellous machine made of interlocking rhymes, rhythmic pulses and transcendent singing. Soon enough, people would be wondering what became of that Bob Dylan.

*

Some of the reviews for the album wouldn't help. In New York's *Village Voice* (29 November 1983), quantifying artistic success and failure with a helpful B-minus on his critic's pocket calculator, Robert Christgau would judge that the artist had managed a 'complexity of tone' but nevertheless 'turned into a hateful crackpot' with his lectures on industrial relations, Israel and the risks of space travel. 'Jokerman' would not even be mentioned by the voice of the *Voice*. Others, such as the reviewer for *Rolling Stone*, were cheered by the album, excessively so, but the Christgau view would not disappear. Michael Gray, that most notable of writers on Dylan, grants everything to the opening track, but still finds *Infidels* giving off 'feigned emotion wrapped in a fog of mere professional competence'. As for the artist, Gray has written, this 'dissembling demeans him'. The album is 'a small, shifty failure', failing 'in a small-minded, cheating way'.[31]

Such talk might be enough to persuade the unwary to prefer *Saved* and *Shot of Love*. That would be a big mistake. Those who greeted *Infidels* as a relief and heard its merits were not so far wrong. It would be a long while before they were again allowed even a notable-if-shifty failure from this artist. Nevertheless, the largest and most important fact, then as now, was that Dylan disfigured one of his better efforts in the studios for reasons that even he has struggled to explain. Mark Knopfler went off to Europe on tour with his band and the artist was left alone to overdub, mix the album and make his own choices. They were bad choices. Afterwards, Knopfler would be baffled, dismayed and just a little peeved by what became of all his exertions on behalf of *Infidels*. Once again, Dylan's attitude towards his own work raised questions. Did he know what he was doing? More to the point, did he know why?

No tour was planned for 1983. Dylan went back to Malibu, messed around with some young local musicians and in March 1984 put in an appearance on NBC's *Late Night with David Letterman*. The performance was both chaotic – for want of the right harmonica the singer was momentarily lost – and enthralling. The video for 'Jokerman' had been released during the previous month to much media chatter and acclaim. Predictably, the version of the song thrashed out for the TV audience with just bass, drums and guitar by Dylan and three under-rehearsed youngsters was barely a second cousin to the album track. The artist seemed invigorated, nevertheless, by his pick-up band and the company of a new generation of musicians.

Nothing came of it. Those four words could stand as the epitaph for most of Dylan's endeavours in the years ahead.

CHAPTER NINE

World Gone Wrong

THE CLEVER COMMERCIAL MOVE WOULD HAVE BEEN TO FOLLOW *Infidels* in short order with another polished, professional and mostly 'secular' album, one laying to rest the obnoxious allegation put about by supercilious hacks that Bob Dylan had suffered a midlife creative crisis. In theory, such a task should have posed no serious challenge. Four albums had appeared in just over four years since the release of *Slow Train Coming* in August 1979. They had ranged from decent to dreadful, but a song such as 'Jokerman' demonstrated even to the artist's worst enemies among the critics that, despite everything, his essential talent was intact. In his born-again moment he had been furiously productive. What hindered Dylan now? There was surely no good reason to doubt that he could deliver product if required. *Infidels* had meanwhile repaired most of the damage done by *Saved* and *Shot of Love*, reaching number twenty in America and number nine in Britain. Columbia had recouped a large part of whatever vast sum they had paid out for a five-album contract. There was a moment to be seized.

It didn't happen. Some 13 long months would elapse between the appearance of *Infidels* and a new Dylan album. The artefact when it arrived would amount to little more than a stopgap, a desperately poor one at that. *Real Live* would seem only to justify the perennial suspicion among fans that cynical performers stick out concert albums when they have nothing better to offer. Dylan's effort would be treated with the disdain it deserved – even the title would seem lazy – but miserable sales figures would not spur him into action. Evidence for a loss of appetite, interest, will, desire, concentration and creativity would mount. Another seven months would go by after *Real Live* before Dylan's twenty-third studio album reached the stores. Celebrations would be muted when they were even audible. All the ground regained with *Infidels* would be lost, and lost, so it would seem, irretrievably. Even the last of all possible excuses, 'better than nothing', would be hard to sustain. And the album called *Empire Burlesque* would not be the worst of it.

*

For some who remember the period, the 1980s tend to call W.H. Auden's contemptuous epitaph for the '30s to mind. Here was another 'low, dishonest decade', its clever hopes soon expired. If the coke habits, booze, ugly fashions, ostentatious wealth and gaudy politics of the few were insufficiently distracting, the '80s counted for everyone else as a time when it made rational sense to be uncertain and afraid amid global 'waves of anger and fear'.[1] It was a decade that seemed to baffle Dylan even as it all but destroyed him as a writer.

Both America and Britain had acquired right-wing governments as conservative as any they had seen. The absolutist free-market policies promoted by these administrations would make a minority rich and leave the majority to worry about jobs and the uncertainties of a post-industrial world. Both countries had elected leaders, in Reagan and Margaret Thatcher, with a marked taste for Cold War rhetoric and an eagerness to risk a confrontation with the Soviet Union. Both leaders liked to preach a stern economic discipline that somehow they failed to practise. While increasing the defence expenditure of the United States by 40 per cent in real terms between 1981 and 1985, Reagan, that enemy of 'public spending', was piling up the national debt as though assembling an oozing toxic layer cake. No matter how hard he hacked away at the programmes intended to aid the poor, the Republican president could not balance the books. By the time he left office early in 1989, the debt burden would have almost tripled, from $997 billion to $2.85 trillion. While the better-off were enjoying his tax cuts and *Infidels* was being released, the unemployment rate in 1983 for ordinary Americans, according to the official numbers, was touching 10.4 per cent. By borrowing to cover Reagan's budget deficit, their country had become the biggest debtor the world had seen. Times had indeed changed.

Unabashed neo-liberalism had arrived in the democracies of the West. Country to country, the family resemblance was unmistakable. Trade unions, the public realm, left-idealism under the banner of the bleeding heart, the 'permissive society': these were to be prepared for history's dustbin. To justify an agreeable theory, Thatcher's British 'economic miracle' had torn the vitals out of manufacturing and turned the country into a net importer of goods for the first time. In January 1982, if you believed figures based on ever-changing, politically useful methods of calculation, the average rate of joblessness in the United Kingdom was 12.5 per cent. In the old industrial regions of the country, one in five were out of work. In the most afflicted areas, the figures were still worse as Thatcher prepared to pick a fight with Britain's coal miners and divide her country utterly. Dylan might have tired of 'issues' – though 'Union Sundown' had seemed to say otherwise – but he could not ignore the world in which he found himself. He could try, though.

On one reading of events, the advent of Reagan and Thatcher was proof enough that the progressive forces which once had claimed Dylan as a figurehead had failed completely. Not a lot of overcoming had been done by those who liked to sing reassuring anthems. The 'foes' mentioned in the youth's 'When the Ship Comes In' when he performed the song at the Washington civil rights march in August 1963 had not chosen to 'raise their hands / Sayin'' we'll meet all your demands'. Moreover, Reagan and Thatcher were the democratic choices of their peoples, elected and re-elected. The only alternative explanation, still being heard more than 20 years after those early-'60s songs, was that the battle had been lost because Dylan and others besides had deserted the fight. The criticism could have been developed further. By the early '80s born-again Bob had seemed to forget even the reasons for the conflict. Where morality was concerned, especially the moral failure he defined as sin, that Dylan had been on the side of the conservatives. The single telling fact might be that such insights, if insights they were, had done his art no good.

In music, as in real life, the 1980s were proving to be a charmless decade. If, for argument's sake, year zero was 1956 and the Big Bang in a small universe the release of 'Heartbreak Hotel', maximum entropy was achieved within three decades. What began with Elvis Presley at an afternoon recording session on Nashville's McGavock Street on 10 January in '56 was over and done, never to be renewed, when Dylan was releasing *Empire Burlesque* and preparing the folly he would call *Knocked Out Loaded*. Presley had brought him to consciousness as a 14-year-old. A decade later Dylan was contending with the hanging judges at the Manchester Free Trade Hall. A decade after that, barely a month before the anniversary of the 'Heartbreak Hotel' session, he was on stage at Madison Square Garden in New York, singing for the freedom of Hurricane Carter. Yet by the time one more decade had elapsed Dylan would be telling a journalist from the Australian TV programme *60 Minutes* that he didn't know much about anything. By the sound of things, he wouldn't care a great deal either.

In January 1986, the programme's George Negus would ask the artist if the times had truly changed as once he had predicted. The answer: 'I don't know. I've no answer.' Had he believed, then, in the imminence of those great changes when he wrote the song? 'I would have no way of knowing,' replied the oracle. His religion, Dylan would claim, 'has more to do with playing the guitar'. As to possessing anything as risky as an actual opinion about anything at all, the response from this *fin de siècle* performing artist would be worthy of a suspect under interrogation, or of a coma victim regaining consciousness. 'I mean,' he would say, 'it would be pointless for me to go out and say how I feel about this and how I feel about that.'

One popular theory, attractive because it is impossible to prove, holds that everything Elvis began ended with punk. The rest, including Dylan's career from the mid-1980s onwards, has been a dull, irrelevant footnote, or a species of nostalgia. The explosive energy of the primeval moment had dissipated by the time the '80s arrived; the music, as one of the singer-songwriters Dylan permitted said, had 'died'. So the story goes. But the belief that pop was flawless and unimpeachable once upon a time is founded on a myth. The idea that innovation ended was being mocked by new-school hip hop even as Dylan was turning *Infidels* into a jigsaw with most of the important pieces missing.

The 1980s were peculiarly decadent, much of the time, for reasons of their own. Some of it had to do with the nature of that low, dishonest decade; some of it had to do with the likes of Dylan and his surviving contemporaries, the odd species known as rock stars, befuddled people with too much money and too little remaining artistic sense. Music was in decline in the middle of the 1980s for the simple and profound reason that those who had once made the great records settled for inferior stuff, even risible stuff. The buying public seemed to have no complaints, after all.

In Britain in 1984 Paul McCartney would score a number one with 'Pipes of Peace'; Stevie Wonder would do the same with 'I Just Called to Say I Love You'. Lionel Richie would enjoy a gargantuan British hit with the frankly creepy and musically redundant 'Hello'. Most of the rest would involve drum machines, Wham! and Duran Duran. If Dylan was in need of a hint, meanwhile, the essential American response in

1984 would be Bruce Springsteen's vastly successful valediction to the Vietnam generation and their music, *Born in the USA*. That album would sell more copies, upwards of 15 million of them, than most of Dylan's releases put together. He had always been a minority taste. In 1984, he seemed determined to stretch the definition of that category to its limits.

In a suddenly conservative world, a subgenus of the self-involved called *yuppies* occupied a lot of column inches and airtime. Credit and the consumption justified by credit were the new preoccupations of those in work and, as they perceived it, on top of the heap. There was a lot of talk, on both sides of the Atlantic, about individualism and liberty, rather less about communities and freedom. In this era, Reagan and his bosom friend Thatcher shared a taste for moralistic homilies. They seemed to stress that any difficulties in life were due to personal character flaws, or to a society that had lost its 'values'.

This kind of conservatism could be comical, never more so than in 1987 when a wandering right-wing academic named Allan Bloom would decide that America had boarded the handcart to hell because its colleges had succumbed to relativism and the exotic allure – Thomas Jefferson was not available for comment – of Enlightenment thought. Bloom's book, *The Closing of the American Mind*, would provide an emblematic cultural moment by picking on music, 'rock music' that is, as the reason for young America's 'spiritual void' and the failure of youth to attend to all the things Allan Bloom had to say about the books Allan Bloom had decided were eternally canonical. To read *The Closing of the American Mind* in 1987 was like spinning a dial and picking up 1957, loud and clear. Rock music, Bloom wrote in the '80s, 'has one appeal only, a barbaric appeal, to sexual desire – not love, not *eros* – but sexual desire undeveloped and untutored'.[2] It was, indeed, 'the beat of sexual intercourse' and it was helping to lay waste the nation's intellectual capacities, its capitalism and its democracy. Bloom would have Plato and Nietzsche on his side, whether they knew it or not, but he would make no mention of Bob Dylan. The book was a big success, meanwhile. In its aftermath, as one journal would record, 'Conservative cultural commentators burst forth from all corners, rhetorical cudgels in hand.' Their list of pernicious trends 'was long and varied: political correctness, multi-culturalism, deconstruction, cultural and moral relativism, feminism, rock & roll, television, the legacy of the Sixties . . .'[3]

That last decade was long over and done, as the artist knew better than most. The 1970s had given him a tantalising encore. In the 1980s, most of the time, he would struggle and fail to find a Bob Dylan adequate to the occasion. That once reliable conveyor belt of identities had ground to a halt. Suddenly his art, what remained of it, had neither purpose nor meaning.

*

So much was evident during a brief, catastrophic European tour, the last Dylan would countenance before the early weeks of 1986. The only apparent motives for this 1984 exercise were the sums of money that could be taken on the gate at big football stadiums and Olympic arenas across the continent. Band introductions aside, Dylan barely spoke a word to the vast crowds. The veteran musical crew assembled by Mick Taylor might have been designed, meanwhile, to illustrate just how redundant this version of 'rock' had become. As often as not, the hired hands had no idea what Dylan intended to play on a given night and no understanding of how, if at all, they were supposed to follow his butterfly instincts. For whatever reason, Carlos Santana and his band were hired as one support act; Joan Baez as another. Soon disillusioned, yet again, she failed to stay the course. Later, the experience would be recalled as 'one of the most demoralising series of events I've ever lived through'. Baez would also record how it felt to be groped, it seems for old time's sake, by an enervated, half-aware superstar whose character she could barely recognise.[4]

Dylan was knocking out old hits for big money, yet talking, when he deigned to talk, as though he lived for art alone. On 27 June, in a café in Madrid, he would tell Mick Brown of England's *Sunday Times* that 'I don't think I'm gonna be really understood until maybe 100 years from now'.[5] The next night he would be doing 'Maggie's Farm', 'Ballad of a Thin Man', 'Like a Rolling Stone', 'Knockin' On Heaven's Door' and all the other old songs he had begun to regard as perfunctory offerings to those who still thought it a treat to glimpse from several hundred yards' distance someone who might once have been Bob Dylan. The 'stadium-rock experience' was another of those 1980s phenomena to which he had consented. Here was the deified artist, beyond reach and almost beyond sight; here too were the multitudes who would take what they were given. Any belief in the communicative function and power of art and artist was boiled away while the band, the contract labour, played on.

By the time the tour reached the inverted pit of London's Wembley

Stadium on 7 July, Dylan was littering his stage with 'guest stars'. An honest groundling might have glimpsed Van Morrison, or heard a guitar that might have been played by Eric Clapton. The alert ticket-holder probably noticed that the artist had messed around with the words to 'Simple Twist of Fate' and, as ever, decided that 'Tangled Up in Blue' stood in need of revision. The worth of all this would be revealed when *Real Live*, with tracks recorded in London, Newcastle and Dublin, was released in November of the year. It is possible, just about, to argue that the album does not represent the better moments of the tour, but it still gives a fair account of the average show in Europe in '84. American record-buyers – which is to say non-buyers – would make *Real Live* the least successful of all of Bob Dylan's albums. Number 115 on the *Billboard* chart would be its reward and its requiem.

Back in America, he returned to the studios and began the long, tedious process of casting around for inspiration in the hope that an album would emerge. Songs, suddenly, were coming hard, but that was not the whole story. The fact that Dylan's very first studio sessions would revolve around material that had found no place on *Infidels* was revealing. The fact that he tried (and failed) to make something out of 'Clean-Cut Kid' rather than 'Foot of Pride' or 'Blind Willie McTell' is beyond curious. It was as though he no longer understood how a great song sounded.

The standard excuse for Dylan's working methods, an excuse he has used often enough in his own defence, is that he does not return to the scene of previous defeats. If a song is deemed a failure, he forgets it and moves on. In Dylan's telling of the legend, fantastic unheard works float between possible universes. With *Empire Burlesque*, nevertheless, he would return twice to the *Infidels* discard pile, consciously and deliberately, yet take an interest only in one fine song and one minor piece. No issue of principle as to the reuse of previous work was at stake, therefore. Dylan nevertheless took an avid interest in some songs and ignored other, better works. It is almost as if he was keeping 'Blind Willie McTell' in reserve for the rainiest of days.

That blasphemous suggestion can be heard among fans, now and then. The basic allegation, the conspiracy within the grand conspiracy, is that Dylan's many outtakes, known to the world of 'collectors' almost from the instant a recording console switch is reset, are no accident, that since the Bootleg Series he has salted tracks away for the sake of a secondary, if highly profitable, outlet. This, it is argued, is how he allows himself to think twice, to make amends, and to take no responsibility for what might have gone wrong with all those 'official' albums. With the Bootleg Series as a safety net, there is no longer a pressure to get things right first time around. All albums become, in a sense, provisional. A judicious release of outtakes can repair the reputational damage of any number of past failures. A new album can be revised, in effect, almost as soon as it has been released. It is a pleasing idea, but silly. No one wastes material the way Dylan has wasted material, sometimes in moments of dire need, if his calculations are so cold-blooded. Equally, no one has worked as he has worked, amid a virtual posterity, for quite so long.

So: when did discussions truly begin over the creation of the *Biograph* box set, the one that would be released to the world at the end of October (or the beginning of November) in 1985? When did Dylan, who had failed for years to make anything useful out of the basement tapes, decide to feed on his own corpus? A great deal of work on copyrights and permissions, not to mention a lot of archival labour and audio restoration, must have been undertaken before the 'unprecedented retrospective' (and so forth) *Biograph* collection of five vinyl discs or three CDs gained Columbia's approval. A certain amount of thought on the artist's part must also have taken place. The first of the big, lucrative box sets dedicated to a living artist, a concept that would give the music industry a second lease on life, didn't just happen.

Dylan's tendency to regard himself and his work as entities existing outside the present moment has never been accidental. Equally, no one begins to curate his own life inadvertently, least of all in the trough of a writer's despond. Yet the most remarkable sleight of hand conducted by this artist down the years has involved persuading the world (himself included, it sometimes seems) that stuff just happens. Songs somehow get written, albums somehow get made and fame – none of this is Dylan's doing – somehow descends. Yet by allowing the *Biograph* set he did not just give permission for still another greatest-hits package. With this little casket he altered his perspective on his own work. In fact, he would alter everyone's perspective, even when they thought they knew every possible angle. Accepting the past, and with it all those accumulated identities, he could never be the same unencumbered artist again. He would make a fair few bucks from *Biograph*, though, and go on insisting that none of it was his idea.

In the mid-1980s, no one had yet realised that you could, in essence, flog a bunch of old, near-forgotten stuff to the middle-aged demographic and screw the tape thieves, as it were, to boot. For that matter, you could repackage a career, an artist or an entire self-conscious 'legendary' existence. Dylan's public position was then, as it remains, to disdain all his missing back pages. He still pretends that his hugely lucrative Bootleg Series releases have somehow just materialised while his back was turned. In November 1985, talking to *Time* magazine about *Biograph*, he would state:

> It wasn't my idea to put the record out. This record has been suggested in the past, but I guess it just didn't come together until recently. I think it's been in the works for like three years. I had very little to do with it. I didn't choose the songs. A lot of people probably had a hand in it. The record company has the right to do whatever they please with the songs. I didn't care about what was on the record. I haven't sat down and listened to it.[6]

Dylan would go on to boast that if someone had made it 'worth my while' a compilation twice the size might have been forthcoming. It could, he said, have contained nothing but his unreleased songs. In a slight if inadvertently truthful slip, however, the line about 'the record company has the right to do whatever they please' would be undermined by the artist's flat statement: 'I'm the final judge of what goes on and off my records.' So who had sanctioned the box set? Columbia might have been entitled to another greatest-hits package, but not to *Biograph*. Like everyone else in his business, Dylan signs contracts. These specify the number and nature of his releases. Sony/Columbia, as the conglomerate is these days more accurately styled, cannot just empty its vaults of his material as it sees fit. To this day, the planning of Bootleg Series releases is subject to continual revision according to choices made, if the record company is to be believed, only by the artist or his representatives. If nothing else, uncertainty and fascinating rumours keep the hardcore fans interested.

Biograph had been in the planning, nevertheless, 'for like three years' as of November 1985. So the intention to memorialise Bob Dylan in a lavish if unproven format, if with no more than his tacit consent, had come into existence just after *Shot of Love* was dying its deserved death. The artist was regarding himself – his life, his writing, his career – as an artefact as early as 1982. To see his monument being erected while he was trying to make a new record, even if he 'didn't care' about the contents of *Biograph*, must surely have had an inhibiting effect on his writing. The evidence of Dylan's mid-1980s albums suggests that the effect was near-paralysing. Even today, the continuing archaeological excavations represented by the Bootleg Series must make for an odd existence, like reading your own obituary day after day. 'Bob Dylan', that mirror within a mirror, is a work forever in progress for the man who bears the name.

Back in 1985, the accusation that he aimed for a 'disco' sound with *Empire Burlesque* was perhaps the most half-witted of all the criticisms the artist has ever encountered. A lot of things can be done, no doubt, to the accompaniment of a Dylan soundtrack, but dancing has never been one of them. The same was true of the album he made in fits and starts, with a changing cast of musicians, between the summer of 1984 and March 1985. The aim was to achieve what was then a 'contemporary' sound with the help of the fashionable engineer and producer Arthur Baker, an individual who had worked, as Dylan was no doubt aware, with Bruce Springsteen. It is not a sound – cluttered, top-heavy, full of manipulated drum machine effects, synthesisers, horns and over-assertive bass lines – that has improved with age. It is as though a template was created before anyone listened to the songs. But then, the album itself can probably be summed up by the fact that its best track, 'Tight Connection to My Heart (Has Anybody Seen My Love)', was in essence a leftover from *Infidels*.

In this song, as elsewhere on the album, Dylan had begun to incorporate snatches of old movie dialogue into his writing, anticipating techniques he would adopt wholesale in the twenty-first century. Yet while the ventriloquising of hard-boiled Humphrey Bogart works brilliantly in 'Tight Connection' – 'Well, I had to move fast / And I couldn't with you around my neck' is lifted almost intact from a picture called *Sirocco* (1951) – other borrowings are less successful. Songs, it turned out, could not be assembled from found art alone, though criticisms of Dylan's technique are sometimes based on a deep misunderstanding of what plagiarism means. Who could have resisted 'I'll go along with the charade / Until I can think my way out', even if its source was a less than perfect 1949 Bogart movie called *Tokyo Joe*? If the audience is ignorant of the source, what does it matter? The issue is one of intent and artistic resources. Could a writer be culpable because he lifted a few lines while stuck for ideas, yet innocent of theft if, consciously and artistically, he was trying to create a particular verbal resonance? Dylan would have to deal with that persistent question at a later date.[7]

Of the rest of the *Empire Burlesque* songs, or rather the best of the rest, the mesmerising 'Dark Eyes' was a simple, acoustic affair, blessedly free of Baker's 'production' and relying on just Dylan's guitar, his harmonica and his words. Supposedly inspired by a late-night encounter in a hotel lobby, it sounds like a lament for all women who stray in the dark, for the writer himself, and for lost souls everywhere.

Oh, the French girl she's in paradise
And a drunken man is at the wheel
Hunger pays a heavy price
To the falling gods of speed and steel

Oh, time is short and the days are sweet
And passion rules the arrow that flies
A million faces at my feet
But all I see are dark eyes

Typically, Dylan would discard a thundering version of a song entitled 'When the Night Comes Falling From the Sky' that he had recorded with Steve Van Zandt and Roy Bittan of Springsteen's E Street Band. It would be resurrected – for everything the artist did could now be revised or restored to life – on 1991's *The Bootleg Series Volumes 1–3*. The same luck would not befall another, better and far more important track that emerged, as though from nowhere, during a session in Los Angeles during the second week in December 1984. Written with the playwright Sam Shepard, 'New Danville Girl' is one of the most structurally complex narratives ever to bear Dylan's name. As such, it is also one of the most sophisticated meditations on identity, fate and memory ever attempted in popular song (or in any other art form). All that being the case, it was almost inevitable that the track would not make the *Empire Burlesque* album. When Dylan later returned to the piece he failed to improve it and used the song, renamed 'Brownsville Girl' and still a riveting creation, to pad out a miserably poor album. For now, that's another story.

The complicated history of *Empire Burlesque* does not make the album any more interesting unless your taste runs to the analysis of outmoded production techniques. Yet again, like a man calling heads and getting tails a statistically improbable number of times, Dylan had misjudged – and therefore misunderstood – his own best songs. In 1985, he had few enough of those. Too many of the pieces that survived his haphazard culling were probably better read than heard. That was not, presumably, the judgement an artist in need of a hit record wanted to hear. If *Empire Burlesque* caught a break from the critics when it was released that was mostly because of continuing relief that God remained a backseat driver. As Clinton Heylin has observed, the artist had stripped religious allusions from 'Someone's Got a Hold of My Heart' – Christ's blood and so forth – when turning the song into 'Tight Connection to My Heart'.[8] Overt religiosity was behind him finally. It might say something about the open-mindedness or otherwise of critics, but any Dylan album without born-again overtones had a head start in the mid-'80s.

Record-buyers would be more pragmatic, raising *Empire Burlesque* no higher than number 33 in the American chart. British fans, loyal as ever, allowed the album to rise briefly to number seven, but in Dylan's homeland the public was more perceptive than some of the critics who allowed undimmed hope to be father to their thoughts. At this distance in time it is hard even to understand what *Rolling Stone*'s Kurt Loder thought he was hearing when he wrote of

a blast of real rock & roll, funnelled through a dense, roiling production – custom-chopped-and-channelled by remix wiz Arthur Baker – that affords Dylan more pure street-beat credibility than he has aspired to since . . . well, pick your favourite faraway year. Could there be actual hits hunkering here? Is Dylan 'back'? Again? One is tempted to trumpet some such tidings.[9]

History would judge it to be a trumpet solo. For his next trick, in any case, the artist would join the chorus. In January of 1985, whether because of some species of industry peer pressure or a sincere belief in celebrity-endorsed charitable endeavours, an unmistakable voice could be heard peppering an unremarkable if well-meaning singalong called 'We Are the World'. This was the American response to the Band Aid project launched in Britain a few months earlier by Bob Geldof and Midge Ure to succour the oppressed in Ethiopia. USA for Africa, as the American ensemble called itself, involved a large and absurdly 'diverse' group of singers and show-business types. Dylan found himself in a Los Angeles studio alongside everyone from Willie Nelson to Ray Charles, Springsteen to Diana Ross, Paul Simon to Kenny Rogers. He delivered his closing chorus with a certain growling gusto, but at the time he seemed not to wonder why a song dedicated to the downtrodden failed to ask about the reasons for their plight. 'We Are the World', banal and sentimental, was certainly not a Bob Dylan song, far less a human-rights anthem. On the other hand, it did raise tens of millions of dollars and, presumably, saved some lives.

In the aftermath, Dylan was persuaded to take part in the gigantic transatlantic Live Aid event in July. Of all the mistakes he made in the 1980s, this would be among the worst. It would certainly be the best remembered. The idea was to stage two vast concerts, one at London's Wembley Stadium, the other in Philadelphia's JFK Stadium, and to link them by satellite with other shows around the planet. In one mark of his continuing eminence in American music, Dylan was asked to close the concert on his side of the Atlantic before the massed ranks of celebrity sympathisers gathered for a rendition of 'We Are the World'. In theory, there should have been no problem. Anyone who saw Dylan's performance at the time, or has seen it since, will recognise the ghastly fascination experienced by a TV audience estimated at 1.9 billion as grim reality unfolded.

One idea had been for Dylan to perform 'Blowin' in the Wind' with the reassembled Peter, Paul and Mary. Whether because the symbolism was too much for him – the trio's version of his song had long been a mixed blessing – or because his voice was no longer up to the job, the artist took against that proposal. He decided instead that he would perform with Ronnie Wood and Keith Richards of the Rolling Stones. Contrary to appearances in Philadelphia, the three *did* rehearse before facing the global audience. On stage, however, the Englishmen gave the distinct impression that perhaps they had killed time while waiting to go on by sharing a bottle or two. Dylan, sweating and strained, didn't look good. His companions looked as though they were lounging in the back room of an after-hours club as time was being called. The improvised sound was pitiful while the artist's choice of songs was hardly calculated to tug heart strings or open wallets around the world. 'The Ballad of Hollis Brown' and 'When the Ship Comes In', a pair of songs from his earliest days, were not the sunniest works in Dylan's repertoire. The inevitable 'Blowin' in the Wind' meanwhile failed to suggest that 'the answer' had ever involved regiments of rich, self-regarding superstars wheedling cash from common folk for the sake of the starving. The impression given by the louche trio – to be strictly fair, they had been denied the onstage monitors that would have allowed them to hear how they sounded – was not helped when the singer decided to speak. After 'Hollis Brown', Dylan said:

I'd just like to say I hope that some of the money that's raised for the people in Africa, maybe they could just take a little bit of it, maybe one or two million maybe, and use it, say, to pay the . . . pay the mortgages on some of the farms . . . the farmers here owe to the banks.

It was as though there was a near-audible intake of breath from households around the world, followed by a vast global thought bubble. It said: why don't *you* find 'one or two million' for those farmers? Dylan, so it seemed, had failed even to bother to inform himself of the purpose of the event for which he was supposed to be the inspirational headline act. The little speech was naive, at best, and the effect on what remained of his reputation among the general public was catastrophic. Here, it seemed, was a choice example of just how detached from reality a spoiled emperor of rock could become.

Dylan would redeem himself somewhat, at least in American eyes, by inspiring Willie Nelson to mount the Farm Aid concert later in the year in Champaign, Illinois. The artist would put in a near-sensational performance with Tom Petty and the Heartbreakers at that event, as though making amends for Philadelphia. When the time came, Dylan would take unusual care with rehearsals and technical matters. The privations being suffered by rural America were real enough and he would more than do his bit. Nevertheless, to many among the enormous TV audience who saw him perform in Philadelphia on 13 July, the verdict was obvious. Bob Dylan was utterly redundant, a dismal and decadent joke who couldn't even give a respectable performance of one of his oldest and most famous songs.

*

At the beginning of November, *Biograph* appeared. As though to emphasise the paradox of a living artist's status as a historical artefact, Columbia staged a big reception at New York's Whitney Museum of American Art. The triumphs of a bygone era would be celebrated to honour a songwriter who had not enjoyed a hit in a while.

Dylan had meanwhile published a revised edition of his *Writings and Drawings* (1973). Though this time around he had settled for the arguably less pretentious *Lyrics: 1962–1985* as his title, there was no denying the irony attending his situation. Aged only 44, the poet of popular song had somehow managed to become both canonical and washed up. His private life remained chaotic, involving several women simultaneously, but that kind of turbulence had not impeded Dylan in the past. Something else, the times or passing time itself, was afflicting him. Interviewed by Cameron Crowe for the booklet that accompanied *Biograph*, he had said, 'Actually I'm amazed that I've been around this long. Never thought I would be.' Meanwhile, with nothing much to sell save an inferior album, he was turning up in prestigious publications all across America as the paterfamilias of pop-music art in the 'rock' style. Almost without fail, journalists wanted to ask the legend about his legend, or question the myth-maker, as they would call him, about the myth.

> Well, people tell me about the myth, you know? Some people are in awe. It doesn't penetrate me for some reason. I wish it did because then I might be able to use it to some advantage. I mean, there must be some advantage to it. I haven't been able to figure out what it is as yet. [He laughs.][10]

Among other things, the box set, with its earliest tracks dating all the way back to 1962, was a reminder that he had already spent more than half of his entire life in fame's hot glare. Robert Allen Zimmerman, his legal existence long since eradicated, was barely even a memory. Bob Dylan, his manifestations arrayed like a group portrait on the *Biograph* track listings, was the only reality the artist could hope for in 1985. Nevertheless, the elegant box set had the effect of turning his life into a historical event even as he tried to live that life. His relationship with time had been altered by what was represented on some pieces of brittle plastic. He was historic and actual, present and gone, this artist with the invented name. Amidst it all, art was deserting him. Whatever else he thought about while he made a play for yet another woman at the Whitney reception – apparently a Susan Ross by name – he must have begun to wonder what would become of Bob Dylan if his writing failed once and for all, if there were no more songs. He had suffered the affliction before and called it 'the amnesia'. In 1985, as the years piled up behind him, it must have resembled extinction.

Biograph would do exactly as well as *Empire Burlesque* in the American charts, but reaching number 33 with a box set was vastly more impressive than pulling off the feat with a single album. Given that *Biograph* went for $30 a pop and involved no recording costs, the artist and his record company did far better out of the old Dylan than the new model. The compilation would also have a far longer shelf life than *Empire Burlesque*, an album whose reputation has not improved with time. Neither outcome counts as unfair to the works involved. Even granting all the usual fan arguments over what is and what is not represented by *Biograph*, it illuminates the sheer scale of Dylan's achievement in 24 years. He was not far wrong when he claimed that he could have filled the box twice over with original but unreleased music. Not one of his contemporaries could have made the same claim. Columbia had not filled *Biograph* with every last scrap of detritus; anything but. The bulk of the material was familiar, but it set an entire career in a new context. The 'previously unreleased' songs served only as a reminder that there was a lot more to Dylan than his hits – the term is used loosely in his case – might have suggested. Others in the music industry whose self-regard would before long cause them to demand an equivalent testimonial had no such abundance of riches stored in the vaults. *Rolling Stone*'s reviewer would not be far wrong when he referred to the 'mere ten sides' contained in *Biograph*. Within the box, as the magazine's Tim Holmes would say, was 'incontrovertible evidence of a continuing explosion of genius'. No one had said that about *Empire Burlesque*. The single word in the *Rolling Stone* encomium inviting a quibble was 'continuing'.

*

On the last day of January 1986, Dylan became a father again. Three days later he went back on tour. The simple facts are eloquent. He was by instinct a family man, but by nature a travelling musician. He loved children, but he was most content, or at his least vulnerable, out on the road. There is plenty of romanticised nonsense in the history of pop, blues, R&B and rock and roll to explain and justify the dichotomy, but Dylan has endured (and deserved) doses of disruptive truth at intervals during his career. As his life with Sara had shown, a faith in domesticity had conquered him more than once. He had surrendered willingly to the idea of a (mostly) normal life, one he had not experienced since childhood. But he had also accepted every promise implicit in the devil's music and failed, time after time, to honour even the idea of fidelity. By the beginning of 1986 he was at the centre of multiple relationships. By that time, equally, the singer Carolyn Dennis, with whom he had resumed an affair, was about to have his sixth child. The little girl, named Desiree, would subsequently have the kind of 'secret' existence best understood by tabloid newspapers fond of seeing the word in 84 point sans bold. The only truly relevant fact is that parenthood had once intruded forcibly on Dylan's public life and altered his behaviour. In 1986, mother and newborn child remained at home while he flew to New Zealand.[11]

It would be known as the True Confessions tour. The Farm Aid show had convinced Dylan that he, Tom Petty and Petty's band were made for one another. That would turn out to be a matter of opinion. They had gone through the motions of rehearsals, but in reality they knocked the performances together by trial and error at the expense of paying customers. The first shows, in Wellington and Auckland, were dire; the opening night in Sydney, Australia, the first in a run of four concerts, might have passed as adequate if the artist had not been Bob Dylan. Rambling chatter to do with Jesus being 'my hero' was the new father's only coherent statement on life as he understood it. A few nights later he was introducing his song for Lenny Bruce by talking about the playwright Tennessee Williams and misunderstood artists generally. In Melbourne on 20 February, Dylan said in a song introduction: 'We're in Lonesome Town, learning to forget. Sometimes you got to do that. God knows, there's enough to remember.'

He could not have known or guessed, but that strange little aside might have passed for a premature epitaph for a friend. When the tour reached Japan, Dylan was informed that Richard Manuel had hanged himself with his belt in the early hours of 4 March in some lousy Florida motel after another lousy gig on the endless highway. The end had come after a performance in an 'upscale' joint called, of all things, the Cheek to Cheek Motel, but it had been a long time coming. Manuel had been drinking too much and doing too many bad drugs for too many years. The collapse of The Band after the *Last Waltz* movie had been his signal to subside, piece by broken piece, into incoherent misery. Long before the end, the sublime falsetto and the writing had been reduced to scrap. Dylan was entitled to remember the piano player and drummer who had provided the melody for 'Tears of Rage' back in Woodstock in 1967, but he kept any fury for the lost Band member to himself. There would be no onstage eulogies from the artist, just more chatter about Tennessee Williams. Manuel, born a lost soul, had in any case left no note. There had been nothing left to say. The shy man might have provided his own last words, in any case, on one overlooked song from The Band's second album: 'When you awake,' it went, 'you will remember everything.' Sweet Richard had chosen to forget it all.

The Pacific leg of Dylan's tour was brief enough. On 10 March, back in Tokyo's Nippon Budokan hall, he was still paying tribute to 'a guy who died pretty miserably', but he was still talking about Lenny Bruce, not Richard Manuel. As he had on every night, the artist was still closing the main part of the show with 'In the Garden', a defiantly born-again song from *Saved*. Where religion was concerned, Dylan had reached the point of all but teasing his audiences, as though asking them to guess what he did and did not believe. Introducing this rewrite of the tale of Christ's betrayal in Tokyo, he had talked yet again about 'my hero', but had also said, as though for the avoidance of doubt, 'I write songs about all kinds of things.' That wasn't factually true, not any more. He was not writing any kind of song worth speaking about, far less songs worth recording.

He had always been a high-wire act. For most of his career it had been no sort of test for Dylan to enter the studios with only the bare bones of a handful of songs at his disposal. Nor had his preparedness provided any sort of guide, for him or anyone else, to the quality of the album he was liable to make. In late 1967 he had gone to Nashville with *John Wesley Harding* written and ready in its entirety. The album had come off beautifully. In a few days in February and March 1966, in contrast, he had kept musicians waiting for ten hours at a time in the same studios while he scribbled away to conjure up the songs for *Blonde on Blonde*. The result was hardly one of his lesser works. The conditions necessary for Dylan's gift to function had rarely depended on the external circumstances in his life. If something was amiss within him, on the other hand, no amount of bravado or improvisation could redeem the work. The puzzle of the 1980s and the succession of flawed, misconceived, or simply bad albums Dylan made in that period lies in deciding what ailed him.

A complicated life? There was nothing new in that. In June of 1986 he would marry Carolyn Dennis and attempt, for a while, to straighten out his tangled existence and raise another child. Though he would make extraordinary efforts to keep wife and baby out of the public eye, he was not entirely indifferent to his responsibilities. Bad habits, then? Estranged friends and lovers, Susan Ross in particular, would later make allegations of alcoholism. Other types of possibly illegal behaviour would be, in slippery tabloid parlance, 'rumoured'. Even if every story was true, each would amount to a small hill of beans besides the existence Dylan had endured in 1966. *Blonde on Blonde* had emerged from that hell. Two decades later, the only apposite word would be supplied by the French. Ennui would seem to hang over

Dylan like a low, dark cloud. He had been too many people, too often. He had lost himself and recovered himself time and again, but the effort had come at a cost. If his work is any guide, it had all become familiar to him and the returns were diminishing. Even resurrection becomes repetitive, after a while: a triumph is a triumph is a triumph. The same formulation can be applied, no doubt, to catastrophe. The first best guess is that in 1986 Dylan was simply bored with his several selves, bored with the duty of creativity, jaded by spectacle, fatigued by the relentless insistence that he could exist only within the fiction of myth and legend. He had seen that movie before, more than once.

The second best guess at the reasons for Dylan's very bad albums in the 1980s imposes a liability on God. The artist had given his all to those derided born-again albums. From where he stood, he had placed his art in the service of eternal truth and been mocked and spurned for his pains. That must have been disheartening. But Dylan's faith had also provided him with a precise measure of what mattered in life and what did not. If you happen to believe sincerely in the Book of Revelation and imminent apocalypse, it must be difficult to take the making of an album of popular songs too seriously. Inevitably you must think that such things are, by definition, pretty trivial. If you have meanwhile given every ounce of your commitment to a profound belief and seen belief and commitment alike rejected, you might cease to give much of a damn for critics, audiences, record companies and a pop-music career founded on a burdensome media 'myth'. The Bible said, in essence, that Bob Dylan, his ego, art and career, didn't matter much. So why would the artist strain every nerve for the sake of a mere album?

Besides, for all their bleating and behind-the-hand carping, Columbia were never going to drop him. *Biograph* was the final proof of that. Even if the company never saw another chart-straddling, revolutionary album, Dylan's back catalogue was by the middle of the '80s a semi-official national treasure. That was the whole meaning of the box set. The fact that the artist made no money to speak of for the shareholders counted for little against his intangible but real worth as the final guarantor of Columbia's pretensions. The bosses might not fall over themselves to promote his latest efforts, but having Dylan on the roster was a prize in itself. Executives who guaranteed his creative freedom could glow in his lustre and congratulate themselves on their discernment. Even when his work failed to justify the fond belief, he represented quality, art, *class*. He knew it and the suits knew it. The only fly swimming in the soothing ointment was the fact that this shared knowledge bred utter complacency.

Hence the third best guess at Dylan's dire efforts in the 1980s: he was under no pressure whatever to succeed. None of his superstar fan-friends whispered the harsh truth about his self-evident decline. No corporate automaton asked about the meaning or purpose of the latest piece of crap to emerge from the studios. Journalists could sneer now and then. Fans could grumble at a sloppy concert while the artist, Petty and the Heartbreakers spent half the show sorting themselves out. Record-buyers could decide that the latest instalment of half-realised Dylan nonsense wasn't worth the price being asked. But all knew, for a certainty, that he had proved them dead wrong several times before. Few wished to be behind the next curve, however he might choose to describe the arc. So Dylan was indulged. For those astonished by his behaviour, his methods and his risible output in the 1980s, it became a kind of incantation to lift all curses. 'But,' someone would always say, 'he's Bob Dylan.'

It would not be even slightly surprising, therefore, when better than two years of intermittent effort resulted finally, in July 1986, in the piece of crap he would choose to call *Knocked Out Loaded*.

*

In the aftermath, he would flog the legend almost to death. That was not necessarily a bad idea. If a myth was what was desired, onlookers would be given an education in how such a thing was made and unmade. He would demolish the monument. There was probably no conscious intent involved, but an act of purgation was required. Dylan would have to destroy himself utterly as a performer and as a recording artist before summoning the will, yet again, to start afresh.

He had staged a few recording sessions in California in the spring of 1986, apparently still convinced that a modern album could be made in a week. The old belief in spontaneity persisted, but apathy also exerted its enervating negative energy. The artist had put in a lot of time, by his lights, on *Empire Burlesque*. He had tried to make his peace with modern technology and modern techniques. Where had it got him? His 24th attempt was, in that favourite phrase, 'just another album', of no great importance in the cosmic scheme of things. Most of the tracks recorded at Skyline Studios in Topanga Canyon on the edge of the Santa Monica Mountains at the end of April and the beginning of May had been cover versions. There had been no other choice. Dylan had failed to come up with songs of his own that were worth the name. He had messed around instead, so it had seemed, with anything that came to mind, as though hunting for one bright needle of inspiration in a big, rickety haystack.

After close to a month's worth of sessions, an album, a real album, had failed to materialise. Dylan had done a lot of work to no avail and a fair bit of drinking in the process, though whether for consolation or inspiration's sake it is impossible to say. In the end, the thing he called *Knocked Out Loaded* – alcohol did his talking even in the title – had been compiled rather than created. Bits and pieces from previous sessions, leftovers from *Empire Burlesque*, cover versions: it was, save in one particular, a pitiful affair. Had it not been for an eleven-minute remake of 'New Danville Girl' that he called 'Brownsville Girl', *Knocked Out Loaded* would have amounted to twenty-five minutes of residue containing only two poor songs, 'Driftin' Too Far From Shore' and 'Maybe Someday', that Dylan had succeeded in writing without help. The two he had contrived with Tom Petty and the lyricist Carole Bayer Sager were equally bad. The best way to describe *Knocked Out Loaded* is to say that it took either nerve or sheer, demoralised indifference to release the thing. What once would have been unacceptable to the artist was by mid-1986 the best he could manage.

'Brownsville Girl' was the only beacon in the gathering darkness. The phenomenon it represented would become another feature of Dylan's work in the 1980s. No matter how awful the album, there was always *something*, always a track or two to set you wondering what might have been. You had to be a resolute and determined fan, however, to buy an entire record for the sake of a couple of songs. By this point, most of the artist's long-lost former admirers were not prepared to be short-changed so outrageously. *Knocked Out Loaded* would get no higher than number 54 in America. In Britain, where fans had been so reflexively loyal for so long, it became the first of Dylan's works since 1973's *Dylan*, a collection for which he could not be held responsible, to fail to penetrate the top 20. The British had taken *Saved* and *Shot of Love* to their trusting hearts, but not this. Those who did bother to purchase *Knocked Out Loaded*, the thrawn coterie who bought new Bob Dylan albums simply because they were new Bob Dylan albums, spent a long time listening, over and over, to a single track.

By one description, 'Brownsville Girl' is a movie within a movie about a movie. It draws a parallel between a life's faltering memories and half-remembered films. One voice begins by talking about standing in line to see an old Gregory Peck picture, *The Gunfighter* (1950), and then lurches off into his own disjointed road movie, one in which stories seem to begin and fall apart time and again. Everything is visual, a mental picture: 'I keep seeing this stuff'; 'I can still see the day'; 'There was a movie I seen one time'. In the original 'New Danville Girl' the idea was deepened, yet perhaps made too obvious, with an explicit evocation of Plato's analogy of the cave, the philosopher's account of how we perceive and understand reality, and a reference to people 'busy talkin' back and forth to our shadows on the old stone wall'. This is a song, furthermore, 'about' the experience of loss that connects the idea of emotional distance with physical distances travelled. Borders (and lines) are crossed. The travelling is meanwhile desperate and apparently aimless. The haunted – and hunted – couple are seen tearing over the Rockies at sunrise, driving all night to San Antonio, heading for Amarillo, in flight from the law in Corpus Christi, parting in New Orleans. All the while, the singer is drawn back to Peck's movies, to some lost code of honour from a time 'long before the stars were torn down'.

This recitative, sung only in choruses that seem to intervene in no fixed pattern, is beautifully written and performed, for the only time on *Knocked Out Loaded*, as though Dylan actually believes in the material. Great lines are scattered throughout the song. Lines such as, 'Oh, if there's an original thought out there, I could use it right now.' Lines such as, 'The only thing we knew for sure about Henry Porter is that his name wasn't Henry Porter.' 'Brownsville Girl' is arguably a lesser work than 'New Danville Girl', but that is ultimately a matter of disputable opinion. The production, according to taste, can sound overloaded; the backing singers – named the Queens of Rhythm by Dylan – can seem too intrusive. On the other hand, these gospel and soul performers are acting as a chorus in the Greek style: there is a point to their presence. Sometimes their mocking interventions are very funny. Dylan's own speaking/singing is meanwhile masterly. Wonderful lines in the song only truly make sense when he delivers them. Shepard, as a playwright and scriptwriter, understood as much. At one point in the writing process, it seems, he asked wonderingly how Dylan could possibly perform the enormously long lines of 'New Danville Girl'. The artist simply told him not to worry about it. In either version, he justifies that confidence.

Who wrote what? As with *Desire* and Dylan's collaborations with Jacques Levy, it is impossible to say. Neither writer has spilled those beans. Much of the ambience of 'Brownsville Girl' is reminiscent of Shepard's *Motel Chronicles* (1982) and of *Paris, Texas* (1984), the Wim Wenders movie (appropriately enough) partly inspired by the book and co-written by the playwright. Equally, much of the dialogue in the song and its delivery could be no one else but Dylan. That aspect of his art, its sheer inimitability, was what he stood to lose as he drifted rudderless through the 1980s. It would be a long time before he produced anything as fine as 'Brownsville Girl' again.

*

He was back on the road with Petty and the Heartbreakers in the summer of '86. *Knocked Out Loaded* appeared and disappeared and no one much cared. The concerts, on the other hand, went pretty well. Dylan's choices among his songs were odd enough to be intriguing, with everything from 'Positively 4th Street' to 'I Dreamed I Saw St. Augustine' surfacing alongside 'In the Garden' and numerous cover versions, familiar or obscure. The artist seemed to be enjoying himself, too, as though happy to be hiding out in the wide open spaces of anonymous amphitheatres. Dylan was barely a recording artist in any serious sense and had all but ceased to be a songwriter. He had reason to prefer hedonism. By no accident, a favourite encore on the tour was the venerable 'Let the Good Times Roll'.

In the early autumn of the year he travelled to England to participate in a catastrophe of a movie entitled *Hearts of Fire*, a drama intended by its director, Richard Marquand, as a 'study' of stardom. Instead, it resembled a parody of every lame rock and roll movie cliché ever to stain celluloid, one in which Dylan played a parody of himself as the reclusive veteran superstar 'Billy Parker'. It soon became clear that his acting had not improved much with the years, but the malformed script was no aid to performance. In America, the feature went, as industry shorthand had it, 'straight to video', sparing discerning customers the waste of a night out. Of more immediate importance was the fact that Dylan had agreed to come up with at least four and possibly six new and original songs for the film's soundtrack. In the event, he managed, barely managed, just two. The best way to describe 'Had a Dream About You, Baby' and 'Night After Night' is to say that they could cause you seriously to doubt that Bob Dylan actually wrote them. The second of the pair begins: 'Night after night you wander the streets of my mind.'

Towards the end of the *Hearts of Fire* shoot the artist traded dialogue with a BBC crew for a piece the documentary makers would entitle *Getting to Dylan*.[12] It was a clever title. He had acted out the role of the unapproachable star and made it devilishly hard for his interrogators to get anywhere near him for weeks, finally dragging them all the way to Toronto, where parts of his movie were being shot. They retaliated slyly with the suggestion that some of the things getting to the artist were not necessarily doing him a world of good. At times Dylan seemed to have a bad cold, for example, a condition that came and went unpredictably. At other moments the idea that anyone could get through to him on any real human level, person to person, straight question and straight answer, was mocked by his affectless demeanour while he sat fidgeting in his movie-star trailer. Just as in the mid-'60s, Dylan's entire effort went into remaining resolutely unforthcoming, but on this occasion his idea of postmodern mockery was to sketch his interviewer, fail to take enquiries about his work seriously, and affect no interest in anything, in general or in particular. The impression given was that it was no affectation.

The first of two encounters for the documentary team had barely begun before Dylan was laying down his perverse rules. 'Well,' he said, 'you know, I'm not gonna say anything that you're gonna get any revelations about . . . It's not gonna happen.' His songwriting? 'I just write 'em.' Politics? Yet again, Dylan claimed to be baffled by the very meaning of the word. His public? 'Nobody knows me and I don't know them.' By the end, he was resorting to old press-conference tricks from a previous life. 'Well, gimme an answer,' he demanded at one point, 'and I'll say it.'

Once upon a time, that kind of thing had seemed like a street-smart tease in the face of fatuous enquiries. This time around Dylan looked and sounded as though he truly had no answers, as though jadedness had become pathological. Worse, he behaved as if he was perfectly, coldly content with his condition. At no point did he attempt to explain why this poor, put-upon star, this legend (and so forth) reduced to playing in a second-rate melodrama because his albums no longer sold, was bothering to talk to anyone at all. The fires had been doused.

In February 1987, Dylan turned up in Los Angeles at a Taj Mahal concert, then at a Warren Zevon session where there was a need for a harmonica player. In March, he sang a George Gershwin song, 'Soon', at a Brooklyn Academy of Music affair to mark the half-century that had passed since the composer's death. Dylan was by then four years older than Gershwin had been at his passing. The paradigmatic Jewish musical genius had composed *Rhapsody in Blue* when he was only 26, *An American in Paris* before he was 30 and *Porgy and Bess* when he was just 37. Dylan was not the only dazzling meteor ever sighted in the American firmament. In his short life, Gershwin had not wasted a day and had never succumbed to self-indulgence, to self-pity, or to lethargy. Dylan's creative inertness had become his public image.

The only important mystery attached to the recording sessions for the work Dylan would call *Down in the Groove* is why he bothered. It was an album made to fail, predestined, if that's the word, to have not a prayer. The artist could only have justified this exercise if his intention had been to inform the world that his talent was extinguished. At least 30 musicians were called to the scene of the crime, but not one among them could crack the case. The likes of Mark Knopfler and Sly and Robbie, who knew something about the artist and his methods, could not provide him with a clue. Superstar peers such as Eric Clapton and Jerry Garcia could not revive the corpse. Paul Simonon and Steven Jones, those jobbing punk survivors of The Clash and the Pistols, could shed no light on the mystery. Unlike *Knocked Out Loaded*, the nadir before the nadir, there would not even be that one song to treasure, that single sliver of hope, in the wreckage named *Down in the Groove*.

Even Columbia paused over this one. In fact, the company paused for an entire year. Efforts to record the album began in March and ended in June, but the 32 minutes retrieved from the debacle would not see the light until the end of May 1988. Dylan would juggle with what he had during that long hiatus, altering the running order, inserting a couple of previously discarded failures of his own as though throwing damp twigs onto dying embers. It made no important difference. The album would reach number 61 on the American album chart and only get so high because, miraculously, there were still handfuls of customers refusing to believe that Dylan was incapable, finally, of repaying their faith.

It is almost redundant to discuss *Down in the Groove*, like recycling waste paper for a thesis on waste paper. Of ten tracks, only two were the artist's own work. One was 'Death Is Not the End', the song that buyers of *Infidels* had been spared for the sound reason that the writer had insulted the memory of his talent before getting around to insulting the audience. It begins:

WORLD GONE WRONG

When you're sad and when you're lonely
And you haven't got a friend
Just remember that death is not the end

The other original piece offered by the world's greatest songwriter was 'Had a Dream About You, Baby', one of the works he had struggled to contrive for *Hearts of Fire*. It no more needs to be quoted here than it needed to be recorded. Remarkably, however, neither song is quite as bad as the pair Dylan devised with Robert Hunter of the Grateful Dead when he was trying to mend the mesh in his shredded net. The artist would come to have a bizarre attachment to the piece called 'Silvio', even sanctioning its release as a single in 1988. It seems he liked it. An alternative view is that the track is objectively hateful and infallibly, almost supernaturally irritating. It is redeemed somewhat only by the fact that its companion piece is worse. Officially, Dylan was to blame for just the music, but he was entirely responsible for performing a song called 'Ugliest Girl in the World' and putting it on an album. The full measure of what *Down in the Groove* signified is that he could come up with nothing, nothing at all, better than this piece of stupefying nonsense.

The album's cover versions are blameless by comparison. The fact that Dylan discarded a couple of those while tinkering with the sequencing has even allowed a few of his blindly loyal fans to misapply the weasel's favourite word to the entire farrago. *Down in the Groove* is, apparently, 'underrated', a misunderstood and overlooked 'classic'. One answer to that claim would be this: underrated only by anyone who has heard several hundred other Bob Dylan recordings. The album's single saving grace is a good performance of the traditional 'Shenandoah'. There was a clue in that fact, had Dylan been paying attention.

*

His legal contest with the hovering ghost of Albert Grossman, that other reminder of past glories, was dragging towards its end while the flotsam of *Down in the Groove* was being lashed together. The Bear himself had died of a heart attack on a Concorde flight to London in January 1986, but his widow, Sally, had elected to carry on the fight on behalf of the Grossman estate. In May 1987, Dylan sanctioned an out-of-court settlement that cost him a couple of million dollars but got him what he truly wanted, the publishing rights to his own work.

In essence, the deal was a recognition of the familiar distinction between justice and law. Albert's moral right to own any part of those songs had been as questionable as the percentages he had extracted at every turn from his young client's earnings. On the other hand, as the settlement in effect recognised, the contracts had been sound enough in law. Grossman had been ruthless, but not stupid. Dylan, trapped all those years later in an era when he was barely able to string a verse together, had won full ownership of the art he had made when songs had flowed from him like prophecies from an entranced oracle. That must have made for a strange moment in the spring of 1987.

His next move was stranger still. Fans of the Grateful Dead were, as they remain, almost as fixedly dedicated as fans of Bob Dylan. Among devotees, for whom the name Deadheads has long seemed apt both as a description and a definition, the band possessed a significance – arrived at through a lot of drugs, a lot more hippie twaddle and a seemingly infinite tolerance for the zero-sum pastime called jamming – beyond any music they happened to play. On a good day, that was pedestrian, sometimes achieving the heights of tiresome. On a bad day, what with the drugs, the Dead were inept, relentlessly so. They talked a good song, however, and there is no denying their inexplicable popularity. Some of those stoned Deadheads spent their lives travelling from show to show.

Like everyone else for whom credibility mattered, the band were big Bob Dylan fans. The artist meanwhile counted the band's guitar player, Jerry Garcia, as a friend. He also had a respect, for reasons best known to himself, for the lyrics of Robert Hunter. None of these facts counted as a sound enough basis for a collaboration. Nor was the money, even the very large amount of money, that Dylan accepted for agreeing to six shows with the Dead collective in the biggest stadiums available in July much of an excuse. We can only presume that he wanted cash quickly to pay off the widow Grossman. That kind of motive is not often worth confusing with artistic inspiration.

There are, as usual, bootleg recordings of the tour rehearsals staged at a place called Club Front in San Rafael, California, in June. Copies of these are often extensive, not to say endless – in such matters, the word 'complete' on packaging counts as fair warning – but they have the merit of showing Dylan being nudged into attempting songs he had long ignored. Left to his own devices, he would probably not have considered *John Wesley Harding* songs such as 'The Ballad of Frankie Lee and Judas Priest' or 'The Wicked Messenger'. Equally, for whatever reason, he had never paid attention to the likes of 'Queen Jane Approximately' or 'Stuck Inside of Mobile'. At San Rafael he was even talked into essaying 'Joey', the disputable *Desire* song he had written with Jacques Levy. That was the good news, all of the good news. From the desultory bootleg recordings can be heard the approaching sounds of a disaster in the making.

In this period the artist had at least one vice in common with his new colleagues. They had always been relaxed in their attitude towards what was good enough for the public, apparently believing that if they were entranced by their ramshackle efforts the customers would feel the same way. A faith that, some of the time at least, things would somehow 'come together' on stage was part of the price audiences were expected to pay. By 1987, Dylan had acquired the same view. Add the fact that the Grateful Dead loved his songs but seemed utterly incapable of understanding how the artist achieved a performance, in his better moments, and the script for a real farce was written. Deadheads were numerous; big crowds could be guaranteed. But the alliance was so inherently foolish, its basis so fragile, a humiliation for Dylan was certain.

So it proved. On the inevitable concert bootlegs the following can be heard: one famous songwriter struggling to find the melodic line, never mind the heart, of song after song; one cult band operating below even their modest best; and two acts occupying the same stage who each seem, often enough, to be unaware of the presence of the other. A decent live album might yet have been salvaged. Six big shows would surely have yielded seven tracks fit to be released. In one set of post hoc excuses that claim would be made and Dylan would get the blame for dumping some of the least-bad recordings. The truth is that nothing in the material discarded would have improved the album entitled *Dylan & the Dead* when it was released finally in February 1989. The critical consensus then would be uncomplicated: if this was the best, God help the rest. Should you ever wish, with malign intent, to deter a prospective young fan from taking an interest in Bob Dylan, play him or her a couple of the San Rafael bootleg tracks, then this dead-and-barely-alive set.

*

Years later, Dylan would say that 1987 was almost the end of him as a performer. He might have been trying to fool the public, but he was not fooling himself. In 2001, John Farley of *Time* magazine would be told: 'At that point, I was just going to get out of it and everything that entails.' Steve Inskeep of National Public Radio would hear in 2004 of how 'I really didn't feel like my heart was in it much any more.'[13] Perhaps so, but Dylan still crossed the Atlantic to spend September and half of October on tour once again with Tom Petty and his band. During an interview with Rolling Stone's Kurt Loder in Jerusalem on the eve of the second concert the artist was observed to be drinking with relentless, practised ease. On stage that night he looked haggard and uncertain in his movements. The concerts were not well received in Israel, though they would improve as the artist dragged himself across Switzerland, Italy, Germany, Denmark, Finland, Sweden, back to Italy and Switzerland, then to France and Belgium, and finally to England. But even the improvements would not be to every taste.

Bob Dylan could still justify three nights in Birmingham and four nights at the Wembley Arena. Whether he could still justify himself, or do justice to songs he no longer understood, was another story, a tale growing darker as age and time pressed in upon him. As he would confess in due course in his 2004 book Chronicles: Volume One, the songs had become 'strangers' to him. Why, in truth, did people continue to turn out for concerts by this performer? Just for a glimpse of what still passed for a legend? And was that enough, in turn, for him?

He had called the tour Temples in Flames, as though passing his own judgement on desecrated monuments. In Locarno in Switzerland on 5 October, while concealing himself among the backing vocalists, he had experienced what he would remember as a strange, daunting moment of self-awareness. Years later, one who was present at one of the Wembley shows would describe Dylan's performance as 'an inspired vandalisation, brutal and challenging, a scorched earth triumph, charred and astonishing', but admit that many other fans were appalled or infuriated by what had been done to the songs.[14] In The Observer, the BBC disc jockey John Peel would write: 'Being an enigma at 20 is fun, being an enigma at 30 shows a lack of imagination, and being an enigma at Dylan's age is just plain daft . . . From the moment the living legend took to the stage, it was evident that here was business he wanted accomplished with the minimum of effort.'[15]

He was pulling the temple down around his ears. It might have counted as creative destruction, as an artist's defiant gesture, but sometimes explanations are no better than rationalisations. In Chronicles: Volume One, Dylan would explain that after the European concerts he had planned a touring schedule with the deliberate intention of alienating his older fans. Somehow they were to be replaced with a younger crowd on the grounds – you can only admire the gall of this rationalising writer – that his traditional audience was no longer up to the task of appreciating his shows. If that was the plan, it would be postponed. As the book tells it, Dylan sustained a 'freak' injury that left his hand gashed. The wound is described as serious and painful, injurious to his body and his hopes, but the dates and details are vague.

Early in 1988, Dylan would distract himself for a while as a member of the Traveling Wilburys, a kind of musical club for superstar hobbyists of a certain vintage, as though to prove there was nothing more pressing on his mind than messing around with George Harrison, Roy Orbison, Petty and Jeff Lynne. The gang would give themselves silly names – Dylan would be 'Lucky', supposedly – and manage to come up with an album full of inoffensive music that would fare far better than any of the artist's recent works. *Traveling Wilburys Vol. 1* would in fact sell many more copies than any album Dylan had ever made. His chief contribution would be a fairly sharp song, its lyrics a parody of Bruce Springsteen, complete with the appropriate allusions, entitled 'Tweeter and the Monkey Man'.

It was out on Thunder Road, Tweeter at the wheel
They crashed into paradise, they could hear them tires squeal
The undercover cop pulled up and said everyone of you's a liar
If you don't surrender now it's gonna go down to the wire

The song was adequate, if that was your taste, though clearly the writer did not take it seriously. Why would he? In January 1988 he had been 'inducted' into the Rock and Roll Hall of Fame at a big ceremony in New York. Springsteen had given a passionate speech in tribute that had sounded only a little like a requiem. For all his rhetoric and for all his affected disdain, the artist accepted the world's baubles readily enough. He seemed not to notice that such honours sometimes come at the end of a career.

These things filled up his time. In essence, it was all little better than displacement activity. Dylan's real problem was that he was going through these motions because he did not know what else to do.

CHAPTER TEN

Born in Time

NOTHING MUCH WAS EXPECTED OF INTERSTATE 88, THE TOUR inaugurated on 7 June 1988 out in the golden west. To begin with, it seemed that nothing much would be delivered. The Pavilion amphitheatre in the city of Concord, in San Francisco's suburban East Bay, though designed by Frank Gehry and prestigious enough, was just another oversized open-air entertainment space. Given the choices available to him, it was not the most appropriate or intriguing venue Dylan could have picked to commence a run of 71 concerts in the United States and Canada that summer. For one thing, the appeal of his name alone could no longer fill the wide and open expanses of a place like the Pavilion.

What was the average casual fan entitled to expect, in any case? In Europe in 1987 Dylan had too often crashed and burned amid those pseudo-mythic temples in flames. Any Californian observer who had read reports of the four shows at London's Wembley Arena would have noted only insinuating tales of an artist in bad shape and, as most reviews insisted, wretched voice. Once again, the omens were poor. None of the 6,000 or so people who saw Dylan return to work after his vacation with the Traveling Wilburys – at a venue capable of containing 12,500 – could have expected something historic. Quite how historic remains a matter of dispute, not least if the artist is offering an opinion. In his version, nothing particularly unusual happened at the Pavilion, or in its long aftermath, not at his behest. He had pulled himself together, that was all.

Second on the bill that evening were The Alarm, a briefly popular, well-meaning Welsh band who might just have been mistaken for The Clash on a bad day if there was plenty of static on the radio and you weren't listening too hard. Who knows who chose them, big hair and big pretensions, for the tour? The Alarm were better suited to providing the introductory bombast for U2, as they had done in 1983, but such was the price Dylan fans had to pay for the stadium-rock experience. If nothing else – and truly there was precious little else – the support act provided a handy illustration of the nature of the decade in which the artist had been cast adrift.

Given all that had gone before, these were not popular music's finest hours. Another of heavy metal's Monsters of Rock tours was soaking up the middle-American youth dollar when Dylan took the stage at Concord. Michael Jackson was, it seemed, everywhere that year. George Michael had commenced his campaign for hearts, minds and sundries that very week with the single 'I Want Your Sex', an introduction to what would become the year's most successful album. If the aim was to fill stadiums, the high-end competition was Guns N' Roses. As ever, the charts tell their story.

Dylan might have been the agent of his own artistic decline in the trough of this low, dishonest decade. He might have made some very foolish moves. But how, in truth, was he supposed to react in such an environment? By courting slow, sure artistic death as a nostalgia act? By accepting that his moment in the spotlight was long gone? It amounted to a further series of questions. Did he still know what he wanted? Did he still care? Did he still know how to achieve what he wanted? For most listeners, *Down in the Groove*, released just a week before the Concord show, was providing dispiriting answers.

*

Almost a decade later, in September of 1997, Dylan would sit down with David Gates of *Newsweek* in a hotel room in Santa Monica, California, for an interview designed to publicise the album *Time Out of Mind*. In the course of the conversation the singer would make a couple of statements that were frank by most standards, far less by the infinitely pliant standards of the entertainment business.

Those who had judged him finished and done by 1987 had not been far off the mark. 'I'd kind of reached the end of the line,' Dylan would tell Gates. 'Whatever I had started out to do, it wasn't that. I was going to pack it in.'

As he told the tale, the performer had been left with very little choice. Decadence, carelessness, bad habits and cynicism have been adduced often enough by critics, friendly or hostile, to explain Dylan during this late '80s period. In his own recollection, something more profound was going on. The inability to write much of anything, easily or often, was by then well established. But as Dylan told Gates, he had lost even the ability to perform his songs. A decade on, he mimicked and relived his dread: 'I can't remember what it means, does it mean – is it just a bunch of words? Maybe it's like what all these people say, just a bunch of surrealistic nonsense.'

Later, in his 2004 book *Chronicles: Volume One*, Dylan would return to the memory of the burned-out relic of 1960s folk-rock – a term he had always despised – who found himself empty and wrecked in the middle of the '80s. This erstwhile 'troubadour' – a word he had once found comical – was heading for cultural oblivion. Above all, as the book would record, he had nothing much left to say.

Only rarely does self-doubt go deeper. Nothing had remained of that old '60s swagger, that instinctive certainty, the knowledge that one song would thread itself seamlessly to the next whenever he chose. More than Dylan's confidence had disappeared by the end of 1987. A decade later, the remembered emotion sounded like nothing so much as the despair of a man who had gone blind by stages.

Jerry Garcia and the Grateful Dead had managed to coax Dylan back to a kind of life, for a while at least, but the respite had been no cure. As represented on the miserable *Dylan & the Dead* album, those half-dozen stadium appearances in July 1987 had demonstrated only that the foremost songwriter of his generation could get up on a stage, if needs must, and remember some of the words. The performances had been dire; rumours questioning the star's physical condition had circulated. As often as not, great songs had been shorn of verses and meaning while the Dead treated their eternally faithful fans to the usual grimly predictable minor-league rock.

As he told the story to Gates, Dylan's luck turned at last on a foggy, windy night while he peered at an audience spread across the damp cobblestones of the Piazza Grande in Locarno, Switzerland. He would return to the tale several times in subsequent interviews. Deep-dyed fans would meanwhile give the anecdote a pseudo-religious tint by talking, in all apparent seriousness, about an epiphany. Whatever happened, it mattered to Dylan the storyteller. Locarno became part of his personal mythology, the moment when the long withdrawing tide began to turn.

It's almost like I heard it as a voice. It wasn't like it was me thinking it. *I'm determined to stand whether God will deliver me or not.* And all of a sudden everything just exploded. It exploded every which way. And I noticed that all the people out there – I was used to them looking at the girl singers, they were good-looking girls, you know? And like I say, I' had them up there so I wouldn't feel so bad. But when that happened, nobody was looking at the girls any more. They were looking at the main mike. After that is when I sort of knew: I've got to go out and play these songs. That's just what I must do.

So it came to pass. Doubters might struggle to find much of a difference between minor bootlegs such as *Locarno 1987* and snatched recordings of the following night's show such as *Paris, France*. Only a minority in the Wembley Arena left the building at the tour's end convinced that Dylan had redeemed himself. Connoisseurs of the numerous illicit *Temples in Flames* recordings can point to fine performances, here and there, both before and after the 'epiphany'. It is also self-evidently the case that we only have Dylan's word for this life-changing Locarno experience, this moment of understanding. He believed, in any case, that words of defiance and resolution had come unbidden into his head, as though from nowhere, and he believed in what they meant. As he knew better than most, faith is a powerful thing.

Recasting the story for the benefit of *Rolling Stone*'s Mikal Gilmore at the end of 2001, Dylan said: 'That night in Switzerland it all just came to me. All of a sudden I could sing anything. There might've been a time when I was going to quit or retire, but the next day it was like, "I can't really retire now because I really haven't done anything yet", you know? I want to see where this will lead me, because now I can control it all. Before, I wasn't controlling it. I was just being swept by the wind, this way or that way.'[1]

All that remained was to persuade disillusioned audiences to believe it too. A Bob Dylan who could still sing 'anything'? Proof of the proposition would not be the work of moments. The 1980s had produced a mountain of lousy reviews for which amends were required. One of the decade's many glib formulations was as applicable to Dylan as it was to any beleaguered politician: he had a credibility problem, a big one. Just 'to go out and play these songs' would not be enough.

Whatever took place in Switzerland, the alleged Locarno incident became a declaration of faith. It has been used since by fans to explain everything about Dylan the dedicated, even obsessive, public performer. The phenomenon known as the Never-Ending Tour, 2,480 concerts in 24 years as of the end of 2012, is always said to have begun in

California on 7 June 1988, and is always explained by what happened to the artist in Switzerland. There remains the sense, nevertheless, that a few things are missing from the story.

*

On paper, the 13-song Concord set list does not these days seem like anything out of the ordinary for a Dylan show. A little brief at 70 minutes, perhaps, certainly when compared with the concerts of '66 and '76, and with concerts since, but that's of no account: with this artist, only quality is supposed to matter. Dylan opened with 'Subterranean Homesick Blues' and closed with 'Maggie's Farm' for an encore. He gave the crowd 'Like a Rolling Stone', second to last. Along the way there was a fair enough résumé of his career, from the first album's traditional 'Man of Constant Sorrow' through 'Absolutely Sweet Marie' and 'Gates of Eden' to 'You're a Big Girl Now' from *Blood on the Tracks* and God's own 'Gotta Serve Somebody'. Most of the choices were not startling. The American Civil War 'Irish' ballad 'Lakes of Ponchartrain' – Creole would be a better description – made for an interesting preface to 'Boots of Spanish Leather' in an acoustic sequence. It introduced, or rather reintroduced, traditional music to the concerts: thereafter one obscure piece or another would feature in the set. But the rest of the songs performed at Concord would have been familiar to anyone who knew anything about Dylan.

The first real surprise had come, in fact, when he took the stage. The girl singers, the star accompanists, the instrumental paraphernalia and the rest of the supporting cast were gone. Aside from an appearance by Neil Young – barely audible on the recording – it was just Dylan and three musicians. The intention, like the musical setting, was stark. For the first time in years, he was leaving himself with no place to hide.

He was meanwhile refusing to employ his famous harmonica while granting the first public performances to 'Subterranean Homesick Blues' and 'Absolutely Sweet Marie'. That was worth noting. But the important fact, faintly astonishing in 1988, was that Dylan was audibly performing as though he cared, as though his songs meant something once more. Whatever the excuses made for the Temple in Flames 'scorched earth' approach – and some of those are elaborate – this new demeanour amounted to an acknowledgement of how low he had sunk. Now he was a serious performer again.

It didn't make for a flawless first show. Dylan's rehabilitation had barely begun. Equally, Concord's implicit manifesto was no guarantee that every performance would be unimpeachable in the years ahead: anything but. In Sacramento two nights later the tour's next stop saw another half-empty amphitheatre and a set drastically curtailed for reasons only Dylan could explain. Press reviews were poor, in the main, perhaps because journalists had closed their minds instead of opening their eyes and ears. Nevertheless, Dylan still gave them a certain amount of ammunition, not least with his perverse decision to perform one fairly new song from *Down in the Groove*, the lamentable 'Had a Dream About You, Baby', amid the purest products of the songwriter's art. Assembled for *Hearts of Fire*, that gutted turkey of a movie, and inserted between 'Girl From the North Country' and 'Just Like a Woman', a song that counted as close to the least in Dylan's canon did no more than remind listeners of how good a writer he once had been.

It was a minor detail. The recording says that the crowd, though sparse, was enthusiastic. The Sacramento audience had reason. Dylan's trio of musicians had begun to carve a little piece of legend for themselves. G.E. Smith, guitarist and bandleader from TV's *Saturday Night Live* satire show, was intuitive, empathetic and sure of himself. The artist had meanwhile found in Kenny Aaronson (bass) and Christopher Parker (drums) a rhythm section that would never let him down, no matter what might transpire. A lot could yet transpire, but Dylan had made his choices. What remained to be seen was their effect, if any, on his writing, the core of his art.

*

Devotees of the tour-without-end don't necessarily see things that way. They are avid, year upon year, for word of a new song being performed somewhere in the world, but their fascination with a cultural phenomenon has as much to do with the supposedly ever-changing manner of Dylan's renditions as it has to do with a body of recorded work. For these believers, the public stage is the true locus of his art. The appearance of another Bob Dylan album is, in a strange way, secondary. Predictably, the artist doesn't see things that way. He despises the idea that he is adrift, like some musical Ancient Mariner, on a never-ending voyage, but he also rejects the claim that he is forever rearranging his songs. In 2006, he said as much to the writer Jonathan Lethem.[2]

I've heard it said, you've probably heard it said, that all the arrangements change night after night. Well, that's a bunch of bullshit. They don't know what they're talkin' about. The arrangements don't change night after night. The rhythmic structures are different, that's all. You can't change the arrangement night after night – it's impossible.

Undaunted, some of his fans possess hundreds of bootleg concert recordings. In legend, a few have collections numbering in the thousands, of show after show after show. The inner circle of adherents think nothing of crossing America, Europe, or the ocean between to follow Dylan from place to place when he tours. They have seen the 'nightly ritual' dozens of times and have never tired of him, despite all his failures and provocations. At venues across the world this fraternity, by now old friends, will gather. Set lists from far-flung cities circulate among them, each one pored over for evidence of 'revealing' choices (or a veteran singer's whims).

So in Brittany on 22 July 2012, he performed 'This Wheel's On Fire' for the first and only time in 86 shows that year? He did 'Absolutely Sweet Marie' and 'Under the Red Sky' only once in the entire tour? Fascinating; tell me more. These days, internet databases, Dylan's own not least, keep track of such important facts. Those for whom the statistical record is better than a hobby find nothing peculiar in the endless pursuit of details. They are less likely to remember that Dylan endured booing at Brittany's Festival Vieilles Charrues in Carhaix from a section of the crowd apparently demanding more modern (or more intelligible) entertainment. Committed fans do not long discuss the fact that Tour 2012 – 'Don't You Dare Miss It', as the poster said – went through some rough patches.

The art-in-progress failed to sell out at most stops along the way, even in the United States. In a few places, concerts were cancelled, apparently because of a lack of local interest. Media critics were meanwhile, it is fair to say, divided. Some things had not changed since 1988.

Of a performance at the Hop Farm Festival in Kent on 30 June 2012, the reviewer from London's *Daily Telegraph* wrote: 'Somehow between the magic of his fantastic songs, the liquid groove of his superb band, the mysterious charisma of the legend himself and the will of the crowd to enjoy the moment, something strange and truly spectacular happens, a thrilling performance that nobody, perhaps not even the man at its centre, can really explain.' Elsewhere it was recorded that in Toronto that November, 'The 71-year-old Dylan spent the bulk of [the show] seated behind a piano at stage right, barking, braying and hoarking [sic] unintelligible linguistic formations into the microphone and banging out ill-disciplined boogie-woogie licks on the keys.'[3]

At Concord in 1988 Dylan was making his stand, fending off retirement, and attempting to save his career. A quarter of a century on, even those who found his ruined voice ridiculous had given up asking why he refused to quit. Were his overheads so high and his record sales so low that he needed to keep going, night after night? Surely songwriting royalties, his songwriting royalties above all, would maintain him in comfort and style?

It seemed that the Dylan who had once been able to transform himself in an instant, to astonish with the speed of his changes, was chained to an idea. He could protest all he liked that his working habits were misrepresented. For the media, for his audience, he was the man on the never-ending tour.

His exasperated response has become familiar since he advised readers of the sleeve notes to 1993's *World Gone Wrong* album to avoid becoming 'bewildered by the Never-Ending Tour chatter'. That particular tour had ended, he wrote, 'in '91 with the departure of guitarist G.E. Smith'. Since then, Dylan has treated interviewers to variations on the theme of 'Playing is a job. My trade' (to Sweden's *Aftonbladet* in 1997), or to discourses on longevity in the performing arts. A typical example of the latter appeared in *Rolling Stone* in May 2009.[4]

You never heard about Oral Roberts and Billy Graham being on some Never Ending Preacher Tour. Does anybody ever call Henry Ford a Never Ending Car Builder? Is Rupert Murdoch a Never Ending Media Tycoon? What about Donald Trump? Does anybody say he has a Never Ending Quest to build buildings? Picasso painted well into his 90s. And Paul Newman raced cars in his 70s. Anybody ever say that Duke Ellington was on a Never Ending Bandstand Tour? But critics apply a different standard to me for some reason. But we're living in an age of breaking everything down into simplistic terms, aren't we? These days, people are lucky to have a job. Any job. So critics might be uncomfortable with me. Maybe they can't figure it out. But nobody in my particular audience feels that way about what I do.

The intensity of this rebuttal suggested a man who was sick and tired of being buried under still another pile of legend. There was also a hint, however, of something like fear, fear of retirement, fear of the road's end, fear of having to decide what else he might do with himself. He wasn't going to let that happen without a fight.

> Anybody with a trade can work as long as they want. A welder, a carpenter, an electrician. They don't necessarily need to retire. People who have jobs on an assembly line, or are doing some kind of drudgery work, they might be thinking of retiring every day. Every man should learn a trade. It's different than a job. My music wasn't made to take me from one place to another so I can retire early.

This otherwise unimpeachable defence overlooks the fact that the speaker had spent the best part of eight years (1966 to 1974) staying as far away from the public stage as possible. Even when he was performing in the years before and afterwards, the former 'song and dance man' did not talk about his work in terms of a trade or a vocation. And what did Dylan mean, exactly, by claiming that his music 'wasn't made to take me from one place to another so I can retire early'? It sounded as though he was lashed to the wheel, forbidden by the music itself to alter course. At the time of the interview he was 67, about to turn 68, and well beyond the usual age for early retirement.

He won't allow the adjective 'never-ending' to be attached to his concert schedule and yet he describes his annual peregrinations as a task to which he is bound. He has millions of miles under his belt. After a quarter of a century a map of Dylan's travels across the continents would probably resemble a chart of the planet's prevailing winds and ceaseless tides. As 2013 began, plans were being laid for his return to Japan and Australia. For those who track Dylan in perpetual motion, the fun quiz game in the twenty-first century is to name a city he has not yet visited. For all that, the idea that he is forbidden from retiring by the demands of art is, at best, an appropriately poetic conceit.

He doesn't have to do this. Sometimes he sounds as though he has neither a desire nor a taste for it, but he certainly has the wealth and the opportunities to allow him to take up any other pursuit he might fancy. Yet touring is what he does. More precisely, it seems that today, after everything, Bob Dylan only truly exists through and within public performances. He has been known to make a virtue of the fact. But when yet another innocent dope of a journalist tells this Ancient Mariner that his voyage is unending, he recoils. Just when did Dylan shoot the albatross?

Neither did he label his touring schedule 'never-ending' nor once conspire in the elaborate accompanying mythology. That much is true. As Michael Gray has demonstrated in his *Bob Dylan Encyclopedia* (2006), it was a helpful journalist for *Q* magazine who turned a question about tours into a printed statement by his subject.[5] All that Dylan said in an interview on Rhode Island in October of 1989 was, 'Oh, it's all the same tour.' From a single casual remark an edifice of speculation and theory has been constructed. Yet even while knowing full well that Dylan detests and rejects the adjective, journalists, authors and diehard fans still refuse to relinquish their Never-Ending Tour. Sometimes a legend is too good to waste.

*

In 1988, the featured artist and his band picked up speed soon enough. Even as he struggled to sell records, Dylan began to acquire a new reputation as a concert performer. His choices from his vast catalogue of songs became more eclectic. For those who remembered Dylan the folk singer – and for plenty of those who did not – the traditional pieces performed with only Smith as an accompanist provided another source of fascination. Reviewing one show towards the end of the tour, Michael Gray would observe that 'Dylan's avid alignment with such material, for the first time in more than two decades, holds out tantalising possibilities as to where he might land next time he jumps'.[6] In the meantime, shows grew longer, the critics warmer. At the end of July, Edna Gundersen of *USA Today* was writing of the tour as 'the sleeper hit of the season' and quoting *Rolling Stone* magazine's welcome for the performer's 'extraordinary no-frills rock & roll'.[7] At Berkeley, on the third night, Dylan enjoyed the first of several triumphs. Soon enough, the tour was being extended.

The emerging argument in the artist's defence was that, with his vast stock of songs, record sales no longer really mattered. He began to make the point himself: he was a performer, first and foremost. His real work happened on stage. The recordings were sketches, at best, mere glimpses of the art attempted and frustrated in the alienating confines of the cursed recording studio. Only in performance could the songs be fully realised. Before July was out, Dylan was telling *USA Today*'s readers:

> Touring is part of playing. Anybody can sit in the studio and make
> records, but that's unrealistic and they can't possibly be a meaningful

performer. You have to do it night after night to understand what it's all about.

Almost a decade later, in September of 1997, as the tours rolled on endlessly, he was sticking to his theme, explaining to the *New York Times* that 'A lot of people don't like the road, but it's as natural to me as breathing'.

> I do it because I'm driven to do it, and I either hate it or love it. I'm mortified to be on the stage, but then again, it's the only place where I'm happy. It's the only place you can be who you want to be. You can't be who you want to be in daily life. I don't care who you are, you're going to be disappointed in daily life. But the cure-all for all that is to get on the stage, and that's why performers do it. But in saying that, I don't want to put on the mask of celebrity. I'd rather just do my work and see it as a trade.[8]

Such claims were plausible, for a while, but they failed to answer every question. Was the occasional reworking of old material a true substitute for creativity, for a lost songwriting gift? If his records didn't sell, what size of an audience was he entitled to expect? In the notes for *World Gone Wrong* Dylan would write of 'learning to go forward by turning back the clock'. It would be a necessary step, perhaps. The album and its predecessor, 1992's *Good As I Been to You*, would represent a reimmersion in the original sources of his music. In some sense, Dylan would repeat the course of study he had undertaken back in Greenwich Village, in his early days. But how could the wandering life of a touring performer allow him to 'go forward' if it involved nothing more than the endless reshuffling of his back pages? That didn't seem feasible. After all, *World Gone Wrong* would appear almost at the mid-point of a seven-year creative intermission in which Dylan released not a single new, self-written song. His habit of performing ancient folk and blues tunes during his concerts no doubt had a salutary effect, but it did not count as any kind of substitute for original work.

Still, for a star down on his luck in 1988 a small band was relatively cheap to run and easy, if the only issue was music, to lead. Freeing himself from the paraphernalia of previous years also forced Dylan once again to pay real heed to the songs he was performing. Sacking the backing vocalists (wife included) forced everyone's attention, not least his own, back to the person whose name was on the tickets, big and bold. It also helped that the artist had reached the point at which, ironically enough, his choices carried few risks. Since his critical stock was on the floor when he took to the stage in Concord on 7 June, Dylan was in one sense liberated. Nothing was expected of him. It therefore didn't much matter what he did.

The beginnings of a like process, the first glimmerings, might have been at work in the part of his brain where songs began. They would be slow to emerge, but after the crushing failures of his recent albums there was, perversely, nothing to inhibit them. The intense pressure always to perform as a writer had been all but guaranteed to leave Dylan making elaborate excuses for failure when potency deserted him. But after *Down in the Groove*, how much worse could things become? Defeat was, weirdly, an opportunity. He had been written off so thoroughly it hardly mattered what he wrote. Finally he had been freed of that crushing 'legend', the great and forever matchless Bob Dylan. There was something to be said for burning bridges.

The artist certainly understood the logic. He had applied it himself to excuse the *Self Portrait* album when that odd, disconcerting work was derided after its release in 1970. In one of the stories he had told back then, the project was presented as a deliberately self-destructive act. It had been intended, supposedly, to free him from the burden of expectations. An entire double album sacrificed just to correct a few misperceptions? You don't have to believe the tale to grasp that, by the middle of 1988, fate and a bunch of shoddy releases had indeed left Dylan with next to nothing by way of reputation and with nothing left to lose. It was entirely logical for a voice in his head to say, 'What the hell.'

The contrary version can be found in *Chronicles: Volume One*.[9] By his own account, Dylan had stopped even thinking of himself as a writer of songs. By 1988, supposedly, he had no desire to pursue the art. He had written enough and had nothing more to prove. In his recollection, he had reached the point at which he no longer expected to write another song. Somehow, nevertheless, he did just that. Typically, Dylan's book fails to explain just what changed or why the change took place. By the beginning of March 1989 this artist, the one who had been planning his retirement, would have enough material for another album, with plenty to spare. And plenty to waste.

You could just as well believe, of course, that once again bits of song simply began to come to him, as so often before, as if from out of the air. He had no other explanation for his creativity. By and large, he did not attempt to tamper with the mystery, to force himself or force the process. Nevertheless, after he and his three-piece band had rolled across the republic between June and October in 1988 to end up with a final triumph on their hands during a four-night stand at Radio City Music Hall in New York – causing a regiment of critics to perform a smart if inelegant about-face – he might just have begun to dare to dream again. Clearly, he had begun to scribble.

In *Chronicles: Volume One*, Dylan would describe writing perhaps 20 songs while he recovered from his hand injury. He would say they had come very easily in the end, but he would not bother to explain the reasons for this sudden upsurge from what had seemed a long-dry well. *Chronicles* is elusive by design. The sole piece of dating evidence given in the text is a reference to the presidential election of 1988 as a possible background to a song called 'Political World'. That scarcely narrows the range of possibilities. The last Dylan concert of the year took place on 19 October; the nation chose George H.W. Bush in preference to Michael Dukakis on 8 November. In other words, the artist started writing when the year was almost at an end. Though he regarded the first song that came to him as a kind of reawakening, like the first sign of a dreaming patient emerging from deep sedation, the author was not exactly punctilious in documenting such matters.

Equally, it is not known when Dylan decided that the bruises inflicted after *Down in the Groove* had healed sufficiently for him to risk a return to the studio. It is not known, though it involves a decent guess, if all the praise he had won for the tour known as Interstate 88 restored his confidence after so many dismal years. A lot isn't known. For facts, we can mention the release of *Dylan & the Dead* in February 1989, an event that rendered any thought of an album drawn from his more recent concert work impossible, more's the pity. We can remember, too, that it wasn't remotely feasible for this recording artist just to stop recording. In order to tour he needed product, preferably product of some small merit, to keep himself in the public eye. He also had an obligation, as ever, to Columbia. Despite all the later talk of a planned retirement, Dylan had accepted a new contract from the company just as it was being taken over by the Japanese conglomerate Sony. Thanks presumably to fans of his collaborators, *Dylan & the Dead* would not fail as catastrophically as *Real Live*, but it would get no higher than 37 on the American chart. Like it or not, a degree of commercial pressure remained a fact of life for anyone, legendary or not, who hoped to sell concert tickets. Finally, there is the fact that over dinner one night the U2 singer Bono had recommended the producer Daniel Lanois to Dylan.

He had watched this 37-year-old Canadian at work in New Orleans with the soul-singing Neville Brothers when the tour reached the city towards the end of September. Dylan had liked what he heard. It seems he had also enjoyed the kind of ambience Lanois tried to create when he was recording. It was not quite the Woodstock basement, but it was based on the semi-subversive idea that technology should come to the artist, not the other way around. In essence, Lanois championed a sophisticated version of the kind of mobile recording set-up that Dylan had tried and failed to provide for himself while making *Street-Legal* at Rundown in Santa Monica. The mock-domestic setting the producer offered in New Orleans with his 'Studio on the Move' was vastly preferable to the usual music-industry padded cells that had given the artist the horrors for years. Perhaps this time Dylan could make an album that actually sounded the way he wanted it to sound. If, that is, he knew what he wanted.

In Dylan's eyes, Lanois also had the advantage of being a musician, not unsuccessful, in his own right. Furthermore, the Quebecker was an advocate of 'atmosphere', of the inherent worth of a great performance over anyone's arbitrary notion of technical perfection. He detested the practice of separating the control console from the musicians. He liked 'organic' sound, ambient reverb and big, natural drum noises. Lanois would call the sound he created for *Oh Mercy* 'swampy'. If it meant anything, the word would recognise the fact that there was no point in trying to turn a Bob Dylan album into an audiophile's dream. That was no reason, equally, to allow it to sound, as certain of the artist's albums had sounded, like a cheap radio heard through a mattress. Lanois took a great many pains to make his recordings sound 'natural'.

Dylan would tell the story of the making of *Oh Mercy* in *Chronicles: Volume One*. It would be a puzzling narrative, one that would not accord in every last particular with other accounts. It would describe the artist's state of mind scrupulously, however. Here was a man who hesitated to begin work when he arrived in New Orleans, keeping Lanois and everyone else waiting. Here, too, was a Dylan who had a notebook full of songs, just for a change, but no real opinion, none he could articulate, about how they should sound, or any clear thoughts about the kind of album he wanted to make. As it transpired, he liked the idea of working with Lanois in New Orleans better than he liked the reality. A process that should have gone smoothly became, in Dylan's later telling, a slow, difficult and fraught business. He wanted to believe he had left the aggravations of album-making behind, but before long his relations with Lanois grew tense as the two failed to agree over issues large and small. A friendship survived, but it was tested severely. Such circumstances were never conducive to clear-headed decision-making on Dylan's part.

During the first couple of weeks of recording he was as difficult as only he could be, rejecting every last thing attempted by the producer and his trusted local musicians. Dylan sat around strumming his guitar while Lanois struggled, temper fraying, to get any sort of useful contribution out of him. To those present, it wasn't clear why or if this artist even wanted to make an album. As Mark Howard, the engineer, would remember, 'there came this one point when Dan [Lanois] finally had a freak-out. He just wanted Dylan to smarten up. It became . . . not a yelling match, but uncomfortable.' The artist nevertheless imposed his will in ways that could seem arbitrary, selfish, or designed just to show who was in charge. Dylan was a veteran of studio power struggles, though why he should have set out from the start to make life impossible for the producer he had chosen, a lauded professional who had accepted the job having heard only fragments of a few songs, is inexplicable. The legend's aim seemed to be, in any case, to inflict as much inconvenience as he could on those around him, as though to test their obedience. Lanois, more than a little star-struck, was ready to put up with almost anything for the sake of a Dylan album. 'Bob had a rule,' he would recall. 'We only recorded at night. I think he's right about that: the body is ready to accommodate a certain tempo at night-time. I think it's something to do with the pushing and pulling of the moon. At night-time we're ready to be more mysterious and dark. *Oh Mercy*'s about that.'[10]

So it began, yet again, the making of an album that *should* have been great. As with *Infidels*, the artist embarked on the production of a body of work that these days can only be appreciated if you take account of the songs Dylan chose – wilfully, perversely – to leave aside from the album he would release for sale. *Oh Mercy* would still turn out to be a very good set. It would return Dylan to that state of grace called critical favour, at least for a time. But once again it would leave anyone who cared about his art to put together a home-assembly kit from bootlegs and Bootleg Series releases. It remains the only way to get a clear idea of what was achieved in March and April 1989. Either

BORN IN TIME

Dylan was still refusing to put everything he had into a single album, or his understanding of what he was doing was a secret he didn't care to reveal. In either event, he would seem like an artist with a peculiar ambivalence towards his work. For him, it seemed, even the best of his songs remained disposable and replaceable. That attitude relied on the conviction that there were plenty more where those came from. The songwriter who had barely survived a long spell on short rations would behave, in short, as though a brief season of plenty could never end.

Dylan has never been straightforward about his understanding of his gifts, perhaps because his relationship with them is complicated, perhaps because the relationship has changed over the years. He takes an expert interest in the craft of songwriting, as you might expect, yet in *Chronicles* can be found describing himself as utterly bereft of interest in writing before, all of a sudden, he began to write the *Oh Mercy* songs. He has often denied being a disciplined writer, the kind who clocks in dutifully at a desk each day. In some of his descriptions of his art he truly does jot down notes that could as easily come to nothing as form the makings of a song. Equally, in some phases of his career – before recording *Highway 61 Revisited* or prior to *Blood on the Tracks* – he has indeed sat down and done his best to fill a notebook. At other times he has embarked on albums with little better than a handful of scraps at his disposal.

The fragments of songs Lanois heard before the recording sessions that became *Oh Mercy* were accompanied by plaintive-sounding questions from the writer. Did the producer think this or that bit of verse and basic piano melody could make a song? Clearly, Dylan didn't know. You are inclined to believe him, then, when he denies having much understanding of his own talent. Sometimes songs just come. He accepts or refuses the power of an idea according to his mood. That kind of claim makes his gift sound like a fragile thing, despite all the evidence to the contrary. The inference remains, therefore, that if Dylan can't tell whether a fragment has the makings of a song he is liable to be a poor judge of the finished product.

The largest crime he committed during the making of *Oh Mercy* was the omission of a song entitled 'Series of Dreams', closely followed by the decision to drop another work called 'Dignity'. A third piece, 'Born in Time', would turn up on a subsequent Dylan album, but in a rendering that would sound undistinguished when set beside the track discarded from *Oh Mercy*. When the magnificent *Tell Tale Signs*, volume eight in the Bootleg Series, appeared in October 2008 with its outtakes and 'previously unreleased' tracks, anyone with an interest in Dylan could just about piece together the work that might have been. It would cost the fan the price of two albums, the second running to three discs if you felt extravagant, for the privilege. In effect, though *Oh Mercy* still contained songs of rare quality, songs such as 'Most of the Time', 'What Was it You Wanted' and 'Ring Them Bells', it had been deprived of 30 per cent of its power.

The grievous loss was 'Series of Dreams', a song unlike any that Dylan had produced before, one that proved he was no extinct creative volcano and vindicated the Lanois method. By the artist's standards the skeletal lyrics were nothing special, yet the song truly did manage to capture the haunting power of a dream. Furthermore, it was a vivid illustration of a theme that had long underpinned Dylan's work and thought, less a question of 'What's truly real?' than an enquiry into our ability ever to experience reality as anything more than a succession of overlapping dreams. On one reading, the speaker in the song could simply be describing what seemed to go on in his head while he slept. In one dream

. . . numbers were burning
In another, I witnessed a crime
In one, I was running, and in another
All I seemed to be doing was climb

Yet these dreams, twisted one within the other, might also be happening in a dream-like reality. Lanois has drums that pound like an insistent question as the singer in the first verse describes himself thinking about his series of dreams, but then saying that the thinking itself, about nothing 'specific', also felt 'Like a dream, when someone wakes up and screams'. In this human condition, as Dylan observes, there is 'no exit in any direction' and no way to break out: 'the cards are no good that you're holding / Unless they're from another world.'

So brilliant was the track, Dylan clearly had no choice – or so the jaundiced listener is left to conclude – but to leave it off the album. The best of the songs that survived his veto – and the best are very good – were enhanced by that 'swampy' Lanois production, a design for the album's overall sound that seemed to manipulate light, shade and ambient temperature within the verses. Some still find the producer's method too fussy, the results contrived and artificial, but it suited Dylan's words. 'What Was It You Wanted' sounded sepulchral; the lovely 'Shooting Star' *felt* elegiac; 'Most of the Time' was in its essence nocturnal. So much could be taken for granted, you might think, as part of a producer's job. Yet Lanois and his musicians complemented Dylan's lyrics in their arrangements and playing with an assurance that no one else had achieved, the artist least of all in his attempts to manage his recording sessions, in a very long time.

In parts, *Oh Mercy* would have a kind of Southern Gothic quality. The mysterious if melodramatic 'Man in the Long Black Coat', the tale of a Bible-quoting stranger with whom a woman disappears leaving no explanation or clue, showed that Dylan had not lost his interest in punishment and sin. 'Most of the Time', the stoical confessions of a man no better than 'halfway content', sounded like evidence that age had begun to take its toll on a writer approaching his 48th birthday. The title 'What Good Am I?' spoke for itself: one writer, at least, was not impressed by Bob Dylan. 'What Was it You Wanted', solemn as a walk in a graveyard, was the artist at his most icily dismissive, and his most commanding.

> What was it you wanted
> I ain't keeping score
> Are you the same person
> That was here before?

Yet still he lacked the crucial ability to make important decisions and get them right. Worse, indecision only made Dylan stubborn. With his unparalleled record of achievement, who was to tell him he was wrong? He was not, in any case, some gauche teen idol to be commanded by a producer; all the power was his. Lanois had been granted as much of a say as anyone Dylan had worked with since Jerry Wexler during the *Slow Train Coming* sessions, but when push came to shove only one person called the shots. By all accounts, Lanois argued hard for 'Series of Dreams'. It was the one song above all others he hoped to protect from the artist's reckless self-censorship. The producer was proud of his contribution to the track, in each of its several incarnations, and rightly so. He had understood instantly that Dylan was embarked on a new kind of writing. Lanois had sensed the possibilities and had struggled to bring them to fruition. As far as he was concerned, *Oh Mercy* could and should have been the start of something. In the end, Dylan was once more the chief obstacle to what could have been one of the finest of Bob Dylan albums. He still managed to emerge with an album that was pretty fair. Above all, it was no *Down in the Groove*.

Rolling Stone would decide that '*Oh Mercy* explores moral concerns and matters of the heart with a depth and seriousness Dylan has not demonstrated since *Desire*'.[11] The habit of measuring the artist against a yardstick he himself had shaped was, as ever, near pointless, but it at least served to affirm the truth that there was some flame of creative life left in him. *Oh Mercy* would reach number 30 on the American chart, a showing that was both indifferent and far better than anything *Down in the Groove* had managed. British buyers meanwhile placed the new album at number six, a more reasonable verdict. If still another comeback was required, *Oh Mercy* was surely a start.

*

In May 1989, Dylan once again toured Europe. Afterwards, he set running the tale of the never-ending odyssey by playing on in America from July until September. That autumn he reorganised his management, giving the job of handling his concert bookings to one Jeff Kramer in Los Angeles and responsibility for his New York office to another Jeff named Rosen. Dylan also turned up, incongruously, at a telethon in LA for Chabad-Lubavitch, scaring up a whole new flock of 'rumours', which is to say guesses, about the nature of his religious beliefs. In the spring of 1990, meanwhile, he busied himself once again with the largely pointless if lucrative Traveling Wilburys project. Roy Orbison had died suddenly during the previous December. The ageing ad hoc celebrity boy band were deprived of a guiding spirit, but the survivors pressed on regardless. They were rewarded, if that's the word, with a flaccid little album that would come nowhere near to matching the sales of its predecessor.

Amid all this, with plans being laid for a year of touring that would encompass 92 shows, the artist was attempting to make another album of his own. This time the fashionable Was brothers, David and Don, joined the list of music industry Dylan fans who thought they could master the job of producing his work. The brothers hired the likes of Al Kooper and the guitarist Stevie Ray Vaughan as the core of a top-heavy if illustrious musical crew. George Harrison, Elton John, David Crosby, Bruce Hornsby and other famous names put in appearances in the studio, but the added scattering of glitter did nothing to improve *Under the Red Sky*. After the album's release in September, Robert Christgau of the *Village Voice* would decide to 'rate' the album more highly than *Oh Mercy*, apparently because the new set showed 'post-punk' tendencies, whatever those might be, but most attentive reviewers would be as dismissive as most record-buyers. Dylan's downward slide would resume: 38 in America, number 13 in Britain. With one good leftover from *Oh Mercy*, a fine mock children's song that gave the album its title and one terrific track inserted to compensate the diehards, *Under the Red Sky* would get what it deserved in the marketplace. Loyal buyers deserved some small recompense, in whatever shape or form, for a set that began with a thing called 'Wiggle Wiggle'.

> Wiggle, wiggle, wiggle in your boots and shoes
> Wiggle, wiggle, wiggle, you got nothing to lose

A piece of fun? Just a nonsense song for the sake of it? Those are comforting thoughts, no doubt. Instead, a track that has pole position in any contest to find the worst thing Dylan ever recorded sounds like a demonstration of his contempt for his industry, for his work and for the album-making process. To choose the 'Wiggle' horror as the album's opening number smacked of something more than carelessness. With this, so it seemed, the artist was defying enemies and allies alike. Along with a second-best version of the marvellous 'Born in Time', the song called 'Handy Dandy' was the compensation, a piece in which Dylan described and adopted a fascinating, funny and devilish persona, part gangster, part Cotton Club bandleader, part demonic presence. It was, in essence, a recasting of 'Like a Rolling Stone' with a few rough grains of the Kingsmen's 'Louie Louie' from 1963 thrown in, but none the worse for that. Dylan at least sounded as if he was briefly happy in his work. For the rest, it was an ill-written album, one from which plenty of 'analysis' could be derived, but precious little real listening pleasure. For what it's worth, Dylan himself has never had good things to say about *Under the Red Sky*.

He went back on the road as though going on the run. Performance now truly did seem to be the entire point of this artist's existence. In January, after the first sessions for the album, he had made a dash for Brazil, France and England, finishing up with six long-remembered nights at London's Hammersmith Odeon. Once *Under the Red Sky* and the last Traveling Wilburys sessions were complete, he was gone again, to Canada and the northern United States. In midsummer he could be found at any European festival anyone cared to name. By August he was hitting the homeland once more and still touring – sometimes for better, sometimes for worse – by the middle of November. The idea that Dylan was doing all of this to promote an album he disliked and the public disdained was laughable. Whatever the reality of the 'Locarno epiphany', that mythologised moment of truth, it was obvious that he could not or would not stop performing. Another trait was becoming plain. Some shows could be incandescently brilliant, others utterly risible. Those who bought tickets for a Dylan concert were given no guarantee as to the version of the artist liable to turn up.

So much was becoming common knowledge within his industry. What was not yet known was the significance of *Under the Red Sky*, an album that would remain 'underrated' for very good reasons. Of itself, that needn't have mattered. Dylan's lyrical gift had ebbed since *Oh Mercy*, but he had still managed to come up with ten original songs for the *Red Sky* project. He had made poor albums often enough before, in any case, and hauled himself out of the pit. There was nothing to say he wouldn't recover again. His riposte to those who had gathered for his wake after *Down in the Groove* had been robust enough, after all. The several failures of *Under the Red Sky* would surely be forgotten in time. What no one knew was that those were to be the last songs, good or bad, that Dylan would write and record in seven years.

*

It was as though he went underground. No one still hoped to hear this artist voice any sort of comment on the nation's affairs, or ever again reset the compass for popular music, but the absence of his songs would become almost disorienting for those who had followed his career. The lacuna would have no precedent. Dylan had endured a savage writer's block before and survived. He had suffered 'amnesia' like an actual neurological wound. In the early 1970s he had struggled long and hard to find creative alternatives to the miraculous, unforced spontaneity of the '60s. But even the hiatus between *New Morning*'s release in October 1970 and the *Planet Waves* 'comeback' of January '74 had not been wholly barren. There had not been much writing to underpin the *Pat Garrett & Billy the Kid* soundtrack in July 1973, but 'Knockin' on Heaven's Door' had still counted as a lot better than nothing. What began after *Under the Red Sky* was a crisis of a different order, one that seemed only to deepen when Dylan talked amiably, expertly, about the art of songwriting to Paul Zollo of *SongTalk* magazine in April 1991, or when he claimed to a journalist in April 1994 to have 'a bunch of papers and notes and things lying around. Only time is going to tell when those things come out.'[12] Year after year, nothing would 'come out'. If a couple of sparse albums of old folk and blues tunes were meanwhile to be Dylan's oblique judgement on modern times, the statement made would prove hard to decipher. Beyond those enigmatic offerings he would fall silent as a recording artist, as though one part of him had ceased to exist.

Instead, he would be out there somewhere, ceaselessly in motion, entirely public and utterly inscrutable, somehow barely visible under all the blazing stage lights. You could catch him if his tour came to your town – and there was always a good chance of that – but save for an outbreak of strangeness, a performance of the Beatles' 'Nowhere Man' or Otis Redding's 'Dock of the Bay', it would become hard to describe what he was doing or why. Witnesses at some of his shows would begin to claim that he wasn't necessarily sober during every performance. One city would report that the concert was dire, another that their Dylan had been magnificent. In part, the tale of the never-ending tour would be born of the self-evident fact that for fans there would be nothing else to go on during seven lean years. An entire aesthetic would be devised, one that persists to this day, to justify the claim that Dylan's creativity survived and thrived in the stark, undeniable absence of new songs.

The America he traversed in the early 1990s had decided to remain conservative. The Iran-Contra scandal, the fascinating tale of the Reagan White House flogging missiles to Iranian hostage-takers in order to fund murderous Nicaraguan insurgents, had not harmed the Republican cause in the slightest during the 1988 election. Barely half the electorate had bothered to vote, but George H.W. Bush had still put the Democrats and his opponent, Michael Dukakis, to disorderly flight. By 1990, some 15 per cent of Americans were still failing to graduate from high school, yet that was exactly the percentage of their fellow citizens who had been smitten by 'home computing'. An alliterative mouthful, the World Wide Web, was about to go public while conservative commentators fretted over porn, public morality and the subversive habit they called political correctness. Inspired by Robert Bly's book *Iron John* a few stout men were off in the woods hunting for masculinity while a few others were being handcuffed for crimes committed in the Wall Street undergrowth. In Iraq, a place that could be found on most maps, a former American ally named Saddam Hussein would spend the summer of 1990 preparing to invade a kingdom built on oilfields called Kuwait. The United States had not been in a real war for a while.

In 1990 and 1991, nevertheless, a Bob Dylan fan was plotting to remove Bush from the Oval Office. The connection between Bill Clinton's New Democrats and the old New Left as the artist once had known it was remote, by no accident, but a lot of things had changed. The breaching of the Berlin Wall in 1989 had seen the Soviet regime begin to unravel like a threadbare banner. On the day after Christmas in 1991 the USSR would be gone, formally and for good. Republicans would claim most of the credit on Reagan's behalf, and even allow a little of it to Bush, but at first they would fail to notice that much of their self-declared purpose and a lot of their rabble-rousing opportunities had disappeared with the Russian reds. A short war over Kuwait had done Bush's opinion-poll ratings a power of good in the early part of 1991, but suddenly the ground was shifting, all but unnoticed, under Republican feet. If there was no longer a need to fear the nuclear war that had sometimes seemed inevitable when Reagan was in charge, what need was there for a war party addicted to defence spending? Political territory that had seemed secure for conservatives was put at risk while the evil empire folded and the economy struggled. A Democrat who represented youth, change, hope and other non-specific virtues while tending to the concerns of middle America might be in with a shout: such was Clinton's insight, even if his own party needed a lot of convincing.

This candidate was certainly young enough. Dylan's junior by five years, Clinton was the first presidential contender in the artist's career who did not regard him as the perplexing voice of a coming generation. In 1991, Dylan would be 50, no one's idea of the voice of youth, rebellious or otherwise. Yet what was Clinton if not proudly, even aggressively youthful, though 'moderate' in all things (save his sexual behaviour)? He could command a stage and inspire a crowd as well as any famous singer. Clinton was, after all, a performer first and last. He had a genius for it. He also knew what he was talking about, down to the last abstruse detail, but he could speak as though talking personally to each and every member of an audience. The candidate had charisma, 'voice of a generation' charisma.

Against this master politician planted firmly on the centre ground a new strain of conservatism was beginning to organise even as Bush luxuriated in his poll ratings after the first Gulf war. Right-wingers of this variety hated Clinton's guts. They hated him most of all simply because he was brilliant. Their loathing became frantic when it became obvious in the summer of 1992 that this Democrat was dangerous, that he could win and go on winning. Conservatives turned on Bush, the traitor in the Oval Office with his effete talk of common ground, but their real impulse was a fear of losing power. The '80s had been a good time to be rich and right wing. That was – wasn't it? – the American way of life, to be defended at all costs. Clinton was no more left wing than he was celibate, of course, but that didn't matter. There was the risk that he would preside over the return of ungodly liberalism if his party gained control of the government. While Dylan turned the corner into middle age, old battle lines were being redrawn. A fact was rapidly becoming a cliché. Amid Clinton's victories in the 1990s the country would divide evenly and, it seemed, beyond hope of reconciliation into the so-called 50–50 nation. Where would an artist stand in that kind of American landscape? Dylan the songwriter would be silent for years on end, as though lost in a fog, but reality would find him in the end. The present, as he would realise, begins in the past.

*

Those who track the artist's activities have a job on their hands when they list, tabulate, annotate, adumbrate and otherwise pore over the first half of the '90s. Unless you have the philosophical serenity of a data-entry clerk, it must be tedious work. Tour after tour after tour, musician following musician, one-night stand following one-night stand in city after city, country after country: the bare historical facts of places and dates are not, of themselves, enthralling. Whatever the level of art created, the statistical record of the unending tour is the opposite of fascinating reading. Eleven musicians were on retainers from Dylan between the summer of 1988 and the autumn of 1992. Some of them were crucial to his performances; not one played a significant role in his life. He worked almost ceaselessly. It left the rest of his existence all but empty of incident.

In August 1990, his marriage to Carolyn Dennis had ended. Since the final dissolution in 1992 she has barely said a word about the relationship and nothing about the reasons for the split. In 2001, provoked finally by revelations in the Howard Sounes biography *Down the Highway* that a child had been born and a wedding had taken place, Dennis did release a brief statement. Plainly unhappy that her privacy had been breached, she said: 'To portray Bob as hiding his daughter is just malicious and ridiculous. That is something he would never do. Bob has been a wonderful, active father to Desiree.' Dennis went on to explain that she and Dylan had taken advantage of a California law that allowed them to seal their marriage certificate from public scrutiny. 'Bob and I made a choice,' the singer said, 'to keep our marriage a private matter for a simple reason – to give our daughter a normal childhood.' Finally, in an attempt to kill off a persistent piece of speculation over Dylan's motives for his ceaseless travels, Dennis added: 'To say I got a huge settlement that forced Bob to do concert tours is fictitious, irresponsible and hurtful.'

In the first three years of the 1990s he put on an average of 95 shows annually during those tours, taking his music to all corners of North America, to Europe, to Central and South America, and to Oceania. It didn't leave much time for a marriage, or for anything else. For most of the period there was room only for bad habits and peculiar incidents. In February 1991, for example, the organisers of the Grammy Awards had the actor Jack Nicholson present Dylan with one of those obituaries disguised as a 'lifetime achievement' prize at a ceremony in New York. First he sang 'Masters of War' very badly just as American troops were preparing to retake Kuwait. Then he gave a strange, halting little acceptance speech to the audience at Radio City Music Hall. 'My daddy,' Dylan said, 'he didn't leave me too much.'

You know, he was a very simple man and he didn't leave me a lot, but what he told me was this . . . [Here Dylan allowed himself a lengthy pause while some in the crowd laughed.] He said, 'You know it's possible to become so defiled in this world that your own mother and father will abandon you, and if that happens God will always believe in your own ability to mend your ways.'

It was the statement of a man who considered himself to be a Jew: Dylan was paraphrasing a passage from a nineteenth-century rabbinical text.[13] It was no joke, either; despite the laughter of a puzzled audience, he didn't joke about his father or rabbinical texts. Why he would also have considered himself to be 'defiled' is, however, as puzzling as his reasons for sharing his guilt with an audience full of rich, sleek and bewildered music-industry types. Perhaps a reported case of flu had left him in poor spirits. Equally, it might be that spirits of another sort had given him an existential hangover.

Life on the road was hardly likely to have rendered Dylan pure in body and mind. The shows he had given just days before in Scotland, Ireland and in London had left even hardcore fans shocked by his demeanour and his grisly performances. Reviewers were writing openly that the star appeared to be drunk. In the *Guardian*, Michael Gray had observed that at the start of the first show in Glasgow Dylan 'shuffled onstage wearing a tartan jacket and looking like he'd had a drink'.[14] Another who was there would report that the next night's burlesque was no more reassuring. The artist 'certainly seemed to be the worse for alcohol at the second Glasgow show, dropping his guitar a couple of times and wandering off stage during "Positively 4th Street", leaving his astonished band to continue without him'.[15]

These were not isolated incidents. All the credibility Dylan had accumulated with his return to touring was being dissipated by a drunk and an unrehearsed group of confused musicians who were sometimes worse while sober than the boss deep in his cups. In London, people walked out. Those who stuck around, real fans almost by definition, had the disconcerting (not to say unsatisfactory) experience of being unable to recognise the songs Dylan thought he was singing. The Grammy Awards audience reported the same technical difficulty. These were not 'creative reworkings', not deliberate attempts to reawaken interest in familiar pieces by demolishing preconceptions. These were atrocities.

If there was anything to the claim that this artist defined himself in performance, that his real art was the product of the concert stage, both the singer and the songs were being defiled. Had the story ended there, as many thought it might, Dylan would be remembered as just another superstar casualty in the Elvis Presley memorial ward. As it was, Joe Queenan, writing in *Spy* magazine, would describe the figure who appeared at the televised Grammy awards.

> If any of the tens of millions watching had not already realised that Bob Dylan, poet, wit, heart-rending vocalist, hipster, scourge, had turned into Bob Dylan, somewhat pathetic kook – well, now they knew.[16]

So he felt 'defiled'. So the question becomes: why carry on disgusting and destroying himself? In his book, Sounes asserts that Dylan was in need of cash because of his divorce. His recent albums had certainly sold badly and he had nothing new, nor even the hope of something new, to offer Columbia. It makes no sense, however, to believe that an individual with Dylan's instinct for survival would annihilate himself in public once and for all. He had a precious asset, in any case. That he allowed the asset to be exploited just at the moment he was supposedly in dire need is probably an encouragement to cynics, but a few facts are worth bearing in mind. One is that the reports of drunkenness sound nothing like a superstar's decadence. Alcohol might have crept up on Dylan, but the worst of his behaviour coincided with the aftermath of a divorce and the misery that tends to accompany such an event. He wasn't in a mess because he was on the road. He was in a mess when he happened to be on the road. Second, even if he allowed Columbia to issue choice parts of his back catalogue at an opportune moment, he wasn't quite out of a job as a performer. He didn't quit that job, either, even when all his previous Bob Dylans were supplying the record company with revenue and his alimony had long been covered. Drunk or sober, Dylan wasn't forced out onto the road.

The next premature obituary arrived, in any case, around a month after the weird affair at Radio City Music Hall. It was welcomed by all save a rueful few capable of making comparisons between the Dylan who had stumbled insensibly around British concert stages and the writer represented by *The Bootleg Series Volumes 1–3 (Rare & Unreleased) 1961–1991*. The worst that could be said of the compendium was that it laboured under a title better suited to a dusty manuscript folio hidden in library stacks than to one of the great achievements in modern art. Bootleg collectors deprived of their bragging rights would quibble, of course, over the choices made. Many fans would meanwhile wonder about the implicit comment made by this box set on the status of *Blood on the Tracks* and *Infidels*. Finally listeners were given the chance to encounter 'Blind Willie McTell', or to hear a drastically different account of 'Idiot Wind', but that only deepened the mystery of the original albums. There would be frustration, too, that despite the appearance at long last of 'I Shall Be Released', the basement tapes were still being denied proper representation. The 58 tracks did not tell the whole story about any period in Dylan's career. The story they did tell, one only hinted at by the *Biograph* release, was a tale of startling, enduring achievement that dwarfed *Down in the Groove* and *Under the Red Sky*. In fact, it made them look ridiculous.

That might have played on Dylan's mind, whether he needed the money or not, while the box set was in preparation. On the one hand, *Volumes 1–3* was testimony to 30 years of matchless work. No songwriter of Dylan's or any generation ran it close. On the other hand, this piece of the historical record stopped, much as he had stopped, in 1989, with a debatable remix of the marvellous 'Series of Dreams'. Even if he had thought to extend this collection, what could he have offered to represent the rest of his labours in the 1980s and 1990s? A 'Brownsville Girl', a 'Born in Time', or a 'Handy Dandy'? Add all those and a few others together and you would have a fine album. Count it as the fruits of better than a decade, without the malformed *Infidels* and the botched *Oh Mercy*, and it looks like slim pickings. Besides, in March 1991 the 58 tracks on the box set only served to remind Dylan and the world that he had ceased to write anything at all. He showed no signs of resuming the old, addictive habit. Talking to Paul Zollo in April, he would not mention *Volumes 1–3*. Sounding wistful, the artist would say, however, 'It's not to anybody's best interest to think about how they will be perceived tomorrow. It hurts you in the long run.'[17]

If so, it helps if you can stay one step ahead of the obituarists. Dylan was having no luck with that. In April and May he trekked up and down America's east coast; in June he was in mainland Europe for more amplified debacles. Some of these shows were legendarily awful. The only undefiled virtue to which Dylan could still lay claim was his pride. Perhaps the advent of his 50th birthday, the one he said meant nothing to him, had registered after all. Perhaps he simply grew tired of humiliation and self-disgust. Perhaps the sense that he had polluted his talent was truly profound. It might be easier to believe that the old, thrawn tenacity, the bloody-minded stubbornness that had seen him through so many crises, began to reassert itself. He had never knuckled under easily.

Whatever the truth, at some point in the second half of the year, as he travelled America's highways once more, Dylan found the ability to stay sober for longer. He stayed straight long enough, at least, to give paying customers a glimpse of what they sought. Bootlegs say that late in 1991 the public began once again to get what they had paid for. More than a few of the shows were very good. The only thing Dylan could not offer these people in Texas, Indiana or Ohio was a new song.

There was a contract he had yet to fulfil, with two albums owing, whatever the blockage in his creative plumbing. As 1992 began, Dylan had to solve the problem of supplying Columbia with *something* while knowing he possessed nothing, nothing at all, of his own. All he could do, therefore, was make a record of other people's music, but he knew that strategy was risky. Much as he enjoyed covering the songs of others, and as often as the practice had spurred him back to writing in the past, Dylan had never managed to create a successful album as the interpreter of his favourite tunes. *Self Portrait*, that brave but ill-served experiment, had given him one of the worst moments of his young life. *Down in the Groove* had not been saved from critical perdition by his variations on themes supplied by other hands. Nevertheless, one fact seems to have made Dylan pause and think straight.

In some of his worst, least coherent concerts the only redeeming moments had come while he performed his brief 'acoustic' interludes. In the better shows, as his thirst subsided, Dylan's explorations of traditional songs had become more than a gesture to a few of the old folk devotees dotted around the halls. These songs were his assertion of faith and belief in something that could never be defiled. 'Trail of the Buffalo', 'Golden Vanity', 'Two Soldiers', 'Roving Gambler', above all 'Barbara Allen', that early love from Dylan's youth: these and others like them were the songs he understood best and could still perform as well as anyone.

The irony was profound, even poetic. The artist who had once been given so much grief by the guardians of tradition in Greenwich Village would seek his redemption in traditional song. His decision as it formed was also a kind of confession. Whatever else Dylan had made of himself as a writer and performer, whoever he had been or had seemed to be, folk and blues still formed the core of his identity as a musician and as a person. The great revolutionary hadn't really changed at all. There was wisdom in the old songs, things that could be trusted, a sense both of history and of mystery. This music was life as he understood it.

The beginnings of an insight came to him just as Bill Clinton was spinning glib, comforting tales to the American people. Dylan would make his first attempt to record some of the older songs on 3 June, when the newly confirmed Democratic Party nominee was on a popular TV show playing a bad if exuberant 'Heartbreak Hotel' on his saxophone. When Clinton accepted the nomination as candidate at his party's convention in New York in July, he would tell delegates that he had in mind a 'new covenant' with America's people. Dylan sought only a new contract with himself.

Simplicity would be achieved amid complications. First, irrespective of any theories over his motives, Dylan was committed to play plenty of concerts. There would be 92 of those, appropriately enough, in '92, but they would be scattered across the planet. The artist's first task in

March and April was to show Australia and New Zealand that reports of his living death as a performer were not to be trusted. Then there were engagements on the American west coast to be fulfilled. Europe, then Canada, then another swing through the American Midwest – with no fewer than five nights amid his old Minneapolis haunts – would follow. Dylan would thereafter perform on the east coast of his country before finishing up in November, as had become almost traditional, with a run of dates in Florida. Even amid the insanity of 1966, when he had flown from concert to concert in a ramshackle old jet while trying to write and record *Blonde on Blonde* before setting out to conquer an obdurate world, he had never tried to make an album under these conditions.

First Dylan somehow found time for sessions in Chicago. Less than a fortnight after finishing up a spring tour of the western states in Las Vegas, of all benighted places, he was working with David Bromberg and a disparate group of musicians at the Acme Recording Studio. The two men had known one another for better than a couple of decades. Bromberg, one of those musicians with a seeming ability to play just about anything, had contributed to *Self Portrait* and *New Morning*. As he remembered years later, he had been performing at the Bottom Line in Greenwich Village one February night when Dylan and Neil Young came in. According to what Bromberg was told, 'Neil had said to Bob' that a collaboration would be an idea worth considering. At Acme, with a full band, a horn section, fiddle and mandolin players, he and Dylan worked on perhaps 30 songs. What's striking is that the selection would not necessarily have appealed in every respect to a folk or blues purist. A couple of the numbers were Bromberg's songs, several others were songs he had made his own. 'Lady Came from Baltimore' was a very well-known piece by Tim Hardin, a writer Dylan admired greatly who had died after a long-postponed heroin overdose in 1980. For one track, described as a 'contemporary Christian' piece, an entire gospel choir was brought in; for another a zydeco accordion player was hired. Plenty of traditional songs, blues of various vintages, country songs and folk tunes were attempted. But the aim was certainly not to recreate a Dylan performance from the Gaslight Cafe *circa* 1962.

Reputedly, the artist had driven to Chicago in 'a truck', though the description is unlikely to be an exact match for the vehicle. He is also said to have yet again sought a 'live' sound. From what has emerged of the tapes, it's hard to tell whether his wish was granted. By all accounts, nevertheless, these were productive sessions and enough was achieved, in Bromberg's telling, for an album he believed was worth the effort. Dylan didn't agree. He was due to play festivals in Europe, starting in Sweden on 26 June, and decided to leave the mixing work to his producer. If that was the case, an album was close to completion. But as Bromberg would explain in 2008:

> He left me to mix things and he told me before he left, 'I've usually been on every mix I've done, but I trust you. Go ahead and mix it.' And I think I did a bad job. I didn't understand what he wanted . . . When he came back and listened to it, he said, 'That's awful. Go back and listen to the roughs.' I went back and listened to the rough mix and I saw what he was talking about, but he had lost interest . . . It's unfortunate that we didn't get to mix it together because it might have come out.[18]

Two tracks from the Chicago sessions, 'Duncan and Brady' and 'Miss the Mississippi', would be made available in 2008 to anyone prepared to buy the three-disc version of the Bootleg Series release *Tell Tale Signs*. Those recordings fail to make it clear why Dylan would be so dissatisfied with what was done at Acme, but Bromberg probably guessed right: the artist lost interest. For whatever reason, what could have been his best attempt at an album of cover versions had failed to enthuse him, or at least had failed to enthuse him for long.

In July, having concluded his touring business for the moment at the Jazz à Juan festival amid the whispering pines of the French Riviera, Dylan retreated to his Malibu garage, where there was room enough to spare for a modest home studio. In Europe, he had continued his practice of featuring traditional songs such as 'The Roving Blade' and 'The Girl on the Greenbriar Shore' in his sets. (The latter, performed at Dunkirk on 30 June, would also turn up on *Tell Tale Signs*.) Back in California, he proceeded to delve far deeper into this heritage than he had been prepared to attempt in Chicago. In one version of events, the initial plan was simply to supplement the recordings he had made with Bromberg. That notion seems to have been discarded quickly. Dylan also forgot any idea of covering contemporary songs. He reverted, in effect, to being a hardcore, uncompromising folk musician. In his own terms, he became a purist.

Good As I Been to You could give the impression that it was recorded at the kind of speed that was customary in the days when Dylan first entered a recording studio. Columbia would certainly make the claim that a disconcertingly ragged-sounding set had been captured in single takes, but that was far from the case. While the engineer, Micajah Ryan, might have been guilty of exaggeration when he said that after the sessions began 'I didn't get back to my family until a couple of months later' – Dylan was on stage in Toronto by 17 August – the technician saw enough of the artist at work on *Good As I Been to You* and the companion piece *World Gone Wrong* to dispel any belief that there was busking going on. Dylan would 'come in each day with at least a couple of songs to work on', the engineer would remember. 'He'd do several takes in every key and tempo imaginable; speeding up or slowing down, making it higher or lower in pitch until he felt he got it.' Ryan would also state that it was the album's producer, Debbie Gold, who had 'convinced Dylan to record with just acoustic guitar and vocals'.

Generally described as a 'long-standing friend' of the artist, this music industry professional clearly enjoyed his trust. Having been hired as a teenager in 1975 by the Grateful Dead's Jerry Garcia after the guitarist was impressed by her work at Philadelphia's Tower Theatre, Gold had also served on Bruce Springsteen's immense 1978 tour to promote his *Darkness on the Edge of Town* album. She had first worked for Dylan as 'production co-ordinator' on *Shot of Love*, presumably having met him through the Dead, given that he had been a friend of Garcia since 1972. Dylan valued her, it seems, because she was honest and failed to keep her opinions to herself. She for one – and she might have been the only one – was not intimidated by the legend. According to Ryan, the artist

> consulted Debbie on every take. He trusted her and I got the feeling that was unusual for him. She was never afraid to tell him the truth, and, boy, was she persistent, often convincing him to stay with a song long after he seemed to lose interest in it.[19]

If that was the case, Gold could probably count herself Dylan's most successful producer since John Hammond. Unlike Bromberg, she was not prepared to allow this reborn folk singer to 'lose interest'. Equally, if Gold had seen the artist at work during *Shot of Love* she probably had a fair idea of where the source of certain problems might lie. The suggestion that it was 'unusual' for Dylan to deal with someone he could trust might explain a number of things about his '80s albums. How many of those fine, lamented songs were discarded because he had no faith in the pliant opinions of those around him?

As it was, not one of the old songs Dylan had performed on his tours made it to *Good As I Been to You*. Nor did he have to perform the mundane task of learning the songs he did perform: he knew them all. The memory that once had allowed him to recall 'hundreds' of Woody Guthrie numbers was intact in an artist who only a few years before had been incapable of remembering his own lines. Dylan responded viscerally to those aged, often anonymous songs of love, betrayal, revenge and loss. Above all, it seems, he responded to stories, to narrative. For him, emblematic and symbolic tales had always been at the heart of folk. The songs endured, decade after decade and century after century, precisely because of what they had to say about an unalterable human condition. That was why he would talk about them as somehow beyond time, as ancient as myth, as modern as the nightly news. The album kicked off with 'Frankie & Albert', for example, in an arrangement that owed everything to the version Mississippi John Hurt had first recorded for Okeh Records in 1928. The story told in the song had been unfolding for *centuries* – though the specific killing has been located in St Louis in 1899 – and it was probably unfolding somewhere, in one doleful form or another, even while Dylan was recording his album.

For him, it was as much a matter of human continuity as of human history. His 'Blackjack Davey' is the descendant of a ballad that was being sung in the Scottish Borders before Robert Burns began to scribble. Dylan's 'Hard Times' – Stephen Foster's 'Hard Times Come Again No More', to be exact – is sepia-tinted antebellum America, but its sentiments in the face of brutal poverty are as contemporary as any. 'Arthur McBride' has its origins in Ireland, probably at around the time of the Napoleonic wars, yet is still a better protest against militarism's deceits than most. Even 'Froggie Went a-Courtin'', a song that should have been destroyed by banal performances long ago, has its roots in sixteenth-century Scotland and has endured despite everything the ages have contrived. Dylan probably wouldn't use a phrase like 'eternal verities' to describe his work on the album, but those are at the heart of *Good As I Been to You*.

The artist was also asserting that all tradition, no matter how ancient its roots, exists in the present, informs the present and shapes the present. In fact, folk music could serve as a metaphor for the perpetuation of all of humankind's vices and virtues. The mechanism of folk 'transmission', of 'folkways', the handing down of songs to be reshaped by each successive generation, could as easily be applied to the truths contained within the songs as to any 'folk process'. There is more to it, equally, than a William Faulkner line that has become a truism in American discourse. In a novel cross-bred with a play, he wrote: 'The past is never dead. It's not even past.'[20] Dylan's album says that the entity called folk music, a kind of collective unconscious, somehow knows this and has always known it. Folk exists, despite everything, because of that knowledge.

Dylan would go back to the well within ten months. *World Gone Wrong* would draw deep, once again, on the songs that had called him to the fountainhead of American music from the moment he first heard Lead Belly in 1959 and exclaimed to a friend, 'This is the thing, this is the thing!'[21] Perhaps because it leaned more on the country blues and on songs necessarily less ancient than before, *World Gone Wrong* would seem more immediately accessible than its predecessor, both murkier and wittier, more obviously like the Bob Dylan with whom album-buyers – those who remained loyal, at any rate – were familiar. Yet the second set would do less well than the first, perhaps because the novelty of hearing the artist with just his guitar and harmonica had worn off, perhaps because too many reviewers found too much to say about 'production'. Neither collection would sell in significant quantities. In sales terms, these brave and unflinching albums would languish with *Down in the Groove*.

Dylan placated a lot of critics, however, chiefly by giving them a lot of high-flown things to say – as above – about folk tradition and such. On *World Gone Wrong* he offered up a Blind Willie McTell song, 'Broke Down Engine', as though to make an explicit connection with his own 'Blind Willie McTell', newly liberated with *The Bootleg Series: Volumes 1–3*. The artist's decision to make these albums of 'traditional' material would cause a good deal of semi-scholarly comment. Any number of issues, some of them fascinating, would be raised for those with a discursive turn of mind. That was the real risk in the exercise: Dylan would yet again be discussed for what he seemed to signify, rather than listened to for what the songs said. No one ever managed to say quite enough about his version of 'Delia', another turn-of-the-century tale of death and loss in which the past haunts the present. Its refrain – 'All the friends I ever had are gone' – is like a living and continuing memory, one of those links with universal meaning that can't be severed.

Conventionally, *Good As I Been to You* and *World Gone Wrong* are taken to mark Dylan's reawakening from an artistic coma. Convention has the right idea, but it overlooks the fact that the best part of four long years would pass before any of the lessons learned from the making of a pair of albums were applied. Those much-admired *World Gone Wrong* notes, those defiant boasts of 'revival, getting a new lease on life', of not seeking 'immortality thru public acclaim', of going against 'cultural policy', of 'learning to go forward by turning back the clock', made nothing happen. Instead, close to four years would be filled with a *Greatest Hits Volume 3* that would contain only one modest hit, with an *MTV Unplugged* that would fail to assert itself as the live album it should have been, and with still another *Best of*. The Dylan who found his roots in his garage studio would not begin to flourish, not for a very long time, thanks only to *Good As I Been to You* and *World Gone Wrong*.

They did not inspire him to write. Musically, perhaps personally, they enforced a conservative view of art and existence. In that sense, at least, Dylan did not decide 'to go forward'. Henceforth, as though to confuse semanticists, everything that mattered to him would lie in the past. Even when he found a way to write again, all of Dylan's reality would be historical reality. In one sense, he would surrender to a truth that had been obvious since the end of the '60s. As much as anyone, as much as Blind Willie McTell or a Border ballad, 'Bob Dylan', too, was becoming a part of tradition.

The artist might have owned the copyright, but in reality 'Blowin' in the Wind' and 'The Times They Are a-Changin'' were already in the public domain. The fact marked an end, finally, to the promise of modernity, perhaps even of Modernism, as the '60s had understood that promise. The idea, albeit the fictive idea, that pop music must always be new was finished. Instead, with *Good As I Been to You* and *World Gone Wrong*, Dylan played his part in formulating the ground rules for what was becoming known as Americana, nostalgia's niche market. He could and did scorn the term, but the implications would be hard to ignore. Embrace ancestral 'roots' and, one way or another, you neglect progeny. While belief in the possibility of progressive politics was withering in America amid Clinton's sunny opportunism, music was turning its back on the future. Pop's key word had once been 'tomorrow', but that was yesterday. In recording *Good As I Been to You* and *World Gone Wrong*, Dylan was leading the way, but this time he was leading the retreat towards the reliable past.

He had not solved the old Greenwich Village conundrum, the one posed by all the old and implacable guardians of purity. Tradition was essential; tradition was life; but dogged traditionalism could crush the life from art. One way or another, in any case, none of it made a practical difference to Dylan's own career in 1992 and 1993. Whatever else has been said about his reimmersion in the wellsprings of his music, the fact remains that close to four years would pass before he managed to record a single new song in his own name.

Something else had been made obvious by *Good As I Been to You* and *World Gone Wrong*. It had already been noticeable in some of the cold, rumbling echoes of *Oh Mercy*. His voice was going, if it had not already gone. The range and fluidity of that once-extraordinary instrument was reduced drastically on *Good As I Been to You* and on its successor album. By 1993, Caruso's ghost had nothing more to fear when it came to hitting notes or holding them. The endless touring, the ritual nightly fight to perform his kinds of song, had done truly fearful damage to Dylan's most distinctive instrument. Sometimes the noises coming from his throat resembled the echoes of a scouring storm in a dry canyon, sometimes the sound of ice cracking, sometimes of weary, rusted girders parting. Sometimes, against the odds, it all still worked wonderfully well; sometimes nothing worked. He tried to pick songs and arrangements of songs that did not exceed his diminishing capacities, but tour by tour he was losing ground. Smoking and hard liquor had done him no good, of course, but the effects of so many shows were proving to be brutal. There would be speculation in due course about emphysema and any other substance-related, attenuating condition you could name. To some ears the vocal changes were so sudden there had to be a complicated explanation, whether exotic or sinister. The likeliest truth remains that an untrained singer with an uncompromising style had failed to take elementary precautions and pushed his equipment beyond its limits. As the years passed, guesses would neither matter nor help. Dylan's voice had always been part of his art. From the beginning, one part of the fundamental meaning of any Bob Dylan song had been in its delivery. By the early 1990s, some of that art was already forfeit.

Just before *Good As I Been to You* appeared, Columbia came up with another obituary. The 30th Anniversary Celebration, staged on 16 October 1992 at Madison Square Garden in New York, was a little casual as to dates – the first album had appeared in March 1962 – but lavish in its use of celebrity names. Some parts of a long evening were a lot of fun. Lou Reed's knowing performance of 'Foot of Pride', that song dropped from *Infidels*, compensated for several of the witless acts of fealty committed on the Garden's stage. It was oddly cheering, meanwhile, to see the Clancy Brothers and Tommy Makem return with 'When the Ship Comes In'. George Harrison's choice of 'Absolutely Sweet Marie' at least showed some imagination. For all that, this was a record-company 'tribute' with top-dollar ticket prices and a pay-per-view TV audience. It served only to invite a question: was Dylan so far gone as to require obsequious last rites? He had the wit, while performing only a brief, three-song set, to look wholly uninterested in the entire affair.

*

His own concerts continued, show after show, year after year. There are useful databases listing every last one. Collate the lists with each season's bootleg efforts and you can access a record of the deterioration in Dylan's once-exquisite voice, if that's your taste. There are good things recorded amid the debris, but there is a lot of debris. There is also a clear sense that by 1993 and 1994 Dylan was simply going through the motions once again. The shock and awe provided by Interstate 88 were long gone.

Surveying all of this you can also note, with a certain wonderment, that by the autumn of 1993 the artist could be found touring with Santana, a band so dull they seemed to make an entire art form out of the many possibilities of tedium. In reality, Dylan needed that tasteful entertainment-industry noise because he could no longer hope to draw big crowds on his own behalf. He would repeat the trick as the decade wore on, touring South America with the Rolling Stones, or offering counter-culture vaudeville to the heartland with Joni Mitchell and Van Morrison. Most tellingly, Dylan would end the decade trailing around arenas with Paul Simon, an artist towards whom he had long exhibited a certain ambivalence, let's say.

This spectacle would take place, it should be remembered, even after the artist had won back the cold, tiny hearts of the reviewing fraternity with a lauded album of his very own songs. Whatever the financial imperatives – could any still remain, could he *still* need the money? – touring would become an end-without-end in itself. While indecent quantities of semi-creative writing would be expended on the meaning and significance of the never-ceasing concert phenomenon, the damage to Dylan's vocal folds would be profound.

In November 1993, he took what might have been his last chance to record a late-period concert album that could have stood the test of time. The idea, it seems, was for a TV special that would capture Dylan in the kind of 'intimate' setting he said he liked best. To that end, he booked an upmarket, velvet-draped, 'retro' Manhattan venue called The Supper Club, hired a TV crew and digital recording gear – all of this was coming from his own pocket – rehearsed hard and played four shows over two nights. It was, no doubt, his last remaining alternative to an album of original songs, given that *Good As I Been to You* and *World Gone Wrong* had not exactly raced up the lower slopes of the charts, but bootlegs say the artist was vindicated. Some of his performances at The Supper Club were far better than anything he had managed on stage in 1993; some were the best things he had done since his voice began to disappear.

The fact that only bootlegs of the full shows can be had – the newer, 'soundboard' versions are excellent – tells the rest of the story. In January 1994, having seen the last of a large amount of his cash, Dylan scrapped the whole project. No explanation was given. A single track, a marvellous rendition of *Oh Mercy*'s 'Ring Them Bells', would appear, predictably, on 2008's *Tell Tale Signs*. But as with the Bromberg sessions in Chicago, another chance to put a respectable face on Dylan's career in the 1990s was let slip for reasons only he understood.

A year later, Dylan and his band were to be found participating in an MTV Unplugged exercise. The artist had wanted to perform a set consisting of only traditional songs, but the cable pop-loop channel, having no interest in anyone's cultural roots, insisted on 'hits'. Dylan obeyed and produced a fair enough set that sold surprisingly well, almost gracing the top 20 in America and touching number 10 in Britain. For all that, it was just another interlude in the perennial round of tours upon tours. By 1994, even diehards were finding those pretty dull. The younger crowd that Dylan had set out to convert with Interstate 88 were turning up, it seemed, out of simple curiosity. Hordes of them had been present in August for Woodstock '94, the self-conscious, not to say money-conscious, attempt to reproduce the famous 1969 festival in New York State that multitudes of their parents had embraced and Dylan – that year's Dylan – had despised. On this occasion, mercifully, young America witnessed the artist at something like his best, but such miracles were becoming rare. As a rule, the performances were no longer catastrophic. They were simply nothing out of the ordinary. Special pleading offered in elaborate justification for all the ceaseless tours had become implausible.

Dylan pressed on, as though convinced that stubborn determination would get him to where he wanted to be, wherever that was. At the end of 1993 he had been granted a new contract by Sony, the Japanese corporate behemoth by then in possession of the Columbia brand. This time Dylan had signed up for no fewer than ten albums. No one seems to have raised the delicate question. *Greatest Hits Volume 3* and *MTV Unplugged* were all very well – though the former would in fact do very badly – but how did the artist intend to fulfil the rest of the contract? There would be a glut of repackaged Dylan material on the market in the years ahead, but his willingness to make a blind bet on his vestigial writing skills counts as remarkable. Whether he truly needed the money, or simply wanted the money – there are two schools of cynical thought – he was living beyond his artistic means.

*

Some of those wedded to the idea of the never-ending tour – or N.E.T., as initiates persist in calling the phenomenon – do a fine line in theoretical constructs. Some elect to believe that the concerts have more to do with Dylan's art than any piece of plastic, that his songs are not held in a single moment, or locked into any one recorded version. (The word 'version' is itself often called in evidence.) Some further contend, in a properly post-postmodern way, that what an artist might intend by a song or a performance is neither here nor there.

This last argument becomes authentically comical when Dylan rejects the idea of a never-ending tour and derides even the phrase, as he has done many times. The statement (of fact, as far as he is concerned) is simply ignored. There is an N.E.T., whether he likes it or not. Reality as Dylan understands it is a minor detail within the great art event. What he says he is doing on stage is but one part, not an especially important part, of the never-ending deconstruction. In that exercise, as the reliable joke goes, the only thing we know for sure about Bob Dylan is that his name isn't Bob Dylan.

He has no voting privileges, even if we agree on who 'he' might think he is. The audience will have their own ideas, based on their own experiences, of what is taking place and what it might mean (especially if they have trouble making out the words). The insight can be refined to serve the claim that Bob Dylan, in numerous manifestations, is merely a 'text' to be interpreted through an understanding of what might be going on during performances. Both meaning and identity, say the fruits of one low-hanging branch of critical theory, are neither fixed – given the subject, this is handy indeed – nor stable phenomena. Jacques Derrida, the loquacious French 'post-structuralist' philosopher, has a lot to answer for, in short (but you can take him at his theoretical word that any written remark of his is not to be trusted).[22]

No matter. This version of chatter became fashionable among those who wrote about Dylan, by no coincidence, at a time when he was doing a lot of touring and no writing worth the name. He and his never-ending performance schedule suited interlocking postmodernist theories only too well. Biographical approaches, the treatment of songs as literary objects, the artist's intent: these could be rejected or denied 'authority'. If 'Bob Dylan' had no fixed identity and persisted in 'reinterpreting' his songs out of all recognition, what remained but performed art, forever mutable, forever in flux? As Michael Gray wrote, perhaps a little wearily, a quaint notion of 'anti-text', as it might be called, 'has become the main cliché of Dylanology in the 1980s and 1990s. . . Dylan's constant "reinterpretation" of his work in performance is insisted upon as showing – and actually as itself *arguing* – that there is no finished text of any individual song.'[23]

Gray's fatigue, if such it was, is understandable. As a matter of mere biographical fact, Dylan doesn't 'reinterpret' his songs *constantly*. Often enough, you wish he would, but he denies doing any such thing and he's right. He has sometimes revised his lyrics, as poets do, and more often tried to freshen up his musical arrangements, as musicians will. He has expressed dissatisfaction with his albums and on occasion has described his recorded songs as 'blueprints'.[24] His attempts to improve on the originals are therefore unsurprising. In any case, he was never one to attempt to reproduce a recording. That's traditional, and no big deal.

To state the obvious, you cannot 'reinterpret' anything unless there is a text prepared for reinterpretation. In Dylan's case, that will be found on an album somewhere. It is original, fixed (remixing aside) and enduring. The same argument applies to the rejection of biographical approaches and to the claim, useful to certain kinds of critic, that authorship is mostly incidental to art. The problems of biography are familiar and ancient. Facts are slippery, people lie, impressions conflict, memories fade, witnesses are unreliable, most interpretations differ, editorial choices are made: and so what? To leap from these self-evident truths to the claim that any description of a life is irrelevant to a piece of art neglects the obvious: *someone* did the work, at a certain place, under certain circumstances, for certain reasons. Life, as a song would soon enough mention, is hard.

The attempt to relegate reality to footnotes can have some amusing consequences. So it is that in a truly illuminating book, Lee Marshall's *Bob Dylan: The Never Ending Star* (2007), you can find a consideration of the biographical approach and why it has been rejected by certain writers, followed by this statement: 'Dylan himself has criticised those who offer biographical readings of his songs.'[25] Who has done this criticising? What do we know about this critic and why should it matter? You could repeat the questions when the issue of the author and his irrelevant intentions is raised. You could return to the table and lay down a couple of chips when the claim is made that meaning and identity are never 'stable'. Dylan's identities – not roles, not masks, not aliases – have come and gone throughout his life. So much is true and such has been his abiding problem. That has nothing to do with meaning. Meaning remains available.

The belief that concerts without end offer the only authentic insights into Dylan's art has also led to assaults on anyone who spends time treating the songs as literary works. Granted, the lit-crit approach has its problems. It gets bogged down, inevitably, in spurious debates over whether a songwriter who sings his works and messes around with text and delivery can be a poet. (The better question is to ask what poetry is made of and where the argument lies.) But the rebuttal remains: in the beginning, there was a piece of work, written down, revised and rewritten before it was performed. *Someone* made *that*. Once the song was recorded it became a text, with an author who was not 'privileged' but still, you can be sure, picking up an author's royalties. Even the endless arguments over 'folk process' do not alter the truth that a person who calls himself Bob Dylan makes Bob Dylan songs before any of the art-in-performance can even begin.

Sometimes the performances have been vile: there's that small detail. If the artist on occasion disdains to play in the same key as his musicians, critical theory might be superfluous. Naturally, tour devotees have their answers ready. Marshall writes, disarmingly, that 'Fans of the N.E.T. do not attend multiple shows because the performances are consistently magnificent'. Instead, these tours 'create an environment in which special moments can occur'.[26] Those 'outside of the N.E.T. cocoon' – a revealing word – might not grasp the logic of this, but once you escape 'the tyranny of recording' things become easier. So the recorded songs that drew people to Dylan in the first place become secondary to the communal experience of those inside the cocoon. On a good night.

A bystander might wonder how Dylan gets away with this. A truly thoughtful bystander might then wonder why it is that Dylan, alone among performers, gets away with selling tickets, decade after decade, to a coterie that does not expect him necessarily to be any good. The sheer weight of intellectual effort to understand his work and career has something to do with it, no doubt. The apparent artistic worth of songs whose authorship is, apparently, scarcely important might be another factor. But as Michael Gray has also observed, 'never-ending-text theory' can be damned convenient for a writer who is blocked solid.[27]

Such was Dylan's chronic condition for most of the 1990s. What's fascinating, as a banal biographical detail, is that he persisted with his never-ending tours even as his literary gifts returned, as time and age encroached, as his shredded voice made a nightly mockery of his poetry – an irony rendered as performance art, then – and as his relationship with history, his own history and the history of his country, was altered.

In 1995, Dylan put on 116 shows in Europe and America. In 1996, he roused himself for just 84 concerts. One of those, for which the press received no invites, was staged in an improvised 'nightclub' created within the Biltmore Hotel in Phoenix, Arizona, at the beginning of February '96. The writer who thought up a famous line about money preferring expletives to straight talk performed at the Biltmore, in a voice without complaint, before 250 of the guests of Nomura Securities International Inc., the American arm of a transnational high in the empyrean of international finance. Clearly, an author's intentions had no bearing on any art created that night. For those who trade in financial instruments, it was a $300,000 expense. He opened with 'Jokerman'.

*

Far from the realms of redundant theory, Dylan was making crateloads of money. Howard Sounes arrives at the slightly improbable gross figure of $35 million as the artist's annual earnings from his tours in the mid-'90s, implying $350,000 nightly and every show a sell-out, but the point stands.[28] Even after the crew, the bodyguards, the dependants, the musicians, the functionaries, the management, the accountants, the promoters, the motels, the taxes, the office staff, the transport, the broken guitar strings and all of Mr Dylan's domestic utility bills had been accounted for, a lot remained. Much of that was earmarked, it seems, for a property portfolio that by mid-1998 would embrace 17 'substantial' pieces of real estate around the world.[29] The artist had begun to seem avid for what his brand could earn.

In October 1996, 'The Times They Are a-Changin" could be heard advertising a Canadian internet bank. In the years to come corporate offers – for the benefit of Apple Inc., for Victoria's Secret lingerie, for the Cadillac Escalade 'luxury sport utility vehicle' – would not be resisted. 'The Times' had already been sold off once, early in 1994, to the tax-efficient accountants at Coopers & Lybrand for the purposes of company self-congratulation before Bank of Montreal was given its bite of the ethical cherry. Perhaps this was Dylan's idea of subversive social comment. Perhaps he was confirming the death of the author, as demanded by semiotic theory. Or perhaps he just wanted the money. What can be said for certain is that he more closely resembled the CEO of a multimedia enterprise than the person who in 1985 had told Cameron Crowe that rock music had become 'a highly visible enterprise, big establishment thing'.

> You know things go better with Coke because Aretha Franklin told you so and Maxwell House Coffee must be OK because Ray Charles is singing about it. Everybody's singing about ketchup or headache medicine or something. In the beginning it wasn't anything like that, had nothing to do with pantyhose and perfume and barbecue sauce . . .[30]

Later in the interview, Dylan had told the journalist: 'I'm not selling breakfast cereal, or razor blades or whatever.' In 2009, nevertheless, he would sell a brutally mashed-up version of his heartfelt song 'Forever Young' not to Coke but to Pepsi – slogan: 'Every generation refreshes the world' – for a Superbowl half-time advertising spot. Things go better, it transpires, with Bob.

The biographical approach, lacking rigour, allows for ideas such as presentiment. On 19 November 1995, at the Shrine Auditorium in Los Angeles, Dylan could be found singing 'Restless Farewell', a song he had not performed in public since 1964. The number was a request. The person doing the requesting, so it is said, was Frank Sinatra himself on the occasion of a 'star-studded' 80th birthday event in the great singer's honour. His knowledge of Dylan's back catalogue had not been noted previously.

The artist, on the other hand, had always admired Sinatra, Bing Crosby, the late Presley and the rest of the old-style crooners and balladeers who could always hit all the notes. At the Shrine, Dylan sang sincerely and well. He finished up with an infinitely modest and infinitely deferential 'Happy birthday, Mr Frank!'

So one possible future was glimpsed, perhaps, by the artist who had once written 'Like a Rolling Stone'. The way things were going, he too was destined to wind up inside the museum, a national treasure, while his posterity went on trial. Dylan was at risk of becoming the author of his own obituary as, unstoppably, the years slipped away.

CHAPTER ELEVEN

Things Have Changed

ACUTE PULMONARY HISTOPLASMOSIS IS ABOUT AS MUCH FUN AS IT sounds. Europeans don't often run the risk of acquiring the ailment, but in parts of America, especially around the Ohio and Mississippi rivers, the fungal histoplasmosis infection is common enough, generally because of bird or bat droppings in the soil and the microscopic spores the crap generates. Inhale the spores and you might get sick. If you are unlucky, you might get very sick. Dylan was unlucky.

After he was hospitalised on 25 May 1997, the severity of his illness was explained by a delay in the diagnosis. That's entirely possible. He had complained of chest pains and inadvertently set running the tale that a heart attack had occurred. Instead, struggling for breath, he was enduring pericarditis, a painful swelling of the fibrous sac around the organ. Since a formal diagnosis of histoplasmosis can often take weeks, during which the fungus is cultured in the lab, the delay wasn't necessarily surprising. If properly treated with antibiotics, the infection is rarely fatal, but what soon became known as Dylan's 'brush with death' was unusually nasty.[1] Histoplasmosis 'ranges from the totally asymptomatic or a mild flu-like illness through acute and chronic pulmonary forms' to (it says here) 'a severe disseminated involvement primarily of the reticuloendothelial system [by which foreign particles are otherwise cleared from the blood] which may spread to the heart, central nervous system, gastrointestinal tract, and other organs'.[2]

In plain language, while most people have no symptoms, or very mild symptoms, Dylan was at the upper end of the unpleasantness scale. Pericarditis in such cases tends to afflict the very young, the elderly, or those who have a compromised immune system. The artist had just turned 56 when he was hospitalised in Los Angeles. He was no kid, but hardly ancient. He was released after just a week, though concerts scheduled for Britain, Ireland and Switzerland in June were cancelled. Yet even by August, when he had returned to touring in the United States, the Dylan who spoke to Edna Gundersen of *USA Today* was not exactly back to his old self.

I'm doing as good as I can under the circumstances. I'm still taking medication three times a day. Sometimes it makes me a little light-headed and dizzy. And I need to sleep a lot. I did get the doctor's OK to do this tour. I guess I'll make it through . . . I don't have the energy I usually have, so I have to save it all to perform. Outside of that, I'm doing as well as I can.[3]

Dylan also admitted that he had been off his feet for six weeks, barely able even to walk. 'When I got out of the hospital, I could hardly walk around my yard,' he told Gundersen. 'I had to stay in bed and sleep all the time. I guess it's a slow process of recuperation.' Clearly, it had been no minor affliction. At another moment in the interview, Dylan told the journalist that the sheer pain of pericarditis 'stopped me in my tracks and fried my mind. I was so sick my mind just blanked out.' Given such consequences, you wouldn't wish a delayed diagnosis on anyone. Nevertheless, it is impossible not to wonder about the shape Dylan's immune system was in before he fell sick. Constrictive pericarditis, it seems, is usually a complication of viral infections, less frequently of influenza, rheumatic fever, HIV or tuberculosis. Even for the experts, reasons can be hard to name. Dylan's brief statement on leaving hospital had made a lot of people smile, but caused a few to wonder. 'I'm just glad to be feeling better,' he had said. 'I really thought I'd be seeing Elvis soon.'

*

Presley's sequinned shade might have been amused to hear that Dylan had contemplated the final curtain after recording his first album of new songs in seven years. Had he taken his last bow, the crepuscular mood of *Time Out of Mind* would alone have been enough to keep believers in presentiment and grim fate talking long after the event. Since his histoplasmosis had intervened between the recording and release of the longest piece of work he had produced since *Blonde on Blonde* – the vinyl version would be a double album – these songs 'about death' gave a lot of people the wrong idea.

Some reviewers were certain Dylan had received his intimations of mortality, looked up the number for the King's celestial direct line, and recorded *Time Out of Mind* as an acknowledgement of how fragile life can be. Who writes songs with titles such as 'Tryin' to Get to Heaven', 'Not Dark Yet' and 'Cold Irons Bound' if he hasn't had his interview with the Reaper? Where histoplasmosis was concerned, those who jumped to conclusions landed badly. The coincidence of illness and songs of melancholic fatalism was arresting, but coincidence it remained. Still, the album that inaugurated the most thrilling of all Dylan's recurring comebacks was not a work designed to spread sunshine and happy thoughts. The author himself would call *Time Out of Mind* 'spooky'. It was as good a one-word description as any. Dylan used the word, he would say, 'because I feel spooky. I don't feel in tune with anything.'[4]

If thoughts of death had inspired the album, however, they might have had less to do with the artist's inevitable fate than with the passing of Jerry Garcia on 9 August 1995. The guitarist had barely turned 53 when years of drug abuse and obesity shut down his worn body and distressed mind while he was residing, appropriately or not, in a rehab clinic. Dylan, ever attuned to the larger meaning of loss, had been badly shaken. In a press statement he had said that Garcia 'wasn't only a musician and friend, he was more like a big brother who taught and showed me more than he will ever know'. In point of fact, the guitarist had been the younger man by better than a year.

Garcia's Grateful Dead, it is worth observing, had been famous, or infamous, for their own 'endless tour', that gesture against changing times, fashion, common sense and a cynical age. They had defied every problem, personal and professional, just to keep on keeping on. The band toured because the band toured, year after year. Much good it had done Garcia. Music had not been his salvation. Despite Dylan's eulogy, 30 years on the road had taken the guitarist nowhere in particular save on a version of life's fated journey. That must have been a thought for the artist to ponder. In an album full of songs of aimless movement, of endless walking, of travel without purpose or end, of images of sickness, love and death, *Time Out of Mind* would place a higher final value on stoicism than on any other human virtue. It would be droll in places, but only, it seemed, because humanity's vanity in the face of futility was comical. Dylan's writing began again, at a best guess, just a few weeks or months after Garcia's death.

THINGS HAVE CHANGED

I was born here and I'll die here
Against my will
I know it look's like I'm moving,
But I'm standing still
Every nerve in my body
Is so vacant and numb
I can't even remember what it was
I came here to get away from

Interviewing the artist for a *Newsweek* cover story after the album's release, the second, third and fourth things David Gates saw fit to notice were 'the white hairs among the curls, the two days' worth of stubble and the 30 years' worth of lines'.[5] The first thing mentioned was a face still capable of spooling through the cycles of inscrutability. The message of the piece was that, despite 'a near-fatal illness and a near-terminal career slump', the artist – whose attitude towards 'the media' had been poisoned by a 'hatchet job' interview with the selfsame magazine in 1963 – was still a figure of cultural importance. It was as though by 1997 a collective decision had been taken that it was necessary for Dylan to matter again. Another comeback was required after all the derision and near-contempt. *Time Out of Mind* was being greeted with sheer, exultant relief even before Gates sat down with his questions ready in a fine hotel by the Los Angeles shore. Several critics had been extravagant in their praise for the album.

Early in the interview, Dylan made a remark that would attract a lot of attention from those still trying to work out where he stood on issues of faith and belief. He would return to the theme several times in other encounters with journalists. Speaking to Gates, it sounded as though he was attempting to explain the album – and therefore to explain himself – by calling a halt to questions about God. Instead, inadvertently or not, Dylan simply confused matters.

Here's the thing with me and the religious thing. This is the flat-out truth: I find the religiosity and philosophy in the music. I don't find it anywhere else. Songs like 'Let Me Rest On a Peaceful Mountain' or 'I Saw the Light' – that's my religion. I don't adhere to rabbis, preachers, evangelists, all of that. I've learned more from the songs than I've learned from any of this kind of entity. The songs are my lexicon. I believe the songs.

It seemed to explain everything and yet it explained nothing at all. Dylan was not prepared to give allegiance to a particular creed, but that was hardly news. In fact, any half-attentive listener to *Time Out of Mind* would be left wondering about the lazy claim, persistent still in 1997, that he had long before returned to 'secular' music. He might have sounded world-weary; he might have seemed obsessed with mortality and the passing of time; but his album was another deeply religious piece of work. 'Tryin' to Get to Heaven' was unambiguous, but there were plain declarations of faith scattered everywhere throughout the recordings, obvious enough even for those who cared nothing for the 'biographical approach'. Thus: 'I know God is my shield and He won't lead me astray' ('Til I Fell in Love With You'). Thus: 'I know the mercy of God must be near' ('Standing in the Doorway'). Thus: 'It's mighty funny, the end of time has just begun' ('Can't Wait').

As with Dylan's born-again albums, there was nothing about any of this that sounded remotely like joy. Equally, there was nothing that didn't sit easily with messianic Judaism. The only way to argue otherwise is by dismissing any possibility that the songs contain autobiographical content while simultaneously ignoring the artist's previous declarations on God and related topics. *Time Out of Mind* might have marked the start of one last, startling resurgence in Dylan's creativity, but religious faith endured. His 'late period' work, as remarkable as anything he had achieved, would be at least as devout as the charmless proselytising songs of 1979–81. *Time Out of Mind* was filled, as the writer would tell the *New York Times*, 'with the dread realities of life'.[6] He would employ the adjective with care. Dread can mean fear, in the usual usage, but it also has an older sense, meaning awe. For a man in a certain frame of mind, it could mean two things at once.

*

Dylan had begun to write again, so it appears, while snowed up at his Minnesota farm during the winter of 1995–6. What isn't clear is what spurred him to begin to write then and there, or caused him to write in a new way. In his own mind, as he would tell the story, he had given up on the art. The need had disappeared. No song demanded to be written, no creative urge was so overwhelming it could not be denied. The death of Jerry Garcia and his own darkening mood, one that caused Dylan to seem to shun most of the normal forms of human contact, are therefore only partial, proximate explanations for the *Time Out of Mind* songs. There had been plenty of other trials in his personal life that might have caused him to pick up pencil, his second divorce and some very public drunken misery above all, but nothing had forced new work. Suddenly the songwriting began again, just like that, despite all the long, arid years. Perhaps, for these things happen, Dylan enjoyed a kind of spontaneous remission in which his gift was restored miraculously to health. Perhaps the belief that he was running out of time provided inspiration. It might also be that sheer necessity forced him back to work.

He could tell Edna Gundersen that it 'mortifies me to even think that I am a celebrity', that losing anonymity 'short-circuits your creative powers'. True enough, no doubt, but these were problems that went with the territory of stardom, a landscape he understood as well as anyone.[7] The parallel fact was that unless he chose to retire entirely, unless he decided to give up performing along with writing, Dylan had a choice. Either he could come up with something new, or he could become the fading star of a touring nostalgia show, 'reinterpretations' and all. One way or another, he was running out of road.

Dylan had done his two albums of old folk and blues songs. He had failed, for whatever reason, to extract anything he wanted to use from fine performances at The Supper Club. The greatest-hits packages could arrive at intervals (and with increasing frequency) in the hope that the eyes and ears of still another generation might be caught, but that was a game of diminishing returns. Unless he could record a new album, 'Bob Dylan' would become a performer represented only by the marvels of the Bootleg Series, those tell-tale signs of an encroaching history, and by concerts dependent on the old songs, each performance appropriated the instant it happened by real bootleggers. The shows meanwhile varied horribly in quality and they catered, too often, to a self-selecting niche audience.

One myth of the unending tour rests on Dylan's declared intention to find himself new customers who did not wish simply to gawk at the legend and demand the old hits as they thought they remembered them. In the 1990s, his concert crowd were often younger, it's true, than the fans attracted by most of his peers. For better or worse, he also managed to inherit a choice collection of Deadheads after Jerry Garcia's passing. Nevertheless, a great many among the college-age generation were still turning out at Bob Dylan shows just to see what all the fuss had *once* been about. Without new songs it was not, as marketing folk say, a sustainable strategy. That left only the problem of actually writing and recording those new works. It was one thing to decide what had to be done, quite another to carry it off.

By Dylan's own account – one account, at any rate – none of the above bears any resemblance to the truth. In 2006, he would tell the novelist Jonathan Lethem blithely that *Time Out of Mind* had come about almost against his will. Someone had pointed a loaded cheque book at him. The album wasn't personal, just business. And seven wasted years of his artistic life had been his choice. Dylan would say:

> They gave me another contract, which I didn't really want. I didn't want to record anymore, I didn't see any point to it. But, lo and behold, they made me an offer and it was hard to refuse. I'd worked with Lanois before, and I thought he might be able to bring that magic to this record. I thought, 'Well, I'll give it a try.'[8]

In another version of events, he showed some songs to Daniel Lanois in June 1996. 'I had the songs for a while,' Dylan would say, 'and I was reluctant to record them, because I didn't want to come out with a contemporary-sounding record.'[9] Contrary to the suggestion that he had written the album while on the farm, in this interview the artist would claim that the *Time Out of Mind* works had been assembled on the road, enabling him to run through material with the band and 'hear it right'. In all probability, lyrics were drafted in Minnesota and refined in rehearsals and at soundchecks. There had also been at least one informal recording session before Lanois was called in. Thereafter a lot of serious rewriting would take place while the album was being made at the Criteria studios in Miami, Florida, in January 1997.

Talking to the *Irish Times* in October, just after the album's release, the producer would remark, perhaps a little disingenuously, that Dylan had 'slowed down writing for a while, then came back at it with a vengeance'. Lanois would also remember that 'when we first got together he didn't play me any songs; he read me the songs. He read twelve lyrics back-to-back for an hour and it was like listening to someone reading a book. Then later, in the studio, he modified the lyrics.' Nevertheless, Dylan would tell *USA Today*: 'There was no pressure on me to write these songs. There was no one breathing down my neck to make this record.' The album had just 'happened when I had the time'.[10] So much for the contract offer that couldn't be refused, then.

In one way, the euphoric reviews and the Grammy awards it earned – Album of the Year, 'Best Contemporary Folk Album', 'Best Male Rock Vocal Performance' – did *Time Out of Mind* a disservice. They gave the appearance that an album containing greatness was itself, in the round, a great piece of work. Where Dylan was concerned, people were beginning to hear what they wanted to hear. Lustre was granted to some mediocre tracks simply because of the refulgent things around them on the album, because Dylan was 'back', because all was somehow right with the world. The acclaim was also a distraction. As it transpired, seven years of silence as a writer had taught the artist nothing useful about assembling a collection of diverse songs and resolving any contradictions, thematic or musical, that might exist between them. *Time Out of Mind* was not, by a dirt-road country mile, the album it should have been. By 1997, the statement had so many antecedents it was becoming either redundant, annoying, or the only insight worth possessing. In due course the set would be better understood than it was on first hearing, thanks partly to the bootleggers and thanks, belatedly, to Dylan's own Bootleg Series. That would not solve all the proliferating riddles. Perceptions of this artist were becoming peculiar, dislocated in time, dependent on who heard what and when they heard it. The Bob Dylan story had acquired a set of conflicting time schemes and a host of complicated themes.

*

Think back. There was the artist of public record who had first sung into John Hammond's microphone on a couple of cold November days in 1962 and gone on to create a catalogue of available works of which, in studio-made album form, *Time Out of Mind* was the 30th. There was the artist who had disrupted every media narrative with his unpredictability and his tendency to mock anyone who tried to understand what he was about. There was the artist whose work had been chopped and diced – seasoned, too – a thousand times over according to the tastes, intuitions and prejudices of those who 'interpreted' and understood his work in a myriad ways. There was the artist whose glorious past had been locked in synchronous step with his difficult present since the release of *Biograph* in 1985.

Then there was the semi-secret artist, the one who existed in parallel dimensions, supposedly, alongside the public works. Bootleg Dylan, off-the-record Dylan – for some, 'the real Dylan' – had been haunting art and artist ever since word of the basement tapes first got out in the summer of 1968. His own *Bootleg Series Volumes 1–3* had only added another couple of lengths of rope to the big, tangled Gordian ball. One mass of people heard a Dylan song every now and then and sometimes bought an album if he didn't sound too weird. Another tribe were plain Bob Dylan fans who bought most of the records most of the time. A third group, small but growing, were ever-present. These fans possessed, so they believed, a larger idea of what this artist had done thanks to all the recordings he had failed to complete or failed to release. Finally, welcome at every party, there were assiduous scholars representing the meta-universe of criticism in which significance always trumped a mere song. A few of these were folk whose fluid sense of reality had long since gone down the drain, such was their need to confuse private obsessions with Dylan's utterances. By 1997, in short, things had become messy.

Dylan had done more for bootleggers and the idea of bootlegging than any other performer. This had not been his choice, but a few faintly absurd beliefs about the prophetic voice of a generation had got out of hand long before the '60s were done. In essence, those beliefs had become specimens of the irrational urge for 'alternatives' that had turned Carlos Castañeda into a bestseller, seen gurus taken seriously, or caused millions to decide they were born again. Crudely put, the ramshackle argument went as follows. If Bob Dylan was a true poet, insightful and prophetic, privy to an understanding denied to all others, everything he said, did or put on tape was, by definition, a big deal. *Everything.*

The fact that the prophet denied this nonsense, or just made his professional, creative choices, right or wrong, was neither here nor there. 'Bob Dylan' did not belong to Bob Dylan. A.J. Weberman's somewhat sinister and mostly comical 'Dylan Liberation Front' had been founded at the start of the 1970s thanks entirely to this circle-jerk consensus. It was cult thinking, if thinking is the word, but it was not much worse than some of the never-ending tour chatter, or those postmodern critical fads that allow no houseroom to the idea of authorship. *Great White Wonder*, first of the bootlegs, had justified itself in the summer of 1969 with the implicit claim that 'Bob Dylan' was too important to be impeded by some mere breadhead superstar just because he wrote, recorded and imagined he owned the art. That he gained not a penny piece from his 'liberation' while counter-culture entrepreneurs did very nicely was a detail beneath consideration. That he was being denied any say in the fate of his work was barely considered. This art belonged to all. Theft was an act of love.

The number of Dylan bootlegs is impossible to estimate. Plenty were available before he began to tour relentlessly in 1988. Since then, judging by list upon endless list of titles, he has been honoured by illicit taping far more often than anyone else in the music business. That statement has been made often enough. Few pause to ask just why it should be true when there are plenty of rock stars vastly more popular than this artist. Yet if Dylan opens his mouth on a public stage, recordings will circulate within hours or days. Things will 'leak' from his offices; tapes will 'appear' whenever he enters a recording studio. In one madcap conspiracy theory the wily genius is complicit in all of this, giving his tacit permission to the bootleggers just to advance the sales of his own Bootleg Series and perpetuate all the legends he claims to despise. No one needs to enlarge bootlegging's excuses to that extent. The security measures imposed by his management would shame the CIA. Through it all the convenient idea persists that Dylan's art is not his own, that no creative choice over this track or that truly matters, that no album is ever complete just because he says so.

The fans who cannot resist bootlegs – let's call that a motes and beams discussion – not only deny Dylan ownership and earnings in his work, they deny him an artist's right to decide when a recording is complete, good enough or not good enough, a piece he will claim in Bob Dylan's name or reject. To be a writer in such a circumstance must be tricky. For a writer who cultivates mystique as a matter of personal psychological need, the tape thief hovering always at his shoulder must be an unabating royal pain. Yet what leaves every argument stalled is that bootleggers have been dead right from the start about one thing. You can't begin to see the scale of his achievement unless you know about the songs that were left off Dylan's 'official' albums. Such is the implicit justification, after all, for his own Bootleg Series.

Time Out of Mind was no different from albums that had gone before. Some of the people who had worked on the project were dismayed, to say the least, by the choices Dylan made. Most listeners, informed by bootlegs or the Bootleg Series, arrive at the same view. The chorus sounds: what was he thinking? What gets forgotten is the small truth that if Bob Dylan was like everyone in the chorus he would not be Bob Dylan. The frequently heard claim that he has 'borrowed' too often from the works of others faces a similar objection. Which song has he not improved in the process? So why then shouldn't he know better when it comes to his own albums than those who write big books and couldn't find the light switch in a recording studio? Still, scribblers and fans demur.

To complicate matters further (yet again), some of the bootleggers had acquired the sheen of professionalism and entrepreneurial gall by 1997. In certain offerings they were doing a better job of representing the artist and the art than his planet-crushing Japanese media contract-owners were managing. In 1995, conspicuously, the person-behind-the-people at an outfit calling itself Scorpio had answered Dylan's *Bootleg Series Volumes 1–3* with an impertinent thing entitled *The Genuine Bootleg Series*. Along with some taunting images of macaws on your discs, you got three CDs full of outtakes and live recordings that in some important respects made the Dylan-Columbia release seem a little grudging.

Much of the material had been bootlegged before, but this package was high-quality contraband for a general audience. There were some fascinating photographs and a wealth of documentary information. Each and every stage in Dylan's career was sampled, with the totality presented in an expensive-looking 'glossy full-color' box. So here was the other 'Blind Willie McTell', here was 'New Danville Girl' and a chance to hear the version of 'Hurricane' pulled from *Desire* by a record company's fretful lawyers. The quality of the sound was mostly impeccable: some serious work had been done. Then, in 1997, *Genuine Bootleg Series* volume two appeared. Remarkably, it was even better than its predecessor, embracing the likes of 'Lay Down Your Weary Tune' from Carnegie Hall in 1963, a lovely 'Wild Mountain Thyme' from the Isle of Wight Festival, and the always-preferable 'Born in Time' from the *Oh Mercy* sessions. This was no longer exotica and trivia for obsessed and obsessive collectors. An alternative version of Dylan's reality was arguing against him. His history was being written and rewritten while his back was turned.

*

It might sound odd, even mean-spirited, to say that *Time Out of Mind* was the best album he had made in years, yet nowhere near as good as many people wanted to believe. Nevertheless, that still feels like the truth of the matter. Songs such as 'Dirt Road Blues' and 'Million Miles' are routine, if that, and not much more than padding. 'Cold Irons Bound', as a matter of personal taste, is a tough song to like or respect, a piece of overproduced melodrama that seems utterly discrepant on this album. 'Make You Feel My Love' should have been shipped off instantly, gratis, to Billy Joel, Garth Brooks and the rest of the balladeers who would take the vapid thing to their sentimental hearts: the cover versions explain the problem. "Til I Fell in Love With You' and 'Can't Wait' might have amounted to something had they been handled differently, but in neither case was much achieved with them, either by Dylan or Lanois.

That leaves five tracks from an album of eleven songs. It also leaves two songs better than most of the rest that the artist declined to share with his public. Of the five, two or three can probably be called great, one can be called interesting, and one is best described as fascinating but, put kindly, a little problematic. In other words, there are what critics like to call difficulties with this album, despite the garlands and awards, despite its great songs, despite its importance in restoring Dylan's gifts and his claim to public attention. On its release, *Time Out of Mind* had the benefit of being compared with its immediate predecessors, some truly miserable specimens among them, not with those '60s and mid-'70s albums that were the artist's transformative contributions to the canon. The praise for *Time Out of Mind* amounted to a suspension of historical judgement. A few second thoughts would soon prove that the decade he refused to call his own still had prior claim on Dylan's artistic posterity. Five very fine songs, a couple of them better than fine, was a hell of a lot more than he had managed on a single album since *Blood on the Tracks* and *Desire*, of course. Anyone who found *Time Out of Mind* 'disappointing' on first hearing was employing a very strange yardstick. Nevertheless, the work done in 11 days in January 1997 remained a start, a very good start, not the last word in every argument over Dylan's rehabilitation.

The first issue is straightforward: how much better would *Time Out of Mind* have seemed had 'Mississippi' and 'Red River Shore' been included? Four songs were discarded from the fifteen recorded for the album, but these two mattered most. Anyone who has heard any of the several versions of the pair will struggle to understand what was going through Dylan's head. These are works of real literary cunning, both in their deployment of folk ancestry and in their use of narrative personae. On these songs, Dylan speaks in several voices: his own, that of his characters, that of everyman. The titles, by no accident, are plain invocations of an American past, one of the Mississippi Delta under the old apartheid when sometimes a black man's only crime was to be in the wrong place at the wrong time, the other of a West that might be a backdrop to the 1948 Howard Hawks film *Red River* (though the song and the movie have no clear relationship), or just a fable set anywhere along the enormous length of a Mississippi tributary, the Red River of the South (though there are plenty of other Red Rivers). Dylan's collagist methods have been well researched, from the old blues in the refrain of 'Mississippi' to the folk commonplaces that are rearranged and reilluminated, like old mnemonic epithets, all the way through 'Red River Shore'. A preoccupation with 'borrowings' is beside the point, however. Dylan is justifying the claim he began to make decades before: the folk tradition, in style and substance, contains universal truths.

Both songs can be read – as you are obliged to say of all the artist's best songs – in a multiplicity of ways. Most obviously these are tales of love lost, of the girl from the river's banks who can never be found again, of the woman who is told, 'I know you're sorry, I'm sorry too.' These are also, unmistakably, songs drenched in a sense of resignation, of choices exhausted. In 'Mississippi', Dylan sings of the inevitable acceptance of life's realities. He also manages to add what might be a sly reference to the cycles of his own career:

> Well, the emptiness is endless, cold as the clay
> You can always come back, but you can't come back all the way

'Red River Shore' contains much the same sort of thought:

> Well, we're living in the shadows of a fading past
> Trapped in the fires of time
> I've tried not to ever hurt anybody
> And to stay out of the life of crime

There is something more, however, that is held in common by this pair of great songs. It is fairly well disguised. It had become Dylan's habit not to sound this particular horn after he quit his gospel ways. Nevertheless, there are parts of 'Red River Shore' and of 'Mississippi' that only make sense if these two songs of men on life's journey are considered in terms of religion. Even given Dylan's taste for the poetic non sequitur, both songs contain verses that at first seem oddly out of place. The penultimate verse of 'Red River Shore' is plain enough in itself. But then you ask: what is *that* doing in this love song?

THINGS HAVE CHANGED

Now I heard of a guy who lived a long time ago
A man full of sorrow and strife
That if someone around him died and was dead
He knew how to bring 'em on back to life

'Mississippi' is less overt, but one of its verses sticks out, both in terms of its quality and its placing within what is, at its plainest, a song of love gone astray. We have already heard that 'the devil's in the alley / Mule's kickin' in the stall'. Then:

Well, my ship's been split to splinters
And it's sinking fast
I'm drownin' in the poison
Got no future, got no past

A metaphor, then. Even if a Mississippi riverboat founders, or if a ship is wrecked in the Gulf of Mexico, no one is left drowning in the kind of poison that eradicates an identity. Dylan is talking about the Ship of Faith and/or the old allegory of the Ship of Fools, another version of life's journey. That the writer probably means the former rather than the latter seems clear enough from the next couplet. 'Drownin' in the poison' or not, he sings:

But my heart is not weary,
It's light and it's free
I've got nothin' but affection
For all those who've sailed with me

For once, the cliché will do: most writers would have sold their nearest and dearest for these two songs. Either Dylan let his weariness get the better of him when he failed to realise the works to his satisfaction – it wouldn't have been the first time – or he failed to hear what everyone else can hear. One argument goes in his favour, for all that. Given all the versions since issued of these songs, it is perfectly clear that their inclusion in any form would have caused the whole album to sound entirely different, certainly less cohesive. The 'swampy', layered production that seemed to be the only bag of tricks Lanois had to offer would have made no sense for 'Red River Shore' and done little justice to 'Mississippi'. Had Dylan got the kind of sound design he thought he was getting – 'like an old record you put on a record player', as he told a French journalist in October – the two songs would have been perfect.[11] Instead, an album in which 'Red River Shore' sat anywhere near 'Cold Irons Bound' or 'Make You Feel My Love' would have sounded ridiculous. Yet if that was the case, why did an artist perfectly capable of getting his own way not put the songs before the producer's tastes?

One answer, perhaps, is that he had been deferring to others for too long. As soon as someone promised Dylan the latest thing in production any ancient-sounding songs became obstacles. This was paradoxical, given that the sound he wanted on *Time Out of Mind* was old and gramophone-like. Besides, it wasn't Lanois who insisted on dropping the better tracks and keeping the likes of 'Make You Feel My Love'. Not until Dylan despaired of the professionals and began to produce his own sessions would he begin to find a solution to these problems. The fact remains that substantial parts of a long album were flawed in their execution. Dylan realised as much, or came to the realisation in due course. In 2001, talking about *Time Out of Mind*, he would say:

> Repeatedly I'd find myself compromising on this to get to that. As a result, though it held together as a collection of songs, that album sounds to me a little off. There's a sense of some wheels going this way, some wheels going that, but 'Hey, we're just about getting there.'[12]

Sometimes he got there. 'Not Dark Yet' is unquestionably one of the great Dylan songs. Lanois served it well too, to be fair. Had this been played to despairing fans hearing *Knocked Out Loaded* or *Down in the Groove* for the first time, it would have been hard to distinguish relief from gratitude. Above all others, this *Time Out of Mind* song gave rise to the conviction that Dylan was meditating on age, mortality and regret. There is, if nothing else, that key statement: 'time is running away'. In this dark night of the soul, you conclude, the artist's faith is less sure than in other songs. Faith persists, but the singer is in a place where he can't 'even hear a murmur of a prayer'. Then, inevitably, you wonder: why? At the time of the album's release, even after the histoplasmosis scare had distracted the world's attention, the evidence of the lyrics seemed to say that Dylan had been in a bleak mood long before he was hospitalised. Because he had lost dear friends? Because he had been overtaken, not for the first time, by ennui? Neither possibility quite explains this song. Equally, there are odd things going on throughout *Time Out of Mind* that do not quite serve the age-and-mortality thesis.

There is a risk, in any case, in assuming that a song such as 'Not Dark Yet' is necessarily autobiographical. Dylan has contradicted himself often enough down the years when the subject of self-portraits has come up. Sometimes he has warned journalists against taking personal pronouns too seriously, reminding them of the nature of art and the liberty imagination needs and demands. At other moments he has said that the songs are 'always' about him. Then he has placed a thick layer of ambiguity over what he might mean by 'about'. In 2001, nevertheless, he would dismiss the idea that *Time Out of Mind*, undeniably sombre as it was, amounted to a glimpse of his innermost thoughts as he entered the last stretch of middle age.

> People say the record deals with mortality – my mortality, for some reason! [Laughs] Well, it doesn't deal with my mortality. It maybe just deals with mortality in general. It's one thing we all have in common, isn't it? But I didn't see any one critic say, 'It deals with my mortality' – you know, his own. As if he's immune in some kind of way . . .[13]

It's a fair point. Would 'Not Dark Yet' be any less of an achievement if it failed to fit a biographical narrative? Part of the profound appeal of the song is that it contends with the second fundamental fact of every existence. The theme is by definition universal. Bob Dylan will die one day? Who won't? One essential part of his gift as an artist, present from the very start, has been his understanding of the dangers of confessional writing. The crude appetite for the 'true story' diminishes art, artist and audience. This writer had spotted the risk of autobiographical banality many years before. All those 'interpretations' telling us that the majestic 'Mr. Tambourine Man' is 'about' Dylan dropping acid didn't just insult the intelligence of the writer, they insulted his song. That had been one reason for a habit of self-concealment.

Still, no writer is immune to circumstance. No artist is wholly, coldly impersonal, supremely dispassionate. The prevailing mood of *Time Out of Mind* is dark. It turns, too, on particular images. Its better songs – this song above all – tend to come at the close of day. These works have their own weather, thundery or wet, and their own cheerless landscape. Then there is the weird, wired, dislocated mood familiar to insomniacs, when sleep won't come or is resisted, and there's nothing to do but walk and think the thoughts that will allow no rest. In song after song on this album the voice is that of a man who is exhausted and ill. Always, inexorably, time is passing.

You can pick out these motifs, if that's the adequate word, easily enough. Thus 'Love Sick': night, walking, air full of thunder, 'the clouds are weeping', 'I hear the clock tick'. The sickness might be more than emotional: 'you destroyed me with a smile / While I was sleeping'.

Thus 'Standing in the Doorway': another night, still walking, time playing tricks, he's 'sick in the head' and worse, contemplating the final mortal moment at which 'the flesh falls off my face'. Thus 'Million Miles': 'voices in the night', he's 'drifting in and out of dreamless sleep' and risking psychic infection from 'every mind-polluting word'. Thus 'Tryin' to Get to Heaven': still another hot night, more thunder, more walking before the struggle to sleep in an effort to 'relive my dreams'.

Thus 'Can't Wait': 'it's way past midnight', 'the air burns', skies are grey, 'things disintegrate', his mind is a 'lonely graveyard' and he knows he won't be 'spared this fate'. Thus ''Til I Fell in Love With You': night again, 'my nerves are exploding and my body's tense', beyond healing save for a redemptive human touch, expecting rain, wondering if he'll still be 'among the living' when the next night comes, and showing symptoms that sound all too real:

Junk is piling up, taking up space
My eyes feel like they're falling off my face
Sweat falling down, I'm staring at the floor
I'm thinking about that girl who won't be back no more

The effect, inevitably, is cumulative, but it is also specific in its details. Weather, walking and sickness are either key metaphors or a poet's plain reports from the ravaged front lines of body and mind. Love and women have failed him, or betrayed him, at every step of the way and nothing else remains. 'Not Dark Yet' is at the heart of all of this. The song is retrospective: it happens after all struggles have ceased. The last darkness hasn't quite arrived, but the body is shutting down, every nerve 'vacant and numb'. For this speaker, the end is close. Dylan had every right to say that none of this had much to do, in truthful essence, with him. On the other hand, the average listener is entitled to wonder what it was that put the writer in this frame of mind.

The best of the rest of the songs, by personal choice, are 'Standing in the Doorway', 'Tryin' to Get to Heaven' and 'Love Sick'. They are variations, inevitably, on the theme. The first renders inner desolation as film noir, the tough guy vigilant in the doorway but weeping inside, with lines such as

> Don't know if I saw you, if I would kiss you or kill you
> It probably wouldn't matter to you anyhow

Or

> Maybe they'll get me and maybe they won't
> But not tonight and it won't be here

'Tryin' to Get to Heaven' reaches the same viewpoint – for almost all of these songs reach that viewpoint – but the style this time is Dylan's version of a spiritual. He takes the standard, even stereotypical idea of the sinner who must make his peace with God before it's too late, but he transforms it into another kind of statement. This protagonist has suffered the trials of Job. At the song's end he will be left to wonder 'if everything is as hollow as it seems'. In the Hebrew Bible Job asks the fundamental existential question 'Why do the righteous suffer?' only to discover that God isn't answerable to His creation. The song yields an equivalent truth: 'When you think that you lost everything / You find out you can always lose a little more.' Faith guarantees nothing in this world. Hence the unmissable – because Dylan doesn't mean you to miss it – adaptation of Woody Guthrie's adapted 'This Train Is Bound for Glory':

> Some trains don't pull no gamblers
> No midnight ramblers, like they did before

'Love Sick' comes across as Gothic R&B. Perhaps only Dylan would have chosen to open his first album of original music in seven years with the line 'I'm walking through streets that are dead', but why bother to pretend that 73 minutes of jolly noise lie ahead? Two things are then apparent. One seems trivial, but cannot be accidental. This, the opening to the latest comeback album, is entitled 'Love Sick', not 'Lovesick'. The condition alluded to is not the fey pining of romantic convention. This is love as a physical affliction, an enervating venereal assault that has left its victim sick to his soul, attracted and yet repulsed by his desires, first declaring 'I wish I'd never met you' before surrendering at the last: 'I'd give anything to be with you.' Few songs in the pop field with the word love in their titles sound anything like this.

The second striking aspect is a matter of writing style. It marks out the entire album as something new in Dylan's work. He had been struggling against his glorious youthful eloquence since 1967's *John Wesley Harding*. It seems he came to distrust his effortless ability to forge those chains of flashing images. In 'Love Sick', as with the rest of *Time Out of Mind*'s best songs, he is rigorous with his language. In places it is spare-to-skeletal. Equally, given several accounts of the rewriting Dylan did in the studio, even when it meant returning to a song that had already been recorded, we can assume that the album contains few casual remarks. Even the clichés are intentional. 'Love Sick' is written, with great precision, to echo the rhythms of a man walking the streets. Its minimal melody pulses as though to match his breathing. All the while the song's end rhymes and internal rhymes circle like the speaker's thoughts, caught in their obsessive loops. 'Love Sick' is one of Dylan's works that can cause you to forget what is being said while you wonder at the sheer craft that allows it to be said.

Then there is 'Highlands', conventionally 'the longest song Dylan ever recorded'. That's perfectly true, but what of it? The tendency to invest a piece with significance simply because the writer is demanding more of your time than usual is a strange quirk among Dylan's fans and critics. It's akin to saying that if an airport novel is as long as *War and Peace* it must be as important as *War and Peace*. 'Highlands' is not Dylan's sixteen-and-a-half-minute masterpiece. Ironically, in fact, its qualities have nothing to do with its vast length and everything to do with its smallest details. The problems arise, meanwhile, because Dylan attempts the difficult feat of welding two contrasting songs into one, or rather of interrupting one song with a comic (mostly comic) dialogue 'bridge'. A lot of people have found the result enchanting or intriguing. This writer is less enthusiastic. 'Highlands' is more often a piece to be admired rather than enjoyed.

The compensations, and they are numerous, are in those details. One, obvious enough, is to hear Dylan pay his respects to Robert Burns, one ballad-maker (and borrower) to another, by adapting 'My Heart's in the Highlands'. Here is the 'folk process' with a vengeance. Dylan's 'Highlands' lifts one of the most famous lines by the Scottish poet, despite the fact – surely not because of the fact? – that it was the one line in the famous song that Burns himself didn't write when he was rescuing the fragments of a culture almost destroyed by imperial England. As the Scot's note to the song had it: 'The first half stanza is old, the rest is mine.' In other words, the key line 'My heart's in the Highlands' came from an old thing called 'The Strong Walls of Derry' (itself in part derived from a song called 'Boys of Kilkenny'). So Dylan is borrowing a borrowed fragment from a poet who not only adapted older works but felt he had a patriotic duty to do so in order to preserve relics. If rescue often involved stripping multiple sources for spare parts and adding a Gaelic melody just because it seemed to fit, Burns didn't care. In fact, he would not even have understood the problem. He was a greater poet than any of the anonymous peasants from whom he borrowed. That statement might have made for a few arguments in Greenwich Village in the early 1960s. As to the grand question of folk 'authenticity', Burns was in no sense a Highlander. His song of 1790 begins:

My heart's in the Highlands, my heart is not here
My heart's in the Highlands a-chasing the deer,
A-chasing the wild deer and following the roe
My heart's in the Highlands, wherever I go

Dylan commences, to his own adapted melody:

Well my heart's in the Highlands gentle and fair
Honeysuckle blooming in the wildwood air
Bluebells blazing where the Aberdeen waters flow
Well my heart's in the Highlands
I'm gonna go there when I feel good enough to go

Fantasy? If not strictly of the Scottish variety, bluebells certainly blaze in gloomy Highland woods in May. A pedant could protest, however, that the coastal city of Aberdeen is a good distance from the mountains. That's certainly true. So is Dylan letting his romantic imagination run wild just to provide images of purity to contrast with the rest of his blackly comical talking blues? No doubt. But Aberdeenshire's main rivers, the Don and the Dee, do in fact rise in the Highlands, the latter at a great height in the western Cairngorms. Equally, though a later line in the song invoking 'the beautiful lake of the black swan' might have been created just to achieve a rhyme with 'break of dawn', there are a couple of Aberdeenshire lochs where black swans are sometimes seen. With Dylan, you never quite know. We do know, however, that late in 2006 the artist and his brother David spent a reported £2 million buying a mansion called Aultmore House near Nethy Bridge in the Cairngorms foothills. Nethy Bridge is known, for what it's worth, as 'the village in the forest'. In the right season there are bluebells in the woods. There's honeysuckle, too, at other times.

Dylan might have made some good guesses, then. It is a fact, on the other hand, that in his earliest days in Greenwich Village he was well acquainted with the Scottish traditional singer Jean Redpath. She arrived in New York in March 1961 and sang at Gerde's Folk City to great acclaim. She also won one of those precious rave reviews from the *New York Times* that could launch a career back then. Redpath, it should be added, is the world's best-known interpreter of the songs of Robert Burns. She has recorded at least 180 of them.

You could speculate a little more. The first play by the Armenian American writer William Saroyan was a comedy entitled *My Heart's in the Highlands* (1939). Aside from the presence of a octogenarian Scottish ham actor and escapee from an old folks' home by the name of Jasper MacGregor, it has more to do with a poverty-stricken self-styled poet and his Armenian family struggling to survive in Fresno, California, in 1914 than it has to do with Burns. Nevertheless, the play takes its title from the song for much the same reason that Dylan and the Scottish poet saw fit to borrow a line: for an idea of a lost but remembered Eden, far from the squalor of present reality. The point of this kind of borrowing is the fact that the words appropriated are familiar to the audience. Was the artist familiar with Saroyan's work? It would be surprising if a literate person of Dylan's generation was ignorant of a writer who influenced the Beats and was furiously prolific, if by then unfashionable, throughout the '50s and '60s. As to the little play, there is no way of knowing, though Dylan is full of surprises where literature is concerned. At one point in Saroyan's comedy, in any case, a character remarks, 'In the end, today is forever, yesterday is still today, and tomorrow is already today.' *Time Out of Mind* says much the same thing. Time had become Dylan's chief preoccupation.

'Highlands' begins among the mountains and streams. Then the singer awakens from his bad dreams to 'the same old page / Same ol' rat race / Life in the same ol' cage'.

THINGS HAVE CHANGED

I don't want nothing from anyone,
Ain't that much to take
Wouldn't know the difference
Between a real blonde and a fake
Feel like a prisoner in a world of mystery
I wish someone would come
And push back the clock for me

All is phoney and time is running away. While someone is yelling at him to turn the music down – the music of Neil Young, in Dylan's little joke – the speaker's mind drifts back again to a place where the heavens take their cue from the old spiritual in 'Big white clouds like chariots that swing down low'. Along the way, Dylan gives a brief nod to another poet. 'The Circus Animals' Desertion' was first published in 1939, just months after the death of W.B. Yeats. It ends:

Now that my ladder's gone
I must lie down where all ladders start
In the foul rag-and-bone shop of the heart.

Dylan sings:

If I had a conscience, well, I just might blow my top
What would I do with it anyway?
Maybe take it to the pawn shop

Most writers would settle happily for the oppositions Dylan has set up in the first third of the song. On the one hand are those (apparently) imagined idyllic Highlands, the 'Only place left to go'; on the other, raw and alienating urban life. Here's heaven against daily hell. Perhaps, indeed, it's the actual paradise of Dylan's faith set against his miserable mortal existence. After all, these Highlands are a place the singer can only get to 'one step at a time'. This is more than enough, surely, for a song with which to end an album imbued throughout with 'dread realities'? Dylan isn't satisfied.

The seven verses of what is sometimes called 'the restaurant scene' interrupt and disrupt 'Highlands'. They involve a dialogue between the singer and a waitress in a near-empty joint somewhere in Boston. In part, they are Dylan's reflections, very funny reflections too, on art, the artist and the audience. It is almost as though he is pausing mid-song to tell you about songwriting. Or rather, to explain why he can't tell you much about songwriting.

She knows he's an artist, a visual artist, and demands a portrait. He has no drawing book; she says – for what is art really worth? – that a napkin will do. As blues innuendo demands, he can't locate his pencil, but when she helps him out and he draws her picture she's disgusted: 'That don't look a thing like me!' By this point in his life Dylan had spent years listening to mockery of his 'incomprehensible' songs and impossible voice. Relentlessly, the conversation switches to books. She decides that he 'don't read women authors'. We can take this to mean that the songwriter has idealised or despised women but never truly understood them. He disagrees and in the best pure joke in the song bathetically names Erica Jong, the self-appointed authority on female sexual desire, as one author he knows something about. The artist and his entirely unimpressed audience have failed to establish any sort of contact. When her back is turned, he slips away.

By the song's end, his Highlands are the hills of the Scottish Borders. Dylan is taking his geography from a confused reading of a couple of Sir Walter Scott's novels, or glimpsing a landscape from the back of a limousine as it returns from the north of Scotland. Back in Boston, crossing the street, 'Talking to myself in monologue', wishing he could trade places with the young, he knows himself to be ageing. Dylan might deny it, but if 'Highlands' had anything at all to do with his life – the restaurant scene has a strong flavour of a superstar's reality – those intimations of mortality are everywhere. Before he's 'Over the hills and far away', following a songline far older than his own country, the penultimate verse is plain enough. If it is even slightly autobiographical, the critics Dylan would dismiss, the ones who talked about age and a sense of mortality, perhaps had a point.

> The sun is beginning to shine on me
> But it's not like the sun that used to be
> The party's over and there's less and less to say
> I got new eyes
> Everything looks far away

'Highlands' might be structurally unsound, but give Dylan credit. To begin an album with 'Love Sick' and close it with a sixteen-and-a-half minute song after so long a silence was audacious. *Time Out of Mind* was brave as well as bold. Dylan had not hesitated to follow his art wherever it led, however dark and forbidding the destination. He had not pandered to anyone. Greil Marcus, reviewing the album for the *San Francisco Chronicle*, said as much: 'This is as bleak and blasted as any work a major artist in any field – and by major artist I mean an artist with something, a reputation, an audience, to lose – has offered in ages.'[14] A writer who had followed Dylan's career from the very beginning was taken aback, observing: 'At first the music is shocking in its bitterness, in its refusal of comfort or kindness.' Though it no doubt suited a few of his theses, the critic went on to say something that was equally important. 'Verbal, melodic, and rhythmic signatures from ancient blues and folk songs fit into the songs on *Time Out of Mind*,' he wrote, 'as naturally, seemingly as inevitably, as breaths.' In case anyone had missed the point about 'the reappearance of the forgotten past in an empty present', there was also the fact that Dylan had induced Columbia to revive its 1920s 'Viva-Tonal Recording' label for his album, a label that had once been reserved for 'race' records and poor-white country music.

'Learning to go forward by turning back the clock,' Dylan had written in his *World Gone Wrong* notes. Like everyone else, Marcus had only glimpsed what the artist was about. It was not nostalgia for nostalgia's sake, or a retreat into older ways of making music in an effort to revive his interest and career. *Time Out of Mind* was not, in any case, quite as obviously 'ancient' as the reviewer meant his readers to believe. Lanois would be criticised by other writers for too often creating an ambience that was anything but natural. Nevertheless, with a sense of mortality comes a sense of history. Dylan had seen the future often enough, generally when he was busy inventing it, and it didn't work. All the clues to his present, and to America's present, were in the past. If that was where enduring reality was to be found, that was where Dylan was heading.

*

Bill Clinton had won his second presidential election with decisive ease on 5 November 1996. In January 1997, while Dylan was still deep in the struggle for *Time Out of Mind* in the Criteria studio in Miami, the 42nd president took the oath of office once again. That was when his troubles really began.

Trouble had followed Clinton doggedly for years, like some personal weather front forever threatening a catastrophic deluge. He seemed to have a talent for turning triumphs into squalid disasters before always managing, always at the last, somehow to beat the odds and the rap. Sex was his abiding problem. Clinton had a seemingly incorrigible taste for adulterous sex and a knack for the lies that are the soundtrack to philandering. The other small blight on his presidency was that America's conservatives detested him viscerally. Their loathing was awesome, even pathological, an animus less political than wholly personal. The politics was mostly trivial. Having shed any pretence of progressive intent after a couple of rough years in office, Clinton's team had huddled defensively around the centre ground, making a virtue of the vice of 'triangulation' – in effect, campaigning against friends and enemies alike to avoid seeming partisan – and eschewing anything with a hint of ideology or risk. To the new breed of media Republicans, shouting into microphones, hectoring their readers, spreading tales of Clinton's crimes without number, none of that mattered. They had a vendetta going. With a passion that approached obsession, they hated this Democrat because they feared his political gifts. They wanted him destroyed. In a truly tawdry scandal that erupted almost exactly a year after his second inauguration, Clinton's enemies thought they had him.

At times it seemed he was giving them all the help they needed. His wife, Hillary, would blame a 'vast right-wing conspiracy' for all the woes of the first family. There would be evidence enough for the claim. First amendment rights had long made America fecund ground for the propagation of outrageous libels. Clinton, as though driven by a secret need to be caught and condemned, acted as though he was only too happy to oblige his antagonists. Yet he broke no law save when lying under oath about his private and legal, if unsavoury, affairs, above all his casual liaison with a young White House intern named Monica Lewinsky. His real crime was to hand too much material to stand-up comedians, for nothing else of importance could be made to stick. When compared with Nixon, he was constitutional small fry. Yet it was Bill Clinton who would become the first American president since the unlamented Andrew Johnson in 1868 to face impeachment proceedings for providing 'perjurious, false and misleading testimony' to a grand jury.

This was a peculiar moment in American politics. It meant that something fundamental had changed. There was poison in the air and vitriol in every argument. The rest of the democratic world looked on amazed as its self-proclaimed leader, 'the essential nation', embarked on a virtual civil war over a head of state's problems with his marriage vows. That morality American-style was merely an excuse was well understood. But an excuse for what, exactly? The hysteria and hatred seemed to speak of a profound instability within society. Dylan would record a song for a movie just after Clinton's impeachment. 'People are crazy,' the refrain would say, 'and times are strange.'

Despite everything, as his admirers still recall, Clinton would leave office with the highest approval ratings of any president since the Second World War. One sign of strange times was that his enemies would simply ignore the fact. Clinton was more popular during his second term, amid the blizzard of scandal, than during his first. If a 61 per cent Gallup average rating for his second period in office bore any resemblance to reality, millions of Americans who voted against him in the presidential election were still prepared to say he had done a good job.[15] On 23–24 January, one week after the Lewinsky scandal broke, 58 per cent of those polled said they approved of the job Clinton was doing. Thereafter, his popularity *increased*. On 19 December 1998, while the House of Representatives was voting to impeach their president on charges of perjury and the obstruction of justice, his approval rating rose to 73 per cent. Not only did the vast majority of Americans refuse to care about Clinton's private sexual behaviour, they objected to anyone trying to make an issue out of his failings.

Instead, they were grateful to him. Clinton had disappointed liberals systematically, but middle America chose to see existence through the bright prism of the economy. Three weeks after the second inaugural the Dow Jones Industrial Average had closed above 7,000 for the first time in its history. With a couple of blips along the way, it went on rising. In May 1997, unemployment fell below 5 per cent for the first time since 1973. To Bill Clinton's 266,489,999 fellow Americans, such facts trumped any sexual impropriety. In that year, 81.7 per cent could declare that they had completed high school; 23.6 per cent had finished four years of college. They had 212 million motor vehicles and 192 million firearms between them, but possession of the latter, confined to 25 per cent of adults, was in decline. True, 13.8 per cent of Americans, fully 36.4 million souls, were still living below the poverty line, but the country had seen worse. Most had not seen better times since the 1960s. 'Slick Willie' Clinton, glib and grinning, soulful when required, solemn when the occasion demanded, happy to be all things to all the voters he could convince, was delivering.[16]

Conservative loathing for the President of the United States would not abate. The more popular he grew, the more the right fumed and raved. It didn't matter what the opinion polls said. One America, with one idea of the country's nature and purpose, held the other in contempt. The feeling had been growing for a while. Before long the belief would become a cliché. Politically, culturally, socially, by geography and sometimes by ethnicity, the republic had become divided against itself. What one of his aides would call 'the Clinton wars' were the public expression of a deeper truth.[17] He was the symbol, the lightning rod, simultaneously a sworn enemy and the people's champion.

In himself, this president was a kind of parable. The man from Hope, Arkansas – a town that might have been created for a campaign slogan – could seem like the embodiment of the old dream that encouraged every kid from a modest, difficult background to aim for the White House. In the right light, he could look like the last best hope (indeed) of '60s liberalism. But he had a bad habit of betraying those who believed in him most. Morally, his outlines were as blurred as a silvery fog. Personally and politically, he was a mass of contradictions, both idealistic and cynically expedient, inspirational and capable of producing a deep disillusionment.

Even the apple of prosperity Clinton gave to the American people had a worm at its heart. A lot of cheap, dangerous credit had bought his popularity. When in November 1999 his signature brought an end to the Glass–Steagall Act that had hindered banks from playing roulette with depositors' money, consequences followed. One was the near collapse in 2008 of the entire banking system, with it the economy of the western world. Clinton achieved federal budget surpluses, it is true, but private individuals were borrowing all they could and spending all they could. When the banks were 'liberated', with his enthusiastic support, a disaster was set in train. Like the president's affairs, the '90s were only good while they lasted.

It was an apt moment, whether he realised it or not, for Dylan to have his mind filled with the music of the 1920s and 1930s. The truth about what was to befall America in the twenty-first century could be found, had anyone bothered to wonder at the end of the '90s, in those bygone eras. That music was the story of how the people had behaved in hard times.

*

Dylan didn't pause for long after finishing his album. By the second week in February 1997 he was back on tour for a round of concerts in Japan. Unless you have an unnatural taste for endless lists of the which-songs-were-played-where variety, the narrative for this and most of the following few years becomes predictable, not to say tedious. The known story of a life involves some public events, some private matters, an interview here and there and the wait, generally a long one, for an album of new work while Dylan toured on and ever on. In 1997, his shows would scarcely differ in format or style from the shows of 1996. Even after recovering from his encounter with histoplasmosis Dylan would sometimes seem exhausted on stage – during several concerts in August he was forced to sit down between songs – but nothing, so it seemed, would keep him from girdling the planet to play his shows.

Back in the real world, his contemporaries were disappearing, one by one. By default, and by dint of sheer, stubborn perseverance, a 56-year-old Dylan was becoming a grand old man. He was to issue a lot of brief obituaries and sing numerous songs in tribute to the dead in 1997 and in the years after. The pop world he had transformed a generation before had made a virtue of transience, of always moving on, of forever discarding its brief past for the sake of an alluring, insistent future. By the '90s, the remaining pioneers, hucksters, wounded saints and one-hit wonders of the 1960s were discovering what transient really means. Richard Manuel and Jerry Garcia had already quit the field. On 5 April another private matter intruded when Dylan was told that Allen Ginsberg had died at his home in Greenwich Village of liver cancer and its complications.

Perhaps America's bravest post-war poet, if not its best, the older man had managed to be both besotted with Dylan and one of the most alert, dispassionate observers of the Dylan phenomenon. Ginsberg had been a profound inspiration for the artist long before their first meeting at a party above a Village bookshop late in December 1963. At minimum, much of what Dylan wrote in the mid-1960s would have been very different had he never read *Howl* and *Kaddish*. Not many hours after Ginsberg's death, the set list for a concert in Moncton, New Brunswick, was altered. That night, Dylan performed 'Desolation Row'. After it was done, he told the audience: 'A friend of mine passed away, I guess this morning. That was one of his favourite songs. Poet, Allen Ginsberg.'

Unlike others, that poet had never lost his faith in the possibility of radical change. He had been carried away, ecstatically so, by what he supposed to be the mind-altering epochal significance of the Rolling

Thunder Revue. For all his nonsense, Ginsberg had never surrendered his devout belief that Dylan was a revolutionary force. There had been a reason, equally, why the poet had been given the role of 'The Father' in *Renaldo and Clara*. As to art, Ginsberg saw in Dylan the embodiment of what he called 'poetry-music', the essence of each recombined in a way that was both ancient and modern. There was an irony in the fact that one man had personified the counter-culture even as the other was rejecting its grandiose claims and messy thinking, but that had never tainted their friendship. The artist had owed a lot to Ginsberg.

With his Buddhist friend gone, Dylan added another creed to his collection by making an appearance at Italy's 23rd National Eucharist Congress in Bologna on 27 September, three days before *Time Out of Mind* was released. The event was a Catholic 'youth festival' involving two less-than-youthful men and some 300,000 young Italians. Pope John Paul II oversaw events from a throne above the stage, or rather called the shots (though apparently half-asleep for much of the time), while a nervous-looking Dylan offered up 'Knockin' On Heaven's Door' and 'A Hard Rain's a-Gonna Fall'. Then the artist climbed the staircase, removed his cowboy hat, kissed the pope's ring and exchanged a few private words, prophet to pontiff. Finally, John Paul did as all good pastors must and took 'Blowin' in the Wind', that most ambiguous of songs, as the basis for an unambiguous sermon. The pope said to Italy's young Catholics: 'You asked me: how many roads must a man walk down before you can call him a man? I answer you: just one. One only.' You get the gist. Then Dylan finished up with 'Forever Young'.

There are only two possible explanations for his motives in accepting the engagement. They are not mutually contradictory; quite the reverse. One is that Dylan was not entertaining a dozing pontiff as a charitable gesture. By all accounts, a fee of several hundred thousand dollars was secured from those arranging the show for all those Italian kids. A second explanation is that it did not trouble Dylan in the slightest to sing for a pope who took a dim view of contraception, abortion, gay marriage, left-wing priests and several other things of this world. It is worth mentioning, however, that John Paul had established formal relations between the Holy See and the State of Israel just four years before the Bologna congress. For Dylan, that might have counted for something. Whatever the reasons, this strangest of all his performances was another reminder that any naive souls still hankering after the subversive, mercurial and politically progressive artist of years long gone needed to reset their preconceptions once and for all.

In London, a week later, he would tell *Mojo* magazine that Bologna had been a 'great show'. Asked if he was involved in 'world affairs', however, Dylan would once again reply, 'No, I can't really say that I am.' Despite histoplasmosis, he was about to face a final run of 32 American dates in a concert schedule that would total 94 performances by the time 1997 was done. In the year ahead, Dylan would surpass even his accountants' expectations by fulfilling no fewer than 110 engagements across the planet. Yet in talking to journalists he persisted in giving the impression that none of it had much to do with him, or with his wishes. If this was a man bent upon perpetual art-in-performance, he seemed to have no good idea of what his motives might be. Not for the first time or the last, his remarks gave credence to the suspicion that the grand artistic ritual of the alleged tour without end had become aimless, a tedious commercial venture. As he sometimes liked to claim, it was just a job.

> I don't know why people talk about never-ending, because I don't really consider myself on tour. We just go out and play a certain amount of shows every year, so it isn't really a tour. It could stop any time. Part of me doesn't want to do it all. Part of me would just like to be done with it all.[18]

Roughly a year earlier he had been nominated, finally, for the Nobel Prize in Literature due to be awarded in 1997. Though Dylan laughed off the whole idea when any journalist asked for his reaction, even pretending to be ignorant of what the Nobel signified, it was the beginning of a contest over the nature of literary art that would persist (with ample opportunity for laughter) into the twenty-first century. Allen Ginsberg, stalwart as ever, had written in support of the claim being made on Dylan's behalf, calling him 'a major American Bard & minstrel of the XX Century, whose words have influenced many generations throughout the world'. The artist deserved his Nobel, according to Ginsberg, 'in recognition of his mighty and universal powers'. Professor Gordon Ball had made the formal nomination, stating: 'In our modern era Bob Dylan has returned poetry to its primordial transmission by human breath and body . . . in his musical verse he has revived the traditions of bard, minstrel, and troubadour.'[19]

Nice try. The 1997 prize went instead to the Italian playwright Dario Fo. He was not a popular choice among *littérateurs*, ironically enough, because the keepers of high culture regarded him as a performance artist rather than a real writer. The Nobel committee recognised this difficulty in their press release announcing the award. It was full of high-flown verbiage about 'texts' that were 'always open for creative additions and dislocations, continually encouraging the actors to improvise, which means that the audience is activated in a remarkable way'. Dylan's better-read fans could and would take encouragement from that. A playwright whose work depended on performance rather than the printed page? Surely one more obstacle to their candidate's elevation had been removed.

It might seem like a neat if inadvertent touch, meanwhile, to have had the nomination go forward when finally there was a Dylan album capable of backing up the claims being made for his art. In reality, *Time Out of Mind* arrived in the stores just a week before the Nobel selectors announced their winner on 7 October. There is therefore the grisly if entertaining possibility that a bunch of nonplussed eminent Swedes believed they were being asked to judge the creator of *Knocked Out Loaded* and *Down in the Groove*. In any case, Dylan's backers hadn't thought the problem through. Understandably, they took it for granted that everyone had heard of, and heard, their candidate. He is certainly well-respected in Scandinavia, where English-speakers are commonplace. But what was the committee being asked to judge? Printed lyrics in place of their sacred 'texts'? A group of recordings containing things that sucked along with things that were sublime? And where stood the vaunted Dylan of evolving live performance whose audience 'is activated in a remarkable way' (on a good night)?

The persistent belief that the artist's never-ending candidacy is the victim of snobbery and prejudice towards popular culture, not to mention towards Americans, is probably well founded. Other factors should not be ignored. It is less a question of whether purblind Swedish professors can understand Dylan's work than of explaining what it is they are being asked to understand. Plenty of reluctant witnesses to his career have had that problem down the years. Calling him an artist is easy. Stating the nature of the art is a trickier task. Ginsberg's 'poetry-music' had been a good stab at a definition, but it was not a complete description.

In January 1998, Dylan did a few shows with Van Morrison. In February, he dispatched another note of condolence and praise, this time to a funeral mass in Jackson, Tennessee. Carl Perkins, peer to Elvis, writer of 'Blue Suede Shoes', had died of throat cancer, aged just 65. Dylan's note read: 'He really stood for freedom. That whole sound stood for all degrees of freedom. It would just jump off the turntable. We wanted to go where that was happening.' If there is an art to writing such things, Dylan was becoming adept.

March found him in South America, taking the money (presumably very good money) and swallowing whatever pride was involved in serving as an opening act for the Rolling Stones. In May, as though to prove that finding a new, younger audience was not at all times his priority, he was performing concerts jointly with Joni Mitchell. That month he also found another set of fine and sincere words for the recently deceased Frank Sinatra. None of this activity was of any real significance. As in the aftermath of *Oh Mercy*, Dylan seemed already to have decided that a creative renaissance could wait. Room had been found in his concerts for songs from *Time Out of Mind*, but if he was eager to write more, he showed no urgent sign of desire. Patently, making albums was an afterthought.

While Dylan marked fully ten years back on the road and took less-than-onerous superstar gigs with fellow artists of a certain age, October provided a thunderous, bracing echo from his past. It also offered a rebuttal to the never-ending chatter about a never-ending tour. If brevity was the criterion, a title like *The Bootleg Series Vol. 4: Bob Dylan Live 1966, The 'Royal Albert Hall' Concert* deserved no prizes. In every other respect the double CD was, as legend and all the real bootlegs had long said, impeccable. Anyone who bought this when it went on sale on 13 October and then caught Dylan's show in a town called Duluth, Minnesota, just nine days later was invited to contrast and compare. The tour that took the artist to the city of his birth saw some pretty fair performances along the way. It had nothing to compare with a slice of the historical record as it pertained to the events of 17 May 1966.

Dylan would tell interviewers, reasonably enough, that he could no longer be the person who had given that Manchester show, or write those songs, or occupy that near-impossible role, or endure the killing pressures once imposed on a young man not yet 25. All his complaints and explanations were fair. They nevertheless invited the question: who could he be, then, and what could he do as the century approached its end? *Time Out of Mind* had provided the beginnings of an answer. Yet as the months and the tours came and went he seemed to have no interest in pursuing a conclusion.

In 1999, he would give 119 public performances, breaking his own record once again. Four dozen of these 'arena experiences' would be shared with Paul Simon, for reasons probably best explained by the prices the two legends felt entitled to charge. They would not ask for an arm and a leg at every stop along the way while one short man alternated with a shorter man – Dylan won that contest, just for a change – in opening or closing the show. Some customers would get away with surrendering just the contents of a wallet with a couple of fingers attached, depending on what the local nostalgia market would bear. In Raleigh, North Carolina, a loyal fan of one or other star would contemplate a top price of $75; in Camden, New Jersey, the costliest ticket would be $100. A fan in Concord, California, who wanted the best seat in the house could expect to pay $127.50, while in Vegas the top-end entry fee was $150. At Madison Square Garden, New Yorkers who refused to settle for less than the finest accommodation would pay $123. To put this in context, the most expensive ticket for an Eric Clapton show at the Garden two years later would be $80. The highest price demanded by U2 during their blockbusting 2001 tour would be $130.

Money aside, it is hard to identify the purpose and point of the joint-tour exercise. For the most part, predictably, dedicated Dylan fans would enthuse over his performances – though bootlegs say these were nothing special – and pay little attention to Simon. Even those wholly enamoured of the artist would become just a little sceptical, however, about this particular detour on the endless highway. One fan, having attended six shows in a week, would remark after the last night at the Jones Beach Amphitheatre in Wantagh, New York, on 31 July that though the concerts had been 'very good' it was all 'kinda uneventful'.[20] Seth Rogovoy, journalist and prolific writer on Dylan, would open a review of a show in Albany, New York, with these words:

> Lightning didn't strike nor did fireworks ignite when Sixties icons Bob Dylan and Paul Simon joined forces on a handful of songs at the Pepsi Arena on Tuesday night. In fact, what on paper might have seemed like a stroke of promotional genius – putting the two folk-rock visionaries together for the first time in their careers for a barnstorming tour of the nation – turned out to be anti-climactic from the get-go.[21]

Rogovoy, another finding few flaws in Dylan's own performances, would finish up by remarking that the concert was a failed attempt to produce 'something new and unique'. Presumably that was not the aim. Nevertheless, when the usual story says that the artist was in the throes of a creative renaissance by the end of the '90s, it is worth bearing in mind how he chose actually to spend his time. *Time Out of Mind* and all the publicity engendered by the latest 'comeback' were causing a renewed interest in Dylan and his works by the century's end. The album had sold a million copies. Yet for most of the time this artist reborn was just playing the arena circuit, spinning on a wheel.

The spring of 1999 had seen him return to Europe for the 11th year in succession; the next dozen years would be no different. It would matter greatly to handfuls of devoted people, no doubt, to know who had joined or left the 'Never Ending Tour Band', which musician had stayed the course and which one could tolerate the experience the least. In the bigger scheme of things all the theories and tales did not alter the fact that the tours were a poor substitute for creative work. Yet the odd fact remains that Dylan would revive his reputation as a recording artist, and do so emphatically, while treating the making of albums as little more than a necessary chore. The income from concerts meant that he would no longer be in thrall to the despised studio. He could play live and tell some journalists that it was his first and only love, his artistic reality, his whole existence. Others would be told that he could take it or leave it. Did he notice, then, that a big part of his usual crowd were the same people, night after night, following him from venue to venue?

On 10 December 1999, Rick Danko died in his sleep of heart failure, aged 56 and a day. The weight, his own physical weight, had proved too much after a lot of booze and a lot of drugs. The singer and bass player – or trombonist, or fiddle player – who had helped Dylan to write 'This Wheel's On Fire' and harmonised with him during several of the songs on the basement tapes, had been in poor shape for a while. He had last played briefly with Dylan in August 1997, when the artist's tour halted for a concert in Connecticut. Danko had been the Band member who in 1967 spotted that a big pink house in the middle of 100 acres was available in Saugerties, New York. By the late '90s he and Garth Hudson, the last men standing, had been reduced to travelling from little show to little show in a motorhome. Levon Helm, who had found better things to do with himself, would forever maintain that Danko had worked himself to death because he had never received his fair share of money from *The Last Waltz* and other Band ventures.

In the summer of 1999, the little town of Hibbing, Minnesota, had begun to lay plans for a new exhibit in its public library. The municipality already had a museum dedicated to its claim to fame as the birthplace of the Greyhound bus line. The Hibbing Historical Society also had a museum to call its own. By the century's end, nevertheless, the need was felt to recognise another piece of local history. The Zimmerman kid, still remembered by a few older residents, was to be memorialised while he yet lived. Meanwhile, the news that his beloved mother had been diagnosed with cancer would remind Dylan that time and mortality could not be denied. Beatty Zimmerman would die on 27 January 2000 at the age of 84.

*

In 1999 there had been one moment of clarity in a fog of concerts. That summer, tempted by Hollywood, Dylan had gone into a New York studio for a day and turned out a recording of a song called 'Things Have Changed'. Typically, it was better than at least half the stuff on *Time Out of Mind*, a cynical song from the world's end that also somehow managed to make sense within the context of the movie for which it had been designed. It made some sense of the era, too. For a change, the film, entitled *Wonder Boys*, would also be a pretty fair effort. 'Things Have Changed' would win Dylan an Academy Award.

Film music had come to his attention, no doubt because it paid very well. The piece he wrote for *Wonder Boys* cannot be dismissed cynically, however. It is as sharp and penetrating a sketch of human vanity as anything he ever created. The song, compelling proof that he could still write when the need arose, also contains another of those fragments of evidence, if such was still required, that Dylan's fascination with an apocalyptic ending for humankind had not been extinguished. 'If the Bible is right,' as he sang, 'the world will explode.' The real point offered in this work is that the speaker, or the artist, couldn't care less.

People are crazy and times are strange
I'm locked in tight, I'm out of range
I used to care, but things have changed

'Things Have Changed' might also have contained a hint that not only could Dylan still manage a new song at short notice, but that, amid another lengthy pause between albums, there might be more to come. In point of fact, there is no evidence that he was not writing all the while. His problems with writer's block are well-enough established. The paucity of new songs between 1969's *Nashville Skyline* and 1974's *Planet Waves*, from an artist who had spent most of the '60s in a ferment of creativity, had been impossible to ignore. The seven lean years between *Under the Red Sky* and *Time Out of Mind* told their own story. The long silences between albums during Dylan's later years are a different matter. If he was making excellent money out on the road, felt no creative need to make yet another album and despised the recording process, it makes sense to believe him if he says a piece of work was done when he 'had the time'. No doubt his record company had some say in the matter, but in 2000 Sony would make do with no fewer than three compilation albums titled, almost comically, as a *Best of . . . Vol 2*; a *Very Best of*; and an *Essential Bob Dylan*. As though to mock every sceptic and critic, the last of these would do very well indeed, in due course being 'certified platinum' in America, Britain and Australia and as a 'gold' record elsewhere.

Touring continued regardless. In 2000, while the American market was assaulted once more, Europe got two separate visits from Dylan. In February 2001 he was off to Japan and Australia once more, pausing along the way to accept his 'best original song' Oscar by satellite link from Sydney. The year would end with the death of George Harrison, the Beatle of whom Dylan had been most fond. That much was plain from the statement in which the artist made his farewells. Touchingly, it was written as though to suit the beliefs and the character of the deceased. Of Harrison, Dylan said:

> He was a giant, a great, great soul, with all of the humanity, all of the wit and humour, all the wisdom, the spirituality, the common sense of a man and compassion for people. He inspired love and had the strength of a hundred men. He was like the sun, the flowers and the moon and we will miss him enormously. The world is a profoundly emptier place without him.

That year it became known that Dylan had indeed returned to the recording studios. He was finishing work in May at Clinton Recording in Manhattan, in fact, when he reached the age of 60. When had he ever imagined that birthday? It would not prevent journalist after journalist asking a man in his 60s what he thought about the '60s. Yet in July, astoundingly, it transpired that despite every denial he might have been thinking about that confused and intoxicating decade himself.

In Italy, during a press conference held at the De La Ville InterContinental Roma Hotel to publicise the release of his new music, Dylan remarked, it seems out of the blue, that he was working on a book to 'be published in an article form, but as a book, a book of articles, because they're ongoing'. At first he said that this was 'as much as it is at the moment'. When pressed about 'articles', however, Dylan went on:

> Oh, I think that with this type of writing I was just trying to find the right way to get into it, rather than making it some kind of self-serving story of my particular past. If it seems to happen that way, it's actually dissimilar in a lot of ways. I can do it because I'm a famous person, so I use that fame, because a lot of the things I might write about other people know about anyway. So with a person like myself, the process of doing it this way works.
>
> I mean, I'm not really making a real attempt to do this. I just do it in my spare time.[22]

*

'Love and Theft' keeps the promise made by *Time Out of Mind*. With this album it becomes possible to talk seriously of a Dylan who was not only renewed but, at 60, reborn creatively. Here all the claims made for his late period are not only plausible but undeniable. Only controversy over his methods – charges of plagiarism, bluntly – would stain the achievement, at least for nature's tenacious pedants. Most of those charges were and remain specious, trivial, irrelevant to the great mass of listeners and born of a profound ignorance of artistic method, far less of 'folk process', but they have clung to Dylan ever since 'Love and Theft' appeared. In fact, the hunt for evidence against the accused has become a tiny, if furiously busy, cottage industry. Where once it was a critic's delight to cite those among the quick and the dead who could be named as a Dylan 'influence' or somehow just associated with his themes and manner – Keatsian, Rimbaldien, Poe-like and the rest – in the twenty-first century the game has become one of spot-the-pilfering. The always-implied justification is that with this album Dylan began to adopt an underhand method by which to eke out a waning creativity. Some hasten to add that they just knew it all along. Given his free and easy manner with other people's material down the years, not least his old habit of claiming as his own that which was 'traditional', this doesn't cause many presses to be stopped. But these days, if you believe those who are most vehement, the issue is more serious, less excusable, sometimes inexplicable. Plagiarism, a word liable to cause every writer since Chaucer to look shifty, is the subtext of 'Love and Theft'.

Dylan knew it, too. He got his mockery in first: hence those quotation marks around his title; hence his title. Others might prefer collage, cut-and-paste, modernist technique, a sophisticated system of allusion and invocation, or a statement about a form of writing that makes no bones over how inspiration and tradition really work. The fact remains that the artist was perfectly self-aware. Grant him this much, then: it is an unusual thief who advertises his theft. Dylan took his title wholesale from a book and stuck it between quotation marks.

The book itself, Eric Lott's *Love and Theft: Blackface Minstrelsy and the American Working Class* (1993), is a sophisticated analysis of the cultural transactions down the decades between African Americans and a white world. It does not for an instant deny the thefts from black artists that have formed the basis of much of white American culture, but it spends a great deal of time unravelling the complicated impulses in its title's first word. Dylan knew all about that. His joke, a sly and brilliant joke, was to acknowledge everything, all the music that had made him, by stealing the very name of Lott's book. For some of his most dogged pursuers that wouldn't do. To them it would seem like a fancy, postmodern excuse for plagiarism and a piece of misdirection to boot. In their indictment, Dylan was admitting to a lesser crime in order to conceal truly heinous offences.

If you knew none of this, *'Love and Theft'* could give many years of unalloyed pleasure. If you knew it all, down to every last musical 'quotation' and lyrical 'allusion', would it matter? Those who can't grasp why this is one of Dylan's finest albums, who have quaint ideas about originality and imagine that literary art must function like a variety of (respectable) journalism, miss not only the pleasure of the thing, but fail to see how Dylan's 'plagiarism' functions within his larger purpose. If part of your aim is to examine and revivify your country's history, what else would you bring to bear if not historical materials? If, meanwhile, you come to terms with the idea of found art and the resetting of found materials for poetic effect, the charge of plagiarism is almost puerile. In Dylan's method things old and new echo within the landscape created, as they do in memory, as they do in the real world of which we hear so much. Things overlap and interconnect, change meaning in juxtaposition, acquire a significance they would not otherwise possess. When Dylan does it, some pretty good tracks also become available.

Take the following verse from 'Tweedle Dee & Tweedle Dum'. Is it possible, do you think, that Dylan stole those two characters? Never mind. Assiduous textual detectives, those who seem to believe that all true art is entirely pristine and wholly original, would track the first pair of lines to a Civil War poet called Timrod. The lit dicks would not make quite as much fuss over the second pair, or explain how those lines function in relation to the lines that precede them.

> Well a childish dream is a deathless need
> And a noble truth is a sacred dream
> My pretty baby, she's lookin' around
> She's wearin' a multi-thousand dollar gown

Some lines are borrowed, but the result is wholly original. Robert Burns pulled this trick time and again. Elsewhere Dylan might quote F. Scott Fitzgerald's *Gatsby* – nothing minor, just the unmissable 'You can't repeat the past' – or a Japanese memoir. In 'Lonesome Day Blues', for one example, there's a big portion of Mark Twain. There are jokes, too, from the Marx Brothers and W.C. Fields. Conceivably, there are also classical allusions. But then, the classics themselves are stuffed with allusions. In this variety of critical argument, a big point is being missed.

To get the sound he wanted, finally, the artist – 'Jack Frost', for his purposes – produced the album himself. The sound he secured is the first and most obvious clue to the relationship between *'Love and Theft'* and American history. Dylan had indeed moved forward by turning back the clock. Using his touring band for the first time – having grasped finally that people who played with him every other night knew his little ways better than any expensive session crew – the album resembled an aural scrapbook of the pre-history of pop. Its reference points were the '20s, '30s and '40s. None of the songs shout masterpiece; that wasn't the point. In an odd way, the album was all the better for it. Dylan's greatest works, the big songs, have a habit of diminishing everything around them. With *'Love and Theft'* the listener is granted an *apparently* relaxed, sunny suite of songs in the vernacular, full of little jokes – some even have punchlines – and eccentricities. This is one of those rare things, a loveable Dylan album.

THINGS HAVE CHANGED

The loose (very loose) literary equivalent to Dylan's structural method might be William Faulkner's tales of Yoknapatawpha County. The songs are not interlinked, not explicitly, but journey almost from scene to scene. Even the darker pieces are somehow smoothed out to fit the overall pattern. So the great 'Mississippi' is revived, but here it sounds nothing like the versions attempted for *Time Out of Mind*. With *'Love and Theft'* Dylan also finds a style that suits his ever-diminishing voice. The 60-year-old sounds even older, in places, than his age should allow. At all times he sounds as though his first album in the twenty-first century is being broadcast from some Alabama radio station in the late 1940s with Hank Williams and Bukka White hanging around outside.

As observed, *'Love and Theft'* is saturated in 'influences'. There's plenty of blues, some of it so familiar and obvious Dylan was all but pleading with listeners to notice what he was doing. If on one song he sings 'it's all in vain' and on another 'I believe I'll dust my broom', he is making the most overt reference possible to Robert Johnson. You can discover the blues even in song titles such as 'Lonesome Day' or 'Po' Boy'. If most of his audience has meanwhile never heard of Charley Patton, to whom 'High Water' is dedicated, what does it matter? The blues and what the blues has signified in American history is a main tributary for *'Love and Theft'*. The African American experience is what truly matters in 'High Water', not the fact that Dylan quotes from an ancient song called 'The Cuckoo' that he used to sing back in the Gaslight club in 1962.

> High water risin', six inches 'bove my head
> Coffins droppin' in the street
> Like balloons made out of lead
> Water pourin' into Vicksburg
> Don't know what I'm going to do
> 'Don't reach out for me,' she said
> 'Can't you see I'm drownin' too?'
> It's rough out there
> High water everywhere

The idea that Dylan was supposed to cite every source, confess to every appropriation and submit to being treated as a desiccated folklorist was absurd. Worse, it was banal. Yet to read some subsequent comment, confess was exactly what he was supposed to do. If he was reassembling found art with this album, a perfectly respectable technique was involved. This was not the young Dylan who had passed off melodies and more as his own. This was not the master thief, the sponge. This was a conscious (and self-conscious) artist. The distinction would escape several people whose only apparent desire is to have the artist document every last facet of his life and work. And then apologise.

The sunny mood of 'Love and Theft' is deceptive, of course. The songs in this album have as their trademark the sting in the tail, the jab that seems to come from nowhere. They are once again driven by religion, but also by the curious conviction, as in 'Things Have Changed', that resigned acceptance of this world means the singer no longer has to care about anything much. On this album, it's almost a side issue. Above all, these are stories, fables, episodes from what Greil Marcus identifies as the 'old, weird America'. One fine joke in this album is that despite all the literary allusions every voice is the voice of the common people. Irrespective of anything the songs might have to say, Dylan was making the claim that America exists in its voices and its music, in cultural geneaology, in tradition as it evolves and mutates. His critics crawled all over the thefts and forgot about the love.

*

No one in Mahattan bought 'Love and Theft' on the day of its release. New York had other things to worry about on 11 September 2001. The coincidence was grim, but grim coincidence it remained. Unlike so many others in his trade, Dylan did not rush to write a song, patriotic or otherwise, about the attacks on the World Trade Center and the Pentagon. His views about what any piece of art was worth amid a cataclysm were well developed. Besides, his creativity had long before lost the reflexive speed needed for so-called 'topical songwriting'. In any case, '9/11', as it soon became known, seemed existential rather than just another pressing issue of the day. By another brutal coincidence, Dylan's old boyhood friend Larry Kegan, comrade of the Herzl summer camp and beyond, had succumbed to a heart attack on the day America was assaulted. Death happened, as life happened, without politics or poetry. Musicians could only make music. Dylan kept going.

CHAPTER TWELVE

Sketches from Memory

AT NO POINT IN ITS 293 PAGES IS THE BOOK PUBLISHED BY DYLAN IN October 2004 described as a memoir. Even the dust cover's encomium does not risk the word 'autobiography'. Instead, the buyer is offered explorations and elegies, intimacy, insight and the briefest stab of punctuating memory. On second sight, the advertisement seems to have been constructed with some care. What is claimed is tantalising; what is left unsaid more tantalising still. The publisher's commendation for *Chronicles: Volume One* promises only glimpses, as through a dusty window, of an author's thoughts and the influences exerted on those thoughts. This is not chapter and verse, then.

A chronicle, says the dictionary, is 'a continuous record of events in order of time; a history'. Dylan's *Chronicles* propose no such thing. The significant word in the blurb, the reader will soon enough learn, is 'storytelling'. The book is not corroborative evidence for anyone's case. Yet when the first printing hit the *New York Times* bestseller lists – and remained there for 19 weeks – it was classified as non-fiction. It is part of Dylan's method, in prose or verse, to question whether such a claim can be made of anyone's life.

The critical reception, as he would tell the novelist Jonathan Lethem in the late summer of 2006, moved him almost to tears.[1] This author, so long in the making, had the fond belief that literary critics must know what they are talking about, unlike their colleagues on the music (rock and pop) beat. Dylan seemed to believe – each to his own – that book hacks can't be fooled. If they said *Chronicles* was vital and valuable, the writer was hugely gratified. It was as though the youth who struggled so hard and long with his *Tarantula* experiment 40 years before had been vindicated at last.

The confession to Lethem was a reminder that, after everything,

411

Dylan still cared about the reception his work received. It suggested he must have been nervous indeed about appearing in this manner in the court of critical opinion. It told his audience – as though they needed telling – that he understood exactly what to expect with his name above the title. By publishing *Chronicles* he had once again placed himself under investigation. That fact, in turn, said something about the careful, artful way the seemingly nonchalant book was constructed. You could even call it cunning. Not for the first time, Dylan took preconceptions and juggled with them in a piece of writing that no one had ever expected to see.

Chronicles is not a memoir, not in the usual sense. It is certainly not a cradle-to-the-present autobiography, not a Rousseauian *Confessions*, an apologia, or the definitive explanation for a life. In 2012, Dylan would remind readers, via his usual *Rolling Stone* conduit, that the book does not, in fact, contain the very meaning of existence, his 'or anyone else's'. The text, he would say, 'doesn't attempt to be any more than what it is'.[2] The modest disclaimer could leave the reader to wonder what, in that case, *Chronicles* does attempt. A lot *is* explained, but most of that happens allusively, between the lines. The choices made in the narrative, or rather narratives, were meanwhile surprising to many fans in 2004 and downright baffling to those looking eagerly for Dylan's frank remembrances of famous times past. The omissions seemed wilful. For all that, the blurb did not lie: what you got for your bestseller was as fine a piece of pure American storytelling as most readers had recently seen.

*

There are no direct quotations from *Chronicles: Volume One* in this book, just as there were no direct quotations from the singer's prose in its predecessor. For once, the overworked word ironic can stand in plain sight. As my *Once Upon a Time* was nearing completion, someone in Dylan's office – and who knows? – declined to grant permission for the use of selected passages. Such is the artist's right and copyright.

The simple idea had been to allow the subject to speak for himself, now and then, while warning the reader, here and there, that alternative accounts were available. Judging by the message relayed from New York through Simon & Schuster, Dylan's publisher, umbrage was taken by someone at a few illustrative samples from my text. Scepticism towards the idea that *Chronicles* provided any kind of full documentary record of events and conversations from four decades back and more, human memory being what it is, was taken as an assault on Mr Dylan's 'veracity'. (I place the word in quotation marks to signify quotation: it's a habit worth acquiring.) Close readers of his book might therefore begin to see where irony comes in. I was being forbidden to quote from a volume richly and demonstrably stuffed with quotations, very few of them acknowledged. The subject, it turns out, is a sensitive one. It is also fascinating.

Perhaps, first time around, I should have mentioned the reviews of *Chronicles* instead. One, written by the film critic and novelist Tom Carson and published in the Sunday books section of the *New York Times* on 24 October 2004, had plenty to say about veracity. There was 'the voice Dylan has devised for his youthful self, which is spellbinding in its hokum'. That voice was 'transparently fraudulent'. The writing offered 'some of the best fake *Huckleberry Finn*' Carson had ever read. The reviewer further observed, correctly, that 'the book's larger purpose is mythographic', but he went on to note its 'reality-distorting priorities and revealing omissions', not least in Dylan's failure to address his 'square peg' Jewishness in 1950s middle America. To point out, said Carson, 'that *Chronicles* is designed to manipulate our perceptions is simply to affirm that it's genuine Dylan. The book is an act, but a splendid one . . .' The memoir was deemed 'self-serving', but also – I had laboured the same point – a marvel. 'This is a veteran carny's magic show,' observed the man in the *New York Times*, 'not a confessional.' Precisely.

Other reviewers who knew their Dylan had reached very similar conclusions. A few had been needlessly stern on the subject of veracity. My account argued, somewhere along the line, that the kind of truth being offered did not depend much, if at all, on specific facts. To me, those didn't matter alongside Dylan's version of the truth. You could call that truth deeper or higher; I would have said 'artistic'. And that was while setting aside until this volume most of the arguments over precise words, precise phrases and their precise origins.

Chronicles is a marvel. It counts as a significant piece of American literary art, one all the better for its solid craft in the age of celebrity tell-all-tell-nothing confessions. Pulling it apart like a questionable witness statement is about as useful as denying the power of 'The Lonesome Death of Hattie Carroll' just because Dylan was shaky – as he was – on the facts of that celebrated tragedy. But where *Chronicles* was concerned the issue of honesty cut a little deeper, it transpired, than any argument over whether the writer had got his stories straight.

Suddenly the topic for discussion became the nature of his art in the twenty-first century.

By 2004, it wasn't exactly a whole new symposium. Noises had been made before about Dylan's methods, his influences, inspirations, sources, borrowings and the uses to which sometimes he put them. Back in the 1960s he had dismissed all such questions with a famous crack to the effect that influence was impossible to avoid. You open your eyes and ears, he had said, and you're influenced. That had not been the sole basis for an avid student's speed-learning in the art of songwriting. It didn't make him guilty of the glib charge that he was 'a master thief'. It didn't establish his unsullied innocence, either. It did help to explain him, however.

Dylan had come to fame by way of a Greenwich Village scene and a folk tradition that saw nothing wrong with 'borrowing', adaptation, imitation and the subtle (or not so subtle) shaping of 'influences' into a style the artist could call his own. In an important sense, that process *was* the folk tradition. It amounted to the casual, communal effort continually to remake songs that had been handed down from generation to generation. For some, folk was inspirational on that account alone. Its problems arose only when the old egalitarian hootenanny habits began to run up against a capitalist entertainment industry with a vested interest in copyright and ownership.

Dylan, always remembered as a 'sponge', even by those who had done plenty of sponging themselves, had his share of trouble on that score in the first half of the '60s. His management were obliged to pay off Jean Ritchie, the Appalachian 'Mother of Folk', when her arrangement of the ancient 'Nottamun Town' turned up as the basis for Dylan's 1962–3 'Masters of War'. His 'Don't Think Twice, It's All Right' was born, indisputably, from a version of the traditional 'Who's Gonna Buy You Ribbons (When I'm Gone)' developed and placed under copyright by his friend Paul Clayton. For what it's worth, the publishing companies settled that argument out of court. As Dylan had admitted in a 1962 radio interview and would cheerfully admit again in *Chronicles*, he had also lifted the tune for 'The Ballad of Emmett Till' from Len Chandler, another Village colleague. Amidst all this it hardly required perfect pitch to hear that 'A Hard Rain's a-Gonna Fall' was built around the Child ballad 'Lord Randall', or that 'It Ain't Me, Babe' owed its existence to an early-twentieth-century recasting by John Jacob Niles of the old work song 'Go 'Way From My Window'. The scruffy prodigy's borrowings from 'obscure' black blues players were meanwhile extensive and wholly unselfconscious. It was what everyone did, after all. Copyright arguments aside, the folk scene amounted to a nightly test case for the proposition that originality of authorship, pure, protean and sufficient unto itself, was a myth.

The musicologist Charles Seeger, father to Pete, had devised the phrase 'folk process', though the idea was far from original, aptly enough.[3] The International Folk Music Council had already attempted to codify the whole business in 1954 with a few lofty-sounding rules involving 'oral transmission', reinterpretation and 'transformation'. It didn't solve every problem. Interviewed in 2001, Pete Seeger would remember his father describing the folk process as akin to cooks adapting recipes, or to legal systems devising new laws for each new generation.[4] The analogies were neat, but they failed to explain, for one conspicuous example, how Pete Seeger himself could wind up as one of the copyright holders to the civil-rights anthem 'We Shall Overcome'.

The refrain originated in an early gospel song, 'I'll Overcome Someday', written by the Rev. Dr Charles Tindley and published in 1901. By 1947, that piece formed the basis for a song published in its turn as 'We Will Overcome'. Taken up by the Highlander Folk School in Tennessee, it was heard by Pete Seeger and others who then joined in the process of (slight) adaptation. Four individuals or their heirs today hold the copyright, along with various publishers, for this product of the 'folk process'.

In a 1993 book, Seeger explained that he had taken out the copyright as a purely defensive measure to protect the song from music-business predators.[5] It is worth noting, too, that all royalties from 'We Shall Overcome' have gone to a fund that bestows grants to aid the cultural efforts of African Americans in the Southern states. The simple fact remains, nevertheless, that only the rectitude of Seeger and his friends prevented the most famous of all folk songs from ending up as a spectacular example of how ridiculously easy it was in the 1950s and 1960s to abuse the fabled 'process'. Dylan's Greenwich Village knew all the arguments. Everyone was a staunch believer in folk's ancient uncorrupted practices until they had a song, or even an arrangement, they could call their own. Claiming to have 'arranged' some old, familiar piece in fact became a favourite device in the copyright game.

In his youth, Dylan was also inhabiting another '60s entirely. In this universe adolescents and students across the western world were reading T.S. Eliot's *The Waste Land* (1922) and discovering that it was perfectly OK – fascinating and revolutionary, in fact – to bulk up one's text with big chunks of imported writing by other hands. The New Criticism, of which Eliot was a household god, was then infesting the English departments of American colleges with the delightful (to critics) notion that an author's intentions, therefore his 'authorship', didn't really count for much. In France, the critic Roland Barthes was working towards an essay, 'The Death of the Author' (1967), in which readers and the 'liberated' text would be judged to matter more than any writer with a byline. Dylan didn't know much about all of this, if he knew anything at all, but it was part of the era's background noise.

If creativity could not happen in isolation, if authorship was therefore a disputable idea, how could a line be drawn? For some, easily enough. Copyright protection was sought for the many songs of Bob Dylan, as standard practice, almost as soon as they were written. On a few occasions even songs to which other writers had prior claims were filed under his name. Since the early '60s all of Dylan's many works – albums, art, films, even acclaimed books – have been protected as a matter of course. Like any artist, he has his rights.

In pop art in the '50s and early '60s collage and photomontage, adapting and juxtaposing 'found' or borrowed images, were fashionable techniques. By 1962, Andy Warhol's Factory was up and running on New York's East 47th Street, mass-producing copies of mass-produced imagery and offering the results, at excellent prices, as artworks. Pop music, the other art with the name, had long been excusing plagiarism and theft as the name of the creative game. While Warhol was challenging international art buyers to question their preconceptions towards authenticity and the role of the artist, fans of the *Billboard* Hot 100 were taking precious little interest in the names of the Tin Pan Alley hacks who wrote or rewrote the hit songs.

Dylan, like his generation, had come to adulthood amidst all of this. In an affluent age the cultural chatter said that anything found, borrowed, remade or copied was justifiable as art simply because of the choices made in the act of appropriation. Authorship was an arguable matter. But for one writer who would later assert his right 'to be identified as author', the issue was a little more complicated. From the start, Dylan had been uncertain, deeply so, about his identity. He couldn't get a fix on himself. As he mentioned in a 1991 interview: 'Yes, well, what can you know about anybody?'[6] In *Chronicles* he would write of a missing person, a person missing 'inside', who had to be found. Pronouns confuse the matter, but he needed to find 'him'. So who really did the making and who did the taking? When the time came to unmask the author, he told some Bob Dylan stories instead.

*

In a book of five long chapters, Dylan composed three concerning the near-year straddling his blizzard-blown arrival in New York in January of 1961 and the making of his first album in late November. He conjured up a long-gone city, its streets, rooms, speech, textures and preoccupations, with a rare sensitivity to the peculiarities of memory, how it looms unexpectedly and fades unpredictably across the span of the decades. Patently, Dylan mythologised his younger self, just as the critics alleged, but that seemed apt. Who looks back with perfectly clear eyes? For his part, the artist was attempting to look backwards through the deep murk of fame and myth at a long-lost youth with a fragile sense of himself who had laboured under the self-imposed burden of an invented name and a heap of juvenile fabrications. Was clarity even possible?

Dylan's storytelling, the *faux* reminiscences, wry asides and sly humour that provoked all the flattering comparisons with Twain, made an insistent point. In a proper celebrity memoir he would, for starters, have got his chronology straight and paid due attention to the usual arc of fame. Then he would have hosed his pages with superstar secrets and notable names. His publishers must have prayed nightly for such a manuscript. Instead, the author ignored all the stuff of legend, all the controversies and all the moments, famous and infamous, that had been written about so often by others. He gave his readers tales of old New York – almost a distinct American genre, as it happens – and episodes involving two of his less-celebrated later albums. This, Dylan seemed to be saying, is what I remember when I choose to remember. This is *how* I remember. For encounters with God or 'going electric' (and all that) readers would have to look elsewhere. Or wait.

Late in the autumn of 2012, he would admit that volumes two and three of *Chronicles* were gestating. If nothing else, there was a contract to be honoured. His readers might yet be allowed to share his thoughts on his moments of high fame, or they might receive nothing much from the horse's mouth. His original scheme, it appears, had been to anchor his memories to particular albums, but that had already gone awry. The matching idea had been somehow to inhabit the past and the future simultaneously. But with *Volume One* Dylan had lost one thread and found another, surprising himself in the process. His own youth and his early days in New York had become 'extremely interesting. When you start doing that, it amazes you what you uncover without even trying.'[7]

It was not a promise to dish the dirt. *Chronicles*, properly understood, was of a piece with the music Dylan had been making since *Time Out of Mind*. The past was in the present; all time was present. Plainly, he found it impossible to say what those future non-memoirs might contain. In any case, as he informed his *Rolling Stone* interviewer in September 2012, his memory wasn't great. He remembered what he *wanted* to remember. 'And what I want to forget, I forget.'[8] His book writing, Dylan said, followed links in a chain. Allen Ginsberg, dying in the year *Time Out of Mind* was released, had once invoked chains of flashing images to describe the singer's art. In his songs, as in his book, Dylan followed an associative logic that was not always readily apparent to the listener or the reader. Imagery provided the syntax of the songs. In prose, or so it seemed, he allowed wandering memory to make the connections. A standard autobiography would have followed a linear chronological path. *Chronicles* was informed by the knowledge that memory simply doesn't work that way, that to pretend otherwise is a kind of fraud. Then again, a writer who remembers only what he wants to remember, who throws aside the restraint of a chronological structure, can write whatever he likes and call it the truth.

The pair of least-expected chapters devoted to two of Dylan's less-famous albums, *New Morning* and *Oh Mercy*, were disconcerting when set amidst all the engaging reminiscences of Greenwich Village in the early days. Why Dylan would be hung up 30-odd years after the fact on what had passed between him and the aged patrician poet Archibald MacLeish as they attempted to add songs to a play was mystifying. It had been, by any measure, one of the least significant episodes in the singer's career. His account of his dealings with the producer Daniel Lanois during the making of the *Oh Mercy* album, aside from raising certain questions of 'veracity', also seemed near-redundant. For the reader, the chapters became a puzzle in their own right. Perhaps that was the idea. But why were these events on Dylan's mind, of all the events in his life, early in the twenty-first century?

If you needed to know, the *New Morning* section would tell you that he had never cared to be regarded as any generation's spokesman, that demented fans had ruined his Woodstock idyll, that the conferring of an honorary doctorate by Princeton in 1970 had left him angry enough to want to rend flesh. Set beside riveting accounts of his creative origins, the story of his first encounter with the music of Robert Johnson above all, tales of hard labour in a New Orleans studio, or of strange days under siege in his own home, were almost pointedly beside the point. The episodic anecdotes were beautifully told, but why tell these of all stories?

It was impossible to say how or if the episodes connected with one another, far less with Dylan's memories of his Greenwich Village youth. In his *New York Times* Sunday review Tom Carson wrote that 'the major surprise of *Chronicles* is its literary cunning, which is partly structural'. The reviewer argued that vignettes of Dylan 'beleaguered' in 1970 and as the 'weary lion' of 1987 were deliberate counterpoints to the tales, placed before and after, of New York and the Village in 1961. This was a generous interpretation. What the reviewer called this 'narrative ploy, this convolution' might have echoed movie flashbacks – Carson nominated a famous sequence in *The Godfather Part II* – but in film that technique is intended to make plain the connections between past and present. If that was what Dylan was doing, he didn't bother to make any of his aims clear.

Most reviewers didn't mind in the slightest. Given only *Tarantula* to go on, they were taken aback by the fact that the singer had turned out to be such an accomplished prose stylist. Fake or not, the authorial voice was a real achievement, a convincing blend of cunning, wit and conversational tone. In the *New York Times*, Janet Maslin welcomed a book of 'amazing urgency'.[9] Nevertheless, a journalist who had been observing Dylan for as long as most people in her trade was not deceived by the author's guile.

> Deliberately, no doubt, *Chronicles: Volume One* beggars the efforts of biographers to reconstruct Mr Dylan's inner workings. With no great interest in the supposed landmark events of his life or even in the specific chronology or geography of his movements, he prefers to mine a different kind of memory. And he once again makes his homage to Woody Guthrie – another figure not known for autobiographical exactitude – with a writing style both straight-shooting and deeply fanciful.

The tale told by the 'Holden Caulfield of Hibbing, Minn', as Maslin styled the author, was 'lucid without being linear, swirling through time without losing its strong storytelling thread. And it begins and ends at more or less the same place: the calm before the storm . . .' Approbation for the book was all but universal. In *The Guardian*, Mike

Marqusee, having written extensively on the subject's 1960s career, said that 'with this rich, intermittently preposterous, often tender work, Bob Dylan has delivered more than many of us dared hope for'. In the *Sunday Times*, Bryan Appleyard said, straightforwardly, that *Chronicles: Volume One* was 'an extremely good book indeed, actually a great one'. In the *Boston Globe*, Carlo Wolff argued that the work 'affirms Dylan's idiosyncrasies and his mastery of the vernacular. As his best songs also show, he's a great reporter with a talent for vivid detail.' *Chronicles*, Wolff added, is 'packed with ruminations on musical theory, sharp and humorous commentary, flashes of poetry – and facts filtered and colored to flummox, entertain, and illuminate'.[10] It was enough to make any author weep tears of gratitude.

*

Almost two years after the release of *'Love and Theft'* in September 2001, a curious tale had appeared on the front page of the *Wall Street Journal*.[11] It involved a 62-year-old Japanese writer and doctor and the then 62-year-old Dylan. Junichi Saga had only a slight knowledge of the American singer – 'I'm not familiar with these things,' he told the paper – but the American, it was suggested, had clearly come to know something about Saga's oral history of a Japanese mobster and former patient, a book translated into English in 1991 as *Confessions of a Yakuza: A Life in Japan's Underworld*. In fact, as the article proceeded to explain, there were some striking similarities between passages in certain songs on Dylan's *'Love and Theft'* album and the dying gangster's story of the loves and life of a thief. The resemblances did not seem accidental.

It had been noticed back in 2001 that the artist had set the title of his album in quotation marks. The gesture had been treated as an acknowledgement, playful or rueful, that Dylan had borrowed a phrase from Eric Lott's 1993 book *Love and Theft: Blackface Minstrelsy and the American Working Class*. That study had attempted to untangle the complicated, century-long story of white responses to black culture, as represented by the white 'minstrels' who had once performed in preposterous 'negro' costumes with banjos on their knees and burnt cork on their faces. It was incidental to Lott's main point, but the salience to Dylan and all the other young white men who took up – or stole away – the blues in the 1950s and 1960s was obvious. As the author had mentioned in passing, 'Every time you hear an expansive white man drop into his version of black English, you are in the presence of blackface's unconscious return.'[12]

If it did not amount to an acceptance of the charge, Dylan's use of Lott's title – itself a theft, obviously enough – had been a tacit admission that the accusation had force. He didn't feel guilty about it, necessarily – he venerated the blues and blues musicians – but Dylan had raided black culture at every step of his career. Who had not? Like a lot of his contemporaries, from Elvis to the Rolling Stones, oblivious to every contradiction, he had seen no problem with that. In 2003, however, the *Wall Street Journal* seemed to be saying that contemporary issues of love and theft might be at once more straightforward and more troubling than the artist's fans realised.

The *Journal's* headline had gone to the point: 'Did Bob Dylan lift lines from Dr Saga?' If he had not, similarities between *'Love and Theft'* songs and odd passages in the Japanese book (as translated) were near-impossible to explain. 'My old man would sit there like a feudal lord . . .' ran the book. 'My old man, he's like some feudal lord / Got more lives than a cat,' went the song entitled 'Floater (Too Much to Ask)'. 'Actually, though, I'm not as cool or forgiving as I might have sounded,' a sentence in *Confessions of a Yakuza* began. 'I'm not quite as cool or forgiving as I sound / I've seen enough heartaches and strife,' Dylan sang in 'Floater'.

There were other examples in the *Journal* story, some rather less convincing as examples of alleged plagiarism. The book: 'If it bothers you so much,' she'd say, 'why don't you just shove off?' 'Floater': 'Juliet said back to Romeo, "Why don't you just shove off / If it bothers you so much?"' *Confessions*: '"Break the roof in!" he yelled. [He] splashed kerosene over the floor and led a fuse from it outside.' Dylan's 'Summer Days': 'Yes, I'm leaving in the morning just as soon as the dark clouds lift / Gonna break the roof in – set fire to the place as a parting gift.'

In those cases, the worst that might have been said of the singer was that, consciously or unconsciously, he had adapted a few images and common phrases. One or two of the examples marshalled against him could even have been dismissed entirely as inevitable coincidences in the wide, busy world of literature. What's a writer to do if he wants to describe trees without echoing someone else's description of trees? Saga: 'They were big, those trees – a good four feet across the trunk . . .' Dylan's 'Floater': 'There's a new grove of trees on the outskirts of town / The old one is long gone / Timber two-foot-six across / Burns with the bark still on.'

The affair had come to light when Chris Johnson, a young American teaching English in Japan – but originally from Dylan's home state of

Minnesota – had chanced upon a copy of *Confessions of a Yakuza* in a bookshop in the city of Fukuoka. The Japanese edition of Saga's work was by then out of print; the English version had sold a reported 25,000 copies. It was the 'feudal lord' line on the first page of the gangster's narrative that had caught Johnson's eye. A Dylan fan, he had begun to search, so the *Journal* reported, for further examples of imitation, adaptation or theft. What struck him was that Dylan had not taken 'the most poetic or most powerful lines from the book'. In fact, the borrowings appeared to the young teacher to have been almost random. Interviewed by the newspaper, Johnson had nevertheless offered up what must have sounded to the newsroom like the perfect disingenuous quote. 'I kind of wondered if he had done a lot of that before on other albums,' he had said. 'But if he'd been doing this all along, somebody would have caught him a long time ago.'

What had Dylan been doing exactly? 'Floater' is 16 verses and 64 lines long. It is set in the rural American South. It has nothing whatever to do, in tone or theme, with Japan or Japanese gangsters. A quotation from F. Scott Fitzgerald's *The Great Gatsby* had already been spotted lurking within *'Love and Theft'*. Was that also an act of plagiarism, or precisely the sort of homage you would expect from one American writer to another, an invocation of shared experience, a deepening of the national literature? A piece of verse by the little-read Civil War poet Henry Timrod, the catchily titled 'Vision of Poesy', would also be linked with Dylan's *'Love and Theft'* track 'Tweedle Dee & Tweedle Dum'. In the '60s, the singer would have been lauded to the skies for the breadth of his literary knowledge. Journalists and academics would never have tired of quizzing the cultured pop poet about his book habits. By the twenty-first century, thanks to plagiarism scandals of its own involving thefts more flagrant than anything of which Dylan stood accused, thanks to the internet's corrosive effects on copyright, thanks to corporate media's increasingly hysterical efforts to defend intellectual property against any unlicensed use, fair or otherwise, all unacknowledged quotation was being treated by the press as theft. It became, as it remains, an obsession for America's cultural arbiters. Yet this was in the era, ironically enough, of sampling, of the mash-up, the era born of the pop-art collage and Warhol's Factory. Eliot's *The Waste Land* would have been put to the sword – 'Did Nobel Prize winner lift lines from St Augustine?' – in such a fervid climate of opinion. Dylan stood no chance. He had not heard the last of it, either.

In the writing of 'Floater' stray pieces of Saga's text had helped him to achieve rhymes. That detail had been overlooked: the good doctor had not attempted poetry. There is not much doubt, equally, that Dylan helped himself to a few words, but their true worth and weight, their real significance, is arguable, at best. One verse of his song, nothing special by his standards, goes:

My grandfather was a duck trapper
He could do it with just dragnets and ropes
My grandmother could sew new dresses out of old cloth
I don't know if they had any dreams or hopes

You could call it American pastoral, an invocation of rural poverty in former times, a scene from a folk tale. You would have to call it culturally specific: tattooed Japanese gangsters are nowhere heard or seen. The *Wall Street Journal* made no mention in its front-page story of what 'Floater' might be about, or of Dylan's possible artistic purpose in the song. An admirer might regret that he was careless enough to throw in a few images and phrases he had picked up, but the charge of plagiarism only sticks if it involves intentionally passing off substantial parts of another's work as your own. Dylan seems to have come close – his *Lyrics 1962–2001* (2004) makes no mention of sources – but not close enough for conclusions to be drawn. You have to ignore the songs entirely to call the offence heinous.

Consider this comparative exercise. *Confessions*: 'My mother . . . was the daughter of a wealthy farmer . . . [She] died when I was 11 . . . I heard that my father was a travelling salesman who called at the house regularly, but I never met him. [My uncle] was a nice man, I won't forget him . . . After my mother died, I decided it'd be best to go and try my luck there.' The frequent ellipses are interesting, let's say. Now here's Dylan's 'Po' Boy':

My mother was a daughter of a wealthy farmer
My father was a travelling salesman, I never met him
When my mother died, my uncle took me in – he ran a funeral parlor
He did a lot of nice things for me and I won't forget him.

Mother dies, travelling salesman, nice man, 'did a lot of nice things': that's the sum total of the evidence. Dylan had taken cues from stray passages in a book he had picked up and used them to make a distinct piece of art, yet he stood accused not of creativity but of plagiarism. Another very funny passage in 'Po' Boy', especially when delivered in Dylan's deadpan voice, goes as follows:

> Othello told Desdemona, 'I'm cold, cover me with a blanket
> By the way, what happened to that poison wine?'
> She says, 'I gave it to you, you drank it'
> Poor boy, layin' 'em straight –
> Pickin' up the cherries fallin' off the plate

Plagiarism from Shakespeare, then? That bard knew the game of beg, borrow or steal better than anyone. Given that Dylan's po' boy has a shaky knowledge of the Moor's tragedy, or a sly appreciation of the comic potential of acting dumb, it would be silly to say that something underhand is going on in this part of the song. It would be no sillier, however, than a suggestion of theft that paid not the slightest attention to what the artist had done with the allegedly stolen goods. There are several clear examples of Dylan appropriating Saga's translated words. Amid this small fuss, however, there were very few instances of the artist's accusers mentioning what Dylan was attempting in the finished songs of 'Love and Theft'. The bigger game, evident since Newsweek had printed the wholly false 'rumor' that he was not the author of 'Blowin' in the Wind', was to prove that Dylan was, in some way, a fraud.[13] Saga's 'feudal lord' line, the one that would be quoted repeatedly as some sort of clincher, will serve as a final example. In isolation, the use of the phrase seems lethal to any defence of Dylan. But what happens to it in the context of the song?

> My old man, he's like some feudal lord
> Got more lives than a cat
> Never seen him quarrel with my mother even once
> Things come alive or they fall flat

An old-fashioned husband behaving like a feudal lord: there's a novel idea. If this was the best that could be managed to catch out Dylan, it was trivial stuff. Interestingly, those who seized on a handful of words also failed to mention their original use in Saga's text. The words appear on the first page of a chapter entitled 'Oyoshi' and have nothing important to do with the verse in Dylan's song.

My old man would sit there like a feudal lord, with his back to some fancy flower arrangement. The staff would be sitting in front of him, red-faced from bowing down till their foreheads touched the floor.[14]

In his September 2012 interview with *Rolling Stone*, Dylan would explain and complain. 'In folk and jazz, quotation is a rich and enriching tradition,' he would say (while failing to deny the accusation of borrowing). 'It's true for everybody but me. There are different rules for me.' The *Confessions of a Yakuza* controversy would blow over soon enough – Dr Saga enjoyed *'Love and Theft'* and had no intention of suing – but Dylan was not yet off the hook.

*

When the *Modern Times* album appeared at the end of August 2006, any lingering doubts that he had restored his reputation and his career would be eradicated. Album number 32 would become his first since *Desire* 30 years before to top the charts and his first in any era to go directly to the summit of *Billboard*'s rankings. A fortnight later, a story would appear in the *New York Times*.[15]

'Perhaps you've never heard of Henry Timrod, sometimes known as the poet laureate of the Confederacy,' the article began. 'But maybe you've heard his words, if you're one of the 320,000 people so far who have bought Bob Dylan's latest album, *Modern Times*.' Under the headline 'Who's This Guy Dylan Who's Borrowing Lines From Henry Timrod?', the reporter, Motoko Rich, would then describe what seemed to be copious borrowing by Dylan from the works of a poet of whom, it was possible to guarantee, very few Americans had heard.

Walter Brian Cisco, a biographer of Timrod, would be brought in to pronounce that beyond doubt 'there has been some borrowing going on'. Verses would be contrasted and compared; a brief account of Timrod's life would be given. Born in 1828; private tutor on plantations before the Civil War; medically discharged by the Confederate Army because of tuberculosis; too frail to last as a war correspondent; editor of a South Carolina newspaper; occasional poet who took as his themes the war between the states and its effect on the South; dead at 39. Timrod managed only a single volume of posthumously published verse. The *New York Times* article would mention his 'Ode Sung on the Occasion of Decorating the Graves of the Confederate Dead at Magnolia Cemetery, Charleston, South Carolina 1866' on the apparent grounds that it was one of only a couple of anthologised Timrod poems liable to be even half-familiar to a non-scholarly American reader. No cribbing by Dylan from those couple of works would be detected, however. Nevertheless, the contrast-and-compare exercise between his *Modern Times* songs and the versifier's works would leave little doubt: Dylan had built parts of some songs with recycled masonry. For the benefit of those who knew no better, meanwhile, the *Times* would further explain that because Timrod was long dead and his works out of copyright, there was 'no legal claim that could be made against Mr Dylan'.

In an undistinguished poem entitled 'A Rhapsody of a Southern Winter Night', Timrod had written:

These happy stars, and yonder setting moon,
Have seen me speed, unreckoned and untasked,
A round of precious hours.
Oh! here, where in that summer noon I basked,
And strove, with logic frailer than the flowers,
To justify a life of sensuous rest,
A question dear as home or heaven was asked,
And without language answered. I was blest!

In his 'Vision of Poesy', meanwhile, the luckless Confederate bard had offered this:

. . . and at times
A strange far look would come into his eyes,
As if he saw a vision in the skies.

Among other examples of borrowings from Timrod, part of Dylan's *Modern Times* song 'When the Deal Goes Down' runs as follows:

The moon gives light and it shines by night
Well, I scarcely feel the glow
We learn to live and then we forgive
O'er the road we're bound to go
More frailer than the flowers, these precious hours
That keep us so tightly bound
You come to my eyes like a vision from the skies
And I'll be with you when the deal goes down

426

The matter had come to the attention of the *Times* thanks to Scott Warmuth, described as 'a disc jockey in Albuquerque and a former music director for WUSB, a public radio station in Stony Brook, on Long Island'. In the months and years to come, this keen student of the artist and his methods was to cause no small commotion among Dylan's most dedicated fans and critics. In September 2006, after what the *Times* called his 'judicious Google searches', Warmuth agreed he had not been surprised by the fact that the singer had 'leaned on a strong influence'. Quoted directly, Warmuth said: 'I think that's the way Bob Dylan has always written songs. It's part of the folk process, even if you look from his first album until now.' He had found ten echoes of Timrod in *Modern Times*, but did not question Dylan's originality. In fact, Warmuth made an excellent point: 'You could give the collected works of Henry Timrod to a bunch of people, but none of them are going to come up with Bob Dylan songs.'

Three days later, the *Times* invited the singer Suzanne Vega to cast an eye over the case. She argued, first, that it is 'modern to use history as a kind of closet in which we can rummage around, pull influences from different eras, and make them into collages or pastiches. People are doing this with music all the time.' Vega wondered, however, whether it was truly part of the 'folk process' to lift 'a few specific metaphors or phrases whole from someone else's work'. That was a proposition she couldn't accept. Graciously, she doubted that Dylan had raided Timrod on purpose, speculating that the artist might be in possession of an eidetic memory – he doesn't think so – or that he had immersed himself so completely in Civil War literature – a better bet – as to render the absorption of Timrod's work unconscious. In any event, by one definition of the offence, Dylan seemed to be guilty as charged. One essential question remained to be answered. What of it?

In an article for the Poetry Foundation's website published on 6 October, the poet Robert Polito, director of creative writing at the New School in New York, would respond almost despairingly to the 'controversy'.[16] In his view, to reduce the connection between Dylan and Timrod to a 'story of possible plagiarism is to confuse, well, art with a term paper'. After mentioning the advent of sampling in pop music, Polito pointed out that *Modern Times* also 'taps into the Bible' while revisiting the music and words of 'Robert Johnson, Memphis Minnie, Kokomo Arnold, Muddy Waters, Sonny Boy Williamson, Blind Lemon Jefferson, the Stanley Brothers, Merle Haggard, Hoagy Carmichael, Cole Porter, Jerome Kern, and standards popularised by

Jeanette MacDonald, Bing Crosby, and Frank Sinatra . . .' Polito also noted, as dedicated fans had noted, the shadows laid across the album by old folk songs such as 'Wild Mountain Thyme', 'Frankie and Albert' and 'Gentle Nettie Moore'.

The writer intended to vindicate Dylan as an artist who was 'rearranging the entire American musical and literary landscape of the past 150 years' with *Time Out of Mind*, *'Love and Theft'* and *Modern Times*. Reading Polito's lists of the great and gone, however, a reader was liable to wonder if the case for the defence might not hang the accused in the end. The abundance of 'sources' was daunting. Here they were, like a celestial greatest-hits package or the perfected version of what Dylan had attempted back in 1970 with his *Self Portrait*: 'Crosby, Sinatra, Charlie Patton, Woody Guthrie, Blind Willie McTell, Doc Boggs, Leroy Carr, Bessie Smith, Billie Holiday, Elvis Presley, Blind Willie Johnson, Big Joe Turner, Wilbert Harrison, the Carter Family, and Gene Austin alongside anonymous traditional tunes and nursery rhymes.'

Polito wasn't done. He had noticed a range of reference in the so-called Dylan trilogy that had already been spotted, as a collective effort, by other avid fans, but the writer called Dylan's use of 'fragments' a revelation, not plagiarism. So here were more famous names and famous titles: 'W.C. Fields, the Marx Brothers, assorted film noirs, *As You Like It*, *Othello*, Robert Burns, Lewis Carroll, Timrod, Ovid, T.D. Rice's blackface *Otello*, *Huckleberry Finn*, *The Aeneid*, *The Great Gatsby*, the Japanese true crime paperback *Confessions of a Yakuza* by Junichi Saga, Confederate general Nathan Bedford Forrest, and [Flannery O'Connor's novel] *Wise Blood*.'

Polito also talked about 'folk process', but accepted that the term was inadequate as a description of Dylan's methods. T.S. Eliot and Ezra Pound were therefore recruited once again to the artist's cause. The three albums were thereby defined as 'Modernist collages', as 'verbal echo chambers of harmonizing and clashing reverberations'. Within this elaborate verbal machinery, in Polito's account, Timrod's presence 'works as a citation we're ultimately intended to notice, though no song depends on that notice'. For Polito, none of this 'conjuring' counted as plagiarism.

Nevertheless, one remark made by the writer almost as a joke would intrigue Scott Warmuth. Of *'Love and Theft'*, Polito wrote that he 'wouldn't be surprised if someday we learn that every bit of speech on the album – no matter how intimate or Dylanesque – can be tracked back to another song, poem, movie, or novel'. Warmuth returned to his listening, his reading and his Google searches.

For his part, Dylan would in due course tell *Rolling Stone*'s Mikal Gilmore that when it came to the appropriation of nineteenth-century texts, only 'wussies and pussies complain about that stuff'. The artist would challenge the journalist, asking, 'as far as Henry Timrod is concerned, have you even heard of him?'

> Who's been reading him lately? And who's pushed him to the forefront? Who's been making you read him? And ask his descendants what they think of the hoopla. And if you think it's so easy to quote him and it can help your work, do it yourself and see how far you can get . . . It's an old thing – it's part of the tradition.

After conflating those who laid plagiarism charges with those who had called him Judas for taking up the electric guitar in the mid-'60s – 'All those evil motherfuckers can rot in hell' – Dylan stuck to a bold and simple claim. The most interesting thing about his defence, the most important thing, was the simple fact that in making use of Timrod or of anyone else he had known exactly what he was doing. Dylan was not taking refuge in the excuse that the habit was remotely 'unconscious'.

> I'm working within my art form. It's that simple. I work within the rules and limitations of it. There are authoritarian figures that can explain that kind of art form better to you than I can. It's called songwriting. It has to do with melody and rhythm, and then after that, anything goes. You make everything yours. We all do it.[17]

*

Cast your mind back to the young man who set out late in the 1950s to turn himself into Bob Dylan, folk singer. The word sponge, so often used, is probably inadequate, as is the word dedication. His intensity in the pursuit of musical knowledge more closely resembled an obsession. One of his college contemporaries would tell Robert Shelton in 1966, for example, that Dylan was 'the purest of the pure' where folk was concerned, that while living a version of the bohemian life in the Dinkytown area of Minneapolis he 'had to get the oldest record and, if possible, the Library of Congress record, or go find the original people who knew the original song'.[18] It sounds less like fascination than a kind of need, less like a desire for knowledge a young singer could use than a desire to know everything there was to know. Dylan was greedy: he wanted it all.

He was in love with folk and blues music, of that there is no doubt. It has remained the one enduring, unquestioned affection in his existence for better than half a century. It is hard, nevertheless, to escape the feeling that Dylan's desperate thirst for knowledge arose from an equally desperate need to complete himself, to give substance to the identity he was attempting to inhabit. Either there was more to it than just an instinct for art, or the instinct was central to the evolution of the figure called Bob Dylan. Even the fantastical tales the kid would tell about himself in his earliest days in Greenwich Village required documentation, background knowledge, as complete as he could make it or fake it. The stories of the musicians he would claim to have met and played with out on the road – to complicate matters, a few of the stories were true – needed a deep understanding of what they played and how they played. Above all, for Robert Zimmerman himself to believe in Bob Dylan called for the kind of knowledge only that unlikely character could possibly possess. Study, obsessive study, was a way of giving authority to the identity the young Dylan was trying to mould around himself.

But why would the ageing man wall himself behind quotations, allusions, borrowed texts and lifted phrases? It might be, for he has said so often enough, that he finds writing harder now than he found it when he was creating automatically and unselfconsciously in the '60s. But as we have seen with a song like 'Floater', a big pile of verses only depends to a very limited degree – as best we know – on what has been borrowed. You can understand why he might want to add texture for poetic effect by drawing on a variety of sources. As Polito argued, it is a legitimate stratagem. As Vega described matters, it is also commonplace and acceptable within limits. It troubles a lot of Dylan's fans, however. They wonder if he lards his song with the work of others as an artistic choice or because, these days, he lacks the resources to manage a Bob Dylan song unaided. His defence of the habit when talking to Mikal Gilmore – 'You make everything yours' – has an echo throughout literature. There remains the distinct possibility, nevertheless, that Dylan is still completing himself with the gleanings of his relentless studies, that it is a way of maintaining the edifice of his identity and the bigger, ever-present cultural edifice that bears his name.

Perhaps Polito had a point. Perhaps Dylan expects his borrowings to be 'noticed'. Perhaps, too, he expects the people who buy his albums either to understand the folk process and the tactics of Modernism, or – and why not? – to fail to give a damn about a song's origins if it's a song worth hearing. Dylan is right about one thing. If simple plagiarism was the only issue, anyone could pull a book from the shelf and manufacture a Bob Dylan song. Whether *Chronicles* can be justified in the same manner is another question.

*

In the summer 2010 issue of the *New Haven Review* there appeared an essay by Scott Warmuth. You must presume the title was his. It amounted to the boldest headline yet where Dylan and his multiplicity of sources were concerned. 'Bob Charlatan,' it read, 'Deconstructing Dylan's *Chronicles: Volume One.*' Clearly, Warmuth had moved on from defending the artist as an exemplar of 'folk process'. The notion that a bunch of people armed with *The Poems of Henry Timrod* couldn't come up with Bob Dylan songs no matter how hard they tried was no longer a relevant detail, it seemed, where the artist's book was concerned. Charlatan is a word with no positive connotations.

On his blog, Goon Talk, much as in the September 2006 *New York Times* piece, Warmuth describes himself as a writer, musician and disc jockey.[19] He scarcely does himself justice. Along with another blogger, Edward Cook, Warmuth has subjected a major artist to the kind of extensive crowd-sourced textual analysis that attracts attention. The attention, in turn, raises some serious questions where Bob Dylan's art is concerned. After all, another word for charlatan is fraud.

Warmuth had made an appearance on the Dylan fan website Expecting Rain at the end of July 2009 with a series of observations on *Chronicles: Volume One*. It is fair to say they caused a good deal of interest among the faithful and a good deal of consternation. Warmuth observed, first, that a March 1961 issue of *Time* magazine had obviously been used to plug a great many gaps in Dylan's memory while providing the basis for certain *Chronicles* anecdotes and the phrases employed in the telling. The blogger went on to explain that Ed Cook had been hard at work unearthing the debts owed by Dylan to a well-known book called *Really the Blues*, an autobiography written by the horn player Mezz Mezzrow with the help of the novelist Bernard Wolfe and published in 1946. Warmuth had added to the list of borrowings. Then the two men had uncovered more than a few traces of Sax Rohmer's Fu-Manchu stories, and of a book called *Raised on Radio*, and of a volume entitled *Daily Life in Civil War America*, and of numerous lines from Jack London. Walt Whitman, Herman Melville and Timrod would be added to the list. Links with Marcel Proust and several Robert Louis Stevenson stories would be made. Most of the examples were better than plausible. As a certain kind of detective used to say, the game was afoot.

In his *New Haven Review* article, Warmuth came to the point quickly. Between them, he and Cook – entirely appropriately, a co-author of *The Dead Sea Scrolls: A New Translation* – had discovered in *Chronicles*[20]

> an author, Bob Dylan, who has embraced camouflage to an astounding degree, in a book that is meticulously fabricated, with one surface concealing another, from cover to cover.
>
> Dozens upon dozens of quotations and anecdotes have been incorporated from other sources. Dylan has hidden many puzzles, jokes, secret messages, secondary meanings, and bizarre subtexts in his book.

Warmuth called it 'autobiographical alchemy'. To penetrate the mystery, he had 'studied cryptography and puzzle-solving', he had 'explored techniques used by crossword-puzzle solving champions' and then 'keyed in on how code-breakers look for patterns and anomalies, try to find a way in, and then build on their successes'. Warmuth had studied 'sideshow talkers and pitchmen', books on poker strategy and cheating at cards. He had looked at the interlinked worlds of magic, carnivals, medicine shows, minstrel troupes and con men. Whether he had enjoyed listening to Bob Dylan albums while all this was going on was not mentioned. To begin with, as Warmuth admits in the essay, he did not know how any of his researches could be applied to the study of the artist's work. *Chronicles* was, it appears, a gift.

Warmuth and Cook would come up with a dozen pages covering the Jack London connection alone. In his essay, the disc jockey would attempt to deal with the issue of whether plagiarism matters by conceding that London's own wholesale thefts had done his reputation no lasting harm. Once the idea of codes and hidden meanings was established, at least to the writer's satisfaction, the next question had become obvious: what was being concealed? Warmuth would end his article by concluding that an 'initially invisible second book' existed within the covers of *Chronicles* amid the 'amalgam' of voices that constituted Dylan's singular American voice. On the way to reaching that judgement, the essay observes:

In reading *Chronicles: Volume One*, it may be worth ignoring the perception of motion and looking instead at individual frames as puzzles in their own right. While creating what is read as a narrative, Dylan, with all his samplings and borrowings, may have been seeking to freeze-frame his image and suggest shadows of his possible self.

Warmuth's work continues. On the Goon Talk blog and elsewhere he continues to add to the stock of alleged Dylan borrowings. Others have joined him in the hunt. The search engine hits just keep on coming and the research effort is impressive, the results undeniably intriguing. Warmuth believes they add up to a kind of 'treasure map'. You could as easily call them a schematic diagram of the inner Dylan. Sometimes the books cited are obvious enough, sometimes oddly discrepant. So here stand the shades of Juvenal, Hemingway, Ovid, Conrad, Baudelaire, Orwell, H.G. Wells, Homer, Carl Sandburg, Henry Miller, Willa Cather, Strindberg, Pynchon, Tennessee Williams and others besides. Here are Civil War histories, here an encyclopedia of desks. Here, as though to show that Dylan knows his pre-Beat stuff, is Kenneth Patchen's *The Journal of Albion Moonlight* (1941).[21] One incidental service performed by Warmuth and Cook might be to have brought to a halt finally the game of speculative allusion hunting where Dylan is concerned. What point remains when a bibliography has been supplied? At the time of writing, Warmuth and like-minded souls are already hard at work unpicking *Tempest*, the artist's 2012 album. On 12 August of that year, the blogger wrote:

Dylan's *Chronicles: Volume One* is a vast palimpsest, with the words of many other writers coming through the text, hundreds and hundreds of times. When you are aware of what the original source material is you find that the subtext often subverts the surface text or adds another meaning to it that you could not be aware of initially.

If that is what the artist is doing, another small question remains to be answered: why he is doing it? Not, surely, for all the grief he has received. In April 2010, Joni Mitchell, veteran of the Rolling Thunder Revue, set Dylan watchers abuzz across the internet by telling an interviewer, 'Bob is not authentic at all. He's a plagiarist, and his name and voice are fake. Everything about Bob is a deception.'[22] For the record, Mitchell's given name was not Mitchell, nor did her parents know her as Joni, but she doesn't answer to Roberta Joan Anderson. Still: 'a deception'.

So again you wonder: to what purpose? Just to keep the money coming in? Or because the deceit, if that's what it is, has gone on for so long Dylan has passed the point of no return? So where stand the songs against which no allegations have been laid? Plagiarism and deception, funnily enough, are not always as they seem. If Warmuth is right about *Chronicles* functioning as a palimpsest, you can as well argue that in all of his twenty-first-century creations the artist is simply doing what he has always done. He is turning the invented figure of Bob Dylan into an artwork. If that's the case, and if borrowing is part of the method, why on earth would he list his sources?

In his own blog, Ralph the Sacred River, Edward Cook has tried to deal with the entire issue of plagiarism, sorting through definitions of allusion, 'uncredited use', the borrower's intention or consciousness of the borrowing, passing off – presenting the work as the borrower's own – and the 'presumption of originality'. Cook accepts that the last of these is 'weak' within a folk process that depends, or once depended, on continual reuse and adaptation. He believes, however, that originality is presumed and expected in written work. Dylan is therefore 'arguably guilty of plagiarism' in *Chronicles*. Cook, a fan, believes furthermore that in 'the last ten years or so [Dylan] has compensated for the waning of his creative powers by over-indulging in this borrowing habit, which reaches a high point in his own autobiography'.[23] The conclusion is that he should therefore own up to the habit. You can only wonder what would then remain of the work created, shorn of the illusions that are supposed to be at the heart of the great conjuring trick.

As previously observed, neither Dylan nor his publishers calls *Chronicles* an autobiography. It 'explores critical junctures in his life and career', it is described as 'an intimate and personal recollection of extraordinary times', but it is nowhere identified as autobiographical. An interested reader might be entitled to ask what on earth the book is, in that case, but it remains safe to call it a work of literary art. Dylan tells a good story. He incorporates essential elements of the American experience. He functions as an artist. The point made by Warmuth and Dylan himself about the Timrod borrowings is another statement worth adapting. You could hand the keys to the artist's apparently extensive library to thousands of people and each of them would fail to produce *Chronicles*. That might be the most important fact of all.

*

Chronicles: Volume One will tell you a lot about Dylan. It won't tell you what it appears to tell you. Even the deceits are not what they seem. You don't need to go to the extravagant lengths of Warmuth and Cook – the former would call it 'thoroughness' – to grasp the degree of artifice in the book. Then again, anyone who finds Dylan a slippery memoirist should cast an eye over *Roland Barthes par Roland Barthes* (1975). This so-called postmodern autobiography mocks the idea of the story of a life truly told and offers up instead a seeming jumble of (possibly) connected fragments. French literature has been awash since the 1970s, in any case, with *autofiction*, the fictionalised autobiography, the autobiographical fiction. America has had its parallel 'faction' genre since Truman Capote's *In Cold Blood* (1966) with Tom Wolfe, Norman Mailer and others following along behind. Some people glory in the ensuing complications. They better represent reality, it is argued, than anyone's 'true story'. In that context, Dylan's book is a wholly modern exercise. And surely he knows it.

There is nothing new about seemingly autobiographical writing founded on the belief that all autobiography is a kind of fiction. The joke has been around at least since Laurence Sterne's *Life and Opinions of Tristram Shandy* (1759–67) (a book also misunderstood because of plagiarism charges). There is nothing new, either, about the conviction that all modern celebrity memoirs are hogwash, self-serving, mere inventions of the public-relations industry. Dylan has taken that dismal truth and turned it into something valuable. His peculiar dilemma, after all, is that he has spent half a century confronting people who demand 'the truth' about him when no such truth is available and when, as often as not, they begin from the conviction that he is forever playing games. Warmuth and Cook maintain that *Chronicles: Volume One* is the most elaborate game of all. They fancy that it can be played and won.

It is, of course, a hell of a way just to read and enjoy a book. Some of the arguments over Dylan's borrowings and thefts could leave the impression that there is nothing more to *Chronicles: Volume One* than the writer's unacknowledged debts. But the con artist, if that's what he is, remains an artist. Among others things, the book contains a real sense of America's past – the past from which we learn and borrow – and of the people who lived there, from Walt Whitman to Robert Johnson. It reminds you, if you needed reminding, that the writer is very well read, that books, borrowed or not, inform his art in unusual ways. Above all, *Chronicles* shows you what it is like to see the world through Bob Dylan's eyes.

If a book that turns on the private world of memory means anything, this one gives you the author's sense of himself, or at least his sense of the character whose name is on the cover of the book, the one identified as the real author. Expecting Bob Dylan to write the last word on Bob Dylan is like expecting a child to catch his own shadow.

*

Despite all controversies, *Chronicles* remained a bestseller in the years after its publication. One way or another, that should have been the end of Dylan's difficulties with vigilant fans and the press. In September 2011, however, there came a postscript to all the arguments over use and misuse when an exhibition of 18 of his acrylic paintings opened at the Gagosian Gallery in New York. The affair would give even the staunchest defender of Dylan and postmodernist stratagems pause.

In 1994, he had published a book entitled *Drawn Blank*. It involved a collection of drawings he had made while on tour between 1989 and 1992. Several of the images – portraits, interiors, landscapes, still lifes, nudes, street scenes – were not at all bad. Dylan, it transpired, had developed his art to considerable effect since his lessons with Norman Raeben all those years before. He had an eye for composition, a seeming gift for rapid transcription. He could catch a moment.

In 2006, a woman by the name of Ingrid Mössinger, curator of the Kunstsammlungen Museum in Chemnitz in Germany, had come across the book during a visit to New York. Subsequently she had secured Dylan's agreement for an exhibition and also inspired him to turn the drawings into paintings. So our artist had become an artist. Not only that, he had become, perhaps predictably, a bestselling artist, with his own www.bobdylanart.com at the forefront of the marketing effort. More prestigious exhibitions had followed in galleries around the world. Collections of prints and books had begun to appear annually. They had sold very well indeed. In fact, given a rough calculation of the limited-edition runs and the 'sold out' notices on his art website, Dylan the artist has to date sold perhaps 20,000 prints at £1,500 a time. Everyone should have such a hobby.

The artist's Asia Series was described initially by its promoters as a 'visual journal of his travels in Japan, China, Vietnam, and Korea'. It was composed, supposedly, of 'first-hand depictions of people, street scenes, architecture and landscape'. Within days some of those viewing the works in the Madison Avenue gallery were pointing out that such claims did not so much stretch the truth as twist it into elaborate knots.

Yet in this case, just for a change, things were exactly as they seemed.
Briefly, as many as ten of Dylan's 'first-hand' works had been copied,
and copied slavishly, from photographs. There was no possible way to
deny the fact. There was no good way to explain it, either, when some
of the images had been looted from Henri Cartier-Bresson, Dmitri Kessel
and Léon Busy, an intrepid camera *opérateur* who had captured colour
('autochrome') images in South East Asia on behalf of Albert Kahn's
early-twentieth-century 'Archives of the Planet' project. These victims
of Dylan's acquisitiveness were not mere Sunday snappers. Their
photographs were not overlooked works or internet detritus, though
Dylan was also accused of 'borrowing' six images from the Flickr stream
and private collection of a fan named Okinawa Soba. Within days,
the Gagosian had ceased to call the show a 'journal', preferring instead
'a visual reflection'. What could not be undone was an interview with
the artist staged for the exhibition's catalogue. Dylan had said:

> I paint mostly from real life. It has to start with that. Real people, real
> street scenes, behind the curtain scenes, live models, paintings,
> photographs, staged setups, architecture, grids, graphic design. Whatever
> it takes to make it work. What I'm trying to bring out in complex scenes,
> landscapes, or personality clashes, I do it in a lot of different ways. I
> have the cause and effect in mind from the beginning to the end. But
> it has to start with something tangible.

So had he somehow been in the room in Vietnam in 1915 when Léon
Busy was conducting an exercise in photographic colonialism entitled
Indochine/Woman Smoking Opium, a picture whose composition and
details exactly – as in, 'in every respect' – anticipated Dylan's *Opium*?
Was there any important difference between Henri Cartier-Bresson's
1948 photograph of a Chinese eunuch once of the court of the Dowager
Empress Tzu Hsi and the painting bearing Bob Dylan's signature? How
about the artwork of a pair of Yakuza gangsters lighting a cigarette
and the monochrome Bruce Gilden photograph from 1998? What of
the Kessel? It had once existed as a 1950 *Life* magazine cover shot
bearing the caption 'Boys playing Siamese chess in front of the
Trocadero Hotel'. Was Dylan's painted facsimile truly just an example,
then, of 'Whatever it takes to make it work'?

A few members of the New York art crowd capable of mistaking
theory for artistry attempted to defend Dylan by talking about 'reference
photographs'. The excuses had a hollow sound. Given everything that

had gone before, the humour of the situation lay in the fact that each of those photographs were (and are) protected by the iron laws of copyright. Whether Dylan paid to use the images is not yet clear. That he simply copied or traced them, for whatever 'artistic purpose', is beyond argument. The last line of defence, it seems, was that they became art, if they became art, simply because Dylan decided to make paintings of them. For those accustomed to treating him as a singular talent, it was a poor return on a long-standing investment.

Looking at the evidence in 2011, it was hard not to be reminded of every previous debate over plagiarism. Then, yet again, you were left to ponder motives. Perhaps Dylan had been too arrogant to realise or care that the Asia Series invited exposure and humiliation. Perhaps, hiding in plain sight, he had fully expected to be caught out. That possibility counted as bizarre but not, on balance, impossible, given the debate over Chronicles. Cartier-Bresson is one of the most important names in the history of photography. His images are near-impossible to disguise. Surely Dylan knew as much?

If the paintings were examples of love and theft why, yet again, had Dylan made no attributions, given no credit, and invited the unwary to believe that each and every image was his own, unaided and original work? The rhetorical question was fast becoming his most important contribution to every argument about the nature of his creativity. If the Asia Series was intended as a complicated statement about art and originality – the last possible plea in mitigation – it didn't work. This time the charge of plagiarism was impossible to refute.

Then she says, 'I know you're an artist, draw a picture of me.'
I said, 'I would if I could but I don't do sketches from memory.'[24]

CHAPTER THIRTEEN

Hand Me Down My Walkin' Cane

IN THE MIDDLE OF AUGUST 2002, FANS ATTENDING A DYLAN SHOW at the Erie County Fair in Hamburg, New York State, were treated to a novel piece of entertainment just before the artist and his band took the stage. It was almost sunset on the tenth night of that year's summer tour of the United States and Canada. For those stuck on the idea, it was concert number 1,440 of the everlasting road trip. It was also just another show. As Aaron Copeland's 'Hoe-Down' played, the voice of Al Santos, Dylan's road manager, boomed out over the fairgrounds in a perfect stentorian parody of every cornball stage announcement ever made. It might as well have been Ed McMahon opening the old *Tonight* show with his 'Heeere's Johnny!'

Ladies and gentlemen, please welcome the poet laureate of rock 'n' roll. The voice of the promise of the '60s counter-culture. The guy who forced folk into bed with rock, who donned make-up in the '70s and disappeared into a haze of substance abuse, who emerged to find Jesus, who was written off as a has-been by the end of the '80s, and who suddenly shifted gears, releasing some of the strongest music of his career beginning in the late '90s. Ladies and gentlemen, Bob Dylan!

The introduction would be retained for a decade to come. In due course, it would be adapted slightly to make sardonic mention of 'Columbia recording artist Bob Dylan', but the joke would survive. It was a good joke, given that it was mostly true. What made it funnier was that Dylan had not invented this baroque spiel. It had been taken, more or less wholesale, from an article that had appeared in the *Buffalo News* less than a week before. Fully 40 years before that, the artist had been in the middle of recording *The Freewheelin' Bob Dylan* with no possible idea of the fate that awaited him. In 2002, he was making a nonsense of those who still made a nonsense of his life and times. And mocking himself, too, trading cliché for cliché. If they wanted a caricature, they could have a caricature. A joke is as good a place to hide as any.

*

Dave Van Ronk, mentor-in-chief in the Village all those decades before, had died earlier in the year at the age of 65. He had never left the district. At the end of June 2004 the City of New York would rename the little street where he had lived near Sheridan Square in honour of the blues player. A lot of old friends would show up for the ceremony. Dylan, who no longer stood around on street corners listening to speeches, would be touring in Europe, as usual.

He had spent many nights sleeping on a couch in Van Ronk's West 15th Street apartment during his first year in the city. Later he had repaid the hospitality by stealing his host's arrangement of 'House of the Rising Sun' for the sake of the *Bob Dylan* album. Van Ronk had meant to record the piece himself. Relations had become strained for a while, less because of the betrayal than because of what the theft – unambiguous, on that occasion – had seemed to reveal. Craft and career, art and its imperatives, had mattered more than friendship. Van Ronk, self-styled Trotskyist, had never been capable of the ruthlessness an entertainer needs if his desire is a big name or big money. Dylan would remember the older man fondly in *Chronicles*.

In his American concerts early in 2002 the artist had opened, as often as not, with the old murder ballad 'Duncan and Brady', a song that had appeared as the first track on Van Ronk's first album, *Dave Van Ronk Sings Ballads, Blues and a Spiritual*, in 1959. By coincidence or choice, Dylan had performed the ballad in Charleston, West Virginia, on the night after his old friend's death on 10 February. Given all that he had learned, absorbed and borrowed from a Greenwich Village autodidact, you could count the performance as a perfect example of the eternal folk process. The song belonged to no one save the singer of the moment. Unless he made it his own, of course.

All Dylan did was play. It was as though he was working his way through the population centres of the developed world one by one. In Europe, there was still some glamour attached to his appearances in London, Paris or Zurich, but in the heartland a Bob Dylan show was commonplace by 2002. He came and went with the seasons; sometimes fair, sometimes foul. Most of the fans who saw him year after year, or who travelled from place to place to witness multiple performances, had become as tolerant of Dylan's failures as they were eager for a memorable night. They took their chances. This show might be bad, but tomorrow's might become part of the enveloping legend. Few other performers, if any, had achieved this kind of relationship with their audiences. Judging by online fan chatter, some of the most devoted even found a strange connoisseur's fascination in seeing Dylan perform badly, as though it only made the next triumph sweeter. This audience, the initiates within the cocoon, were as much a part of the never-ending phenomenon as the artist. Arguably, since they clung to the name despite all his scorn, the tour belonged to them, not to him.

Nevertheless, year after year, in city after city, there would be walkouts at Dylan's shows. Those who refused the contract, who expected to hear an artist who resembled his recorded work, believed they were entitled to more than pot luck for the price of a ticket. Sometimes they had a case. It was one thing to reject the idea that the artist should repeat himself, another to use the legend of perpetual creativity to excuse substandard shows. Those aficionados who defended Dylan at all costs – for he rarely bothered – were still taking refuge in the 'reinvention' argument when he was doing no such thing, when the performances sucked, when he seemed tired, surly, or simply uninterested. In 2002, amid 77 shows in North America and 29 in Europe, no one was entitled to expect perfection every night. Equally, no concert-goer should have been naive enough still to believe that Dylan, of all people, would attempt to reproduce note for note some track he had recorded in 1965 or 1975. But even in a year when he was putting on good shows with a good band – and 2002 often resembled such a year; London had seen at least one very fine performance – there was a sense of mechanical repetitiveness about the tours. Dylan would sometimes answer journalists who asked why he worked so hard by pointing to some other musician – Willie Nelson and B.B. King were favourites – who toured constantly and did more concerts in a year than he ever contemplated. It was true enough. He has never come close to matching the 250 to 300 dates King was fulfilling annually well into his 70s. But no journalist seems ever to have asked the follow-up questions. Was that the sort of revered, mummified figure he wanted to become? If so, why?

It led him to strange places for unexplained reasons. The Erie County Fair, 'America's Fair', was one such. Essentially an agricultural show with a carnival and other entertainments attached, the event saw Dylan and his band playing to a racetrack grandstand in western New York State. Even the hardcore fans didn't think it was anything special as a concert. All agreed that it was a bizarre place to be watching this artist in action. The best you could say is that a racetrack on a hot night made a change from another carbuncular sports arena custom-built to shrivel the soul. Almost a year had passed since the release of 'Love and Theft'. Another four years would elapse before a new Bob Dylan album emerged.

In the meantime, reports concerning the artist had begun to appear in the Hollywood movie papers just after Dave Van Ronk's death. They said Dylan was in 'discussions' over a possible starring role in a picture that might be called *Masked and Anonymous*. It seemed someone still believed he could be turned into an actor. Someone certainly seemed to believe, at any rate, that his name remained potent enough to get a film project off the ground and attract the sorts of talent who could turn cachet into cash.

There was a little more to it than that. In fact, there was a lot more to it. No one was wooing Dylan for this piece of work, nor was he being tempted with big money. He was one of the co-writers, a moving force behind the entire picture. The itch he had felt before attempting *Renaldo and Clara* needed to be scratched again. Dylan was in the mood to make a statement. Yet on 8 June the *Hollywood Reporter* would confirm that Angela Bassett had been added to the cast and state:

> Written by Rene Fontaine and Sergy Petrov, *Masked* is based on the unpublished short story 'Los Vientos del Destino', written by Enrique Morales. It follows the story of Dylan's character, Jack Fate, a wandering troubadour brought out of prison by his former manager for one last concert, a charity benefit. Bassett would [sic] play Mistress, who has a past with Fate. The cast also includes Jessica Lange, Luke Wilson, Penelope Cruz, and Jeff Bridges.

In Paris, a hapless and actual Enrique Morales was obliged to point out that whichever way *los vientos del destino* (the winds of fate) were blowing, they were not coming from his vicinity. The Italian-Argentinian actor, playwright, director and teacher knew nothing about any such 'short story', or any such movie project. The *Hollywood Reporter* had not bothered to ask questions, meanwhile, about Rene and Sergy/Sergei, the unheralded writing team who were to put words into the mouth of the Dylan oracle. 'Petrov' was the artist himself, of course. 'Fontaine' was Larry Charles, formerly a sitcom writer best known for his contributions to *Seinfeld*. He was to direct the picture, despite the fact that his only previous experience in such a role had been with the show *Curb Your Enthusiasm*. The star of *Masked and Anonymous* would need no encouragement in that regard.

So: Jack Fate? The echoes of *Renaldo and Clara*, its 'Father', 'Son', 'Woman in White' and the rest, were not reassuring. Sometimes, especially those times when movie cameras were present, Dylan's sense of ambiguity deserted him. It could be pointed out, rightly, that *Masked and Anonymous* is allegorical. It could also be observed that Hollywood, as though to prove poetic justice yet exists, doesn't get allegory. Reviewers reared on its cheesy diet also seem to have trouble digesting that kind of art-house conceit. So it would prove. Dylan's decision to give himself so pretentious a fictional name while speaking in aphorisms would all but subvert any points he wanted to make about attitudes towards performers and fame.

Wearing a black fender-fold cowboy hat, red-striped trousers and a pencil moustache that made him look like an anaemic Vincent Price or a gnarled Cisco Houston, he gave the second of two shows at London's Docklands Arena on 12 May. On 2 July, principal photography began in Los Angeles for what would become *Masked and Anonymous*. By that time the cast list had begun to resemble an agent's address book. In addition to those already mentioned who were prepared to work for 'scale' (union rates) on Dylan's behalf, John Goodman had agreed to take on the central role of Uncle Sweetheart, venal former manager to Fate, the washed-up rock legend. The list of other notables for whom parts were somehow found included Val Kilmer, Mickey Rourke, Ed Harris, Bruce Dern and Cheech Marin. A lot would be asked of the script assembled by Rene and Sergei. Enough dialogue to go around would be one requirement.

Masked and Anonymous is undeniably a strange film. At its centre is a star who does a fine basilisk stare, but very little of what is otherwise known as acting. It seems we are supposed simply to know that this is Bob Dylan, one gigantic performance in his own right, and adjust our assumptions accordingly. If that was the idea, it doesn't work. In the usual Hollywood parlance, Dylan is meant to carry the film. Instead, he too often resembles a diffident presence, the approximate locus for something or someone the real actors can talk at. In scene after scene, the cliché 'less is more' is taken to its illogical conclusion.

Around Dylan/Jack Fate turns a plot that is not often detained by the need for exposition or explanations and a bunch of characters whose purpose, half the time, seems to be to engage the semi-absent hero in psychotic-Socratic exchanges. A lot of the dialogue is cryptic; much of it wears its presumed profundity like a ball and chain. Kinder critics and the distributor, Sony Pictures Classics, would attempt to suggest that part of the effect being attempted was to create dramatic correlatives to Dylan's songs. No one seems to have thought that one through. Those songs are in essence monologues; the speaker is not interrogated. Most movies, in contrast, are driven by their dialogue, by interplay and exchange. The expedient of allowing Fate to address us in voice-over is a sign, as some film purists will always insist, of cinematic failure.

That said, *Masked and Anonymous* is awash with ideas, good and bad. The picture offers a lot to talk about and analyse. Whether it returns the same investment in terms of viewing pleasure is, let's say, disputable. The *idea* of Bob Dylan and what that might mean is much in evidence. There are countless jokes for fans and students of the music business. There is an entire character, Tom Friend (Bridges) – another blunt-edged joke of a name – whose purpose for much of the time is to illustrate Dylan's misfortunes at the hands of dishonest journalists (especially those who are obsessed with the '60s). This is supposed to lead us, it seems, into an argument over truth, reality and art. Instead, it gives the appearance of a star demanding attention by complaining about all the attention.

And yet the thing is fascinating. It has levels the way an M.C. Escher architectural fantasy has levels. If the measure of a piece of art is that it repays attention, *Masked and Anonymous* is worth a lot of attention. Its effects are cumulative, its ambitions large. *Les Enfants du Paradis* it is not, but the contrast between a contained theatrical world and life's bigger stage, between conscious performance and a world full of lies, disguises and political performances – masked and anonymous, in short – is very effective. Some of the music, if not all, is terrific.

Uncle Sweetheart (Goodman) has pulled Fate from a Mexican jail for the sake of a TV benefit – supposedly for the poor and needy, as ever – with Sweetheart as the beneficiary. In a dilapidated, ramshackle America torn apart by economic failure and an incipient civil war, it's every hustler, demagogue and thief for himself. On the way to the gig, Fate pauses to visit his dying father, who happens to be the dictatorial 'President', one who is about to be overthrown by Edmundo (Rourke), the next caudillo in line. Democracy is a thing of the past. Such is one subtext in search of a plot.

In fact, it might be the most interesting theme of all. Dylan the scriptwriter has cast his eyes beyond the 'Clinton wars' and America's sense of infinite entitlement to peace and prosperity. He has packed one corner of his film with allusions to one great Civil War – an Abraham Lincoln impersonator and the ghost of a blackface minstrel turn up, 'Dixie' is played – and asked himself why another conflagration is out of the question. Death squads roam the land; TV executives go armed; peonage has returned; corruption is commonplace. When a little girl (Tinashe Kachingwe) sings 'The Times They Are a-Changin'' for Fate's sake, there is a world of poignancy in the moment. The truth is in the eyes of all the grown men who are listening: the times have changed, but for the hellish worst, not for the better.

The film seems to say that the United States is deluding itself, that infernal forces are never far from its bright, complacent surface. All that's required for understanding, as Fate explains before the closing titles, is an altered perspective. In short, though the country is never named, Dylan imagines the end of America. This time the prophet ventures a prophecy. Once he preached of apocalypse and end times; this is a glimpse of what he meant.

Masked and Anonymous is not the typical all-American dystopia. It could be set in anyone's future and is not, in any case, remotely 'futuristic'. The misery of daily life could be unfolding in one of those Third World countries to which all 'low intensity' wars are supposed to be confined. But one memorable and moving slow panning shot offers a dismal vista of a recognisable contemporary Los Angeles. On the soundtrack Dylan sings his 'Blind Willie McTell': 'See the arrow on the doorpost / Saying, "This land is condemned."' All ambiguities aside, the artist has not been as 'political' as this in many years.

He also has something to say about religion, art, dreams, friendship, families and lies. What makes the film complicated – what makes it impossible as a Hollywood production – is that Dylan is not trying to say just one, two or half a dozen things. He also seems be insisting that the things he is trying to convey cannot be isolated, one from the other. As writing, the film is tightly woven. Contrary to what would be said by critics who understood only the standard Hollywood three-act brain-killer, it is not without structure. It is certainly not 'formless'.

Some of the allusions to Shakespeare make you wonder, for example, if Fate, Sweetheart, the TV producer Nina Veronica (Lange) and the rest are not just actors in a play within a play. Oscar Vogel, the ghost of the blackface minstrel who opened his mouth once too often – Vogel is the German word for bird – makes the obvious statement: 'The whole world is a stage.' The Bob Dylan we think we know is meanwhile both a performer and a performance. In one of its aspects that performance is mistaken for reality. In another sense it has been reality, one reality, ever since Robert Zimmerman adopted a fictitious name. In this stretch of celluloid, Bob Dylan plays a Bob Dylan figure. He plays himself as a character forever playing himself. If the movie confused some people, that was no accident.

It is equally possible to ask whether the outside world of civil wars, death squads and murderous politicians in *Masked and Anonymous* is not just another of history's hellish perpetual re-enactments. Edmundo, the President, the insurgents and counter-insurgents could as well be players in some Elizabethan drama of regicide and betrayal done in modern dress. You can have a third bite at the cherry by wondering how much of what is going on is happening in and through the mind of Fate. The film's closing sequence sees him being driven back to his prison. Dylan's immobile face is held for almost a minute and half, resigned or accepting, in essence disinterested, while the voice-over says, 'I was always a singer and maybe no more than that.' His last words are: 'Seen from a fair garden, everything looks cheerful. Climb to a higher plateau, and you'll see plunder and murder. Truth and beauty are in the eye of the beholder. I tried to stop figuring everything out a long time ago.' The film all but invites you to come up with your own guesses as to what it was he had once tried to understand.

When it was released in July 2003, the film did not impress many reviewers. No one should have been too surprised. Yet again, Dylan had made a piece of cinema that required too much thought and too many explanations. His non-acting, even in a movie that justified passivity and a few non sequiturs, did not make for the kind of sense the critics wanted to understand. Most agreed that the star was a mumbler, wooden, taciturn to a fault – all too true, unfortunately – who had indulged in yet another of his well-known ego trips. Thanks to *Renaldo and Clara*, Dylan was never again going to catch a break in the world of movies. It was also said, reasonably enough, that too many of the big names who had queued for a chance to be in the picture had been reduced to cameo performances. So Val Kilmer turned up as an animal trainer apropos of nothing, it seemed, beyond an incoherent speech on the fate of species and because he was Val Kilmer.

Equally, the possibility that tiny roles were sometimes crucial was not considered by busy reviewers. A common reaction to Ed Harris playing the ghost of Vogel the blackface minstrel was expressed by the *San Francisco Chronicle*'s man in the free seats. 'Why? I don't know,' said the critic helpfully. 'It's best to not think about it.'[1] The picture might have made a bit more sense had the cineaste bothered to do his job.

A 'lot of long-winded gobbledygook', said the *Los Angeles Times*. Proof 'that what is towering genius in one medium can go insanely wrong in another', observed the *Boston Globe*. 'An incomprehensible Bob Dylan vanity project that is not only nearly impossible to sit through, but embarrasses a long list of stars who lined up to work for scale opposite the legendary musician,' judged the *New York Post*. 'Simply painful to watch as the doomed vehicle . . . comes whistling toward a fiery crash landing,' concluded the *Washington Post*. An 'unholy, incoherent mess', said the *New York Times*.

The *New Yorker* made an effort, its critic deciding that the picture was 'knowing without always being knowledgeable, darkly humorous, full of wisdom both faux and real, and genuinely mysterious'. Ann Hornaday gave the *Washington Post*'s second opinion on its own review, granting that *Masked and Anonymous* was 'uneven', but nevertheless judging the picture to be 'a fascinating, vexing, indulgent, visionary, pretentious, mesmerising pop culture curio'.[2] These pleas in mitigation did nothing to alter the damning verdict. As a commercial proposition, the movie was dead within days.

What was interesting, in a ghoulish sort of way, was the extent to which Dylan was held in contempt or attacked just for being Bob Dylan. Some people had grown very weary of the legend. The *Village Voice*, for one example, warned those liable to be guided by its opinions that the movie was 'first and foremost a trash-can monument' to the 'ageing coolness' of this 'pop Mahatma'.[3] The hostile reviews had one other thing in common. The political content of *Masked and Anonymous* was dismissed or just ignored. Here was Dylan, for a miracle, addressing politics and a possible American future and no one wanted to know. It seems that radical views had gone out of style since his first adventures in ideology. Perhaps if he had made the picture a few years later, when the truth about warmongering conspiracies was known to all, when banks were brought to their knees and capitalism trembled, the critics might have been a little more attentive.

*

On 3 August 2002, of all the festivals in all the world, Dylan performed at Newport. The event at which he had made his name in 1963 and made some enemies in '65 was as much a part of the received narrative of his career as the 1962 Fender Stratocaster with a three-tone sunburst finish that, back in olden times, had infuriated those with an inflexible idea of how folk music was supposed to sound. Thirty-seven years later, the organic-fruit-juice-vending sponsors were calling it the Apple & Eve Newport Folk Festival. In the late afternoon of a ferociously hot day, Dylan opened with a traditional song, 'Roving Gambler'. He didn't do so to make a point about ironies, but simply because it had become his habit. He had outlasted all the arguments.

In fact, many of the critics and fans who had listened hard to *Time Out of Mind* and *'Love and Theft'*, who had pored over all the verses, unpicked the quotation-collages and tracked down every fragment of borrowed melody, said *he* had become the keeper of tradition's flame, the archivist of the American experience. The idea was already in danger of becoming a cliché. Reviewing *'Love and Theft'* in the *New York Times*, Greil Marcus had remarked that Dylan's new music opened up a window in time.[4] That was no more strictly true than the accusations of betrayal in 1965 had been wholly true. But it contained truth enough. Dylan was not quite the last person in his country still capable of remembering a few things about the republic's history. He was hardly alone among performers in trying to pierce the veil of cultural amnesia. Americana, a term he would mistrust until he claimed it nonchalantly for his 2013 Americanarama tour, had been thriving without his help during the 1990s. Somehow, for all that, Dylan's explorations hinted at a bigger statement than anything that could be contained in a revivalist pastiche. Walt Whitman was being invoked increasingly often by admirers. The artist, it was asserted, was finding a way to articulate a sense of the past in the present, alive and active. He too had become part of the American tradition, lodged in the collective memory he was mapping.

Dylan returned to Newport less than a fortnight after the death of Alan Lomax, the left-wing folklorist who had been among those shouting loudest for less volume back in the middle of the '60s. The artist had chosen to forget about that. On being 'inducted' to the Rock and Roll Hall of Fame in New York in January 1988, Dylan had picked out the folk-song collector – along with Little Richard, no less – for special thanks. During a show in Vienna, Virginia, in August 1997, Dylan had once more expressed his gratitude to the 'father of world music'. The artist would also make respectful mentions of Lomax in the pages of *Chronicles*, as though all the fuss of 1965 had never happened.

There was an odd sense in which that was almost true. By 2002, the three albums of rococo R&B and opaque verses that had forged Dylan's reputation in the middle years of the '60s looked increasingly like aberrations, however brilliant they might have been in conception and execution. Journalists writing about him were still talking of *Bringing It All Back Home*, *Highway 61 Revisited* and *Blonde on Blonde* in terms of 'rock and roll'. He had said often enough, correctly but in vain, that the term had never been descriptive of his music. The other truth was that those three monumental albums did not represent the dominant strains in his art. Strange as it sounds, they had been a phase.

By the end of his life, Lomax had long since come to terms with popular music, though he never lost his contempt for homogenised mass culture. Dylan had travelled in the opposite direction. His thanks from the stage at the Wolf Trap Farm Park for the Performing Arts in Vienna in 1997, just after singing 'Blind Willie McTell', had included the following statement: 'Alan was one of those who unlocked the secrets of this kind of music. So if we've got anybody to thank, it's Alan.' That had been as explicit as the artist ever gets, even if it overlooked the fact that the Lomax version of love and theft had sometimes involved dubious methods, not least a tendency on the collector's part to behave like a condescending patron towards black performers. Dylan had always talked of folk song in terms of mystery and secret knowledge. In thousands of field recordings, in *Folk Song Style and Culture* (1968), in *The Land Where the Blues Began* (1993) and in many other publications besides, Lomax had spent 70 years making the connections that had helped others to solve the riddles. He had helped white boys to sing the blues, at any rate. Dylan's twenty-first-century approach was more sophisticated. As with borrowed words and phrases, he laid himself open to the charge that he had built a career by appropriating the creations of overlooked or anonymous artists. In his defence was the fact that he had, in essence, perpetuated tradition more surely than any other performer. So dominant was he in the art of American song, it was hard to say where tradition ended and Dylan began. His late recordings were meditations on that truth.

Still, when he returned to the stage in Newport after 37 years it seemed to most members of a huge audience that he had been taking his ethnomusicological researches a little too far. Either that or he had landed a job playing third villain from the left in a particularly bad western. The big white Stetson was in place, but there the resemblance to any known Bob Dylan ended. His hair was shoulder length, straight and unkempt. He wore a beard that looked as though it had been drawn on by an impish child. What made this all the more bizarre was that some fans knew he had looked entirely different, which is to say more or less normal, during the previous night's show in Worcester, Massachusetts. At Newport, Dylan made no attempt to explain himself. As was often the case, he said not a word to the crowd, but carried on as though nothing whatever was amiss. His eccentricities had long been proverbial; this – the weird hair like a stringy curtain around his head, the billy goat beard-thing – invited diagnosis. When photographs got out, a small frenzy would ensue among those who worry over What It All Means.

It meant that Dylan had been shooting a video for a new song called "Cross the Green Mountain'. The mystery lay in the fact that he had not bothered to take even ten minutes to remove a silly wig and a fake beard before going on stage. Perhaps it was his oblique comment on expectations and the return to Newport. Perhaps he thought it was funny. When a *Rolling Stone* journalist asked a couple of years later, 'What was up with the wig and fake beard?' Dylan's answer almost gave the game away. 'Is that me who you saw up there?' he asked.[5] Perhaps he just liked the look, or the idea that photographs of what seemed to be late-period Howard Hughes in a cowboy hat would certainly find their way around the world. He didn't look much better in the video, but at least the get-up was appropriate to the subject.

Behind all the nonsense, typically, lay one of his finest songs. That the piece would be relegated for better than five years to the soundtrack album for a failed Civil War movie called *Gods and Generals* is almost too predictable to be worth stating. It was the kind of perverse decision that had also become typical. "Cross the Green Mountain', a majestic threnody for those who fell in the war between the states, vindicated Dylan's literary borrowing habit. It confirmed, too, that his attempts to address a century and a half of American history, to contain its strands and contradictions within his work, were not whims.

Ted Turner, the billionaire 'media mogul' and founder of CNN, had financed *Gods and Generals* with tens of millions of dollars from his own pocket. The exact number of millions is open to dispute. By the time the picture was released in February 2003, an original budget of $56 million had grown to what the *Los Angeles Times* understood to be $90 million; others said anywhere between $60 million and $80 million. In the end, this 'prequel' to the movie *Gettysburg* took just $12.9 million at the box office. Some of the many critics who dismissed the epic as mannered, verbose and far too long would think the receipts generous. One result was that Dylan, apparently intent on a second career as a composer of songs for films, would sacrifice one of his most affecting statements to a risible piece of Southern ancestor worship. Thanks to *Tell Tale Signs: Rare and Unreleased 1989–2006*, the eighth volume in the Bootleg Series, the song survives and still manages to say more about America's Civil War in just over eight minutes than *Gods and Generals* achieved in three hours and forty-nine minutes.

It's a song without a chorus, dolorous as a funeral march, couched in a fair facsimile of the language of the period, religious yet clear-eyed, and streaked through with the found poetry of historical truth. "Cross the Green Mountain' also manages to be a movie song that is cinematic in its own right. The work is complete and self-contained. It has no need of the picture's thunderous battle re-enactment scenes, or of promotional videos of famous singers in fright wigs. From verse to verse it moves across 'the ravaged land' with a more penetrating gaze than any feature film.

Across the green mountain
I slept by the stream
Heaven blazing in my head
I dreamt a monstrous dream
Something came up
Out of the sea
Swept through the land of
The rich and the free

Dylan's method is immediately apparent. 'Heaven blazing in my head' has been connected by several critics, rightly, to the W.B. Yeats of 'Lapis Lazuli', he who speaks of 'Heaven blazing into the head'. What's often forgotten is the connection Dylan is making. The next line of the Irishman's 1938 poem follows a punctuating colon with 'Tragedy wrought to its uttermost'. In the succeeding verse there is the line 'Old civilisations put to the sword', then 'All things fall and are built again'. This being Dylan, meanwhile, the thing emerging from the sea and a monstrous dream no doubt originate in Revelation 13:1: 'And I stood upon the sand of the sea, and saw a beast rise up out of the sea, having seven heads and ten horns, and upon his horns ten crowns, and upon his heads the name of blasphemy.' This being Dylan, the 'Star-Spangled Banner' formulation, 'land of the free and the home of the brave', is shorn of bombast. The 'land of the rich and free' has lost its prosperity and liberty to carnage and the beast within. Blasphemy will meanwhile reappear in the song 'on every tongue', as though to say that the conflict itself is blasphemous. Yet 'virtue lives / and cannot be forgot'.

The wonder of the piece is the quantity of imagery Dylan manages to condense. An entire nineteenth-century notion of sacrifice on the 'altar' of war, of the 'good' Christian death for one's country, is caught in a few bare lines. Then the entire scene of a coming battle, with all its bathetic pretensions to honour and gentlemanly conduct before the slaughter, is laid out in 20 words.

> Altars are burning
> with flames far and wide
> the foe has crossed over
> from the other side
> They tip their caps
> from the top of the hill
> You can feel them come
> More brave blood to spill

Throughout the song, Dylan sticks to his brief. *Gods and Generals* was an attempt both to tell the story of a decisive period in the Civil War and to portray General Thomas 'Stonewall' Jackson, the insanely devout hero of the Confederacy. The song, like the movie, intends to give an idea of vast loss on both sides, but for much of the time, inevitably, its perspective is Southern. Jackson was shot three times by the pickets of his own rebel army towards the end of the battle of Chancellorsville early in May 1863. After an arm was amputated, pneumonia set in and he died of its complications. The South greeted the loss of a brilliantly audacious general with a keening panic. Some historians of the struggle argue, in fact, that Jackson's death was the war's turning point. Without his aid, Robert E. Lee was unable to beat the odds at the battle of Gettysburg a few weeks later. After that, it is claimed, the Confederacy's defeat was inevitable. Dylan's song takes no interest in any of this. By contrasting veneration and banal, bloody reality, he gives instead a working definition of war's infinite stupidity.

> Close the eyes
> of our captain
> Peace may he know
> His long night is done
> The great leader is laid low
> He was ready to fall
> He was quick to defend
> Killed outright he was
> by his own men

"Cross the Green Mountain' has the gravitas of a hymnal, the brooding undertones of a graveside eulogy. Dylan's abraded voice becomes the only conceivable instrument for this kind of mourning. His touring band provide still more evidence, meanwhile, that he has no need to draft in big-name session players. The violin of Larry Campbell and the organ of Benmont Tench are the only counterpoints the lyrics require. Within the words the restless shades of nineteenth-century American poetry move at a steady, ponderous pace. Dylan's reliable Henry Timrod is there, with both a line from a verse and an echo of the rhetorical style of the poem 'Charleston'. In part, that reads:

> Meanwhile, through streets still echoing with trade,
> Walk grave and thoughtful men,
> Whose hands may one day wield the patriot's blade
> As lightly as the pen.

Herman Melville's poem 'Running the Batteries' has been heard in Dylan's song; Whitman's 'When Lilacs Last in the Dooryard Bloom'd' has been adduced; part of Henry Wadsworth Longfellow's 'Killed at the Ford' could almost have been one of the verses in the song.

> Sudden and swift a whistling ball
> Came out of a wood, and the voice was still;
> Something I heard in the darkness fall,
> And for a moment my blood grew chill . . .

Anyone who fails to see the point of the allusions and borrowings, who prefers hunt-the-plagiarist and elects to 'deconstruct' a piece of art as though it were a clockwork toy fit only to be taken apart, will find plenty to work with in "Cross the Green Mountain'. This is Dylan:

> A letter to mother
> Came today
> 'Gunshot wound to the breast'
> Is what it did say
> 'But he'll be better soon
> He's in a hospital bed'
> But he'll never be better
> He's already dead

This is Whitman (from 'Come Up From the Fields, Father'):

> All swims before her eyes, flashes with black, she catches the main words
>   only,
> Sentences broken, *gunshot wound in the breast, cavalry skirmish, taken to*
>   *hospital,*
> *At present low, but will soon be better.*

Again, Dylan's ability to edit and condense is startling. Whitman goes on for two more verses before reaching the point:

> Alas poor boy, he will never be better, (nor maybe needs to be better,
>   that brave and simple soul,)
> While they stand at home at the door he is dead already . . .

Dylan's source is obvious enough, then. What's worth remembering is that while he intermingles unassuaged grief from both sides of a warring nation – his 'Captain' could as well be Lincoln as Jackson – he fuses the poetry of North and South, Whitman and Timrod. Dylan also traces a cultural continuity. His lines 'Stars fell over Alabama / I saw each star' are, aptly, a luminous evocation of extinguished Southern lives. But they are also adapted from a 1930s jazz song, 'Stars Fell on Alabama'. That tune, in turn, borrowed its title from a book describing a never-forgotten Leonid meteor shower over the state in 1833. The past is in the present; the present is somehow within the past. By its tone the song seems to say, meanwhile, that the war between the states has never truly ended. Grief has never been forgotten; the reasons for grief and enmity have yet to be addressed; nothing is healed. Modern America was born of this conflict and modern America, as Dylan knew perfectly well, remains a house divided against itself.

Finally, there are those verses which, though no doubt unearthed from someone's prose, become purest Dylan. They leave you to wonder what all the charges of plagiarism can truly mean. So the merest hint from an old jazz song becomes a verse remarkable for its concision and precision. The writer does not have to state all that has been lost. There is a world of mourning in a few words:

Stars fell over Alabama
I saw each star
You're walking in dreams
Whoever you are
Chilled are the skies
Keen is the frost
The ground's froze hard
And the morning is lost

*

The government of the United States was threatening war while Dylan was recording "Cross the Green Mountain'. George W. Bush, the latest president, did not mean to be deterred from his ambitions for a conflict in the Middle East, least of all by the facts. An elaborate plot to exploit the 9/11 atrocity for the sake of a strategic incursion was in train. The fiction of an Iraqi dictator's weapons of mass destruction was being spun out across the media, all outlets. If he cared, Dylan got still more points for prescience: *People are crazy and times are strange . . .*

Another movie song, the ancient-sounding one that had plenty to say about futility and loss, had made no comment about the manner in which wars are sometimes contrived, or about the kind of people who fix things so that others do the dying. That had been the younger Dylan's style. But the older man still knew, as he had known in his youth, that politicians will lie reflexively to achieve their ends. That understanding had never disappeared from Dylan's thinking and he had not relinquished every right to an opinion. 'Summer Days' on the *'Love and Theft'* album had offered a sour, minor joke:

Politician got on his jogging shoes
He must be running for office, got no time to lose
He been suckin' the blood out of the genius of generosity

The adventure known simply as 'Iraq' would be constructed upon a mound of calculated deceits and do America no credit in the world. Americans themselves would find much of it shameful and most of it troubling. Many citizens of allied countries would feel the same. Worst of all, the war when it came in March 2003 would see all the old ideas of duty, honour and country despoiled by cynics once again. Dylan – patriotic enough and certainly no pacifist – had said all he needed to say in "Cross the Green Mountain' about the terrible things done in virtue's name. Interviewed in the autumn of 2001, he had tried to make a distinction between being simply 'anti-war' – impossible for a supporter of the State of Israel – and his abiding distrust of those who 'manipulated' patriotism.

> Take 'Masters of War'. Every time I sing it, someone writes that it's an anti-war song. I'm not a pacifist. I don't think I've ever been one. If you look closely at the song, it's about what Eisenhower was saying about the dangers of the military-industrial complex in this country. I believe strongly in everyone's right to defend themselves by every means necessary . . .
> I think something changed in the country around 1966 or so. You'll have to look at the history books to really sort it out, but there are people who manipulated the Vietnam war. They were traitors to America, whoever they were. It was the beginning of the corporate take-over of America.[6]

The one-word debacle called Iraq would be a sharp lesson for those still prepared to learn. The notion that there could be untrammelled American power in a 'unipolar' world would be refuted. Grandiose boasts of 'the second American century' would come apart like cheap cement amid a welter of excuses. The claim that democratic 'values' could be pressed on peoples whose desire for liberation was taken for granted would dissolve in the keen light of reality. Meanwhile, the 'corporate take-over' would be extended to the very business of war-making as private enterprises made fortunes from Pentagon contracts, much as fortunes had been made during the Civil War. In Iraq, the military-industrial complex, Eisenhower's nightmare, would emerge defiantly from the shadows. Yet when the official lies became too obvious to ignore, trust in America's government would be shaken once again. For the last superpower and for those still attempting to redeem history, Vietnam above all, Iraq would become a bloody mess. Dylan gazed upon all of this with the eyes of one who regarded war as fallen mankind's perpetual condition. Bloody Chancellorsville or irradiated Fallujah: the only real difference was that in the modern atrocity Americans were not killing one another.

You cannot assemble an opinion on Dylan's behalf just from the evidence of his public statements. He has had decades in which to master the arts of evasion and self-contradiction. You must go to the art instead. He appears always to say that it is beside the point for some mere singer to pontificate, that poetry, as W.H. Auden insisted, 'makes nothing happen'. All the wars meanwhile say that humankind isn't altered in the slightest by art, however passionate, however moving, however true. That had been the youngster's insight in the '60s. Protest songs made people feel better about themselves, but they didn't truly change anything. The cities of the western world would erupt in protest against the Iraq conspiracy. Brave songs would be sung and brave words spoken, but the military machine would roll on regardless. Besides, if you cleave to Revelation, as Dylan does, your belief in immutable prophecy is liable to make everything else seem like trivia. But.

The coincidences that saw this artist writing *Masked and Anonymous* and "Cross the Green Mountain' within the same brief span allow for the sketching of a rough composite picture of part of Dylan's thinking. The idea of a war in the Middle East no doubt revived a few of his high-definition apocalyptic fantasies. Nevertheless, his movie said he had a precise idea of the forces at work within his country. His movie song said he had understood what becomes of essential humanity when it is exposed to pitiless warfare. Together, two overlooked works testified to the fact that, despite everything, he was clear-eyed and undeceived. Radical, too.

*

In October 2002, as though for the hell of it, Dylan's performances in concert began to amount to something again. Whether this was because he had taken to playing the electric piano on stage, or because he had begun to tackle other people's songs more often than before, there was a vitality to the shows, first on the American west coast and then in the east, that had not been evident in years. Renditions of works by Warren Zevon, who had just been diagnosed with terminal cancer, became a speciality. Dylan had not known the writer of 'Lawyers, Guns and Money' and 'Werewolves of London' especially well. He had played a little harmonica at a Zevon session in 1987, but did not claim to be a friend. Nevertheless, it seems the artist felt compelled to honour a dying man whose work he admired by performing his songs, often three in a night, at show after show.

As more than one Dylan fan noticed, he took pains to get his performances right when works that were not his own fell into his care. Amid all the exculpatory talk of 'reinvention', few had paused to ask how many times the feat could be attempted or accomplished with Dylan songs that were 30 and 40 years old. This would be his 15th year out on the road in a touring programme that had been interrupted just once, unavoidably, by the histoplasmosis infection scare. What was left to be squeezed from 'Mr. Tambourine Man' or 'It's Alright, Ma'? So it was that on 19 October the crowd at San Diego State University heard not only Zevon's 'Mutineer' but Van Morrison's 'Carrying a Torch', Neil Young's 'Old Man', Buddy Holly's 'Not Fade Away' and, remarkably, a version of the Rolling Stones' 'Brown Sugar'. Arguably, the last of these was the best of the lot. Dylan was testing himself with songs he didn't know inside out, asleep or awake, in every conceivable improvised variant reading. It did him a power of good to sing what others had written.

For all that, the exercise also served to prove that he was once again in need of new material. Each of the songs of 'Love and Theft' had by this point been performed in concert, with varying degrees of success. Dylan was meanwhile turning to a few of his less-obvious older pieces to keep the customers satisfied. But if the tour never-ending had truly won him a new audience, the customers seemed strangely content with the same core set of the same old songs from the '60s at show upon show. Perhaps, in the main, they were the same old customers. Still there was no sign of a new album. It seemed that Dylan could happily produce work if there was a Hollywood cheque attached, but could not be galvanised by any other means.

The consolation for fans late in 2002 was the release of The Bootleg Series Vol. 5: Bob Dylan Live 1975, The Rolling Thunder Revue. It was a very fine double CD set that nevertheless managed to annoy a few people by giving only a partial and misleading account of a typical revue concert. The album, a memento of idealism and high passion long gone, was nevertheless the best Dylan had to offer. For all his complaints about bootleggers, the appeal of 'rare and unreleased' recordings was his sole commercial proposition in the absence of new work. *The Bootleg Series Vol. 5* would sell in respectable quantities, neither a golden goose nor a turkey.

In January 2003, *Masked and Anonymous* received its premiere at the Sundance Film Festival in Utah and went to meet its maker. Dylan was at risk, not for the first time, of becoming a world-famous cult figure. He toured Australia and New Zealand once again, went through the Southern American states in April and May, covered most of the rest of the country in July and August, reached Europe in October . . . And so on. If touring was not just a job, it looked very like one. On 12 September, after a good deal of hard living and the loss of his beloved and stalwart wife June, Johnny Cash died in Nashville at the age of 71. Dylan prepared still another of his eulogies. This one was longer and more heartfelt than most.

Cash, he wrote, 'was and is the North Star; you could guide your ship by him'. Dylan remembered how his friend had sent a letter of support in the mid-'60s when the dogmatic editors of *Sing Out!* were 'chastising me for the direction my music was going'. At that point, he and Cash had not actually met, but 'the letter meant the world to me. I've kept the magazine to this day.' Johnny Cash, said Dylan,

> is what the land and country is all about, the heart and soul of it personified and what it means to be here; and he said it all in plain English. I think we can have recollections of him, but we can't define him any more than we can define a fountain of truth, light and beauty. If we want to know what it means to be mortal, we need look no further than the Man in Black. Blessed with a profound imagination, he used the gift to express all the various lost causes of the human soul. This is a miraculous and humbling thing. Listen to him, and he always brings you to your senses.

These were honourable sentiments. Dylan's affection and respect for Cash had deep roots. Those who admired either or both of these men could ingest a little of their essential nobility vicariously from the artist's words. A touching moment, then. It was slightly difficult, however, not to notice the disjunction sundering the Dylan who wrote so movingly of those 'various lost causes of the human soul' from the Dylan who materialised in Italy, handy and undeniably dandy, in

January 2004. The ghost of John Cash had not brought this individual to his senses.

Dylan was in Venice to stand around in a rented palazzo for a couple of days, more or less alive and apparently in person, to shoot a minute-long commercial for the Victoria's Secret lingerie company. The song sold for the occasion, along with the artist's services, was 'Love Sick'. The first self-evident fact, therefore, was that not a soul involved in the exercise save the writer could have listened to the track beforehand. The existential significance of undergarments is not, even at a stretch, one of its themes. Was this Dylan's private joke? Hardly. He was there for the cheque.

As a provocation, as an art event staged with subversive intent to wring some comedy from commerce, it might have engendered all sorts of scholarly chatter. Instead, there was the sight being prepared for American TV audiences of a 62-year-old Dylan and a model almost 40 years his junior posing their way through a series of meaningful looks and sultry stares. She wore angels' wings and examples of the company's products; he wore his best rueful old devil empty face. Skin crawled on five continents. Even Salvador Dali, who had not been called Avida Dollars for nothing, spun gently in his unquiet grave. But what was a poor boy to do? Victoria's Secret had thrown in an offer to sell a $10 Dylan compilation 'exclusively' at their outlets.

The online magazine *Slate* gave the artist a headline precisely as crass as his behaviour. 'Tangled Up in Boobs', it said. The *Wall Street Journal*, on most mornings predatory capitalism's handmaiden, reported that it was all 'part of a move to bring Mr Dylan's music to new audiences'. Quote: 'A moustachioed Mr Dylan, 62-years-old, appears in a new television ad for the sexy chain's "Angels" line while models cavort to a remixed version of his 1997 song "Love Sick".'[7] The problem with all of this, dispassionately, for anyone who cared even slightly, was not that the artist had sold himself, but that he had sold the song. *Slate* invited its readers to ask themselves 'why Bob Dylan, respected counter-cultural artist, would choose to sell panties'. The sole available answer was straightforward: he got paid.

Questioned by *Rolling Stone* later in the year, the artist would attempt a familiar trick and affect oblivious ignorance of the whole affair. As with all inconvenient events in his life, it somehow had nothing to do with him. 'Was I not supposed to do that?' he asked the journalist innocently. Why, he hadn't even seen the ad.

I wish I would have seen it. Maybe I'd have something to say about it.
I don't see that kind of stuff. That's all for other people to see and make
up what they will.[8]

In any terms, by anyone's biographical method, it counts as another
puzzle. The Dylan who had written *Masked and Anonymous*, who had
recorded "Cross the Green Mountain', who had paid homage to the
integrity of Johnny Cash and done a few other useful things in his
time, was taking the cheque – grabbing the cheque – to play an aged
roué in some adman's wipe-clean fantasy while Ms Adriana Lima
looked celestial in underwear, feathers and his handmade cowboy hat.
Everything Dylan owned was his to sell, but he was forcing the ethical
issue. If he didn't care, why should anyone else? It seemed that every
ounce of his famous mystique, every last fragment of the latest self-
determined identity, had become a commodity. One excruciating
thought was that the entire Victoria's Secret debacle had happened
just because it appealed to the vanity of an ageing man. The other
explanation, more plausible by the year, was that anyone could hire
Bob Dylan if the money was right. The money, it seemed, was of
consuming importance.

It made no sense. Those who had claimed that he toured because
of alimony commitments were as erratic in their arithmetic as the
Dylan who tried to pretend – talking to his old Village friend Izzy
Young in Stockholm in October 2003 – that he worked just because 'I
have 14 grandchildren!' Thousands of singers, actual thousands, had
covered his songs. Lennon and McCartney aside, no one could match
Dylan's music publishing empire. Having bought off Albert Grossman's
estate, he owned everything he had ever written save the titles in which
Sara had a share. Thanks to the Bootleg Series and a reliable back
catalogue, meanwhile, his albums and 'greatest-hits' packages still
turned a pretty fair profit. Those 100 or so shows a year still delivered
a multimillion-dollar gross, season after season. Yet he would betray
a great Bob Dylan song, and make himself seem like a sleazy ancient
mask for hire, just for the money? Yes, he would.

It counts as one context for his late renaissance. The identity being
defended in the first years of the twenty-first century was paradoxical.
He was least true to himself in the moment he truly did bring it all
back home as a writer. In parallel with any art he might be creating
ran a money-making juggernaut to which he was at all times
subservient. No one ever said a genius is obliged to be likeable, but

the best excuse loyal fans could manage for the grisly Victoria's Secret affair was that old Bob was 'just having fun'. Few among his less-slavish admirers were able to share the pleasure. Dylan had called his own enduring integrity into question. His right to assail anyone had been rendered suspect, let's say, by a single minute of the softest soft porn.

In March, as though the younger artist was mocking his older self across the decades, another volume in the Bootleg Series, volume six, was released. This was the Halloween concert from New York's Philharmonic Hall in 1964, the one with the joke about the singer wearing his Bob Dylan mask. The album, bootlegged for years, had an eleven and a half minute version of 'It's Alright, Ma' on its first disc. You could play it while waiting for the Victoria's Secret ad to come on. On the other hand, if you happened to have bought a ticket for the show at Philadelphia's Electric Factory on the night *Bob Dylan Live 1964, Concert at Philharmonic Hall* was released, you could catch the 62-year-old's contemporary version. The words didn't alter much: 'Advertising signs they con / You into thinking you're the one / That can do what's never been done.' *Live 1964* also contained several examples of what had once been called protest songs from a 23-year-old who was getting ready to move beyond *that* kind of thing. Adventures in the advertising industry had been no part of his plans.

In June, just before a couple of shows in Glasgow, Dylan found his way to St Andrews, the little university town and golf resort on Scotland's east coast. He had agreed to accept the degree of doctor of music, *honoris causa*, from an ancient institution that had only recently shed a reputation for disdaining anything smacking of modernity in literature. On the other hand, as usual, Dylan was being honoured for his work in the field of music, not poetry, but he donned his robe with no obvious reluctance. He had a soft spot for Scotland, as the laureation (big speech) recognised. That was delivered by Professor Neil Corcoran – of the department of English, not music – who managed to say most of the right things without collapsing into the usual clichés. The professor, a fan with scholarly credentials, had organised the whole affair. On a wet Scottish day, he captured the essence of Dylan better than a lot of the big books.

> Bob Dylan's life as writer and singer has the aspect of vocation, of calling, and his is an art of the most venturesome risk and the most patient endurance. He's spent a lifetime applying himself to such long-sanctioned

forms of art as folk, blues, country, and rock music. And, partly by transfusing them with various kinds of poetic art, he's reinvented them so radically that he's moved everything on to a place it had never expected to go and left the deepest imprint on human consciousness. Many members of my generation can't separate a sense of our own identity from his music and lyrics. He's been for us an extension of consciousness – a way of growing up, and a way of growing more alive. And his work acts like that for succeeding generations too . . .[9]

It was, as these things go, a nice affair. It also marked another aspect of Dylan's life in his late pomp. The honours were coming thick and fast. A surly reviewer could still observe that 'his voice hovers between that of a shrill housewife and Yoda, and he teeters around the stage with the elegance of the Elephant Man', but within what had once been known as the establishment it no longer mattered.[10] Dylan had been certified as a figure of substance and significance, in part because a '60s generation had taken charge of the prize-giving machinery. He was about to justify their faith, but not, to the evident delight of purely literary types, with songs alone. Those still waiting for a new album could pass the time reading.

Chronicles: Volume One was published on 4 October, *Lyrics 1962–2001* a week later. Dylan meanwhile submitted to a round of interviews with what were still known as major publications to explain himself as an author. As an offering to the reading public, *Chronicles* would scarcely need the help. The book with the biblical title would sell in quantities sufficient to justify any publisher's hyperbole. Simon & Schuster's main task was to print enough copies. Inducing Dylan to explain what had caused him to attempt the work after so many years spent refusing to explain himself was, predictably, a trickier matter.

John Preston of the *Sunday Telegraph* was told: 'In part, I guess I wanted to set the record straight.' For contrast, Edna Gundersen of *USA Today* was informed: 'I wasn't trying to explain anything to anybody.' David Gates of *Newsweek* heard, in a third version, that something resembling serendipity had guided the author. 'It's like I had a full deck and I cut the cards and whatever you see you go with that,' Dylan said. 'I realise there's a great gap in it.'[11]

The author told Preston, in all apparent seriousness, that he had been 'determined to write a book that no one could misinterpret'. He had found the writing 'quite an emotional experience in places', but had also discovered the bitter truth about the 'tedious process' of making books. To Gundersen, he confessed that 'I was just trying to charm my way through it, really', but he insisted that in no sense was the book 'an open confession'. Gates was another who heard that the splendid isolation of authorship was not 'that splendid'. In this round of interviews a few semi-secrets were revealed. Dylan admitted to the *Sunday Telegraph* that in the 1980s 'I was just above a club act'. Close to two years before an album existed to substantiate the claim, Austin Scaggs of *Rolling Stone* heard that new songs were being written: 'I have a bunch of them. I do.'[12] For all that, none of the journalists who were invited to these meet-the-author sessions seems to have come to grips with a simple question: why a book?

After the laudatory reviews began to arrive, the idea would gain ground that *Chronicles* was just another Dylan performance, albeit one of his finest. When the close, forensic reading commenced the book would come to be viewed either as a sustained exercise in appropriation and worse, or as a kind of postmodern parody of autobiography. Most of these approaches still seem fantastically over-complicated. Who gains when literature is treated like evidence extracted under oath? To regard *Chronicles* as a piece of documentary reportage to be challenged and rebutted at every turn was to show a certain honed talent for missing the point. What got overlooked was a perverse fact: you could doubt Dylan and still believe him.

You could doubt the author's understanding of what was taking place when he told John Preston that in the process of writing his memory, to his surprise, 'seemed to unlock', allowing him to visualise people, clothing and furnished rooms from days long gone. You could doubt that he remembered conversations word for word. You could certainly doubt that he got all his facts right. It was not a question of decrying Dylan's veracity (saints preserve us). Doubts arose from common reality. After four long decades memories that seem brilliantly clear are still liable to be deceptive. Certainty, the sense of recovered truth, is no guarantee of anything.

Dylan's description of memories being unlocked, of a book that 'took on a life of its own' as he wrote, was akin to Marcel Proust's celebrated account in *Swann's Way* (1913) of 'involuntary memory'. This was the instinct set free on the instant, supposedly, that the novelist dipped a little cake into his tea. In modern psychological theory, the speculation runs that memories awakened in such a manner set off a chain reaction, much as Dylan described the experience during the writing of *Chronicles*. For his part, Proust got better than 3,000 pages out of this 'chaining effect' as one remembrance led to another. Yet *In Search of Lost Time* is, avowedly and triumphantly, a work of fiction. No one ever said that every vivid memory the writer described was factually accurate.

Dylan might have believed that every last word in his book (even the borrowed, embedded words) involved the honest truth. Belief wasn't relevant. Read Proust attentively and you discover him describing the sheer effort he made to remember the past after the cake was dunked in the tea; the process was not spontaneous. Read *about* Proust and you find that the memorialised madeleine started out, in a 1910 draft of *Swann's Way*, as *biscottes*.[13] If the great novelist dithered over his memories of bakery products, what else can be trusted? Some of the techniques Dylan employed for his book suggest he understood perfectly well that memory is never a simple, dispassionate recording device. The one thing he failed to remember clearly, nevertheless, was his motive for putting the truth down on paper.

There is a lot of truth in *Chronicles*. Some is the kind you can check – this place, that event, those characters – and some derives from the ineffable coherence of art. In one important sense Dylan made it all true. The boys (always boys) in the literary forensics labs can run all the tests they like. The artist had been investigating the way past and present entwine long before he sat down to write. History might be the dream and nightmare from which we cannot awaken, but in this regard Dylan tends to side with Gatsby. You can't repeat the past? Of course you can. Proust did it; our artist did it in the pages of his *Chronicles*. If he had not, he would have been overwhelmed by his own history.

That was piling up, year upon year. In 2005, while Dylan toured with Willie Nelson, or pulled together another song for another movie (an interesting song called 'Tell Ol' Bill', a picture with some integrity entitled *North Country*), the artist's management were hard at work. The project would turn out to be the grandest monument yet. Filmed interviews for what would become a three-and-a-half-hour documentary had been going on, without publicity, for the best part of a decade. In 2000, Dylan had talked at length to his manager, Jeff Rosen, under the camera's quizzical eye. Yet after the finished work was broadcast in two parts in the United States and Britain in the last week of September, the subject would pretend to know little about it and care less.

'I've never seen it,' he would tell an interviewer in 2009. 'Well, a lot of that footage was gathered up from the '60s. So I'd seen that and

I thought that was like looking at a different character. But it certainly was powerful. And I don't, or can't, do that anymore.'[14] His management, his name, his office, his music, his life: nothing to do with Bob Dylan, apparently. Presumably the fact that the film omitted all mention of certain topics – drug use, say, or a first marriage – was also none of his doing. It was as though he could only support an identity through periodic denials. Somehow the rejection of every previous self was a perverse affirmation of who Dylan thought he was. For all that, *No Direction Home*, 'A Martin Scorsese Picture', was a landmark.

It was not without a few problems, however. For one thing, the famous director's chief contribution seemed to be to truncate the filmed performances fans wanted most to see. Above all, the startling long-lost colour footage shot on 17 May 1966 at Manchester's Free Trade Hall was cut short, apparently for the sake of 'dramatic effect' and some by-the-numbers film-school editing. The viewer was granted the infamous 'Judas' moment, but just a taste of the music that ensued. Once a fan had recovered from the astonishment of seeing a visual record of the fabled incident, a certain resentment followed. Given the dramatic structure of the entire documentary, with Dylan accelerating towards an almighty psychological crash, the miserly use of footage from Sheffield, Newcastle and Manchester seemed self-defeating.

Scorsese had been brought in to make sense of all the material, new and archival, that Rosen had compiled. In exchange, the director had been allowed to put his million-dollar brand on the finished picture, though his actual role was in essence supervisory. Scorsese shaped the narrative, the 'Bob Dylan story', with great skill, but it was Rosen who asked the crucial questions. Inevitably, many choices were then made. The decision to end the film in 1966 was in one sense obvious, in another sense too obvious. That's how the story of Dylan's life and career is always told, but in *No Direction Home* it had the effect of locking the artist into an era, an era of which he tends to speak with a well-rehearsed disdain. Anyone coming to Dylan's work for the first time thanks to the documentary would have received a sample of the 'voice of a generation' legend and little else. The only dissenting, gently sceptical voice to be heard was that of the artist himself. Some of his contemporaries, it's true, were fascinating. Suze Rotolo, consenting to a very rare interview, was refreshingly dispassionate. Joan Baez was nicely acerbic. But everything was fashioned to preserve the orthodox view of the 'poet laureate of rock 'n' roll', the one parodied in all those Al Santos stage introductions.

That said, Scorsese brought an unerring sense of period to the work. His depiction of Dylan's childhood in Minnesota's North Country – crucially, his use of Dylan's own memories of childhood – was a marvel. Arguably, the viewer got a better idea of a man's sense of himself from those early sequences than from any other part of the film. Scorsese also managed to document the tumults of the '60s, the struggles and the rupture with all that had gone before, in a way that avoided most of the clichés. As a documentary record of a period, Dylan or no Dylan, *No Direction Home* was a corrective to a lot of glib pseudo-historical chatter. If Britain was swinging in the '60s you wouldn't guess it from the dreary scenes of a glum brown world captured in this film.

As Michael Gray, suitably indignant, puts it in his Dylan *Encyclopedia*, the documentary gives only a minimal account of one part of its subject's musical education. The desultory treatment of the blues, that crucial formative influence, is indeed 'scandalous'.[15] The misjudgement on Scorsese's part spoke of a willingness to accept without argument the old 'folk singer' label and ignore the complicated roots of Dylan's affections and art. This director, of all directors, should have known better. But then, you could also observe that the documentary does not delve deeply or often into its subject's literary background. If Dylan is the near-unique product of musical circumstances – he and Elvis had that much in common – the same could be said of his development as a writer. That he is very well-read is well known, but he is well read in unusual ways. *No Direction Home* does not begin to explain what this autodidact made of himself when he began to make verses.

The film remains a wonderful piece of work. Its release raised Dylan to the American pantheon while reminding you that despite everything, the honours and the awards, the veneration and the three and a half hours of airtime, he remained discrepant. Somehow he still didn't fit with the larger culture, high or low. That might have been one reason for his importance, of course. Nevertheless, though no one has admitted as much, least of all the figure at the centre of it all, the release of *No Direction Home* on the heels of *Chronicles* looked like an attempt to reclaim Dylan's history. Or rather, to shape and control perceptions of that history. A memoir that was not a memoir, a biographical film with just one contestable version of a life, above all the old illusion of a figure forever slipping off into the shadows: along with the Bootleg Series, these were offered as the approved, official record. Any idea that Dylan had at last decided to confess all was spectacularly wide of the mark.

Even the movie's 'soundtrack' album was no sort of soundtrack, though none the worse for that. Instead, *The Bootleg Series Vol. 7: No Direction Home: The Soundtrack* was another large trove of treasures, with a couple of outtakes apiece from *Highway 61* and *Blonde on Blonde* to surprise even the most avid of bootleg collectors. The point was control, control of the past as it loomed over the present, control of reputation, work and image. Dylan knew everything there was to know about the myth of Bob Dylan.

Product continued to appear, each release a seeming exercise in coming to terms with historical memory, the problem of a vast 'legacy' and the demands of the bottom line. So it was that in August 2005 Columbia released *Live at the Gaslight 1962*, an artefact from the beginning of recorded time. Since this album captured the coffee house singer in the last days before fame's hurricane, someone thought it clever to strike an 'exclusive' distribution deal with the Starbucks beverage chain. Depressingly, revealingly, this kind of thing had become standard practice for the 64-year-old artist. As though to balance the historical accounts, still another *Best of* was issued for the American market in November. Providing the sleeve notes, the author and TV executive Bill Flanagan had the good grace to call the unremarkable release 'a sampler for new listeners . . . a starting point'. There was no other excuse. Those listeners might have been better advised to begin, meanwhile, with *Live at Carnegie Hall*, a promotional 'EP' or mini-album that also appeared in November.

Quite why Columbia/Sony chose to release just half a dozen tracks when they had the full 19-song concert recording in their possession was, as ever, baffling. The show Dylan gave on 26 October 1963 had been taped in preparation for an *In Concert* album that was abandoned for unexplained reasons. Two tracks had since turned up on *The Bootleg Series Volumes 1–3* and two on the *No Direction Home* soundtrack. This *Carnegie Hall* made use of the artwork designed for *In Concert* decades before, but it amounted to another 'sampler'. As a response to the bootleggers, it was close to useless, even if the handful of tracks did demonstrate just how powerful a performer the young Dylan had been. Predictably, an illicit double CD set of the full 1963 show entitled *Unravelled Tales* would appear in the summer of 2008.

*

February 2006 found him back in the studios in New York. This time, finally, he was at work on his own behalf. Whether he knew it or not,

Dylan was about to make his most successful album since *Desire* 20 years before. All the attention earned by *Chronicles* and *No Direction Home*, all the journalism expended since *Time Out of Mind* on the alluring theme of the impossible creative renaissance: all of that was about to pay off handsomely. As any number of reviewers around the world would soon confirm, the artist was about to complete his late-period trilogy with a masterpiece. Someone should have told the artist.

The point is less trivial than it seems. Dylan's recorded work is classified persistently in terms of 'trilogies' even when he denies having any such notion. As with the tour that never ends, helpful critics tell the artist what he has done when their favourite theory has been no part, so he says, of his intentions. So the three albums that appeared like lightning flashes between March 1965 and May 1966 are described as a trilogy when the differences between the works, thematic and musical, are obvious. Nothing on *Bringing It All Back Home* would sit easily on *Blonde on Blonde*, but that detail is ignored. Similarly, the albums made while Dylan was in the throes of Christian evangelical belief get called his 'gospel trilogy', despite the fact that *Shot of Love* pays attention only intermittently to the obsessions of *Saved*. Neither album involves gospel music in the proper sense, in any case, but that too is forgotten. To some ears, 'trilogy' sounds irresistibly impressive. The evidence says Dylan doesn't think that way.

He certainly did not think that way about the album he would call *Modern Times*. It was not intended to complete a design commenced with *Time Out of Mind* because there had been no such design. Talking to the novelist Jonathan Lethem late in the summer, the artist would 'demur' at the word trilogy.

> *Time Out of Mind* was me getting back in and fighting my way out of the corner. But by the time I made *'Love and Theft'* I was out of the corner. On this record, I ain't nowhere, you can't find me anywhere, because I'm way gone from the corner. I would think more of *'Love and Theft'* as the beginning of a trilogy, if there's going to be a trilogy . . . If I decide I want to go back into the studio.[16]

In other words, he had paid no attention to the idea before it was put to him. By 2006, the attempt to give his work the formal unity of a trilogy, to ascribe to it a fixed set of themes, ideas and interests, was in danger of becoming another of the labels he had always detested.

The truth of the work was at risk of being submerged by the latest clichés. Chief among those was the one that confused Dylan with a historical figure just because he wasn't getting any younger and because he was fascinated with origins and roots, sometimes as ends in themselves, sometimes as explanations for modern times. He was being consigned to the archives while he yet lived. In 2006, the *New York Times* would call him 'an emissary from a reinvented yesteryear, where he finds clues to eternal truths in both the blues and the Bible'.[17] The description would be fair enough, but it would carry a noxious whiff of obituary, as though better voiced in the past tense. The idea that history could and should be deployed for a modern purpose was being lost. The specific idea that an older America mired in hard times might have something to say to the country after 9/11 was being missed entirely. Instead, too often, the artist was being treated as a revered antique.

A kind of unthinking cultural nationalism was also beginning to emerge. By 2006, Dylan was being described as one of those great, quintessential Americans, a maker of culture and history, a figure who seemed to contain the country's whole spirit and character. Again, this was not too far from the haphazard truth. He approached the *idea* of America much as Whitman, Twain, or Scott Fitzgerald had approached it. But he was also a living, working performer in the twenty-first century, with all that implied, not some exhibit trapped inside the museum of collective memory. As Dylan aged, the urge to treat him as a national monument, the last American hero, was becoming a little perilous for his art.

You can take it, then, that he did not name his album *Modern Times* for nothing. He had been called Chaplinesque often enough in his youth; one of the allusions made by the album's title was therefore plain. Chaplin's 1936 comedy had mocked the modernising pretensions of capitalism and satirised its dehumanising effects. First and foremost, it was a movie about exploitation. The running gag was that industrialisation was crazy and liable to drive people crazy. Modern times were bad for the human race. One of Dylan's responses would come in language of a kind he had never before employed.

There's an evenin' haze settlin' over the town
Starlight by the edge of the creek
The buyin' power of the proletariat's gone down
Money's gettin' shallow and weak

470

HAND ME DOWN MY WALKIN' CANE

The place I love best is a sweet memory
It's a new path that we trod
They say low wages are a reality
If we want to compete abroad

The artist's interest in the buying power of the proletariat had not been noted hitherto. On the other hand, Dylan was straightforwardly correct: real wages for American workers had been in steady decline for years while wealth was concentrated in fewer and fewer hands. The verse quoted is not one he has been accused of stealing, a fact that is interesting for its own sake. By 2006, the obsession with plagiarism among those who watched over Dylan meant that much of his work, the work for which no handy antecedents could be found, was being neglected. What was being said in the songs was being ignored studiously. 'Borrowing' had become the only topic when it ought to have been a footnote. The statement made by 'Workingman's Blues #2' and by the rest of the album was not unimportant, after all.

Praised extravagantly as it was, *Modern Times* would turn out to be a victim of some truly purblind scholarship. Even now, the album tends to be discussed in terms of what it owes to ancient blues, old popular songs, or poetry. What Dylan did with his sources somehow becomes a secondary issue, perhaps because he did complicated things with found materials. It is a lot easier to investigate alleged thefts from Henry Timrod, Robert Johnson, or Bing Crosby – Dylan is nothing if not eclectic – than it is to talk about an artist's belief in biblical prophecy and the precarious lives of the downtrodden poor. Some seemed to think the title *Modern Times* was merely whimsical. In reality, it signifies a deeply political piece of work by an author still inclined to believe that these times are the end times. He might have sneered endlessly at party hacks, but he had not stopped thinking about power and powerlessness.

Politics in the plain sense is far from dominant on the album, of course, but here and there Dylan could pass for Jim Casy, the faithless preacher of Steinbeck's *Grapes of Wrath*, oppressed by sex, righteousness and justice. Yet 'Workingman's Blues #2' – number two because the country singer Merle Haggard had used the title first – is more than just a series of oblique observations on current affairs and tough economic times. It ranges across the country's history, speaks the biblical language of revolution straight from Dylan's old song 'When the Ship Comes In', displays a real empathy with poverty's victims, takes a detour by way of classical literature, and yet remains rooted in twenty-first-century realities:

> Now I'm down on my luck and I'm black and blue
> Gonna give you another chance
> I'm all alone and I'm expecting you
> To lead me off in a cheerful dance
> Got a brand new suit and a brand new wife
> I can live on rice and beans
> Some people never worked a day in their life
> Don't know what work even means

If you say that Dylan is full of surprises you have said nothing at all. This is the writer who 'rejected politics'? Nevertheless, all those years of muttering that party politics is meaningless, fraudulent or the work of the Devil led a lot of listeners to assume, even when the contrary evidence was plain, that he took no interest in the woes of this world. All of the people in the songs of *Modern Times* are common folk, distressed, spooked, confused and oppressed. They struggle with life and faith, but their suffering is no accident. As often as not, bad things have been done to them. A lot of vengeance is plotted on this album, even when the rhymes are outrageous.

> Gonna raise me an army, some tough sons of bitches
> I'll recruit my army from the orphanages

'Love and Theft' had a light heart; *Modern Times* wears the organ bloody and ragged on its sleeve. The album exists in a smoky twilight, out on dusty roads, in bare rooms. It contains the nagging sense of ending, perhaps for America, perhaps for the world. Hence that odd line in 'Workingman's Blues', 'I can see for myself that the sun is sinking.' It is as though the speaker has just noticed the approaching darkness for the first time.

The producer, this 'Jack Frost', knew his business. When he told journalists that doing the job himself simply saved a lot of time and 'rigmarole', Dylan was being too modest. *Modern Times* was solid evidence for the claim that some of his previous albums had been ruined by eager industry pros convinced they understood the needs of his music better than he ever could. Even if they did not justify his erratic decision-making, the new recordings were proof that the artist could achieve the sound he wanted without anyone's help. 'I know my form of music better than anyone else would,' as Dylan put it in 2009.[18] It was just a pity that it had taken him so long to grasp this self-evident fact. *Modern Times* sounded wonderful.

The opening track, 'Thunder on the Mountain', all but painted a picture. However the effect was achieved, it was like listening to some supernatural roadhouse band crowded onto a tiny, ill-lit stage in the early hours with a singer who sounded as though he was facing his last night on earth. This, though, was rockabilly, 'primitive' rock and roll, a source code invested with the spirit of Carl Perkins and carried by two guitar players (Stu Kimball and Denny Freeman) performing as though they have just heard Chuck Berry for the first time. Meanwhile, the vocalist – there is no other word for it – *declaims*.

I've been sitting down studying the art of love
I think it will fit me like a glove
I want some real good woman to do just what I say
Everybody got to wonder
What's the matter with this cruel world today

In due course it would be pointed out that Dylan had slipped in a reference to Ovid's *Ars Amatoria* ('The Art of Love') and that there were other lines from the Roman poet's works scattered throughout the album. A snatch of Virgil's *Aeneid* had already turned up in 'Lonesome Day Blues' on *'Love and Theft'*. In New Zealand, the poet Cliff Fell would write in the *Nelson Mail* in October of his amazement on discovering several lines from Ovid's *Tristia* and *Epistulae ex Ponto* ('Black Sea Letters') in the songs of *Modern Times*.[19] In most cases, the correspondences were exact, dead ringers in fact. For example, the seventh verse of 'Workingman's Blues' has the lines 'No one can ever claim / That I took up arms against you.' In the translation used by Fell, *Tristia* (2.52) runs: 'My cause is better: no one can claim that I ever took up arms against you.' Scott Warmuth would duly add to the tally of Ovidian echoes and Richard Thomas, professor of classics at Harvard, would contribute half a dozen more.[20]

This would be interesting, just as the citations derived from the works of Berry, Bing Crosby, Robert Johnson, Memphis Minnie, Timrod, Howlin' Wolf, Muddy Waters, the Stanley Brothers, Lightnin' Hopkins and others besides would be interesting. Whether the discoveries could be called significant was another question. If the desire was simply to run up an indictment of Dylan for theft, the game was as banal as ever, founded in ignorance. On the other hand, anyone who wanted to ask why the artist was laying claim to a near-spiritual connection with Ovid, old and sick, exiled to Tomis on the war-torn edge of the empire (and therefore of civilisation) by a ruler's inscrutable whim, was entering fascinating territory. What Dylan had done mattered far less than why he had done it.

Cut off from the world, family and friends, Ovid believed that exile had destroyed him as a poet. In his *Metamorphoses* he had described the ages of humankind as golden, silver, bronze and iron. The last of these – faithless, savage, lost to truth – was for Ovid his modern times. Dylan was borrowing these lines for a specific poetic purpose. By the time he made *Modern Times* he almost certainly knew that every last example of 'intertextuality' would be netted and pinned to someone's tray of specimens. Cliff Fell, who believed the 'homage' to Ovid was something to celebrate rather than bemoan, probably put it best. Dylan, he wrote, had 'cast the songs as a modern lament, in the mask of a new Ovid, a kind of modern exile in the modern world'. Fell used the handy word *bricoleur* and pointed out what should have been obvious: 'Ovid, himself, stole lines and stories from Homer, as did Virgil. And Dante, Chaucer and Shakespeare all stole ideas and lines from Virgil and Ovid. It goes on. It's a part of the poetic process.'

For whatever reason, that process was not well understood. As David Kinney would observe in a *New York Times* op-ed piece in 2012: 'For the past decade, a great debate has been boiling about the authenticity of Mr Dylan's work.'[21] Out in the 'blogosphere', where Joni Mitchell's blunt allegation of plagiarism had raised temperatures, the pot had boiled over. The media's headlines would meanwhile arrive clad in protective question marks, but their very ambivalence would be suggestive. 'Plagiarism in Dylan, or a Cultural Collage?', said one. 'Is Bob Dylan a Phony?' ran another.[22] The witless charge of simple plagiarism, like the demand that Dylan should have named all his many sources, ran up against a familiar but fundamental question. Who else could have shaped all of those found materials into these songs?

Even 'Rollin' and Tumblin'', at first hearing the most blatantly imitative and derivative track on *Modern Times*, is intended to be understood as the artist's contribution to a piece of blues heritage held in common by a host of musicians. Dylan made no attempt to disguise what he was doing. Listeners might think of it as a familiar Muddy

Waters tune – he had the hit and took the credit – but old McKinley Morganfield also 'stole' the song. The sole issue of real substance arose when anyone asked if one rich man deserved every cent of the royalties from an album whose credits announced, 'All songs written and composed by Bob Dylan.' Still, if plagiarism is defined as 'passing off', what does the artist's 'When the Deal Goes Down' have in common, in meaning and intention, with Crosby's 'When the Blue of Night (Meets the Gold of the Day)'? A melody has been adapted; the lyrics are worlds, universes, apart.

The artist's 'Spirit on the Water' sounds at every turn like *something* you've heard before. We can take that to be Dylan's intended effect. It's western swing; it has stride piano, a walking bass, some lines you could sing in church and some you certainly would not. But you need hear neither the voice nor a rather pretty harmonica break to know that this could be no one else but Dylan. Nor is this one of those 'American songbook' exercises that seem to attract unthinking praise as often as this artist has attracted suspicion. All the borrowings littering the album are mere cues, musical and rhetorical. Dylan's way with words is utterly distinctive.

> I wanna be with you in paradise
> And it seems so unfair
> I can't go to paradise no more
> I killed a man back there

Is that last line an allusion to Johnny Cash and 'Folsom Prison Blues' ('I shot a man in Reno just to watch him die')? Or does Dylan get to it by way of a hundred murder ballads, country laments and blues songs? The Cash song was itself based on a movie and a stolen melody, but who still knows or cares? One of the great achievements of *Modern Times* springs from the artist's refusal to give a damn for arguments over method. He knows that songwriters, songmakers, have always operated in the manner he has adopted. They faced less scrutiny than Bob Dylan, but that's another story. His lovely 'Nettie Moore' shares a title and a few words with a nineteenth-century song. It takes a cliché – 'They say whiskey will kill ya, but I don't think it will' – from 'Moonshiner', a traditional piece he had performed in his days in the Village. Numerous blues singers had also found the line irresistible. But the 'Nettie Moore' of *Modern Times* bears no resemblance whatever to its sources. In any sense that matters, it's a new song. With its antique language intended to evoke a sense of lost time, it exists for the sake of the last line of its chorus:

Oh, I miss you Nettie Moore
And my happiness is o'er
Winter's gone, the river's on the rise
I loved you then and ever shall
But there's no one here that's left to tell
The world has gone black before my eyes

The fact that *Modern Times* amounts to a full-spectrum analysis of pre-modern American music would be noticed by all. Every style that went into the making of popular song, and therefore of the country's native culture, was there. Dylan would be applauded for his range of reference, the ease with which he made it all seem his own, the fact that he understood what tradition involved. Any comparison with Presley as a one-man pop-music melting pot, fusing every influence, was justified by the album. It would sometimes be forgotten, however, that Dylan's pursuit of pre-rock and roll styles was not a species of nostalgia or some antiquarian hobby. The concerns of *Modern Times* are eternal and *therefore* contemporary. The final track, 'Ain't Talkin'', stands out from the rest as the summation of everything the album has been about: faith and the loss of faith, failure, the urge to vengeance, hard times and injustice. Still the pilgrim keeps on walking. No single verse gives an adequate idea of the whole. It is enough to say that while critics prepared to celebrate the triumphant conclusion to a so-called trilogy, Dylan ended the album with words that were as bleak as they were unflinching.

Ain't talkin', just walkin'
Up the road around the bend
Heart burnin', still yearnin'
In the last outback, at the world's end

Cliff Fell yielded to no one, it seems, in his admiration for what Dylan had achieved. He did make one point, however: 'Section 13 of *Tristia* begins with Ovid sending greetings from "his outback" and section 14 speaks of Ovid's wife being known "to the world's end".'[23] In terms of poetic method, this was fascinating, but of no greater consequence than that. It should have given pause, nevertheless, to anyone still

476

inclined to treat Dylan's lyrics as specimens of purest autobiography.

When the album was released at the end of August it would go straight to number one in America and in several other countries. At 65, Dylan would achieve the curious feat of being recognised as the oldest performer ever to have topped the US album charts. But that was apt. Though a few critics carped that *Modern Times* did not justify all the fuss, or argued that the artist was being lauded less for the music than for his improbable longevity, it was impossible to maintain that he had failed to achieve his 'renaissance'. It was hard, too, to ignore the fact that Dylan had re-emerged with a new kind of songwriting, writing less flamboyant than it had been once upon a time, but more acute and more considered. Allied to his innate talent was the kind of editorial intelligence required to make sense of all those sources. Words, his own or borrowed, no longer spilled from him in torrents, but the songs were none the worse for that. Some of them stood comparison with his greatest works of the 1960s. It would soon be possible to argue, in fact, that some among them might prove more enduring than the magical songs of his youth. As to quality, this listener holds to the belief that there are six truly terrific pieces of work in the ten tracks of *Modern Times*. Very few albums, in any period, achieve that kind of ratio. As it happens, most of those are Bob Dylan albums. He had not merely recovered creatively. By the end of 2006 it was clear that as a writer he was as good as he had ever been, and in some respects better. If the charge ran that he was assembling and arranging fragments, they were glittering fragments turned into a glittering whole. These too were compositions.

All that was truly lost, never to be recovered, was the voice, once his chief instrument. In *Modern Times*, as in *Love and Theft*, Dylan employed several stylistic tricks – elisions, stresses, slurs, abrupt pauses – to distract attention from the fact that there were notes he would never hit again. Sometimes he achieved remarkable effects. Sometimes, in fact, there were things emerging from those corroded pipes – 'Nettie Moore' is one good example – of which the young Dylan, always desperate to sound older than his years, had never dreamed. Vocally, nevertheless, the artist was covering his losses as best he could. Somehow the fact made the success of *Modern Times* seem all the more remarkable. Dylan wasn't raging against the dying of the light. He was treating the diminution of his powers as just another creative problem to be solved. Jonathan Lethem put it well when describing his meeting with the artist just before the album's release.

What we do understand, if we're listening, is that we're three albums into a Dylan renaissance that's sounding more and more like a period to put beside any in his work. If, beginning with *Bringing It All Back Home*, Dylan garbed his amphetamine visions in the gloriously grungy clothes of the electric blues and early rock & roll, the musical glories of these three records are grounded in a knowledge of the blues built from the inside out . . .[24]

In staking his claim to the deep soil of American music, Dylan ceased to be a figure beyond the mainstream. At the start of the twenty-first century he was reordering the criteria by which both music and literature were understood, much as he had once 'put an end' to Tin Pan Alley. He would never be conscripted by the academies, but he was being accepted, even embraced, by the arbiters of what was important. Hence all the awards, hence all that 'cultural nationalism'. There was no longer a qualm over describing him as the most significant artistic figure, or perhaps just the most significant American, of his age. Having been down and almost out, having been reduced – having reduced himself – to a performer barely one thin cut above a club act, he had confounded friends and enemies alike. No one, in any field, had come back in this manner before. He had defied age, time and, above all, every prowling, mocking ghost that had ever borne the name Bob Dylan.

*

Just before his 65th birthday, he had consented to become a disc jockey. The deal had been done with the XM Satellite Radio subscription service in December 2005, but the first broadcast from Studio B in the fabled Abernathy Building (which didn't exist) was not heard until 3 May 2006. *Theme Time Radio Hour with Your Host Bob Dylan* would become one of the most quixotic and charming episodes – or rather, 100 episodes – in his career. Who couldn't love a DJ who followed Jimi Hendrix and 'The Wind Cries Mary' with Judy Garland? Who, save those who ran radio by computer program and the hokum of market research, could not warm to someone who fashioned his broadcasts around off-the-wall 'themes'? 'Mother', 'Jail', 'Flowers', 'the Devil', 'Dogs', 'Sleep', 'Luck': only when an unavoidable event such as Christmas intruded did the host deviate from his plan of having no plan.

The first show, for no immediately obvious reason, was entitled

'Weather'. Eighteen tracks, dating from 1928 and the Carter Family to Hendrix in '67, pursued the topic of meteorological events wherever it happened to lead. Dylan seemed to enjoy every minute. After all those years and all those concerts spent saying absolutely nothing to his audiences – 'Nobody gives a shit how you're *doin' tonight* in Cleveland' – he turned out to be a natural broadcaster. The kid who once listened avidly in the small hours to 50,000-watt clear-channel stations for music 'blastin'' in from Shreveport' had become an older gentleman with the freedom to play any record that took his fancy. As a youth he had listened out for Muddy Waters. The first record played on the first *Theme Time* was Waters and 'Blow Wind Blow'.

Dylan was often wickedly funny in these weekly broadcasts. Most people knew about the wit; he was famous for that. Few had been exposed to the artist as a shameless stand-up, purveyor of sensationally bad jokes and sheer whimsy. Yet on tour, if in a good mood, he had been known to crack some awful gags. In the days when he was using back-up singers he had on occasion introduced the women as 'my ex-wife, my next wife, my girlfriend and my fiancée'. The drummer George Receli had once been described as 'probably the best drummer . . . on the stage'. If Dylan was feeling particularly jolly, no joke was too juvenile. Thus, to the good folks of Wisconsin's metropolis: 'Nice to be here. One of my early girlfriends was from Milwaukee. She was an artist. She gave me the brush-off.' Between records, *Theme Time* could involve an hour or more of this sort of drollery interspersed with poetry readings, ancient jingles, cocktail recipes, fake calls and invented emails, advice on divorce and any odd if unreliable fact Dylan's researchers had managed to dig up. There would be speculation, inevitably, that he was working to a script supplied by the TV writer and producer Eddie Gorodetsky, from whose vast collection many of the deeply obscure tracks broadcast on the show were taken. *Theme Time* rarely sounded as though it had been scripted.

Only Dylan, you thought, could have uttered the irrefutable statement, 'Few things go together as well as country and western music and crazy people.' Only he could have spoofed his listeners – and be taken seriously by some of them, journalists included – by claiming he was thinking of hiring out his sandblasted voice to the makers of satellite navigation systems. 'I think it would be good if you're looking for directions,' Dylan muttered on the 'Street Maps' show, 'and you heard my voice saying something like, "Take a left at the next street . . . No, a right . . . You know what, just go straight."

I probably shouldn't do it because whichever way I go I always end up at the same place . . . on Lonely Avenue.'

The first show began with the voice of the actor Ellen Barkin as the somewhat-mysterious 'Lady in Red'. 'It's night-time in the big city,' she said, exhaling each word. 'Rain is falling. Fog rolls in from the waterfront. A night-shift nurse smokes the last cigarette in her pack . . . It's *Theme Time Radio Hour* with your host, Bob Dylan.' Barkin and the DJ would keep this glorious nonsense going for the best part of three years. The introductions would vary a little from week to week, but the parody of long-gone radio links would remain a beloved vignette within the show. Episode ten, 'Summer', commenced with 'It's night-time in the big city. Angry prostitutes fight over a street corner. A man gets drunk and shaves off his moustache.' Show 13, 'Rich Man, Poor Man', began: 'It's night-time in the big city. A guilty man goes home to his wife. It's time to make the doughnuts.' The introduction to the two-hour episode broadcast for Christmas and New Year in 2006 might count as Barkin's finest moment. 'It's night-time in the big city. A department store Santa sneaks a sip of gin. Mistletoe makes an old man sad. Eight reindeer land on the roof of the Abernathy Building.'

In dull reality, Dylan recorded the show in his spare moments while touring the world. When the first episode went out he was nowhere near Washington DC, where the temporaneous Abernathy Building was alleged to be situated, but out on the road between Davidson, North Carolina, and Knoxville, Tennessee. When the ninth show was aired, Dylan was performing in Bournemouth on England's south coast. During the next broadcast he was in transit between Clermont-Ferrand in France and Cap Roig in Spain. It made no difference to the fiction of the nodding night owl in Studio B who seemed to say whatever came into his addled head while playing records no other station would recognise, far less touch.

Amid the entertainment, the show offered an unimpeachable musical education. Whether the tracks were picked by Dylan, Gorodetsky or by some collaborative process was neither here nor there. When Episode 14, 'The Devil', opened with Robert Johnson's 'Me and the Devil Blues' it wasn't hard to guess who had made the selection. The DJ played a lot of his well-known favourites and took the listener on an inimitable journey through the history of American popular culture. It was another way, more playful than his albums, of explaining a country's past. When *Theme Time* was picked up by the BBC and Ireland's Phantom FM in 2007 it was in recognition of the fact that something unique in broadcasting had been achieved by the ever-eccentric host and his omniscient producer. Something very funny, too.

During an early show entitled 'Father', Dylan reported: 'We got an email from Johnny Depp from Paris, France. He wants to know "Who was the father of modern communism?" Well, Johnny, Karl Marx was the father of modern communism. He also fathered seven children.' Apropos of the Tom Waits song 'On the Nickel', the host said: 'Waits has a raspy, gravelly singing voice, described by one fan as like how you'd sound if you drank a quart of bourbon, smoked a pack of cigarettes and swallowed a pack of razorblades after not sleeping for three days. Or as I like to put it, beautiful.' At one point during the 2006 Christmas broadcast, Dylan sent out his idea of season's greetings: 'To all of our friends listening in behind bars, we know you made mistakes, we're sorry you have to be there, but Merry Christmas to all of you, from all of us here at *Theme Time Radio Hour.*' When the theme was 'Flowers', the host began: 'Tonight we're going to be talking about the most beautiful things on earth, the fine-smelling, colourful, bee-tempting world of flowers – the Bougainvillea, the Passion Flower, the Butterfly Cleradendron, the Angel's Trumpets, the Firecracker plant. We're going to be talking about Rosa rugosa, the Angel Face, All That Jazz, the Double Delight . . .' So it went on, plant after plant, the names no doubt plucked from the internet by a researcher, yet turned into a weirdly hypnotic Dylan performance.

If *Theme Time* ever had a serious point – the proposition is open to question – it might have had something to do with the DJ's belief in music's deeper meaning and importance, in the galvanic force that had once propelled him unstoppably out of Hibbing, Minnesota. No one knew better than Dylan that music could change lives; no one believed more sincerely that something important was being lost from the culture. When he grumbled about modern recording technology and its failure to capture the pure truth of a performance, he might as well have been bewailing the decline and fall of the West. It made him sound like a crusty reactionary, but Dylan believed he was defending something precious, something irreplaceable. So for three years the essence poured forth from the Abernathy Building of his mind: Muddy Waters and Buddy Holly; Ray Charles and George Jones; Van Morrison and Charlie Parker; Johnny Cash, John Lee Hooker, the Beatles, the Drifters, Bo Diddley, Elvis, Robert Johnson, Big Joe Turner, Sonny Boy Williamson. There was an implicit question in all of this: why did no one else ever play these things? Amid it all, the artist did what he did best: he told stories to strangers. That said, only Dylan could have illustrated the theme of 'Birds' with Leonard Cohen's 'Bird on the Wire' followed by Al Jolson singing 'When the Red, Red Robin (Comes Bob, Bob, Bobbin' Along)'.

*

He bobbed. In addition to recording an album and launching his radio show, Dylan gave 98 concerts in the United States and Europe in 2006. *Modern Times* was released on 29 August and its songs soon began to appear on set lists for performances on the West Coast. Despite all his talk about quitting the recording studios, Dylan was quick to embrace the new material. Clearly, the idea that he could go on playing the same old songs 'forever' was no longer self-evident.[25] In February 2007, though he declined to put in an appearance at the event, the artist was given another pair of Grammy awards thanks to *Modern Times*. It brought the running total of those honours to ten. In May of the year, he reached the age of 66 in the briefest of breaks in a touring schedule that saw him return to Australia and New Zealand amid the usual campaigns in North America and Europe.

Grammy awards or not, the shows continued to divide audiences. While the success of the album attracted new crowds, walkouts were still being reported. By any normal standards, Dylan's voice was beyond any hope of recovery. Despite his complaints, the detested recording studio offered the protections and second chances that were unavailable in the middle of a ball park. As ever, those who were prepared to grant Dylan licence in all things didn't seem to care. Often enough they could persuade themselves they had witnessed something truly remarkable – 'historic', 'awesome' and the rest – when the recorded evidence said they were deluded. For the casual customer or the fan returning to Dylan after years of indifference, the game of name-that-song was too often infuriating. Another, more thoughtful section of the audience had meanwhile arrived at a new reason to bear with the artist. There might not be another chance, they told themselves, to see Bob Dylan perform.

It was not yet dark. By any decent estimate, in fact, the artist was hardly classifiable as old. *Modern Times* had displayed an unmistakable vitality. It hadn't felt like any sort of valediction. Nevertheless, a lot of reviewers began to wonder how much useful life was left in the performing artist when his voice was utterly ravaged and his interest in the job at hand often seemed slight. His band was professionalism itself, on stage or in the studio. Millions of people were still fascinated by his work, past and present, and by the mutations of what they took to be his personality. Books, the endless infernal books of study, criticism and reportage, continued to appear. But the concerts and the bootlegs that materialised after almost every show continued to raise the question of whether Dylan remained viable as a live performer. His voice, it was observed, was far more reliable at the start of a tour than at its end. That voice needed to be rested, but in the concert season – generally from March or April until the middle of November – he allowed it no respite. Doubts were raised constantly and Dylan ignored every one of them. For him, it seems, the good nights eradicated every memory of the bad. In 2006, just after the release of *Modern Times*, he could be found exulting that his band were 'the best band I've ever been in, I've ever had, man for man'. He could be heard talking of the shows as though performance was an obligation, a kind of vocation, but he gave no hint of reservations about his fitness for the task. That wasn't his way. Every word he spoke gave credence to the belief that these tours would never end.

> You do care, you care in a big way, otherwise you wouldn't be there. But it's a different kind of connection. It's not a light thing . . . It's alive every night, or it feels alive every night . . . It becomes risky. I mean, you risk your life to play music, if you're doing it in the right way.[26]

In the same conversation, Dylan made an odd remark about writing the songs for *Modern Times* in a 'trance-like, hypnotic state' and of questioning himself as he wrote: 'This is how I feel? Why do I feel like that? And who's the me that feels this way?' It was the old and perennial enquiry: *who's the me?* A man in his middle 60s was still posing the question. No one had provided him with an answer.

The belief that Dylan simply 'reinvented' himself periodically was wearing very thin. The notion that his career was best represented by a series of masks didn't seem so credible after a religious fervour that had been only too real. The talk of continual reinvention had always been a little glib. How does a person manage such a thing and keep any kind of grip on reality? The equivalent idea that Dylan dealt in riddles, that his entire body of work was some giant puzzle full of clues to be unravelled, was another test of credulity. It was one thing to argue, as Scott Warmuth was arguing, that a single text such as *Chronicles* was best understood as a precision-made enigma, but even that clever thesis ignored the life lived, the life described. However he had come into existence, this 'Bob Dylan' was not just an evolving piece of art or a self-created conundrum. There was a person in there. That character continued to intrigue a lot of people.

The movie *I'm Not There* was less an attempt to solve the mystery than to depict it. When shooting began in Montreal at the end of July 2006, six actors were on hand to give life to aspects of the artist in his several manifestations. In one sense, the picture's director, Todd Haynes, was employing some of the known, multiple Dylans much as the artist had done. In the film-maker's hands they became devices for asking questions of the audience. The result was vastly entertaining for fans, with some fine performances (and some not so fine) from the cast, but it was a little way short of the greatest movie ever made. The film was a biopic that attempted to fuse several contending biographies into one while leaving room for myths, legends and whatever illumination there was to be had from an eclectic selection of Dylan songs. It made for a crowded two hours and fifteen minutes. Haynes tried to get the contents of Dylan's imagination onto the screen alongside the public record of the artist's career, some suggestive fictions and a meditation on the nature of identity. *Masked and Anonymous* had already seemed to prove that film probably wasn't the best medium for this kind of effort, but Haynes had other ideas.

He had lots of ideas. The most eye-catching was to have Dylan in his mid-'60s pomp played, and played brilliantly, by Cate Blanchett. Her performance became an exquisite act of impersonation, one that said more about identity than anything in the script. The film's title, lifted from one of the venerable basement tapes songs Dylan refused to take seriously, was another unambiguous statement. The subject of the film was as elusive as any final judgement on the subject. (The track proved to be elusive, too. Neither Columbia nor the artist's management possessed the tape. It had been loaned to Neil Young years before and somehow forgotten. The writer truly didn't care about his song.) Nevertheless, the picture would remain a challenge, as they say, for mainstream audiences. A movie about a person who could be present and absent simultaneously, known to millions and yet somehow unknowable, essentially impersonal yet capable of making audiences feel as though he had touched each one of them personally: what could go wrong?

When *I'm Not There* was released in November 2007 most of the movie critics would rise to the occasion with more agility than they had summoned for *Masked and Anonymous*. The idea of having six actors attempt different aspects of a single person wouldn't bother the reviewers too much. A messy, confusing western sequence involving Richard Gere as 'Billy the Kid', an alias for Dylan's Alias in *Pat Garrett and Billy the Kid*, would be tolerated because Blanchett's hypnotic acting was going on, so to speak, next door. Even the idea of having a young African American (Marcus Carl Franklin) represent 'Woody Guthrie' would fail to test hard-working journalists unduly. It made a kind of sense. Much of the film made plenty of sense, in fact, but only if one key condition was fulfilled: you had to know *something*, ideally any number of things, about Bob Dylan. A fan would not have blinked to hear the character called 'Arthur Rimbaud' (Ben Whishaw) answer questions with verbatim quotations from interviews Dylan had given down the years. The uninitiated were liable to wonder what was going on and ask why some nineteenth-century French poet was being subjected to intense official interrogation in what looked like the middle of the 1960s.

In due course, the artist would give the picture what passed for his seal of approval. Talking to *Rolling Stone* in 2012, Dylan would at first say, 'I don't know anything about that movie. All I know is they licensed about 30 of my songs for it.' Pressed, he would concede that *I'm Not There* was 'all right'. He seemed slightly impressed by the fact that Haynes had appeared not to care whether his picture was understood or not. Asked about the film's investigations into 'phases and identities', however, Dylan resorted to his usual answer: 'I don't see myself that way. But what does it matter? It's only a movie.'[27]

The director had told a writer from the *New York Times* magazine that Dylan's 'refusal to be fixed as a single self in a single voice [was] a key to his freedom. And he somehow escaped this process of being frozen into one fixed person.'[28] For all the movie's stratagems, that 'somehow' would form the basis of a question left unanswered by *I'm Not There*. Yet as brave tries go, the film was among the bravest. Haynes was asking the audience to submit to a piece of cinema much as they would submit to Dylan's music. The film, effectively six short films yoked together, was an attempt to reproduce a phenomenon rather than describe a life. As the director had said to the *New York Times*: 'What would it be like to be in that moment when it was new and dangerous and different? You have to do a kind of trick almost to get people back to where Dylan did what he did, or Mozart did what he did.'

Haynes had been trying to put his disconcerting movie together for years. As far back as the summer of 2000 he had been invited to send a single-page proposal to the artist by way of Dylan's 'representative', Jeff Rosen. The invitation had been extended with the advice that there should be no mention whatever in the pitch of the word genius. The phrase 'voice of a generation' had also been placed beyond bounds. The text had commenced with the old Rimbaud 'I is another' quotation. Haynes had written of making a film 'in which the breadth and flux of a creative life could be experienced'.

> The structure of such a film would have to be a fractured one, with numerous openings and a multitude of voices, with its prime strategy being one of refraction, not condensation. Imagine a film splintered between seven separate faces – old men, young men, women, children – each standing in for spaces in a single life. [A seventh, Chaplin-type character was cut from the script.]

Dylan had known a little bit more about the picture beforehand, then, than his recollection of a request to license some songs would suggest. On the other hand, he had made no effort to become involved in the production. The first serious attempt to fictionalise his life directly was complicated enough without that kind of contest between perceived realities. *I'm Not There* would go on to win the Grand Jury Prize at the Venice Film Festival and gain Blanchett an Oscar nomination, but fail at the box office. As Richard Goldstein observed in a doleful article in *The Nation* in 2006, Dylan was 'cruising towards sainthood' among those who subscribed to the cult. 'We're witnessing a consecration,' said the writer. The artist had acquired 'enduring status as a fetish' irrespective, it was argued, of the quality of the music.[29] Haynes had made his picture as a fan, apparently forgetting that the cult was not universal. A lot of non-aligned movie-goers would decide that *I'm Not There* offered a challenge they didn't care to meet.

In a notebook, the director had jotted down his 'governing concepts/ themes' for the film. The notes had read: 'America obsessed with authenticity/ authenticity the perfect costume/ America the land of masks, costumes, self-transformation, creativity is artificial, America's about false authenticity and creativity.' The result, as Blanchett described it, was an impenetrable script 'completely and utterly inside Todd's brain'. Haynes would tell the *New York Times* that his movie was 'intimate and panoramic, the story of a personality and a nation'.

One of the director's friends added, for the journalist's benefit, that 'it's no less than a history of American conscience and American soul . . . It's a movie about Bob Dylan as the President of America.'

*

In 2008, that job would become available. In fact, a candidate had declared himself on 10 February 2007, in Springfield, Illinois, picking his spot outside the Old State Capitol where Abraham Lincoln once had stood to notify an interest in the position of head of state. Barack Hussein Obama didn't have a stovepipe hat, or a fund of tall tales. He was 45, personable and articulate, a rising orator among Democrats, highly intelligent and, some said, effortlessly and ineffably cool. Amid an eclectic collection, he kept 30 Bob Dylan songs on his iPod. He wasn't white.

That aside, Obama was another all-American politician whose time was almost upon him. Few realised as much on a cold February day. It was not a perception the former junior senator intended to foster when he told a boisterous crowd about his 'different kind of politics'. Obama had written a couple of very successful books, one with the word dreams in its title, a second, newly published, invoking audacity and hope.[30] Those words would play a big part in the nomination campaign he would win against the odds, and in the presidential race he would win easily. In a country tired of war and George W. Bush, Obama would portray himself as the personification of faith in the idea, whatever it meant, of 'change'. He would also create expectations that were impossible to fulfil, even for a candidate who meant every word he said.

According to reporters from the *Washington Post*, Obama had declared in a statement before the announcement of his candidacy that he would emphasise 'traditional Democratic goals such as lowering health-care costs, providing college-tuition assistance and developing new energy sources. He only briefly mentioned the Iraq war, the issue that could well drive the 2008 election.'[31] The new candidate said, in fact, that America was 'mired in a tragic and costly war that should never have been waged'. By 2007, his was not an unpopular position.

The Bush administration was persisting with its attempts to portray the Iraq incursion as a victory-in-the-making for liberty and democracy. Even among conservatives, few were still falling for that. According to Gallup polling in July 2007, only 29 per cent of Americans could be found to approve of the way their president was doing his job.[32]

Bush's ratings would sink lower still before he was done. Despite a 'surge' involving an additional 30,000 troops in the second half of the year, 2007 would inflict a bloody toll, with 899 American lives lost. According to surveys conducted by the Associated Press, 18,610 Iraqi 'non-insurgents' would also perish. The news agency's figure would be a conservative estimate for the year, but since the occupiers chose not to keep records of civilian deaths it stood as an entry in history's ledger. Here were modern times, just like the old Vietnam times.

In Springfield, Obama had invoked Lincoln shamelessly. The young black candidate possessed the oratorical gifts to make the association sound plausible, at least for those who wanted most to believe that 'there is power in hope'. The possibility that hope could be disappointed was a thought not fit for a modern political campaign. Thanking his audience for turning out on a freezing day, Obama had said:

> It's humbling, but in my heart I know you didn't come here just for me. You came here because you believe in what this country can be. In the face of war, you believe there can be peace. In the face of despair, you believe there can be hope. In the face of a politics that's shut you out, that's told you to settle, that's divided us for too long, you believe we can be one people, reaching for what's possible, building that more perfect union.

The Periclean triplets had been sonorous – Dylan knew all about that kind of rhetoric – but manipulative. Like all inspirational poetry, they made nothing happen. Anaphora, the trick of repeating a phrase at the start of successive statements, had been a device favoured both by Lincoln and by Martin Luther King. Obama's fine words had also had the effect of seeming to address an issue without once naming that issue. He wasn't white. Nevertheless, that Saturday in February he had stood where the liberator of black slaves once had stood, claiming Lincoln's mantle and sounding very like King. The symbolism had been deliberate yet deliberately vague.

By 2007, Dylan had seen 11 men occupy the Oval Office. He had even met a couple of them. But he had also performed on 28 August 1963, during the Great March on Washington. He had sung 'When the Ship Comes In' before a quarter of a million people, most of them black, who had marched that day 'for jobs and freedom'. Dylan had listened while King preached of his dream of human, social and racial justice. The artist had done more for civil rights, for a brief while, than most white entertainers. He had made a career from the legacy of the blues and married a black woman for love. He had drawn a cordon around himself for protection against politicians and their slogans, but he had never lost his political intelligence or, more importantly, his gift for empathy. Still, Dylan must have wondered what would become of Barack Obama in twenty-first-century America. Election results might say in due course that the civil-rights movement had won its victory with the election of a black citizen to the White House. The unremitting hatred of Obama from an unreconciled portion of the nation would say something else entirely. As president, the black lawyer would turn out to be the least radical of Democrats, with a near-suicidal instinct for compromise, a willingness to indulge the military, a tendency to betray 'hope' whenever its meek head appeared, and a strange need to appease Wall Street. It would make no difference to his enemies. Obama would inspire in them an attempt to 'reclaim America' from the upstart and his supporters. Sometimes the diehards would make the democratic process sound like an irrelevance. As the artist would describe the state of the nation just before the 2012 election:

> This country is just too fucked up about color. It's a distraction. People at each other's throats just because they are of a different color. It's the height of insanity and it will hold any nation back, or any neighborhood back. Or anything back. Blacks know that some whites didn't want to give up slavery – that if [whites] had their way, they would still be under the yoke. And they can't pretend they don't know that.[33]

Dylan would take to the young, black and eloquent candidate. Judging by the news coverage, the fact that the artist was even prepared to say so counted as a surprise, but the reaction was naive. His distrust of machine politics ran very deep, but so did his understanding of American history. Besides, Obama was not the average politician. Dylan, by his lights, had plenty to say. Interviewed by *The Times* in the summer of 2008, he would remark:

> Well, you know, right now America is in a state of upheaval. Poverty is demoralising. You can't expect people to have the virtue of purity when they are poor. But we've got this guy out there now who is redefining the nature of politics from the ground up . . . Barack Obama. He's redefining what a politician is, so we'll have to see how things play out.
> Am I hopeful? Yes, I'm hopeful that things might change. Some things

are going to have to . . . You should always take the best from the past, leave the worst back there and go forward into the future.[34]

On election night in 2008, Dylan and his band were playing at the University of Minnesota, the college to which he had given a few rare moments of his precious time almost half a century before. Perhaps that memory influenced what became the closest thing the artist had given to a political endorsement in many a year.

Tony [Garnier, Dylan's bass player] likes to think it's a brand-new time right now. An age of light. Me, I was born in 1941. That's the year they bombed Pearl Harbor. Well, I been living in a world of darkness ever since. But it looks like things are gonna change now.

A year later, talking of his new president as 'Barack', Dylan would come up with a dizzying, near-poetic description of his reasons for being 'intrigued' by the black man who seemed to have fulfilled Martin Luther King's fervent hopes. The artist, that insatiable reader, had come across Obama's book, *Dreams From My Father*. True to art, Dylan had responded first to the story. In the interview, a history lesson followed. What had 'struck him' about Obama?

Well, a number of things. He's got an interesting background. He's like a fictional character, but he's real.

First off, his mother was a Kansas girl. Never lived in Kansas, though, but with deep roots. You know, like 'Kansas bloody Kansas'. John Brown the Insurrectionist. Jesse James and Quantrill. Bushwhackers, guerrillas. Wizard of Oz Kansas. I think Barack has Jefferson Davis back there in his ancestry someplace.

And then his father. An African intellectual. Bantu, Masai, Griot-type heritage – cattle raiders, lion killers. I mean, it's just so incongruous that these two people would meet and fall in love. You kind of get past that, though. And then you're into his story. Like an odyssey, except in reverse.[35]

In the years to come, Dylan would resist every attempt to persuade him to offer anything as banal as a real celebrity endorsement. In 2012, a *Rolling Stone* journalist would put his tortured head against a metaphorical brick wall in a doomed effort to extract a statement from the artist. Of Obama, Dylan would concede only, 'I like him.'[36] This citizen would do things in his own way. On a Monday night in November in Madison, Wisconsin, just after an Obama rally in the city and just before voters were due to pass judgement on the president's hopes for a second term, the usual 'Blowin' in the Wind' encore was interrupted.

> Thank you everybody. We tried to play good tonight, after the president was here today. You know, we just had to do something after that. It's hard to follow that. I think he's still the president, I think he's still gonna be the president . . . Yeah, we know . . . You know, the media's not fooling anybody. It's probably gonna be a landslide.

A renewal of his all-knowing roving prophet's licence was assured when Dylan predicted the result in a race that had left pollsters and pundits floundering. Most of them were still maintaining that the contest between Obama and Mitt Romney, the Republican challenger, was far too close to call. On the following day, the artist activated the Facebook account he had hitherto ignored to repeat his statements and ensure that no one had misunderstood him.

In Madison, the audience would cheer Dylan's prognostications. In contrast, the 'white nationalist' fascists of Stormfront would commence an online discussion under the rubric 'Jew Bob Dylan Predicts Obama Landslide'. That wasn't even the half of it. The artist steered clear of party politics: this much was known. But in picking out the black candidate with the 'interesting background' in 2008, and by sticking with Obama in 2012, he had placed himself on one side of a deep divide. The loathing that had engulfed Bill Clinton was as nothing to the passions aroused in one part of the American soul by the sight of a black man in the White House. The more the president's opponents denied that their contempt had anything to do with race, the more obvious the motivating force became. In coded terms mystifying to the average European, some tried to accuse the commander-in-chief of 'socialism', but the tactic was a feeble distraction. Certain things didn't change, even if civic America had a horror of 'the race issue'. Each halting discussion was hedged around with euphemisms. Yet as the votes of minorities flooded in for Obama and swept away the complacency of a white conservative world, the reaction was furious, transparent and ugly. For Dylan, some old memories must have been awakened. Half a century had passed since he had performed 'When the Ship Comes In' beneath the shadow of Lincoln's marble memorial, but the path picked out by the March on Washington and Obama's election still went by some old, dark and muddy roads.

The statistical evidence would arrive in due course. Seth Stephens-Davidowitz, an ingenious Harvard economics scholar pursuing his PhD, would set aside what dishonest people told the pollsters and look, first, at their Google searches and the language they used, then at how the votes fell. In March 2013, the researcher would publish a paper to show that 'Continuing racial animus in the United States appears to have cost Obama roughly four percentage points of the national popular vote in both 2008 and 2012'. What's more, the black man 'lost substantially more votes from racial animus . . . than he gained from his race'.[37] Publishing in the *Journal of Politics*, meanwhile, an assistant professor at Brown University on Rhode Island named Michael Tesler would assert that the sight of a black president had produced the effect, in one grim sense ironic, of reawakening 'old-fashioned racism' – the biological 'superiority' kind – in a non-trivial portion of the electorate.[38]

In 2008, Obama's campaign would be approaching its end just as capitalism in America and around the world seemed to fall apart. Dylan's 'Workingman's Blues' would turn out to have been more prescient than most economists. The baby boomers were hitting their 60s as all the familiar American dreams of prosperity passing between the generations began to unravel. A historic national debt that had been condemned by Obama in 2007 when it stood at $9 trillion would explode after 2008. Families whose real median income had fallen by 3 per cent between 2000 and 2004 (in 'the good times') were about to be crushed as the bills came in for Wall Street's sins.[39] A few, a very few, were immune to dread: the phenomenon began to be noticed. According to estimates published by Forbes.com in September 2007, the 25 richest people in the country, few of whom made or built things for a living, had a collective 'net worth' of $490.8 billion.

The crisis caused by banking's robber barons would be international. In terms of jobs lost and national wealth destroyed, some European countries would suffer more profoundly than the United States. Nevertheless, in Dylan's country, in the country whose collective memory he tried to preserve in his songs, the psychological scars ran deep. Obama would be entitled to claim credit for relative success in propping up the system and coping with the slump, but he would receive few thanks, least of all from Republicans who began to talk as though debt had nothing to do with bankers and everything to do with minimal welfare spending. For Dylan, modern times must have contained innumerable echoes of the past. But that was how history functioned, or so he had long believed.

His imagination had first been set aflame by the songs of Woody Guthrie, quintessential witness to the Great Depression. In many places in America, and for much the same reasons as in the 1930s, the old sour smell of hard times had returned. For all that, the parallels were not exact. Dylan's awakening had come late in the gaudy 1950s when the country was still rich, powerful and generally admired around the world. Just before the banking crash of 2008 the Pew Global Attitudes Project was reporting that, thanks chiefly to Bush, the United States was mistrusted abroad if it was not despised. By then, the reaction to the exercise of military power had spread far beyond Muslim countries. In Germany, for one example, 'favourable attitudes' towards America had slipped from 78 per cent in 2000 to 37 per cent in 2007. Among the British, those most reliable of allies, the equivalent figures were 83 per cent and 56 per cent.[40]

Like some mythical island lost in a peculiar fog, America seemed to be drifting off from the rest of the world. There was no longer a consensus over the values being disputed or defended. It was not just a question of military might and its uses. One finding by the Pew researchers might have struck Dylan and his compatriots as odd, for example, but in Europe it seemed to explain a great deal. A majority of Americans (58 per cent) believed their country was 'not religious enough'. Among the Europeans, American religiosity was regarded as a defining problem. As one result, the hope promised by Obama and his election victory on 4 November 2008 was greeted with frank relief in Europe and beyond. Millions chose to believe that somehow America had come to its senses. No one could quite say what they meant by that, however.

As pandemics of optimism go, this one would prove brief. During his 2008 campaign Obama had promised to shut down the Guantanamo Bay prison in Cuba where America was holding numerous 'detainees' without charge or trial amid its war on terror. When the president then failed to keep his word, and continued to fail to keep his word, 'liberals' and assorted supportive believers began to suffer doubts. When Obama then seemed reluctant to do much more than lecture those responsible for the banking crisis, the idea that he embodied change started to look a little implausible. Fear of Romney, the Republican alternative, would win the president his re-election in 2012, but that victory would serve only to conceal a larger crisis, political and moral, within the administration. Dylan and many others would discover that 'redefining the nature of politics from the ground up' had not meant much more than presidential business as usual.

In May 2013, Obama would give a speech to explain that he meant to alter 'what has been a global war into a more targeted assault on terrorist groups threatening the United States'.[41] He would say that he also intended to 'curtail the use of drones', the robotic airborne devices that had become the vehicles for his presidential 'signature assassinations'. George Bush had ordered 52 of those drone attacks. By 2013, Obama had selected personally the targets for 318 assaults, most aimed at individuals and groups in Pakistan. By mid-2011, according to one study, 385 civilians, 160 children among them, had died thanks to these remotely controlled weapons.[42] Four American citizens had also been assassinated by their president, his 'kill orders' and his drones. To many, there was no moral justification for any of this. Nevertheless, in his May address at the National Defense University in Washington DC, Obama would still feel able to invoke the theological doctrine of the just war.

A lawyer's training would be of little use to the commander-in-chief when it was revealed that the Internal Revenue Service had been victimising his opponents in the right-wing Tea Party movement, or when it was disclosed that his justice department had been seizing the telephone records of Associated Press journalists. Even progressive sorts, specialists in disillusionment, would find it hard to explain how their liberty-loving candidate had turned into a president bent on extending the arm of the state into every corner of life. Yet if May 2013 would come to feel like the cruellest month for Obama's fans, June would be worse. On this president's watch, the headlines would say, the National Security Agency had been given licence to spy upon the communications of hundreds of millions of Americans. 'Prism', as this vast attempt at digital martial law was called, collected data from every major telephone, internet and GPS network in public use. The charge would be one of mass covert surveillance with the thinnest of legal justifications. As even the liberal media would notice, it went against every ethical and constitutional principle that Obama, the liberator, had ever espoused. He had never said, 'Yes we can . . . hack your phone.'

Dylan had written 'Masters of War' as his response to Dwight Eisenhower's warnings against the military-industry complex. Half a century later, he had spoken up, if haltingly, for the young black president who was going to change everything. Instead, the artist had given his backing to an architect of what was better described as the national security-industrial complex. By 2013, according to one estimate by budgetary analysts, 'defence' in its various manifestations would be costing America $931 billion a year, a sum approaching 25 per cent of all federal spending.[43] The young singer who had once turned his back on political idealism and fine-sounding hypocrites might have been right all along.

CHAPTER FOURTEEN

Pay in Blood

IN OCTOBER 2007, DYLAN WAS GIVEN THE PRINCE OF ASTURIAS AWARD, an honour created in the name of the heir to the Spanish throne. The artist was staging a concert in Omaha, Nebraska, and unable to show up in the city of Oviedo for his diploma, medallion, 50,000-euro cheque and a fine piece of Joan Miró sculpture. Once again, Dylan's excuse was reasonable. Just finding the time to pick up all the awards on offer was becoming a problem. August institutions around the world seemed to be competing to burden the artist with their superlatives. Aside from sometimes saying politely how very honoured he was, Dylan had no real response to these grand affairs. He was proud, no doubt, to be taken so seriously, proud that the boy who had once been patronised in dingy coffee houses for his out-of-tune guitar and his Guthrie impersonations was being exalted after half a century of work. But there was something odd, nevertheless, in the spectacle of Bob Dylan becoming canonical. Some of the orotund citations sounded like obituaries. Some of them seemed to have been written by people who had not heard many of the songs.

As 2008 began, Episode 62 of *Theme Time Radio* was broadcast. The languid Lady in Red was her familiar self: 'It's night-time in the big city. Temptation is on every corner. A man rents a hotel room under an assumed name.' The show's theme on 2 January was 'Number One', or as Dylan put it: 'For the next 60 minutes, we're gonna be talking about one-horse towns, one-track minds, one-armed bandits, one false move, one in a million, one too many, one way or another, one brick shy of a load, and one and only. So stay here one and all and listen to songs on a singular subject, that subject being . . . number one.' After playing 'I'm the One Who Loves You', a 1963 track by The Impressions, Dylan allowed himself another of his little jokes. 'The

Impressions had Curtis Mayfield at the helm,' said the host. 'Curtis was a triple treat. He wrote the songs, he played guitar on the songs, he sang on the songs.'

A month later, the *Theme Time* theme was 'Mail'. As Dylan explained to his listeners, this involved 'love letters, pen pals, going postal, ransom notes, letters to Dear John and Dear Abby, Miss Lonelyhearts . . . We'll be returning things to sender, and we'll be telling you that your cheque's in the mail.' In his case, the next cheque was never far away. The early shows of the year would take Dylan to Mexico, Brazil, Chile, Argentina and Uruguay. Later he would be in Canada, then back in Europe. In the summer, the artist would criss-cross America once more before finishing up back in Canada. The European leg of the annual trek was a little more interesting than usual. In June, audiences in Russia, Estonia, Lithuania, the Czech Republic and Croatia were granted their first encounters with the legend. Even tiny Andorra, a speck on the maps, was not forgotten. Dylan's booking agents were exhausting the land masses still untouched by their artist.

He would manage 98 concerts in 2008, a modest enough achievement by his standards. On the other hand, James Brown had thought nothing of putting his Revue through 330 one-nighters in a year. Charles Dickens, star of the Manchester Free Trade Hall and other tough venues, had once given 129 of his scintillating readings in a few brief months on the road. Harry Houdini had picked his locks in every vaudeville house in America and traversed the continent of Europe. Buffalo Bill and his Wild West show had kept going for a quarter of a century and done their stuff, their version of equine Americana, for all the crowned heads. Frank Sinatra had retired at the age of 55 and staged comebacks often, many said too often, as his great voice diminished and his memory ebbed away. There were meanwhile many thousands of honest performers, as Dylan knew well enough, who had never made a record and would never make a record. Cash on the nail aside, performance was a kind of addiction, satisfying a need that could not be met in any other manner. It was a way of life and it, too, was enmeshed in tradition. Performance was a part of an artist's contract with the public. For all his complaints, for all his ambivalence and his contradictory explanations, it seemed that Dylan still felt a need to stand before an audience.

He ploughed on, for better or worse, when some of the younger stars in his business were making no apologies for miming on stage to pre-recorded backing tracks. Their audiences wanted spectacle and music that sounded exactly like the downloaded noises in their headphones. Why risk screwing up? Dylan risked it year in and year out. At some point, therefore, he deserved to be taken at his word. Performance, he argued, was central to his artistic being. Why then would he do anything else? The trouble was that this artist's public performances were sometimes bad and often, at this point, no better than dull. Only rarely did the shows reveal anything new about the songs. The desire to be on stage was less an artistic imperative than an end in itself.

By 2008, it was inconceivable that the annual tours were being staged to meet a financial need. He didn't put on all those concerts, as most of his surviving contemporaries put on concerts, just to plug a new piece of product or to celebrate some so-called reunion. He didn't do it for the sake of critical appreciation. Despite all the complicated theories, he wasn't out there, in country after country, simply to remake his songs or reinvent his art. No one needed to go all the way to Andorra to mess around with a melody. The judgement remains, nevertheless, that while the obdurate spirit was only too willing, the voice was weak and growing weaker. On any estimate not clouded by the conviction that Dylan could do no wrong, he had not staged an interesting tour in five years. Even the shop-worn claim that each attempt to reconfigure a melody or switch a few words in a lyric counted as a creative act no longer held up. Sometimes it seemed like a game, a mere distraction from the fact that in reality Dylan had nothing much else to offer. Yet still he needed to be Bob Dylan, showing himself to the world.

In April 2008, the author of *Chronicles* would find himself on the receiving end of a 'special' Pulitzer Prize. This one was for his impact on popular music and American culture. Mention was also made of 'poetic power'. His son Jesse collected the citation on Dylan's behalf, but amid general applause a few doubts were raised. The artist was the first 'rock musician' to be honoured with a prize meant for writers and journalists, yet the Pulitzer people had failed to give him the award for poetry, or to select his prose work for attention. John Coltrane, too, had been given a posthumous 'special citation', not the music prize. Writing in the *New York Times*, Dave Itzkoff wondered how many people were 'ambivalent, or even uneasy, and fretted that the grizzled troubadour's authenticity was being co-opted'. The journalist contended that 'Dylan aficionados' were 'apprehensive' and called in aid the novelist Jonathan Lethem as one of those 'who see the Pulitzer as another chapter in [Dylan's] complicated history with the establishment, an ongoing dance of distancings and détentes'.[1] Clearly, the artist had no such qualms.

In the following month, Suze Rotolo would publish her memoir, *A Freewheelin' Time: A Memoir of Greenwich Village in the Sixties*. The smiling girl on the second album's cover had kept a resolute near-silence for decades, but having been misrepresented so often by strangers she had decided it was her turn to tell a few stories. Her relationship with Dylan had been brief enough, three years at the most, and as nothing to the forty-year marriage Rotolo had enjoyed with the film editor Enzo Bartoccioli, but no reviewer of her book would pause over those facts. Such was the way Dylan's supereminence warped reality around anyone touched by the nimbus. Encroaching fame had been one reason for the failure of the affair, his juvenile selfishness aside, after Rotolo had refused to surrender her independence to the impossible demands of his career. Her book was more than a collection of superstar anecdotes, but it too was caught still in Dylan's orbit, what with its title and its cover image taken from that famous *Freewheelin'* photo-shoot on Jones Street, near the little apartment they had shared at 161 West 4th Street before the storm carried him away. Despite her best efforts, one brief episode had cast its shadow over Rotolo's entire life. So how could anyone hope to live with this man? And where, as a human being, did that leave him?

Like Dave Van Ronk, Rotolo had never left the Village. She would tell one interviewer that she and Dylan had kept in 'occasional' touch over the years, but that was all.[2] Respect for their shared history had endured and he had made no attempt to interfere with her book. Nevertheless, she knew and he knew that the things his audiences wanted from songs such as 'Don't Think Twice' were long lost in the deep past. Only the legends remained, but the legends were all-consuming. For decades, Suze had been an artist, teacher and activist in her own right, but when she died of lung cancer on 25 February 2011, obituaries would be published around the world for a single reason. That Rotolo had taught Dylan a little about politics and poetry and introduced him to the habit of sketching during a short romance in a bygone decade counted for more than a life well lived. Once upon a time, for a brief while, Suze had been privy to a handful of the secrets of which 'Bob Dylan' was composed. For most of those who would mark a woman's death, nothing else would really matter. But then, she is not remembered in these pages for any other reason.

Dylan would offer no public response to her book or, when the moment came, to a former lover's passing.

At some point between 7 September and 23 October, between the ending of one tour in Santa Barbara, California, and the resumption of performances in Victoria, British Columbia, he went back into the studios yet again. Jackson Browne's Groove Masters in Malibu was about as close to home as Dylan could get, but the circumstances in which an album came about were as odd as any in his long recording career. With a certain impertinence, the French film director Olivier Dahan, fresh from the Oscar-winning success of *La Vie en Rose*, had asked the artist to contribute not one but 'ten or more' songs to a new picture to be called *My Own Love Song*. As he would tell the writer Douglas Brinkley, Dylan didn't quite know what to make of this Gallic gall.

> At first this was unthinkable. I mean, I didn't know what he was actually saying. [In faux French accent] 'Could you write uh, ten, twelve songs?' Ya know? I said, 'Yeah, really? Is this guy serious?' But he was so audacious! Usually you get asked to do, like, one song, and it's at the end of the movie. But ten songs? Dahan wanted to put these songs throughout the movie and find different reasons for them. I just kind of gave the guy the benefit of the doubt that he knew what he was doing.[3]

Dylan would call on the Grateful Dead lyricist Robert Hunter for help with all but one of the songs on what became *Together Through Life*. Once again, a collaborative effort would be treated as though it was all the artist's own work. While Dylan was in the studio, meanwhile, another instalment in the Bootleg Series appeared that made the need for a co-writer seem faintly ludicrous. The set called *Tell Tale Signs: Rare and Unreleased 1989–2006* was volume eight in the never-ending project and the most striking chapter in what amounted to a counter-factual history of Dylan's career. It was also, in any one of three released forms, a remarkable album in its own right. Those who talked of trilogies forgot to take this large piece of work into account. It was, as it remains, easily the equal of *Modern Times* and *'Love and Theft'*. There is a good case for saying that, whether as a single, double or horribly overpriced three-disc set, it was better than either of those albums.

In part, nevertheless, it was another episode in the old story. Here were the works, sometimes in several forms, that Dylan had elected to discard or neglect. Here finally was 'Red River Shore' twice over. Here was "Cross the Green Mountain', two tracks from the 1992 sessions with David Bromberg, the better attempts (three of them) at 'Mississippi' and a taste, albeit just one track, from the shows at the Supper Club in New York in 1993. Critics, it is fair to say, were delighted and perplexed, irritated and approving. Most of the irritation would arise from the fact that someone, whether within Columbia or the artist's management, had let greed's mask slip. While the two-CD *Tell Tale Signs* would be sold at a normal sort of price - $18.99 in America, £10 or so in Britain – the fans devoted enough to want the three-disc 'deluxe edition', with its flimsy book and a two-track piece of 'bonus' vinyl, would have to find $129.99 or its equivalent in their local currency. Most fans were furious. Even the diehards understood that they were being exploited simply because of their willingness to buy anything with Dylan's name attached. These were the people most likely to covet the 'deluxe' package, after all, and these were the people being gouged. For some, the price seemed to mark what the artist really thought of his most devoted admirers.

The chance offered late in October by the Hohner musical instrument company to purchase a ludicrous limited edition 'complete set of seven Marine Band harmonicas in the natural keys of C, G, D, F, A, B, and E which have been played and hand-signed by Bob Dylan' was taken as an insult added to injury, even by those with no aspirations to attempt a tune. Neither wit nor elegance was involved in this joke. Yet in the summer of 2013 bobdylan.com was still offering the 'Bob Dylan Signature Series Harmonica', gold-plated reed plate and all, for $120. Should anyone have desired the 'Individually Hand-Signed Harp in a Carved Ebony Box', the price given was $5,000. For those interested in owning the full seven-harmonica set, one of only twenty-five known to 'exist worldwide', with each instrument guaranteed to have felt the warm breath of the artist himself, the tab was $25,000.

Tell Tale Signs was a mesmerising piece of art with a lot to say about the human condition. By 2008, the marketing effort for the Dylan brand also said something unmistakable about human nature. Fans who had stuck with the artist for four decades found the realisation hard to take. Those struggling to balance the poetry with the price tags found it impossible to explain. Yet the obvious explanation was probably the right explanation. *Tell Tale Signs* contained a couple of versions of the song called 'Dignity', the *Oh Mercy* piece that Dylan had failed to record to his satisfaction in New Orleans in 1989. Two lines run:

I went down where the vultures feed
I would've gone deeper, but there wasn't any need

The last *Theme Time*, broadcast on 15 April 2009, also carried a whiff of corporate manoeuvring, coming as it did after XM Satellite Radio fell under new ownership. The reasons for the show being brought to an end were never made clear, though it had probably run its course in any case. The final theme, naturally enough, was 'Goodbye'. Dylan said: 'It's one thing to make an entrance, it's another thing entirely to get out alive. So for the next hour we'll be checking all the exits, finding our way outta here . . . And this show might run a little long this week, but that's OK. What are they gonna do, fire me?' He was approaching the age of 68, but all the familiar talk of packing things in, of giving up on recording or touring or meeting the demands of the expanding Bob Dylan corporate enterprise, had disappeared. Like some monarch without an heir, he had no intention of abdicating. His life had become a bizarre mixture of high art and low commerce, of thoughtful statements on the state of man and the modern world interspersed with textbook examples of the kind of behaviour that gives stardom its disreputable name.

*

Together Through Life would turn out to be a big hit. Most critics would esteem it less highly than *Modern Times*, but most album buyers would pay no mind to another round of media *feuilletons* describing the writers' long, personal and fraught relationships with the slippery art of Bob Dylan. Among reviewers there was a sense that the creative renaissance thesis had run its course. They had worked the idea almost to death, after all, without coming to terms with what it might truly signify. Memories of the depths to which the artist once had descended were beginning to dissipate. By May 2009 he was rich, famous, legendary, garlanded with awards and with his name on an album that had charged up the charts to number one in America, Britain and a host of other countries. According to the weird logic of music journalism, Dylan was therefore fair game for reviewers prepared to hit all the notes on the gamut between level-headed and empty-headed. One even managed to say that while the album offered 'many great things' it was 'rendered underwhelming' simply by the fact that some of the writer's peers had praised it too highly.[4]

Together Through Life contained fewer appropriations, borrowings and obvious thefts than hitherto. This reduced the opportunities for learned prosecutorial statements on the difference between intertextuality and dishonesty. On this album, Dylan sounded both droll and righteously angry. That tested critical systems in which a reviewer's little printed stars were supposed to be worth a thousand words. Self-evidently, the artist had taken some 1950s Chicago blues standards for his templates and reworked songs associated with Muddy Waters, Willie Dixon, Otis Rush and the like. Then the Tejano accordion of David Hidalgo, leader of the Chicano band Los Lobos, had been featured prominently, inevitably lending a Southern, borderland ambience to the songs. In Dylan's poetic universe, borders are the places where things fall apart, where rules and laws break down and madness looms. Those presentiments ran through every track on *Together Through Life*.

Even the songs which *sounded* affable drew on the belief that in the modern world social order is precarious. The title of the first track, 'Beyond Here Lies Nothin'', was another borrowing from Ovid in his exile. The next song was the scarcely ambiguous 'Life is Hard'. 'If You Ever Go to Houston', its melody and chorus lifted wholesale from the traditional 'Midnight Special' that Lead Belly had made his own, seemed jolly enough until you gave some attention to the words. The speaker, this eternal tipsy wanderer, was not cheerful.

I know these streets
I've been here before
I nearly got killed here
During the Mexican war

Similarly, 'I Feel a Change Comin' On' seemed almost optimistic when set beside some of the album's other offerings. It appeared to be a raffish love song, testimony to the enduring emotions apparently implied by the album's title. 'Life is for love,' Dylan sang, welding clichés together, 'and they say that love is blind.' The next verse said something else entirely.

Well now what's the use in dreamin'?
You got better things to do
Dreams never did work for me anyway
Even when they did come true

If a single song characterised Dylan's mood on *Together Through Life* it was the final track, the mocking, defiant, contemptuous 'It's All Good', a cliché transformed into an indictment. It would be fascinating to know who actually composed each line of this lyric, but the artist performed the whole as his own. Those who still assumed that he had put 'topical song' behind him long before would have some difficulty explaining this rackety number.

> People in the country, people on the land
> Some of them so sick, they can hardly stand
> Everybody would move away if they could
> It's hard to believe, but it's all good

> The widow's cry, the orphan's plea
> Everywhere you look, more misery
> Come along with me, babe, I wish you would
> You know what I'm sayin'. It's all good

For the most part, the album worked well, flagging only when Dylan allowed his readings of the blues to become a little perfunctory, as in the pointless 'Shake Shake Mama', or the truly tiresome 'Jolene'. At its best, *Together Through Life* possessed both an aura and a swagger that the artist had not displayed for a long time. The issue of authorship would not be resolved, least of all by Dylan, but certain of the best lines were invested with his familiar tone, even when he was leaning on a favourite writer such as Edgar Allen Poe. In 'Forgetful Heart', for example, there was the brief but lovely conclusion 'The door has closed forevermore / If indeed there ever was a door'. In 'I Feel a Change Comin' On', meanwhile, Dylan (or Hunter) came up with a brilliant, gnomic verse that so delighted the country singer named he emblazoned it across his website.

> I'm listening to Billy Joe Shaver
> And I'm reading James Joyce
> Some people they tell me
> I got the blood of the land in my voice

One dim-witted listener (this one) spent a week convinced that Dylan was making reference to the blood of the Lamb, though why it would be in his voice was never obvious. On the other hand, 'blood of the land', whatever it might mean, has no clear connection with country singers. There might be something involving Joyce, 'blood and ouns' and Ireland, but that's a stretch. Dylan mentioned the novelist in *Chronicles* only to say that as a youth he had failed to make much headway with the prose. He recited the Joyce poem 'Sleep now, O sleep now' during Episode 28 ('Sleep') of *Theme Time*, but he recited a lot of poetry on the show. The Dubliner was a gifted piano player with a deep interest in music. Any help? On the other hand, 'Joyce' is one of the better rhymes for 'voice'.

As is often the case when Dylan offers a non sequitur, it doesn't seem to matter much. The performance imposes its own logic. One large part of his gift has always been the ability to turn statements whose meanings are private (or mysterious even to him) into a kind of sense beyond sense. There is nothing accidental about how the effect is achieved. As David Hidalgo would remember the *Together Through Life* sessions, Dylan 'was always rewriting the lyrics'. Robert Hunter seems to have played no part in this procedure. The idea that the artist had taken on a collaborator because he was once again stuck for words is therefore nonsensical. In the studio, as the songs were shaped and reshaped, the only writer was Dylan. As Hidalgo would describe the process, 'he has, you know, 20 verses that he's got laid out, and he'll pick and choose and rewrite while he's going. It's amazing to watch him work.'[5]

In the end, Olivier Dahan got more Bob Dylan music for his wayward Renée Zellweger road movie than he could have dreamed possible. In addition to five tracks from the album, the artist came up with sixteen bits and pieces of incidental music and allowed cover versions of older songs such as 'What Good Am I? and 'Precious Angel' to be used. On his own behalf, meanwhile, Dylan turned *Together Through Life* into a memorable oddity, a set that was vivid, energetic and, unmistakably, an old man's album. In this case, the aged individual was dismayed by the world yet furiously defiant of all it could throw at him. Dylan was ageing on his own terms. In an account of an interview given in Paris to promote the album, he was described as a kind of tenacious anachronism, out of step with the times and proud of the fact.

Like the dour-faced farmer in Grant Wood's *American Gothic*, Dylan seems to have the [Great] American Songbook in one hand and a raised pitchfork in the other, aimed at rock critics, politicians, Wall Street financiers, back-alley thieves, the world wide web – anything that cheapens the spirit of the individual . . . If Dylan had his way, there'd be Sousa bands on Main Street and vinyl albums instead of CDs. Teenagers would go on nature hikes instead of watching YouTube.[6]

It was a slight exaggeration, but not too far wide of the mark. He who had once sailed effortlessly into a future only he could discern had put down his anchors. On the other hand, *Together Through Life* could make even Dylan's eccentricities sound rational. There were plenty of those. In May, just after the album's release, he was in the fair city of Liverpool for a show. To the evident astonishment of the National Trust, keepers of the modest house called Mendips in Woolton where John Lennon had been raised by his Aunt Mimi, one of the 14 curious tourists paying £16 for a bus trip and tour could claim to have known the dead Beatle personally. 'He spent ages going through photo albums and was thrilled at all the memorabilia,' reported a representative of the trust.[7] Dylan had been spotted previously at Neil Young's childhood home in Winnipeg, but this excursion to Mendips and to Strawberry Fields was odd even by the artist's standards. There he was, a performer who claimed to be sceptical of fame and fans, goggling at 'memorabilia' like a true prying fanatic. The artist who had asserted that there is no difference between nostalgia and death might even have seemed a little wistful. At least no one in Liverpool tried to arrest him for it.

That honour would fall to Officer Kristie Buble in Long Branch, New Jersey, in July. The 'eccentric-looking old man' was causing no trouble as he strolled around in the rain on a summer's day. On the other hand, the officer was only 22 and unfamiliar with the names and faces of people who were famous long before she was born. As Buble would tell ABC news: 'I wasn't sure if he came from one of our hospitals or something.' Locals had reported 'an old scruffy man acting suspiciously'. The young cop would confirm that detail, more or less. 'He was acting very suspicious,' she would say. 'Not delusional, just suspicious. You know, it was pouring rain and everything.' The suspect had no useful ID on him. When Buble therefore took him back to his hotel to investigate his paperwork, she felt it necessary to call her precinct to 'check who Bob Dylan was'. After the laughter down the line from the station house had subsidised, the artist was free to go about his business.

Journalists who thought they knew their man tried to turn a guess into a weird 'fact' by deciding that he had been wandering around looking for the house in which Bruce Springsteen had written *Born to*

Run. Asked about the incident in an interview three years later, Dylan's explanation was mundane: he had simply gone for a walk. 'I guess in that neck of the woods they're not used to seeing people walking in the rain,' he said. 'I was the only one on the street.'[8] His ID was missing simply because 'I wear so many changes of clothes all the time.' Dylan's mistake, if that's the word, had been to forget that in a country obsessed with crime no one could act as though it was still 1958 in Hibbing, Minn. But even his run-in with Officer Buble was not the strangest episode in 2009 for one globally famous complete unknown.

Towards the end of the summer, a rumour began to circulate within the Dylan-watching fraternity to the effect that he was recording again. Given his limited productivity in the twenty-first century, this was a surprise in itself. As ever, speculation and amateur investigations commenced. When the facts were established, they were treated by some earnest fans as a worse betrayal than a $129 price tag for a box set. A Christmas album: how could Dylan even contemplate such a surrender to the worst kind of crass commercialism, far less carry it through?

He could and he did, much to the benefit of the charities Feeding America and Crisis in the UK, to whom all the album's royalties were directed. *Christmas in the Heart*, a seasonal affair played (almost) entirely straight, was a gift to anyone who enjoyed the holiday and retained a sense of humour. It was no great surprise to discover that a lot of Dylan fans were lacking in that department. Quite what they had made of *Theme Time Radio* was therefore anyone's guess. How they squared Dylan's complicated religious affiliations with the discovery that, where Christmas was concerned, he was a middle-of-the-road Middle American who loved the entire affair is also likely to remain mysterious. But why would he not cherish the festival? The birth of his messiah was of no small importance to the artist.

Christmas in the Heart – by David Hidalgo's account entirely Dylan's idea – did not labour that point when it appeared in October. Religiosity was notable by its absence. Equally, there was little of his usual sardonic bite to the artist's treatments of standards and carols. Even when he cut loose with 'Must Be Santa', filming a truly demented video to accompany the track, he seemed to be evoking, not mocking, the polka bands of his Minnesota childhood. A few would remember that the song had once been a hit for Mitch Miller, the professionally bland Columbia producer who had led the old school's chorus of contempt for 'Hammond's folly' back in Dylan's early days, but that had nothing to do with the spirit of the track, or of the album.

On the internet, nevertheless, scandalised fans reacted as though the artist had contrived another *Self Portrait* (as though that would have been a bad idea). Not for the first time, many missed the point. Not for the first or the last time, their reluctance to accept that Dylan was entitled to autonomy, or just to his whims, was striking. Elvis had made Christmas albums; Springsteen had done Christmas songs: where was the by-law forbidding a wistful messianic Jew with a taste for tales of the apocalypse from participating in an all-American tradition? That such recordings, good or bad, were meanwhile as traditional as anything contrived by 'folk process' was a truth some fans were never likely to concede. *Christmas in the Heart* was fun: wholly innocent, daft and incongruous, but fun. It would get nowhere near to number one in America, but number 23 was a sight better than the result achieved by *Under the Red Sky*. And those charities, granted royalties in perpetuity, would benefit for many years to come.

*

On 9 February 2010, Dylan was back in the White House, this time to perform – he had never played the hall before – during a concert entitled 'Songs of the Civil Rights Movement'. He sang 'The Times They Are a-Changin'' in a gentle, piano-backed version with an unusual air of quiet pride and even, though he claimed to despise the emotion, of nostalgia. An old man stood for a few minutes in a young man's shoes. A veteran, voice cracking and striving, sang the words of a beginner for the sake of an African American president. It was an affecting moment, but it was also a reminder of just how much time had slipped away. In the second decade of the twenty-first century Dylan remained a modern artist, perhaps the most modern of them all, but he was also becoming a piece of history. There was no way to escape the contradictions lodged in that truth.

Early in the summer, undaunted, he found a few more fresh pastures. Touring took him to Greece, Bulgaria, the republic that called itself Macedonia, Romania, Serbia, and the Slovak Republic. In most of these concerts the artist who had made his earliest marks during the worst of the Cold War's paranoia was bringing his music to formerly Communist countries for the first time. It made for an odd disjunction. In America and western Europe people were still turning up at Dylan concerts just to complain that he sounded nothing like his records. In

Bucharest and Sofia, Skopje and Zagreb, they were trying to match the image of the aged man on stage with the tale of the most significant artistic figure in half a century. Just to complicate matters further, he gave them 'Jolene', trivial and dull, as an encore.

Past and present were entangled. Bob Dylan, every last one of him, existed in a weird continuum. Each new instalment in the Bootleg Series – new for many, ancient for the artist – imposed its echoes on his existence, his image and his reputation. At every turn, all those previous Dylans infiltrated his life. The question of identity, personal and artistic, was more complicated than anything Todd Haynes had imagined when he was writing *I'm Not There*. Bob Dylan seemed to exist at numerous points in time simultaneously.

In September 2010, an exhibition of the 40 canvases he called the 'Brazil Series' opened at the National Gallery of Denmark. In October, another volume in the Bootleg Series, one entitled *The Witmark Demos: 1962–1964*, made its appearance. Anyone who knew nothing about the makers of these works would have had problems connecting one with the other. No amount of learned argument over 'pictorial' songs and narrative paintings – and there would be plenty of that until the uproar over the Asia Series commenced – solved this puzzle. Brutally, you could observe that the rough, mud-hued canvases shown in Denmark lacked clarity, drama and any real instinct for composition. That wasn't often said about Bob Dylan songs, even the minor pieces taped at the start of the '60s just to satisfy the youth's publishers. Yet something more than lost time or a gulf in technique separated the two collections. The young singer getting his work down as fast as he could scribble the verses might have amounted to little more than a found identity, a personality assembled or imposed by circumstance. His songs, even the earliest, had chiselled out the contours of individuality with a madcap intensity. The 69-year-old painter displayed no personality of any kind. His canvases were less dispassionate than disengaged, less objective than inert. If Dylan had put his heart and soul into these images, evidence for the sacrifice was nowhere to be seen. Perhaps that was what had attracted him to painting in the first place.

The Copenhagen exhibition, though spared a fuss over plagiarism, was given what is known among polite critics as a mixed reception. Which is to say that those who staged the show at the Statens Museum for Kunst spoke proudly of their achievement and highly of their artist. The Danish press, on the other hand, were less than kind.

Writing in the exhibition catalogue, the gallery's curator, Kasper Monrad, reckoned that Dylan's work had 'ties to a figurative tradition that has remained vibrant up through the twentieth century'. The 'painterly mode' identified was meanwhile placed in line of descent 'from French modernist painting of the 1920s'. John Elderfield, the Englishman who had served as chief curator of painting and sculpture at the Museum of Modern Art in New York and who would become Dylan's ambassador in the world of high-end galleries, wrote about 'the imperatives of his visual imagination as it travels back and forth across the borderline between painting and song'.[9] The names of famous artists, Matisse chief among them, were thrown around. Judging by press comment, the critics must have looked at different pictures entirely.

According to agency reports, the daily *Berlingske Tidende* said: 'When we talk about music, Bob Dylan is one of the great Picassos of the twentieth century, but this is not the case for his painting.' The newspaper also believed that the Statens Museum had staged the exhibition 'not because his canvases are good, but because he is Bob Dylan'. The financial journal *Boersen* was also unhappy with the national gallery for putting 'financial interest ahead of artistic judgement', knowing that the name would be a draw regardless of the quality of the work. In *Information*, an art history specialist named Peter Brix Soendergaard offered the opinion that 'Bob Dylan paints like any other amateur, using a rather oafish figurative style. He is what we used to call a Sunday painter.'[10]

In conspicuous contrast, bad reviews for *The Witmark Demos* were hard to find. Sales were pretty satisfactory too, taking Dylan to number 12 on the American chart. It was as though critics had forgotten just how good the young singer had been. That said, the 47 tracks possessed a ragged, unquenchable vitality that would have deserved success at any time. Among the juvenilia were sketches of some of the works – 'Blowin' in the Wind', 'Times They Are a-Changin' and 'Tambourine Man' among them – from which agreeable Albert Grossman had for years extracted fully 50 per cent of Dylan's publishing earnings. The fact did not diminish the quality, or the sense of remembered and imagined excitement, of the *Witmark* set. Even those who knew the performances well enough from bootlegs were startled by the freshness after more than 40 years of the refurbished recordings. Once again, the Bootleg Series was demonstrating the extent and durability of Dylan's achievement. The claim that he was an artist bigger than any era was becoming hard, if not impossible, to dispute. He had outlived many of his contemporaries and outlasted them all.

The beginning of 2011 brought news that he was, in his own mind, a long way from done. Anyone who signs a six-book deal with his seventieth birthday approaching either has ambitions for longevity, or no interest in the issue of age. Dylan's claims in 2006 that he was contemplating a second *Chronicles* volume were in any case confirmed. But half a dozen books? It seemed that the Proustian knack, once acquired, can become a habit. As it transpired, the artist had signed with Simon & Schuster to provide not one but two more books in the vein of *Chronicles*. A third book would 'reportedly' comprise samples of the wit and wisdom of *Theme Time Radio Hour*'s DJ, but details of the other promised volumes were not disclosed. That might have been just as well. No news report was indelicate enough to make much of the fact that almost seven years had elapsed between the appearance of *Chronicles: Volume One* and the signing of the six-book agreement. At that rate, the third book was liable to arrive as the author celebrated his eighty-fourth birthday. Asked in September 2012 if there would even be a second volume, Dylan's first reply was 'Oh, let's hope so'.[11] He then said that he was 'always working on parts of it', that he didn't mind the writing, but found making time for rereading difficult. By the middle of 2013, in any case, there was no sign of *Chronicles: Volume Two*.

He was an author, then, and he was a figurative artist. He was a stage performer and a living historical project. He was the recipient of more awards than you could fit into a U-Haul trailer, a movie composer for hire, available for acting jobs, radio, documentaries and TV advertising. He would blow briefly into very expensive harmonicas for sale and resale. He could be hired for the most select private engagements. In short, the making and recording of albums was just one line of work among many. The revenue stream it represented was a minor tributary, even if the flow had increased slightly since the appearance of *Modern Times*. But then, no one still produced records pell-mell, year in and year out, as they had in the 1960s. The few remaining conglomerates no longer wanted product in that kind of quantity. A specialist back-catalogue line such as the Bootleg Series, with no recording costs at stake and a guaranteed market of willing buyers, was a welcome exception. The fact remained that albums had ceased to be the cornerstones of Dylan's business plan. They mattered only as works of art, for whatever that was worth.

In this, he was no different from other stars of popular music in the early twenty-first century. There was no money *to speak of* in album sales, or so they said. The big bucks, the customary rewards, were to be had from the concert circuit: hence the extraordinary ticket prices being charged by the acts making their laser-lit homes in gigantic arenas.[12] By the time Michael Jackson died of a self-inflicted heart attack in June 2009 he had sold 100 million records and blown hundreds of millions of dollars on toys and trash. At the end, his intended solution to his fantastically complicated financial problems was a scheme to stage no fewer than 50 concerts in succession at London's 20,000-seat O2 Arena. According to promoters, Jackson would have made £5 million a show. Dylan had never been in that league. Equally, there was no sign that he had ever squandered his earnings in the style of the screwed-up maker of *Thriller*. (If anything, the artist had a certain reputation for being 'careful' with cash.) Yet the detail overlooked in all the award citations straining for eloquence with their talk of poetry and culture was that Dylan's most profound gift had long been a secondary concern. When he felt moved to make an album he would apply himself, most of the time, with the same concentration he had brought to the task in his greatest days. But art was no longer his main business. Those who wrote the big books or argued over allusive imagery too often forgot an obvious truth.

Nothing interrupted the tours. Time that could not be spared for prose revisions could always be found for those. At the beginning of April, Dylan set off on a month-long trip to the Far East, Australia and New Zealand. He began with another new country, known to most as Taiwan, known to itself as the Republic of China. No one in the western media was troubled by this choice of destination. In contrast, the artist's next stop three days later, in another Chinese republic, the vast empire that claimed to be in the sole possession of its people, would set off one of those miniature typhoons of controversy that seemed to engulf Dylan periodically. Most of those involved, not least the artist himself, would miss the point of the argument entirely.

According to some press reports – reports Dylan would later dismiss convincingly – shows in Beijing and Shanghai had been cancelled during the previous April after permission was refused by China's Ministry of Culture. *The Guardian*, acting on information from Taiwanese promoters Brokers Brothers Herald, had said that the ministry 'appeared wary of Dylan's past as an icon of the counter-culture movement'.[13] Yet on 6 April 2011, there he was on stage at the Workers' Gymnasium in Beijing. This time *The Guardian* reported that the artist was 'singing to the culture ministry's tune'. In a story that was part report and part review, datelined on the night of the show, the paper ran an unsourced quote stating that the performance was 'strictly according to an approved programme'. In other words, Dylan had allowed himself to be censored. If the story was true, he had agreed not to perform songs deemed provocative by an oppressive one-party regime. Worse, as the tale told by the *Guardian* and others stressed, this surrender had taken place in the week in which the admired dissident artist Ai Weiwei had been locked up.

The paranoia of the 'Communists' controlling totalitarian capitalism in China was not the world's biggest secret. They had censored the Rolling Stones (who, typically, had lost no sleep over that). They had refused entry to the 'unsuitable' Oasis. They had been furious, supposedly, when in 2008 the Icelandic singer Björk had shouted (or muttered, depending on who you believed) 'Tibet! Tibet!' during a song called 'Declare Independence'. In November 2012, Elton John would be visited by police in Beijing after he announced that his show in the city was dedicated 'to the spirit and talent of Ai Weiwei'. In March 2013, the veteran German electronic music pioneers Kraftwerk would be denied a visa because, according to Agence France-Presse, they had agreed to participate in a Free Tibet benefit in Washington a decade before. The regime had long made its views on the liberties it would allow to performers very clear. 'Paltry and few' just about covered it.

Had Dylan submitted to these controls? The *Los Angeles Times*, with a correspondent on the spot, reported that 'at a time when many other American performers would have been banned from China', the concert at the Workers' Gymnasium 'omitted Dylan's most famous ballads of dissent'. The newspaper also stated as fact that the artist's 'set list had to be sanctioned beforehand by the Ministry of Culture'. In this version, the demand that Dylan should 'conduct the performance strictly according to the approved programme' had been part of the 'formal invitation' to play in China. This was going on 'in the midst of a crackdown on Chinese intellectuals, activists and artists in which dozens of people have been arrested or investigated'. The story filed by the correspondent for the *Washington Post* made much the same points. The concert was 'devoid of any numbers that might carry even the whiff', it said, 'of anti-government overtones'. Dylan had played 'Desolation Row' and 'Blowin' in the Wind' in Taiwan, but dropped them for the show in China's capital. 'There was no "Times They Are a-Changin'" in Beijing,' reported the *Post*. 'And definitely no "Chimes of Freedom".'[14]

Across the West, comment followed. Conspicuous among the artist's critics was Maureen Dowd of the *New York Times*, who began her op-ed piece with an unequivocal statement: 'Bob Dylan may have done the impossible: broken creative new ground in selling out.' For Dowd, his long-standing refusal to engage with America's impeccably democratic politics was not worth mentioning. The failure to perform certain songs in the heart of totalitarian darkness was 'a whole new kind of sell-out'. As the columnist put it:

> Dylan said nothing about Weiwei's detention, didn't offer a reprise of 'Hurricane', his song about 'the man the authorities came to blame for something that he never done'. He sang his censored set, took his pile of Communist cash and left.[15]

The fact that Dylan had not performed 'Hurricane' on any stage since the days of the Rolling Thunder Revue in the middle of the 1970s slipped Dowd's mind, as did the fact that he had given a rendering of 'A Hard Rain's a-Gonna Fall' in Beijing, though not in Taiwan. That piece of evidence was also overlooked by most of those who seemed as intent on dictating the artist's set list as any Chinese bureaucrat. For that matter, the country with the somewhat famous wall, the one built to keep nervous autocrats safe, had also heard 'All Along the Watchtower'. In a *New Yorker* blog, Sean Wilentz waded in on Dylan's behalf. To the professor, it was all just like the bad old '60s days when the artist was arraigned by purblind leftists for failing to do his progressive duty. Wilentz argued that there was plenty of subversion, if few slogans, in some of the recent work Dylan had performed in China. The old nonsense yet prevailed: 'He is not allowed to be an artist, he must be an agitator. And he can only be an agitator if he sings particular songs.' Wilentz added:

> Depending on whatever agreement he made with them, I'd argue Dylan made a fool of the Chinese authorities, while getting paid in the bargain. He certainly made a fool of Maureen Dowd – or she has made a fool of herself.[16]

Just for a change, Dylan decided to speak for himself. Clearly, the charge that he had been pushed around by a few dour men in suits had rankled. Presumably an artist who had stood up to censorious lawyers for *The Ed Sullivan Show* in 1963 needed no lectures on how to handle the People's Republic of China. Dylan, to be fair, was just setting the record straight, more or less. In a statement headed 'To My Fans and Followers' published on bobdylan.com on 13 May, he said there had been no shows planned for China in 2010; therefore, 'we were never denied permission to play in China'. The whole tale had been 'drummed up by a Chinese promoter'. Then Dylan denied that there had been a lot of empty seats at the Beijing show and rebutted claims that the audience were mostly foreigners. (The majority of press reports in fact said that there were *some* vacant seats and a significant minority, though still a minority, of non-Chinese in the crowd.) Then the artist stated:

> As far as censorship goes, the Chinese government had asked for the names of the songs that I would be playing. There's no logical answer to that, so we sent them the set lists from the previous three months. If there were any songs, verses or lines censored, nobody ever told me about it and we played all the songs that we intended to play.

Set lists had indeed been demanded, then, and duly provided. On the other hand, there remained the demonstrable fact that Dylan had been altering his nightly programme to suit his mood for decades, no matter the venue, no matter the country. 'Desolation Row', one of the two songs that supposedly 'disappeared' in Beijing according to the *Washington Post*, reappeared in Shanghai. Were the censors less vigilant in China's most populous city? 'Blowin' in the Wind', allegedly 'dropped' in China, was also omitted during each of nine subsequent concerts in Australia. Were the totalitarians of Oz at work? Dylan was entitled to be taken at his word. In Beijing, 'we played all the songs that we intended to play'.

And so what? Amid all the arguments over censorship, sell-outs, the songs he could have played and the songs he should have played, no one asked an obvious question of Dylan. What was he doing in China in the first place? What possessed him to believe that a police state like that – if there is a police state 'like that' – was just another place to play, another region to be conquered, another patch on the map to be checked from the list while the box-office take was calculated? For Dowd and certain other journalists it would have been enough if Dylan had taken all the Chinese money he could scoop up just as long as 'a statement' was made. Rhetoric was the issue, not the fact of doing business with a regime with an unspeakable human-rights record.

In 1985, Dylan had signed up for a campaign called Artists United Against Apartheid alongside Bruce Springsteen, Steve Van Zandt, Miles Davis, Lou Reed, U2, Gil Scott-Heron, Run DMC, Peter Gabriel, Pete Townsend and many more besides. Their chief object had been to make a campaign record called 'Sun City', a track declaring their refusal to perform at that all-white resort while apartheid remained. Dylan had added his voice. So why was China different? His statement didn't say. Much of the criticism the artist attracted over the Beijing show was simplistic; Wilentz was right about that. But in the commotion over the failure to sing some journalist's favourite protest songs the moral choice involved in agreeing to appear in China was ignored. One commentator (this one, it so happens) had no interest in the choice of material, but wrote: 'The point in dismissing politics is to grant freedom from every politician. Had you happened to be called Dylan, and written "Chimes of Freedom", and then found yourself in the middle of Totalitarian Central, that might resonate.'[17] Dylan, it was argued, had donated a little of his credibility to an obnoxious regime just by his presence in the Workers' Gymnasium. For once, the songs were not the issue.

*

On 24 May 2011, he reached the age of 70 and induced another spasm of media interest around the world. Some writers wondered what had become of their youth, some their idealism. Many contemplated a world gone wrong with the failure of the counter-culture, even if the artist had never subscribed to that confused and confusing notion. There were a multitude of assessments, reassessments, reminiscences and profiles amid the celebrations. It was a rare publication that had nothing to say. (This writer's drop in the ocean: 'Bob Dylan's real triumph at 70? He's a twenty-first-century artist and the central American poet of his age. I should probably wish him happy birthday, but the old miscreant wouldn't thank me.'[18]) There was also general wonderment that Dylan was still around to rack up his three score and ten, what with one thing and another. That the survivor remained 'relevant' in a world that was losing its collective attention span as fast as it was losing its ozone layer counted as another miracle. In the end, most agreed that the grand puzzle set by the artist and his career endured. Some wondered, reasonably enough, if the man could endure as an artist for very much longer.

Taking a break after his return from New Zealand at the end of April, Dylan was not foolish enough to be standing on a public stage when his birthday moment arrived. The celebrations would not spare him the Asia Series fiasco in September, in any case, or free him from the attentions of the plagiarism industry. The more his achievements were proclaimed, the greater the effort became, so it seemed, to cut him down to size, to make him fit, to render him comprehensible within someone's idea of religion or politics, history or literature. On 4 November, he was playing in Stockholm when an anniversary more significant than his birthday was reached. According to the stakhanovite work done by Olof Björner, this was show number 2,382 in the unending tour.[19] It also marked fully 50 years to the day (or night) since Dylan had given a real concert, his first, at the Carnegie Chapter Hall in New York City. He had measured out his life in songs. For him there had been no other existence, no existence in any normal sense, for better than half a century. The art of songmaking and all it had brought him, good and bad, had shaped those many identities, those serial lives. The all-consuming habit of art had consumed each life one by one. Dylan had never 'reinvented' himself, adopted roles, or put on 'masks' to bewitch, deceive or confound. Those appearances had been the effects of 50 years and more of writing songs, of following where the songs led. A detestation of the recording studio had altered nothing. There had never been a choice in the matter. When 2012 arrived it was time to make another album. All other bits and pieces aside, this would be number 35.

Dylan went to work at Jackson Browne's Groove Masters in January and continued to work until March. In July, Columbia would announce that an album of 'ten new and original Bob Dylan songs' – an interesting form of words – was scheduled for release on 11 September. It would be called *Tempest*. On the internet, the reaction would be instantaneous, as though someone had pushed a starter button. For months, the hum of online chatter would be almost audible. A one-word title would produce a chain reaction of speculation ending in the conclusion that this must surely be Dylan's last album. *Tempest*, ran the thinking: just like Shakespeare's play (not quite). Just like Shakespeare's *last* play (not exactly). Just like the play in which Shakespeare made his farewell to his art and to the stage (not if you prefer one of a dozen other interpretations of the drama). In due course, our artist would become a little peeved at being pensioned off in this manner. First, however, he had a real farewell to make.

We can probably guess that a collection of Dylan's valedictory messages for friends and heroes was not among the volumes he promised to Simon & Schuster. Nevertheless, taken together these notes of acquiescence to age and mortality would make for interesting reading. His remembrances might be the closest anyone gets to the unguarded Dylan, the 'real' Dylan. There are no riddles in his eulogies. When Levon Helm, singer and drummer with The Band, was taken by cancer on 19 April after almost 14 years of intermittent struggle, Dylan's response was released within hours. He was in Belo Horizonte in Brazil, on the third stop of a tour through South and Central America, but he caught the essence of a friendship in a few words. He even sounded a little lonely.

> He was my bosom buddy friend to the end, one of the last true great spirits of my or any other generation. This is just so sad to talk about. I still can remember the first day I met him and the last day I saw him. We go back pretty far and had been through some trials together. I'm going to miss him, as I'm sure a whole lot of others will too.

At the end of May, one leg of the now-familiar spin around the globe completed, Dylan paused in Washington DC to suffer the distress – or so it appeared – of receiving the Presidential Medal of Freedom from Obama. It might have counted as his nation's highest civilian honour, but the artist looked as though he was being fitted for a noose. His dark glasses reflected the East Room of the White House back upon itself and kept his thoughts, if any, penned within. The rest of Dylan's face, both drawn and blank, seemed only to hint that if he could be anywhere else he would be back out on the road, or just – for how often had he expressed the hope? – left alone at home. But where was that exactly? Sometimes he said that he could make his home wherever he happened to be. At times he even spoke like a song. In reality, he had European festival engagements to complete over the summer.

'Reportedly', 'apparently', 'reputedly' – for not a word of it had been confirmed – arthritis in his hands would once again prevent him from attempting the guitar. Another tale said that a bad back made the weight of a solid-body instrument too much to bear. Dylan's age was beyond concealment. No one who wrote about his concerts forgot to mention the passage of time, what it had done, what had been won and lost. Yet he seemed spry enough at the first show, part of the Hop Farm Festival in Kent, as he laughed and joked with his band, or postured, sometimes comically, through songs whose broken bones and gleaming entrails were scattered across the stage. Reviews were favourable, for the most part, but even the writers who still found something spellbinding about a performance by this artist had to couch their praise in strange language. For example, the critic from the *Daily Telegraph*, invariably supportive, first observed: 'At 71, the great troubadour is still out there, presenting his works of genius in weird, garbled, sometimes barely recognisable forms, for reasons that nobody can really understand but himself.' But then:

> Dylan delivers his highly charged lyrics with three-note melodies that don't necessarily bear much resemblance to the originals, chopped up into short rhythmic phrases that frequently seem to baffle his own band, who watch him like hawks throughout, looking for clues and cues.

And then again:

> Somehow between the magic of his fantastic songs, the liquid groove of his superb band, the mysterious charisma of the legend himself and the will of the crowd to enjoy the moment, something strange and truly spectacular happens, a thrilling performance that nobody, perhaps not even the man at its centre, can really explain.[20]

Others present failed to detect this supernatural event. That, though, had become the way of things. The stratagems Dylan had been forced to adopt to compensate for the disintegration of his voice had grown ever more elaborate, ever more extreme, inventive or preposterous according to taste. To say this divided audiences is like saying that some people are colour-blind and some are not. But which was which, in this case? At Carhaix in Brittany, three weeks after Hop Farm, the booing and the heckling directed at Dylan was impossible to ignore. The racket raised questions. Should those who saw merit in everything he did just have told themselves that it was ever thus, that it was worse in '66? Or should they have grasped that loyalty had become blind (or deaf)? By the summer of 2012, those who stuck by Dylan tended to say, almost blandly, that anyone who didn't get it should go elsewhere and find something else to misunderstand. As an answer, it felt incomplete. The artist was about to release an album that would become still another of his big twenty-first-century hits. The praise from reviewers would be as lavish as any he had ever received. Yet a lot of people who would buy and admire *Tempest* would still emerge baffled from many of his shows. That counted as strange to everyone save those inside the cocoon.

*

Tempest is one of the finest things he has ever done: add it to the list. At this stage in the game the stock of superlatives is almost exhausted. Most of the things said in praise of Dylan have been said many times before. That's a problem, if it matters, for the reviewer's trade. The habit of asserting that album A is the 'best since' album B might do for a five-year pop career, but not for a career more than half a century long, one tangled up in arguments that often have nothing to do with music. In the case of *Tempest* the 'best since' yardstick would be extended, regardless, even unto *Blonde on Blonde*. You would be better off talking instead of Picasso in his final years of raging turmoil, remaking Old Masters obsessively, mocking death, locked in a futile combat with age and libido. You will not have said much about Dylan's album, but you will have located the territory.

Tempest is a work of grim relish and flamboyant recklessness. Dylan has spent most of his long career seeming not to give a damn what anyone thinks, but with this set the contempt for restraint is ostentatious. Whether the issue is artistic method, politics, age, truth, women, religion, or a profound desire for revenge against allcomers, this Dylan doesn't care what you think. He's pretty sure that God doesn't care, either. The world represented in the ballad-stories and movie-stories of *Tempest* contains little for your comfort, nothing for your enlightenment. Even the album's one, uncertain eulogy, the song for John Lennon that was perhaps inspired by Dylan's strange visit to Aunt Mimi's house in Liverpool, all but says, 'So it goes.' *Tempest* is an album, as the old oath has it, of blood and thunder. In these songs the skies darken and the corpses pile up thanks to betrayal, fate, or because the artist is offering to do the job himself. Those who chose to see Dylan as Shakespeare's Prospero got the wrong character. Lear would have been a better fit.

Besides, as the exasperated artist took pains to point out to *Rolling Stone*, Shakespeare's enchanted castaway play has the definite article in its title. The difference might be no more than a nuance, but for Dylan it mattered: 'The name of my record is just plain *Tempest*.'[21]

There was nothing plain about the contents. Even the opening track, 'Duquesne Whistle', is another of those tricks of misdirection at which the artist had long been adept.

It opens with the sunny, gentle sounds of what could be an old western swing band reaching the end of a number, as though we have just tuned in to some local Texas radio station back in the '40s. That's one clue to this album: amid the rockabilly, folk, blues and country most of the music is drawn from a time before there was the sound of someone called Bob Dylan. Then the song proper kicks in. It's a train song, a jolly-sounding uptempo piece that could be in the lineage of all the old gospel train songs pointing down the track to redemption. But there's something a little off here. Why is the train's whistle blowing 'like the sky's gonna blow apart' when the voice the singer says he can hear 'must be the mother of our Lord'? Why, if that's what is in his head, would the whistle sound 'like it's gonna kill me dead'? Dylan isn't telling, but this jaunty roadhouse number is utterly deceitful. Even its promotional video would attract a little spurious controversy for a scene of notable mock brutality amid a scenario that had nothing whatever to do with trains of any description. In his ritual *Rolling Stone* interview to mark the album's release, Dylan would manage to explain everything and nothing.

> *Tempest* was like all the rest of them: the songs just fall together. It's not the album I wanted to make, though. I had another one in mind. I wanted to make something more religious. That takes a lot more concentration – to pull that off ten times with the same thread – than it does with a record like I ended up with, where anything goes and you just gotta believe it will make sense.[22]

So: *anything goes and you just gotta believe it will make sense?* Dylan is describing both his method and the moral universe of the songs. The two are connected, in any case. It has nothing to do with God's presence or absence; the artist continues to testify, here and there, to his faith. But one subtext of *Tempest* – in the title song it becomes explicit – is that anyone expecting explanations from the deity is wasting time and effort.

Several of the album's songs tell stories; all are fabulistic in one way or another. A couple of the longest pieces, 'Scarlet Town' and the title track, are modelled explicitly on the old, endless folk ballads, shot through with supernatural mystery, that had once entranced the young

Dylan. Indeed, 'Barbara Allen', the Scottish ballad he had sung at the Gaslight in the Village back in 1962, begins 'In Scarlet Town where I was born'. 'Roll On, John', the song for Lennon, is constructed like a movie, opening on the murder scene before tracing moments in the victim's life and work in a series of flashbacks. The death ballad 'Tin Angel' is meanwhile a hybrid of folk and film. Its immediate ancestry lies in the song 'Love Henry' that Dylan had performed on *World Gone Wrong*, but its origins stretch all the way back to one of the Child ballads first known in old Scotland. The tale of love, infidelity and murder – in which by the end bodies are actually piled up – could nevertheless be taken from a bloody western movie. That said, even a song such as 'Pay in Blood', which sounds like nothing so much as one of Dylan's mid-'60s revenge songs, is a parable of a people enslaved – in biblical bondage, perhaps – rather than just the artist's curse on those he happens to despise. Though the works sound utterly dissimilar, the nearest thing there is to *Tempest* in Dylan's back catalogue is, in fact, the fable-laden *John Wesley Harding*.

Needless to say, the comparisons are anything but exact. For one thing, the obsession with enemies is harder to detect in the older album; for another, *Harding*'s treatment of women involves none of the sheer malevolence that recurs in *Tempest*. What Dylan intends by these themes is hard to puzzle out. Who are these 'foes'? Is he serious when he gives free rein to vitriolic misogyny? By the time he made this album he had spent half a century picking fights in song. He had also been accused, often enough, of sexism as an artist and as an individual. 'When the Ship Comes In' from 1964 was a mock-biblical call to class war; 'Positively 4th Street' from the following year was a young man settling scores on his own behalf. As for his attitude towards women, pick an album. Dylan's inability to see beyond his precious Madonna/whore caricatures has been criticised for decades. For many tastes, it has created odd undertones, let's say, even in some of his best and loveliest songs. But something more is going on in *Tempest*.

> You got too many lovers
> waiting at the wall
> If I had a thousand tongues
> I couldn't count them all
> 'Narrow Way'

Set 'em up Joe, play 'Walkin' the Floor'
Play it for my flat-chested junkie whore
      'Scarlet Town'

You got the same eyes that your mother does
If only you could prove who your father was
Someone must've slipped a drug in your wine
You gulped it down and you crossed the line
      'Pay in Blood'

I can dress up your wounds
With a blood-clotted rag
I ain't afraid to make love
To a bitch or a hag
      'Early Roman Kings'

Had Dylan been a hip-hop act – and in another time and place, who knows? – the denunciations would have come thick and fast. It is a fact, nevertheless, that violent language is thrown in all directions in most of the *Tempest* songs. It is also worth remembering that in these moods, for better or worse, the artist isn't seeking approval. More importantly, the picking out of a handful of words here and there obscures the fact that statements function differently within different songs, that sometimes they act as a counterpoint to an entirely different sentiment, often within the space of a few lines. The raw accusation of fantastic promiscuity in 'Narrow Way', for example, takes us to an odd refrain: 'If I can't work up to you, / You'll surely have to work down to me someday.' The cheap insult has come from a man who thinks better of her than he thinks of himself. Another couplet manages the same effect. It is vicious by any measure – 'Your father left you, your mother too / Even death has washed its hands of you' – but it reaches that same refrain. Similarly, the poor 'flat-chested junkie whore' of 'Scarlet Town' is followed directly by that marvellous song's marvellous conclusion:

I'm staying up late, I'm making amends
While we smile, all heaven descends
If love is a sin, then beauty is a crime
All things are beautiful in their time

The black and the white,
The yellow and the brown
It's all right there in front of you
In Scarlet Town

Here and there in the songs you can hear Dylan, or the speaker, trying to come to terms with his perceptions of women and womanhood. He responds to what he takes to be different aspects of femininity, for good or ill. So much is recognised in a verse in 'Soon After Midnight' that manages to toy with the whore/Madonna cliché and introduce a mythical note with a nod to Elizabethan poetry and Edmund Spenser:

Charlotte's a harlot
Dresses in scarlet
Mary dresses in green
It's soon after midnight
And I've got a date with the Fairy Queen

Perhaps only this artist could meanwhile combine lechery and sanctity in the same verse. Once again, the song is 'Narrow Way':

I've got a heavy stacked woman
With a smile on her face
And she has crowned
My soul with grace

The lines from 'Pay in Blood' and 'Early Roman Kings', in brutal contrast, are hurled at enemies, at parasites and the makers of slaves, no matter the gender. In neither song does the singer intend to mind his language in the presence of 'foes'. Dylan is at war. He has a lot of enemies. He treats them all badly. Again, however, they are not the same enemies in every context. In one song the singer is 'armed to the hilt', in another he threatens to drag a man's corpse 'through the mud'. But there is a difference between vengeance, rebellion and honour.

Night after night, day after day
They strip your useless hopes away
The more I take the more I give
The more I die the more I live

PAY IN BLOOD

I got something in my pocket make your eyeballs swim
I got dogs could tear you limb from limb
I'm circlin' around the southern zone
I pay in blood, but not my own
        'Pay in Blood'

In Scarlet Town, you fight your father's foes
Up on the hill, a chilly wind blows
You fight 'em on high and you fight 'em down in
You fight 'em with whiskey, morphine and gin
        'Scarlet Town'

'Early Roman Kings' is a prime example of Dylan's ability almost to hear history as a series of echoes. Interviewed by *Rolling Stone*, he was clear about how his understanding had affected the writing of *Tempest*, far less forthcoming, as ever, about any specific conclusions he was prepared to identify or share with a journalist:

> The thing about it is that there is the old and the new, and you have to connect with them both. The old goes out and the new comes in, but there is no sharp borderline. The old is still happening while the new enters the scene, sometimes unnoticed. The new is overlapping at the same time the old is weakening its hold. It goes on and on like that. Forever through the centuries.[23]

'Early Roman Kings' therefore treats its imperial figures as mere gangsters in 'Their sharkskin suits / Bow ties and buttons / High top boots'. Historically, it makes for a neat connection: ancient Rome's rulers, with their clans and casual murders, were like nothing so much as the Mafia. But Dylan's 'kings' are also America's nineteenth-century robber barons 'Blazin' the rails / Nailed in their coffins / In top hats and tails'. They are, too, the slouching figures of organised crime, heading for 'a Sicilian court'. They are the bankers, the lawyers, the politicians, the corrupt ruling elite of modern life. If Dylan calls them the kings of old Rome he is saying that, when power and money are at stake, nothing important ever changes.

They're peddlers and they're meddlers
They buy and they sell
They destroyed your city

They'll destroy you as well
They're lecherous and treacherous
Hell-bent for leather
Each of 'em bigger
Than all them put together
Sluggers and muggers
Wearing fancy gold rings
All the women goin' crazy
For the early Roman kings

Dylan's hyper-awareness of history as an active presence has been one of the distinguishing features of his 'late period'. It explains many, if not all, of his acts of alleged plagiarism. But as interesting as the awareness of the past is the use to which he has put his understanding. Rarely does he content himself with just the facts. For him, everything has a mythical dimension. The past is a dream state, sometimes the nightmare, as James Joyce's Stephen Dedalus says in *Ulysses*, 'from which I am trying to awake'. 'Narrow Way', far from the best *song* on the album, has yet another extraordinary verse.

Ever since the British burned the White House down
There's a bleeding wound in the heart of town
I saw you drinking from an empty cup
I saw you buried and I saw you dug up

The album's most obvious point of contact with history is in its title song, 'the *Titanic* song'. Yet again, the sheer length of a work would guarantee the attention of reviewers ever quick to assume that if Dylan was taking 45 verses to say something it must, almost by definition, be something important. 'Tempest' in fact competes for the title as the least of the album's songs, 'epic' or not, and length has nothing much to do with its flaws. Too many of the verses are redundant, several are clumsily written and the song does not count, for this listener at least, as a musical treat. 'Tempest' is too self-conscious, even obvious, as an excursion into folk tradition. Talking to *Rolling Stone*, Dylan was entirely aware, as always, of his musical antecedents.

If you're a folk singer, blues singer, rock & roll singer, whatever, in that realm, you oughta write a song about the *Titanic*, because that's the bar you have to pass.[24]

In part, Dylan was explaining the fact that his work begins with an almost straight lift from 'The Titanic', a Carter Family song from the early 1950s. Before that there had been Lead Belly's song of the same name, one that Huddie had chosen to call his own. Before *that* there had been *Titanic* songs by the dozen, some reputedly composed within days or weeks of the great ship's sinking in 1912. What interested musicologists for long enough was that many of the early performers were black, despite the fact that the only non-white passenger allowed on the vessel had been a French Haitian with a white wife. African American singers, Lead Belly not least, took a certain grim satisfaction in the disaster as retribution for racism. Some chose to detect a divine judgement. In his *The American Songbag* (1927), in a note to a version he called 'De Titanic', Carl Sandburg asserted that 'Negro troops sang the song crossing the submarine zone and in the trenches overseas'.[25] In other words, there was a sardonic black song in circulation within five or six years of the tragedy. Equally, it has been claimed that the *Titanic* song group drew on African American folk tradition and a ballad describing the sinking of a long-forgotten Mississippi river-steamer.[26] Dylan knew a lot about these things, but neither his borrowings from the Carter Family, nor his several shameless references to James Cameron's risible 1997 *Titanic* movie, greatly aided an interminable song. To these ears 'Tempest' comes perilously close in places to sounding like something poor William McGonagall might have cherished.

It is a ship-of-fools song, an allegory. While the watchman sleeps and catastrophe approaches, humanity goes about its petty business. When disaster strikes, people show themselves for what they are, good or bad. Dylan's point, the repeated theological note struck throughout the album, is that none of it sways an indifferent God whose purposes are not to be judged by His creation. One oddity is that an iceberg is never mentioned, perhaps because the writer thought there was no need to state the obvious. On the other hand, Dylan calls his song 'Tempest' while history relates that *RMS Titanic* met her fate on a clear, calm night. The artist gets to the burden of his tale, in any case, in three verses rather than forty-five. Yet again, Dylan's favourite scriptural thriller justifies all.

In the dark illumination
He remembered bygone years
He read the Book of Revelation
And he filled his cup with tears

When the Reaper's task had ended
Sixteen hundred had gone to rest
The good, the bad, the rich, the poor
The loveliest and the best

They waited at the landing
And they tried to understand
But there is no understanding
Of the judgement of God's hand

The phrase 'dark illumination' probably does not count as Dylan's finest moment, just as 'Roll On, John' is a long way short of his finest song. Would so many reviewers have found it quite so affecting if its subject had not been quite so famous and so beloved? Dylan quotes Lennon songs – no problems over 'attribution', then – and throws in some of William Blake's 'The Tyger', for reasons that are not entirely clear. Because Lennon was fond of Blake? Because there was both primal ferocity and gentle beauty contained within the former Beatle? Because it's a jungle out there? But then, long delayed mourning aside, the song's motives are not clear. You are given the uneasy sense, in fact, that this is a communion between superstars, those burdened souls. A long album would still have run for over an hour if Dylan had decided against this song. As it is, what with the near-fourteen minutes of the title piece and this seven-and-a-half-minute eulogy, *Tempest*'s concluding passages feel like a long haul.

Miraculously, the album is not greatly diminished on that account. 'Pay in Blood', 'Scarlet Town', 'Long and Wasted Years', 'Early Roman Kings' and 'Soon After Midnight' more than prove that 'late Dylan' lacks nothing whatever in fire, power and poetry. The touring band, once again the studio band, are exemplary. Dylan's eroded rock formation of a voice sounds wonderful, which is to say right, and once again the producer, this cool Jack Frost, has done a better job in producing a Bob Dylan album than most others have managed. If the artist had chosen to drown his books and break the spell with *Tempest*, disavowing Shakespeare all the while, it would have been a fitting ending. But there was no sign of any such intention.

*

He was on the road again in April and the first half of June. Touring took up most of July, all of August and the first half of September.

In October, Mark Knopfler joined him on the trail for the first of 33 North American concerts. Read cold, the reviews seemed to depend on who was doing the writing. The critics who had observed Dylan for years allowed a benefit to every doubt. The *New York Times* sent the vastly experienced Jon Pareles to the reopening of the Capitol Theater in Port Chester, New York, at the beginning of September. 'A current Dylan concert is always a matter of shifting expectations,' he wrote.

> At first his voice sounds impossibly ramshackle, just a fogbound rasp. But soon, at least on a good night, his wilful phrasing and conversational nuances come through. While he has – for decades – rearranged many of his songs so that only the words are immediately recognizable, his musical choices aren't exactly arbitrary. They lead listeners, and Mr Dylan as well, to grapple with the songs anew.

The *Times* man conceded, nevertheless, that the artist was not 'courting new fans with anything that's easily appealing. Nowadays Mr Dylan is singing, and cackling, to loyalists.' In Vancouver in October the *Sun* reported that two types of fan had been in evidence, one 'completely enchanted', the other 'fairly disappointed' by the performer's 'mumble-jumble rambling style'. The *Los Angeles Times* reviewer called one concert in the city an 'unimpeachable' 15-song display of the artist's work. But the critic added: 'Way up in the Hollywood Bowl's cheap seats on Friday, it was hard to tell whether the guy with the gutter-nasal voice was actually Dylan or a monster with indigestion.' The *Chicago Tribune*'s veteran Greg Kot stuck, meanwhile, with the fable of reinvention that had seemed to explain everything once upon a time. 'He treats his songs as portable, mutable works in progress – forever subject to change,' wrote Kot. It was therefore impossible to write the artist off or 'embalm' him in his own history.[27]

Perhaps so. Perhaps, in a weird way, it no longer really mattered. If he still wanted to play and if people still wanted to pay, that was a matter for the artist and his audience. All the possible explanations for touring became irrelevant, in any case, as the 25th continuous year of concerts began. On 1 May 2013, according to bjorner.com (also unstoppable), Charlotte, North Carolina, saw show number 2,500 on the unending pilgrimage. As this is being written, the annual European tour is being announced. So here he goes again: Scandinavia, Germany, Switzerland, the Netherlands, Italy, Belgium, France, Luxembourg. Then three nights in Glasgow in November? You never know. You can tell for certain, though, which city will draw most attention. His sense of history – or is it humour? – is intact. In 2013, Dylan means to finish up with three nights at London's Royal Albert Hall. That's almost where we came in.

*

In his interview with Mikal Gilmore of *Rolling Stone* in September 2012, Dylan said one of the strangest things he has ever said. It could all be explained – survival, belief, the ability that 'allows you to crawl out from under the chaos and fly above it' – by transfiguration. Or as the artist said to the writer, 'I'm not like you, am I?'

Since Dylan had been expounding on his perfectly truthful *Chronicles* tale about a character named Bobby Zimmerman, the Hell's Angel dead thanks to his own stupidity at the start of the '60s, Gilmore wanted to know if they were talking not about transfiguration but about the transmigration of souls, metempsychosis. (You suspect the journalist also wanted desperately to ask if Dylan was kidding.) The artist denied it, though he seemed a little unsure, suspiciously so, about his terms, far less his theology. He certainly affected not to realise that by claiming transfiguration he was placing himself among the Old Testament prophets – finally – and the mother of God, and the Christ Himself. In the usual version, we humans get our transfiguration, if we're lucky, only in the life eternal. The artist's real point seemed to be that Gilmore was asking his questions of a person who 'doesn't exist'. Dylan went on: 'But people make that mistake about me all the time.'

He doesn't exist; the truth sets him apart. In some strange, beguiling sense, there is no Bob Dylan. After all those lives, all those incarnations, all the years under so much scrutiny, you can just about see why it might make sense to him. Perhaps it also imparts a truth about poor human existence to the rest of us.

Transfiguration does not explain art. An artist's gift might amount, though, to a kind of transfiguration. If there is truth in art, each and every Bob Dylan might count as a product of the imagination, with Robert Allen Zimmerman its first page and its first canvas, not invented but made real, time and again, time out of mind, like a folk tale told and retold. The tale is American, of course, and probably the oldest story of them all.

Chants of the prairies;
Chants of the long-running Mississippi, and down to the Mexican Sea;

Chants of Ohio, Indiana, Illinois, Iowa, Wisconsin, and Minnesota;
Chants going forth from the centre, from Kansas, and thence, equidistant,
Shooting in pulses of fire, ceaseless to vivify all.[28]

Acknowledgements

A number of Bob Dylan's songs, as listed below, have been quoted for purposes of criticism and review:

pp. 26, 522, 523, 524, 526, 'Narrow Way' (Copyright © 2012 by Special Rider Music); pp. 26, 523, 524–5, 'Pay in Blood' (Copyright © 2012 by Special Rider Music); pp. 26, 527–8, 'Tempest' (Copyright © 2012 by Special Rider Music); pp. 34, 199, 462, 'It's Alright, Ma (I'm Only Bleeding)' (Copyright © 1965 by Warner Bros. Inc.; renewed 1993 by Special Rider Music); p. 35, 'Wedding Song' (Copyright © 1973 by Ram's Horn Music; renewed 2001 by Ram's Horn Music); p. 36, 'Idiot Wind' (Copyright © 1974 by Ram's Horn Music; renewed 2002 by Ram's Horn Music); p. 45 'Shelter from the Storm' (Copyright © 1974 by Ram's Horn Music; renewed 2002 by Ram's Horn Music); pp. 58, 68, 84, 87, 89, 'Isis' (Copyright © 1975 by Ram's Horn Music; renewed 2003 by Ram's Horn Music); pp. 61, 89, 'One More Cup of Coffee' (Copyright © 1975, 1976 by Ram's Horn Music; renewed 2003, 2004 by Ram's Horn Music); p. 67, 'Rita May' (Copyright © 1975 by Ram's Horn Music; renewed 2003 by Ram's Horn Music); pp. 68, 91, 92 'Joey' (Copyright © 1975 by Ram's Horn Music; renewed 2003 by Ram's Horn Music); pp. 71, 73, 74, 75, 78, 82, 83, 'Hurricane' (Copyright © 1975 by Ram's Horn Music; renewed 2003 by Ram's Horn Music); p. 90, 'Oh, Sister' (Copyright © 1975 by Ram's Horn Music; renewed 2003 by Ram's Horn Music); pp. 95, 96, 'Black Diamond Bay' (Copyright © 1975 by Ram's Horn Music; renewed 2003 by Ram's Horn Music); pp. 96–7 'Romance in Durango' (Copyright © 1975 by Ram's Horn Music; renewed 2003 by Ram's Horn Music); pp. 98, 99, 'Sara' (Copyright © 1975, 1976 by Ram's Horn Music; renewed 2003, 2004 by Ram's Horn Music); p. 113, 'She's Your Lover Now' (Copyright © 1971 by Dwarf

ACKNOWLEDGEMENTS

Music; renewed 1999 by Dwarf Music); p. 116, 'Bob Dylan's 115th Dream' (Copyright © 1965 by Warner Bros. Inc.; renewed 1993 by Special Rider Music); pp. 117–18, 'When I Paint My Masterpiece' (Copyright © 1971 by Big Sky Music; renewed 1999 by Big Sky Music); p. 162, 'Is Your Love in Vain?' (Copyright © 1978 by Special Rider Music); p. 163, 'Señor (Tales of Yankee Power)' (Copyright © 1978 by Special Rider Music); p. 165, 'Changing of the Guards' (Copyright © 1978 by Special Rider Music); pp. 166, 167, 'Where Are You Tonight? (Journey Through Dark Heat)' (Copyright © 1978 by Special Rider Music); p. 176, 'Gotta Serve Somebody' (Copyright © 1979 by Special Rider Music); p. 178, 'Do Right To Me Baby (Do Unto Others)' (Copyright © 1979 by Special Rider Music); p. 182, 'I'd Hate to Be With You On That Dreadful Day' (Copyright © 1964, 1968 Warner Bros. Music, renewed 1992 Special Rider Music); pp. 183, 475, 'Spirit on the Water' (Copyright © 2006 by Special Rider Music); p. 193, 'Chimes of Freedom' (Copyright © 1964 by Warner Bros. Inc.; renewed 1992 by Special Rider Music); p. 195, 'Ain't Gonna Go to Hell for Anybody' (Copyright © 1980 by Special Rider Music); p. 197, 'One Too Many Mornings' (Copyright © 1964, 1966 by Warner Bros. Inc.; renewed 1992, 1994 by Special Rider Music); p. 202, 'Covenant Woman' (Copyright © 1980 by Special Rider Music); p. 213, 'Love Minus Zero, No Limit' (Copyright © 1965 by Warner Bros. Inc.; renewed 1993 by Special Rider Music); p. 215 'Trouble in Mind' (Copyright © 1979 by Special Rider Music); p. 215, 'Gonna Change My Way of Thinking' (Copyright © 1979 Special Rider Music); p. 216 'Precious Angel' (Copyright © 1979 by Special Rider Music); p. 216, 'I Believe in You' (Copyright © 1979 by Special Rider Music); pp. 217, 220, 'Slow Train' (Copyright © 1979 by Special Rider Music); p. 217, 'When You Gonna Wake Up' (Copyright © 1979 by Special Rider Music); p. 218, 'When He Returns' (Copyright © 1979 by Special Rider Music); pp. 241, 242 'Every Grain of Sand' (Copyright © 1981 by Special Rider Music); p. 257, 'Trouble' (Copyright © 1981 by Special Rider Music); pp. 257, 264, 'Dead Man, Dead Man' (Copyright © 1981 by Special Rider Music); p. 257, 'Property of Jesus' (Copyright © 1981 by Special Rider Music); pp. 257, 260, 261, 'Shot of Love' (Copyright © 1981 by Special Rider Music); p. 258, 'Caribbean Wind' (Copyright © 1985 by Special Rider Music); p. 259, 'The Groom's Still Waiting at the Altar' (Copyright © 1981 Special Rider Music); p. 260, 'Lenny Bruce' (Copyright © 1981 Special Rider Music); p. 266, 'Ballad of Hollis Brown' (Copyright © 1963 by Warner Bros. Inc.; renewed 1991 by Special Rider Music); pp. 272, 290, 'License to Kill' (Copyright ©

ACKNOWLEDGEMENTS

2001 by Special Rider Music); p. 426, 'When the Deal Goes Down' (Copyright © 2006 by Special Rider Music); pp. 451, 452, 453, 454, 455, "Cross the Green Mountain' (Copyright © 2003 by Special Rider Music); pp. 470–1, 472, 473, 'Workingman's Blues #2' (Copyright © 2006 Special Rider Music); pp. 472, 473, 'Thunder on the Mountain' (Copyright © 2006 by Special Rider Music); pp. 475, 476, 'Nettie Moore' (Copyright © 2006 by Special Rider Music); p. 476, 'Ain't Talkin" (Copyright © 2006 by Special Rider Music); p. 502, 'Dignity' (Copyright © 1991 by Special Rider Music); p. 503, 'If You Ever Go to Houston' (Copyright © 2009 by Special Rider Music and Ice-Nine Publishing); pp. 503, 504, 'I Feel a Change Comin' On' (Copyright © 2009 by Special Rider Music and Ice-Nine Publishing); p. 504, 'It's All Good' (Copyright © 2009 by Special Rider Music and Ice-Nine Publishing); p. 504, 'Forgetful Heart' (Copyright © 2009 by Special Rider Music and Ice-Nine Publishing); p. 521, 'Duquesne Whistle' (Copyright © 2012 by Special Rider Music); pp. 523, 523–4, 525, 'Scarlet Town' (Copyright © 2012 by Special Rider Music); pp. 523, 525–6, 'Early Roman Kings' (Copyright © 2012 by Special Rider Music); p. 524, 'Soon After Midnight' (Copyright © 2012 by Special Rider Music)

Notes

CHAPTER ONE – TIME IS AN ENEMY

1. According to the indefatigable fans who insist on keeping count, Dylan's last concert of 2012 – in Brooklyn, New York, on 21 November – was performance number 2,480 in the unending tour. The first show is dated to 7 June 1988. The lives devoted to these studies are not refundable.

2. The Hearst Greek Theatre, 19 October 2012. Madonna had just picked up $7 million for a couple of nights' work in Las Vegas during the previous week.

3. Edition of 27 September 2012.

4. 'We're all familiar with Fitzgerald saying that there are no second acts in American lives and this clearly disproves that.' (Greil Marcus, nbcnews.com, May 2011.) 'When F. Scott Fitzgerald declared that "there are no second acts in American lives," he obviously hadn't envisioned the existence of Bob Dylan.' (Douglas Heselgrave, www.musicbox-online.com, January 2009.) And so on.

5. 'Bob Dylan's Invisible Republic: Interview with Greil Marcus', Paolo Vites, *Jam* magazine (Italy), 1997.

6. *Allen Ginsberg: Beat Poet* (2010), p. 460.

7. The verses come, respectively, from the songs 'Narrow Way', 'Pay in Blood' and 'Tempest'.

8. Edition of 27 September 2012.

CHAPTER TWO – WRITTEN IN MY SOUL

1. See Bert Cartwright's 'The Mysterious Norman Raeben' in *Wanted Man: In Search of Bob Dylan* (1990), ed. John Bauldie.

2. That Dylan made an editorial choice is not seriously in doubt. Two or three of the notebook's unused blues songs would have given him enough for a double album. *Blonde on Blonde*, the most famous double-disc set of them all, runs to just under 73 minutes. Clearly, the notebook overmatter was not up to scratch, or a distraction from Dylan's purpose. In years to come he would be less scrupulous. In 1988, in

arid times, *Down in the Groove*, barely 32 empty minutes long, would be deemed fit for release.

3. *Down the Highway* (2002, paperback ed.), p. 332.

4. Dylan's 1964 poem acquired a curious history of its own. The actor-singer Ben (Benito) Carruthers, who had travelled with him in Europe that year, set an adapted version of the piece to music and released it as a UK single in the summer of 1965. The Dylan/Carruthers 'song' was in turn recorded by Fairport Convention for their eponymous first album in 1968. Richard Thompson was still performing this version in 2004.

CHAPTER THREE – A WANDERER BY TRADE

1. Foreword to Sam Shepard's *The Rolling Thunder Logbook* (1977, reissued 2004), p. viii.

2. 'Patti Smith' by Barry Miles, from the anthology *Wanted Man: In Search of Bob Dylan* (1990), ed. John Bauldie.

3. The first pair of quotations appeared in the issue of 18 December 1975. Ginsberg's remark was reported by Nat Hentoff in the issue of 15 January 1976.

4. 'Jacques Levy and the *Desire* collaboration', first published in the British fan magazine *The Telegraph* in April of 1983, reprinted in *All Across the Telegraph: A Bob Dylan Handbook* (1987), edited by Michael Gray and John Bauldie.

5. www.reddit.com. The exchanges, in one of the site's regular 'Ask Me Anything' features devoted to almost-live exchanges between notable individuals and the public, appeared on 14 November 2012.

6. *On the Road with Bob Dylan* (1978, reissued 2002), Chapter 1.

7. *SongTalk*, winter issue, 1991.

8. See, if you truly must, *The Holy Blood and the Holy Grail* (1982) by Michael Baigent, Richard Leigh and Henry Lincoln. Dan Brown's *The Da Vinci Code* (2003) takes certain of these speculations to their preposterous conclusions. An equally good Provençal fairy tale holds that the Romani are survivors of Atlantis who clambered ashore locally.

9. See, for example, p. 247 of Tim Dunn's daunting *The Bob Dylan Copyright Files 1962–2007* (2008) as it concerns the ownership of the song 'Isis'. Since Dylan would surrender 'an undivided fifty percent (50%) of his fractional interest' in such works in January 1978 as part of the settlement made on Sara Dylan, he actually wound up making less from the writing deal than Levy. In 2012, equally, the director's son would tell his online audience that his father had earned little for his efforts.

10. Edition of December 1977.

11. Sam Shepard, *The Rolling Thunder Logbook* (1977, reissued 2004).

12. 'Rita May' would also turn up on the 1978 three-disc compilation *Masterpieces*, a 'greatest-hits' package sold to Dylan fans in Japan and Australia – and to

those among us prepared to pay absurd import prices for a couple of unfamiliar tracks.

13. See the *Desire* session notes at Olof Björner's inestimable resource bjorner.com.

14. Dr Rubin 'Hurricane' Carter LLD (with Ken Klonsky), *Eye of the Hurricane: My Path from Darkness to Freedom* (2011). Klonsky's introduction to the tale of a 'spiritual journey' concedes of Carter: 'There are those who focus on his character flaws, his difficult past, his long-windedness. He owns up to it all, often good-naturedly.'

15. *The Sixteenth Round*, p. 15.

16. *Ibid.*, p. 42.

17. Larry Sloman, *Rolling Stone*, issue of 4 December 1975.

18. See Paul B. Wice's *Rubin 'Hurricane' Carter and the American Justice System* (2000), p. 90.

19. 'Algren in Exile', *Chicago* magazine (February 1988). Carter appears in *The Devil's Stocking* as 'Ruby Calhoun'.

20. Artis spent 14 years in prison before his parole in 1981. He was sentenced in August of 1987 to six years by a New Jersey court for 'conspiracy to distribute cocaine and to receiving a stolen handgun'. According to the *New York Times* (9 August 1987), Artis accepted one drug charge 'in exchange for dismissal of two other drug counts'. He would later work as an articulate 'juvenile counsellor'.

21. 'Early in 1966 the reform mayoral candidate, Laurence "Pat" Kramer, declared, "Paterson doesn't need a mayor, it needs a referee."' Wice p. 1, 'Prologue'.

22. See 'Hurricane Carter: The Other Side of the Story', www.graphicwitness.com, or 'Top Ten Myths about Rubin Hurricane Carter and the Lafayette Grill Murders', members.shaw.ca/cartermyths.

23. 'The Real Record on Racial Attitudes' by Lawrence D. Bobo, Camille Z. Charles, Maria Krysan and Alicia D. Simmons. The paper appears as Chapter 3 in *Social Trends in American Life: Findings from the General Social Survey* (2012), ed. Peter V. Marsden.

24. See the Human Rights Watch website: www.hrw.org/reports/2000.

25. Bruce Western: 'The Impact of Incarceration on Wage Mobility and Inequality', *American Sociological Review*, August 2002.

26. 1985 U.S. Dist. LEXIS 14085.

27. Wice, p. 2.

28. Later supplied as an 'extra' to early purchasers of *The Bootleg Series Vol. 5: Bob Dylan Live 1975, The Rolling Thunder Revue* (2002).

29. *On the Road With Bob Dylan*, p.13.

30. *Rockline* with Bob Coburn, 17 June 1985.

31. *The Golden Bough: A Study in Magic and Religion* (abridged ed. 1922), p. 383.

32. *The Hero with a Thousand Faces*, p. 1.

33. Pages 424 and 147 respectively.

34. Chapter 2.

35. Pages 186f and 175 respectively.

36. *On the Road with Bob Dylan*, p. 14.

37. From the Uniform Crime Reporting Program database maintained by the FBI at www.ucrdatatool.gov. Clearly, America's population had increased greatly over the intervening years, but the trend was indisputable. In 1960, 5.1 homicides were reported per 100,000 of the population; by 1975, the figure was 9.6.

38. 'Joey Gallo Was No Hero', 8 March 1976. A slightly different version would appear in the April 1976 edition of the magazine *Creem*, for which Bangs acted as 'senior editor'.

39. *Still on the Road: The Songs of Bob Dylan Vol. 2: 1974–2008* (2010), p. 79. Dylan's website disagrees with Heylin, stating that the song was performed in Salt Lake City, Utah, on 25 May 1976, during the last of all Rolling Thunder concerts. Les Kokay's *Songs of the Underground: A Collector's Guide to the Rolling Thunder Revue 1975–1976* (privately published, 2003) notes the supposed performance but accepts that the claim is based on a single unsupported report of a show for which no bootleg tapes exist. One performance or no performance, Dylan hasn't exactly embraced 'Black Diamond Bay'.

40. *Song & Dance Man III*, p. 185.

41. *Still On the Road*, p. 84.

42. *Song & Dance Man III*, p. 83; *The Bob Dylan Encyclopedia*, p. 589.

43. p. 19.

44. 'In *Blonde on Blonde* I wrote out all the songs in the studio. The musicians played cards, I wrote out a song . . .' (Interview with *Newsweek*, published 26 February 1968.) 'I just sat down at a table and started writing ['Sad Eyed Lady']. At the session itself.' (*Rolling Stone*, November 1969.)

CHAPTER FOUR – THUNDER ON THE MOUNTAIN

1. *Rolling Stone*, 4 December 1975. Roger McGuinn would later be quoted in Sloman's book *On the Road with Bob Dylan* (p. 149) stating 'slyly' that the noises Dylan had heard were 'probably' sonic booms from aircraft at Vanderburg Air Force Base near Malibu, California.

2. *On the Road with Bob Dylan*, p. 71.

3. *Rolling Stone*, 15 January 1976.

4. *Down the Highway*, p. 341.

5. See Clinton Heylin's *Behind the Shades Revisited*, p. 394.

6. *No Direction Home: The Life and Music of Bob Dylan* (1st ed., 1986), p. 450.

7. *Bob Dylan in America* (2010), Chapter 5. The McGuinn tale can be found under the title 'Roadie Report 31' at http://rogermcguinn.blogspot.co.uk/2007_12_01_archive.html.

8. *People*, 10 November 1975.

9. Hank Reineke, *Ramblin' Jack Elliott: The Never-Ending Highway* (2010), p. 225.

10. Shelton, p.15.

11. Barry Miles, *Allen Ginsberg: Beat Poet*, p. 457.

12. *The Rolling Thunder Logbook*, p. viii.

13. *Songs of the Underground*, pp. 8–10.

14. Sloman, *On the Road with Bob Dylan*, p. 20.

15. *Rolling Stone*, 15 January 1976.

16. *Shelter from the Storm: Bob Dylan's Rolling Thunder Years* (2010), p. 35.

17. Reineke, p. 226.

18. *And a Song to Sing With*, Part 5, Chapter 1.

19. The details come largely from a 1998 interview with a local witness conducted by Dave Conlin Read. See http://www.berkshirelinks.com/bob-dylans-rolling-thunder-revue-party-mama-frascas-dream-lodge/.

20. Lucian K. Truscott IV, edition of 28 August.

21. Just before he hanged himself on 9 April 1976, in Far Rockaway, in the New York borough of Queens, Phil Ochs was diagnosed finally as suffering from bipolar disorder.

22. *And a Voice to Sing With*, Part 5, Chapter 1.

23. Barry Miles, *Allen Ginsberg: Beat Poet*, p. 458. Miles also says that Dylan, playing the piano, went down very well among the mah-jong players with a version of 'Simple Twist of Fate'.

24. *On the Road with Bob Dylan*, p. 70.

25. *Ibid.*, p. 71. In July 1963, having just turned 13, Larry Sloman hadn't yet heard – by his own admission – of Bob Dylan.

26. *Ibid.*, pp. 117–18.

27. *Rolling Stone*, 18 December 1975.

28. In 1975, for the purposes of comparison, it would have cost a fan $10 to see the Rolling Stones and $8.50 to catch Led Zeppelin. The Kinks, on the other hand, were available in smaller halls for $4.50. The issue of ticket prices is complicated by the additional fees imposed by many venues.

29. Sloman, *On the Road with Bob Dylan*, pp. 177–8.

30. Barry Miles, *Allen Ginsberg: Beat Poet*, p. 469.

31. Peter Guralnick, *Careless Love: The Unmaking of Elvis Presley* (1999), pp. 587–8.

32. Sloman, *On the Road with Bob Dylan*, p. 379.

33. *New York Times*, 9 December 1975.

34. Edition of 4 February 1977.

35. *On the Road with Bob Dylan*, p. 404.

36. Interview with Allan Jones, published in *Uncut* magazine, 8 January 2013. Ronson died of liver cancer on 29 April 1993, aged 46.

37. *People*, 10 November 1975

NOTES

CHAPTER FIVE – THE PALACE OF MIRRORS

1. 22 January 1978.
2. 11 March 1976.
3. *Rolling Stone*, 24 February 1977. 'Night of the Hurricane (Or Was It Just an Idiot Wind?)' ran the magazine's headline.
4. Issue of March 1978.
5. Issue of 26 January 1978.
6. Interview with Gregg Kilday, 22 January 1978.
7. Interview with Philip Fleishman, 20 March 1978.
8. Issue of 11 September 1976.
9. 'The State of the Union: 1975', first published in *Esquire*, May 1975, reprinted in *United States: Essays 1952–1992* (1993).
10. John Micklethwait and Adrian Wooldridge, *The Right Nation: Why America Is Different* (2004), p. 72.
11. Levon Helm and Stephen Davis, *This Wheel's On Fire: Levon Helm and the Story of The Band* (1993, 2000), p. 312. Danko had been arrested in Japan in 1996 for possession of heroin. The multi-instrumentalist Richard Manuel, co-writer with Dylan of 'Tears of Rage', had hanged himself in Florida in 1986. Over time, Robertson bought out the interests of each member in The Band save Helm.
12. The incident is discussed in David Fricke's sleeve notes to the 2002 reissue of *The Last Waltz* album, broadly confirming the account given in Helm's book.
13. Joel Selvin, *San Francisco Chronicle*, 4 April 2002.
14. See Sounes, *Down the Highway*, p. 360.
15. *Careless Love: The Unmaking of Elvis Presley*, p. 638.
16. *Melody Maker*, 29 July 1978.
17. As recalled in an article by J. Hoberman in the *Village Voice*, 13 November 2007.
18. As republished in the wholly self-effacing *Teenage Hipster in the Modern World: From the Birth of Punk to the Land of Bush – Thirty Years of Apocalyptic Journalism* (2005), pp. 132–4.
19. Issue of 13 February 1978.
20. Interview with Robert Hilburn, published 28 May 1978.
21. *Masterpieces*, valued by many fans thanks to the inclusion of a handful of previously unreleased tracks, would soon be imported to Britain and America at horribly inflated prices.
22. In 1999, the album would be remixed and remastered by Don DeVito, once again Dylan's nominal producer. The result was a great improvement, but the exercise did not solve all of *Street-Legal*'s technical problems.
23. *The Bob Dylan Encyclopedia*, p. 643.
24. *Rolling Stone*, 24 August 1978.
25. *Song & Dance Man III*, p. 216.

26. The versions of Dylan's lyrics preserved by bobdylan.com and by his *Lyrics 1962–2001* are often unreliable guides to the words as he has performed them on the albums. To put it kindly, the process of transcription – by whose hand, we don't know – has been erratic. It may be that Dylan himself has rewritten passages. Again, we don't know.

    Similarly, the arrangements of the words in verse form in *Lyrics* and at bobdylan.com are often at odds with the recordings. Sometimes, in fact, book and website disagree. All that being the case, I have used the words as they are heard on the albums and ordered the lines to reflect Dylan's performance.

    This verse is a case in point. Book and website say 'But Eden is burning, either brace yourself for elimination . . .' There is no 'brace yourself' on the *Street-Legal* album and the backing vocalists provide a clear line break after 'burning'.

27. *Melody Maker*, 29 July 1978.

28. *Rolling Stone*, 13 July 1978.

29. Issue of 1 July 1978.

30. The monologue, as contained in 'circulating' bootlegs, is derived from a necessarily abysmal mono recording made by a member of the San Diego audience. Contrary to the impression given in a couple of biographies and disseminated in various reference sources, there is no extant Dylan interview in which the story is told.

CHAPTER SIX – GOD SAID TO ABRAHAM . . .

1. The description of a presence in the hotel room, the room moving, Dylan's claim to have been 'relatively content' and the declaration that he was 'willing to listen' are statements taken from an interview with Robert Hilburn, *Los Angeles Times*, 23 November 1980. The descriptions of an unseen hand, of trembling and of being 'knocked down' are from an interview conducted by Karen Hughes in Dayton, Ohio, on 21 May 1980 during Dylan's third gospel tour. The Hughes piece was published in New Zealand's *The Star* on 10 July 1980.

2. Hilburn, *Los Angeles Times* interview, 23 November 1980.

3. *Ibid.*

4. From the Dylan fan magazine *On the Tracks*, autumn issue, 1994.

5. Karen Hughes, *The Star*, 10 July 1980.

6. According to Cameron Crowe's booklet for the 1985 *Biograph* compilation, Dylan devoted five months to Bible studies in the first half of 1979. The claim is nowhere corroborated.

7. Bert Cartwright, *The Bible in the Lyrics of Bob Dylan* (1985, rev. and expanded 1992).

8. Interview with Mikal Gilmore, *Rolling Stone*, 27 September 2012.

9. *On the Tracks* magazine, autumn issue, 1994.

10. www.tempevineyard.com.

NOTES

11. With Gulliksen no longer involved, the contemporary Vineyard Association has an interesting habit of describing Wimber as its 'founder'.
12. Interview with Kurt Loder, *Rolling Stone*, 21 June 1984.
13. Interview with Dan Wooding for the ASSIST ('Aid to Special Saints in Strategic Times') Christian news service in Anaheim, California, 25 April 1999.
14. *The Right Nation: Why America Is Different* (2004), p. 325.
15. *Ibid.*, pp. 83–5.
16. 'Satan had mobilised . . .' The Reverend Jerry Falwell, Southern Baptist evangelical founder in 1979 of the Moral Majority. Mickelthwait and Wooldridge, p. 84.
17. In its issue of 14 April 1980, *Time* magazine reported Reagan's declaration during a televised interview. The magazine observed, however, that he 'seemed shaky about the evangelical concept of personal belief'. Reagan's best guess was 'I suppose I would qualify'.
18. The Barna Group is a self-described 'research and media development organisation'. It has also been called 'an evangelical Christian polling firm'. Its methods are both respectable and rigorous, however, and its findings are not always welcomed by born-again creeds.
19. Joan Acocella, 'Seeing and Believing', *The New Yorker*, 2 April 2012.
20. Interview with Mikal Gilmore, *Rolling Stone*, 17 July 1986.
21. John S. Dickerson, senior pastor of the Cornerstone Church in Prescott, Arizona. The piece was published in the *New York Times* Sunday Review, 15 December 2012.
22. In Britain in 2010, according to a Eurobarometer poll, 37 per cent reported a belief in God; in France the figure was 27 per cent. Both countries found majority support instead for an impersonal 'spirit' or 'life force'. The 2011 census in England found 59.4 per cent professing Christianity while 'no religion' was given as 24.7 per cent.
23. www.vineyardusa.org/site/task-forces/blessing-muslims
24. Nicholas de Lange, *Judaism* (1986).
25. Report by the ASSIST News Service, 10 March 2011.
26. The interview appeared via continentalnews.net, a news service specialising in Christian issues, on 1 October 2012.
27. ASSIST News Service, 10 March 2011.
28. Interview with Karen Hughes, *The Star*, published on 10 July 1980.
29. See *Introduction to New and Alternative Religions in America*, ed. William M. Ashcroft and Eugene V. Gallagher (2006), *Vol. 2: Jewish and Christian Traditions*, pp. 193–7.
30. *Dylan Redeemed: From Highway 61 to Saved* (2006), p. 81.
31. *Ibid.*, p. 11 and p. 16.
32. Interview with Kurt Loder, *Rolling Stone*, 21 June 1984.
33. www.umjc.org.
34. *Daily News*, 8 June 1986.
35. 13 January 1984.

36. In a videotaped interview posted on YouTube in January 2013, Friedman cast doubt on whether sexual abuse was a significant *averiah* (sin). He also questioned why victims should feel damaged. The rabbi further stated that 'there is hardly a kid who comes to a yeshiva [religious school], to a program, that hasn't been molested'.

37. 21 June 1984.

38. Interview conducted in September of 1985 and published in the December issue of *Spin*.

39. 'Don't You Ever Pray?', Chris Cooper interview with Helena Springs, published in *Wanted Man: In Search of Bob Dylan*, ed. John Bauldie (1990), p. 125.

40. See, generally, *Revelations: Visions, Prophecy and Politics in the Book of Revelation* (2012) by Elaine Pagels.

41. See Adam Gopnik's review of Pagels, 'The Big Revival', *New Yorker*, 5 March 2012.

CHAPTER SEVEN – WADE IN THE WATER

1. Interview with Bert Kleinman and Artie Mogull for the Westwood One network. First broadcast on 17 November 1984.

2. Jerry Wexler and David Ritz, *Rhythm and the Blues: A Life in American Music* (1993), Chapter 2.

3. *Mojo* magazine, January 1997.

4. See Colleen McDannell and Bernhard Lang, *Heaven: A History* (1988), pp. 335–41.

5. 12 July 1979.

6. See Matthew Zuckerman's essay, 'If There's an Original Thought Out There, I Could Use It Right Now: The Folk Roots of Bob Dylan' (1997). It can be found at http://www.expectingrain.com/dok/div/influences.html.

7. See Robert V. Wells, *Life Flows On in Endless Song: Folk Songs and American History* (2009), p. 112.

8. Chris Bohn, *Melody Maker*, August 1979.

9. 'Amazing Chutzpah', *New West* magazine, 24 September 1979.

10. *Rolling Stone*, 20 September 1979.

11. Interview with Scott Cohen, September 1985, published in *Spin* magazine in December 1985.

12. Interview with Scott Marshall for the Dylan fan magazine *On the Tracks*, issue 17, autumn 1999.

13. 'Don't You Ever Pray?', Chris Cooper interview with Helena Springs, published in *Wanted Man: In Search of Bob Dylan*, ed. John Bauldie (1990), p. 125.

14. http://www.tonywright-art.com/Pages/AlbumDetails/Dylan-Saved.html

15. The first Dylan quotation comes from an interview with Paul Zollo published in the 1991 winter issue of *SongTalk* magazine. The second fragment – in which Dylan also said that 'Every Grain of Sand' was a 'very painless song to write' – comes

from an interview with Robert Hilburn published in the *Los Angeles Times* on 9 February 1992.

16. Interview with Robert Hilburn, 23 November 1980.

CHAPTER EIGHT – JOKERMAN

1. Micklethwait and Wooldridge, *The Right Nation*, p. 71. The National Elections Studies database at the University of Michigan is cited.

2. *New York Times*, 19 April 2005.

3. Erich Goode and Nachman Ben-Yehuda, *Moral Panics: The Social Construction of Deviance* (1994), Chapter 12.

4. Address to the Conservative Political Action Conference, Washington DC, 20 March 1981.

5. *Rolling Stone*, 15 October 1981.

6. The last of three complete takes captured at that session according to Michael Krogsgaard's painstaking 'Bob Dylan: The Recording Sessions (Part 5)' published in *The Bridge* (Issue 1, summer 1998).

7. *Still on the Road*, pp. 187–95.

8. See Krogsgaard, as before.

9. See Howard Sounes, *Down the Highway*, pp. 394, 400–2.

10. *New York Times*, 9 March 2013, citing the General Social Survey.

11. From the introduction to Faye D. Ginsburg's *Contested Lives: The Abortion Debate in an American Community* (1989, rev. ed. 1998), pp. 1–2. As an intriguing, if inadvertent, sidelight on Dylan's North Country upbringing, the anthropology professor at one point remarks that her Jewishness was regarded as 'culturally strange' in Fargo. This was in 1981, not 1941.

12. 13 January 1984.

13. Many accounts continue to insist, for as much as it matters, that the son in question was Jacob (later Jakob) Dylan. Since Jewish law says that a boy becomes a *bar mitzvah* on reaching the age of 13, this doesn't seem likely. Jacob didn't reach that age until 9 December 1982, whereas Samuel was 13 until his birthday on 30 July. *New York* magazine's informant had also made it clear that the ceremony was to take place in LA and not in Israel, as has sometimes been reported. Dylan was leaving New York in March 1982 because 'He has to be in California by the 20th for his son's *bar mitzvah*'.

14. Christopher Connelly, 24 November 1983.

15. At some point, Dylan grasped that his verse was liable to leave half the species unimpressed. Should you check his website these days, you will find that 'Taking care of somebody nice' has been replaced by the less egregious, if clumsy, 'Watching out for someone who loves you true'.

16. 'The life and crimes of the music biz', *The Observer*, 20 January 2008.

17. To be fair to Asher, he had by this time earned a reputation for fighting corruption

within the industry. In 1983, his stance would cost him his job. Described as 'a company man', 'blunt and a bit awkward', the former Marine was no diplomat. Asher had been promoted to deputy president to cut costs, a fact that might have a bearing on any clash with Dylan. Asher's claim to fame as a hit-maker was the success of Julio Iglesias. See Frederic Dannen's *Hit Men: Power Brokers and Fast Money Inside the Music Business* (1991), pp. 1–13, 'The Education of Dick Asher'.

18. Interview conducted on 5 July 1983 and published in Britain by the *New Musical Express* on 6 August 1983.

19. Interview with Robert Hilburn, *Los Angeles Times*, 30 October 1983.

20. Bootleggers tend towards the opposite extreme. At their most extravagant, they turned this single Dylan album into *The Complete Infidels Sessions*, a seven-CD box set with a concert DVD from 1984. If six versions of 'Neighborhood Bully' and seven of 'Don't Fall Apart On Me Tonight' are what you seek, the capacious set answers most prayers.

21. In December 2001, the Associated Press (AP) news agency published a three-part investigation into the theft of land from black Americans that began even before the Civil War and had continued almost to the present. 'Torn From the Land' established that property worth hundreds of millions of dollars, if not billions, had been stolen.

    Amid a mass of documentation, AP noted: 'In 1910, black Americans owned at least 15 million acres of farmland, nearly all of it in the South, according to the U.S. Agricultural Census. Today, blacks own only 1.1 million acres of farmland and are part owners of another 1.07 million acres . . . [Black] ownership has declined two and a half times faster than white ownership according to a 1982 federal report.'

22. Merline Pitre, *In Struggle Against Jim Crow: Lulu B. White and the NAACP, 1900–1957* (1999), pp. 5–6.

23. Texas State Historical Association (http://www.tshaonline.org).

24. *Song & Dance Man III* (2000), pp. 527–45.

25. *Bob Dylan in America* (2010), Part 3, Chapter 6: 'Many Martyrs Fell'.

26. See, generally, the marvellous *Hand Me My Travelin' Shoes: In Search of Blind Willie McTell* (2007), to which I am indebted for biographical information and much else besides.

27. *Rolling Stone*, 7 September 2006.

28. Edition of 21 June 1984.

29. Interview with Kurt Loder, *Rolling Stone*, 21 June 1984.

30. Interview with Martin Keller, *New Musical Express*, 6 August 1983. Asked the same question by the Australian writer Karen Hughes in 1978, Dylan had replied that he believed in reincarnation 'In a casual but not astonishing way'. (*Rock Express*, April 1978).

31. *Song & Dance Man III* (2000), p. 464.

NOTES

CHAPTER NINE – WORLD GONE WRONG

1. 'September 1, 1939', *The English Auden: Poems, Essay and Dramatic Writings 1927–1939*, (ed. Edward Mendelson) (1977, pb. 1986), pp. 245–7.

2. *The Closing of the American Mind: How Higher Education Has Failed Democracy and Impoverished the Souls of Today's Students* (1987), p. 73.

3. Scott Stossel, *The Atlantic*, 2 September 1998.

4. *And a Voice to Sing With* (1987, repub. 2009), Part 5, Chapter 1.

5. *Sunday Times*, 1 July 1984.

6. Edition of 25 November 1985.

7. Michael Gray deals with this issue in fascinating and exhaustive detail in his *The Bob Dylan Encyclopedia* (2006), pp. 225–31. Gray also points out that the album's title derives in part from the fact that there once were movie houses called Empire Burlesques. One such pops up in Philip Roth's 1983 novel *The Anatomy Lesson*.

8. *Behind the Shades Revisited* (2000), p. 575.

9. 4 July 1985.

10. Interview with Denise Worrell, *Time*, 25 November 1985.

11. Howard Sounes, the biographer who brought the Dylan of secret marriages and love children to public attention, has more in Chapter 9 of his *Down the Highway: The Life of Bob Dylan*.

12. The film, part of the BBC's Omnibus strand, would not be broadcast until September 1987.

13. The Farley interview was published on 17 September 2001; the Inskeep interview

14. Allan Jones, 'Editor's Diary', *Uncut*. www.uncut.co.uk/blog/uncut-editors-diary/the-greatest-shows-on-earth

15. 18 October 1987.

CHAPTER TEN – BORN IN TIME

1. Edition of 22 December 2001.

2. *Rolling Stone*, 7 September 2006.

3. Ben Rayner, *Toronto Star*, 15 November 2012.

4. Interview with Douglas Brinkley, published 14 May 2009.

5. *Encyclopedia*, pp. 173–4.

6. *The Independent*, 21 October 1988.

7. Edition of 29 July 1988.

8. Interview with Jon Pareles, 28 September 1997.

9. *Chronicles*, p. 165.

10. Both quotations come from interviews given to *Uncut* magazine, November 2008.

11. 21 September 1989.

12. Interview with Ellen Futterman, *St Louis Post-Dispatch*, 7 April 1994.

13. See Ian Bell, *Once Upon a Time: The Lives of Bob Dylan* (2012), p. 101.

14. 4 February 1991.

15. Andrew Muir, *Razor's Edge: Bob Dylan & the Neverending Tour* (2001), p. 71.

16. Published in July 1991.

17. The interview was conducted in Los Angeles on 14 April but not published until the winter 1991 edition of the magazine *SongTalk*.

18. Interview with Ryan Cormnier, Delaware Online, 9 October 2008. Retrieved from www.delawareonline.com/blogs.

19. The Ryan quotations are from an interview published online by *Uncut* magazine in October 2008.

20. *Requiem for a Nun* (1950).

21. See Bell, *Once Upon a Time*, p. 138.

22. See, generally, three books by the late Paul Williams: *Bob Dylan: Performing Artist 1960–1973* (1990); *Bob Dylan: Performing Artist: The Middle Years 1974–1986* (1992); *Bob Dylan: Performing Artist 1986–1990 and Beyond* (2005). Each is admirable, learned and somehow beside the point. See also Stephen Scobie's fine *Alias Bob Dylan Revisited* (2003).

23. *Song & Dance Man III*, p. 389.

24. Interview with David Gates, *Newsweek*, 5 October 1997.

25. *Bob Dylan: The Never Ending Star*, p. 21.

26. *Ibid.*, p. 209.

27. *Song & Dance Man III*, p. 389.

28. *Down the Highway*, p. 475.

29. *Ibid.*, pp. 488–9.

30. *Biograph* booklet.

CHAPTER ELEVEN – THINGS HAVE CHANGED

1. The melodrama began to get out of hand when Barry Dickens, Dylan's British agent, described the infection as 'potentially fatal' (*The Independent*, 29 May 1997). The New York *Daily News* (29 May 1997) preferred 'potentially deadly'. By 8 June, *Newsweek* had reported claims from the previous week that Dylan 'might be dying'. By 16 October, *Der Spiegel* was stating that he had 'almost died of a heart disease'.

2. *The Oxford Companion to Medicine*, Volume I, p. 546.

3. Edition of 26 August.

4. Interview with David Gates, *Newsweek*, 5 October 1997.

5. *Ibid.*

6. Interview with Jon Pareles, 28 September 1997.

7. *USA Today*, 29 September 1997.

8. *Rolling Stone*, 7 September 2006.

9. Interview with Edna Gundersen, *USA Today*, 29 September 1997.

10. *Ibid.*

NOTES

11. Serge Kaganski, *Mojo* magazine, February 1998 edition.

12. Alan Jackson, press-conference report, *Times* magazine, 8 September 2001.

13. Interview with Mikal Gilmore, *Rolling Stone*, 22 November 2001.

14. *San Francisco Chronicle*, 2 November 1997.

15. While it is true that only 49 per cent of eligible voters bothered to turn out for the election in November 1996, giving 49.2 per cent of the popular vote to Clinton and 40.7 per cent to his opponent, Bob Dole, polling organisations weight their findings to take account of participation, party affiliation, if any, and other factors besides. Clinton was popular.

16. The population statistics come from a Bureau of the Census document entitled *Population Profile of the United States 1997*. The firearms figures are from a National Institute of Justice survey published in May 1997.

17. Sidney Blumenthal, *The Clinton Wars: An Insider's Account of the White House Years* (2003).

18. *Mojo*, February 1998. The piece was provided by Serge Kaganski of the French magazine *Les Inrockuptibles*. He had been part of a group of European journalists who had interviewd Dylan in London on 4 October 1997.

19. A Norwegian committee and John Bauldie, editor of the Dylan magazine *The Telegraph*, were equally important to the campaign. Bauldie died in a helicopter crash just after the nomination was submitted. Contrary to some reports, the submission, though lodged in 1996, was made too late for consideration that year.

20. From Bill Pagel's Bob Links, a website 'dedicated to providing Bob Dylan concert information'. (http://www.boblinks.com/dates11.html.)

21. *Berkshire Eagle*, 22 July 1999.

22. Reported by Dave Fanning, *Irish Times* magazine, 29 September 2001.

CHAPTER TWELVE – SKETCHES FROM MEMORY

1. *Rolling Stone*, issue of 7 September 2006.

2. Interview with Mikal Gilmore, 27 September 2012.

3. Charles Seeger put some of his thoughts on process and plagiarism in print in the journal *Western Folklore* in April 1962. See Bell, *Once Upon a Time*, pp. 374–5.

4. Interview with Seth Rogovoy, *Berkshire Eagle*, 8 June 2001.

5. Pete Seeger and Peter Blood (eds), *Where Have All the Flowers Gone?: A Singer's Stories, Songs, Seeds, Robberies*, (1993) p. 33.

6. Interview with Paul Zollo, *SongTalk* magazine, 1991 winter issue (Vol. 2, Issue 16). Republished in *Singers on Songwriting* (1993, rev. and expanded 2003).

7. *Rolling Stone*, 14 September 2012.

8. Mikal Gilmore interview, 27 September 2012.

9. 5 October 2004.

10. The Marqusee review appeared on 16 October 2004, the Appleyard piece on the following day. Carlo Wolff's notice was published on 5 October.

11. 8 July 2003.

12. Lott, p. 5.

13. Edition of 4 November 1963. Dylan had in fact taken his inspiration from the spiritual 'No More Auction Block/Many Thousands Gone', but its resemblance to 'Blowin' in the Wind' was not self-evident.

14. Junichi Saga, *Confessions of a Yakuza* (trans. John Bester, 1991), p. 6.

15. 14 September 2006.

16. 'Bob Dylan: Henry Timrod Revisited': www.poetryfoundation.org/article/178703.

17. Issue of 27 September 2012.

18. *No Direction Home*, Chapter 2.

19. To be found at swarmuth.blogspot.com.

20. As a specialist in Aramaic and Hebrew, Cook was probably more alert than most to the biblical connotations of Dylan's title. Cook's translations of the Scrolls, with Michael O. Wise and Martin G. Abegg, were published in 1996 with a revised edition in 2005.

21. See Bell, *Once Upon a Time*, pp. 348–9.

22. *Los Angeles Times*, 22 April 2010.

23. The blog can be found at ralphriver.blogspot.com. The relevant entry is for 30 July 2011.

24. 'Highlands', *Time Out of Mind* (1997).

CHAPTER THIRTEEN – HAND ME DOWN MY WALKIN' CANE

1. 1 August 2003.

2. 4 August and 5 September 2003, respectively.

3. 29 July 2003.

4. 2 September 2001.

5. Interview with Austin Scaggs, *Rolling Stone*, 26 October 2004.

6. Interview with Robert Hilburn, *Los Angeles Times*, 16 September 2001.

7. Seth Stevenson, www.slate.com, 12 April 2004. Brian Steinberg, *Wall Street Journal*, 2 April 2004.

8. Interview with Austin Scaggs, *Rolling Stone*, 26 October 2004.

9. Corcoran, who first saw Dylan in Newcastle in 1965, was the editor of the useful collection *Do You Mr Jones?: Bob Dylan With the Poets and Professors* (2002). With contributions from Paul Muldoon, Simon Armitage, Sean Wilentz and an impressive legion of others, the book contains more sense about its subject than is usually available.

10. From the *Guardian*'s notably vicious review of a 'bizarre' performance at London's Wembley Arena (17 November 2003). It seems the paper was having another of its little turns where Dylan was concerned.

NOTES

11. *Sunday Telegraph*, 26 September 2004; *USA Today*, 4 October; *Newsweek*, 4 October.

12. Edition of 26 October 2004.

13. See, for example, 'The Sweet Troubles of Proust', a *New York Review of Books* blog by Colm Tóibín, 22 February 2013 (www.nybooks.com/blogs/nyrblog/2013/feb/22/sweet-troubles-proust/)

14. Interview with Douglas Brinkley, *Rolling Stone*, 14 May 2009.

15. *The Bob Dylan Encyclopedia* (2006), p. 497.

16. *Rolling Stone*, 7 September 2006.

17. Jon Pareles, 20 August 2006.

18. Interview with Douglas Brinkley, *Rolling Stone*, 14 May 2009.

19. 7 October 2006.

20. See Richard F. Thomas, 'The Streets of Rome: The Classical Dylan' in the journal *Oral Tradition*, Vol. 22, No. 1, pp. 30–56 (March 2007).

21. 2 August 2012.

22. The first headline comes from the *New York Times* (12 July 2003), the second from the online *Daily Beast* (30 April 2010). What's interesting is that in both cases the writers, Jon Pareles and Sean Wilentz respectively, found the charges groundless. As mentioned previously, Joni Mitchell staged her attack in an interview with the *Los Angeles Times* published on 22 April 2010.

23. *Nelson Mail*, 7 October 2006.

24. *Rolling Stone*, 7 September 2006.

25. In an interview with *Rolling Stone*'s Mikal Gilmore (22 December 2001), Dylan once again said that he had lost the desire to make albums, that 'It was clear to me I had more than enough songs to play. Forever.'

26. Interview with Jonathan Lethem, *Rolling Stone*, 7 September 2006.

27. Interview with Mikal Gilmore, 27 September 2012.

28. Robert Sullivan, 'This Is Not a Bob Dylan Movie', 7 October 2007.

29. 15 May 2006.

30. *Dreams From My Father* (1995); *The Audacity of Hope: Thoughts on Reclaiming the American Dream* (2006).

31. 17 January 2007.

32. www.gallup.com/poll/116500/presidential-approval-ratings-george-bush.aspx.

33. Interview with Mikal Gilmore, *Rolling Stone*, 27 September 2012.

34. 5 June 2008.

35. The promotional interview was conducted by Bill Flanagan and published on bobdylan.com. The excerpt was published by *Newsweek* on 6 April 2009.

36. Interview with Mikal Gilmore, *Rolling Stone*, 27 September 2012.

37. 'The Cost of Racial Animus on a Black Presidential Candidate', 24 March 2013. www.people.fas.harvard.edu/~sstephen/papers.html.

38. 'The Return of Old Fashioned Racism to White Americans' Partisan Preferences in

the Age of Obama', *Journal of Politics*, Vol. 75 (1), pp. 110–23 (January 2013).

39. Lawrence Mishel, Jared Bernstein, Sylvia Allegretto, *The State of Working America 2006/2007* (2007), p. 2.

40. 'America's Image in the World: Findings from the Pew Global Attitudes Project', released 14 March 2007.

41. *New York Times*, 23 May 2013.

42. Chris Woods, Bureau of Investigative Journalism, August 10, 2011 (http://www. thebureauinvestigates.com/2011/08/10/most-complete-picture-yet-of-cia-drone-strikes/)

43. See The National Priorities Project (Mattea Kramer, Chris Hetman *et al.*), *A People's Guide to the Federal Budget* (2012), pp. 134–6.

CHAPTER FOURTEEN – PAY IN BLOOD

1. 13 April 2008.

2. Richard Williams, *The Guardian*, 16 August 2008.

3. *Rolling Stone*, 14 May 2009.

4. Alexis Petridis, *The Guardian*, 24 April 2009.

5. *Uncut* magazine, January 2010.

6. Douglas Brinkley, *Rolling Stone*, 14 May 2009.

7. *Mojo* magazine, January 2010.

8. Interview with Mikal Gilmore, *Rolling Stone*, 27 September 2012.

9. Kasper Monrad, 'The Painter Bob Dylan: An Introduction'; John Elderfield, 'Across the Borderline'. In the catalogue/book *The Brazil Series* (2010).

10. Agence France-Presse, 7 September 2010.

11. Interview with Mikal Gilmore, *Rolling Stone*, 27 September 2012.

12. In the United States, ticket prices increased by more than four times the rate of inflation between 1996 and 2008. (Associated Press report, *Billboard*, 27 December 2010.)

13. 4 April 2010.

14. Both stories published 7 April 2011.

15. 9 April 2011.

16. 10 April 2011.

17. *Sunday Herald*, 10 April 2011.

18. *The Herald*, 21 May 2011.

19. This book, like its predecessor, like almost every book written about Dylan over the last two decades, owes eternal gratitude to the Swede for his extraordinary researches, tracking both public performances and recording activities from 1958 until (at the time of writing) 2013. See, in all circumstances, www.bjorner.com.

20. Neil McCormick review, 1 July 2012.

21. 16 August 2012.

22. Interview with Mikal Gilmore, 27 September 2012.

23. *Ibid.*

24. *Ibid.*

25. *The American Songbag* (1927 edition), pp. 254–5.

26. *Ozark Folksongs Vol. IV: Religious Songs and Other Items – Collected and Edited by Vance Randolph* (1946–50; reprinted 1980), p. 144.

27. *New York Times*, 5 September; *Vancouver Sun*, 13 October; *Los Angeles Times*, 27 October; *Chicago Tribune*, 12 November.

28. Walt Whitman, 'Starting from Paumanok' ('Protoleaf').

Bibliography

Books

Ashcroft, William M., and Eugene V. Gallagher (eds), *Introduction to New and Alternative Religions in America, Vol. 2: Jewish and Christian Traditions* (2006).

Auden, W.H., *The English Auden: Poems, Essay and Dramatic Writings 1927–1939*, ed. Edward Mendelson (1977, pb. 1986).

Baez, Joan, *And a Song to Sing With* (1987).

Bauldie, John (ed.), *Wanted Man: In Search of Bob Dylan* (1990).

Bell, Ian, *Once Upon a Time: The Lives of Bob Dylan* (2012).

Bloom, Allan, *The Closing of the American Mind: How Higher Education Has Failed Democracy and Impoverished the Souls of Today's Students* (1987).

Bradford, Adam, *Out of the Dark Woods: Dylan, Depression and Faith* (2011).

Carter, Rubin, *The Sixteenth Round: From Number 1 Contender to Number 45472* (1973).

Carter, Dr Rubin 'Hurricane', LLD, with Ken Klonsky, *Eye of the Hurricane: My Path from Darkness to Freedom* (2011).

Campbell, Joseph, *The Hero with a Thousand Faces* (1949).

Campbell, Joseph, *Primitive Mythology* (1959).

Campbell, Joseph, *Occidental Mythology* (1964).

Cartwright, Bert, *The Bible in the Lyrics of Bob Dylan* (1985, rev. and expanded 1992).

Conrad, Joseph, *The Nigger of the Narcissus* (1897).

Conrad, Joseph, *Victory* (1915).

Corcoran, Neil, *Do You Mr Jones? Bob Dylan With the Poets and Professors* (2002).

Dannen, Frederic, *Hit Men: Power Brokers and Fast Money Inside the Music Business* (1991).

BIBLIOGRAPHY

de Lange, Nicholas, *Judaism* (1986).

Dettmer, Kevin J.H. (ed.), *The Cambridge Companion to Bob Dylan* (2009).

Dunn, Tim, *The Bob Dylan Copyright Files 1962–2007* (2008).

Dylan, Bob, *Chronicles: Volume One* (2004).

Dylan, Bob, *Lyrics: 1962–2001* (2004).

Epstein, Daniel Mark, *The Ballad of Bob Dylan: A Portrait* (2011).

Flanagan, Bill, *Written in My Soul* (1986).

Frazer, J.G., *The Golden Bough: A Study in Magic and Religion* (abridged ed. 1922).

Ginsburg, Faye D., *Contested Lives: The Abortion Debate in an American Community* (1989, rev. ed. 1998).

Goode, Erich, and Nachman Ben-Yehuda, *Moral Panics: The Social Construction of Deviance* (1994).

Gray, Michael, *Song & Dance Man III* (2000).

Gray, Michael, *The Bob Dylan Encyclopedia* (2006).

Gray, Michael, *Hand Me My Travelin' Shoes: In Search of Blind Willie McTell* (2007).

Griffin, Sid, *Shelter from the Storm: Bob Dylan's Rolling Thunder Years* (2010).

Guralnick, Peter, *Careless Love: The Unmaking of Elvis Presley* (1999).

Helm, Levon, and Stephen Davis, *This Wheel's On Fire: Levon Helm and the Story of The Band* (1993, 2000).

Heylin, Clinton, *Behind the Shades Revisited* (2000).

Heylin, Clinton, *Still on the Road: The Songs of Bob Dylan Vol. 2: 1974–2008* (2010).

Jacobson, Mark, *Teenage Hipster in the Modern World: From the Birth of Punk to the Land of Bush – Thirty Years of Apocalyptic Journalism* (2005).

Kramer, Mattea, Chris Hetman, *et al.*, *A People's Guide to the Federal Budget* (2012).

Kokay, Les, *Songs of the Underground: A Collector's Guide to the Rolling Thunder Revue 1975–1976* (privately published, 2003).

Lawrence, D.H., *The Man Who Died* (1929).

Lindsey, Hal, with Carole C. Carlson, *The Late, Great Planet Earth* (1970).

Lott, Eric, *Love and Theft: Blackface Minstrelsy and the American Working Class* (1993).

McDannell, Colleen, and Bernhard Lang, *Heaven: A History* (1988).

Marcus, Greil, *Bob Dylan: Writings 1968–2010* (2011).

Marshall, Lee, *Bob Dylan: The Never Ending Star* (2007).

Micklethwait, John, and Adrian Wooldridge, *The Right Nation: Why America Is Different* (2004).

Miles, Barry, *Allen Ginsberg: Beat Poet* (2010).

Mishel, Lawrence, Jared Bernstein, Sylvia Allegretto, *The State of Working America 2006/2007* (2007).

Muir, Andrew, *Razor's Edge: Bob Dylan & the Neverending Tour* (2001).

Obama, Barack, *Dreams from My Father: A Story of Race and Inheritance* (1995).

Obama, Barack, *The Audacity of Hope: Thoughts on Reclaiming the American Dream* (2006).

Pagels, Elaine, *Revelations: Visions, Prophecy and Politics in the Book of Revelation* (2012).

Pitre, Merline, *In Struggle Against Jim Crow: Lulu B. White and the NAACP, 1900–1957* (1999).

Randolph, Vance, *Ozark Folksongs Vol. IV: Religious Songs and Other Items* (1946–50; reprinted 1980).

Reineke, Hank, *Ramblin' Jack Elliott: The Never-Ending Highway* (2010).

Ricks, Christopher, *Dylan's Visions of Sin* (2003).

Rogovoy, Seth, *Bob Dylan: Prophet, Mystic, Poet* (2010).

Rotolo, Suze, *A Freewheelin' Time: A Memoir of Greenwich Village in the Sixties* (2008).

Sandburg, Carl, *The American Songbag* (1927).

Scobie, Stephen, *Alias Bob Dylan Revisited* (2003).

Seeger, Pete, and Peter Blood (eds), *Where Have All the Flowers Gone? A Singer's Stories, Songs, Seeds, Robberies* (1993).

Shelton, Robert, *No Direction Home: The Life and Music of Bob Dylan* (1986, rev. ed. 2011).

Shepard, Sam, *The Rolling Thunder Logbook* (1977, reissued 2004).

Sloman, Larry, *On the Road with Bob Dylan* (1978, reissued 2002).

Sounes, Howard, *Down the Highway: The Life of Bob Dylan* (2002).

Webb, Stephen H., *Dylan Redeemed: From Highway 61 to Saved* (2006).

Wells, Robert V., *Life Flows On in Endless Song: Folk Songs and American History* (2009).

Wexler, Jerry, and David Ritz, *Rhythm and the Blues: A Life in American Music* (1993).

Wice, Paul B., *Rubin 'Hurricane' Carter and the American Justice System* (2000).

Wilentz, Sean, *Bob Dylan in America* (2010).

Williams, Paul, *Bob Dylan: Performing Artist 1960–1973* (1990).

Williams, Paul, *Bob Dylan: Performing Artist: The Middle Years 1974–1986* (1992).

Williams, Paul, *Bob Dylan: Performing Artist 1986–1990 and Beyond* (2005).

BIBLIOGRAPHY

Yaffe, David, *Bob Dylan: Like a Complete Unknown* (2011).

Yeats, W.B., *Collected Poems* (1985, revised ed. 1990).

Articles

Bauldie, John, 'Jacques Levy and the *Desire* collaboration', *All Across the Telegraph: A Bob Dylan Handbook* (1987), ed. Michael Gray and John Bauldie.

Acocella, Joan, 'Seeing and Believing', *The New Yorker*, 2 April 2012.

Bangs, Lester, 'Joey Gallo Was No Hero', *Village Voice*, 8 March 1976.

Bobo, Lawrence D., Camille Z. Charles, Maria Krysan and Alicia D. Simmons, 'The Real Record on Racial Attitudes', *Social Trends in American Life: Findings from the General Social Survey* (2012), ed. Peter V. Marsden.

Krogsgaard, Michael, 'Bob Dylan: The Recording Sessions (Part 5)', *The Bridge* (Issue 1, summer 1998).

Pintauro, Joe, 'Algren in Exile', *Chicago* magazine (February 1988).

Tesler, Michael, 'The Return of Old Fashioned Racism to White Americans' Partisan Preferences in the Age of Obama', *Journal of Politics*, Vol. 75 (1) (January 2013).

Thomas, Richard F., 'The Streets of Rome: The Classical Dylan', *Oral Tradition*, Vol. 22, No. 1 (March 2007).

Vidal, Gore, 'The State of the Union: 1975', *United States: Essays 1952–1992* (1993).

Vites, Paolo, 'Bob Dylan's Invisible Republic: Interview with Greil Marcus', *Jam Magazine*, 1997.

Western, Bruce, 'The Impact of Incarceration on Wage Mobility and Inequality', *American Sociological Review*, August 2002.

Index

INDEX

INDEX

INDEX

INDEX

INDEX